Mare Clausum

Legal History Library

VOLUME 77

Studies in the History of International Law

VOLUME 28

The titles published in this series are listed at *brill.com/shil*

Mare Clausum

The Formation of the Law of the Sea in Pre-modern State Practice and Legal Doctrine (c.1350–1650)

By

Stefano Cattelan

BRILL | NIJHOFF

LEIDEN | BOSTON

Cover illustration: The Voyage of the Cardinal Infante Ferdinand of Spain from Barcelona to Genoa in April 1633, with Neptune Calming the Tempest by Peter Paul Rubens (1635). Conserved at the Harvard Art Museums, object number: 1942.174. Photo: © President and Fellows of Harvard College.

Library of Congress Cataloging-in-Publication Data

Names: Cattelan, Stefano author
Title: Mare clausum : the formation of the law of the sea in pre-modern
state practice and legal doctrine (c.1350-1650) / by Stefano Cattelan.
Description: Leiden ; Boston : Brill Academic Publishers, Inc, 2025. |
Series: Legal history library ; volume 77 | Includes bibliographical
references and index.
Identifiers: LCCN 2025029963 | ISBN 9789004741393 hardback |
ISBN 9789004741409 epub
Subjects: LCSH: Mare clausum | Law of the sea--History | Freedom of the
seas--History | Maritime law--History
Classification: LCC KZA1340 .C38 2025 | DDC 341.4/50903--DC23/ENG/20250708
LC record available at https://lccn.loc.gov/2025029963

Typeface for the Latin, Greek, and Cyrillic scripts: "Brill". See and download: brill.com/brill-typeface.

ISSN 1874-1793
ISBN 978-90-04-74139-3 (hardback)
ISBN 978-90-04-74140-9 (e-book)
DOI 10.1163/9789004741409

To my nephew Jacopo – may your curiosity be as boundless as the ocean and the freedom of the seas always inspire your adventures, big or small

Contents

Foreword

The Turn of the Tide in the Debate on the Law of the Sea

The question of who owns the sea and how regimes to govern it should be established and managed has been a subject of debate among lawyers and scholars for centuries. Following the 'discovery' of America by Christopher Columbus in 1492 and the first circumnavigation of the globe by Ferdinand Magellan and Juan Sebastian Elcano, completed by the latter in 1522, the full extent of the ocean planet was first realised in Europe. The subsequent intensification of exploration and commerce led to a growing entanglement of ocean spaces, making questions surrounding 'the law of the sea' more pressing than ever on a global scale.

The Dutch jurist Hugo de Groot, also known as Hugo Grotius, is widely credited with launching the great debate on the freedom versus the dominion of the seas through his work *Mare liberum* (1609). This brief treatise argued that ocean areas were immune from claims of dominion and that freedom of navigation was a natural right of all peoples and nations. Grotius' thesis was countered by John Selden's *Mare clausum* (1635), which justified the possibility of national occupation of, and dominion over, ocean spaces. This debate, which from the late nineteenth century onwards became known as the 'battle of the books', continues to dominate modern scholarship on the early modern law of the sea.

The extensive historiographical output sparked by the battle of the books has placed *Mare liberum* and its arguments for a free sea at the forefront. Consequently, scholars advocating sovereign claims over the sea are often portrayed as merely responding to Grotius' work and its legal arguments. This dominance of the Grotian perspective in scholarship on the law of the sea is frequently taken for granted. Not so by the Italian legal historian Stefano Cattelan, whose aim is not to view arguments in favour of exclusive maritime rights simply as reactions to the notion of *mare liberum*, but to trace their development on their own terms. To do so, he introduces the concept of 'claimed seas', encompassing what Selden would later explicitly term *mare clausum*, or the closed sea. According to Cattelan, both the development of claims over the sea in the 'pre Grotian' period as well as the scholarly production defending the notion of *mare clausum* in the seventeenth century have been 'obscured' due to 'a bias considering the development of the law of the sea as a complete victory of the freedom of the seas' and 'by the long-lasting ascendancy of the Dutchman among later generations of jurists and the central place he acquired in the western legal tradition canon'. (p. 21)

Cattelan's approach to the 'claimed seas' encompasses a range of legal and political concepts, including for example 'jurisdiction' (*jurisdictio*), 'occupation' (*occupatio*), 'power' (*imperium*), 'ownership' (*dominium*), prescription (*praescriptio*), and 'sovereignty'. Legal and political questions relating to the sea, its governance and its legal underpinnings shaped various and sometimes conflicting or even adverse definitions of these concepts. Cattelan's principal aim is to explore how the 'claimed seas' principle and its historical variations were employed in legal argumentation to justify claims over maritime spaces. The present book, which is the fruit of this endeavour, delivers several important contributions to the historiography on the law of the sea. Four of these will be touched upon here. They concern time, maritime space, the wider context of power politics, and present-day relevance.

First then, the book puts the freedom versus the dominion of the seas debate in a much wider time frame than usually is the case. The book crosses both the traditional boundary between the Middle Ages and the early modern period, and the cesura created by the publication of *Mare liberum* in 1609. The former crossing fits well in a current tendency in the historiography of the early modern period, which extends the early modern era backward, including part of the fourteenth and fifteenth centuries, as Hamish Scott recently observed in his introduction to the *Oxford Handbook of Early Modern History, 1350–1750* (2015). International legal historians have embraced this approach, including Martti Koskenniemi, whose magnum opus *To the Uttermost Parts of the Earth. Legal Imagination and International Power 1300–1870* (2021) starts in the early fourteenth century.

By also crossing the 1609 cesura, Cattelan wants to emphasise that 'the notion of 'claimed seas' continued to be central in state practice in the decades following the publication of *Mare liberum*' (p. 21–22). This is crucial as the distinction between the territorial and the free sea is not just an intellectual construct of the seventeenth century. This distinction has a much longer history which is rooted in customary law. Both classical and medieval scholars influenced the thinking of early modern international lawyers on the law of the sea, even though the revival of classical scholarship in the Renaissance often hid the support from customary law for the law of nations. Claims over specific sea areas were quite common in the Middle Ages: Venice claimed the Adriatic and Genoa the Ligurian Sea. Baldus de Ubaldis (1327–1400) referred to these pretensions as 'inveterate custom'. The count of Flanders claimed control of the sea in front of the Flemish coast, known as the *Vlaamse stroom* (Flemish stream), from at least the middle of the fourteenth century. Further north, Denmark-Norway claimed the northern seas from Norway to Greenland. How these claims were originally recognised by foreign powers and how the latter's attitudes changed over time is one of the many aspects of the medieval 'law of the sea', which is highlighted in this book, and which show its relevance for the subsequent period.

Second, Cattelan's study extends beyond a single maritime region to encompass three different maritime spaces, which he refers to as 'macro-regions': the seas of northern Europe, the Mediterranean, and the oceans. Often, the discussion of the 'battle of the books' is limited to Grotius and Selden and their respective works in the context of Anglo-Dutch rivalry on the North Sea and the English Channel. This is partly due to the Anglophone domination of academia. Whereas a vast amount of literature is available on Grotius, Selden, and Anglo-Dutch maritime rivalry in English, both the French and Italian historiography on the Mediterranean and the Portuguese and Hispanic historiography on the Iberian division of planet ocean have not been fully integrated in Anglophone literature on the history of the law of the sea. This is especially true for the Venetian/Adriatic and Nordic/Scandinavian dimensions of the debate. Thanks to his mastery of many languages, Stefano Cattelan has been able to integrate these different historiographies into a single analysis, which greatly broadens the scope of understanding the development of legal thinking on how the sea could or should be governed.

Third, the author does not study the development of the 'claimed seas' principle in a legal vacuum but in the context of power politics. He investigates the constant interplay between the development of doctrine around the 'claimed seas' on the one hand and state practice on the other. This allows him to fully appreciate the globalisation of the law of the sea as a process which began in the late Middle Ages and which remained relevant for the early modern battle of the books. After all, the oceans became involved in a power struggle between Spain and Portugal in the late fifteenth century, which generated debate among legal scholars. The papal bull *Inter caetera* and the treaty of Tordesillas at the end of the fifteenth century and the treaty of Zaragoza in 1529, dividing the Pacific, are often considered in the historiography on international law as the starting point for the debate on the law of the sea. Portuguese and Hispanic historiography emphasise that the papal bulls of 1493 were the culmination of a whole series of papal bulls, dating back to pope Clement VI's attribution of the Canary Islands to a Castilian prince in 1344. Both Portugal and Spain originally sought and received papal recognition to legitimise their respective claims to vast maritime spaces. In this respect, the Treaties of Tordesillas and Zaragoza marked a new phase, as they were concluded without papal intervention. Nevertheless, both the papal bulls and the treaties remained significant throughout the sixteenth and seventeenth centuries. The division of the oceans between the two Iberian powers remained a central ideological dispute, not only between them but also with their European rivals. The pope and the Iberian monarchies thus played a crucial role in shaping the closed sea principle, applying it on a global scale, more than a century before the publication of *Mare liberum*.

Lastly, Stefano Cattelan's book on the 'claimed seas' principle is highly pertinent for understanding contemporary trends and developments in the law of the sea. While it is true that the notion of the open sea as inherently free and beyond the sovereignty of any single state has been a cornerstone of modern international law – culminating in the 1982 United Nations Convention on the Law of the Sea – there exists an equally important counter-narrative. Maritime freedoms are enumerated in numerous treaties and an extensive body of regulations worldwide, governing areas such as fisheries, biodiversity, and the Polar regions. Yet, the 'claimed seas' principle (or *mare clausum*) has gained increasing prominence in recent years, as exemplified by mounting disputes over maritime zones, with particular attention drawn to China's claims in the South China Sea. These claims, underpinned by historical justifications extending back to the Eastern Han dynasty (25–220 CE), underscore the enduring role of history in shaping contemporary legal arguments. Determining the validity of such claims requires a nuanced understanding of history, including distant historical contexts that are often overlooked in Western societies, where fleeting present-day concerns frequently dominate discourse. The writing of history tends to ebb and flow in response to current events, and the historiography of the law of the sea is no exception. The present book delivers a major contribution to the turn of the tide in the current debate on the law of the sea. I expect it to play an important role in shaping ongoing discussions of the history, the present, and the future of the law of the sea.

Louis Sicking
Aemilius Papinianus Professor of History of Public International Law, Vrije Universiteit, Amsterdam

Acknowledgements

The writing of this book has been deeply intertwined with my personal and academic journey over the past seven years. Its publication would not have been possible without the invaluable support, guidance, and encouragement of many individuals and institutions to whom I am deeply grateful. My fascination with international legal history was first ignited during my undergraduate studies at the University of Trento, where I had the privilege of writing my master's thesis under the guidance of Professors Diego Quaglioni and Giuliano Marchetto. What began as an initial exploration evolved into my Ph.D. dissertation, which I defended in December 2020 at the Department of Law, Aarhus University. I am especially grateful to my colleagues in Denmark for fostering a stimulating working environment, and in particular to my supervisors, Professors Per Andersen and Torsten Iversen, for their meticulous feedback of each chapter and for granting me the freedom to pursue my interests. I am also indebted to Professor Ole Terkelsen, who offered me the opportunity to teach international law alongside him. During my Ph.D., I was fortunate to spend valuable months at Tilburg Law School and at the University of Bergen. I take this opportunity to express my sincere thanks to Professors Randall Lesaffer, Jørn Øyrehagen Sunde, and Sören Koch for their warm hospitality, insightful discussions, and sound methodological guidance.

During my postdoctoral research at the Vrije Universiteit Brussel, working closely with Professor Frederik Dhondt has been a constant source of inspiration, shaping my scholarship in more ways than I could possibly convey. Through his example, I have been exposed to the highest standards of our discipline, and I am grateful not only for his mentorship but also for the friendship that has grown from our collaboration. I am also thankful to Professor Louis Sicking for his friendship and for sharing his expertise and keen insights, and to Professors Luisa Brunori and Stefania Gialdroni for their generous hospitality during my research stays in Paris and Padua, respectively, which coincided with the pivotal revision stage of this book's manuscript. Regarding the publication process, I would like to thank Petra Stiglmayer and Alessandra Giliberto at Brill for their professionalism, patience, and kindness, as well as the two anonymous reviewers, whose thoughtful and constructive feedback certainly enhanced the final manuscript. I am also grateful to Professor Randall Lesaffer, editor of this series, for his support and encouragement throughout the publication process.

I am deeply appreciative of the generous financial support provided by Aarhus University, the Carlsberg Foundation (Denmark, Internationalisation

Grant CF 21-0367), the CORE research group at the Vrije Universiteit Brussel, and the Research Foundation Flanders (FWO, Junior Fundamental Research Project G016122N). Their funding has allowed me to pursue this research under the best possible conditions, enabling me to present my work at international conferences around the world – from the Azores and Iceland to South Korea and Japan – where I was fortunate to forge lasting academic and personal connections. I would like to thank in particular Dr Ubaldo Morozzi, Dr Simone Maria Bonin, Dr Raphael Cahen, Professor Lukasz Dziedzic, Dr Andrea Longo, and Dr Daniel Ricardo Villamarin Quiroga for their friendship and for stimulating exchanges on certain aspects of the book. I also thank my students at the Brussels School of Governance for making the course 'International Legal History and Theory' such an enjoyable subject to teach and for being a constant source of inspiration. I am equally grateful to Professor Kristin Henrard, programme director of the BA in International and European Law, for her trust and support, which have enabled me to develop as a lecturer and to bring my passion for international legal history into the classroom.

On a personal note, I am profoundly grateful to my family and all my friends for their support during this journey, and for reminding me to take breaks when needed. Their encouragement, humour, and understanding have been invaluable. I am particularly grateful to my high school and university friends, who have always made me feel at home whenever I return to Italy – reminding me that distance is merely a matter of geography. I also cherish the friendships I have made along the way during this academic journey, and my colleagues at the Vrije Universiteit Brussel, who make every day at the office thoroughly enjoyable. Finally, I owe special thanks to my parents, Anna and Francesco, and to my sister, Silvia, for nurturing my intellectual curiosity from an early age and for their unwavering love and belief in me through every challenge and success. They have always reminded me that life is larger than academic pursuits, encouraging balance, joy, and perspective. This book is, in many ways, a reflection of the values they instilled in me, and I am endlessly grateful for that.

Stefano Cattelan
Ixelles, 10 March 2025

Figures

Introduction

1 Freedom or Dominion of the Seas? Current Issues, Ancient Concerns

The tension between freedom and sovereign claims continues to characterise the evolution of the law of the sea. In September 2018, the American guided-missile destroyer USS *Decatur* and a Chinese warship almost collided in the South China Sea, getting as close to each other as 40 meters. The Decatur had just sailed within twelve nautical miles off two reefs in the Spratly chain of islets as part of the United States' operations intended to enforce the right of free passage in international waters (FONOP).[1] These two reefs are claimed by China, Taiwan, Vietnam, and the Philippines. Similar incidents continue to occur in the waters of the South China Sea.

The Chinese, by now an established world power, have been assertively extending their de facto control on several reefs, islands, and low-tide elevations, from which they uphold maritime claims based on the so-called 'nine-dash line'. Competing claims in the region come from Taiwan, Brunei, Vietnam, Indonesia, Malaysia, and the Philippines.[2] The strategic importance of the South China Sea is clear: it hosts rich, though increasingly depleted, fisheries alongside significant oil and gas reserves. Moreover, one-third of global shipping passes through its waters, making it a critical artery of world trade in an interconnected global economy. Many of the world's largest economies depend on these seaways, and the concentration of commercial routes within this relatively narrow area raises concerns about its vulnerability as a strategic chokepoint – especially if it were to fall under the control of a single power.

During Barack Obama's presidency, the US Navy's Seventh Fleet started to routinely patrol Asian waters with the declared intent of preserving freedom

---

1 Steven Lee Myers, 'American and Chinese Warships Narrowly Avoid High-Seas Collision', *The New York Times*, 2 October 2018, Online Edition; Jesse Johnson, 'Photos confirm U.S.-Chinese warships' near-miss as experts say South China Sea encounter likely to affect allied operations in the region', *The Japan Times*, Online Edition, 3 October 2018. For an overview, see Eleanor Freund, *Freedom of Navigation in the South China Sea: A Practical Guide*, Belfer Center for Science and International Affairs, Harvard Kennedy School, Special Report, June 2017.

2 Yih-Jye Hwang and Edmund Frettingham (eds.), *Maritime and Territorial Disputes in the South China Sea. Faces of Power and Law in the Age of China's Rise* (London-New York: Routledge, 2021); Youngmin Seo, *The South China Sea Dispute as International Law and Politics: Discovering the Role of Law in Times of Power Shift* (Leiden: Brill, 2024).

 | DOI:10.1163/9789004741409_002

of navigation in the region. Today, in a conjuncture marked by tensions between the world's two biggest economies, US warships continue to sail within twelve nautical miles of Chinese claims, challenging what they view as excessive maritime claims. The US government asserts that these operations are conducted globally, including in areas claimed by its allies, to uphold access to international waterways under international law. Both nations accuse each other of escalating the situation: Chinese naval spokespeople frequently contend that freedom of navigation should not be used as a pretext to violate the rights of other nations.[3] As of 2024, China's third aircraft carrier, the *Fujian*, is completing sea trials and will soon be operative, further enhancing the People's Republic of China (PRC)'s power of projection in the region, also in relation to the persisting issue of a potential reunification with Taiwan – and its expansive maritime domain – by force.

In this context, the Philippines filed a case against China regarding the disputed waters of the South China Sea. In July 2016, the Permanent Court of Arbitration in The Hague issued a landmark ruling, declaring that Beijing's expansive maritime claims, based on alleged 'historic rights', had no legal foundation. However, China flatly rejected the decision.[4] The court's ruling was grounded on the provisions of the 1982 United Nations Convention on the Law of the Sea (UNCLOS III), sometimes referred to as 'the constitution of the oceans'. This epoch-making international agreement regulates maritime interactions at sea in a comprehensive manner, detailing the legal status of different pelagic zones. UNCLOS III has been described as a 'package deal' because it incorporates numerous compromises between the differing interests of various groups of states. Striking the right balance between the common use of the oceans and the exclusive rights claimed by coastal states was

3 Ben Blanchard, 'China Navy Chief Takes Dig at U.S. Freedom of Navigation Patrols', *Reuters*, 24 April 2019.

4 PCA Case n. 2013-19, *In the Matter of the South China Sea Arbitration*, before An Arbitral Tribunal Constituted under Annex VII to the 1982 United Nations Convention on the Law of the Sea, between the Republic of the Philippines and the People's Republic of China. Cf. Mary J. Cantorias Marvel, 'The South China Sea arbitration: navigating compliance strategies through the lens of raya and the last dragon', in Christina Voigt and Caroline Foster (eds.), *International Courts versus Non-compliance Mechanisms: Comparative Advantages in Strengthening Treaty Implementation* (Cambridge: University Press, 2024), 471–88; Christian Pogies, 'UNCLOS and the South China Sea Arbitration: Into Lawfare's Abyss?', *The German Journal on Contemporary Asia*, 143 (2017), 93–105; idem, 'Oceans of cynicism? Norm-genesis, lawfare and the South China Sea arbitration case', in Björnstjern Baade et al. (eds.), *Cynical International Law? Abuse and Circumvention in Public International and European Law* (Berlin: Springer, 2021), 143–62.

particularly challenging during the protracted negotiations that led to its adoption.

Following World War II, a new trend towards extending state jurisdiction over adjacent seas gained momentum, resulting in the gradual carving up of the oceans and their subjection to various, more or less exclusive, legal regimes.[5] Following World War II, a new trend towards extending state jurisdiction over adjacent seas gained momentum, resulting in the gradual carving up of the oceans and their subjection to various, more or less exclusive, legal regimes. Despite this, the principle of freedom of the seas remains the prevailing rule concerning the high seas. In essence, the tension between freedom and control continues to shape the evolution of the law of the sea. This volume seeks to explore the deep historical roots of this dialectic in international legal history.

2 Seas and Humans, a Complex Relationship

The sea has always captivated humankind, evoking both irrational fears and a desire for mastery. Throughout history, political entities have recognised the vital role of pelagic spaces in facilitating essential activities such as trade, communication, and fishing.[6] For centuries, ships were the only viable means of transporting heavy and bulky goods across vast distances. Seas and oceans also provided abundant resources, including fisheries and salt, which were central to economic and societal development. Even today, the sea remains indispensable, sustaining a growing global population by offering food and other resources. However, the relationship between humanity and the oceans has evolved.[7] With nearly all the world's oceans now explored and mapped, human activities have intensified, leaving a profound impact on marine ecosystems. Practices such as overfishing, plastic pollution, and carbon emissions

---

5 E.g. with the extension of the territorial sea and to the creation of new institutes such as the exclusive economic zone (EEZ) and the continental shelf. See Donald R. Rothwell and Tim Stephens, *The International Law of the Sea* (Oxford-Portland: Hart Publishing, 2023), 1–17; Yoshifumi Tanaka, *The International Law of the Sea* (Cambridge: University Press, 2019), 25.

6 Pascal Picq, 'La mer est le propre d'Homo sapiens', in Pascal Arnaud and Philip de Souza (eds.), *The Sea in History – Vol. I, The Ancient World* (Woodbridge: Boydell Press, 2017), 9–38; Brian Fagan, *Beyond the Blue Horizon. How the Earliest Mariners Unlocked the Secrets of the Oceans* (London: Bloomsbury Press, 2012).

7 At least regarding the oceans' surface, deep-sea beds remain largely unexplored to this day. It has been estimated that ninety-nine percent of the ocean floor is unexplored. Exploring the depths below the ocean's surface is very difficult, time-consuming and, expensive.

disrupt biodiversity and undermine the ocean's critical role in regulating the Earth's climate. The oceans, once seen as an inexhaustible reservoir, are now under severe strain.

However, it has not always been like this. Humans' capability to govern the seas has been historically feeble. Winds and currents could easily overpower even the most daring captains, crushing wooden hulls and making perilous even the shortest sea route. However, humans never stopped sailing and taking their chances. Therefore, the question of whether humans could possess the sea was bound to emerge with the creation of structured societies and complex legal systems. In the beginning, it mainly represented a question of sea power, such as during the Minoan thalassocracy in the Aegean Sea. For a long time, a legal dimension for the sea did not emerge. Seafaring peoples were more concerned with the ways in which sea power could be used to gain political and economic primacy. Undoubtedly, throughout human history, power, trade, and navigation have been inextricably interrelated. That said, this aspect evolved in various ways across different societies.[8]

With the gradual evolution of the concept of 'law' and the establishment of legal systems, the relationship between humans and pelagic spaces emerged as a critical area of analysis for jurists and scholars. As complex political entities developed, interactions at sea became a fundamental aspect of international relations, necessitating regulations to prevent perpetual chaos. Relying solely on force proved insufficient, prompting the creation of legal frameworks to justify territorial claims, secure resources, and repel competitors. However, the inherently intangible and uncontrollable nature of the sea posed unique challenges for legal analysis. While the sea remains a potential source of danger even today, it was far more formidable during the long age of sailing vessels, when the lack of advanced technology and the use of rudimentary navigational tools amplified the risks of maritime ventures.

Not surprisingly then, throughout history humans have mystically revered the sea as a deity and feared it as an unpredictable killer. Greek mythology, for instance, attributed an important place to Poseidon, the god of the seas. It also provided many examples where gods determined the faith of men and women at sea, somehow offering an explanation to the unpredictable dangers inher-

8 For a broad perspective, see David Abulafia, *The Boundless Sea. A Human History of the Oceans* (Oxford: University Press 2019); idem, *The Great Sea: A Human History of the Mediterranean* (Oxford: University Press, 2013); Christian Buchet, *La grande histoirie vue de la mer* (Paris: Cherche-Midi, 2017).

ent to navigation.[9] A famous example allegedly happened at the onset of the war of Troy. The Greek army was blocked in Aulis by unfavourable winds provoked by Artemis's wrath against the Greek leader Agamemnon. The latter ultimately accepted to sacrifice his daughter, Iphigenia, in order to appease the goddess and gain safe passage to Troy.[10]

Other civilisations, from ancient Polynesia to the pre-modern Caribbean, developed a similarly deep connection with the surrounding waters. They often worshipped marine deities and practised apotropaic rituals to appease the power of the sea.[11] Over time, two distinct ways of perceiving the sea emerged. The first saw it as an untameable force – an expanse of inherent lawlessness and fear. The second reimagined the sea as something that could be tamed and governed, much like the land. A striking example of this latter perspective is found in the writings of the Greek historian Herodotus, who describes events during the second Persian invasion of Greece (480–479 BCE). To facilitate the massive Persian army's crossing of the Hellespont – the strait separating Asia and Europe – engineers constructed a pontoon bridge for troops and animals to march across. However, a storm soon destroyed the bridge. Enraged, Xerxes I (r. 486–465 BCE), the Persian King of Kings, sought to punish the sea itself, ordering it to be lashed and symbolically shackled with fetters.[12] Not by chance then, the human flaw of hubris (ὕβρις) has often been associated with the sea.

3 The 'Claimed Seas': Legal Argumentation and Politics

If the law of the sea today remains one of the most dynamic and debated branches of international law, the concerns it addresses go far back in history. This book seeks to study its historical development in the pre-modern world

9 Sandra Blakely, 'Maritime risk and ritual responses: sailing with the gods in the Ancient Mediterranean', in Arnaud and de Souza (eds.), *The Sea in History*, I, 362–79.

10 There are different endings to the scene, in some Iphigenia was spared by the intervention of the goddess herself. Euripides' play *Iphigenia at Aulis* (408–406 BCE) famously depicts the dramatic scenario surrounding the sacrifice.

11 On early Polynesian navigation in the Pacific Ocean, see Abulafia, *The Boundless Sea*, 3–39.

12 Herodotus, *Histories*, VII, translated by Alfred D. Godley (The Loeb Classical Library, London/Cambridge, MA: William Heinemann Ltd/Harvard University Press, 1938), 34–6. On this passage, see Dominique Briquel, 'The Punishment of the Hellespont by Xerxes: Perception of Religious Behaviour of the Enemy in Conflict Situations', *Graeco-Latina Brunensia*, 21(2) (2016), 51–60.

(broadly understood as comprising the late Middle Ages and the Early Modernity), which in many regards constitute the formative period for this body of law.[13] It focuses primarily on the emergence of what is referred to throughout the book as the concept or principle of the 'claimed seas'. Broadly speaking, it deems acceptable that polities may acquire exclusive rights over marine spaces.

The book explores how this notion evolved in pre-modern legal argumentation as a response to questions about whether and how law could extend its authority over the sea. It frequently served as a justification for a wide range of maritime assertions advanced by ambitious princes and wealthy maritime republics. As a hypernym or umbrella term, I conceive the notion of 'claimed seas' as encompassing diverse maritime assertions from the late Middle Ages and Early Modern Age, ranging from criminal jurisdiction, protection of seafarers, imposition of tolls, imposition of conditions upon entrance and use of the sea, bans on navigation, and exclusive fishing zones. In the fullest sense, it may refer to dominion-sovereignty (*dominium maris*).[14]

Firstly, the notion of 'claimed seas' emerged across the seas bordering the European continent. Secondly, it was applied to the world oceans. It developed in a tense dialogue (or clash) with the opposite principle, i.e. the freedom of the sea. The latter involves the belief that the sea is intrinsically different from land and cannot be owned whether by private individuals or polities, being destined to be shared by humankind. Hence, throughout the book special attention is devoted to tracing the legal arguments conceived to support different forms of exclusive rights over the sea, paying due attention to the specific terminology and concepts deployed in different spatial-temporal coordinates. To this end, the book necessarily delves into the constant interaction between law and politics that underpinned the idea itself of claiming exclusive rights over the sea and its contingent materialisations.[15]

13 For our purposes, the law of the sea can be defined as the set of legal rules that regulates human interactions at sea, with special regard to matters related to what we know term public international law. However, it should be noted that throughout the pre-modern period the boundaries between what we now define as the 'law of the sea' and 'maritime law' (the body of private law which governs relationships between parties and private entities in relation to matters such as transport of passengers, general average, jettison, sea loans, etc.) were almost non-existent.

14 Pitman B. Potter, *The Freedom of the Sea in History, Law and Politics* (London: Longmans, 1924), 65.

15 See Alexander Orakhelashvili, 'International law, international politics and ideology', in idem (ed.), *Research Handbook on the Theory and History of International Law* (Cheltenham-Northampton: Edward Elgar, 2020), 240–79.

Arguments employed in the past to justify preferential rights over the sea are not only relevant as historical phenomena. They also allow us to put in proper perspective today's international dossiers, such as disputes in the South China Sea, post-Brexit fisheries' regulations, overfishing, intentional damages to submarine cables, or the future legal status of a potentially ice-free Arctic Ocean.[16] More than ever, as the law of the sea and ocean governance are concerned a better knowledge of the past can help us navigate the present and the future of this blue planet we inhabit, as 'historical connection(s) allow us to see the inner substance of the present, not just its outward form'.[17] Indeed, it is surprising to see how many parallelisms exist between pre-modern debates on the 'claimed seas' and the concerns of the present. Fisheries and trading routes fuelled temptations of maritime dominion in the Middle Ages as much as they do today. However, over the last two centuries new kinds of resources, such as oil and gas, have assumed primary relevance. New technologies and naval capabilities have also changed the degree of control states can exercise over pelagic spaces and oceans and seas have become more interconnected than ever before.

4 The Oceans, International Law, and Eurocentrism

In general terms, seas are smaller than oceans and are usually located where land and ocean meet. Typically, seas are partially enclosed by land and are less deep than oceans. The term 'ocean' is usually reserved to one of the world's five main bodies of waters: the Atlantic, Pacific, Indian, Arctic, and Antarctic oceans. All combined, these bodies of water cover more than three-fifths of the surface of the globe. They constitute an indispensable connecting link between the continents, as well as an immense reservoir of natural resources. It is then easy to comprehend why the regulation of navigation and maritime interactions has been essential from an early stage.[18]

16 Timo Koivurova, Stefan Kirchner and Pirjo Kleemola-Juntunen, 'The Arctic Ocean: are we ready to govern a new ocean?', in Marta C. Ribeiro, Fernando Loureiro Bastos and Tore Henriksen (eds.), *Global Challenges and the Law of the Sea* (Cham: Springer, 2020), 59–80.

17 Matthew Dyson, 'Comparative legal history: methodology for morphology', in Olivier Moréteau, Aniceto Masferrer and Kjell A. Modéer (eds.), *Comparative Legal History* (Cheltenham-Northampton: Edward Elgar, 2019), 110–38, at 110.

18 David J. Bederman, 'The sea', in Bardo Fassbender and Anne Peters (eds.), *The Oxford Handbook of the History of International Law* (Oxford: University Press, 2012), 359–79.

This book begins with an overview of the late medieval 'claimed seas' tendencies across the seas bordering Europe, both to the South and the North of the continent. Afterwards, it addresses the role played by oceangoing navigation on the further development of 'claimed seas' policies in the Early Modern Age. As soon as European sailors started to systematically challenge the open waters of the Atlantic Ocean, they felt the need to legally justify national-political agendas aimed at seaborne expansion. This formed an unprecedented challenge for early modern lawyers and diplomats as the endless expanses of the oceans gave rise to much greater questions compared to smaller seas such as the Baltic or the Mediterranean. Even though the opposite ideas of the 'claimed seas', and the freedom of the sea (*mare liberum*), had already been outlined in earlier epochs, they assumed a totally new dimension once the oceans became the spatial reference. In other words, I will argue that the oceans played a major role in triggering more profound and radical speculations on the legal status of the sea.

The period taken into consideration by the volume consists of the transitional centuries between the Late Middle Ages and the Early Modern Age.[19] However, within this broad timeframe, particular focus is devoted to the second half of the sixteenth and first half of the seventeenth centuries (Chapters 3 and 4). The choice of the timeframe indirectly relativises the importance of the Peace of Westphalia (1648), traditionally viewed as the starting point of a modern 'international law'.[20] From a geospatial perspective, the book moves across three macro-regions: first, the Mediterranean Sea; second, the seas of northern Europe; and third, the oceans. All these pelagic spaces are here

19 This choice allows to underline changes while acknowledging the significant continuities between the late medieval and early modern inter-polity law (or law of nations). See Oliver Diggelmann, 'The periodization of the history of international law', in Fassbender and Peters (eds.), *The Oxford Handbook of the History of International Law*, 1009–10; Ignacio de la Rasilla del Moral, 'The Problem of Periodization in the History of International Law', *Law and History Review*, 37(1) (2019), 275–308; William E. Butler, 'Periodisation and international law', in Orakhelashvili (ed.), *Research Handbook on the Theory and History of International Law*, 281–95; Heinard Steiger, 'From the International Law of Christianity to the International Law of the World Citizen. Reflections on the Formation of the Epochs of the History of International Law', *Journal of the History of International Law*, 3(2) (2001), 180–93.

20 See, among others, Andreas Osiander, 'Sovereignty, International Relations, and the Westphalian Myth', *International Organization*, 55(2) (2001), 251–87. See also Randall Lesaffer, 'Law and history: law between past and present', in Bart van Klink and Sanne Taekema (eds.), *Law and Method: Interdisciplinary Research into Law* (Tübingen: Mohr Siebeck, 2011), 133–52.

understood as frameworks for historical and legal analysis, first separately (Chapters 1–3) and then with a focus on interconnectedness and comparison (Chapter 4).[21]

This book naturally finds its collocation within the broader subject of the history of international law. If the Early Modern Age represented a time of innovation in European international relations and new geographical knowledge, it also coincided with the rise of the 'law of nations' as a separate branch of legal science and learning.[22] Many changes in the latter field were linked, caused by, or had an impact on the way pelagic areas were legally approached. For instance, the rise of the modern state and the concepts of sovereignty and jurisdiction, the adoption of resident embassies, and the evolution of the laws of war and natural law theories, all eventually feature in this work. It has long been maintained that the historical development of the law of the sea, and more broadly of 'modern' international law, has been remarkably eurocentric.[23] In reaction, authors such as Charles H. Alexandrowitz and Ram P. Anand have highlighted, for instance, the importance of the maritime laws and customs that had evolved across maritime Asia by the end of the medieval period, well before the arrival of the Europeans via the Cape

---

21 Jerry H. Bentley, 'Sea and Ocean Basins as Frameworks of Historical Analysis', *Geographical Review*, 89(2) (1999), 215–24. On spatial frameworks for legal analysis and comparison, see Dag Michaelsen, 'Methodological perspectives in comparative legal history: an analytical approach' in Moréteau, Masferrer and Modéer (eds.), *Comparative Legal History*, 103–4; See Anthony Anghie, 'Identifying regions in the history of international law', in Fassbender and Peters (eds.), *The Oxford Handbook of the History of International Law*, 1058–78.

22 Bo J. Theutenberg, 'Mare Liberum et Mare Clausum', *Arctic*, 37(4) (1984), 481–92, at 484: 'The birth of so called modern international law was closely connected with the law of the sea: in fact, the first rules of modern international law were perhaps the rules governing the use of the sea'. Cf. Randall Lesaffer, 'The classical law of nations', in Orakhelashvili (ed.), *Research Handbook on the Theory and History of International Law*, 410; Alain Wijffels, 'Early-modern scholarship on international law', ibid., 19–57.

23 For an example of this traditional view, see Jan H. W. Verzijl, *Western European Influence on the Foundations of International Law*, in *International Law in Historical Perspective*, I (Leiden: A. W. Sijthoff, 1968), 435–6: 'International law as it now stands is essentially the product of the European mind and has practically been received [...] by American and Asiatic states'. For a more nuanced perspective, see Onuma Yasuaki, 'When Was the Law of International Society Born? An Inquiry of the History of International Law from an Intercivilizational Perspective', *Journal of the History of International Law*, 2(1) (2000), 1–66. See also Alexander Pearce Higgins, 'International law and the outer world, 1450–1648', in John Holland Rose et al. (eds.), *The Cambridge History of the British Empire. Vol 1: The Old Empire. From the Beginnings to 1783* (New York/Cambridge: Macmillan/University Press, 1929), 183–204.

Route.[24] Hassan S. Khalilieh has more recently expounded the contribution of Islamic thought to the law of the sea.[25] These authors have highlighted the not-necessarily Western European lineage of the doctrine of the freedom of the sea, drawing on the long traditions of freedom of navigation and trade in the Indian Ocean and the Islamic Mediterranean.

At the threshold of Modernity, the European law of nations was indeed merely one of several regional systems, coexisting with others such as those of the Muslim world, China, and the Indian subcontinent and Southeast Asia. At the time, the 'rise' of Western Europe was far from inevitable. For example, fifteenth-century Ming China (1368–1644) possessed all the resources necessary to potentially impose a distinctly Chinese way of conceiving the sea. However, the great oceangoing expeditions lead by the Ming Admiral Zheng He between 1405 and 1433 – which by all accounts dwarfed European contemporaries – were soon followed by isolationist policies.[26] In the following centuries, China, Muslim empires (and other Asian polities too) largely left the initiative of long-range navigation and colonisation to European nations.

The Early Modern Age can be conceived as the formative period for the European-made law of the sea that European colonial empires eventually suc-

---

24 Charles H. Alexandrowicz, *An Introduction to the History of the Law of Nations in the East Indies (16th, 17th and 18th Centuries)* (Oxford: Clarendon Press, 1967); idem, *The Law of Nations in Global History*, edited by David Armitage and Jennifer Pitts (Oxford: University Press, 2017); Ram P. Anand, *Origin and Development of the Law of the Sea. History of International Law Revisited* (The Hague-Boston-London: M. Nijhoff, 1983); idem, 'Maritime Practice in South-East Asia until 1600 A. D. and the Modern Law of the Sea', *The International and Comparative Law Quarterly*, 30(2) (1981), 440–54; idem, *Studies in International Law and History. An Asian Perspective* (Leiden/Boston: M. Nijhoff, 2004).

25 Hassan S. Khalilieh, *Islamic Law of the Sea: Freedom of Navigation and Passage Rights in Islamic Thought* (Cambridge: University Press, 2019); idem, *Admiralty and Maritime Laws in the Mediterranean Sea (ca. 800–1050): The Kitāb Akriyat Al-Sufun Vis-à-Vis the Nomos Rhodion Nautikos* (Leiden/Boston: Brill, 2006).

26 Ron Harris, *Going the Distance: Eurasian Trade and the Rise of the Business Corporation, 1400–1700* (Princeton: University Press, 2020), 226–34; Abulafia, *The Boundless Sea*, 236–50; Louise Levathes, *When China Ruled the Seas: The Treasure Fleet of the Dragon Throne 1405–1433* (New York: Simon & Schuster, 1994); Ying Liu, Zhongping Chen and Gregory Blue (eds.), *Zheng He's Maritime Voyages (1405–1433) and China's Relations with the Indian Ocean World: A Multilingual Bibliography* (Leiden: Brill, 2014); Edward L. Dreyer, *Zheng He: China and the Oceans in the Early Ming Dynasty, 1405–1433* (New York: Pearson Longman, 2006); Kuei-Sheng Chang, 'The Maritime Scene in China at the Dawn of Great European Discoveries', *Journal of the American Oriental Society*, 94(3) (1974), 347–59; Robert Finlay, 'The Voyages of Zheng He: Ideology, State Power, and Maritime Trade in Ming China', *Journal of The Historical Society*, 8(3) (2008), 327–47; Craig A. Lockard, '"The Sea Common to All"; Maritime Frontiers, Port Cities, and Chinese Traders in the Southeast Asian Age of Commerce, ca. 1400–1750', *Journal of World History*, 21(2) (2010), 219–47, at 227–8.

ceeded in imposing worldwide, albeit only later, starting from the eighteenth century. From this point of view, it seems undeniable that European legal culture, and understanding regarding what the law actually is, shaped the customary law of the sea that remained the reference until the second half of the twentieth century and the successive codification efforts sponsored by the United Nations.[27] European jurists and decision makers, well before Cristopher Columbus' and Vasco da Gama's times, conceived the possibility of acquiring exclusive rights over sea areas, debating in the strictly intertwined arenas of politics and law. The idea itself of claiming dominion over pelagic areas appears as a product of European legal-political thinking, albeit a fiercely contested one from its inception.

Today, the landscape looks markedly different. European and Western perspectives on the law of the sea and ocean governance now represent only one of many factors shaping their evolution.[28] Political scientists speak of an ongoing process of de-westernisation in the realms of international relations, which may well apply to the law of the sea and ocean governance.[29] Decolonisation, the enlargement of the international community, and the relative decline western states' share of global GDP have shifted the global balance of power. Developing countries now make up the majority of the international community, and (re)emerging great powers such as China and India play an increasingly prominent role in shaping the complex and diverse interests that underpin the law of the sea – just as they did five centuries ago.

5 Methodology and Sources

5.1 *Methodology*

Throughout this volume, state practice and doctrinal works are examined in conjunction to shed light on the development of the law of the sea in general and the concept of 'claimed seas' in particular. State practice played a central

27 Bederman, 'The Sea', 360–1. See also Martti Koskenniemi, 'Histories of International Law: Dealing with Eurocentrism', *Rechtsgeschichte. Zeitschrift des Max-Planck-Instituts für europäische Rechtsgeschichte*, 19 (2011), 152–76.

28 Surabhi Ranganathan, 'Decolonization and International Law: Putting the Ocean on the Map', *Journal of the History of International Law*, 23(1) (2020), 161–83; idem, 'Global Commons', *European Journal of International Law*, 27(3) (2016), 693–717. See also Renisa Mawani, 'The law of the sea', in Peter D. Burdon and James Martel (eds.), *The Routledge Handbook of Law and the Anthropocene* (London: Routledge, 2023), 115–29.

29 Didier Billion and Christophe Ventura, *Désoccidentalisation. Repenser l'ordre du monde* (Agone: Marseille, 2023).

role in the genesis of the corpus of customary rules regulating 'inter-polity' relations at sea, especially as long as a theoretical legal science was not yet developed. What polities and princes did appears critical and tells much about their legal understanding of the sea. As such, the volume participates in a broader 'turn to history' in international law[30] and, within that turn, to the increasing possibilities for a history of the practice of international law.[31] Nevertheless, doctrinal-theoretical works remain essential for the depth of their analyses and the introduction of new concepts. Moreover, they contributed to the establishment of the law of nations (later international law) as a separate subject of study. Seminal works such as Hugo Grotius' *Mare liberum* and John Selden's *Mare clausum* did influence the policies of entire nations.

An analysis of doctrinal works divorced from their politico-historical context would severely limit our understanding, as legal sources are neither autonomous nor self-contained.[32] Many jurists who addressed the legal status of the sea were closely connected to governmental circles, with ardent patriotism often shaping their arguments as they sought to advance national interests. Natural law rules and high principles such as the freedom of navigation were whole-heartedly defended and rapidly abandoned according to changing circumstances. With this in mind, the volume examines state practice and doctrine in tandem, asserting that they influenced one another and offer complementary perspectives on the emergence of the concept of 'claimed seas'. By doing so, it maps the political-legal frameworks deployed to conceptualise

30 Ignacio de la Rasilla del Moral, *International Law and History: Modern Interfaces* (Cambridge: University Press, 2021), 11–40; Raphael Cahen, Frederik Dhondt and Elisabetta Fiocchi Malaspina, 'L'essor récent de l'histoire du droit international', *Clio@Thémis*, 18 (2020), 1–7; Bardo Fassbender and Anne Peters, 'Introduction: Towards a global history of international law', in idem (eds.), *The Oxford Handbook of the History of International Law*, 1–24; Randall Lesaffer and Anne Peters (eds.), *The Historiography of International Law*, vol. 1, *The Cambridge History of International Law* (Cambridge: University Press, 2024).

31 Frederik Dhondt, 'Looking Beyond the Tip of the Iceberg: Diplomatic Praxis and Legal Culture in the History of Public International Law', *Rechtskultur*, 2 (2013), 31–42; Frederik Dhondt, 'The historiography of international law on the European continent', in Lesaffer and Peters (eds.), *The Historiography of International Law*, 244–72; Lesaffer, 'Law and history', 133–52; Cahen, Dhondt and Fiocchi Malaspina, 'L'essor récent', 1–7; Anthony Carty, 'Doctrine versus state practice', in Fassbender and Peters (eds.), *The Oxford Handbook of the History of International Law*, 972–96.

32 Dirk Heirbaut, 'Reading past legal texts, a tale of two legal histories. Some personal reflections on the methodology of legal history', in Dag Michalsen (ed.), *Reading Past Legal Texts* (Oslo: Unipax, 2006), 92–3; de la Rasilla del Moral, *International Law and History*, 41–74.

legal regimes at sea and highlights their instrumental use by political actors as a layer of persuasion for achieving state and non-state objectives.[33] The volume thus seeks to reveal the intricate entanglement of law and politics that continues to underpin the law of the sea, while critically assessing the persistent gap between legal-dogmatic approaches and state practice.

If we accept the distinction between 'traditional legal history' and 'contextual legal history',[34] this volume aspires to be included in the second category. The emergence of the 'claimed seas' in legal argumentation was deeply intertwined with state politics as well as broader historical cycles. Hence, great importance is given to the historical, economic, and political background in which legal developments took place. In other words, contextualisation appears essential to a correct interpretation of what different actors understood as acceptable exclusive rights over the sea.[35] Throughout the following chapters, context is conceived in a broad sense, in no way restricted to the chronologically immediate one. For instance, Chapter 1 includes an overview of Roman law concerning the sea as well as an account of the role played by the papacy in late medieval international relations since they both heavily influenced early modern debates on the 'claimed seas'.

Matthew Craven has identified three different forms of international legal history.[36] First, history in international law; second, international law in history; and third, history of international law. Randall Lesaffer points out that such categories may be applied to general legal history too.[37] The first category (history in international law), consists of an instrumental approach to legal history. It is not interested in the faithful representation of past events, but more in using them to serve present purposes.[38] The second category (international law in history), involves the historical analysis of law within its broader political, cultural, social, and economic backgrounds. The mutual interplay between law and society, in a defined time and place, becomes central. In this case, 'the historical law of that given time and place is studied as a

33 Afterall, international law might still today be characterised as an 'art of persuasion', see Iain Scobbie, 'Rhetoric, persuasion, and interpretation in international law', in Andrea Bianchi, Daniel Peat and Matthew Windsor (eds.), *Interpretation in International* Law (Oxford: University Press, 2015), 61–77.

34 Heirbaut, 'Reading past legal texts', 94.

35 Ibid., 92–4.

36 Matthew Craven, 'Introduction: international law and its histories', in idem, Malgosia Fitzmaurice and Maria Vogiatzi (eds.), *Time, History and International Law* (Leiden: Brill, 2007), 7.

37 Lesaffer, 'Law and history', 133–4.

38 Ibid., 134–5.

phenomenon within the particular society the historian is interested in and not as a phase within the evolution of the law'.[39] The last category of literature (history of international law), follows a middle path between the other two. Even though it is more historical in its approach, it is often evolutionary-genealogical since its main concern is the gradual evolution of the law, or particular legal systems, concepts, and institutions, from past to present.

Lesaffer underlines the danger of approaching history in a genealogic fashion, since it easily presents it as a smooth process of progress, tracing clear lines of connection from the past to the present.[40] The American legal historian Robert Gordon points out that lawyers' temptation to look into the past to find support for the issues of the present can easily bring them to identify historical continuities where there are none.[41] In such cases, the legitimisation of contemporary politics becomes the main aim of the research. Andrew Fitzmaurice also underlines that proper contextualisation is needed to avoid 'the political manipulation of the past' for present purposes. Such manipulation can serve positive aims but also be employed for less noble ends.[42]

In relation to the historical development of claims over the sea, the temptation to write an instrumental and potentially a-historical 'history of international law' may be strong, especially if we consider the economic and geopolitical implications of contemporary debates on ocean governance. Having the legal status of the sea as object of investigation one should be careful not to trace a too-linear evolution of concepts and institutions. For instance, Arnold Raestad, an influential author of the last century, named his major work on the historical development of the law of the sea, *La mer territoriale, études historiques et juridiques* (1913), basically tracing back in time the concept of territorial sea as far as classical Rome. Nowadays, it seems difficult to trace the

---

39 Ibid., 136.

40 Randall Lesaffer, 'International law and its history: the story of an unrequited love', in Craven, Fitzmaurice and Vogiatzi (eds.), *Time, History and International Law*, 34–5. Lesaffer specifies that the issue is not the evolutionary approach in itself, but the fact that it often involves 'evolutional history of the worst kind', which 'leads to anachronistic interpretations of historical phenomena, clouds historical realities that bear no fruit in our own times and gives no information about the historical context of the phenomenon one claims to recognise', besides it describes 'history in terms of similarities with or differences from the present, and not in terms of what it was'. Cf. Craven, 'Introduction: International law and its histories', ibid., 9; Heirbaut, 'Reading past legal texts', 92–5.

41 Robert W. Gordon, *Taming the Past: Essays on Law in History and History in Law* (Cambridge: University Press, 2018), 17–49.

42 Andrew Fitzmaurice, 'Context in the History of International Law', *Journal of the History of International Law*, 20(1) (2018), 5–30, at 13.

modern concept of the territorial sea before the eighteenth century.[43] Another example of a potential anachronistic trap might be a carefree use of the notion of 'maritime sovereignty' while addressing historical periods, e.g. the Middle Ages, during which the concept was yet unknown.

The international law scholar Anne Orford has criticised contextual histories of international law, especially regarding their supposed treatment of anachronism as a 'supreme sin' and what she viewed as 'methodological policing'.[44] In *On International Legal Method*, she identifies a difference between juridical and historical thinking. In her view, international lawyers, being 'trained in the art of making meaning move across time', have the right to approach the past in more flexible terms, focusing on its perceived bearing for present concerns.[45] In other words, she points out the risk that a too-strict contextualisation of the past could make it inconsequential for today's necessities, weakening its power to enlighten the politics of the present. The historian of international law Martti Koskenniemi welcomed Orford's critique, somehow departing from his methodological notes contained in earlier works.[46] In the article *Vitoria and Us. Thoughts on Critical Histories of International Law* he argues that 'even as contextualism opens a necessary avenue for the examination of past legal and political vocabularies, it is not without its difficulties', since it inclines 'to rely on a 'positivist' separation between the past and the present that encourages a historical relativism and ends up suppressing or undermining efforts to find patterns in history that might account for today's experiences of domination and injustice'.[47] Thus, he notes that even though contextualism has its own merits, it cannot be the only focus of international legal history that needs to be relevant for the present.[48]

Lauren Benton vigorously replied to Orford' critique of 'contextualism', reaffirming the importance of context, conceived in a deeper and broader sense, also suggesting that 'historians and lawyers can find a settled foundation for at least two elements of a shared enterprise that do not require particular meth-

---

43 Arnold Raestad, *La mer territoriale, études historiques et juridiques* (Paris: A. Pedone Éditeur, 1913).

44 Anne Orford, 'On International Legal Method', *London Review of International Law*', 1(1) (2013), 166–97.

45 Ibid., 172–4.

46 For instance, see Martti Koskenniemi, *The Gentle Civilizer of Nations: The Rise and Fall of International Law, 1870–1960* (Cambridge: University Press, 2001), 1–10.

47 Idem, 'Vitoria and Us. Thoughts on Critical Histories of International Law', *Rechtsgeschichte, Journal of the Max Planck Institute for European Legal History*, 22 (2014), 123–4.

48 Ibid., 124.

odological commitments'.[49] First, the pursuit of evidence-based history. Notwithstanding training and favoured research questions, all scholars must provide reliable and verifiable grounds for their assertions and interpretation of past sources, allowing evaluation by other scholars. Second, the commitment to analytical coherence.[50] Being aware of these ongoing methodological debates,[51] I chose to structure my book around the notion of 'claimed seas' – and not, for example, *mare clausum*, a term first employed by John Selden in the seventeenth century – in order to stay clear of easily avoidable anachronisms, giving the right historical perspective to concepts that often required centuries to emerge and consolidate.

As already stated, I employ 'claimed seas' as a general 'umbrella' term, encompassing distinct legal-political claims, developed in different spatio-temporal contexts. My primary scope is not to write an evolutionary history of maritime sovereignty over the sea. This book aims to study the various declinations of the 'claimed seas' principle in their own specific context, underlying and comparing similarities and differences.[52] Only at the end of this process it will be possible to evaluate if and how early modern maritime claims influenced the further development of the law of the sea. Approaching the topic differently would simply amount to a 'fictional' relation to the law of the sea and its slow and multifaceted historical development.

After all, in Lesaffer's words contextual legal history is nothing more than what 'legal historians have been doing since the days of humanistic scholarship: the textual and contextual analysis of their written sources. Historians should see to it that their sources are as authentic as possible. They should try

49 Lauren Benton, 'Beyond Anachronism: Histories of International Law and Global Legal Politics', *Journal of the History of International Law*, 21(1) (2019), 7–40.

50 Ibid., 33. Cf. Kate Purcell, 'On the Uses and Advantages of Genealogy for International Law', *Leiden Journal of International Law*, 33(1) (2020), 13–35.

51 See also Fitzmaurice, 'Context in the History of International Law', 5–30; Valentina Vadi, 'International Law and Its Histories: Methodological Risks and Opportunities', *Harvard International Law Journal*, 58(2) (2017), 311–52; idem, 'Perspective and Scale in the Architecture of International Legal History', *European Journal of International Law*, 30(1) (2019), 53–71; Matilda Arvidsson and Miriam Bak McKenna, 'The Turn to History in International Law and the Sources Doctrine: Critical Approaches and Methodological Imaginaries', *Leiden Journal of International Law*, 33(1) (2020), 37–56; Thomas Skouteris, 'Engaging history in international law', in David Kennedy and José M. Beneyto (eds.), *New Approaches to International Law: The European and American Experiences* (The Hague: T.M.C. Asser Press, 2012), 99–121.

52 Dyson, 'Comparative legal history: methodology for morphology', in Moréteau, Masferrer and Modéer (eds.), *Comparative Legal History*, 110–38.

to read them as the contemporaries of the authors would'.[53] Any legal history 'which fails to understand the past in its own terms and on its own merits will probably fail to bring anything to the discussion other than some random factual proof or some arguments of authority for a preconceived notion that roots, not in the past, but in present law'.[54] The Belgian legal historian adds that before we can learn anything from history that might be relevant for today, we first have to allow history to speak for itself. That is, indeed, what humanist jurists already claimed centuries ago with regard to the study of Roman law.[55]

For our present purposes, it is also relevant to recall Koskenniemi's distinction between two broad ideal types of history of international law. Firstly, 'realist' narratives that focus on state power and geopolitics. They view international law's past in terms of the succession of apologies for State behaviour. Secondly, 'idealist' histories that focus on lawyers and philosophers, and view the past through theoretical-doctrinal debates. The Finnish scholar suggests that neither of these approaches is viable in itself and that both are best seen as presumptive positions or biases.[56] The first category foregrounds diplomacy and conflicts, over which law would throw a veil of justification. The second one highlights the development of laws, institutions and doctrines to which the world of diplomacy and State power only provides the background.[57] The present volume balances these two different perspectives, taking into consideration both the utopian theories and the political realities that shaped the early modern emergence of the 'claimed seas' in legal argumentation. Indeed, it is crucial to underline when and where reality and theoretical ideas diverged, and when, instead, they mutually influenced each other.

53 Lesaffer, 'International law and its history', 34–5; Georg Cavaller, 'Vitoria, Grotius, Pufendorf, Wolff and Vattel: Accomplices of European Colonialism and Exploitation or True Cosmopolitans?', *The Journal of the History of International Law*, 10(2) (2008), 207–8; Fitzmaurice, 'Context in the History of International Law', 12.

54 Lesaffer, 'Law and history', 144. Dirk Heirbaut adds that traditional legal history often sees law as 'undisturbed by social, economic, political or religious changes. The context is unimportant. In legal history this leads to a legal history without history'. In 'Reading past legal texts', 92.

55 Ibidem.

56 Martti Koskenniemi, 'Histories of International Law: Dealing with Eurocentrism', 161. See also idem, *From Apology to Utopia. The Structure of International Legal Argument. Reissue with a New Epilogue* (Cambridge: University Press, 2006).

57 Ibidem. Cf. Orakhelashvili, 'International law, international politics and ideology', 240–79.

5.2 *Sources*

Throughout this volume, primary and secondary sources are employed jointly. From this perspective, Chapter 4 constitutes the core of the volume. It proposes a close reading of the works of early seventeenth-century supporters of the 'claimed seas' and *mare clausum*, namely those by Seraphin de Freitas, Paolo Sarpi, Giulio Pace da Beriga, William Welwod, and John Selden. These authors have been chosen because they provide paradigmatic insights on the three 'claimed seas' traditions, which had arisen across the three macro-regions already identified: the Mediterranean Sea, the seas of northern Europe, and the oceans. Furthermore, they all drafted their works in the 1610s in the immediate aftermath of the publication of Grotius' *Mare liberum*, even though Freitas and Selden published their treaties only a few years later.

All these authors wrote in reaction, or straightforward opposition, to the sixteenth-century emergence of the freedom of the sea in the international arena. This development, occurring both in diplomacy and doctrine, forced a re-elaboration of the traditional arguments used to support 'claimed seas' policies, as well as the creation of new strategies of persuasion. The analysis of Selden's *Mare clausum,* seen as the culmination of this process, closes the analysis. Indeed, it was both the last of these works to be published and the one advocating the highest degree of territorialisation of maritime spaces, or *dominium maris*. That being said, further works defending the two opposite principles continued to be published in the following decades. Thus, my selection of authors is by no means to be considered exhaustive. However, I decided to focus my attention on the 'first generation' of 'claimed seas' defences, ending my survey once the notion reached theoretical consistency.

Even though Grotius' *Mare liberum* is not the main object of this volume, it still represents the reference point for the analysis of his opponents' arguments and ideas. In other words, the works of the advocates of the 'claimed seas' can only be appreciated in relation to the opposite idea of the freedom of the seas. Consequently, Chapter 3 examines Grotius' *Mare liberum,* focusing on its historical role as a trigger for the (re)emergence of the 'claimed seas' in legal argumentation, but also on Fernando Vázquez y Menchaca's less known treatise *Controversiarum illustrium*, which in fact anticipated and inspired several of Grotius' arguments.[58] Thus, a substantial portion of the book is devoted to the analysis of the doctrinal works mentioned above. That said, an equally important consideration is given to the development of the 'claimed

58 For the complete list of the doctrinal works analysed in the book I refer to the bibliography, section 1.1.

seas' principle in state practice, diplomacy and politics. In this regard, based on the broad timeframe and different geographical macro-regions taken into consideration, the focus has rested on printed sources. Collections of historical treaties and diplomatic documents have been employed throughout the volume in an interwoven way to reconstruct the state practice related to the 'claimed seas'.

For instance, Wilhelm G. Grewe's selection of documents contained in the two volumes of *Fontes Historiae Iuris Gentium*, offers a valid support through the various 'epochs' of international law identified by the author.[59] Frances G. Davenport's *European Treaties Bearing on the History of the United States and its Dependencies to 1648* and Jean du Mont de Carels-Kroon's *Corps universel diplomatique du droit des gens* have proved crucial for the book's purposes and are copiously referenced throughout the book. Davenport in particular compiles the most relevant international treaties and papal bulls of the Age of Exploration, accompanied by valuable background information.[60] Papal documents, especially Alexander VI's bulls, are also included in Alfonso García-Gallo's, *Las bulas de Alejandro VI y el ordenamiento juriídico de la expansioón portuguesa y castellana en África e Indias*.[61]

In relation to Iberian seaborne expansion, dealt with in Chapter 2, I dived into specialised collections of archival sources. They provided hundreds of relevant documents for reconstructing Iberian 'claimed seas' aspirations over the oceans. Firstly, the one edited by Antonio J. Dias Dinis, *Monumenta Henricina, colectaânea documental relativa ao Infante D. Henrique,* which focuses on Portuguese endeavours at the time of Prince Henry the Navigator. Secondly, José R. Coelho's *Alguns documentos do Archivo Nacional da Torre do Tombo ácerca das navegações e conquistas portuguezas...*, and Vitorino M. Godinho's, *Documentos sôbre a expansão portuguesa.* Thirdly, Martín Fernández de Navarrete, *Colección de los viajes y descubrimientos que hicieron por mar los españoles desde fines del siglo XV,* which includes documents on the

59 Wilhelm G. Grewe, *Fontes Historiae Iuris Gentium*, II vols (Berlin-New York: De Gruyter, 1992).

60 Frances G. Davenport, *European Treaties Bearing on the History of the United States and its Dependencies to 1648* (Washington: The Carnegie Institution, 1917); Jean du Mont de Carels-Kroon, *Corps universel diplomatique du droit des gens; contenant un recueil des traitez d'alliance, de paix, de treve, de neutralité, de commerce, d'échange ...* (Amsterdam: chez P. Brunel, R. et G. Wetstein [etc.], 1726–31) (*CUD* in footnotes).

61 Alfonso García-Gallo, *Las bulas de Alejandro VI y el ordenamiento juriídico de la expansioón portuguesa y castellana en África e Indias* (Madrid: Instituto Nacional de Estudios Juriídicos, 1958).

first phase of Castilian discoveries.[62] Fourthly, *Quadro elementar das relações políticas e diplomáticas de Portugal com as diversas potencias do mundo*, edited by the Visconde de Santarem, notably regarding the diplomatic intercourse between England and Portugal in the second half of the seventeenth century.[63]

In relation to the Nordic kingdoms, primary sources have been consulted through the online versions of the *Diplomatarum Norvegicum* (Norway) and the *Diplomatarum Danicum* (Denmark).[64] The online version of the *Diplomatarum Norvegicum* makes available approximately 20,000 *diplomas*, i.e. letters and documents related to Norway between the years 1050 and 1590. In addition, I consulted Lars R. Laursen's *Danmark-Norges Traktater 1523–1750, med dertil hørende Aktstykker*, to better understand the diplomatic tensions between England and Denmark–Norway at the turn of the sixteenth century, notably Dano-Norwegian legal arguments.[65]

Regarding England, the *Calendars of State Papers Foreign* have been rather useful as a navigation tool. Moreover, I made use of Pierre Chaplais' *English Medieval Diplomatic Practice*,[66] Reginald G. Marsden's *Documents Relating to the Law and Custom of the Sea, 1205–1767* and John Rushworth's *Historical Collections*, which contains documents and related to James VI–I and Charles I's reigns in England and Scotland.[67] In addition, Thomas Rymer's collection *Foe-*

62 António J. Dias Dinis (ed.), *Monumenta Henricina, colectaânea documental relativa ao Infante D. Henrique* (Coimbra: Oficinas Gráficas de Atlântida, 1960–74), 15 vols; Martín Fernández de Navarrete, *Colección de los viajes y descubrimientos que hicieron por mar los españoles desde fines del siglo XV: con varios documentos ...*, II (*Documentos de Colon y de las primeras poblaciones*) (Madrid: Imprimeria Nacional, 1859); José R. Coelho, *Alguns documentos do Archivo Nacional da Torre do Tombo ácerca das navegações e conquistas portuguezas...* (Lisboa: Imprensa Nacional, 1892); Vitorino M. Godinho, *Documentos sôbre a expansão portuguesa*, vols. I–II (Lisboa: Editorial Gleba, 1943–44); idem, *Documentos sôbre a expansão portuguesa* (Lisboa: Edições Cosmos, 1956).

63 Manuel F. de Barros y Sousa, Visconde de Santarem, *Quadro elementar das relações políticas e diplomáticas de Portugal com as diversas potencias do mundo, desde o principio da monarchia Portugueza até aos nossos dias*, vol. XV (Lisboa: Tipographia da Academia Real das Sciencas, 1865).

64 https://www.dokpro.uio.no/dipl_norv/diplom_field_eng.html; https://diplomatarium.dk/.

65 Lars R. Laursen, *Danmark-Norges Traktater 1523–1750. Med dertil hørende Aktstykker*, 11 dele i 12 bind (København: Gad, 1905–49).

66 Pierre Chaplais, *English Medieval Diplomatic Practice* (London: Her Majesty's Stationery Office, 1982).

67 Reginald G. Marsden, *Documents Relating to the Law and Custom of the Sea, 1205–1767*, 2 vols. (London: printed for the Navy Records Society, 1915–16); John Rushworth, *Historical Collections of Private Passages of State, Weighty Matters in Law, Remarkable Proceed-*

dera has been used with its large amount of background correspondence and documents concerning diplomatic manoeuvring between England and its neighbours.[68]

The detailed reports written by early modern Venetian Ambassadors, both in the series edited by Eugenio Alberi and those edited by Nicolò Barozzi and Guglielmo Berchet, have provided yet another valuable source of information.[69] They feature first-hand insights on diplomatic-political relations and princely courts of the time, as seen through the keen eyes of Venetian resident and extraordinary ambassadors. Interestingly for our purposes, Venetian envoys always showed a particular interest in the maritime-naval affairs of the hosting country and the broader geopolitical context.

6 The Historiography of the 'Claimed Seas'

A great deal of literature has dealt with the emergence of the freedom of the seas, and especially with Grotius' *Mare liberum*, to the immediate context that motivated its publication as well as its place in the evolution of the author's legal thought. However, in relation to the principle of the 'claimed seas', things appear different. Firstly, the 'pre-Grotian' development of jurisdictional claims over the sea has drawn less attention, because of the bias of considering the further development of the law of the sea as a complete victory of the freedom of the seas. Secondly, many of the authors who replied to Grotius defending 'claimed seas' pretensions have been generally obscured by the long-lasting ascendancy of the Dutchman among later generations of jurists and the central place he acquired in the western legal tradition canon. However, some of them developed surprisingly modern views concerning the sea, which deserve more consideration. The fact that the notion of 'claimed seas' continued to be

---

ings in Five Parliaments: Beginning the Sixteenth Year of King James. Anno 1618, And Ending the Fifth Year of King Charles [*sic*], *Anno 1629* (London: printed by Thomas Newcomb for George Thomason, 1659–1701).

68 Thomas Rymer, *Foedera, conventiones, literæ, et cujuscunque generis acta publica, inter reges Angliæ et alios quosvis imperatores, reges, pontifices, principes, vel communitates, ab ineunte sæculo duodecimo, viz. ab anno 1101, ad nostra usque tempora habita aut tractate* ... (Hagæ Comitis: apud Joannem Neaulme, 1742); idem (ed.), *Foedera, conventiones, literæ, et cujuscunque generis acta publica, inter reges Angliæ et alios* [...], 4 vols., revised ed. by Adam F. Clarke and Fred Hoolbroke (London, 1816–69).

69 Eugenio Alberi (ed.), *Relazioni degli ambasciatori Veneti al Senato* (Firenze: Societaà editrice fiorentina [etc.], 1839–63); Guglielmo Berchet and Nicolò Barozzi (eds.), *Relazioni degli Stati Europei lette al Senato dagli ambasciatori veneti nel secolo decimosettimo* (Venezia: P. Naratovich, 1856–77).

central in state practice in the decades following the publication of *Mare liberum* is often conveniently neglected for sake of linearity.

In addition, the most influential monographs on the topic are dated, although they remain essential reference works to this day. In 1913, the already mentioned Norwegian scholar Raestad published a study on the historical evolution of the territorial seas.[70] Two other key works are Thomas W. Fulton's *The Sovereignty of the Sea* and Pitman B. Potter's, *The Freedom of the Sea in History, Law and Politics*, published in 1911 and 1924, respectively.[71] Fulton provided an in-depth study focused on the issues of North Sea fisheries and British closed sea claims. However, he also included a valuable historical introduction to maritime claims in general. Potter's work contains several references to closed sea claims, but it remains mostly devoted to the freedom of the sea.[72] Indeed, it was influenced by the historical context of the *interbellum* in which it was published.

More recently, the Indian international law scholar Ram Prakash Anand published *Origin and Development of the Law of the Sea* (1983). In it, he provided a thought-provoking overview of the historical developments of the law of the sea, attempting to balance the long-standing eurocentricity of the subject's historiography by applying TWAIL insights. To do so, he focused on events occurring in Asian waters before and after the arrival of the Portuguese.[73] Michael J. Feakes's unpublished Ph.D. dissertation titled *Formative Influences on the Evolution of International Law: A Case Study of Territorial Waters (1550–1650)* provides a survey of the early modern development of law of the sea, albeit focused on the issue of the breadth of territorial waters.[74]

In 2019, the French historian Guillaume Calafat authored a remarkable volume on the historical development of maritime sovereignty, *Une mer jalousée.*

70 Raestad, *La mer territoriale*.

71 Thomas W. Fulton, *The Sovereignty of the Sea* (London-Edinburgh: William Blackwood & Sons, 1911); Potter, *The Freedom of the Sea*.

72 A similar remark applies to: Francis T. Piggott, *The Freedom of the Seas. Historically Treated* (London: H.M. Stationery Office, 1920); Luis García Arias, *Historia del principio de la libertad de los mares* (Santiago: Editora Universitaria Compostelana, 1946); Gundolf Fahl, *El principio de la libertad de los mares. Práctica de los Estados de 1493 a 1648* (Madrid: Instituto de Estudios Políticos, 1974).

73 Anand, *Origin and Development*. On TWAIL and post-colonial approaches to the history of international law, see de la Rasilla del Moral, *International Law and History*, 117–51. Cf. Alexandrowicz, *History of the Law of Nations in the East Indies*.

74 Michael J. Feakes, *Formative Influences on the Evolution of International Law: A Case Study of Territorial Waters (1550–1650)* (Ph.D. dissertation, University of Hull, 1994).

Contribution à l'histoire de la souveraineté (Méditerranée, XVIIe siècle).[75] Although it focuses on maritime claims and concepts developed across the early modern Mediterranean, it also provides stimulating considerations in a broader perspective, namely the dispute between *mare liberum* and *mare clausum* and the development of central concepts such as *iurisdictio* (jurisdiction). The already mentioned *Islamic Law of the Sea. Freedom of Navigation and Passage Rights in Islamic Thought* by Hassan S. Khalilieh (2019) also includes a substantial chapter on 'offshore sovereignty and the territorial sea'.[76]

In addition to the above-mentioned monographs, numerous journal articles, book chapters, and volumes have been published on some of the topics included in the present work. They provided valuable analyses and inputs that are duly taken into consideration in the following pages. However, they usually address specific authors, regions or topics and do not comprehensively address the long-term development of the notion of 'claimed seas' across different macro-regions as this book has the ambition to do.

7 Outline

The structure of the book is as follows. Chapter 1 delves into late medieval legal discussions and state practice related to the 'claimed seas'. It focuses especially on the Mediterranean Sea and the seas of northern Europe, i.e. the main areas of maritime activity for Europeans at the time. Various polities extended their power over the surrounding seas and were confronted with the issue of legally justifying their pretensions. Such phenomenon interacted with the revival of legal science and the establishment of universities. Two 'claimed seas' traditions developed autonomously from each other in the South (the maritime republics of Venice and Genoa) and the North (the kingdoms of Norway and Denmark). This duality encourages reflections on how two different legal traditions, one very learned and the other more practically oriented, dealt with the phenomenon of maritime claims. The geopolitical background of the Late Middle Ages is outlined to contextualise the analysis, as well as a concise account of Roman legal thought on the sea, due to its long-lasting influence. In other words, Chapter 1 lays the necessary foundations for the following ones.

75 Guillaume Calafat, *Une mer jalousée. Contribution à l'histoire de la souveraineté (Méditerranée, XVIIe siècle)* (Paris: Éditions du Seuil, 2019).

76 Khalilieh, *Islamic Law of the Sea*, ch. 2, 95–169.

Chapter 2 radically enlarges the spatial context taken into consideration. It follows the first endeavours of the 'Age of Exploration', examining how Portuguese and Spanish seafarers opened new routes through the world oceans and how both Iberian crowns sought to monopolise their use. In the beginning, the Atlantic Ocean became a contested frontier between the two neighbours, with the papacy playing a cumbersome role. Only in 1494, the two Iberian kingdoms reached a compromise with the Treaty of Tordesillas. From that time onwards, Spain and Portugal focused on excluding newcomers from their respective spheres of influence. As a result, a new 'claimed seas' tradition developed in relation to the oceans, initially distinct from the two medieval traditions introduced in Chapter 1. It was partially built on different legal grounds since pre-existing legal concepts, conceived having as reference smaller seas, appeared inadequate to regulate the endless oceanic expanses. The nautical maps of the turn of the fifteenth century clearly convey the difficulty of visualising the oceans and related legal claims.

Chapter 3 explores the aftermath of Iberian oceanic expansion. In the first half of the sixteenth century, Spain and Portugal held on to their duopoly in the face of unrelenting attacks by pirates and maritime raiders. In the second half of the century, other seafaring nations, such as France, England, and the Dutch Republic, openly challenged Spain and Portugal and their closed sea claims. They sought to impose a freedom of navigation paradigm by diplomatic, doctrinal, and military means. Consequently, the idea of the freedom of the seas emerged in legal argumentation, applied alike to the open oceans and to European waters. In this context, the Dutch scholar Hugo Grotius published the legal brief *Mare liberum* in 1609. It played a crucial role in crystallising the opposing views on the legal status of the sea, igniting a debate that is influential to this day. More specifically, it forced those who disagreed with Grotius' views to articulate the justifications for the 'claimed seas' in a clearer way than ever before. With its focus on the freedom of the sea, Chapter 3 can be conceived as a sort of fulcrum around which the three chapters devoted to the 'claimed seas' rotate.

Chapters 4 constitutes the core of the present work. It addresses the reactions to Grotius' *Mare liberum* and the (re)emergence of 'claimed seas' discourse in the first decades of the seventeenth century, both in the interpolity and doctrinal arenas. Many jurists, from different backgrounds, reacted to Grotius' pamphlet. They wrote treatises defending the idea that states could acquire exclusive rights over the seas. Generally, these authors have been less studied than has been Grotius, and this volume contributes a new and contextual analysis of their works. The chapter assesses how the principle of the 'claimed seas' confirmed itself as the adversary of the freedom of the seas, gaining new momentum in the immediate aftermath of *Mare liberum*'s publication. This process culminated in 1635 with the publication of *Mare clausum seu de dominio maris* (*The Closed Sea or the Dominion of the Sea*) by the English scholar John Selden. The chapter explores and compares the similarities and differences of the arguments employed by the most prominent authors involved, also showing how opportunism shaped states' policies concerning the 'claimed seas'. Finally, the book's conclusions briefly assess how the opposition between *mare liberum* and *mare clausum* influenced the further development of the law of the sea, as well as the significance of *mare clausum* in present times.

As a coherent whole, these chapters seek to unravel the historical development of 'claimed seas' legal-political argumentation in the pre-modern world across three different macro-regions: the Mediterranean Sea, the seas of northern Europe, and the oceans. They critically discuss how historical events and trends, such as oceanic explorations and the emergence of the freedom of the sea, affected pretensions of exclusive rights over the sea, producing a revival of the principle in the early seventeenth century. Furthermore, they investigate how the three 'claimed seas' traditions identified above (Mediterranean, northern European, and oceanic) developed separately, starting to interact in a consistent way only at the turn of the sixteenth century.

CHAPTER 1

Medieval 'Claimed Seas' Temptations

For doute it nat but that he wolde have be
Lorde and master aboute the rounde see,
And kepte it sure, to stoppe oure enmyes hens,
And wonne us gode and wisely brought it thens,
That no passage shulde be wythought daungere.[1]

1 Premises

1.1 *International Relations at the End of the Middle Ages*

The emergence of the 'claimed seas' in the Late Middle Ages can only be fully understood within the context of the European law of nations system of that era. The geopolitical and legal framework of the time significantly shaped how Europeans perceived the sea and formulated legal arguments to assert exclusive rights over it. Two universalist institutions – the Holy Roman Empire and the papacy of Rome – played pivotal roles in medieval international relations, fostering a relatively coherent western European political community.[2] Throughout the Middle Ages, these institutions exerted varying degrees of influence over the continent's polities, particularly from a legal perspective.[3] The prerogatives of the two institutions were theoretically distinct, respectively focusing on the temporal and spiritual matters. Nonetheless, over the centuries they frequently clashed in their pursuit of hegemony over the *respublica Christiana*, the collective body of European peoples united by the Christian faith.

1 George Warner (ed.), *The Libelle of Englyshe Polycye. A Poem on the Use of Sea Power, 1436* (Oxford: Clarendon Press, 1926), 53.

2 Lesaffer, *The Classical Law of Nations*, 410.

3 Even though, as Grewe noted: 'At no point in time did the universal powers, Emperor and Pope, exercise a power which extinguished the political autonomy and independence of the temporal holders of particular power'. Wilhelm G. Grewe, *The Epochs of International Law* (Berlin-New York: De Gruyter, 2000), 61–74.

 | DOI:10.1163/9789004741409_003

The conflicts between the Holy Roman Empire and the papacy were often fuelled by the hierocratic ambitions of the successors of Saint Peter, who sought to extend their authority into political and temporal matters.[4] Over time, the papacy amassed significant financial and economic power and established overlordship over vast territories, positioning itself as a dominant force in medieval international relations and a true temporal power. Starting from the eleventh century, the Holy See imposed its primacy within the Church, while claiming precedence vis-à-vis temporal princes. Its followers regarded the pope as the sole vicar of God on earth, to whom all secular lords were obliged to submit.[5] This assertion of power sparked intense debate among civil and canon law jurists. While some supported the papacy's primacy, others championed the emperor's authority, and still others called for a balanced coexistence between the 'two swords'.[6] Scholars generally consider the thirteenth century as the golden age of the papacy, a time when 'it reached the peak of the effectiveness, which it had been moving throughout the twelfth century', but during which also appeared the first stirrings of a future 'decline of that effectiveness'.[7]

Medieval pontiffs had many means at their disposal to influence international relations and princely policies. Their declared aim was to preserve the fragile balance of powers characterising Christian societies, maintaining '*pax et iustitia*' among the believers on Earth, in anticipation of the Heavenly Kingdom.[8] Harold Berman stated that the reform movement led by the popes,

4 The basic principles of papal primacy were derived from the exegesis of a passage of Matthew's gospel: '*Tu es Petrus et super hanc petram edificabo ecclesiam meam* [...] *et tibi dabo claves regni coelorum, et quodcumque ligaveris super terram, erit ligatum et in coelis, et quodcumque solveris super terram, erit solutum et in coelis*'. Matt., XVI, 18–9. Two ideas were derived from this passage: firstly, the creation of the Church as an institution gathering all the baptised Christians, both clerics and lays, in the so-called *ecclesia*. Secondly, the foundation of the government of this body, with the bishop of Rome at its head (i.e. the 'Petrine commission'). See Walter Ullmann, *Principles of Government and Politics in the Middle Ages* (London: Methuen and Co., 1978), 32–3.

5 See for example the universalist incipit of the bull *Romanus Pontifex*, issued by Pope Nicholas V on 8 January 1455. For the text, see Davenport *European Treaties*, doc. 1, 9. See also Harold J. Berman, *Law and Revolution, I: The Formation of the Western Legal Tradition* (Cambridge, MA: Harvard University Press, 1983), 94–9.

6 Stephen C. Neff, *Justice among Nations. A History of International Law* (Cambridge, MA: Harvard University Press, 2014), 52–9.

7 J. A. Watt, 'The Papacy', in David Abulafia (ed.), *The New Cambridge Medieval History, vol. V, 1198–1300* (Cambridge: University Press, 1999), 107–63.

8 Neff, *Justice among Nations*, 55; Hans Wolter and Hans-Georg Beck, 'Civitas Medievale, secoli XII–XIV', in Hubert Jedin (ed.), *Storia della Chiesa* (Milano: Jaca Book, 1975), 202–22; Ullmann, *Principles of Government*, 77.

culminating in the Gregorian Reforms and the Investiture Struggle, gave rise to 'the formation of the first modern western legal system, the new canon law of the Roman Catholic Church'.[9] The pope held the power to excommunicate individuals, excluding them from contacts with the other members of the Christian community, and from whatever service or privilege derived from the Church.[10] Medieval popes repeatedly used excommunication to bend recalcitrant princes. The interdict constituted another sanction at the pope's disposal. It prevented church services, such as saying Mass, from being carried out in entire polities, regions, and cities. Both could be highly effective means of exerting pressure within the context of medieval societies, where religion and faith in otherworldly salvation were deeply rooted.[11]

One of the greatest papal claims was the power to proclaim the *de iure* depositions of monarchs and emperors, on the ground of misconduct in 'temporal affairs'. While excommunication targeted a prince as a Christian, deposition directly undermined their status as a holder of public power. In such cases, all subjects of the deposed ruler were released from their oaths of allegiance, as the pope asserted the ability to sever the 'strong ties that bound the subjects to their king'.[12] A vassal or a neighbouring prince, armed with pontifical blessing, could later challenge and defeat the already formally overthrown ruler.[13] Furthermore, for centuries, popes claimed and carried out the function of *iudex superior* in relation to disputes involving princes, feudal lords, and cities.[14] Pontifical mediation occasionally facilitated the peaceful resolution of conflicts, a role generally more palatable to secular rulers than the contentious measures of excommunication or deposition. The papacy's function as

---

9 Berman, *Law and Revolution*, I, 86–7. See also James A. Brundage, *Medieval Canon Law* (London: Longman, 1995).

10 Elisabeth Vodola, *Excommunication in the Middle Ages* (Berkeley: University of California Press, 1986), 12–24; Walter Ullmann, *The Growth of Papal Government in the Middle Ages: A Study in the Ideological Relation of Clerical to Lay Power* (New York: Taylor & Francis, 1955), 300.

11 Pope Innocent III (r. 1198–1216) in particular used this sanction several times. In 1200, he placed France under interdict, in 1203, the duchy of Normandy, and in 1208, the kingdom of England. See Neff, *Justice among Nations*, 55–6.

12 Ullmann, *Principles of Government*, 76–7.

13 For instance, Pope Gregory VII (r. 1073–1185) made extensive use of this prerogative. However, one of the most remarkable depositions took place on 17 July 1245 in Lyon, when Holy Roman Emperor Frederick II (r. 1220-1250) was deposed by Pope Innocent IV. See Neff, *Justice among Nations*, 51

14 Arthur Nussbaum, *A Concise History of the Law of Nations* (New York: The Macmillan Company, 1947), 25; Grewe, *Epochs*, 94–5.

iudex superior as regard to inter-polity conflicts was extensively debated within the framework of *ius commune* doctrine.[15]

The papacy gave momentum to the complex phenomenon of the crusades, the 'holy wars' aimed at recovering the Christian territories that in the previous centuries had fallen under Muslim rule, notably Palestine, 'the Holy Land'. The desire to expand the reach of the Christian faith also led to crusades to the eastern edges of the continent.[16] Popes also imposed bans on trade with pagans and Muslims, especially concerning war materials such as timber and iron.[17] However, as the papacy was reaching the peak of its international influence, profound shifts in European international relations started to arise. From the thirteenth century onward, the authority of the two universal institutions faced increasing challenges. The first significant opposition came from the northern Italian communes, which were leading economic and cultural hubs of the era. In the long term, however, the rise of large national states north of the Alps proved more transformative. Powerful monarchs, such as the kings of France, began asserting greater independence and freedom of action, in defiance of universalist authorities.[18]

The Latin maxim *rex imperator in regno suo* expressed well this aspiration. This political-legal formula refers to the full authority, *plenitudo potestatis*, which each sovereign would enjoy over his state. It represents a reaction to medieval doctrines that considered the world as a legal order (*universitatis humanitatis*) and the Holy Roman emperor as *dominus mundi*.[19] To this end, the collapse of a central imperial authority added an 'indispensable precondition' for the further development of a new European state system.[20] These momentous changes would fully mature only during the Early Modern Age. At the same time, the relative decline of both the universal authorities had an impact on the growing importance of natural law doctrine. The *ius naturale*

15 For instance, Cino da Pistoia excluded that the pope held this power, see Domenico Maffei, *Lectura super Digesto Veteri di Cino da Pistoia* (Milano: Giuffrè Editore, 1963).

16 Kurt Villads Jensen, *Crusading at the Edges of Europe, Denmark and Portugal, c.1000–1250* (London-New York: Routledge, 2017).

17 Ullmann, *Principles of Government*, 84.

18 Neff, *Justice among Nations*, 75; Antonio Cassese, 'States: rise and decline of the primary subjects of the international community', in Fassbender and Peters (eds.), *The Oxford Handbook of the History of International Law*, 49; Jacques Le Goff, *Il re nell'Occidente medievale* (Bari: Laterza, 2006), 5–11.

19 See Kenneth Pennington, *The Prince and the Law, 1200–1600: Sovereignty and Rights in the Western Legal Tradition* (Los Angeles: University of California Press, 1993), 32.

20 Grewe, *Epochs*, 15. See also Penelope Simons, 'The Emergence of the Idea of the Individualized State in the International Legal System', *The Journal of the History of International Law*, 5(2) (2003), 293–336.

was beginning to appear as the only 'force of unity' capable of governing international relations.[21]

A characteristic medieval legal source was *bulla apostolica*, promulgated by the popes. This term, employed already before the fifteenth century, designed all the decretals and letters issued by the pontiffs.[22] Bulls were typically addressed to specific individuals or a limited group, in contrast to encyclicals, which were intended for the broader community of believers. One key use of these legal instruments arose when Christian kings and rulers sought papal endorsement to legitimise political actions, thereby strengthening their standing among other Christian leaders. Frequently, monarchs and princes requested papal confirmation or approval, following conquests, as well as in preparation for explorations or crusades. Their objective was often to transform a tenuous or de facto claim into one that was legally recognised. The Holy See, in turn, leveraged its 'approbation prerogatives' to shape international relations.[23] For instance, Pope Eugene IV (r. 1331–1447) issued the bull *Romanus pontifex*, dated 15 September 1436, in response to King Edward I of Portugal's (r. 1433–1438) request for authorisation to conquer the Canary Islands, not inhabited by Christians. By doing so, the pope intended to reaffirm his role of Vicar of Christ on Earth and successor of Saint Peter, at a time when his authority started to be seriously challenged.[24]

The independence and moral authority of the Holy See positioned it as an arbiter in disputes between polities. Moreover, the papacy's spiritual powers, such as excommunication and interdicts, provided a degree of enforcement to its decisions. When state representatives sought papal approval for ventures

21 Neff, *Justice among Nations*, 59–67; Randall Lesaffer, 'The Grotian Tradition Revisited: Change and Continuity in the History of International Law', *British Yearbook of International Law*, 73 (2002), 103–39.

22 The medieval *ius commune* system was inherently pluralistic, marked by the coexistence of competing jurisdictions within the same political community. Multiple legal sources constantly interacted, including imperial constitutions, canon law, and the increasingly significant *iura propria* – i.e. laws specific to temporal jurisdictions such as city statutes. Additionally, Roman law, as codified in the *Corpus Juris Civilis*, retained significant authority across the continent. See Dante Fedele and Wouter Druwé, 'Introduction. Dossier: Le *ius commune* à la fin du Moyen Âge et au début de l'époque moderne. Notions, méthodes, (dis)continuités', *Clio@Themis*, 27 (2024), 1–15; Ken Pennington, 'Ancient, Medieval, and Early Modern Concepts of the *Ius Commune*', *Clio@Themis*, 27 (2024), 1–16.

23 Grewe, *Epochs*, 77–88.

24 Mamadou Hébié, *Souveraineté territoriale par traité, une étude des accords entre puissances coloniales et entités politiques locales* (Paris: Presses universitaires de France, 2015), 43.

involving maritime, territorial, or commercial expansion, they often emphasised the role these undertakings would play in extending Christendom to secure easier papal endorsement.[25] Chapter 2 of the present book will discuss how this area of activity of the Roman *Curia* reverberated on the upcoming oceanic endeavours. The Portuguese and Castilians, pioneers of Atlantic exploration, placed significant importance on papal authority as a source of exclusive rights over the seas. Consequently, until the seventeenth century, discussions about papal authority were inextricably tied to debates about the legal status of the sea.

1.2 *European Geographical Boundaries*

The gradual transition from the Middle Ages to the Early Modern period brought significant changes to the geographical boundaries of Europe. It also fostered intense interactions between peoples and polities, previously separated by oceans and vast distances.[26] This impacted the Europeans' way of conceiving the world and their place in it, as well as their relations with non-European civilisations. Although substantial interconnections with the Indian subcontinent and beyond existed as early as the Hellenistic-Roman period,[27] the fall of the Western Roman Empire and the Byzantine Empire's prolonged struggle for survival disrupted the geopolitical and economic conditions necessary for regular cultural and commercial exchanges with East Asia.[28]

Throughout the medieval era, Europe experienced alternating periods of economic, demographic, and territorial expansion, interspersed with times of economic depression, devastating plagues, and invasions from the eastern steppes.[29] Nonetheless, Christendom slowly but steadily expanded its outer

25 Ibid., 12; Grewe, *The Epochs*, 229–31.

26 The term 'Europe' is here used to describe the whole of the peoples united by a common faith, a degree of common cultural heritage (e.g. Roman law and Greek philosophy) and comparable customs and practices. Therefore, it is not a mere geographical concept. It is related to the definition of 'West' made by Berman in the introduction to *Law and Revolution*, I, 1–2. Cf. Denys Hay, *Europe: The Emergence of an Idea* (Edinburgh: University Press, 1957).

27 Warwick Ball, *Rome in the East: Transformation of an Empire* (London: Routledge, 2016), 130–56; Raoul McLaughlin, *The Roman Empire and the Indian Ocean* (Barnsley: Pen & Sword, 2014); Vimala Begley and Richard D. de Puma (eds.), *Rome and India. The Ancient Sea Trade* (Madison: The University of Wisconsin Press, 1991)

28 Georg Ostrogorsky, *History of the Byzantine Empire* (New Brunswick: Rutgers University Press, 1986).

29 Jacques le Goff, *La civilisation de l'occident médiéval* (Paris: Flammarion, 1964), 46–87; Jack A. Goldstone, *Why Europe? The Rise of the West in World History, 1500–1850* (New York: McGraw-Hill, 2009), 82.

boundaries in northern and eastern Europe, namely in the Baltic region.[30] Pagan peoples were converted to the 'true faith' by zealous missionaries and bloody wars of conquest and colonisation, conventionally named the 'Baltic Crusades'.[31] Viking-Norse seafarers, meanwhile, had a long-standing tradition of venturing into the North Atlantic, reaching as far as Newfoundland and Greenland – an extraordinary nautical achievement for the time. The Late Middle Ages also witnessed the growing importance of trade in the Baltic and North Sea regions. The kingdoms of Norway and Denmark, strategically situated along major maritime routes, played a central role in this regard. However, the powerful Hanseatic League ultimately dominated the so-called 'Baltic system' throughout the late medieval period. Low German trading cities constituted the core of the Hanse, which evolved in a loose association of trading cities. Centred around Low German trading cities, the Hanse evolved into a loose association of commercial hubs. Consequently, the major trend in the region between the thirteenth and sixteenth centuries revolved around the complex interplay between the Nordic kingdoms, which sought exclusive control of their coastal seas, and other regional actors like the Hanse, who advocated for freedom of maritime movement.[32]

Along southwestern Europe, the Atlantic Ocean continued to prove an insurmountable natural barrier for medieval Europeans, who lacked proper nautical technology to navigate its waters. Medieval mapmakers, such as the Venetian Zuane Pizzigano (see Figure 1.1 below), consistently depicted the *Mare Oceanus* as an undefined vastness, unsuitable for navigation.[33] The confrontation between Christendom and Islam also remained a defining feature of Mediterranean geopolitics throughout the Middle Ages. For centuries, Christians were on the defensive across the Mediterranean, prompting

30 Michael North, *The Baltic. A History* (Cambridge, MA: Harvard University Press, 2015), 28–39.

31 Villads Jensen, *Crusading at the Edges of Europe*; Zsolt Hunyadi and József Laszlovszky, *The Crusades and the Military Orders: Expanding the Frontiers of Medieval Latin Christianity* (Budapest: Central European University Press, 2001). From a legal point of view, these crusades were backed by the controversial *dilatatio* doctrine. See Neff, *Justice among Nations*, 102–3.

32 Thomas K. Derry, *A History of Scandinavia* (London: George Allen & Unwin, 1979), 66–7; Jens E. Olesen, 'Inter Scandinavian relations', in Knut Helle (ed.), *The Cambridge History of Scandinavia, vol. I: Prehistory to 1520* (Cambridge: University Press, 2003), 711.

33 John H. Parry, *Europe and a Wider World, 1415–1715* (London: Hutchinson, 1966), 19. Cf. Antonio Musarra, *L'isola che non c'è. Geografie immaginarie tra Mediterraneo e Atlantico* (Bologna: Il Mulino, 2023).

Richard W. Southern to liken medieval western Christendom to a 'beleaguered citadel'.[34]

The development of towns in northern Italy, the Low Countries, and elsewhere between the eleventh and thirteenth centuries, alongside the revival of trade, culture, and curiosity about travel, marked the beginning of a new era of connections with the wider world for the European continent. Even the complex phenomenon of the Crusades was more than a series of wars and bloodshed; it also provided opportunities to strengthen diplomatic and commercial ties between Christian and Muslim powers in the Near East. Dialogue often took the form of international treaties, establishing mutually beneficial economic relationships.[35] Unsurprisingly, an extensive body of literature emerged around the *vexata quaestio* of the lawfulness of the 'impious pacts with the infidels'. The most celebrated jurists of the time debated it and the repeated papal bans concerning trade with the 'infidels' – particularly of war materials – usually proved ineffective.[36]

The powerful Italian maritime republics played a central role, notably Pisa, Genoa, and Venice. From the twelfth century onwards, they became the fulcrum of the trade between the European continent, marked by strong demographic growth, Africa, and Asia. The Far East in particular was seen as a mysterious and distant land, renowned as the source of precious and luxurious goods that commanded high prices in European markets.[37] The Italian seafaring republics attained a dominant position on the Mediterranean communication routes with the Levant. They drew considerable wealth from their role as privileged intermediaries with the Near East Arab potentates, such as the Sultanate of Egypt.

---

34 'Which only survived because its greatest enemy, Islam, had reached the end of its lines of communications, and its lesser enemies [...] were organized only for raids and for plunder', in Richard W. Southern, *Western Society and the Church in the Middle Ages* (London: Penguin Books, 1990), 27.

35 See Giulio Vismara, *Scritti di storia giuridica. 7. Comunità e diritto internazionale* (Milano: Giuffrè, 1989); Neff, *Justice among Nations*, 102–7; Grewe, *Epochs*, 46–7.

36 Nussbaum, *A Concise History of the Law of Nations*, 37; Neff, *Justice among Nations*, 106–7; Dominique Gaurier, *Histoire du droit international* (Rennes: Presses universitaires de Rennes, 2014), 95.

37 Charles H. Parker, *Global Interactions in the Early Modern Age* (Cambridge: University Press, 2010), 72–3; Ram P. Anand, 'Law of the Sea in Historical Perspective', in *Changing Dimensions of International Law: An Asian Perspective* (Leiden/Boston: M. Nijhoff, 2006), 5–6; Basilio Cialdea, *La formazione dell'ordinamento marittimo nelle relazioni internazionali (secoli XIV–XVIII)*, I (Milano: Giuffrè, 1959), 5–12.

Before being loaded on Italian ships, the goods coming from the East had already gone through a long journey along the 'Silk Road(s)'.[38] This ancient network of ever-shifting terrestrial, river, and sea routes started in northern China, transited through the endless expanses of central Asia, and finally reached the Mediterranean emporia like Alexandria in Egypt. The journey, fraught with challenges and hazards, often took over a year for a slow caravan of merchants. One such journey was undertaken by the renowned Venetian traveller Marco Polo (1254–1324), whose accounts vividly captured the extraordinary complexities of this trade network.[39]

Nevertheless, much of East-West trade historically depended on the merchant vessels active along the 'maritime silk road', which typically offered a more efficient, safer, and faster means of transporting goods over long distances.[40] The Indian Ocean constituted the pulsing heart of long-range trade between Asia and Europe, due to its geographical location and predictable wind system. Along its shores, powerful empires and prosperous merchant cities flourished. Arab, Persian, Indian, and Chinese merchants navigated its waters in harmony with the seasonal monsoons, transporting some of the most valuable commodities of the time, including spices, precious stones, silk, and porcelain.[41] By the late fifteenth century, trade in the Indian Ocean fell gradually under Muslim entrepreneurs' control.[42]

The most recent analyses agree in highlighting that, long after the 'second discovery' of America and the circumnavigation of Africa, the importance of European markets in the context of the commercial networks of the time was

38 See Luce Boulnois, *La Route de la Soie* (Paris: Olizane, 2010); Pierre Biarnès, *La Route de la Soie, Une histoire géopolitique* (Paris: Ellipses Marketing, 2014); Eliyahu Ashtor, *Levant Trade in the Later Middle Ages* (Princeton: University Press, 1983); David Christian, 'Silk Roads or Steppe Roads? The Silk Roads in World History', *Journal of World History*, 11(1) (2000), 1–26; Ball, *Rome in the East*, 154–6.

39 Marco Polo, *The Description of the World* [*Il Milione*, 1298] (Indianapolis/Cambridge: Hackett Publishing Co., 2016).

40 Franck Billé, Sanjyot Mehendale and James Lankton (eds.), *The Maritime Silk Road. Global Connectivities, Regional Nodes, Localities* (Amsterdam: University Press, 2022).

41 Derived from the Arabic *mawsim* (season), the term monsoon refer to a large-scale seasonal wind system, which reverses direction every six months with the change of season. See Khalilieh, *Islamic Law of the Sea*, 77; Françoise Vergès, 'Writing on Water: Peripheries, Flows, Capital, and Struggles in the Indian Ocean', *Positions: Asia Critique*, 11(1) (2003), 241–57, at 247–8; Philippe Beaujard, 'The Indian Ocean in Eurasian and African World-Systems before the Sixteenth Century', *Journal of World History*, 16(4) (2005), 411–65.

42 Parry, *Europe and a Wider World*, 33: 'Wherever the European Christians went in the East they found that the Muslims had gone before them, and by 1500 both the production of spices and the trade in spices were largely in Muslim hands'.

overall limited. The goods that reached Mediterranean emporia or the Black Sea harbours, represented only a small portion of global trade.[43] The steady rise of the Ottoman Empire in the Levant, from the fifteenth century onwards, became a powerful driver for change in the region and, consequently, for the paths of long-range Euro-Asian trade.[44] The Muslim potentates of the Middle East fell one after the other into the hands of ambitious Ottoman sultans, such as Mehmed II 'the Conqueror' (r. 1444–1446/1451–1481). In 1453, he succeeded in conquering Constantinople, decreeing the end of the Byzantine Empire.[45] With the subsequent conquest of the Mameluke Sultanate (1516) and North Africa, a massive Muslim empire emerged.[46] It would prove to be a formidable barrier to Christian merchants, capable of interrupting the Silk Road according to the changing wishes of the Sublime Porte.[47] In this regard, it has been argued that:

> Europe's wave of seafaring expansion in the fifteenth century was thus not the result of some new upwelling of European political or military power, but rather a concerted effort to respond to the vigorous expansion of Ottoman power. Europe's age of exploration was driven by the search for another way to reach Asia, a path outside of Ottoman control, to conduct trade.[48]

At the close of the Middle Ages, it was far from certain that Europe, rather than China or one of the Muslim empires, would take the lead in global maritime exploration and subsequent imperial expansion. In the fifteenth century, Europe was neither the wealthiest region in the world nor the most populous or interconnected. Nonetheless, it possessed several characteristics that would ultimately enable European powers to establish seaborne empires and exert a

---

43 Goldstone, *Why Europe?*, 4–15; Parker, *Global Interactions*, 72–3.

44 For more details, see Halil İnalcik, 'The rise of the Ottoman Empire', in Peter Holt, Ann Lambton and Bernard Lewis (eds.), *The Cambridge History of Islam*, vol 1 (Cambridge: University Press, 1977), 293–323.

45 Franz Babinger, *Mehmed the Conqueror and His Time* (Princeton: Bollingen Foundation, 1992).

46 Johnson Brummett, *Ottoman Seapower*, 51–88.

47 The term is translation from the Turkish *Bāb-i'ālī*. European diplomats used it to designate the Ottoman government, namely the Grand Visir offices and the foreign ministry. For an overview, see Robert Mantran, *Histoire de l'Empire Ottoman* (Paris: Fayard, 2003).

48 Goldstone, *Why Europe?*, 53. See also Felipe Fernández-Armesto, 'Exploration and discovery', in Christopher Allmand (ed.), *The New Cambridge Medieval History, vol. VII, c.1415–1500* (Cambridge: University Press, 1998), 175–201.

dominant influence on the development of modern international law.[49] As a result, the question of whether polities could claim control over seas, oceans, and maritime trade routes became one of the most pressing international issues – one that was inherently legal in nature.

1.3 *Development of the Law of the Sea*

The second part of the chapter provides an overview of late medieval state practices and doctrinal debates concerning the sea. Since European seafarers typically preferred to navigate within sight of the coastline, two geographically distinct areas became particularly significant, respectively situated at the southern and northern edges of the continent.[50] First, the Mediterranean Sea, where the influence of Roman law endured strong. In the thriving Italian city-states of the Late Middle Ages, scholars engaged in debates regarding the legal status of the sea and maritime trade. Roman legal thought served as an important reference point, and thus a concise overview of it is provided in the following section. However, it was not the sole factor at play. New concepts and legal trends emerged, along with novel geopolitical actors in the Mediterranean arena. Second, the analysis turns to the seas of northern Europe, where a distinct 'claimed seas' approach developed in parallel.[51] In this region, Roman law exerted far less influence, and legal developments were predominantly original. Instead, state practices and customary laws played a more prominent role in regulating maritime interactions.[52]

The study of these two late medieval 'claimed seas' traditions is essential to fully comprehend the early modern resurgence of the concept of the claimed/closed seas in legal argumentation. Late medieval maritime claims constitute the historical precursors to their early modern counterparts, and the continuities and divergences between the two periods will be examined in subsequent chapters. At this stage, the principle of the freedom of the sea was far from predominant. On the contrary, several polities asserted extensive claims over adjacent seas, and the principle of maritime freedom had yet to be clearly articulated.

Chapter 2 will explore whether and how this legal and geopolitical context influenced Iberian approaches to oceanic navigation in the fifteenth century.

---

49 Anand, 'Law of the sea in historical perspective', 12–5.

50 Grewe, *Epochs*, 257; Lincoln Paine, *The Sea and Civilization, a Maritime History of the World* (London: Atlantic Books, 2014), 316–45; Potter, *The Freedom of the Sea*, 36–40.

51 With the term 'seas of northern Europe', I refer to the Baltic and the North Sea, as well as to the sea area extending between Norway, Oxford, Scotland, and Iceland.

52 Raestad, *La mer territoriale*, 28.

FIGURE 1.1 Portolan chart dated 1424, known as the 'Pizzigano Map', 57 × 90 cm
The chart shows the coasts of western Europe and the portions of north-west Africa known at the time. It well represents the western limits of Europe on the onset of the Age of Exploration.
SOURCE: JAMES FORD BELL LIBRARY, UNIVERSITY OF MINNESOTA.

What is certain, however, is that many legal concepts and ideas employed by early modern commentators and diplomats were initially formulated by their medieval predecessors in relation to the maritime zones bordering northern and southern Europe. The very notion of restricting other peoples' maritime activities – whether fishing or navigation – was firmly rooted in developments that took place in Europe roughly between 1200 and 1500.

2 The Mediterranean Sea

2.1 *Roman Legal Speculation on the Sea*

Since ancient times, the Mediterranean Sea has played a pivotal role for the peoples inhabiting its coasts, serving as the primary connecting route between Europe, Asia, and North Africa. During antiquity, great civilisations such as the Egyptians, Greeks, Phoenicians, and Romans thrived due to the maritime networks it facilitated. These networks enabled the movement of commodities, religions, technologies, and diseases. Great maritime powers, such as Athens and Carthage, expanded their influence by controlling its waters. However, despite the acknowledged centrality of the Mediterranean, a clear and consistent legal status for the sea was not developed, and doctrinal speculation remained limited. Various polities, such as Athens, attained temporary maritime dominance, yet none established a 'right, recognised by independent states, to subject the sea to their authority'.[53] Indeed, it is likely that they did not even aspire to achieve such a claim.

The Ancient Greeks, for example, were deeply connected to the sea but focused primarily on defining certain legal aspects of navigation – mostly related to private and commercial law – without attempting to establish a comprehensive legal framework for maritime interactions. An analysis of one of the most renowned laws from the Hellenistic period, the *Lex Rhodia de Iactu* (The Rhodian Law of Jettison), supports this view. This set of regulations on navigation and maritime trade is believed to have originated in the third century BC in the powerful seafaring republic of Rhodes, an ally of Rome.[54] Historians continue to debate its precise date of enactment and its exact nature. It remains unclear whether it represented a complete juridical framework for the law of the sea or simply codified a collection of customary rules.[55] In ancient Mediterranean practice, the *ius naufragii* (law of shipwreck) allowed coastal inhabitants to claim ownership of ships and their cargo that washed ashore following storms or shipwrecks. Only agreements between polities could impose mutual respect for vessels and their contents. The few surviving fragments of the *Lex Rhodia* include provisions aimed at protecting the owners of distressed ships from plunder. However, it is not possible to determine whether the law had a broader scope.

What we today term the law of the sea was not a foremost concern to the legal speculation of Roman jurists either, who provided solid grounds for the further developments of the western legal tradition in so many areas.[56] Never-

53 Potter, *The Freedom of the Sea*, 34; Jonathan Ziskind, 'The International Legal Status of the Sea in Antiquity', *Acta Orientalia*, 35 (1973), 35–56, at 36–40.

54 The *Lex Rhodia* partially survived through quotes made by classical Roman jurists and due to its incorporation in the Justinian *Digest*, of which it formed the second title of the fourteenth book (D., 14.2). See Walter Ashburner, *Nomos Rhodion Nautikos. The Rhodian Sea-Law* (Oxford: Clarendon Press, 1909).

55 Robert D. Benedict, 'The Historical Position of the Rhodian Law', *Yale Law Journal*, 18(4) (1909), 223–42; Antonio Lozzi, *Codici e consuetudini nella storia del commercio marittimo. Dal Codice di Hammurabi alle repubbliche marinare* (Milano: Mursia, 2010), 126–39.

56 Dominique Gaurier, *Droit maritime romain* (Rennes: Presses universitaires de Rennes, 2004).

theless, as Bo J. Theutenberg noted, in relation to the law of the sea: 'we find that the basic concepts of Roman law are the very foundation of modern concepts and trends', and concepts such as '*mare liberum* – the high seas, open to all nations – and *mare clausum* – the closed sea, under the sovereignty of a power and restricted in terms of use by other states – reflect Roman legal philosophy'.[57]

The relentless expansion carried out by Roman legions across the Mediterranean basin greatly influenced this state of affairs. The Romans primarily considered the sea from the perspectives of private law and anti-piracy measures. Roman jurists generally listed the sea, in the framework of their division of things (*res*) in categories, among the *res communes omnium*. These *res communes* were deemed *extra commercium* (beyond commerce), meaning they could not be subject to legal transactions, and their 'use' was intended to remain open to all.[58] Roman legal thought concerning the sea was crystallised in the Justinian *Institutiones*, which stated that by natural law, the air, the sea, and its shores are common to all humankind.[59] The *Digest* confirms the definition almost to the letter, in a famous fragment of the jurist Marcian therein included:

> Some things belong in common to all men by *jus naturale*, some to a community corporately, some to no one, but most belong to individuals severally, being ascribed to someone on one of various grounds. And

57 Theutenberg, 'Mare Liberum et Mare Clausum', 481. See also Jean Rougé, *Recherches sur l'organisation du commerce maritime en Méditerranée sous l'empire romain* (Paris: Sevpen, 1966).

58 Exemplified by the maxim '*maris communem usum omnibus hominibus*', 'The seas are for the use of Man'. See D., 43.8.3.1. See also Grewe, *Epochs*, 77–88; Potter, *The Freedom of the Sea*, 25–7.

59 The *Institutiones* outlined four categories of *res*: *res publicae, res universitatis, res nullius*, and *res communes* (Inst., 2, *De rerum divisione*). For the latter category, see: Inst., 2.1.1: '*Et quidem naturali iure omnium communia sunt haec: aer, aqua perfluens et mare; et per hoc litora maris*'. English translation by J. B. Moyle: 'Thus, the following things are by natural law common all: the air, running water, the sea, and consequently the seashore', in *Institutes of Justinian* (Oxford: Clarendon Press, 1911): https://amesfoundation.law.harvard.edu/digital/CJCiv/JInst.pdf, 19. In truth, the distinction between *res communes* and *res publicae* is anything but precise in the works of Roman jurists. See also Peter Birks, 'The Roman Concept of Dominium and the Idea of Absolute Ownership', *Acta Juridica*, 31 (1985), 1–38; Andree Kirchner, 'History of Law of the Sea', in *The Max Planck Encyclopedia of Public International Law* (Oxford: University Press, 2012), vol. VI, 733; Percy T. Fenn, 'Justinian and the Freedom of the Sea', *American Journal of International Law*, 19(4) (1925), 716–27, at 723–4.

> indeed by natural law, the following belong in common to all men: air, flowing water, and the sea, and therewith the shores of the sea.[60]

However, we must take into consideration that the *Corpus Iuris*: 'did not really explain the idea of common property' and the legal features of the consequent common use.[61] It is still debated whether the *res communes* category originated in classical, post-classical, or Justinian times. Even though the sea and the air constituted a separate category, the fragments selected by Tribonian and his associates did not explain how their legal regime differed from that of the *res publicae*, such as rivers and roads. It has been suggested that perhaps the compilers did not envisage any tangible difference between the legal regimes of the *res publicae* and *res communes*.[62] Furthermore, the differentiation was elaborated in the context of Roman civil law, the normative body that applied only to Roman citizens, and was not meant to be applied directly to inter-polity relations. Thus, the *Corpus Iuris* only outlined the category without offering further details, placing it at the indefinite boundaries of the legal concept of *res*, being mostly defined by a 'negative' characteristic: their use could not be denied to others.

Roman jurists were clear that the sea was not considered a *res nullius* (a thing belonging to no one), in contrast to fishes, which, as *ferae naturae*, became the property of their captors.[63] Roman jurisconsults agreed that no

60 D., 1.8.2: '... *et quidem naturali iure omnia communia sunt illa: aer, aqua profluens, et mare, et hoc per litoras maris*'. Translation by Alan Watson, *The Digest of Justinian*, vol. I (Philadelphia: Pennsylvania University Press, 1985), 24.

61 Richard Perruso, 'The Development of the Doctrine of Res Communes in Medieval and Early Modern Europe', *The Legal History Review*, 70(1) (2002), 69–93, at 69.

62 For example, Roman jurist sometimes listed the seashore (*lidus*) among the *res publicae*, cf. D., 1.8.6. The *res communes* are listed among the *res publicae* in the scheme created by J. T. Frey, *Partitiones Iuris Utriusque*, Basileae, 1572, f. 10r, reported in Paolo Grossi, *La categoria del dominio utile e gli homines novi del quadrivio cinquecentesco*, in idem, *Il dominio e le cose. Percezioni medievali e moderne dei diritti reali* (Milano: Giuffrè, 1992), 271. See also Ubaldo Robbe, *La differenza sostanziale fra 'res nullius' e 'res nullius in bonis' la distinzione delle 'res' pseudo-marcianea: 'che non ha nè capo nè coda'*, I (Milano: Giuffrè, 1979), 212; Gaetano Scherillo, *Lezioni di diritto romano, le cose, Parte prima: Concetto di cosa, cose extra patrimonium* (Milano: Giuffrè, 1945), 87–8; Mario Fiorentini, *Fiumi e mari nell'esperienza giuridica romana* (Milano: Giuffré 2003); idem, 'L'acqua da bene economico a "res communis omnium" a bene collettivo', *Analisi giuridica dell'economia*, 1 (2010), 39–78; Luigi Garofalo (cur.), *I beni di interesse pubblico nell'esperienza giuridica romana* (Napoli: Jovene, 2016).

63 D., 41.1.3: '*Quod enim nullius est, id ratione naturali occupanti conceditur*'. 'What presently belongs to no one becomes by natural reason the property of the first taker'. Translation by Alan Watson, *The Digest of Justinian*, vol. IV, 1.

one could deny the right to fish to others, whether from the shore or a boat. If a fisherman's rights were obstructed, he could invoke the *actio iniuriarum*, a legal remedy under civil law.[64] The latter constituted a personal action, as the individual prevented from fishing could not bring a property action (such as the *interdictum*) because 'he was deemed to have no property interest in the sea'.[65]

Several Roman literary, poetical, and philosophical works contained references to the idea of property common to all humankind, being sometimes more explicit than their scant juridical counterparts.[66] They show that the idea was relatively popular among the upper echelons of Roman society. Some of those references can be found, for instance, in Cicero's *Topica*, *De officiis*, and *Pro Sexto Roscio Amerino*, Seneca's *De beneficiis*, and Ovid's *Metamorphoses*.[67] Tullio Scovazzi argues that, in antiquity, the freedom of the sea was considered such a self-evident principle that Roman jurists saw no need for detailed legal analysis.[68] The idea that no one could exercise private/public ownership (*dominium*) over portions of the sea arose from the understanding that the sea could not be physically occupied, and thus no property rights could be established over it.

The Roman Empire was arguably not the ideal forum for the development of a comprehensive international law of the sea. Already by the late Republic, the Romans had achieved an unparalleled degree of control over the Mediterranean Sea. Consequently, the coasts of this enclosed sea became increasingly integrated into a complex network of commercial routes. The Romans evocatively referred to the Mediterranean as *Mare Nostrum* ('our sea') or *Mare Internum*, reflecting a political and military assertion (*imperium*) and a de facto reality. Modern scholarship largely concurs that these terms symbolised

64 D., 47.10.13.

65 Perruso, 'The Development of the Doctrine of Res Communes', 70.

66 Ibid., 71–3.

67 Cicero, *Topica*, 7.32; idem, *De Officiis*, I, xvi [51f]; idem, *Pro Sexto Roscio Amerino*, xxvi [71]; Seneca, *De Beneficiis*, IV, xxviii, 3; Ovid, *Metamorphoses*, I, 135.

68 Tullio Scovazzi, 'Libertà o dominio nell'evoluzione del diritto del mare', in Guido Acquaviva and Tullio Scovazzi (cur.), *Il dominio di Venezia sul mare Adriatico nelle opere di Paolo Sarpi e Giulio Pace* (Milano: Giuffrè, 2007), 1–2. See also Percy T. Fenn, *The Origin of the Right of Fishery in Territorial Waters* (Cambridge, MA: Harvard University Press, 1926), 222: 'In considering the doctrine of the Roman jurists on the freedom of the sea, the first thing of importance which appears is the small amount of space their treatment of the subject occupies in Roman jurisprudence […] The people living on the shores of the Mediterranean used the sea in common'.

Roman dominance but did not extend to a legal or theoretical claim of ownership (*dominium*).[69]

By the end of the first century BCE, the only serious challenge to Roman naval supremacy across the Mediterranean basin and commercial prosperity came from pirates.[70] The Roman philosopher, orator, and politician Cicero (106–43 BCE) famously described them as 'enemies of all' (*commun*[*es*] *host* [*es*] *omnium*),[71] as they alone dared to interfere with the imperial peace imposed by Rome (*pax romana*).[72] Moreover, the Roman Empire did not interact with what it perceived as 'barbarian' polities on an equal foot. Therefore, it is difficult to speak of an international community in the Mediterranean basin after the fall of the polities that Rome conceived as its equals, such as Carthage and the Hellenistic kingdoms.[73]

It is also important to note that our knowledge of Roman legal thought on the sea derives largely from the writings of Justinian's compilers, which means

69 Khan, 'Territories and boundaries', in Fassbender and Peters (eds.), *The Oxford Handbook of the History of International Law*, 242; Lozzi, *Codici e consuetudini*, 126–39; Kirchner, 'History of Law of the Sea', 733; Potter, *The Freedom of the Sea*, 27–33; W. Paul Gormley, 'Development and Subsequent Influence of the Roman Legal Norm of Freedom of the Seas', *The University of Detroit Law Journal*, 40(1) (1963), 561–84.

70 Antonio Flamigni, *Il potere marittimo in Roma Antica. Dalle origini alla guerra siriaca* (Roma: Rivista Marittima, 1995); Michele Stefanile, 'The development of Roman maritime trade after the Second Punic War', in Arnaud and de Souza (eds.), *The Sea in History*, I, 258–62.

71 '[*N*]*am pirate non est ex perduellium numero definitus, sed communis hostis omnium: cum hoc nec fides nec ius iurandum esse commune*', Cicero, *De officiis*, translated by Walter Miller (London/New York: William Heinemann Ltd./G. P. Putman's Sons, 1913), III, § 107, 384–5. See also Thomas K. Heebøll-Holm, *Ports, Piracy and Maritime War: Piracy in the English Channel and the Atlantic, c.1280–c.1330* (Leiden/Boston: Brill, 2013), 2–5; Daniel Heller-Roazen, *The Enemy of All. Piracy and the Law of Nations* (New York: Zone Books, 2009), 16.

72 For a comprehensive overview, see Philip de Souza, *Piracy in the Graeco-Roman World* (Cambridge: University Press, 1999). See also idem, 'Rome's Contribution to the Development of Piracy', *Memoirs of the American Academy in Rome*, 6 (2008), 71–96; Manuel Tröster, 'Roman Hegemony and Non-State Violence: A Fresh Look at Pompey's Campaign against the Pirates', *Greece & Rome*, 56(1) (2009), 14–33; Stefan Eklöf Amirell, Hans Hägerdal and Bruce Buchan, 'Introduction', in idem (eds.), *Piracy in World History* (Amsterdam: University Press, 2021), 17–8; Amedeo Policante, *The Pirate Myth. Genealogies of an Imperial Concept* (London: Routledge, 2015), 3–27.

73 The obvious exceptions being the Parthian (247BCE–224CE) and Sasasian (224–651CE) empires centred on Persia, with whom interactions were nevertheless limited to land. See Raestad, *La mer territoriale*, 4; Gaurier, *Histoire du droit international*, 69–70. For further details, see Pierre Grimal, *L'Ellenismo e l'ascesa di Roma* (Milano: Feltrinelli, 1968); Paine, *The Sea and Civilization*, 123–36; Virgilio Ilari, *L'interpretazione storica del diritto di guerra romano fra tradizione romanistica e giusnaturalismo* (Milano: Giuffrè, 1981).

that our understanding of Classical Roman views remains fragmentary at best. In conclusion, the importance of Roman legal thought concerning the law of the sea did not stem from the depth of its speculations and the number of legal cases on the subject. Its role was to bequeath to future generations of European jurists the concepts of *res communis omnium* and *mare nostrum*. From these concepts, would in due time derive the basic principles of the freedom/commonality of the sea (to later become *mare liberum*) and the 'claimed seas' (to later become *mare clausum*). In the following chapters, we will examine how these concepts evolved within the western legal tradition, often diverging significantly from their original meaning and historical-legal context.

2.2 *Medieval State Practice*

With the decline and fall of the Western Roman Empire, the successor states that emerged from its remnants were unable to enforce a general security policy over the waters of the western Mediterranean. In other words, no partition of the Roman maritime *imperium* occurred. The Eastern Roman Empire (i.e. Byzantine) remained a major geopolitical actor; however, its maritime power was centred in the Aegean Sea, and eastern Mediterranean and could extend westward only intermittently.[74] From the seventh century onwards, the rise of Islam introduced a new variable into the Mediterranean international system. Muslim raiders and pirates launched a naval *jihad* against Christian vessels and coastal towns, prompting Christian adventurers to retaliate in a similar fashion.[75] This situation of political pluralism and jurisdictional anarchy in the Mediterranean Sea eventually compelled those polities that were most reliant on seaborne trade to react, providing the input for jurisdictional claims and law of the sea debates.[76]

74 For an overview, see Ostrogorsky, *History of the Byzantine Empire*; Cecily J. Hilsdale, *Byzantine Art and Diplomacy in an Age of Decline* (Cambridge: University Press, 2014); Jean-Claude Cheynet, *Le monde byzantin: Tome 2, L'Empire byzantine, 641–1204* (Paris: Presses universitaires de France, 2006).

75 David Abulafia, *The Great Sea: A Human History of the Mediterranean* (Oxford: University Press, 2013), 249: 'Whereas Roman naval power had been based on the extinction of piracy, Muslim naval power was based on the exercise of piracy'. See also Lozzi, *Codici e consuetudini*, 304–5; Dominique Valérian, 'Lutte contre la piraterie et construction de normes partagées entre chrétiens et musulmans en Méditerranée médiévale', in Louis Sicking and Alain Wijffels (eds.), *Conflict Management in the Mediterranean and the Atlantic, 1000–1800* (Leiden: Brill-Nijhoff, 2020), 147–64.

76 Aldo A. Cassi, *Ius commune tra vecchio e nuovo mondo. Mari, terre, oro nel diritto della conquista* (Milano: Giuffrè Editore, 2004), 101; Giulio Vismara, 'Il diritto del mare', in *La navigazione mediterranea nell'alto medioevo* (Spoleto: Centro italiano di studi sull'alto medioevo, 1978), vol. 2, 689–730; Raestad, *La mer territoriale*, 12; Salvatore Corrieri,

From the eleventh century onwards, especially Italian and Catalan merchants expanded their East-West trade networks to meet the demands of Europe's growing economy and population.[77] Four Italian city-states assumed a pivotal role – Amalfi, Pisa, Genoa, and Venice –, they shared a republican form of government and economies heavily centred on shipping and seaborne trade. Of these, Genoa and Venice ultimately proved to be the most powerful and enduring.[78] Venice, located at the northern end of the Adriatic Sea, and Genoa, situated on the northern coast of the Tyrrhenian Sea, both benefitted from their strategic proximity to the prosperous and densely populated inland regions of the Po Valley. Genoa also enjoyed convenient access to the markets of southern France, while Venice benefitted from natural lines of communication via the Adige River and the low eastern Alpine passes, connecting it to the German markets in cities such as Nuremberg and Augsburg.[79]

The rise to power of these two cities can only be briefly outlined here. Venice initially entered the Mediterranean trading system as a remote province of the Byzantine Empire. Its inhabitants were primarily fishermen and boatmen engaged in riverine and short-range commerce, as well as in salt production.[80] For a series of reasons, such as its unique geographical location and special links with Constantinople, the fortunes of the Venetians gradually shifted seaward. They began to participate in Levantine markets, establishing emporia

---

'Profili di storia del commercio marittimo e del diritto della navigazione nel Mediterraneo: dal periodo statutario all'era delle scoperte geografiche', in Guido Camarda, Salvatore Corrieri and Tullio Scovazzi (eds.), *La formazione del diritto marittimo nella prospettiva storica* (Milano: Giuffrè Editore, 2010), 1–80.

77 Steven A. Epstein, *Genoa & the Genoese, 958–1528* (Chapel Hill: The University of North Carolina Press, 1996), 9–12.

78 Genoa became known as *La Superba*, (the proud one), while Venice as *La Serenissima* (the most serene) and *La Dominante* (the dominant one). See Lozzi, *Codici e consuetudini*, 304–5.

79 Élisabeth Crouzet-Pavan, *Venise triomphante, les horizons d'un mythe* (Paris: Éditions Albin Michel, 1999), 19–73; idem, *Venise, VIe–XXIe siècle* (Paris: Belin, 2021); idem, 'Venice and its surroundings', in Eric Dursteler (ed.), *A Companion to Venetian History, 1400–1797* (Leiden: Brill, 2014), 25–46; Epstein, *Genoa*, 9–12; Frederic C. Lane, *Venice, A Maritime Republic* (Baltimore: The John Hopkins University Press, 1973), 5; Jean-Claude Hocquet, *Venise et la mer, XIIe–XVIIIe siècle* (Paris: Fayard, 2006), 311–8; Giovanna Petti Balbi, *Una città e il suo mare. Genova nel Medioevo* (Bologna: Editrice Clueb, 1991); Geo Pistarino, *La capitale del mediterraneo: Genova nel Mediterraneo* (Bordighera: Istituto Int. di Studi Liguri, 1993).

80 On the role played by the extraction and trade of salt, see Jean-Claude Hocquet, *Venise et le monopole du sel. Production, commerce et finance d'une république marchande*, 2 vols. (Paris: Les Belles Lettres, 2012); Giuseppe Gullino, *Storia della Repubblica Veneta* (Brescia: Editrice la Scuola, 2010), 7–23.

(*fondachi*) in major ports across the region.[81] They also extended their influence along the Adriatic, subduing Istria and Dalmatia on the eastern Adriatic coast. As Byzantine sea power began to wane from the eleventh century onwards, Venice consolidated its control over Levantine trade, displacing Greek merchants. The emperors of Constantinople increasingly relied on the Venetian navy for protection against their adversaries. Venice adopted a highly opportunist strategy, 'whether pro-Byzantine, pro-Moslem, pro-Crusader or anti-Byzantine', to further its interests in the eastern Mediterranean.[82] This approach culminated in the sack of Constantinople during the Fourth Crusade in 1204.

Genoa and Pisa followed a comparable trajectory of seaborne expansion. They were quicker to lease their fleets to crusader lords seeking passage to the Holy Land and to engage in combat against 'infidels' along the Syrian and Palestinian coasts. Consequently, the Tyrrhenian republics secured privileged access to Near Eastern markets and gained sufficient strength to challenge Venetian dominance.[83] Genoa also acquired a leading position in the Black Sea, whose ports were at the time strategical from a commercial point of view. Therefore, it was only a question of time before the most powerful Mediterranean Sea powers clashed. Between 1256 and 1381, Genoa and Venice fought four major wars.[84] As early as 1238, truces and treaties sought to medi-

81 Lane, *Venice*, 5; Crouzet-Pavan, *Venise triomphante*, 75–138; Geoffrey Parker, *Sovereign City: The City-State through History* (London: Reaktion Books, 2004), 82.

82 David S. Chambers, *The Imperial Age of Venice, 1380–1580* (London: Thames & Hudson, 1970), 38; Donald M. Nicol, *Byzantium and Venice. A Study in Diplomatic and Cultural Relations* (Cambridge: University Press, 1992).

83 Epstein, *Genoa*, 28–69; Lane, *Venice*, 5; Nicholas Walton, *Genoa, 'La Superba': The Rise and Fall of a Merchant Pirate Superpower* (London: Hurst & Company, 2015), 14–5. One of the best analyses of Genoese seaborne-commercial expansion is Roberto S. Lopez, *Storia delle colonie genovesi nel Mediterraneo* (Torino: Marietti1820, 1996); John H. Pryor, *Logistics of Warfare in the Age of the Crusades: Proceedings of a Workshop held at the Centre for Medieval Studies*, University of Sydney, 30 Sept.–4 Oct. 2002 (Farnham: Ashgate, 2006), 64–5; Michel Balard, 'Genuensis civitas in extremo Europae: Caffa from the 14th to the 15th century', in David Abulafia and Nora Berend (eds.), *Medieval Frontiers: Concepts and Practices* (London: Routledge, 2002), 143–51.

84 Gherardo Ortalli, 'Venezia-Genova: percorsi paralleli, conflitti, incontri' in idem and Dino Puncuh (eds.), *Genova, Venezia, il Levante nei secoli XII–XIV. Atti del convegno internazionale di studi, Genova-Venezia, 10–14 marzo 2000 (Genova/Venezia: Società Ligure di Storia Patria/Istituto Veneto di Scienze, Lettere ed Arti, 2001)*, 9–28; David S. Kelly, 'Genoa and Venice: an early commercial rivalry', in William R. Thompson (ed.), *Great Power Rivalries* (Columbia: University of South Carolina Press, 1999), 125–52; Antonio Musarra, *Il grifo e il leone. Genova e Venezia in lotta per il Mediterraneo* (Bari: Laterza, 2020); idem., *Genova e il mare nel Medioevo* (Bologna: Il Mulino, 2015); Ermanno Or-

ate their rivalry in the Levant. The 1355 peace treaty in particular imposed restrictions on Venetian navigation in the Ligurian Sea (stretching approximately from Nice to Rome) and on Genoese access to the Adriatic.[85] However, in the intermitting periods of peace, brawls, and acts of piracy and private naval warfare between the two trading communities remained commonplace.[86] Ultimately, Venice obtained an uneasy and costly victory, narrowly avoiding disaster during the War of Chioggia (1378–1381), when Genoa came close to annihilating the lagoon city.[87] The Peace of Turin, signed in 1381, solidified Venetian dominance over Levantine and spice trade routes while reaffirming the reciprocal navigation restrictions established in the 1355 treaty.[88] Following this major setback, Genoa refocused its activities on the western Mediterranean, strengthening its economic ties with the Iberian Peninsula and North Africa.[89]

Of particular interest here is the fact that both Venice and Genoa developed such strong ties to the sea that they felt compelled to construct a legal framework to justify their naval power. As a result, the two republics asserted extensive jurisdictional-territorial control over the seas adjacent to their shores: Venice over the Adriatic, known at the time as the 'Gulf of the Venetians' (*Gulfus Venetiarum*) in maps and international documents (including the Genoese-Venetian treaties of 1355 and 1381), and Genoa over the upper Tyrrhenian (or Ligurian) Sea.[90] Both seas were crossed by important trade and

---

lando, *Venezia e il mare nel Medioevo* (Bologna: Il Mulino, 2014); John Dotson, 'Venice, Genoa and control of the seas in the thirteenth and fourteenth centuries', in John B. Hattendorf and Richard W. Unger (eds.), *War at Sea in the Middle Ages and the Renaissance* (Woodbridge: Boydell Press, 2003), 119–36.

85 The Treaty is printed in *Liber iurium reipublicae genuensis* [=Monumenta historiae patriae 7], vol. 2 (Turin: Officina regia, 1857), columns 617–27 [CCVIII, 1 June 1355].

86 Epstein, *Genoa*, 103–7; Lozzi, *Codici e consuetudini*, 367; Dino Puncuh, 'Trattati Genova-Venezia, secc. XII–XIII', in Ortalli and idem (eds.), *Genova, Venezia, il Levante*, 129–58.

87 Luigi A. Casati, *La guerra di Chioggia e la pace di Torino: Saggio storico con documenti inediti* (Firenze: Le Monnier, 1866), 248–54.

88 Text printed in *Liber iurium reipublicae genuensis* [=Monumenta historiae patriae 7], vol. 2, 858–906 [CCLVI, 8 August 1381].

89 John J. Norwich, *A History of Venice* (London: Penguin Books, 2003), 255–7; Fernand Braudel, 'Venise', in idem and George Duby (eds.), *La Méditerranée. II: Les hommes et l'héritage* (Paris: Flammarion, 1986), 178–9; Walton, *Genoa*, 59–60. The jurist Angelus de Ubaldis expounded the limitation to Genoese navigation in the Adriatic Sea in a *consilium*. See Angelus de Ubaldis, *Consilia D. Angeli de Ubaldis perusini…* (Francofurti: Typis Andrea Wecheli, 1575), *consilium* n. 290, 205–7.

90 Robert Fredona, 'Angelo degli Ubaldi and the Gulf of the Venetians: custom, commerce, and the control of the sea before Grotius', in idem and Sophus A. Reinert (eds.), *New Perspectives on the History of Political Economy* (London: Palgrave Macmillan, 2018),

navigation routes, serving as lifelines for the two city-states. Genoa and Venice sought to control all shipping within 'their' waters and to ensure that cargoes were unloaded and taxed in their harbours.[91] Throughout the thirteenth and fourteenth centuries, Genoa waged numerous wars against the Pisans, the Aragonese, and Muslim potentates to obtain control over Corsica and Sardinia.[92] By the 1280s (Battle of Meloria, 5–6 August 1284), the Genoese had decisively crushed Pisan competition and asserted their exclusive control over the waters between southern France, Sardinia, and the Italian peninsula. For instance, as early as 1174, Count Raymond v of Toulouse (r. 1148–1194), then the most powerful prince in the region, granted Genoa a monopoly over trade and navigation along the southern shores of France:

> I yield to you in favour of the community of Genoa, all customs of the harbours situated between the said place of la Turbie and Narbonne, so that your citizens shall enjoy comprehensive and complete freedom from dues, personally as well as with respect to the goods, which they bring with them, and so that you may receive there and bar from there whom you wish. Nor shall I, contrary to your will, receive or permit to be received any person, except my own people and the inhabitants of my dominions. If it should happen that enemies of yours should be driven off their course into any one of these harbours, I shall not permit them to leave this harbour without your advice and consent [...]. Also I shall forbid the merchants of my dominions from sailing or arranging voyages across the sea for commercial purposes without permission of the consuls of Genoa.[93]

On the opposite side of the peninsula, Venice imposed its supremacy across the upper Adriatic, as early as the eleventh century. Over the following centuries, the Venetians extended their influence further south, across the middle

29–73, at 37–9; Josip Faričić, Orietta Selva and Dragan Umek, 'Geographical Names of the Adriatic Sea on Medieval and Early-Modern Maps and Nautical Charts', *Journal of Historical Geography*, 82 (2023), 68–80.

91 Lane, *Venice*, 61–5; Chambers, *The Imperial Age of Venice*, 38; Lozzi, *Codici e consuetudini*, 362.

92 Epstein, *Genoa*, 24–5; Jacques Heers, *Gênes au XVe siècle: Activité économique et problèmes sociaux* (Paris: Sevpen, 1961), 19–22.

93 'Monopoly of trade and navigation at the French Coast granted to Genoa by Count Raymond of Toulouse', in Grewe, *Fontes*, I, 676–7.

and lower Adriatic.[94] They created a colonial empire *ante litteram* (the so-called *Stato da Mar*), building a network of naval bases, from which the Republic could project its sea power into the Ionian and Aegean Seas. Until the late fourteenth century, Venice deliberately avoided acquiring territories on mainland Italy, focusing all its energies on naval power and the acquisition of strategically located overseas territories.[95] The *Serenissima* substantiated its claims over the Adriatic, despite never fully controlling both its shores, imposing its jurisdiction and positioning itself as the protector of peaceful trade from pirates.

At a later stage, Venetian authorities restricted foreign military vessels from entering the Adriatic without explicit permission. Merchant vessels, on the other hand, were allowed freedom of navigation, although Venetian military galleys reserved the right to inspect them to ensure compliance with Venetian navigation laws. Chief among these was the requirement for ships to dock at the port of Venice, pay tolls, and offer their cargo for sale. As noted by Lane, 'a vital use of Venetian sea power was the channelling of trade through Venice'.[96] These policies made it possible to centralise commerce, beating the competition of other Adriatic ports. Other regional players officially recognised Venetian supremacy after it was imposed de facto. Cities such as Ferrara, Ancona, and Trieste challenged it, without success.[97]

Furthermore, the Venetians always boasted of how the medieval universalist institutions had acknowledged their claims from early on. One precise episode was deemed particularly relevant. Amid the twelfth-century struggles between the papacy and Holy Roman empire, the city hosted the negotiations between the Emperor Frederick I (r. 1155–1190) and Pope Alexander III (r. 1159–1181). The exact role played by the Venetians is still debated; however, the event became soon something in between history and mythical self-celebration.[98]

---

94 Lane, *Venice*, 27; Chambers, *The Imperial Age of Venice*, 44; Ruthy Gertwagen, 'The naval power of Venice in the oriental Mediterranean in the Middle Ages', in Michel Balard (ed.), *The Sea in History – Vol. II, The Medieval World* (Woodbridge: Boydell Press, 2017), 170–83.

95 Freddy Thiriet, *La Romanie vénitienne au Moyen Age. Le développement et l'exploitation du domaine colonial vénitien (XIIe–XVe siècles)* (Paris: De Boccard, 1975); Benjamin Arbel, 'Venice's Maritime Empire in the Early Modern Period', in Dursteler (ed.), *A Companion to Venetian History*, 125–253; Theutenberg, 'Mare Liberum et Mare Clausum', 488.

96 These staple rights were resolutely enforced in the upper Adriatic, but in the middle and lower Adriatic they were less effective. See Lane, *Venice*, 60.

97 For example, after a short war in 1240, Ferrara accepted in a treaty that all goods arriving to Ferrara from the sea had to pass through Venice's port (and custom offices). Ibid., 62.

98 Filippo De Vivo, 'Historical Justifications of Venetian Power in the Adriatic', *Journal of the History of Ideas*, 64(2) (2003), 159–76, at 159–62.

What is certain is that the doge Sebastiano Ziani (r. 1172–1178) facilitated the negotiations, leading to the so-called Peace of Venice, in 1177.[99] In return, the Venetians received from the emperor something close to the acknowledgement of their supremacy in the Adriatic. They obtained free passage across the empire and exemption from imperial tolls. The subjects of the emperor were to receive similar privileges, however only 'as far as Venice, but no further' (*similiter et nostri per mare usque ad eos et non amplius*), i.e. not in the Adriatic.[100]

Additionally, tradition holds that Pope Alexander III presented the doge with a golden ring as a symbolic gesture of goodwill towards the lagoon city. Subsequent generations of Venetians interpreted this anecdote as recognition of Venice's dominion over the sea, providing the foundation of the 'Marriage of the Sea' (*Sposalizio del Mare*), a grand ceremonial event described as 'a carefully orchestrated apogee of the state liturgy'.[101] Each year the doge, accompanied by the republic's highest-ranking officials, reached the sea on board of a sumptuous ceremonial galley (*Bucintoro*), followed by hundreds of boats and greeted by a cannon salute. At the point where the lagoon met the open sea (*bocca di porto*), the doge would cast a gold ring into the waters, solemnly declaring: 'We wed you, sea, as a sign of true and perpetual domination' (*Desponsamus te mare, in signum veri perpetuique domini*).[102]

This ritual formula affirmed the dominion of Venice over the Adriatic and its eternal bond with the sea. It also held a placatory aspect, invoking the favour of the sea for Venetian seafarers. It was an expression filled with legal connotations, such as feudal investiture and the authority of the bridegroom over the bride, derived from Roman law (especially the institute of the *manus*).[103] The ceremony described was performed for centuries, usually in the presence of foreign diplomats, whose attendance the supporters of the Venetian cause in-

---

99 For the English translation of the treaty, see Ernest F. Henderson, *Select Historical Documents of the Middle Ages* (London: George Bell & Sons, 1896), 425–9. See also Andrea Zorzi, *La repubblica del leone* (Milano: Bompiani, 2001), 86–7.

100 Samuele Romanin, *Storia documentata di Venezia* (tomo II) (Venezia: Filippi Editore, 1972), 80–1; Norwich, *A History of Venice*, 116. For a detailed analysis, see Gerhard Rösch, *Venezia e l'impero, 962–1250. I rapporti politici, commerciali e di traffico nel periodo imperiale germanico* (Roma: Il Veltro, 1985), 40–7, 57–75.

101 Edward Muir, *Civic Ritual in Renaissance Venice* (Princeton: University Press, 1986), 121; De Vivo, 'Historical Justifications', 159; Luciano Pezzolo, 'The groom of the sea. Venetian sovereignty between power and myth' in J. D. Davies, Alan James, Gijs Rommelse (eds.), *Ideologies of Western Naval Power, c.1500–1815* (London: Routledge, 2019), 23–7.

102 Theutenberg, 'Mare Liberum et Mare Clausum', 488–9; Romanin, *Storia documentata di Venezia*, II, 82.

103 Romanin, *Storia documentata di Venezia*, vol. II, 82; Fulton, *The Sovereignty of the Sea*, 4.

terpreted as universal recognition of the *Serenissima*'s pretensions over the Adriatic. Therefore, the 'Marriage of the Sea', far from being a mere act of tradition and folklore, bore precise legal and political meanings.[104]

At the same time, art played a crucial role in supporting the Venetian government's long-standing program of public propaganda and myth-building. Through painting, architecture, and other artistic expressions, this program sought to celebrate Venice's exceptionalism, independence, wealth, and maritime dominance.[105] The winged lion of Saint Mark (*leone marciano*) – the symbol of the Republic of Venice – featured prominently on the city's flag and was carved into stone across public spaces, as well as on the walls and gates of dozens of Venetian fortresses stretching from Northern Italy to Cyprus.[106] Notably, painters often depicted the lion with its front paws firmly planted on land and its rear paws standing on water. This imagery symbolised Venice's fifteenth-century expansion into mainland Italy while simultaneously referring to its maritime empire in the eastern Mediterranean and legal claims over the Adriatic Sea, 'the Gulf of Venice'.[107] A striking example of this iconography combining land and sea is the winged lion painted by Vittore Carpaccio in 1516 (see below, Figure 1.2). In this work, the artist also included in the background the Doge's Palace – the seat of the Venetian government – along with various ships and the fortress of *San Nicolo del Lido* guarding the entrance to the lagoon. This composition powerfully reinforces the connection between the winged lion and Venice's political and naval power.[108]

2.3 *Medieval Doctrinal Developments*

The prominence of the Italian maritime republics in the economic and geopolitical sphere interacted with another trend of the time: the revival of the legal science, driven primarily by the rediscovery and reception of Roman law

104 De Vivo, 'Historical Justifications', 159.

105 See David Rosand, *Myths of Venice. The Figuration of a State* (Chapel Hill: University of North Carolina Press, 2001).

106 For an extensive treatment of the subject, see Alberto Rizzi, *I leoni di San Marco: il simbolo della Repubblica Veneta*, III vols. (Caselle: Cierre Edizioni, 2012).

107 Michael Knapton, 'The *Terraferma* State', in Dursteler (ed.), *A Companion to Venetian History*, 85–124; Arbel, 'Venice's Maritime Empire in the Early Modern Period', ibid., 125–253; Edward Grasman, 'A Salute to You: Expansion under the Wings of Saint Mark', *Artibus et Historiae*, 33(66) (2012), 121–31.

108 Daniele Ferrara, 'Carpaccio e lo spazio simbolico del bacino marciano. Il ritratto del doge Leonardo Loredan e il leone di San Marco', in Enrico Guidoni and Ugo Soragni (eds.), *Lo spazio nelle città venete (1348–1509)* (Rome: Edizioni Kappa, 1997), 203–16; Gabriele Matino and Patricia Fortini Brown (eds.), *Carpaccio in Venice: A Guide* (Venice: Marsilio, 2020).

FIGURE 1.2 The Lion of Saint Mark, by Vittore Carpaccio (1516). Tempera on canvas, 130 × 368 cm. Conserved at the Doge's Palace in Venice
SOURCE: FONDAZIONE MUSEI CIVICI VENEZIANI

as crystallised under Justinian and by the establishment of universities across northern Italy and beyond the Alps.[109] Scholars recovered and studied the *Corpus Iuris Civilis* – focusing on the legal texts and neglecting their original historical and cultural context – and Roman law came to its 'second life'.[110] This combination of factors sparked a new wave of legal reflection concerning the sea – the first significant development in this area since Roman times. By the fourteenth century, the maritime republics, having consolidated their power at sea, felt the need to legally justify the functions they were already accustomed to exercising. Consequently, it fell to Italian jurists to craft legal formulas that could reconcile the realities of maritime geopolitics with the Roman legal tradition. This task, however, was far from straightforward and presented considerable challenges.[111]

In addressing these challenges, Italian jurists of the *ius commune* tradition – glossators, post-glossators, and commentators – were confronted with the fact that states were extending their authority over the seas. While medieval jurists generally regarded the extension of political authority to adjacent seas as legally acceptable, the critical debates revolved around the extent of the mari-

109 Jacques Verger, 'The universities', in Michael Jones (ed.), *The New Cambridge Medieval History, vol. VI, 1300–1415* (Cambridge: University Press, 2000), 66–81; Antonio Padoa-Schioppa, *A History of Law in Europe. From the Early Middle Ages to the 20th Century* (Cambridge: University Press, 2017), 9.

110 Randall Lesaffer, *European Legal History: A Cultural and Political Perspective* (Cambridge: University Press, 2009), 252–61; Raoul C. Van Caenegem, *An Historical Introduction to Private Law* (Cambridge: University Press, 1992), 45–55.

111 Raestad, *La mer territoriale*, 12–3; Miguel Á. Ladero Quesada, 'Los debates sobre el Mare Clausum', *Cuadernos de Historia de España*, 74 (1997), 233–54, at 235.

time area that could be subject to exclusive rights and the legal nature of such rights.[112] Legal experts were tasked with interpreting contemporary international practices using the tools and terminology of Roman law. However, the geopolitical realities of the late medieval period – characterised by political fragmentation and the absence of a centralised authority capable of combating piracy or ensuring the safety of seafarers – differed significantly from those of ancient Rome.

In the process, late medieval jurists interacted with the legal legacy of Ancient Rome and began the transformation of Roman property law doctrines into principles capable of regulating relations between nations.[113] In particular, they elaborated the concepts of protection (*protectio*) and jurisdiction (*iurisdictio*), the latter being initially strictly related to the idea of *imperium*, to indicate a position of power.[114] During the fourteenth century, jurisdiction became the primary term to refer to both the right to judge and to punish.[115] In relation to pelagic spaces, most commentators shied away from the Roman concept of ownership (*dominium*), focusing instead on jurisdiction.

Bartolus of Saxoferrato (1314–1357), arguably the most celebrated jurist of his time, addressed the issue of coastal seas in the *Tractatus de insulis* (part of the larger *Tractatus de fluminibus*).[116] The declared aim of the treaty was to determine who could claim jurisdiction over islands, particularly those situated near the coastline. In doing so, it indirectly engaged with the question of

112 Ibid. Here the analysis focuses on the school of the 'commentators' and their immediate successors. See Joseph Canning, *A History of Medieval Political Thought: 300–1450* (London: Routledge, 1996), 161–73; Mario Ascheri, *The Laws of Late Medieval Italy (1000–1500): Foundations for a European Legal System* (Leiden: Brill, 2015), 105–242.

113 Perruso, 'The Development of the Doctrine of Res Communes', 80.

114 Calafat, *Une mer jalousée*, 38; Francesco Calasso, 'Iurisdictio del diritto comune classico', in *Studi in onore di Vincenzo Arangio-Ruiz nel XLV anno del suo insegnamento* (Napoli: Jovene, 1953), 423–43; Fabrizio Fabbrini, *La definizione del potere in Roma antica* (Rome: La Goliardica Editrice, 1983), 63–6; David Armitage, 'The elephant and the whale: empires and oceans in world history', in idem., *Foundations of Modern International Thought* (Cambridge: University Press, 2013), 52.

115 Pietro Costa, *Iurisdictio. Semantica del potere politico nella pubblicistica medievale* (Rome: Bulzoni, 2002), 114–6. The Romans had generally separated the *ius dicere* and *coercere*. Cf. Gilbert Gidel, *Le droit international public de la mer* (Paris: Établissements Mellottee Chateauroux, 1932), vol. I, 28.

116 See Francesco Maiolo, *Medieval Sovereignty: Marsilius of Padua and Bartolus of Saxoferrato* (Delft: Eburon, 2007); Cecil N. Sidney Woolf, *Bartolus of Sassoferrato, his Position in the History of Medieval Political Thought* (Cambridge: University Press, 1913); Carla Frova, 'Le traité de fluminibus de Bartolo da Sassoferrato (1355)', *Médiévales*, 36 (1999), 81–9. On Bartolus and prescription, see Edward Cavanagh, 'Prescription and Empire from Justinian to Grotius', *The Historical Journal*, 60(2) (2017), 273–99, at 282.

the limits of maritime jurisdiction. Bartolus wrote: 'it is to be considered whether the holder of the jurisdiction in a territory bordering the sea holds it in the sea itself and to what extent'.[117] In his analysis, Bartolus applied the Roman tradition in a dialectical and flexible manner. He acknowledged that an affirmative answer to the above question might seem unacceptable due to the principle that: 'the sea is common property of all' (*quia mare est communis omnibus*), and thus showed due respect to traditional Roman conception of the sea. However, he also argued that he did not aim to discuss of property, but jurisdiction.[118] By doing so, he effectively 'circumvented' the limitations inherent to the concept of *res communis*:

> The contrary is true, because in the same way, the head of a provincial administration has to purge this province on land of bad people (D., 1, 18, 13; *De officio praesidis*, fragm., 13), he ought to do this on sea (Cod., 11, 13, 1. *De classicis*). Thus it appears that he likewise holds the jurisdiction on sea and all the more on the islands situated in the said sea.[119]

The first issue Bartolus addressed was the definition of the 'close distance' required to establish *iurisdictio*. He cited various Roman sources to argue that polities could extend their jurisdiction over adjacent seas and the islands within them up to a distance of 100 Roman miles, approximately 150 kilometres. Bartolus justified this claim by referencing the Roman understanding of proximity, where a place was considered 'close' (*vicinum*) if it was located within 100 miles (*per centum miliaria*).[120] Regarding islands, Bartolus added:

> It is common language that those islands situated only a small distance from province belong to this province, just as the islands of Italy do (D. 50,16, 99, 91: »de verborum significatione«, fragm., 99, »notionum«). I am of the opinion that they are situated in modest distance if they lie within a distance up to 100 miles: a place is called vicinal, if it lies within such a distance from a second one. This is in conformity with the Liber

117 Bartolus of Saxoferrato, *Tyberiadis*, 55, reported in Grewe, *Fontes*, I, 692: '*Videndum est, an qui habet iurisdictionem in territorio coherenti mari, habeat in ipso mari, & usq; ad quod spacium*'.

118 Ibidem. See also Raestad, *La mer territoriale*, 12–3.

119 Bartolus of Saxoferrato, *Tyberiadis*, 55, reported in Grewe, *Fontes*, I, 692–3: '*In contrarium est veritas. Imo sicut præses provinciæ debet purgare provinciam malis hominibus per terram, vt. ff. de offic. presid.l.xiij, cogruit, ita etiam per aquam*'.

120 D., 50.16.99. See also Raestad, *La mer territoriale*, 14–5; Ernest Nys, *Le droit international. Les principes, les théories, les faits* (Paris: Weissenbruch, 1912), vol. I, 542.

> extra (V, 1, 3, 28) where it is stated that a place situated within a distance of a two-day journey cannot be called remote. It is notorious, however, that 100 miles on the sea are less than a two-day journey.[121]

Overall, it appears that Bartolus shrewdly interpreted Roman sources to admit *iurisdictio* over the coastal seas, also referencing a canon law source, the *Liber extra*, to strengthen his argument. But what does precisely Bartolus refer to with the term *iurisdictio*? A passage from his *Commentaria* to the *Digest* (D., 5.1.9), where Bartolus offers a legal opinion regarding a case in Pisa, illustrates his view. In this case, pirates who had ravaged the Pisan coastline were eventually captured on an island under Pisan control. Bartolus argued that in such circumstances, the authorities of Pisa had full jurisdiction to investigate the pirates' crimes in the coastal seas and to sentence them to death if those crimes were proven.[122] In another passage of his *Commentaria* (on the *Codex*), Bartolus confirmed his opinion in more general terms: 'It is evident, that, just as it can punish criminals within its territory, so it can do with regard to the sea, adjacent to the city or to the province'.[123] In other words, polities could extend their jurisdiction for the purpose of pursuing and punishing pirates.

Hence, Bartolus imagined maritime *iurisdictio* to be essentially a criminal jurisdiction extending up to 100 miles from the coast. Bartolus' authoritative opinion, and especially the 100 miles limit, was generally accepted by the other Italian scholars of the fourteenth and fifteenth centuries. For example, Paulus Castrensis,[124] Bartholomaeus Caepolla, and Felinus Sandeus.[125] Angelus de Ubaldis (or de Perusio) (1328–1407) put forth the only notable dissenting opinion. He claimed that the crimes committed at sea had to be punished by the authorities of the state that was closer to the *locus commissi delicti*, notwithstanding the distance from the coast.[126] As mentioned above, Bartolus focused its analysis on the criminal jurisdiction *in mari adjacenti*. One of Bartolus' most renowned successors, Baldus de Ubaldis (1327–1400), expanded upon Bartolus' analysis and sought to further clarify the nature of the rights

121 Bartolus of Saxoferrato, *Tyberiadis*, 55, in Grewe, *Fontes*, I, 693.

122 Raestad, *La mer territoriale*, 16; Nys, *Le droit international*, 541; Calafat, *Une mer jalousée*, 38.

123 My translation, Bartolus of Saxoferrato, *Commentaria*, Cod., 11.12.1: '*patet, quod sicut potest punire delinquentes in territorio suo, ita in mari adjacenti illi civitati, vel provinciae*'.

124 Idem, *Commentaria*, D., 39.4.15.

125 Idem, *Commentaria*, Decr., 1.3.35.

126 Angelus de Perusio, *Commentaria*, D. 5.1.9: '*Etiam si illa maris particula esset valde remota, si tamen nulli alii loco terrestri esset propiquor ubi exercetur imperium*'.

that could be exercised over pelagic areas.[127] In his works, Baldus frequently used Venetian and Genoese claims as illustrative examples. In one of his *Commentaria* on the *Digest*, he wrote: 'The sea is for its use common to all, it cannot be anybody's property. The jurisdiction belongs to the Emperor. A threefold distinction is to be made: property, use, jurisdiction, and protection'.[128]

In this passage, Baldus reaffirmed that the sea could not be subject to either private or public ownership, maintaining that its use must remain common to all. However, he also asserted that the sea was subject to the authority and jurisdiction of the Holy Roman Emperor, whom he identified as *dominus mundi* and the successor to the Roman *princeps*. The subsequent question concerned whether polities, such as Venice, could acquire rights over the sea from the emperor. On this point, most commentators reached a consensus, including Bartholomeus Caepolla (1420–1475). Caepolla, a distinguished professor at the University of Padua, was also active in diplomacy, notably serving as an ambassador for the Republic of Venice at the imperial Diet of Regensburg in 1471.[129] In his *Tractatus de servitutibus*, primarily focused on issues of civil law, he also addressed the potential acquisition of exclusive rights over the sea. Of particular importance is chapter 26, entitled *De mari*, 'On the sea'.

Significantly, Caepolla decided to deal with the sea in the section focused on the *servitutes rusticorum praediorum,* or rustic easements. This location suggests that in his opinion, the issue of control over the sea could be solved, applying legal institutes and categories developed, having territory as a reference.[130] Caepolla maintained that the sea, '*quod natura ominibus patet*', could not be subject to private servitudes because its use was common to everyone. However, he suggested that rulers (*princeps*) could acquire such

127 Raestad, *La mer territoriale*, 19. For further details, see Joseph Canning, *The Political Thought of Baldus de Ubaldis* (Cambridge: University Press, 1987); Dante Fedele, *The Medieval Foundations of International Law: Baldus de Ubaldis (1327–1400). Doctrine and Practice of the Ius Gentium* (Leiden/Boston: Brill/Nijhoff, 2021).

128 Baldus de Ubaldis, Comm. I (D., 1.8.2), fol. 51, in Grewe, *Fontes*, I, 693: '*Dico quod (mare) est commune quo ad usum, sed proprietas est nullius* [...] *sed iurisdictio est Caesaris et sic ista tria sunt diversa. s. proprietas usus iurisdictio et protectio*'.

129 Onofrio Ruffino, 'Cipolla Bartolomeo', in *Dizionario biografico degli italiani*, II, vol. 25 (Roma: Istituto della Enciclopedia Italiana, 1981), online edition: http://www.treccani.it/enciclopedia/bartolomeo-cipolla_(Dizionario-Biografico)/; Christian Zendri, '*Mare passim omnibus patet*: il diritto del mare agli inizi dell'età moderna (secc. XV–XVII)', *Archivio Scialoja-Bolla. Annali di studi sulla proprietà collettiva*, 1 (2007), 97–8.

130 Zendri, 'Mare passim omnibus patet', 99–100.

rights.[131] He reaffirmed imperial jurisdiction as a general principle[132] but added that the emperor could transfer his prerogatives 'by donation, i.e., by granting title or privilege'.[133] Additionally, these prerogatives could be lost through non-use or by prescription in favour of a third party.[134] In his *Tractatus*, he expressly took the Venetians and the Genoese as examples of successfully established maritime jurisdictions:

> The Venetians, who have possessed the Gulf of the Adriatic Sea for so long that no memory exists of its beginning, have prescribed jurisdiction over this sea; and likewise, the Genoese have done so with their sea, as noted by learned scholars in the aforementioned places. But the foregoing is understood to be true when it is alleged that a title or privilege of the Emperor is cited, or that they, or their ancestors, believed they had a right over the sea...[135]

Thus, the commentators did not focus on developing a distinct legal status for the *res communes* and its practical implications. Even though they differentiated them theoretically, they partially assimilated jurisdiction to property rights as to their practical functioning. Consequently, the idea that polities could acquire exclusive maritime *iurisdictio* became acceptable, as it could be achieved through the same means of acquisition of property in Roman law – for instance, by donation. These jurists shifted their focus from the legal distinctiveness of the *res communes* category to property law doctrines. The latter seemed more suited for determining what rights could be acquired over the sea and were more favourable to claims of exclusive rights.

Several jurists argued that Venice and Genoa had acquired the emperor's maritime *iurisdictio*. To the commentators, it seemed logical that since

---

131 Bartholomaeus Caepolla, *Tractatus de servitutibus: tam urbanorum, quam rusticorum praediorum* (Coloniæ Agrippinæ: Apud Ioannem Gymnicum, 1616), Tract. II, ch. XXVI, § 1, 643.

132 Ibid., ch. XXVI, § 6, 645: '*Mari, quod natura omnibus patet, servitus private imponi non potest* [...] *quia maris communis est usus omnibus hominibus, ut aeris* [...] *Sed à principe imponi servitus mari potest...*'.

133 Perruso, 'The Development of the Doctrine of Res Communes', 81.

134 Ibidem.

135 My translation from Caepolla, *Tractatus de servitutibus*, ch. XXVI, § 6, 645: '*Veneti, qui gulphum maris Adriatici tanto tempore, cuius non extat memoria, possederunt, ipsum mare quoad eius iurisdictione prescripserunt, & similiter Ianuenses in mari suo, ut not. Doct. in dictis locis. Sed prœdicta intelligo vera, quando allegatur titulus seu privilegium Imperatoris, vel quod credat se, vel maiores suos habuisse ius in mari...*'

the emperor could grant such rights, they could also be prescribed against him.[136] According to Angelus de Ubaldis, the Venetians and Genoese had even acquired ownership of their respective seas by title of prescription from immemorial times.[137] Baldus and Bartolus concurred, stating that both the Venetians and Genoese claimed to have acquired *iurisdictio* over 'their' seas *ex inveteratissima consuetudine* and long-established custom.[138]

It thus became generally accepted that the maritime republics had acquired a legal position over the seas they claimed, whether a use, an easement, a jurisdiction, or ownership. Several leading scholars regarded their entitlements as a sufficient basis for imposing taxes on shipping (*gabellas*) and interfering with foreign navigation.[139] However, Baldus disagreed on this point, arguing that the above-mentioned prerogatives (*regalia*) were not part of maritime jurisdiction and belonged only to the emperor. Nevertheless, he concluded that cities could levy tolls if they did not recognise an overlord (as was the case with Venice);[140] Caepolla concurred with this view.[141] Thus, even Baldus recognised maritime *iurisdictio* as something that could be acquired from the emperor, with or without his consent.[142] Besides, Bartolus had already acknowledged that the authority of the emperors was increasingly becoming a legal fiction in the changing European political context of the time.[143]

As Richard Perruso observed: 'The use sought by the Venetians was not the right to navigate the Adriatic. Rather, the Venetians sought the right to exclude others from navigating the Adriatic, something that was the functional equivalent of ownership'.[144] Indeed, the prerogatives claimed and exercised – especially by Venice – went far beyond mere criminal jurisdiction. While Ven-

136 Perruso, 'The Development of the Doctrine of Res Communes', 81.

137 Angelus de Ubaldis, *Commentaria*, Inst. 2.1 (ed. n. 36, fol. 61va); idem, *Consilia*, n. 290, 205–7. On Angelus, Baldus' brother, see Fredona, 'Angelo degli Ubaldi and the Gulf of the Venetians', in idem and Reinert (eds.), *New Perspectives*, 29–73.

138 Baldus, *Commentaria*, D., 1.8.1 (ed. n. 37, tom. I, fol. 45rb); Bartolus, *Commentaria*, D., 47.10.13.7, *Omnia quae extant opera*, Venice 1615, tom. VI, fol. 130vb.

139 Caepolla, *Tractatus de servitutibus*, ch. XXVI, § 10, 647.

140 Baldus, *Commentaria*, D. 1.8.1 (ed. n. 37, tom. I, fol. 45rb). Venice had never been part of the Holy Roman Empire, as opposed to the rest of northern Italy.

141 Caepolla, *Tractatus de servitutibus*, ch. XXVI, § 10, 647: *'Item quia veneti in eorum imperio habent regalia, & iura fisci, nec superiorem saltem de facto, recognoscunt, ideo in mari predicto possunt imponere gabellas, & confiscare merces, & bona sicut in civitate Venetiarum: quia tantam iurisdictionem habent in mari, quantam in civitate Venetiarum'*.

142 Baldus, *Commentaria*, D. 1.8.1.

143 Sidney Woolf, *Bartolus of Sassoferrato*, 21–7; Grewe, *Epochs*, 43–8; Maiolo, *Medieval Sovereignty*, 231–4.

144 Perruso, 'The Development of the Doctrine of Res Communes', 80.

ice never outright prohibited navigation, it heavily interfered with it, asserting its role as the exclusive *domina* of the Adriatic. However, it is important to note that Venetian legal claims never extended beyond the Adriatic. Even during periods when Venetian maritime power reached as far as Cyprus and the Black Sea, the Republic refrained from formulating broader claims in the eastern Mediterranean, instead confining its assertions to the more manageable Adriatic Sea.[145]

From what has been said above, it appears that Italian scholars formally upheld the principle of the common ownership of the sea throughout the Middle Ages. However, this idea had a limited impact on the doctrinal development of the legal status of pelagic areas. Jurists tended to apply similar legal principles to private, public, and common property, effectively harmonising the treatment of the three categories outlined in the *Corpus Iuris Civilis*. In doing so, they blurred the distinctions between these categories, especially when addressing land territories and coastal seas.[146] Thus, Caepolla considered it natural and reasonable for a sovereign to exercise criminal jurisdiction over the sea within a 100-mile limit to the same extent that such authority was enforced on land (*sicut in terra in suo territorio*).[147] The elaboration of jurisdiction as a legal position theoretically distinct from ownership, particularly concerning pelagic spaces, became a long-lasting legacy that early modern jurists would continue to develop and expand.

To conclude, it is worth recalling Francesco Maiolo's conceptualisation of a medieval, 'embryonic' notion of sovereignty. According to him, medieval sovereignty was not solely tied to raw power (*potestas*) but also to authority (*auctoritas*), which served as the foundation for legitimate rule and sovereignty. This authority derived either from a political community, from God, or from both.[148] Maiolo further notes that: 'A widely accepted hypothesis is that in medieval sources, the term *iurisdictio* appeared as synonymous with *domin-*

145 Lane, *Venice*, 67–72.

146 Perruso, 'The Development of the Doctrine of Res Communes', 80.

147 Caepolla, *Tractatus de servitutibus*, cap. XXVI, § 14, 649: '*Quod habentes iurisdictione etia in mari, & in insulis, quæ sunt in mari vicino usque ad centu miliaria: & possunt ita capere & punire delinquentes in maria usque ad centa miliaria, sicut in terra in suo territorio*'. My transl.: 'Since they also have jurisdiction on the sea, and on the islands to be found in the adjacent sea, up to 100 miles (from the coast): they can capture and punish criminals on the sea up to 100 miles, just like on land, in their territory'.

148 Maiolo, *Medieval Sovereignty*, 70–1; Walter Ullmann, 'The Development of the Medieval Idea of Sovereignty', *The English Historical Review*, 64(250) (1949), 1–33.

ium, as well as *imperium*, and that in both cases, it denoted *potestas*'. These different terms being 'gathered in the semantic area of legal and political discourse that today is occupied by the idea of sovereignty'.[149] In other words, throughout the Middle Ages:

> Jurisdiction played the role of 'synthesis of powers', and, given the needs of feudal society, was one of the most versatile legal tools to exploit. This notion somehow reflected more general concerns, like the concern about the problem of hierarchies of power and their normative foundation.[150]

FIGURE 1.3 The commercial networks of Genoa (red, purple), Venice (blue, purple), and the Hanseatic League (black)
SOURCE: WIKIMEDIA COMMONS

149 Maiolo, *Medieval Sovereignty*, 70–1.
150 Ibid., 143.

3 The Seas of Northern Europe

3.1 *The Nordic Kingdoms and the Hanse*

The seas of northern Europe represent the second significant area for the development of the law of the sea in medieval Europe, particularly the marine areas now known as the Baltic Sea, the Norwegian Sea, and the North Sea. A distinction must be made: the Baltic Sea is a shallow, almost landlocked body of water. Its shores have long been home to diverse peoples and political entities, who equally relied on its waters for communication and resource exploitation. As a result, the Baltic soon became both an area of exchange and a zone of conflict. In contrast, the North Sea is a more open body of water, stretching between Norway, the British Isles, and the continental coasts. The North and Baltic Seas have historically formed a unitary geographical area, or a single maritime trading region; for this reason, they will be treated together in this paragraph.[151] In a broader sense, the term 'seas of northern Europe' can also encompass the waters of the North Atlantic Ocean lying between the Scandinavian Peninsula, Scotland and Greenland, sometimes referred to as the *Oceanus Septentrionalis* in ancient maps and sources. Indeed, following the Viking colonisation of the Hebrides, Shetland Islands, Orkney, Iceland, and Greenland, the geographical scope of the region expanded dramatically.[152]

As previously noted, Roman legal thought regarding the sea had a more limited influence beyond the Mediterranean, particularly in the Baltic region. Nevertheless, far from being a 'lawless' space, the seas of northern Europe witnessed the development of influential regional sea laws and codes such as the *Laws of Visby* (or Gotlandic *water recht*).[153] These laws were named

151 Dirk Meier, *Seafarers, Merchants and Pirates in the Middle Ages* (Woodbridge: Boydell Press, 2009), 10; Geoffrey Scammel, *Preface* to David Kirby and Merja-Liisa Hinkkanen, *The Baltic and the North Seas* (London: Routledge, 2000), ix–x; North, *The Baltic*, 1.

152 Peter Sawyer, 'The Viking expansion', in Helle (ed.), *The Cambridge History of Scandinavia*, I, 106–7.

153 Raestad, *La mer territoriale*, 44; Wolfgang Preiser, 'History of international law, ancient times to 1648', in *The Max Planck Encyclopedia of Public International Law*, vol. IV (Oxford: University Press, 2012), 884; Carsten Jahnke, 'The maritime law of the Baltic Sea', in Balard (ed.), *The Sea in History*, II, 576–84. Edda Frankot convincingly argues that the *Laws of Visby* compiled legal materials that likely did not originate in Wisby but elsewhere. See Edda Frankot, 'Medieval maritime law from Oléron to Wisby: jurisdictions in the law of the sea', in Juan Pan-Montojo and Frederik Pedersen (eds.), *Communities in European History: Representations, Jurisdictions, Conflicts* (Pisa: Edizioni Plus – Pisa University Press, 2007), 151–72; idem, *'Of Laws of Ships and Shipmen': Medieval Maritime Law and its Practice in Urban Northern Europe* (Edinburgh: University Press, 2012).

after the important trading city of Visby, located on the Baltic Island of Gotland. Such sea codes placed particular emphasis on regulating commercial interactions and maritime law issues, such as contracts, shipwreck, and jettison.

Broadly speaking, throughout the Middle Ages, the jurists of the countries bordering the seas of northern Europe did not display a particular interest in defining the legal status of the sea. As a result, customary practices and state actions hold particular importance for understanding legal developments in northern Europe.[154] These developments were largely shaped by the unstable balance of power between two major actors: the Nordic kingdoms – most notably Denmark and Norway – on one hand, and the Hanseatic League on the other. This paragraph focuses on analysing this complex interaction. Similar to the Mediterranean, the legal discourse concerning the sea in northern Europe was deeply intertwined with commercial interests and political hegemony, often making it indistinguishable from the latter two.

From the eleventh century onwards, the Nordic kingdoms evolved into more centralised entities and assumed a leading role in the region.[155] They strengthened their legal-political structures and projected their authority over adjacent seas. Norway, in particular, provides a fascinating case of study. The westernmost of the Nordic Kingdoms developed a special relationship with the vast *Oceanus Septentrionalis*, which extended westward along its long and indented coastline. Norway's economy was heavily reliant on local fisheries, especially cod and herring, which were critical both for domestic consumption and export. This bond with the sea intensified when the islands as far west as Greenland – such as the Shetlands, Faroes, Orkneys, and Iceland – were colonised by Norse settlers and subsequently became 'tax lands' directly subjected to the Norwegian Crown.[156]

Ancient Norwegian laws, such as the *Gulatingslov* and the *Frostatingslov*, outlined the extension of royal authority over the coastal seas.[157] These

154 Raestad, *La mer territoriale*, 28; Meier, *Seafarers, Merchants and Pirates*, 98–104.

155 North, *The Baltic*, 346; Thomas Riis. 'The states of Scandinavia, c.1390–c.1536', in Allmand (ed.), *The New Cambridge Medieval History*, VII, 671–706.

156 Derry, *A History of Scandinavia*, 48–9; Meier, *Seafarers, Merchants and Pirates*, 98–104; Archibald R. Lewis and Timothy J. Runyan, *European Naval and Maritime History, 300–1500* (Bloomington: Indiana University Press, 1985), 86–110; Ryan Sines, *Norse in the North Atlantic* (Lanham: Hamilton Books, 2020).

157 The first one was developed in the south-west of the country, the second one in the northern regions. See Theutenberg, 'Mare Liberum et Mare Clausum', 482; Lozzi, *Codici e consuetudini*, 215–7.

codes established the principle that the king's rule extended up to the median line, drawn at equal distance between the coasts of Norway and neighbouring polities (*Gulatingslov*, III; *Frostatingslov*, IX, 6).[158] It should be noted that medieval Nordic people did not conceive of the Northern Atlantic as an unlimited body of water or an open ocean.[159] Rather, they perceived it as an internal sea, enclosed by land – some already discovered, others were still unknown. Greenland (*Terra Viridis*), for instance, was believed to be connected in some way to north-western Russia. In any case, as Norwegian kings ruled most of the shores bordering the 'Northern Sea', they started to see themselves as 'Masters of the Sea' and 'Lords of Both Shores' in relation to the pelagic spaces stretching between their mainland and island territories.[160] Diplomatic correspondence and treaties from this period suggest a broad acceptance of coastal states' jurisdiction over adjacent seas. However, defining the exact nature and limits of these prerogatives remains challenging. For instance, in 1326, Novgorod and Norway reached an agreement to settle a border dispute in the Finnmark region. In the treaty, the territory of the Norwegian king was described as encompassing both the lands and the seas under his control.[161]

The first legal concept to emerge in this context was likely *protectio*, encompassing the idea that coastal polities were obligated to protect all vessels within their coastal waters from pirates. Norwegian rulers claimed and exercised this prerogative along their coasts and expected other polities to do the same. For example, in 1247, King Haakon IV Haakonsson of Norway (r. 1217–1263) wrote to the city council of Lübeck, protesting that pirates had seized Norwegian merchant ships bound for the Baltic in waters near the Hanseatic city, which were supposedly under its jurisdiction.[162] In retaliation, King Haakon seized German vessels in Norwegian ports, holding Lübeck liable for failing to protect Norwegian merchants in its home waters. In response, German envoys pleaded with the king not to hold their city accountable for

158 Quoted in the *Fisheries* case, ICJ 1951, Counter-Memorial submitted by the Government of the Kingdom of Norway, 237. The original text of these ancient laws is available on the website of the Norwegian National Library: https://www.nb.no/items/b419b872fcc894b62c83d3cce5adc488?page=133.

159 Perhaps it is not hazardous to establish a parallel with the Mediterranean Sea in this regard.

160 Theutenberg, 'Mare Liberum et Mare Clausum', 482.

161 Raestad, *La mer territoriale*, 49.

162 This reaction represents a typically medieval reprisal. John A. Gade, *The Hanseatic Control of Norwegian Commerce during the Late Middle Ages* (Leiden: Brill, 1951), 28–33; Raestad, *La mer territoriale*, 49.

crimes committed by independent pirates. A correspondence ensued between the parties:

> We have received your letter, full of excuses, phrased in polite and detailed words, giving complaints for complaints. But it does not seem to us that you have satisfied our honour or the demands of our subjects, many of whom have suffered grievously on account of your actions, that is, unless restitution should later be made. [...] You who are guardians of the territory of the sea in question, permit our merchants who bring you their wares to be plundered by your people and hires soldiers, almost within your very harbours, and gather at one and the same time both the plunder and the robbers in your city and protect them both. Merchants should be able to travel in peace to, and remain among you, as safely as to a friendly fortress. [...] For you may be certain that we will not fail your men in what is right, but in everything fitting you will find us helpful, if you retain your friendly intercourse with us. Thus, send your ships to us during the summer with the usual goods, necessary to our realm, grain and malt, and allow our merchants the same freedom to purchase the same articles, as long as the scarcity of provisions last in Norway...[163]

The result of the Norwegian-Lübeck negotiations was the signing of a treaty in 1250. It granted freedom of navigation and trade for merchants of both parties, along with mutual assistance in cases of shipwreck. The Norwegian king se-

---

163 English translation from Gade, *The Hanseatic Control*, 32–3. The digitised version of the original Latin text, dated 1247–8, can be found in the online version of the *Diplomatarium Norvegicum*: '*Literas vestras prolixis satis uerbis et politis pro uobis excusaciones multifarie pretendentes et obiectiones obiectionibus proponentes recepimus. Sed in hoc nostro honori uel nostris hominibus tot et tociens a ciuitatibus dampnificatis non uidetur sufficienter satisfactum. nisi melior forte experiencia subsequatur* [...]. *Preterea circumspiciat diligenter vobis cum vestra discrecio, si uere careat scrupulo societatis quod dicitis. Pacem vobiscum et cum uestris habere diligimus. et tamen mercatores nostros ad uos bona sua defferentes quasi in portubus vestris vos illius breuis maris habentes custodiam, a uestris hominibus et uestris guerrariis conducticiis sustinetis spoliari, et spolia simul et spoliatores in vestra ciuitate colligentes quasi omnia benefecerint reseruatis. cum per uos et inter uos pacifice deberent pertransire et ad uos et ad vestros homines si opus haberent quasi ad murum et municionem se transferre* [...]. *Mittatis ergo ad nos naues uestras in estate more solito cum rebus nostro regno necessariis. cum blado et brasio et iddem nostris mercatoribus licenciam emendi concedatis dum caristia in regno nostro durauerit. Quia ea que magis sibi vestri mercatores viderint expedire non negabimus comparare*', vol. v, n. 1, https://www.dokpro.uio.no/perl/middelalder/diplom_vise_tekst.prl?b=4616&s=n&str=.

cured this agreement from a position of strength. However, over the following decades, Norway's international position weakened for various historical reasons. The country grew increasingly dependent on Hanseatic imports, particularly grain, to feed its growing population. In return, Hanseatic merchants received vast quantities of dried fish, which they distributed across Europe through their extensive trading network.[164] German merchants established a trading centre in Bergen – the famous *Kontor* – from which they dominated Norwegian trade, well into the fifteenth century, marginalising competition from England and the Low Countries.[165]

However, the perceived arrogance and wealth of the German merchants in the Bergen *Kontor* periodically provoked resentment among the local population, who grew increasingly hostile to the Germans' privileges and legal immunities. After his coronation in 1280, King Eirik II Praestehader (r. 1280–1299) sought to restrict these privileges. In retaliation, Hanseatic cities closed their ports to Norwegian ships and imposed a de facto grain embargo. By 1285, the Norwegian king was forced to capitulate, signing the Treaty of Kalmar, which not only restored but also expanded the privileges granted to German merchants.[166] Another treaty, signed in 1294, comprehensively addressed navigation and trade between Norway and the Hanse.[167] Hanseatic merchants once again secured liberties and commercial privileges but were officially forbidden from sailing north of Bergen. Only Norwegian subjects were allowed to venture towards Iceland or the rich fishing grounds along Helgeland, Finnmark, and the Lofoten Islands. Given that fisheries were the kingdom's primary source of food and income, it is understandable that Norwegian authorities sought to exclude foreign fishermen. Therefore, the king also established a monopoly over trade between northern Norway's fishing regions and Bergen, which became a staple port and the official gateway to Norway.[168]

Interestingly, a few years earlier, King Magnus VI, the Law-mender (r. 1263–1280), had promulgated the Norwegian Code of the Realm in 1274 (known today as *Magnus Lagabøters Landslov*), which replaced previous regional

164 North, *The Baltic*, 56; Meier, *Seafarers, Merchants and Pirates*, 124–5; Gade, *The Hanseatic Control*, 37.

165 Rolf Hammel-Kiesow, 'The early Hanses', in Donald J. Harreld (ed.), *A Companion to the Hanseatic League* (Leiden: Brill, 2015), 33; Raestad, *La mer territoriale*, 50; Ralph Davis, *English Overseas Trade, 1500–1700* (London: Macmillan, 1985), 28.

166 Gade, *The Hanseatic Control*, 41.

167 *Diplomatarium Norvegicum*, V, n. 23.

168 Nedkvitne, *The German Hansa and Bergen, 1100–1600* (Köln: Böhlau Verlag, 2014), 310; Raestad, *La mer territoriale*, 49; Theutenberg, 'Mare Liberum et Mare Clausum', 482.

codes.[169] The rule of the median line was not expressly mentioned in it, probably because it did not seem a major issue at the time since all islands to the west of Norway (Iceland, Greenland, the Faroes, Shetlands, and Orkneys) were already under Norwegian dominion.[170] The Hanseatic League accepted the limitation concerning navigation north of Bergen, content with its dominant position in trade within and south of the city. Because of the growing Hanseatic influence in the middle of the fifteenth century, a Norwegian law decreed that non-Hanseatic merchants could send to Bergen a maximum of two vessels every year. The Hanse showed a willingness to maintain the freedom of navigation towards Bergen, whenever its commercial routes were endangered, along with its ability to repel competitors.[171]

The 'Bergen limit', renewed in 1313 and 1348, applied to all foreigners. As a result, it frequently appeared in diplomatic negotiations between England and Norway (and later Denmark-Norway). English monarchs repeatedly accepted the restrictions on navigation imposed by the Scandinavian rulers. For instance, in 1429, Henry VI of England (r. 1422–1461, 1470–1471), under pressure from his uncle, the king of Norway, issued a statute forbidding his subjects from sailing north. This statute formally validated Norwegian maritime claims and stipulated punishments for trespassers.[172] In 1432, similar dispositions were included in a treaty between Norway and England.[173] Later, in the treaty of 1450 signed between Henry VI and Christian I, ruler of the Kalmar Union (which included Denmark, Norway, and Sweden). Among other things, the treaty aimed to placate Norwegian protests against English expeditions venturing north of Bergen. In the second part of the treaty, Henry banned his

169 Jørn Øyrehagen Sunde, 'Landslova av 1274 mellom historisk brot og kontinuitet', *Historisk Tidsskrift*, 101(4) (2022), 271–85.

170 The *Fisheries* case, ICJ 1951, Counter-Memorial submitted by the Government of the Kingdom of Norway, 238.

171 Gade, *The Hanseatic Control*, 57; Kirby and Hinkkanen, *The Baltic and the North Seas*, 90–1.

172 The statute is dated September 21: '*Statuimus prohibentes, ne quis ligeorum seu subditorum nostrorum de Regno nostro Anglie, proprie temeritatis ausu, contra ordinationem, prohibitionem et interdictum ipsius Avunculi nostri superius memorata, et in contemptum eorundem, Regna, Terras, Dominia, Districtus, Territoria, Jurisdictiones et Loca dicti Avunculi nostri, ingredi seu intrare presumat; sub pena forisfacture omnium bonorum suorum mobilium, et imprisonamenti persone sue, ad voluntatem nostram. Le Roy le voet*', in *Diplomatarum Norvegicum*, vol. XX, n. 779, online version, https://www.dokpro.uio.no/perl/middelalder/diplom_vise_tekst.prl?b=16756&s=n.

173 Treaty signed on December 24. The text is reported in *Norges gamle Love*, 'Recueil des anciennes Lois de Norvège', 2eme série, I, 135.

subjects from sailing towards *Islandiam, Halgalandiam, and Finnemarchiam,* reiterating the acceptance of Norwegian maritime claims.[174]

A subsequent treaty in 1465 retained these restrictions but introduced a provision allowing English merchants to request a special licence (*speciali licentia*) from the Norwegian Crown. Without such authorisation, offenders risked confiscation of their goods and even death.[175] It was not until 1490 that King Henry VII of England (r. 1485–1509) and John (Hans) of Denmark-Norway (r. 1481–1513) signed a treaty allowing English vessels to sail to the island of *Tyle* (Iceland) for trade and fishing purposes:

> It is also ordered by us that merchants [...], fishermen and all others subjects of the King of England may freely sail, approach, and enter, in the future, for ever, the Island of Tyle (*i.e. Iceland*), with their ships, goods and merchandise, foodstuffs and all other things, to buy, to sell, to fish, or to trade, and there be free to come and to stay, as often as it shall please them, without prohibition, molestation or hindrance from us.[176]

The treaty did not refer to northern Norway (e.g. Finnmark), presumably based on the understanding that the area would remain closed to the English. Moreover, even the freedom of navigation to Iceland was not granted unconditionally and the authority of the Nordic king over the Northern Atlantic (or *Oceanus Septentrionalis*) was still acknowledged. English seafarers wishing to sail north were required to request and obtain licenses from Dano-Norwegian authorities (*proviso semper quod, lapso septennio post datam præsentium immediate currente, licentiam novam a Nobis and Successoribus nostris petant et obtineant*),[177] renewing them every seven years in

174 'Conventio inter Henricum VI, Regem Angliæ, & Christiernum I Regem Daniæ; 9 April 1450', in *CUD*, III.1, 571.

175 'Tractatus Ligæ, Confæderationis & Amicitiae inter Eduardum IV, Regem Angliæ, & Christiernum I Regem Daniæ; 20 November 1465', ibid., 586.

176 'Tractatus Pacis inter Henricum VII, Regem Angliæ, & Johannem Regem Daniæ et Sueciæ; 20 Janvier 1490', ibid., III.2, 245. My translation from the original Latin text: '*Item, ordinatum est per nos quod mercatores* [...], *piscatores, & quicumque alii Regis Angliæ Subditi liberè possint, temporibus futuris, inperpetuùm, ad Insulam Tyle cum eorum navibus, bonis & mercandisis, victualibus & aliis rebus quibuscumque, emendi, vendendi, piscandi, sive mercandizandi causa, navigare, accedere, & intrare, ibique morari & liberere venire, totiens quotiens eis placuerit, absque prohibitione, molestatione, vel impedimento nostro*'.

177 Ibidem.

perpetuity.[178] The matter of the licences would eventually become an incandescent dossier at the end of the sixteenth century, when English merchants and sailors systematically avoided to renew them. As a result, Dano-Norwegian authorities would enforce the treaty's provisions through force. Thus, in medieval Norway, two distinct maritime regimes emerged: north of Bergen, a strict closed-sea policy prevailed, treating those waters as internal to the Norwegian realm, while south of Bergen, freedom of navigation was generally maintained.[179]

As mentioned earlier, the Hanseatic League emerged as another major regional power during the late medieval period. For nearly three centuries, it influenced the policies of neighbouring polities and dominated the regional trade system, stretching from Bruges to Novgorod.[180] Much has been written about the precise nature of the Hansa, and this is not the place to add to those debates.[181] However, it is clear that from its earliest stages, the term *Hansa* referred to associations of German merchants engaged in Baltic-northern trade, who began to unite to protect their shared interests.[182] Starting from the end of the thirteenth century, the term *Hansa* was used to refer to the loose association of merchant cities – mostly German or hosting consistent German merchant communities – located along the Baltic and North Sea. At its height, the League included more than a hundred cities, though it never developed a fixed and hierarchical organisation.[183] The free imperial city (*freie Reichsstadt*) of Lübeck, founded in 1143, gradually became the geograph-

178 Ibidem, '*ut sic, de septennio in septennio, mercatores & omnes predicti nos & Successores nostros, in impetratione novæ licentiæ, inperpetuum recognoscant*'. See also Raestad, *La mer territoriale*, 61.

179 The *Fisheries* case, ICJ 1951, Counter-Memorial submitted by the Government of the Kingdom of Norway, 237. However, it was far from easy to enforce prohibition to sail north, especially considering the irregularity of Norwegian coasts. The many times the ban was restated point out this difficulty.

180 Norbert Angermann and Klaus Friedland (eds.), *Novgorod. Markt und Kontor der Hanse* (Cologne: Böhlau Verlag, 2002).

181 For an overview, see Justyna Wubs-Mrozewicz and Stuart Jenks (eds.), 'Introduction' to idem (eds.), *The Hanse in Medieval and Modern Europe* (Leiden: Brill, 2013), 4–25; Louis Sicking, 'History of the Hanse: Construction and Deconstruction', *History Compass*, e12798 (2024), https://doi.org/10.1111/hic3.12798; Carsten Jahnke, *Die Hanse* (Stuttgart: Reclam Verlag, 2014).

182 Hammel-Kiesow, 'The early Hanses', 38–9; Nedkvitne, *The German Hansa and Bergen*, 12; Meier, *Seafarers, Merchants and Pirates*, 117.

183 Alexander Fink, 'The Hanseatic League and the concept of functional overlapping competing jurisdictions', *Kyklos*, 65(2) (2012), 194–217; Justyna Wubs-Mrozewicz, 'The Late Medieval and Early Modern Hanse as an Institution of Conflict Management', *Continuity and Change*, 32(1) (2017), 59–84.

ical and political centre of this 'association'. However, it was not until 1356 that representatives of the trading towns started to meet periodically in the Hanseatic Diet (*Tagfahrten* or *Hansetagen*).[184] These meetings addressed common interests, trading policies, and collective action against shared threats.

We have already seen how the Hanse imposed a blockade on Norway to pressure the Norwegian court. Such naval blockades were among the League's most effective weapons, as they could exclude their adversaries (or recalcitrant partners) from the Baltic trade network. Throughout the thirteenth, fourteenth, and fifteenth centuries, the Hanse declared blockades against trade partners and neighbours, including Novgorod, England, Flanders, and Denmark.[185] Since maritime trade was the foundation of the Hanseatic economy, its primary concern was maintaining freedom of navigation and countering excessive jurisdictional claims over major sea routes, which would have been detrimental to its interests.[186]

Hanseatic merchants could accept foreign jurisdiction in the coastal seas in relation to piracy but insisted on reserving for themselves, for example, criminal and civil jurisdictions regarding acts happened on board of their ships.[187] In any case, the Hanse did not promote the freedom of navigation as a universal principle for all seafarers. On many occasions, Hanseatic cities attempted to exclude the merchants from the Low Countries and England from the Baltic and were reluctant to extend equal privileges to trading partners.[188]

The eradication of piracy was frequently addressed at the *Hansetagen*. Hanseatic cities periodically united to police the seas and combat piracy,

---

184 North, *The Baltic*, 57–8; Meier, *Seafarers, Merchants and Pirates*, 133–6; Leonard P. Liggio, 'The Hanseatic League and Freedom of Trade', *Journal of Private Enterprise*, 23(1) (2007), 134–41; Carsten Jahnke, 'Lübeck and the Hanse. A queen without its body', in Wim Blockmans, Mikhail Krom and Justyna Wubs-Mrozewicz (eds.), *The Routledge Handbook of Maritime Trade around Europe, 1300–1600* (London: Routledge, 2017), 231–47.

185 They remained highly effective until the Hanse remained commercially dominant, and the member cities maintained a degree of cohesion. See Meier, *Seafarers, Merchants and Pirates*, 122; Jürgen Sarnowsky, 'The golden age of the Hanseatic League', in Harreld (ed.), *A Companion to the Hanseatic League*, 64; Gade, *The Hanseatic Control*, 56–7.

186 Carsten Jahnke, 'The Baltic trade', in Harreld (ed.), *A Companion to the Hanseatic League*, 194–240.

187 Raestad, *La mer territoriale*, 51; Stephen C. Rowell, 'Baltic Europe', in Jones (ed.), *The New Cambridge Medieval History*, VI, 699–734.

188 Kirby and Hinkkanen, *The Baltic and the North Seas*, 116. Regarding the complex Anglo-Hanseatic relationship, see also Henryk Zyns, *England and the Baltic* (Manchester: University Press, 1972), 8–26; Terence H. Lloyd, *England and the German Hanse, 1157–1611. A Study of their Trade and Commercial Diplomacy* (Cambridge: University Press, 1991); Dieter Seifert, *Kompagnons und Konkurrenten. Holland und die Hanse im späten Mittelalter* (Cologne: Böhlau Verlag, 1997).

such as under the 1259 agreement between Lübeck, Rostock, and Wismar, which was later joined by other cities.[189] In 1280, a treaty between the German settlement of Visby and Lübeck, joined by Riga two years later, provided for the joint protection of merchant shipping 'between the Oresund and Novgorod, or across the entire Baltic and all of its ports'.[190] However, like other powers of the time, the Hanseatic cities played an ambiguous role regarding piracy. On multiple occasions, even merchant cities employed maritime predation as a tool of war and commercial policy.[191] The distinction between licit and illicit plunder at sea, always blurred, was particularly so in the spatial-temporal context under consideration. This is well displayed by the events involving the 'victual brothers' (*Vitalienbrüder*), whose depredations almost led to the generalised collapse of Baltic maritime trade at the end of the fourteenth century.[192]

Despite piracy, the greatest threat to Hanseatic dominance came from the assertive policies of the Kingdom of Denmark, which emerged as the wealthiest of the Nordic territorial states.[193] Several factors contributed to Denmark's rise in prominence. Notably, the Danish Crown ruled territories strategically positioned to control the narrow waterways connecting the Baltic

189 'Resolution by Lübeck and other Hanse Cities on the Outlawry of Pirates, 1259', in Grewe, *Fontes*, I, 696. 'To all the faithful subjects of Christ [...] the communes of Lübeck, Rostock and Wismar [...] Since most merchants are not protected on the sea from pirates and robbers, we have, in a common council, decreed, and by this writing declare, that all who rob merchants in churches, in cemeteries, or on the water or on the land, shall be outlawed and proscribed by all cities and merchants. No matter where these robbers go with their booty, whatever city or land receives them shall be held equally guilty with them ...'. See also Hammel-Kiesow, 'The early Hanses', 56–7.

190 Hammel-Kiesow, 'The early Hanses', 32.

191 For instance, during the war against Eric of Pomerania in the 1420s. See Hammel-Kiesow, 'The early Hanses', 90–1; Juhan Kreem, 'Living on the edge: pirates and the Livonians in the 15th and 16th centuries', in Gerhard Jaritz and Juhan Kreem (eds.), *Edges of the Medieval World* (Budapest: Central European University Press, 2008); David K. Bjork, 'Piracy in the Baltic, 1375–1398', *Speculum, a Journal of Mediaeval History*, 18(1) (1943), 39–68. For a later period, see Philipp Höhn, 'La "lutte contre les pirates" comme paradigme. Conflit, concurrence et criminalisation à Lübeck et dans le commerce nord-européen aux XVe et XVIe siècles', *Annales. Histoire, Sciences Sociales*, 77(2) (2022), 293–327.

192 Riis, 'The states of Scandinavia, c.1390–c.1536', 675–6; Gregor Rohmann, 'Did the activity of the "Vitalian brethren" forbid trade in the Baltic Area?', in Balard (ed.), *The Sea in History*, II, 585–94.

193 Even though, in the Middle Ages, Denmark experienced periods of weakness, for example the 1330s. See Sarnowsky, 'The golden age of the Hanseatic League', 64; Meier, *Seafarers, Merchants and Pirates*, 124.

and North Seas – the Skagerrak, Kattegat, and, most importantly, the Øresund (Sound).[194] The Sound, located between the Scandinavian Peninsula and the island of Zealand, was the best suited for navigation. In the narrowest point, between the Danish town of Helsingør (Elsinore), and the town of Helsingborg (today in Sweden), the Sound is only four kilometres in width.

At the time, southern Sweden was part of the Danish kingdom, allowing Danish monarchs to regulate and potentially block navigation through this critical passage, using the Sound 'as a commercial valve, regulating the ingress and egress of Baltic shipping, as it desired'.[195] As Baltic-Atlantic trade routes became some of the busiest in the world, Denmark's relevance grew accordingly. The kingdom's control over the Sound gave it immense leverage over regional powers and significant revenue from tolls. Paul Lockhart aptly summarised the situation: 'it was for this reason that Denmark was both courted and hated by its neighbours. Danish dominion over the Baltic trade occasioned jealousy and resentment in those powers that depended on the trade'.[196]

Realising their strategic advantage, Danish monarchs sought to claim a greater share of Baltic wealth and challenge the Hanseatic League's hegemony. Open conflict erupted in 1361 when King Valdemar IV Atterdag (r. 1340–1375) conquered Scania, Öland, and the strategically important town of Visby. These conquests significantly enhanced Denmark's ability to interfere with Baltic navigation.[197] The Hanseatic League retaliated in 1362, declaring war on Denmark and imposing a trade blockade on Valdemar's territories. However, the Hanseatic fleet suffered a defeat near Helsingborg, leading to the Peace of Vordingborg in 1365. This treaty curtailed Hanseatic privileges and established Danish claims to *dominium maris baltici* – control over the Baltic

194 Concerning the geographical and political importance of straits, see Erik Brüel, *International Straits. A Treatise on International Law: The General Legal Position of International Straits* (vol. I) (London: Sweet & Maxwell, 1947), 17–35. On the Danish straits and their political history, see idem, *International Straits. Straits Comprised by Positive Regulations* (vol. II) (London: Sweet & Maxwell, 1947, 11–105).

195 Paul D. Lockart, *Denmark, 1513–1660: The Rise and Decline of a Renaissance Monarchy* (Oxford: University Press, 2007), 2; Meier, *Seafarers, Merchants and Pirates*, 124.

196 Lockart, *Denmark*, 2. Cf. Wendy Childs, 'Commerce and trade', in Allmand (ed.), *The New Cambridge Medieval History*, VII, 145–60; Thomas K. Heebøll-Holm, 'Medieval Denmark as a maritime empire', in Rolf Strootman, Floris van den Eijnde and Roy van Wijk (eds.), *Empires of the Sea. Maritime Power Networks in World History* (Leiden: Brill, 2019), 194–218; Jan Bill, 'Scandinavian warships and naval power in the thirteenth and fourteenth century', in Hattendorf and Unger (eds.), *War at Sea*, 35–52.

197 North, *The Baltic*, 58; Sarnowsky, 'The Golden Age of the Hanseatic League', 64.

Sea.[198] Emboldened, Valdemar began imposing tolls in the Øresund and disrupting established sea routes.

The Hanse responded by raising a new fleet, with support from its Prussian and Flemish allies, several German princes, and the king of Sweden, all alarmed by Denmark's ascendancy.[199] The Hanseatic cities also lobbied to enlist the support of Emperor Charles IV (r. 1355–1378), who replied he was working to restore the peace.[200] In the ensuing conflict, Valdemar was ultimately defeated, and the Treaty of Stralsund, signed on 24 May 1370, marked the end of hostilities. This agreement is traditionally seen as the pinnacle of Hanseatic maritime power.[201] The Danish Council of the Realm was compelled to recognise the freedom of navigation through the Sound and across the Baltic, as well as the freedom of trade to and within Danish territories:

> 1. Firstly: all citizens, merchants and their servants and those who may be under their rule, may now and in the future visit the kingdom of Denmark and the country of Schonen without any restriction and bring their goods and merchandise by sea and by land to any place unhindered; they may use all they have and they may trade; they must pay the appropriate customs where these are required. 2. In Denmark, Schonen and all other territories of the Danish Kingdom, the sea-shore shall be open to them forever, so that they may salvage shipwrecked goods, wreckages or whatever it is...[202]

---

198 Grewe, *Fontes*, I, 394. The strategic fortress of Helsingborg was at the time besieged by the Hanseatic commander, and major of Lübeck, Johann Wittenborg (1321–1363).

199 See for instance '[The Prussian cities] thank [Lübeck] for a letter to the navy commander with reference to a Danish troop concentration in the Sound and report on the dispatch of forty Dutch and Prussian ships ..., after 11 July 1367' in *Diplomatarium Danicum*, online version, n. 13670711001, URL: http://diplomatarium.dk/dokument/13670711001. See also 'The Prussian cities complain to the Emperor of the damage inflicted on them by the King of Denmark and Norway, February 1368', ibid., n. 13680200001, URL: http://diplomatarium.dk/dokument/13680200001.

200 'Emperor Charles IV responds to the complaints of the Prussian cities ..., 1368, before April 2', ibid., n. 13680402001, URL: http://diplomatarium.dk/dokument/13680402001.

201 Sarnowsky, 'The golden age of the Hanseatic League', 71; David K. Bjork, 'The Peace of Stralsund, 1370', *Speculum, a Journal of Mediaeval History*, 7(4) (1932), 447–76.

202 'Peace of Stralsund between the king of Denmark and the Hanse Cities, 1370', in Grewe, *Fontes*, I, 394–395: '*1. To dem ersten, dat alle borghere, coplude unde ere ghesinde unde de in eren rechte syn, de nu syn unde noch tokomende syn, møghen søken dat rike to Denemarken unde dat land to Schone yn allen enden unde yeghenen; unde dat ze moghen to lande unde to watere varen unde keren in allen yoghenen myd eren gude unde ere copenscap to øvende* [...] 2. *Ok scolen ze den zestrant meynliken vri hebben in alle dem rike to Denemarken unde in alle deme lande to schone unde in allen lande des ganzen rikes to*

The allied towns further demanded the control of Danish fortresses along the Øresund, as reparation for their war expenses and as guarantees for the treaty's enforcement. They retained these fortresses until 1385. In 1388, Valdemar's daughter, Queen Margaret I of Denmark (r. 1387–1412), succeeded in forging a dynastic union between the three Nordic kingdoms, known as the Kalmar Union.[203] While strengthening her position, she maintained a fragile balance with the Hanseatic League, which remained wary of the union's potential to achieve the *dominium maris baltici*. However, open conflict was avoided for the time being. The queen confirmed the traditional trade privileges of Hanseatic merchants.[204] Even concerted Hanseatic-Danish actions against piracy were agreed.[205] Nevertheless, tensions persisted especially on the issue of shipwreck and the salvage of Hanseatic goods.[206] Diplomatic exchanges remained intense throughout her reign.[207]

Queen Margaret's successor, her grandnephew Eric of Pomerania (ruling de facto 1412–1439), adopted a more confrontational approach to international relations. While Margaret acted cautiously, addressing one major issue at a time, Eric had an impulsive inclination for action and tackled new challenges before resolving older ones. His most consequential policy was the permanent

---

Denemarken to ewighen tiden van allem schipbrokyghem gude, it hete wrak edder zevunt edder wo it hete...'.

203 It is only one example of the medieval unions between the Nordic countries, but the most famous. See Steinar Imsen, 'The Union of Calmar – Nordic great power or northern German outpost?', in Christopher Ocker et al. (eds.), *Politics and Reformations: Communities, Polities, Nations, and Empires. Essays in Honor of T. A. Brady* (Leiden: Brill, 2007), 471–89. For further details, see Vivian Etting, *Queen Margrete I (1353–1412) and the Founding of the Nordic Union* (Leiden: Brill, 2004).

204 The *Diplomatarium Danicum* reports three draft agreements, all dated 8 September 1401; n. 14010908004, URL: http://diplomatarium.dk/dokument/14010908004; n. 14010908002, URL: http://diplomatarium.dk/dokument/14010908002; no. 14010908003, URL: http://diplomatarium.dk/dokument/14010908003.

205 Olesen, 'Inter Scandinavian relations', 729; Sarnowsky, 'The golden age of the Hanseatic League', 77. For a different account of the queen's actions, see Bjork, *Piracy in the Baltic, 1375–1398*, 48–50; Riis, 'The states of Scandinavia, c.1390–c.1536', 677–8.

206 Regarding the ongoing tensions, see, for instance, the letter reported in *Diplomatarium Danicum*, 'The Hanseatic cities complain to Queen Margrete about the persistent breaches of their privileges, 14 May 1402', n. 14020514005, URL: http://diplomatarium.dk/dokument/14020514005.

207 *Diplomatarium Danicum*, 'Højmesteren for den tyske orden takker Lübeck, Hamburg og Stralsund, fordi de har lovet at deltage i de kommende forhandlinger i Kalmar med dronning Margrete, og beder om, at deres udsendinge forinden rejser til forhandlinger i Preussen, 16 June 1403', n. 14030616001, URL: http://diplomatarium.dk/dokument/14030616001.

introduction of the Sound tolls (*Øresundtolden*) in 1429. From then onward, all foreign ships passing through the Sound were required to pay dues to the Danish Crown.[208] To enforce this levy, King Eric constructed the imposing Kronborg Castle at the Sound's narrowest point. Control over this critical passage ensured a substantial and stable income for Denmark but also sparked enduring disputes, particularly with the Hanseatic League. The conflict escalated into war between Denmark and the Hanse from 1426 to 1435. Copenhagen was besieged in 1428, and Eric's policies began to unravel due to peasant uprisings in Norway and Sweden and growing tensions with the Danish aristocracy.

In 1435, Eric conceded to the Hanseatic League's demands, exempting Lübeck merchants from paying the Sound tolls. This setback triggered events that ultimately led to his deposition.[209] Nevertheless, Eric's successors, Christopher III (r. 1440–1448), Christian I (r. 1448–1481), and Hans (r. 1481–1513), managed to maintain the Sound tolls. From a legal standpoint, the Sound was increasingly viewed not as open sea but rather as akin to a stream passing through Danish territory, subject to Danish jurisdiction. Although met with resistance, the tolls were generally accepted when kept reasonable, and exemptions were granted whenever external pressures and geopolitical imperatives made it unavoidable.[210]

Only in the late fifteenth century, the Hanseatic League's dominance over Baltic trade began to wane. The League's loose structure and internal disunity – particularly between the Wendish cities (e.g., Lübeck and Hamburg) and the Prussian cities – made coordinated policies increasingly difficult.[211] In addition, many towns fell under the control of emerging territorial states,

---

208 Brüel, *International Straits*, II, 33. See also M. Rubin, 'Sundtoldens Afløning', *Historisk Tidsskrift*, 7(6) (1906), 172–311; Ole Degn (ed.), *The Sound Toll at Elsinore. Politics, Shipping and the Collection of Duties 1429–1857* (Chicago: University Press, 2018).

209 Sarnowsky, 'The golden age of the Hanseatic League', 90; Lockart, *Denmark*, 2. On the Soundtolls, see Jens E. Olesen, 'The right usual waterway', in Degn (ed.), *The Sound Toll at Elsinore*, 29–36.

210 Olesen, 'The right usual waterway', 33–41. In 1452, Christian I prohibited foreign navigation in the Great Belt to maximise the revenues in Elsinore.

211 Raestad, *La mer territoriale*, 61; Meier, *Seafarers, Merchants and Pirates*, 145; Marie L. Pelus-Kaplan, 'De la Hanse aux trois grands ports hanséatiques de Lubeck, Hambourg et Brême: une mutation dans les rapports de forces maritimes en Baltique et Mer du Nord aux XVIe et XVIIe siècles', in Balard (ed.), *The Sea in History*, II, 51–63; idem, 'L'espace hanséatique au début de l'époque moderne (XVIe–XVIIe siècles): entre Europe et Saint-Empire', in Christine Lebeau (dir.), *L'espace du Saint-Empire: Du Moyen Âge à l'époque moderne* (Strasbourg: Presses universitaires de Strasbourg, 2004), 67–81.

which curtailed their independence. Additionally, Dutch and later English merchants posed formidable competition.[212]

Following Sweden's permanent secession from the Kalmar Union in 1523, the union between Norway and Denmark grew tighter. Denmark reasserted control over the Norwegian Sea but strategically prioritised the mastery of the Sound, central to its rivalry with Sweden for the *dominium maris baltici*. For instance, the already mentioned 1490 treaty between England and Denmark-Norway also regulated English access to the Danish provinces of Scania, Zealand, and Dragør (*Scandiæ, Selandiæ and Draghor*) through the Belts and the Sound. The treaty explicitly placed the waterways under the authority and jurisdiction of the Danish-Norwegian king.[213]

In conclusion, throughout the Middle Ages, Danish claims over the Baltic Sea were primarily political in nature and rarely codified into formal legal instruments. Other regional actors, notably the Hanseatic League, often successfully opposed these claims. For example, the Wendish cities played a pivotal role in deposing Christian II in 1523–1524, thwarting his ambitions to dominate Nordic trade and Sweden.[214] However, Denmark's control of the Sound became an enduring fact for extended periods of time. As long as Denmark maintained control over both its shores, the Sound could be regarded as an internal waterway rather than open sea. The tolls levied in Elsinore significantly bolstered Denmark's influence in international relations but also fostered long-term rivalries.[215] Conversely, Norwegian claims encompassing the

212 North, 'The Hanseatic League in the early modern period', in Harreld (ed.), *A Companion to the Hanseatic League*, 102; Alain Wijffels, 'Alberico Gentili and the Hanse: the early reception of the *Iure belli* (1598)', in Pierre-Marie Dupuy and Vincent Chetail (eds.), *The Roots of International Law, Liber Amicorum Peter Haggenmacher* (Leiden: Brill, 2013), 185–6. See also Herman Van der Wee, *The Growth of the Antwerp Market and the European Economy, Fourteenth-Sixteenth Centuries* (The Hague: M. Nijhoff, 1963); Brüel, *International Straits*, II, 19–20; Hanno Brand, 'The diplomatic resolution of the Sound conflicts between the Habsburg Netherlands, Denmark and the German Hanse, 1510–1532', in Degn (ed.), *The Sound Toll at Elsinore*, 193–225.

213 '... *per mare communiter appellatum Oresiund infra potestatem & jurisdictionem regni nostri Daciæ*', in 'Tractatus Pacis inter Henricum VII, Regem Angliæ, & Johannem Regem Daniæ et Sueciæ', in *CUD*, III.2, 245.

214 Already Ernest Nys outlined the role of the Hansa in, *Le droit international*, 497. See also Riis, 'The States of Scandinavia, c.1390-c.1536', 673–4; Waldemar Westergaard, 'The Hansa Towns and Scandinavia on the Eve of Swedish Independence', *The Journal of Modern History*, 4(3) (1932), 349–60.

215 England and the Dutch Republic, the emerging maritime powers in Early Modern Europe, would often support one Nordic Kingdom against the other to keep the Baltic open to navigation and frustrate any attempt to gain or consolidate a solitary *dominium maris baltici*. To a certain degree, they acted as the Hanse had done in the previous age. See

Northern Atlantic (*dominium maris septentrionalis*) were broadly accepted by other regional powers. In the words of Raestad, they constituted '*un article non discuté du code international*'.[216] Scotland, England, and the Hanse all recognised these claims in various international treaties and diplomatic exchanges. It should of course be noted that Norwegian claims covered areas far less trafficked than the Baltic, making them easier for other powers to tolerate compared to their Danish counterparts.

3.2 *England*

In comparison with the claims examined in the previous pages, those put forward by the medieval kings of England appear at first glance less substantiated, if not anecdotal. At the time, England was not a predominantly seafaring nation and remained largely a land-based society, whose fertile countryside produced sufficient food to supply its population.[217] It was not as dependent on fisheries as Norway, nor as reliant as Venice on maritime commerce. Nevertheless, being situated on an island, England was destined to become heavily involved in maritime affairs. By the Late Middle Ages, English authorities were already exercising limited jurisdiction along their coasts to combat piracy, administer justice, and protect peaceful commerce. In the process, institutions such as the 'Cinque Ports'[218] and the English Admiralty were established, with the first 'Admiral of the Sea of the King of England' being appointed in 1297.[219]

Until the second half of the Anglo-French Hundred Years' War (1337–1453), the Plantagenet kings of England held extensive dominions in northern and

---

Leos Müller, 'The growth of Nordic shipping, Scandinavian fleets, their construction, crews and ports', in Christian Buchet and Gérard Le Bouëdec (eds.), *The Sea in History – Vol. III, The Early Modern World* (Woodbridge: Boydell Press, 2017), 30–9, at 33; Jakob Seerup, 'Swedish and Danish rivalry to become great powers seen through the development of naval and merchant fleets', ibid., 496–504.

216 Raestad, *La mer territoriale*, 61.

217 Ibid., 39.

218 The 'Cinque Ports' were a group of port-towns situated on the English Channel that in exchange for commercial privileges were tasked with providing warships and crews to the English monarch in times of war. See Nicholas A. M. Rodger, 'The Naval Service of the Cinque Ports', *English Historical Review*, 111(442), 636–51; Katherine M. E. Murray, *The Constitutional History of the Cinque Ports* (Manchester: University Press 1935).

219 Fulton, *The Sovereignty of the Sea*, 31; Thomas K. Heebøll-Holm, 'Towards a criminalisation of piracy in late medieval England', in Sicking and Wijffels (eds.), *Conflict Management*, 165–86. The 'Black Book of the Admiralty' is the earliest compilation of English admiralty and maritime laws. See Travers Twiss (ed.), *The Black Book of the Admiralty*, vols. 4 (London: Longman & Co. et al.: 1871–1976).

western France, controlling both shores of the Strait of Dover and the English Channel, or the 'Narrow Seas'.[220] As a result, they could rightfully be considered *domini utriusque ripae*, 'Lords of both shores'.[221] English monarchs also claimed that these pelagic spaces constituted an appendage, or frontier marches, of their kingdom. Some even styled themselves as 'Lords of the Sea', occasionally being recognised as such by foreign envoys.[222] However, this title largely remained symbolic, enhancing the personal prestige of the monarch; while the possibility of exacting tolls on navigation through the Channel was at times envisaged, it was never seriously attempted.

Traces of these ambitions can be found during the reigns of Edward I (r. 1272–1307) and Edward III (r. 1327–1377). In 1306, during the Anglo-French negotiations held in Montreuil to settle piracy cases that had occurred 'in times of peace and truce' (*en temps de pees et treves*), English envoys argued that their kings had 'since time immemorial been in the peaceful possession of the sovereign lordship of the Sea of England and the islands in that sea'.[223] The notion of 'peaceful possession' signalled the supposed acceptance by other seafaring nations (*de Genue, Cateloigne, Espaigne, Alemaigne, Selande, Hoy-*

220 The expression 'Narrow Seas' usually referred to the two pelagic spaces lying between England and France (the English Channel) and England and the Netherlands (the southern North Sea). See 'Narrow Seas', in Ian Dear and Peter Kemp (eds.), *The Oxford Companion to Ships and the Sea*, online edition: https://www.oxfordreference.com/view/10.1093/acref/9780199205684.001.0001/acref-9780199205684-e-1664.

221 The English kept hold of the French port of Calais until 1558, and today they still own most of the Channel Islands. See Jeremy Black, *The British Seaborne Empire* (New Haven, CT: Yale University Press, 2004), 22–3; Fulton, *The Sovereignty of the Sea*, 6–7; T. C. Wade, 'The Roll *de Superioritate Maris Angliae*. The Foundation of the Stewart Claim to the Sovereignty of the Sea', *British Yearbook of International Law* (1921–1922), 99–108; Anne Curry, 'Two kingdoms, one king: the Treaty of Troyes (1420) and the creation of a double monarchy of England and France', in Glenn Richardson (ed.), *The Contending Kingdoms: France and England, 1420–1700* (London: Routledge, 2008), 23–42; Thomas Heebøll-Holm, *Ports, Piracy and Maritime War. Piracy in the English Channel and the Atlantic, c.1280–c.1330* (Leiden: Brill, 2013), 183–7.

222 'Agreement reached between Edward II's council and envoys of the Count of Flanders, 14 October 1320', in Chaplais, *English Medieval Diplomatic Practice*, part I, vol. I, n. 234, 414. In the document the Channel is described as the 'Sea of England, and the king of England is referred to as the 'lord of the sea'.

223 '*Du temps qil ny ad memoire du contraire, averoient este en paisible possession de la sovereigne seignurie de la meer Dengleterre et des isles esteans en ycele*', in 'Petition presented by the proctors of the King of England ..., 1306', in Chaplais, *English Medieval Diplomatic Practice*, part I, vol. I, n. 206, 367.

lande, etc.), while the formulae 'since time immemorial' echoed the Romanist concept of *per longam consuetudinem*.[224]

Nevertheless, the English declaration of mastery over the sea was clearly not accepted by the French. In a piracy case involving merchants from la Rochelle (1311), Philip IV of France (r. 1285–1324) asserted that the incident had occurred '*in mari infra districtus nostros*' – that is, in waters under French control.[225] Accordingly, he demanded that the English authorities extradite the pirates, '*in vestro regno degenetes*', so that they could be tried in a French court. Philip IV, therefore, categorically rejected the notion that the seas bordering French coasts were under English exclusive sovereignty or jurisdiction.[226] Edward II (r. 1307–1327), for his part, refused the extradition request but promised that the alleged pirates would face justice in an English court.[227] A few years later, Edward III of England addressed his admirals in the following terms:

> We, calling to mind that our progenitors, the Kings of England, were Lords of the English Sea on every side, and also defenders against the invasions of enemies before these times, and it would greatly grieve us if our royal honour in such defence should be lost or in any or in any way diminished in our time...[228]

However, an earlier ordinance issued in 1201 by John I of England (r. 1199–1216) is generally regarded as the first evidence of something resembling English claims over the adjacent waters. It stipulated that whenever an English admiral or official encountered a foreign ship while patrolling the seas:

> ... which would not stryke and lower their sailes at the command of the king's lieutenant [...], but making resistaunce against those of the fflet, that if they can be taken that they be reputed as enemies, and their shyps, vessels, and goodes taken and forfeited as goodes of enemies, al-

224 Heebøll-Holm, 'Towards a Criminalisation of Piracy in Late Medieval England', 175; On the Montreuil negotiations, see Frederic L. Cheyette, 'The Sovereign and the Pirates, 1332', *Speculum*, 45(1) (1970), 40–68, at 52–3.

225 'Littera regis Franciae, de justicia mercatoribus suis negata, 1311', Rymer, *Foedera*, II.1, 146 (1818 ed.).

226 Heebøll-Holm, *Ports, Piracy and Maritime War*, 189.

227 'Littera ad Regem Franciae super depraedationibus..., 1311', in Rymer, *Foedera*, II.1, 146 (1818 ed.)

228 'Directives by King Edward III of England as Lord of the English Sea, 1336', in Grewe, *Fontes*, I, 680.

> beit that the maysters or possessors thereof should afterwards come and alleadge the same ships, vessels, and goodes to be the goodes of friends of our lorde the kyng, and that the company therein be chastizsed by imprisonment of their bodies for their rebellion at discretion.[229]

This passage represents the earliest evidence of a practice that would later become a contentious issue in the Early Modern Age: 'the striking of the sail'.[230] In an era marked by widespread piracy, English warships claimed the right to stop and verify the identity of foreign merchant vessels. The vessel was required to lower its sails to facilitate the process. The immediate purpose was to immobilise the sailing ship during the verification. If the vessel refused to comply or attempted to escape, it could be treated as an enemy ship.[231] That said, it is difficult to determine how frequently the procedure was enforced; its effectiveness likely varied significantly throughout the Middle Ages, and it never became a recognised custom. Over time, the practice gradually lost its original purpose and transformed into a matter of national prestige, symbolising the recognition of the English Crown's authority by foreign vessels.

More concretely, several international agreements signed by England during the Late Middle Ages demonstrate the English authorities' recognition of broad freedom of navigation and fishing along their coasts, at least in times of peace. Access to coastal fisheries was not restricted, and fishermen from the Low Countries (Flanders, Zeeland, Holland), Picardy, Normandy, and other regions operated without needing licences or being subject to limitations.[232] In other words, navigation and fishing were not restricted based on nationality or political allegiance. For instance, in 1351 and 1353, King Edward III of England signed treaties with the King of Castile and the maritime towns of Portugal, respectively, granting their subjects freedom to fish around the coasts of England.[233]

---

229 'Ordinance by King John of England relating to the Ceremonial of the Sea, 1201', ibid., 679.

230 Fulton, *The Sovereignty of the Sea*, 42–3. See also Sebastian I. Sobecki, *The Sea and Medieval English Literature* (Woodbridge: Boydell Press, 2008), 155; Nicholas A. M. Rodger, *The Safeguard of the Sea: A Naval History of Britain, Volume 1, 660–1649* (London: Penguin Books, 2004), 78–9.

231 Fulton, *The Sovereignty of the Sea*, 6–7.

232 Louis Sicking and Adri P. van Vliet, '"Our triumph of Holland": war, violence, and the herring fishery of the Low Countries, c.1400–1650', in Louis Sicking and Darlene Abreu-Ferreira (eds.), *Beyond the Catch. Fisheries of the North Atlantic, the North Sea and the Baltic, 900–1850* (Leiden: Brill, 2008), 337–64.

233 'Traitè conclu entre Edouard III. Roi d'Angleterre & les Députés des Villes Maritimes du Royaume de Castille & du Comté de Biscaye, 1351', in CUD, I.2, 265–7: '*Item, Pessores de la*

The same liberal approach was also reflected in the so-called 'Burgundy treaties' – a series of political and commercial agreements signed between England and the Dukes of Burgundy (who were also Counts of Flanders and more broadly rulers of the Low Countries) during the fifteenth century.[234] In exchange for political and commercial concessions, England promised not to interfere with Flemish herring fishing activities. Notably, the *Intercursus Magnus*, signed on 24 February 1496 between Henry VII of England and the Duke of Burgundy Philip the Fair (r. 1482–1506), became a cornerstone for relations between England and the Low Countries during the Tudor period. Article XIV of the agreement addressed fishing rights and stated:

> It is agreed, arranged and concluded that the fishermen of both aforesaid sides (in any condition) shall be able to go everywhere, sail through the sea, and fish securely without any hindrance, licence, or safe-conduct.[235]

It should also be noted that Henry de Bracton (c.1210–1268), the leading medieval English jurist and author of *De legibus et consuetudinibus Angliae* ('On the Laws and Customs of England', dated approximately 1235), took a clear pos-

---

seigneurie del roi de Castelle, [...] *peussent venir & pescher, fraunchement & sauvement, en les ports d'Engleterre & de Bretagne, & en touz autres lieux & Portz ou ils vorront, paintz les Droitz & les Custumes*'; 'Traité de Commerce entre Edouard III Roi d'Angleterre & les Députés des Villes Maritimes du Royaume de Portugal, 1353', ibid., 286.

234 Beginning in the fourteenth century, the Counts of Flanders asserted control over the so-called 'Flemish Stream' (*Vlaamse stroom*), which encompassed not only inland waters – such as parts of the Scheldt and the Zwin – but also the maritime area extending from Dunkirk (then part of Flanders) to Zeeland, reaching as far into the sea as the coastline remained visible. The Dutch legal historian Eduard Meijers and historian Louis Sicking and have demonstrated that the concept of the Flemish Stream included the notion of a territorial sea, over which the Flemish Count both claimed and exercised jurisdiction, a claim that was recognised by foreign merchants and governments alike. See Louis Sicking, '*Mare Liberum, Mare Clausum* en de Territorial Wateren. Doctrine en Context van het Zeerecht in de Late Middeleeuwen en de Vroegmoderne Tijd', *Pro Memorie*, 26(2) (2024), 183–210, at 187–9; Eduard M. Meijers, 'Des graven stroom', *Mededelingen der Koninklijke Nederlandsche Akademie van Wetenschappen, afdeling Letterkunde, Nieuwe Reeks* 3(4) (Amsterdam: N.V. Noord-Hollandsche Uitgevers Maatschappij, 1940), 32–49/134–54 (double paging); Fulton, *The Sovereignty of the Sea*, 537.

235 'Tractatus Pacis & Commercii inter Henricum VII Regem Angliae & Philippum Ducem Austria & Burgundiae conclusus, datum Londini 24 Februarii 1495', in *CUD*, III.2, 321. My translation from the Latin original: '*Conventum, concordatum et conclusum est quod piscatores utriusque partis Partium praedictarum* (*cujuscunque conditionis existant*) *poterunt ubique ire, navigare per mare, secure piscari absque aliquot impedimento, licentia, seu salvo conducto*'.

ition concerning the legal status of the sea.[236] Not coincidentally, Bracton employed principles deriving from both Roman (civil) law and canon law to enrich the developing English common law. In the second book of the treatise, titled *De rebus*, he closely followed classical Roman law in enumerating fishes (*pisces*) as *res nullius* and the sea and its shores as *res communis*:

> By natural law these are common to all: running water, air, the sea, and the shores of the sea, as though accessories of the sea. No one therefore is forbidden access to the seashore, provided he keeps away from houses and buildings [built there], for by the *jus gentium* shores are not common to all in the sense that the sea is.[237]

Conversely, one of the most significant early political poems written in English, the anonymous *Libelle of Englyshe Polycye* (c. 1436), presented a passionate argument for England to rule the adjacent seas and establish a strong navy capable of controlling seaborne trade.[238] It did so, somewhat nostalgically, only a few years after the premature death of King Henry V (r. 1413–1422), who had been particularly dominant at sea vis-à-vis France.[239] Although the *Libelle* circulated widely over the following two centuries, it did not significantly influence English maritime policies.[240]

In other words, England did not achieve a control on navigation comparable to that of Venice in the Adriatic, or a military hold on the English Channel comparable to that of Denmark over the Sound. Throughout the fourteenth and fifteenth centuries, English monarchs seemed more inclined towards upholding the freedom to use the sea and its resources, balanced by a vague claim to overlordship concerning the Channel and the adjacent seas. This approach did not impose any serious restrictions on foreign vessels' freedom of movement.[241] Moreover, the boundaries of the so-called 'English seas' were

236 The *De legibus* is one of the oldest and most influential treatises dating to the formative period of English common law. See: Henry de Bracton, *De legibus et consuetudinibus Angliae*, edited by George E. Woodbine, vol. II (Oxford: University Press, 1922).

237 Ibid., II, 39–40.

238 The most recent edition is George Warner's *The Libelle of Englyshe Polycye. A Poem on the Use of Sea Power, 1436*.

239 Ian Friel, *Henry V's Navy: The Sea-Road to Agincourt and Conquest 1413–1422* (Cheltenham: History Press, 2015).

240 The influential editor, writer, and supporter of English colonising projects Richard Hakluyt (1553–1616) included the *Libelle* in his *Principall Navigations* (1589) and John Selden quoted it in *Mare clausum*. See Sobecki, *The Sea and Medieval English Literature*, 145–6.

241 Fulton, *The Sovereignty of the Sea*, 72.

never defined in the Middle Ages, and the expression did not refer to an easily delimited area.[242] In Chapter 4, we will see how this issue evolved into a matter of significant international relevance under the Stuart kings in the early seventeenth century.

4 Concluding Observations

A comparison of the two macro-regions examined in this chapter reveals that both the Mediterranean Sea and the seas of northern Europe witnessed late medieval polities extending their authority over surrounding waters. These polities, however, generally refrained from asserting proprietary rights in the strict legal sense. For example, the English kings failed to substantiate their temporary overlordship of the 'Narrow Seas' separating southern England from the continent. Denmark, by contrast, prioritised control of the Sound and sought – albeit with mixed success – to establish a *dominium maris Baltici*. Its principal concern, however, lay in maintaining the Sound tolls and exerting political influence in the region.

Undoubtedly, the Kingdom of Norway developed the most extensive maritime claims in the North. Norwegian rulers were not only concerned with the sea for communication and trade but also with the preservation of fish stocks, a critical source of food and national wealth. The distinctive 'Bergen limit' imposed by Norwegian authorities heavily restricted foreign *ius navigandi* beyond an imaginary line. By the end of the fifteenth century, Denmark and Norway entered a personal union, which would endure until the Napoleonic era. In Chapter 3, we will examine how this union impacted (Dano-)Norwegian 'closed sea' policies in the sixteenth century.

To the South, the Venetians and Genoese concentrated on controlling limited portions of the Mediterranean Sea and its key trading routes, showing little interest in monopolising fisheries.[243] Similar to the developments in

---

242 Ibid., 16.

243 This is also explained by the fact that North Atlantic fisheries have historically been more productive than those of the Mediterranean due to several factors. The colder waters of the North Atlantic support higher levels of dissolved oxygen, which, combined with strong ocean currents such as the Gulf Stream, promote nutrient upwelling. This fosters abundant plankton populations, forming the foundation of a rich marine food chain. Additionally, the North Atlantic hosts extensive continental shelves, particularly the Grand Banks and the North Sea, which provide ideal conditions for large fish stocks, including cod and herring. In contrast, the Mediterranean is a relatively enclosed sea with lower nutrient levels, limited upwelling, and higher salinity, which collectively

northern Europe, Mediterranean 'claimed seas' pretensions arose primarily from the need to combat maritime anarchy and piracy, viewed as existential threats to commerce. Basilio Cialdea aptly described this 'imperative necessity of security' as the primary stimulus for the extension of jurisdiction over adjacent seas.[244] Thomas Wemyss Fulton identified this aspect as the 'less selfish' explanation to late medieval claims over sea areas.[245] In particular, the Venetians did not claim 'ownership' of the Adriatic as such. However, they regulated so many aspects of maritime interactions that the legal position they claimed came to be functionally close to *dominium*. They restricted access to foreign warships, regulated merchant vessels, and imposed tolls for their protection.[246] In the process, they gained control over a substantial share of Mediterranean trade. The Genoese followed a similar path, although in the early modern period, their capability to project sea power autonomously waned as *La Superba* came into the Spanish orbit.

The main specificity of Mediterranean closed sea claims lies in the presence of a class of university-trained jurists, flourishing as early as the thirteenth century, who scrutinised such claims. Some of the most renowned jurists of the time validated Venetian and Genoese positions, though they upheld the Roman principle of *res communis omnium* in theory. By distinguishing *iurisdictio* (jurisdiction) from *dominium* (ownership), they accepted maritime jurisdiction as a necessary response to the geopolitical realities of their time while rejecting the possibility of ownership over the sea. Many of their terms and ideas would endure into the following centuries, providing the foundation for early modern legal debates. This represented the major contribution of Mediterranean Sea and its jurists of the Late Middle Ages. It is also worth noting that the maritime, commercial, and legal systems of the Baltic-North Sea and Mediterranean regions were not entirely isolated from one another. With the arrival of Genoese galleys in the Low Countries in 1277 and Venetian galleys in 1315, a permanent link was established.[247] Bruges – home to one of

---

result in lower overall fish biomass. See Sicking and Abreu-Ferreira (eds.), *Beyond the Catch*.

244 Cialdea, *La formazione dell'ordinamento marittimo*, 101–2; Zendri, 'Mare passim omnibus patet', 97.

245 Fulton, *The Sovereignty of the Sea*, 72.

246 Ibid., 3–4; Zendri, 'Mare passim omnibus patet', 94.

247 Cialdea, *La formazione dell'ordinamento marittimo*, 17; Roberto Cessi, 'Le relazioni commerciali tra Venezia e le Fiandre nel secolo XIV', *Nuovo Archivio Veneto*, nuova serie, 27 (1914), 5–116, riedito in idem, *Politica ed economia di Venezia nel Trecento* (Roma: Edizioni di Storia e Letteratura, 1952), 71–172; Bart Lambert, 'Making size matter less: Italian firms and merchant guilds in late medieval Bruges', in Dave De ruysscher et al. (eds.), *The Company in Law and Practice: Did Size Matter? (Middle Ages–Nineteenth Century)* (Lei-

the Hanseatic *Kontor* – and later Antwerp and southern English ports became key hubs for the exchange of goods and ideas between northern and southern Europe (see above Figure 1.3).

Nevertheless, the time was not yet ripe for a comprehensive discussion of the legal status of the sea. This state of affairs would eventually change in the aftermath of the 'Age of Exploration'. Only the staggering nature of the world oceans prompted an extensive legal discussion on pelagic spaces and their distinctiveness. In a new global context, the connection between sea and land appeared weaker, and late medieval doctrines and practices failed to offer straightforward solutions. As we have seen, tensions between freedom and control marked the late medieval period, but now they became more polarised than ever. Therefore, in the following chapters, we will discuss how oceangoing navigation influenced the early development of a modern law of the sea. Chapter 2 analyses how Portugal and Spain attempted to impose a new 'claimed seas' approach to the oceans connecting Europe to the 'Indies'. Chapter 3 explores the progressive emergence in legal argumentation of the principle of the freedom of the sea, *mare liberum*. Finally, Chapter 4 considers the evolution of the 'claimed seas' theory as a fully-fledged response to the challenges posed by freedom of the sea arguments.

---

den/Boston: Brill/Nijhoff 2017), 34–48; Justyna Wubs-Mrozewicz, 'De Kantoren van de Hanze: Bergen, Brugge, Londen en Nowgorod', in Hanno Brand and Egge Knol (red.), *Koggen, kooplieden en kantoren: de Hanze, een praktisch netwerk* (Hilversum/Groningen: Uitgeverij Verloren/ Groninger Museum, 2009), 91–107.

CHAPTER 2

The Oceans

> The glorious age, oh lord, approaches
> or has already come in which heaven proclaims
> one shepherd and one flock only on earth,
> and this by fortune reserved for your time.
> [...] and announces to the world, for its greater consolation
> one monarch, one empire, one sword.
> The world partly feels itself to be
> and completely hopes to be your kingdom,
> conquered by you in just war.
> For he to whom Christ has given his standard,
> Christ will give a second, happier day
> on which he will conquer the land, having conquered the sea.[1]

∵

1 The Atlantic Ocean

If already the Mediterranean had seemed disorienting to Roman and medieval jurists, the boundless expanses of the oceans raised far more profound questions.[2] The great seafaring civilisations of the Ancient Mediterranean, such as the Phoenicians and the Greeks, had regarded the Iberian Peninsula and the Strait of Gibraltar as the westernmost edge of the world.[3] The concepts and categories developed over the centuries by Roman law scholars and the *ius commune* doctrine were anchored to the spatial reference of the European continent. At first glance, these legal tools seemed ill-suited for being applied to the new geographical horizons of the 'Age of Exploration'. In other words,

1 Sonnet written by the soldier-poet Hernando de Acuna (1520–1580) for emperor Charles v, celebrating Spanish expansion in the Americas. Cited in Gerard Flynn, 'Padre Las Casas, Literature, and the Just War', *Revista de Historia de América*, 61/62 (1966), 57–72.

2 Cassi, *Ius commune*, 85.

3 Abulafia, *The Boundless Sea*, 322–3.

 | DOI:10.1163/9789004741409_004

the legal approach to the oceans posed an unprecedented challenge for the Europeans of the fifteenth and sixteenth centuries.

Throughout the Middle Ages, both Christians and Muslims viewed the Atlantic – often referred to as the 'green sea of darkness' – as unnavigable. It was conceived as an 'exterior sea' surrounding the known world, fundamentally distinct from the smaller 'interior seas' such as the Mediterranean.[4] Nevertheless, there are reports of attempts to sail west of the Pillars of Hercules, such as the voyage of the Genoese brothers Ugolino and Vadino Vivaldi in 1291, and that of the Catalan sailor Jayme Ferrer in 1346. Tragically, most of these bold adventurers were never seen again.[5]

During the Middle Ages, eastern civilizations had developed a more advanced art of navigation. As reported by Jack Goldstone, the Arab navigator Shibab al-Din Ahmad Ibn Majid, born in Oman in 1430, and the author of numerous works on commerce and navigation, described with these words the state of navigation in Europe on the threshold of the Modern Age: 'We have [...] the measurement of stellar altitudes, but they have not. They cannot understand the way we navigate, but we can understand the way they do; [...] they admit we have a better knowledge of the sea and navigation and the wisdom of the stars.'[6] Asian societies of the time also pioneered superior shipbuilding techniques, such as the use of hulls divided into watertight compartments, the stern rudder, and the lateen sail – features that were essential for oceanic navigation. Up until the fifteenth century, European navigators lagged behind in these advancements, which explains the failure of expeditions like that of the Vivaldi brothers. The brothers had ventured into the Atlantic aboard galleys – flat-bottomed rowing ships perfected over centuries for the quieter waters of the Mediterranean. Designed for cabotage, or coastal navigation, galleys were ill-equipped to face the challenges of the open ocean.[7]

4 Cassi, *Ius commune*, 85; Luis A. Fonseca, 'Portuguese maritime expansion from the African coast to India', in Buchet and Le Bouëdec (eds.), *The Sea in History*, III, 646–7.

5 John R. S. Phillips, *The Medieval Expansion of Europe* (Oxford: University Press, 1998), 147–8; Raymond Mauny, *Les navigations médiévales sur les côtes sahariennes antérieures à la découverte portugaise (1434)* (Lisboa: Centro de estudos históricos ultramarinos, 1960); Charles R. Boxer, *The Portuguese Seaborne Empire, 1415–1825* (London: Hutchinson, 1969), 16–7.

6 Passage taken from the *Book of Useful Information on the Principles and Rules of Navigation*, written in 1490. Quote from Goldstone, *Why Europe?*, 54. See also John H. Parry, *The Discovery of the Sea* (Berkeley: University of California Press, 1981), 139–63; Chang, 'The Maritime Scene', 347–59.

7 Parry, *Europe and a Wider World*, 13–25; Goldstone, *Why Europe?*, 26–9; Philip E. Steinberg, *The Social Construction of the Ocean* (Cambridge: University Press, 2001), 62–3; Fernand Braudel, *Civilization and Capitalism, 15th–18th Century, Vol. I: The Structure of Everyday Life: The Limits of the Possible* (Berkeley: University of California Press, 1981). For further

Only starting from the fifteenth century European seafarers – primarily in the service of the Portuguese and Castilian Crowns – had, at their disposal, improved ship designs such as the nimble caravel and the heavier carrack. These vessels were capable of longer-range expeditions, sailing against the wind, and offered improved seaworthiness and survivability. At the same time, more sophisticated nautical instruments became available, including the magnetic compass (essential for locating the magnetic north) and the astrolabe (used for celestial navigation). These tools enabled long-range voyages without relying on the traditional sighting of reference points, such as islands or capes, as required by cabotage.[8] This combination of advancements ultimately paved the way for the exploration of the entire globe and the establishment of supra-continental colonial empires.[9]

2 Iberian Seaborne Expansion

2.1 *Guinea*

Precisely at this turning point in global maritime history, Portugal, one of the Iberian states emerging from the *Reconquista*, entered the world stage. Although home to renowned navigators and merchants, it had until then remained a relatively poor and peripheral player in international politics.[10] However, from the early decades of the fifteenth century, Portuguese seafarers began systematically challenging the open waters of the Atlantic. They aspired to reach the Far East and its coveted goods, aiming to end the longstanding dominance of Italian and Muslim intermediaries in long-distance Euro-Asian

details, see Robert Gardiner (ed.), *The Age of the Galley: Mediterranean Oared Vessels since Pre-Classical Times* (New York: Book Sales, 2000); Bailey W. Diffie and George D. Winius, *Foundations of the Portuguese Empire, 1415–1580* (Minneapolis: University of Minnesota Press, 1977), 123–4; David Barrado Navascués, *Cosmography in the Age of Discovery and the Scientific Revolution* (Cham: Springer, 2023), 21–2.

8 Mauricio Nieto Olarte, *Exploration, Religion and Empire in the Sixteenth-Century Ibero-Atlantic World. A New Perspective on the History of Modern Science* (Amsterdam: University Press, 2021), 119–85.

9 Daniel R. Headrick pondered on whether it is imperialism that shapes technology or vice versa, in *The Tools of Empire: Technology and European Imperialism in the Nineteenth Century* (Oxford: University Press, 1981), 4.

10 Armindo de Sousa, 'Portugal', in Allmand (ed.), *The New Cambridge Medieval History*, VII, 627–44; Francisco Bethencourt and Diogo R. Curto (eds.), *A expansão marítima portuguesa, 1400–1800* (Lisbon: Edições 70, 2010); Nieto Olarte, *Exploration, Religion and Empire*, 37–54.

trade.[11] Additionally, they sought new trade routes that bypassed the threat posed by the Ottoman Empire and to attack the Muslims in North Africa from the rear.[12]

The geographical position of the Lusitanian kingdom, naturally oriented towards the Atlantic Ocean, acted as a strong incentive, particularly given its small and relatively infertile territory. Members of the Portuguese royal family, most notably Prince Henry the Navigator (1394–1460), played a crucial role in spearheading this initial wave of exploration.[13] Thus began a systematic campaign to explore the African coasts, progressing slowly but steadily until Portuguese sailors finally ventured beyond Cape Bojador. Pre-modern mariners had long considered this cape to be the westernmost navigable limit. The first recorded European to sail south of Cape Bojador was the Portuguese Gil Eanes in 1434. After several failed attempts, he thus overcame one of the greatest ancestral fears of medieval sailors. Before long, Castilian mariners emerged as the main competitors of the Portuguese and a sort of 'race to the East' began between the two Iberian kingdoms.[14] The first area of interest for Portuguese endeavours was West Africa with its already established gold and slave trade.[15]

On 22 October 1443, Prince Henry secured exclusive rights of navigation 'beyond Cape Bojador' and towards Guinea from his brother and regent,

11 Parker, *Global Interactions*, 72–3; Malyn Newitt, *Navigations: The Portuguese Discoveries and the Renaissance* (London: Reaktion Books, 2023), 52–87.

12 Palmira Brummett, *Ottoman Seapower and Levantine Diplomacy in the Age of Discovery* (Albany: State of New York University Press, 1994).

13 The reference works on Portuguese expansion remain Boxer, *The Portuguese Seaborne Empire* and Diffie and Winius, *Foundations of the Portuguese Empire*. More recent works are Malyn Newitt, *A History of Portuguese Overseas Expansion 1400–1668* (London: Routledge, 2004) and Giuseppe Marcocci, *L'invenzione di un impero: Politica e cultura nel mondo portoghese* (1450–1600) (Roma: Carocci, 2011). Traditionally, the figure of Prince Henry dominated the study of early Portuguese explorations; however, contemporary scholars have contextualised and to a certain degree, questioned his role. See Michel Vergé-Franceschi, *Henri le Navigateur et les grandes découvertes du Portugal* (Paris: Édition du Félin, 2016).

14 Nuno Vila-Santa, *Knowledge Exchanges between Portugal and Europe. Maritime Diplomacy, Espionage, and Nautical Science in the Early Modern World (15th–17th Centuries)* (Amsterdam: University Press, 2024), 23–74.

15 In the terminology of the time, the term 'Guinea' became the geographical reference for the coasts south of Morocco. See Bernard Vincent, *1492. "L'année admirable"* (Paris: Champs Flammarion, 1997), 171; John W. Blake, *European Beginnings in West Africa, 1454–1478* (Westport: Greenwood Press, 1969), 16–25; Fonseca, 'Portuguese maritime expansion', 647; Parry, *Europe and a Wider World*, 19; Barrado Navascués, *Cosmography in the Age of Discovery*, 26–34.

Pedro de Aviz (1392–1449).[16] These rights were confirmed later that year by the pope. On 3 February 1446, Henry received a further grant forbidding anyone to sail beyond Cape Bojador, to make war or to trade without Henry's license and without paying him the customary Fifth owed to the Crown.[17] This monopoly was intended to compensate Henry for the significant expenses he had incurred in financing the expeditions (*pollas mujtas despesas que em ello mandou fazer*).[18] Similar restrictions applied to those wishing to sail towards the Canary Islands, as 'no ships ever went to those islands' before Henry's expeditions.[19]

Anyone who sailed past cape Bojador or to the Canaries without a license risked forfeiting both ship and cargo to the *infante*.[20] The king reaffirmed Henry's privileges in October 1448.[21] For instance, in 1454, a Genoese who had been trading in Guinea without a licence was captured aboard a Castilian caravel and had his hands cut off as punishment. Shortly after, a Castilian trader was burned alive as a pirate and heretic for trading weapons with the 'Moors' south of Cape Bojador. The nature of the privileges granted to Prince Henry is reflected in the concessions he made to his captains and subordinates. For example, on 1 November 1446, he granted Captain Bartolomeu Perestrelo extensive rights over the island of Porto Santo. This form of grant would later become a model for subsequent Portuguese colonisation efforts.[22]

---

16 See the text of the *carta* in Coelho, *Alguns documentos*, 8–9. Cf. Blake, *European Beginnings*, 21; Diffie and Winius, *Foundations of the Portuguese Empire*, 59. Pedro of Aviz and Henry the Navigator were two of the most notable members of the socalled *Ínclita Geração* (Illustrious Generation) a term created by Portuguese historians to refer to a group of fifteenth century *infantes* (royal princes) of the Aviz dynasty.

17 Blake, *European Beginnings*, 21.

18 Dias Dinis, *Monumenta Henricina*, vol. IX, 121–3; Godinho, *Documentos sôbre a expansão portuguesa*, I, 201–4; Coelho, *Alguns documentos*, 9.

19 Dias Dinis, *Monumenta Henricina*, vol. IX, 121–3, '*Outrosy, nos disse que, quando elle mandaua asy os dictos naujos aas dictas terras, passauam pollas jihas de Canarea,* [...] *e que, porquanto nos ssabiamos bem como nunca aquellas jlhas destes nossos rregnos forom naujos nehũus atees que elle alla mandou, nem agora geeralmente nom hiam lla ssenom os de ssuas armadas.*'

20 Ibidem; Godinho, *Documentos*, I, 201–4, '*E os que ssem sseu mandado passarem aas dictaa jlhas percam pera o dicto jfante ho naujo ou naujos que leuarem e a mercadaria que trouuerem*'.

21 Dias Dinis, *Monumenta Henricina*, vol. IX, 308–9: '... *nemguem nam pase allem do dito Cabo do Bojador sem seu mandado e liçemça; e os que paasarem nos praz que percam pera o dito jfamte meu tyo ho nauyo ou nauyos que asy la forem e todo o que della trouuerem*'.

22 For the text in question, see Dias Dinis, *Monumenta Henricina*, IX, 254–8; Godinho, *Documentos*, I, 189–92, Coelho, *Alguns documentos*, 10–1. See also Newitt, *A History of Portuguese Overseas Expansion*, 25.

However, in the same period (1449), the king of Castile granted the Duke of Medina Sidonia a trade monopoly covering the region between Agadir and Cape Bojador. In the same year, Afonso v renewed Henry's monopoly from Cape Cantin to Cape Bojador, an overlapping area. The rivalry between Portugal and Castile for control of West African trade was thus intensifying. Following Prince Henry's death in 1460, the Portuguese king directly assumed the authority to confer privileges over Atlantic trade and navigation. By 1469, King Afonso v (r. 1438–1481) had leased a large portion of the Crown's monopoly over the Guinea trade to Fernão Gomes, a wealthy Lisbon-based merchant.[23]

2.2 *The Indies*

In 1492, amidst the ongoing Hispano-Portuguese rivalry, a Castilian-sponsored expedition led by the Genoese mariner Christopher Columbus accidentally reached the Bahamas while attempting to establish a western route to East Asia. Five years earlier, in 1487, Bartolomeu Dias had already reached the Cape of Good Hope for the first time. However, it was only in 1497 that Vasco da Gama successfully navigated around Africa and across the Indian Ocean, reaching Calicut in India.[24] At the time, the Indian Ocean was one of the busiest maritime regions in the world, traversed by merchants of various nationalities whose interactions were regulated by 'customary codes of rules'.[25] Prosperous polities ruled the Indian coasts, where Hindu and Muslim societies had developed advanced systems of international relations and commercial maritime practices.[26]

By the fifteenth century, many of these customs had been codified into written maritime codes, such as those of Malacca (*Undang-undang Laut Melaka*, or 'Maritime Laws of Melaka') and Macassar.[27] The Malacca Code, in

23 Blake, *European Beginnings*, 23–4; de Sousa, *Portugal*, 641.

24 John H. Parry, *The Spanish Seaborne Empire* (London: Hutchinson, 1971), 22–3; David Buisseret (ed.), *The Oxford Companion to World Exploration*, I (Oxford: University Press, 2007), 286; Vincent, *1492. L'année admirable*, 52–72; Newitt, *Navigations*, 190–222.

25 Alexandrowicz, *Law of the Nations in the East Indies*, 64.

26 Alan Villiers, *The Indian Ocean* (Conran: London, 1952), 124–7.

27 Richard Winstedt and Patrick E. de Josselin de Jong, 'The Maritime Laws of Malacca', *Journal of the Malayan Branch of the Royal Asiatic Society*, 29(3) (1956), 22–59; Peter Borschberg, 'The Malaka Empire, c.1400–1526', c.1450–1511', in Strootman, van den Eijnde and van Wijk (eds.), *Empires of the Sea*, 263–93, at 265; Liaw Y. Fang, *Undang-Undang Melaka. The Laws of Melaka* (The Hague: M. Nijhoff, 1976), 32–8; Khalilieh, *Islamic Law of the Sea*, 84–7.

particular, emphasised the prerogatives of the captain, defining him as 'the sovereign at sea'.[28] He exercised jurisdiction over both crew and passengers, resolving disputes and punishing crimes that occurred aboard the vessel. However, the captain's exclusive authority ended once the ship entered a harbour, where jurisdiction was shared with local port authorities. This focus on the captain's powers reflected the limited jurisdictional claims of coastal polities over the high seas, which were regarded as 'distances between places, but not territory'.[29] Charles H. Alexandrowicz observed that the Malacca Code viewed the ship as 'a piece of quasi-territory sailing in the legally undefined vastness of the sea' once it ventured beyond coastal waters.[30] Although all maritime powers were entitled to suppress piracy in coastal waters and on the high seas, such actions did not led to 'claimed seas' ambitions, unlike what we saw in Chapter 1 in relation to medieval Europe. More broadly, the great Asian powers, such as Ming China, did not view the high seas as subject to their jurisdiction.[31]

When the Portuguese entered the Indian Ocean, they immediately sought to dominate its lucrative spice and trade networks, using the superior armament of their ships to overwhelm rivals.[32] By 1499, Vasco da Gama claimed the entire Indian Ocean on behalf of the Portuguese Crown and was rewarded with the grandiloquent title *Almirante da Índia*.[33] King Manuel I of Portugal (r. 1495–1521) quickly wrote to the Castilian court boasting of his *descobridores*' achievements, heralding the discovery of India (*Ymdia*) and pre-empting fu-

28 Ram P. Anand, 'Maritime Practice in South-East Asia until 1600 A. D. and the Modern Law of the Sea', *The International and Comparative Law Quarterly*, 30(2) (1981), 445–6.

29 Steinberg, *Social Construction of the Ocean*, 51–2.

30 Alexandrowicz, *Law of the Nations in the East Indies*, 64.

31 See Timothy Brook, 'China's maritime world', in Buchet and Le Bouëdec (eds.), *The Sea in History*, III, 551–63; idem, 'Trade and conflict in the South China Sea: Portugal and China, 1514–23', in Lucia Coppolaro and Francine McKenzie (eds.), *A Global History of Trade and Conflict since 1500* (London: Palgrave Macmillan, 2013), 20–37; Timothy Brook, *Mr. Selden's Map of China: Decoding the Secrets of a Vanished Cartographer* (New York: Bloomsbury Press, 2013).

32 Anand, *Origin and Development*, 5; Parry, *Europe and a Wider World*, 24; Boxer, *The Portuguese Seaborne Empire*, 44. See also Endang Susilowati, 'Coastal Civilization and Maritime Diplomacy in Premodern Southeast Asia', *International Journal of Maritime History*, 30(4) (2018), 649–63; Anjana Singh, 'Early modern European mercantilism and Indian Ocean trade' in Strootman, van den Eijnde and van Wijk (eds.), *Empires of the Sea*, 245–62.

33 The *carta* in question is dated 10 January 1502. See Coelho, *Alguns documentos*, 127–8.

ture expansion in the region.[34] The Portuguese relied heavily on force to integrate themselves into regional trade networks, as European goods were not easily exchanged for luxurious Chinese porcelain, silks, refined Indian fabrics, or spices from the Moluccas.[35]

Captains such as Pedro Álvares Cabral and Lopo Soares frequently employed violent methods, which from a Muslim-Hindu perspective were tantamount to piracy.[36] Their actions sought to disrupt the pre-existent order and to create a new one, more aligned with their interests. In doing so, the Portuguese seized a significant share of seaborne trade previously dominated by Arab and Indian Muslim merchants, who had been the principal intermediaries supplying Venetian merchants with oriental goods.[37] The arrival of the Portuguese shattered the long-held Indian Ocean conception of the sea as an open space for free navigation and peaceful trade, as local polities had not developed the notion of an extensive maritime jurisdiction.[38]

The Portuguese negotiated trade agreements with the stronger rulers while imposing treaties on the weaker ones, often exploiting regional rivalries to their advantage. Strategic bases such as Goa in India (1510), Malacca in Malaysia (1511), and Ormuz in the Persian Gulf (1515) quickly fell into Portuguese hands. These harbours became the nucleus of the *Estado da Índia*, or the Portuguese Empire in Asia, governed by a viceroy representing the Portuguese Crown.[39] The early participation of Genoese merchants and financers in Por-

---

34 'Carta de El-Rei D. Manuel para os reis de Castella dando-lhes parte da descoberta da India…', in Coelho, *Alguns documentos*, 95–6.

35 For an overview, see Om Prakash, *Bullion for Goods: European and Indian Merchants in the Indian Ocean Trade, 1500–1800* (New Delhi: Manohar, 2004); Kirti N. Chaudhuri, 'European trade with India', in Tapan Raychaudhuri and Irfan Habib (eds.), *The Cambridge Economic History of India, vol. 1: c.1200–c.1750* (Cambridge: University Press, 1982), 382–407.

36 Wan K. Mujani, 'Some Notes on the Portuguese and Frankish Pirates during the Mamluk Period (872–922 A.H./1468–1517 A.D.)', *Jurnal Pengajian Umum Asia Tenggara*, 8 (2007), 18–20.

37 Boxer, *The Portuguese Seaborne Empire*, 45; Anand, *Origin and Development*, 5; George Modelski, 'Enduring rivalry in the democratic lineage, the Venice-Portugal Case', in Thompson (ed.), *Great Power Rivalries*, 31–59; Abulafia, *The Boundless Sea*, 594–610.

38 Alexandrowicz, *Law of the Nations in the East Indies*, 61; Steinberg, *The Social Construction of the Ocean*, 47–8; Khalilieh, *Islamic Law of the Sea*, 3; Frederic C. Lane, 'Pepper Prices before Da Gama', *Journal of Economic History*, 28(4) (1968), 590–7.

39 Alexandrowicz, *Law of the Nations in the East Indies*, 53; Anand, *Origin and Development*, 55.

tuguese endeavours entailed the adoption of colonising techniques originally developed in the eastern Mediterranean.[40]

Given Portugal's limited resources and the geopolitical conditions in Africa and Monsoon Asia, the Portuguese did not attempt to conquer large territories, limiting themselves to the creation of fortified naval bases and trading posts (*feitorias*), strategically located along the coasts of Africa and Asia. This reliance on naval superiority allowed the Portuguese to secure a significant position in the Indian Ocean, particularly in the spice trade.[41] From their bases, they patrolled the region and introduced the *cartaz* system – based on documents granting safe conduct in exchange for payment to the Portuguese Crown. Portuguese captains were instructed to seize any ships not carrying a *cartaz*.[42] The goal consisted of diverting the spice trade towards the newly established Cape route, forcing Asian merchants to buy safe passage – thus acknowledging Portuguese claims over the high seas – while excluding all other Europeans. Nevertheless, from early on the Crown struggled to maintain its monopoly over the Cape Route, contending with private merchants it relied on for cooperation and, later, emerging European competitors.[43]

In contrast, the Spanish in the western Atlantic encountered little naval competition. The absence of heavy, oceangoing vessels among the indigenous civilisations made it relatively easy for the Spanish to regard

40 Carlo Taviani, 'In the shadow of other empires: Genoese merchant networks and their conflicts across the Atlantic Ocean, ca. 1450–1530', in Sicking and Wijffels (eds.), *Conflict Management*, 217–36. Due to the limited financial resources of the Portuguese Crown, other Italian and German financers were involved too, hence the private-public nature of many of the expeditions of the *Carreira da Índia*, see Harris, *Going the Distance*, 236–42.

41 Anand, *Origin and Development*, 57–9; Boxer, *The Portuguese Seaborne Empire*, 47–8; Newitt, *A History of Portuguese Overseas Expansion*, 83.

42 Alexandrowicz, *Law of the Nations in the East Indies*, 64–5; Jan Kieniewicz, 'The Portuguese Factory and Trade in Pepper in Malabar during the Sixteenth Century', *The Indian Economic and Social History Review*, 6(1) (1969), 61–84, at 68. On the *cartaz* system, see Ruby Maloni, 'Control of the Seas: the Historical Exegesis of the Portuguese "Cartaz"', *Proceedings of the Indian History Congress*, 72(1) (2011), 476–84; Luis Filipe F. R. Thomaz, 'Portuguese control over the Arabian Sea and the Bay of Bengal: a comparative study', in Denys Lombard and Om Prakash (eds.), *Commerce and Culture in the Bay of Bengal, 1500–1800* (New Delhi: Manohar, 1999), 115–62; Khalileh, *Islamic Law of the Sea*, 5–7; Kuzhippalli S. Mathew, 'Trade in the Indian Ocean and the Portuguese system of cartazes', in Malyn Newitt (ed.). *The First Portuguese Colonial Empire* (Exeter: University Press, 1986), 69–84.

43 Harris, *Going the Distance*, 234–48; Anand, *Origin and Development*, 57–9. For a historiographical and critical reappraisal, see Cátia Antunes, 'The Portuguese maritime empire: global nodes and transnational networks', in Strootman, van den Eijnde, and van Wijk (eds.), *Empires of the Sea*, 294–311.

the Atlantic as a vast *res nullius* and to sometimes piratically attack the large canoes sailed by native populations.[44] For instance, the Aztecs lacked long-range seafaring capabilities, while the Incas possessed no maps.[45] Soon, a lengthy dispute would arise concerning the legality of Castilian expansion over the Caribbean islands and the Americas, as well as the rights of the natives.[46] Regarding adjacent oceans, the situation appeared instead straightforward (from a Spanish perspective) and Isabella and Ferdinand took steps to monopolise those pelagic spaces and acquire legal titles valid *erga omnes*. In 1513, the Spanish explorer and conquistador Vasco Núñez de Balboa became the first European to reach the shores of the Pacific Ocean, 'the southern sea', after crossing the Isthmus of Panama. Once there, he performed a *toma de posesión*, ceremonially claiming the ocean and the adjacent lands for the Spanish Crown. Balboa's actions mirrored the customary procedure for claiming newly discovered islands and territories. He solemnly walked into the waters in complete armour:

> with a shining helmet on his head, breastplate, greaves, and gauntlets. [...] drawing his sword and taking in his left hand a banner upon which was painted the arms of Castile and Aragon, he waded into the tide, [...] waving both banner and sword, shouted in a loud voice: 'Long live the high and mighty sovereigns of Castile! Thus in their names do I take possession of these seas and regions; and if any other prince, whether

44 Inga Clendinnen, *Ambivalent Conquests: Maya and Spaniard in Yucatan, 1517–1570* (Cambridge: University Press, 1987), 3; Policante, *The Pirate Myth*, 30–1; Kris E. Lane, *Pillaging the Empire: Piracy in the Americas, 1500–1750* (New York: M.E. Sharpe, 1998), 15.

45 Fernández-Armesto, *Exploration and Discovery*, 175–6; Daniel Sandweiss, 'Maritime aspects of early Andean civilizations', in Arnaud and de Souza (eds.), *The Sea in History*, I, 49–53; Heather McKillop, 'Early Maya navigation and maritime connections in Mesoamerica', in Balard (ed.), *The Sea in History*, II, 701–15; Emiliano Melgar, 'The Maya Caribbean: fishing, navigation, and trade', ibid., 716–26; Jorge Ortiz-Sotelo, 'The central Andean peoples and their relationship to the sea', ibid., 727–40.

46 Anthony Pagden, 'Dispossessing the barbarian: the language of Spanish thomism and the debate over the property rights of the American Indians', in idem (ed.), *The Languages of Political Theory in Early Modern Europe* (Cambridge: University Press, 1986), 79–98; Thomas Duve and Heikki Pihlajamäki (eds.), *New Horizons in Spanish Colonial Law: Contributions to Transnational Early Modern Legal History* (Frankfurt Am Main: Max Planck Institute for European Legal History, 2015). On Spanish expansion in the Americas, see John H. Elliott, *Empires of the Atlantic World: Britain and Spain in America, 1492–1830* (New Haven, CT: Yale University Press, 2006), 3–114; Rafael D. Fernández, 'Proceso jurídico del descubrimiento de América (bulas, tratados y capitulaciones)', *Anuario Mexicano de Historia del Derecho*, 2 (1990), 81–114.

> Christian or infidel, pretends any right to them, I am ready and resolved to oppose him, and to assert the just claims of my sovereigns.'[47]

Everything occurred under the watchful eye of the expedition's notary, Andrés de Valderrábano, who meticulously documented the events to provide evidence of the acquisition of possession. Finally, all members of the expedition signed the official record.[48]

3 Legal Titles Involved

3.1 *Early Papal Bulls and Prior Discovery*

As already mentioned, by the end of the Middle Ages, the Roman tradition of conceiving the sea as *res communis omnium* had somewhat faded. Various seafaring powers had asserted control over maritime areas of geoeconomic interest. Now, the rulers of the Iberian kingdoms sought to enforce 'claimed seas' policies on a far grander scale, extending their claims 'over the open, unlimited oceans of the world, the immensities of which were only just becoming apparent'.[49] This marked the opening of a new, global horizon. Their objective was to prevent other European powers from sailing across the oceans, engaging in overseas trade, or establishing settlements. It is important to emphasise that the early modern legal discourse concerning the sea remained deeply intertwined with those related to trade and the acquisition of sovereignty over territories, as exemplified by the *toma de posesión* carried out by Núñez de Balboa. Undoubtedly, 'law' played an essential role in these exploratory endeavours.[50] A notary was usually present in each expedition, to 'legally dress it' and duly document the taking of possession of newly discovered lands and islands.

Spain and Portugal justified their monopolistic claims through various 'titles of acquisition of sovereignty'. One of the most important was the *donatio apostolica*, contained in papal *bullae* that granted privileges over the 'new

47 Frederick A. Ober, *Vasco Núñez de Balboa* (New York: Harper & Brothers Publishers, 1906), 179–80.

48 Ibidem; Henry Kamen, *Spain's Road to Empire* (London: Penguin Books, 2009), 85 (Kindle version).

49 Grewe, *Epochs*, 257.

50 An early version of this chapter appeared as an article in *Historia et ius*, see Stefano Cattelan, 'Iberian Expansion over the Oceans: Law and Politics of *Mare Clausum* on the Threshold of Modernity (XV–XVI centuries)', *Historia et ius*, 18 (2020), 1–28, https://doi.org/10.32064/18.2020.26.

lands and waters'. This aligned with a widespread medieval law of nations practice. European princes sought papal approval or confirmation for military expansion against non-Christian peoples, legitimising their actions vis-à-vis other Christian rulers. Medieval popes had claimed the right to grant new territories and maritime monopolies on various legal grounds, for example, the *Donatio Costantini* in relation to all islands inhabited by heathens and infidels.[51] During the fifteenth century, the Holy See's influence in international affairs remained significant, and Portugal's kings were keen to emphasise their crusading spirit. They framed their expeditions to Africa and the Atlantic as missions to expand the boundaries of Christendom.[52] As a result, on 5 January 1433, Pope Eugene IV issued the bull *Rex regum*, calling upon all Christian princes to unite with Portugal in the fight against the 'African moors' (*mouros de Africa*).[53]

Three years later, King Edward I of Portugal requested that Eugene IV lift the ban on colonising the Canary Islands, inhabited by the Guanches, who were neither Christian nor Muslim. While the king hinted at the possibility of unilateral action, he concluded his letter by reaffirming the pope's supreme authority in such matters.[54] Portuguese arguments proved persuasive at a time when fear of the rising Ottoman Empire was widespread. Consequently, fifteenth-century popes issued numerous bulls legitimising Lusitanian and Castilian maritime expansion.[55] The Holy See granted generous privileges and monopolies, also covering the seas, in return for the spread of the true

51 Bartolus in the *Tractatus de insula* already disputed this prerogative. See Neff, *Justice among Nations*, 55; Hébié, *Souveraineté territoriale*, 43; Luis Rojas Donat, 'La potestad Apostólica en las bulas ultramarinas portuguesas y castellanas', *Revista de estudios históricos-jurídicos*, 29 (2007), 407–20; Ladero Quesada, 'Los debates', 236–7; Sicking, '*Mare Liberum, Mare Clausum*', 189–91.

52 See Raymond C. Beazley, 'Prince Henry of Portugal and the African Crusade of the Fifteenth Century', *The American Historical Review*, 16(1) (1910), 11–23.

53 Coelho, *Alguns documentos*, 7. See also Raymond, *Prince Henry of Portugal*, 11–23.

54 'Letter from King Duarte I of Portugal to Pope Eugenius IV, August 1436', in Dias Dinis, *Monumenta Henricina*, vol. V, 254–8. James Muldoon, *The Expansion of Europe: The First Phase* (Philadelphia, University of Pennsylvania Press, 1977), provides an English translation, doc. 10, 56: 'Although many will strive on their own authority to wage war and to occupy the lands of the infidels, nevertheless, because the earth and its fullness are the Lord's who left to Your Holiness the fulness of this power over the entire world, whatever is possessed by the authority and permission of Your Holiness is understood to be held in a special way with the permission of almighty God'.

55 Hébié, *Souveraineté territoriale*, 67–71; Charles-Martial de Witte, 'Les bulles pontificales et l'expansion portugaise au XVe siècle', *Revue d'histoire ecclésiastique*, 48 (1958), 683–718. Kent McNeil, 'The Papal Bulls Dividing the Americas between Spain and Portugal: A Reappraisal', *Journal of the History of International Law*, 26(4) (2024), 351–82.

faith. In other words, Portuguese kings sought to be adequately rewarded for their 'missionary and civilising endeavour'.[56] Many of these early *bullae* retained a distinctly medieval character, often addressing the legal status of non-Christian political entities and matters relating to the canonistic theory of *bellum iustum* (just war).

At the time, there was considerable ambiguity between titles to territory and titles to dominion over the sea. As Grewe observed, 'the foundations of the Hispano-Portuguese claims to dominion over the oceans of the world were identical with the legal titles on which the overseas colonial acquisitions of these two nations were based'.[57] In any case, both Spain and Portugal seemed inclined to conceive their rights over oceans corridors as *ius excludendi alios* – the right to exclude others from using of something (usually in relation to property), – rather than the more limited *iurisdictio* or *protectio*. More specifically, in West Africa Lusitanian kings relied heavily on the right of prior discovery as additional title to exclusive dominion over the newly discovered regions. This argument also covered the adjacent seas and even the open ocean, since Portuguese seafarers were the first to open new maritime routes in the region.[58]

Castilian monarchs, for their part, asserted claims over parts of Morocco and West Africa by arguing that, as the direct successors of the Visigoth kings, they inherited rights to the Roman province of *Mauritania Tingitana*; by extension, they laid claim to the Canary Islands and the surrounding seas, a justification rooted in an embryonic notion of state succession.[59] King John II of Castile (r. 1406–1454) claimed for his country 'the ancient and exclusive right of sailing in the seas of Guinea' and threatened war if the Portuguese did not stop their journeys southward. Numerous expeditions departed from Andalusian ports towards West Africa. In the words of Alonzo de Palencia, a Castilian chronicler, the Portuguese were 'cruelly preventing all others from cruising off those coasts'.[60]

Thus, Castile initially opposed Portuguese 'closed-claimed sea' policies, reigniting the traditional rivalry between the two neighbouring kingdoms in a

---

56 De Witte, 'Les bulles pontificales', 702.

57 Grewe, *Epochs*, 257.

58 Alfonso García-Gallo, *Las bulas de Alejandro VI y el ordenamiento jurídico de la expansión portuguesa y castellana en África e Indias* (Madrid: Instituto Nacional de Estudios Jurídicos, 1958), 589–90.

59 Michèle Escamilla, *Le siècle d'or de l'Espagne, apogée et déclin, 1492–1598* (Paris: Tallandier, 2015), 45.

60 Alonzo de Palencia, *Cronica de Enrique*, IV, 127–8, quoted in Blake, *European Beginnings in West Africa*, 16–20; Diffie and Winius, *Foundations of the Portuguese Empire*, 59.

new context.[61] This led to a diplomatic triangle between Portugal, Castile, and Rome, with successive popes shifting their support between Castilian and Portuguese interests. However, until the close of the fifteenth century, Portugal remained the primary beneficiary of papal decisions.[62] For instance, in 1452, Pope Nicholas v fully endorsed Portuguese ambitions in the Atlantic, granting King Alphonso v of Portugal significant privileges, including:

> The full and unrestricted right to subjugate the Saracens, heathen and other infidels and enemies of Christ, whoever they may be, to attack, conquer, occupy and subject their kingdoms, duchies, counties, principalities and other dominions, lands, places, cities, castles and other possessions. [...] Furthermore, we concede to you and to your successors in the Kingdom of Portugal the right to appropriate and to annex to your realm their kingdoms, etc. and to use them to your and your aforementioned successors' benefit and pleasure.[63]

3.2 *The Bull* Romanus Pontifex

A further milestone was reached when Pope Nicholas v (r. 1447–1455) issued the bull *Romanus Pontifex* on 8 January 1455, which expanded and consolidated the provisions of the earlier document from 1452. This papal bull officially sanctioned Portugal's monopoly of navigation along the West African coasts, resolving the Castilian-Portuguese dispute over Guinea and the southern seas in favour of King Alphonso v of Portugal, who had petitioned the pope specifically for this purpose.[64] The bull was intended as a reward for the campaigns against the Muslims initiated by the Portuguese. Pope Nicholas v maintained that 'eternal felicity' could best be achieved:

---

61 Ana B. Sánchez Prieto, *La intitulación diplomática de los Reyes Católicos: un programa político y una lección de historia*, in *III Jornadas Científicas sobre Documentación de la Época de los Reyes Católicos* (Madrid: Universidad Complutense, 2004), 292; Antonio P. Voituriez, *Problemas jurídicos internacionales de la conquista de Canarias* (Las Palmas de Gran Canaria: Universidad de La Laguna, 1958), 39–88.

62 For instance, pro Spanish was the bull *Dudum cum*, issued by Pope Eugenius IV in 1436 (31 July). It bestowed upon King John of Castile the right to 'conquest of Africa'. See Blake, *European Beginnings*, 23. The letters wrote by the kings of Portugal and Castile in 1345 to Pope Clement VI, concerning the sovereignty over the Canaries were also part of this 'diplomatic triangle'. They are reported in García-Gallo, *Las bulas*, appxs. 3–4, 747–51.

63 'Enfeoffment of King Alphonso v of Portugal with conquered heathen territories by Nicholas v, 1452', in Grewe, *Fontes*, I, 641.

64 For the text, see Davenport, *European Treaties*, I, doc. 1, 9–26, at 12; García-Gallo, *Las bulas*, appx. 6, 765–775; Dias Dinis, *Monumenta Henricina*, vol. XII, 254–8.

> If we bestow suitable favors and special graces on those catholic kings and princes, who like athletes and intrepid champions of the Christian faith, as we know by the evidence of facts, not only restrain the savage excesses of the Saracens and of other infidels, enemies of the Christian name, but also for the defense and increase of the faith vanquish them [...], though situated in the remotest parts unknown to us, and subject them to their own temporal dominion, sparing no labor and expense, in order that those kings and princes, relieved of all obstacles, may be the more animated to the prosecution of so salutary and laudable work.[65]

The efforts and hardships endured by the Portuguese were recounted in detail within the document. They had ventured for the first time into the 'Ocean Sea', where 'never, or at least not within the memory of men, had it been customary to sail on this ocean sea toward the southern and eastern shores', thereby opening new routes 'as far as the Indians who are said to worship the name of Christ'.[66] What is particularly significant for our purposes, however, is the nature of the privileges bestowed upon the Portuguese. The Lusitanians were granted the right to close off the areas they had explored and to impose the payment of licences on those who wished to follow in their wake.[67] The bull explicitly mentioned the 'islands, lands, ports and seas (*maria adiacentia*)' that were to be exclusively exploited by Portugal. Hence, it appears that the papal court admitted that the seas could be 'possessed' by the Lusitanian kingdom and that Portuguese authorities were authorised to punish all interlopers, who were also automatically subject to spiritual sanctions, i.e. interdict and excommunication *latae sententiae*:

> ... if they be single persons, they shall incur the sentence of excommunication; if a community or corporation or corporation of a city [...] shall be thereby subject to the interdict; and we decree further that transgressors, collectively or individually, shall not be absolved from the sentence of excommunication, nor be able to obtain the relaxation of the interdict, [...] unless they shall first have made due satisfaction for their transgressions to Alfonso himself and his successors, or shall have amicably agreed with them thereupon.[68]

65 Davenport, *European Treaties*, I, doc. 1, 21.

66 Ibidem. Boxer considered the bull as the 'charter' of Portuguese imperialist expansion in the Atlantic. In *The Portuguese Seaborne Empire*, 56. See also Diffie and Winius, *Foundations of the Portuguese Empire*, 75.

67 Maloni, *Control of the Seas*, 477.

68 Davenport, *European Treaties*, I, doc. 1, 25.

Mamadou Hébié argues that the bulls of 1452 and 1455 did not, in themselves, intend to transfer sovereignty or territorial rights. Rather, the Portuguese were still required to effectively occupy or conquer the areas and seas in question. The act of papal concession constituted a precondition, granting the *ius ad occupationem*; however, Portugal was then expected to establish its title to territorial rights through discovery (*inventio*), occupation (*occupatio*) or conquest. In other words, the bulls granted a 'title to territorial sovereignty and not a title of sovereignty'.[69] Thus, the bull implied a twofold acquisitive title: on the one hand, discovery and occupation, and on the other hand, the pontifical donation. The *donatio* aimed to convert a de facto acquisition into a rightfully held legal position.

Portuguese rulers appear to have been aware of the complex nature of the rights granted by the Holy See. This is evident in the letters patent issued to their explorers, as well as in the royal titles used in official documents.[70] They styled themselves as 'kings' of Portugal and Algarve ('on both sides of the Strait of Gibraltar'), while referring to themselves as 'lords' of navigation and commerce, as well as of regions such as Guinea and India. This distinction suggests an acknowledgment of differing relationships between the Crown and its various possessions (real or claimed): full sovereignty in the case of Portugal and the Algarves, while a more limited *ius excludendi alios*, or preferential title, operated in relation to the seas and the distant territories and seas reached by their emissaries.[71]

It must be underlined that, from the outset, the bull *Romanus pontifex* was interpreted by the Portuguese as sanctioning the exclusion of all other Christians from the seas south of Cape Bojador (*ius privativum*) as the legitimate reward for Portuguese missionary efforts and the expenses related to explor-

69 My translation from Hébié, *Souveraineté territoriale*, 51, '*titre à la souveraineté territoriale et non d'un titre de souveraineté*'. See also Cassi, *Ius commune*, 127; Giovanni Distefano, *L'ordre international entre légalité et effectivité: le titre juridique dans le contentieux territorial* (Paris: Pedone, 2002), 32–3.

70 For instance, King Alphonso v in the letter patent given to João Vogado in 1462 (29 February) wrote: 'To all, who shall see this my charter, we make known that in those parts of the ocean whose right to discover has been given to us by the Pope, two new islands have been discovered'. Text reported in David B. Queen, *New American World: A Documentary History of North America to 1612*, vol. I (New York: Arno Press & Hector Bye Inc., 1979), doc. 35, 78.

71 De Witte, 'Les bulles pontificales', 702; Hébié, *Souveraineté territoriale*, 51; Luis Filipe F. R. Thomaz, 'Factions, Interests and Messianism: The Politics of Portuguese Expansion in the East, 1500–1521', *Indian Economic and Social History Review*, 28(1) (1991), 97–109, at 98–100.

ation.[72] The bull *Inter caetera* of Callixtus III, dated 13 March 1456, further reinforced Portugal's exclusive rights along the African coasts. With this document, the pope granted the Portuguese Order of Christ 'all power, dominion and spiritual jurisdiction' over the regions previously reserved to Portugal by the *Romanus pontifex*.[73] If the 1456 bull focused more on the spiritual and ecclesiastical jurisdictional aspect of Portuguese expansion, it also added a significant clarification to its predecessor by more explicitly delineating the areas of exclusive Portuguese expansion:

> … we determine, ordain, and appoint forever that ecclesiastical and all ordinary jurisdiction, lordship, and power, in ecclesiastical matters only, in the islands, villages, harbors, lands, and places, acquired and to be acquired from Cape Bojador and Nam as far as through all Guinea, and past that southern shore all the way to the Indians, the position, number, nature, appellations, designations, bounds, and localities of which we wish to be considered as expressed by these presents, shall belong and pertain to the said military order for all time…[74]

3.3 *Treaty of Alcaçovas*

Despite the clear position taken by the papacy, Castile continued to claim Guinea, with expeditions regularly sailing from Andalusian ports towards West Africa, often resulting in their capture by Portuguese warships. Consequently, various diplomatic crises arose between the two Iberian kingdoms, as Castilian authorities demanded reparations for vessels seized south of Cape Bojador. In 1475, King Alphonso V of Portugal invaded Castile during the War of the Castilian Succession (1475–1479), claiming to defend the rights to the throne of his betrothed, Princess Joanna, against Queen Isabella's alleged usurpation.[75] In response, Castilians forcefully entered the Guinean trade,

72 Davenport, *European Treaties*, I, doc. 1, 25. See Luis Weckmann, *Las Bulas Alejandrinas de 1493 y la teoría política del Papado medieval. Estudio de la supremacía papal sobre islas, 1091–1493* (México: Universidad Nacional Autónoma, 1959), 259–60.

73 For the text, see 'Conveyance of Spiritual Authority upon the Portuguese Order of Jesus Christ by Callixtus III, 1456', in Grewe, *Fontes*, I, 647–8. See also Diffie and Winius, *Foundations of the Portuguese Empire*, 95. Prince Henry was the order's grandmaster, and after his death, the privileges bestowed upon the order would pass to the crown.

74 Grewe, *Fontes*, I, 648. See also Blake, *European Beginnings*, 22–3.

75 Vincente A. Álvarez Palenzuela, *La guerra civil castellana y el enfrentamiento con Portugal (1475–1479)* (Alicante: Biblioteca Virtual Universal, 2006). See also Luis Rojas Donat, 'Dos anális histórico-jurídicos en torno al descubrimiento de las Indias: la accessión y la ocupación', *Revista de estudios históricos-jurídicos*, 19 (1997), 153–66. After the death of

seeking to secure a greater share of its wealth. In June 1478, Isabella sanctioned unrestricted Castilian trade towards the 'Mina de Oro' and instructed coastal cities' authorities to encourage trade with West Africa. This led to intense skirmishing in the Atlantic, culminating in 1478 when a Portuguese squadron intercepted and defeated a Castilian fleet near Mina in Guinea.[76]

Only in 1479, the belligerents reached a comprehensive settlement to solve their 'serious disputes, questions, discussions, and differences' (*grandes debates e quistiones, desençiones e diferençias*), incorporating elements from the previous peace treaty of Medina del Campo (1431).[77] More specifically, two treaties were concluded in the Portuguese city of Alcaçovas. The first resolved dynastic matters, with Alphonso V ultimately accepting Isabella's accession to the throne and withdrawing his wife's claim.[78] The second addressed territorial and maritime issues, with articles eight and nine being particularly significant. Article nine saw the king of Portugal formally acknowledge Castilian sovereignty over the Canary Islands, thereby ending the longstanding dispute concerning them. In return, the 'Catholic Monarchs' (*Reyes Católicos*) solemnly pledged to respect Portugal's monopoly of navigation south of an imaginary line drawn below the Canaries.[79] Portugal thus secured exclusive rights to navigate toward Guinea, Cape Verde, Madeira, the Azores, and the Kingdom of Fez.

As Thomas Duve observes, this international agreement introduced a practice of 'drawing a line dividing the waters, in this case, from east to west, in order to confirm the rights over already existing possessions, and to demarcate the spheres of influence and rights of free navigation and possessions for

Henry IV of Castile (r. 1454–1474), the throne was claimed by Joanna 'la Beltraneja', daughter of the late monarch whose legitimacy was disputed by part of the nobility, and Henry's sister, Isabella. The succession crisis assumed international character, since Isabella had married Ferdinand of Aragon in 1469, while Joanna was married to the king of Portugal.

76 Diffie and Winius, *Foundations of the Portuguese Empire*, 155; Blake, *European Beginnings*, 52. For Isabella's proclamation see 'Seguro á los Marineros de Palos para contratar libremente por mar y tierra con las mercaderías que llevaren y trajeren en su viaje á la Mina del Oro', in Fernández de Navarrete, *Colección de los viajes*, II, 429–33.

77 For the text of the treaty and its English translation, see Davenport, *European Treaties*, I, doc. 3, 37. For the Portuguese version, see Coelho, *Alguns documentos*, 42–3.

78 Sánchez Prieto, *La intitulación diplomática de los Reyes Católicos*, 293; Antonio Domínguez Ortiz, 'La España de los Reyes Católicos', in *España, tres milenios de Historia* (Madrid: Marcial Pons, 2007), 130.

79 The appellation *Reyes Católicos* was formally conferred in 1494 to Ferdinand and Isabella by Pope Alexander VI, in recognition of their actions in favour of the Church.

future discoveries'.[80] The line, based on latitude, passed just below the Canary Islands, effectively separating Portuguese and Castilian exclusive areas of expansion. The portolan charts and nautical instruments of the time already enabled the determination of ships' position relative to the West African coasts and the Canary Islands, or to 'conceive and organize space on the sea between coastlines and known islands'.[81] Isabella and Ferdinand explicitly agreed that neither they, nor their successors and subjects, would:

> ... disturb, trouble or molest, in fact or in law, in court or out of court, the said King and Prince of Portugal or the future sovereigns of Portugal or their kingdoms, in their possession or quasi possession in all the trade, lands, and barter in Guinea, with its gold-mines, or in any other islands, coasts, or lands, discovered or to be discovered, found or to be found [...] from the Canary Islands down toward Guinea. For whatever has been found or shall be found, acquired by conquest, or discovered within the said limits [...], belongs to the said king of Portugal, excepting only the Canary Islands.[82]

Moreover, the Catholic Monarchs agreed to prohibit their subjects from entering Portugal's exclusive area of interest, including navigation towards Guinea and beyond:

> ... if any of the natives or subjects of the kingdoms of Castile, or any foreigners whosoever, shall traffic in, obstruct, injure, plunder, or acquire by conquest the said Guinea, or its trade, barter, mines, lands, and islands, discovered or to be discovered, without the express license and consent of the said king and prince or of their successors, [they do promise] that all such shall be punished.[83]

80 Thomas Duve, 'Spatial perceptions, juridical practices, and early international legal thought around 1500: from Tordesillas to Saragossa' in Stefan Kadelbach et al. (eds.), *System, Order, and International Law. The Early History of International Legal Thought from Machiavelli to Hegel* (Cambridge: University Press, 2017), 418–42, at 425–6.

81 Ibidem. Latitude could be measured relatively accurately with the existing technology – the astrolabe or sextant – as opposed to longitude. The latter could first be determined with certitude in only starting in the 1760s, when the marine chronometer created by the English clockmaker John Harrison (1693–1776) proved accurate.

82 Davenport, *European Treaties*, I, doc. 3, 44. On Portuguese claims over North Africa, see Thomaz, 'Factions, interests and messianism', 98.

83 Davenport, *European Treaties*, I, doc. 3, 44.

On their part, in a document dated 6 March 1480, the king and the crown prince of Portugal reaffirmed their promise not to question Castilian rights and possessions in the Canary Islands (*non turbaran, molesteran ny inquieteram, de fecho ny de derecho, en juizio ny fuera de juizio, por sy nyn por otra*). The aim was to establish a stable peace between the two Crowns, '*para que esta paz sea firme, estable, para siempre duratura*'.[84] Furthermore, both parties promised not to seek absolution or dispensation from the oath contained in the treaty to the pope. Nevertheless, they petitioned Pope Sixtus IV (r. 1471–1484) for a confirmation of the treaty. The pope complied, issuing the bull *Aeterni regis* on 21 June 1481.[85] This document expressly recalled the earlier bulls of 8 January 1455 and 13 March 1456, while incorporating the now-settled matter of Castilian sovereignty over the Canary Islands, and it unambiguously threatened severe consequences for potential violators:

> Let no one, therefore, infringe or with rash boldness contravene this our confirmation, approbation, reinforcement, regulation and mandate. Should anyone presume to do so, be it known to him that he will incur the wrath of Almighty God and of the blessed apostles Peter and Paul.[86]

The king of Portugal's position in West Africa had grown more robust than ever after the conclusion of the treaty, as he now perceived 'Guinea' as undisputedly belonging to his kingdom (*que direitamente a estes rregnos soomemte pertençe*). Consequently, he soon sent a peremptory order to the Portuguese captains cruising in the Atlantic.[87] In the document, dated 6 April 1480, he commanded that the crews of all interloping vessels captured south of the Canaries (*pera baixo e adjante contra Guinea*) were to be summarily thrown into the sea, so that the trespassers would 'die a natural death':

84 Coelho, *Alguns documentos*, 44.

85 For the text of the bull, see Davenport, *European Treaties*, vol 1, doc. 4, 49; García-Gallo, *Las bulas*, 607–10; Grewe, *Fontes*, I, 649–53; Coelho, *Alguns documentos*, 45–56. See also Thomas Duve, 'Treaty of Tordesillas', in *Max Planck Encyclopedia of Public International Law*. Online edition [www.mpepil.com] (Oxford: University Press, 2013); Mario Tedeschi, 'Le bolle alessandrine e la loro rilevanza giuridica', in Simonetta B. Alagna (cur.), *Esplorazioni geografiche e immagine del mondo nei secoli XV e XVI*, Atti convegno Messina 14–15 ottobre, 1993 (Messina: Grafo Editor, 1994), 137.

86 Davenport, *European Treaties*, vol 1, doc. 4, 55.

87 More specifically, the order was directed to the captains who served under the infant *João*, son of Alfonso V, who would succeed him as John II (r. 1481–1495). At the time of the treaty, the infante was already supervising Portuguese endeavours in Guinea. See Blake, *European Beginnings in West Africa*, 54–5.

> By this present letter, we grant power and authority, and special mandate, to the captains who are at any time sent by the Prince, my son, etc., to the said Guinea, that, should they find any caravels or ships of any people from Spain, or from any others who may venture to go, or who may be coming or returning to the said Guinea, or staying there in any manner whatsoever, beyond the limits that have been set and declared by the agreement of the peace treaty made between our kingdoms and those of Castile [i.e. the Treaty of Alcaçovas], which limits and boundaries are marked as lying south of the Canary Islands and onwards towards Guinea, they may, as soon as these people are captured, without any further order or legal proceedings, immediately throw them all into the sea, so that they naturally perish at once...[88]

The king concluded the document by asserting that such harsh measures would serve as a deterrent to those who heard of them. A month later, Alphonso V transferred all rights concerning trade in Guinea and fisheries in the adjacent seas (*pescaria dos seus mares*) to his son, Prince John. Anyone wishing to sail in the region was now required to pay for licences issued by the prince.[89] The chronicler Alonzo de Palencia reported that the Portuguese would often torture and kill the Castilians 'whom they caught beyond the Canaries', commenting that 'in order to instil constant horror in the rest, they used to cut off the legs and arms of others'.[90] While this account may have been exaggerated, it is clear that venturing south of the Canaries had, in practice, become a perilous endeavour. Following the treaty's ratification,

88 My translation from the original Portuguese: '*Nos per esta pressemte carta damos poder e faculldade, e espeçiall mandado, aos capitãees que pello tempo forem emvjados pello Prinçeepe, meu fihlo, etc., aa dita Guineea, que, achamdo ells quaesquer caravellas ou navjos de quallquer jente d Espanha, ou d outro quallquer que seja o user possa, de hida ou vjnda, ir ou virem pera a dita Guineea, ou estar em ella per quallquer maneira quo seja, aallem das marquas que pello ascemto da capitollaçom das pazes feitas amtre os dictos nossos rregnos e os de Castella sam apomtadas e decraredas, as quaees marquas e termos sam das Canarias pera baixo e adjante contra Guinea, que, tamto que os taees forem tomados sem outra majs ordem nem fegura de juizo, possom logo todos ser e sejam deytados ao mar, pera que mouram logo naturallmemte*'. See 'Carta de El-Rei D Affonso V para os capitães dos navios enviados pelo principe seu filho a Guiné tomaren os navios estrangieros que encontrarem fóra dos limites marcados pelas capitulações de paz feitas entre Portugal e Castella' in Coelho, *Alguns documentos*, 45; García-Gallo, *Las bulas*, appx. 9, 784.

89 Ibid., 46. See also de Sousa, 'Portugal', 643.

90 Alonzo de Palencia, *Cronica de Enrique*, IV, 128, quoted in Blake, *European Beginnings in West Africa*, 16–20.

the Portuguese had indeed gained the legal grounds to enforce their claims against Castilian subjects, consolidating their maritime monopoly south of the Canary Islands.[91]

The treaty signed in 1479 triggered another far-reaching development. Isabella and Ferdinand, still eager to access the Indies, realised that the only feasible way to achieve this without infringing on the Portuguese maritime monopoly was to sail westward.[92] Consequently, after considerable hesitation, they agreed to sponsor Columbus' expedition in the famous '*capitulaciones de Santa Fe*'. This document alluded to the royal couple as 'lords of the Ocean Sea' (*vuestras altezas, come Señores que son de las dichas mares Océanas*).[93] Among other privileges, Columbus was granted jurisdiction over the seas of the 'New World' along with the title of 'Admiral of the Ocean Sea'.[94]

The instructions given to the Genoese for his first voyage reaffirmed the prohibition to sail towards Guinea or the Indies via the southern route running along West Africa. Columbus made plans to stop in the Canary Islands and then sail from there into the mysterious western Atlantic. Indeed, the Canaries were located as south as Castilians were allowed to linger under the provisions of the 1479 treaty.[95] Interestingly, as early as 1484 the Genoese explorer had pitched his revolutionary proposal to the king of Portugal, only to be rejected. At the time, Bartolomeu Dias' return had just confirmed the possibility of circumnavigating Africa, prompting the Portuguese king to prioritise that more promising route instead. Eventually, Columbus' voyage resulted in his reaching the Bahamas and the Caribbean Sea, changing the course of history. John H. Parry noted that 'Columbus did not discover a new world; he established contact between two worlds, both already old';[96] indeed, today it is perceived as eurocentric (and factually incorrect) to talk of a 'Discovery of America'. However, the concept of discovery retains its relevance when referring to seaways that crossed previously uncharted oceanic expanses.

91 Blake, *European Beginnings*, 52–6; Rojas Donat, *Dos anális histórico-jurídicos*, 153–5; Newitt, *A History of Portuguese Overseas Expansion*, 37–8.

92 Vincent, *1492. L'année admirable*, 52–72; John H. Elliott, *Imperial Spain, 1469–1716* (London: Penguin Books, 2002), 182–3; Parry, *The Spanish Seaborne Empire*, 54.

93 For the text, see 'Capitulaciones entre los Senores Reyes Catolicos y Cristobal Colon, 17 April 1492', in Fernández de Navarrete, *Colección de los viajes*, II, 11–3.

94 Ibidem.

95 García-Gallo, *Las bulas*, 589–90; Newitt, *A History of Portuguese Overseas Expansion*, 47. On Columbus, see Luís F. Thomaz, *Cristóvão Colombo o Genovês meu tio por afinidade* (Lisbon: Portuguese Navy Academy, 2021).

96 Parry, *The Spanish Seaborne Empire*, 65; Alfred P. Rubin, 'International Law in the Age of Columbus', *Netherlands International Law Review*, 39 (1992), 5–35.

3.4 *The Bulls of Pope Alexander VI*

3.4.1 Premises

With Columbus' arrival in the Americas, the agreement concluded in Alcaçovas suddenly became obsolete, reigniting the heated Iberian rivalry. There was significant uncertainty regarding the identity of the islands reached by Columbus – who believed to have reached Japan (*Cypango y Antillia*) – and whether they lay within the Portuguese area of exclusive interest. In 1493, as Columbus returned from his first voyage, he stopped in Lisbon and engaged in discussions with an irate John II of Portugal. The Portuguese monarch's initial response was to claim the lands discovered by Columbus and prepare a war fleet to seize them.[97]

Moreover, the two crowns offered starkly different interpretations of the 1479 treaty. From Spain's perspective, the treaty applied solely to the eastern Atlantic and West Africa, leaving Castilian expeditions sailing westward unimpeded. This interpretation relied on a literal reading of the treaty's terms. Conversely, the Portuguese government argued that the treaty had established an implicit boundary that prevented Castile from venturing southward, regardless of longitude, thus granting the entire Caribbean region to Portugal.[98] Despite these disagreements, John II prudently refrained from provoking open conflict with Isabella and Ferdinand, whose influence and power were steadily growing. Meanwhile, the Spanish monarchs acted decisively to exploit the legal ambiguity in their favour while striving to avoid a renewed clash with Portugal.[99]

3.4.2 Contents

The papacy again played a central role. Castilian envoys exerted pressure on the Holy See to secure a decision favourable to their interests. Pope Alexander

---

97 Herman Vander Linden, 'Alexander VI and the Demarcation of the Maritime and Colonial Domains of Spain and Portugal, 1493–1494', *The American Historical Review*, 22(1) (1916), 1–20, at 12.

98 Rojas Donat, *Dos anális histórico-jurídicos*, 158–9; Juan Manzano, 'El derecho de la Corona de Castilla al descubrimiento y conquista de las Indias de Poniente', *Revista de India*, 3(9) (1942), 397–427, at 402.

99 'Instrucciones dadas a los embajadores castellanos que se envían Juan II de Portugal, 3 noviembre 1493', in García-Gallo, *Las bulas*, appx. 20, 817–9: '...*la voluntad que dize que tiene a la conservaçion de la paz, amor, deudo e amistad que entre nosotros es, que se quite toda materia e ocasión que algo desto pudiese perturbar, e que desta mesma voluntad estamos nosotros; e de guardar el deudo, amor, amistad que en uno tenemos, e que en ello siempre se conserve*'. See also 'Carta mesangera de los Reyes al almirante Colon, asegurandole de las buenas intenciones del rey de Portugal, 12 June 1493', in Fernández de Navarrete, *Colección de los viajes*, II, 88.

VI (r. 1492–1503), a native of Valencia (Crown of Aragon), issued a series of bulls in 1493, collectively known as the *Bulas Alejandrinas*. Even though the pope declared to be acting '*motu proprio et ex certa scientia, de nostra mera libertate*' – reaffirming his authority and independence – he was adhering to Spanish petitions.[100] In canon law, the term *motu proprio* refers to a document issued by the pope on his own initiative, without a formal request from an external party. These documents were addressed exclusively to Isabella and Ferdinand, leading Antonio García y García to argue that the pope was not functioning as a neutral arbitrator in this matter from a legal standpoint. Notably, Portugal had not sought papal intervention on this occasion.[101]

The bulls in question – technically *brevia bullata* – include the *Inter caetera* and *Eximiae devotionis*, both dated 3 May; the *Inter caetera* of 4 May; and finally the *Dudum siquidem* dated 25 September.[102] Much scholarly debate has centred on the precise nature and implications of these documents. As Grewe observed, their legal significance and interpretation 'remains controversial up the present day'.[103] What is clear is that the bulls strongly favoured Spanish interests, diverging from the steadfast support the Holy See had extended to Portugal in earlier years. Formally, the language and rhetorical style of these bulls echoed the earlier ones granted to Portugal, indicating a continuation of papal discourse.[104] More broadly, they reflect a transitional mo-

---

100 Davenport, *European Treaties*, vol. 1, doc. 5, 59. See also Tedeschi, 'Le bolle alessandrine', 131–2; Álvaro F. de Córdova Miralles, *Alejandro VI y los Reyes Católicos; Relaciones político-eclesiásticas (1492–1503)* (Roma: Edizioni della Santa Croce, 2005); Duve, 'Spatial perceptions', 426.

101 Antonio García y García, *La donación pontificia de las Indias* (Salamanca: Universidad Pontificia, 1992), 23. Cf. Luis Rojas Donat, 'Papal arbitration? Alexander VI and the Portuguese and Spanish Discoveries of the 15th Century', *Imago Temporis. Medium Aevum*, 15 (2021), 363–85; idem, *La potestad Apostólica en las bulas ultramarinas*, 412–6; Hébié, *Souveraineté territoriale*, 55.

102 Opinions have diverged on the original order in which these bulls were issued. Perhaps some of them have been predated or post-dated. See Vander Linden, 'Alexander VI and the Demarcation', 1–2. For a detailed overview of the documents and their background, see García-Gallo, *Las bulas*.

103 Grewe, *Epochs*, 236. See also Duve, 'Spatial perceptions', 426; Paolo Prodi, 'Alessandro VI e la sovranità pontificia', in Carla Frova and Maria G. Ottaviani (cur.), *Alessandro VI e lo Stato della Chiesa* (Roma: Istituto Poligrafico dello Stato, 2003); James Muldoon, 'Papal Responsibility for the Infidel: Another Look at Alexander VI's "Inter Caetera"', *Catholic Historical Review*, 64 (1978), 168–84; Paulino Castañeda Delgado, 'La interpretación teocrática de las bulas alejandrinas', *Anuario Mexicano de Historia del Derecho*, 5 (1993), 20–59; idem, *La teocracia pontifical en las controversias sobre el Nuevo Mundo* (México: UNAM, Instituto de Investigaciones Jurídicas, 1996).

104 García-Gallo, *Las bulas*, 544.

ment between the medieval law of nations and emerging modern frameworks of international relations. While later state practice, particularly from the second half of the sixteenth century, questioned their validity or significance, at the time of their issuance, these bulls provided a robust legal basis for Castile to advance its claims.[105] The first bull issued by Alexander VI on the matter is the *Inter caetera*, dated 3 May 1493. It directly mentioned Columbus' achievements:

> ... you [...] chose our beloved son Christopher Columbus, whom you furnished with ships and men equipped for like designs, not without the greatest hardships, dangers, and expenses, to make diligent quest for these remote and unknown countries through the sea, where hitherto no one had sailed; and they at length, with divine aid and with the utmost diligence sailing in the ocean sea, through the western waters, as is said, toward the Indians, discovered certain very remote islands and even mainlands, that hitherto had not been discovered by others.[106]

The rulers of Castile were then granted the lands discovered or to be discovered by their emissaries (*per nuntios vestros repertas et reperiendas in posterum*).[107] However, a safeguard clause took into consideration Portuguese interests: Castile could take possession of the new lands only if they had not previously belonged to other Christian princes (in other words, Portugal):

> ... and we invest you and your aforementioned heirs and successors with them, and make, appoint, and depute you lords of them with full and free power, authority, and jurisdiction of every kind, with this proviso however, that by no means, that by this our gift, grant, assignment and investiture no right acquired by any Christian prince is hereby to be understood to be withdrawn or taken away.[108]

The pope also entrusted the rulers of Castile with the solemn duty of Christianising the indigenous populations. Additionally, following the precedent established by the bull *Romanus pontifex*, the pope explicitly forbade any

105 Vander Linden, 'Alexander VI and the Demarcation', 1–2; Tedeschi, 'Le bolle alessandrine', 131–2; Hébié, *Souveraineté territoriale*, 55; Weckmann, *Las Bulas Alejandrinas*, 35.

106 For the English as well as the Latin version of the text, see Davenport, *European Treaties*, vol 1, doc. 5, 62. See also Vander Linden, 'Alexander VI and the Demarcation', 14–8.

107 Davenport, *European Treaties*, vol. 1, doc. 5, 59.

108 Ibid., 62.

Europeans from venturing into these newly discovered regions for trade or other purposes without the express authorisation of the Castilian Crown. The second bull, also named *Inter caetera* and dated 4 May 1493, is widely regarded as the most significant of the series. While it reiterated much of the content of the first bull, it introduced a novel mechanism to demarcate spheres of influence.[109] The bull established a north-south demarcation line, set one hundred leagues west of the Azores and Cape Verde Islands. It is possible that Columbus was at the origin of the idea due to his newly acquired geographical knowledge.[110]

More specifically, the bull granted Spain exclusive competence west of this line. Notably, the document did not explicitly reference Portugal or its African-Indian privileges. Instead, it merely delineated the area of Spanish expansion. Despite this omission, it seems that Alexander VI aimed to maintain Portugal's established position, which had been secured by prior papal bulls. Nonetheless, the new demarcation was less favourable to Portugal, as it risked compromising the integrity of its maritime routes around Africa.[111] In the bull, the pope solemnly proclaimed:

> We [...] give, grant, and assign to you and your heirs and successors, kings of Castile and Leon, forever, together with all their dominions, [...], and all rights, jurisdictions, and appurtenances, all islands and mainlands found and to be found, discovered and to be discovered towards the west and the south, by drawing and establishing a line from the Arctic pole, namely the north, to the Antarctic pole, namely the south, no matter whether the said mainlands and islands are found or to be found in the direction of India or towards any other quarter, the said line to be distant one hundred leagues towards the west and south from any of the islands commonly known as the Azores and Cape Verde.[112]

The expression used in the bull, *versus occidentem et meridiem*, 'towards the West and the South', is hard to reconcile with a north-south line. This incon-

109 Scovazzi, 'Libertà o dominio', 12; Vander Linden, 'Alexander VI and the Demarcation', 9; Parry, *The Spanish Seaborne Empire*, 46.

110 'Carta mensager de los Reyes...', in Fernández de Navarrete, *Colección de los viages*, vol. II, n. 71, 131–3, at 132 (n. 34): '[...] *abajo fasta la raya que vos dijistes que debia venir en la Bula del Papa...*'.

111 Weckmann, *Las Bulas Alejandrinas*, 35; Hébié, *Souveraineté territoriale*, 67; García-Gallo, *Las bulas*, 544.

112 Davenport, *European Treaties*, vol. 1, doc. 7, 77.

sistency likely reflects the incomplete geographical understanding of the Atlantic Ocean at the time. It could also represent a refusal of the Portuguese interpretation of the treaty of Alcáçovas. Regardless of intent, the practical outcome of the bull was the establishment of a Spanish monopoly over navigation in an enormous and vastly unknown expanse. All interlopers would face automatic excommunication, '*latae sentetiae et ipso facto*'.[113]

The document of 4 May reaffirmed the provisions of previous bulls, clarifying that it did not intend to invalidate prior grants. It specified that Castile could rightfully possess the newly discovered territories, provided that: 'that none of the islands and mainlands [...], beyond that said line [...], be in the actual possession of any Christian king or prince up to the birthday of our Lord Jesus just past from which the present year 1493 begins'.[114] The bull in question has been generally interpreted, e.g. by Alfonso García Gallo, as intended to provide a straightforward title of acquisition of sovereignty for Castile.[115] The literal language, 'we give, grant to you and your heirs, in perpetuity, together with all their dominions, and all rights, jurisdictions...', appears to leave little doubt about this intention. Under this interpretation, the act of discovery would serve merely to activate an already valid legal title conferred by the bull.

The earlier bulls granted to Portugal derived their legitimacy from a specific legal framework: the right of war against infidels. While applying the medieval theory of the just war (*bellum iustum*) to Sub-Saharan Africa might seem tenuous, it was nonetheless grounded in one of the most thoroughly examined medieval *quaestiones* – 'the right to wage war against the Saracens'.[116] In contrast, the American 'Indians' encountered by Columbus lay well outside the conceptual boundaries of medieval European legal imagination, further complicating the application of established legal frameworks to these new contexts.

Furthermore, previous bulls in favour of Portugal generally followed the principle of effectiveness. Alexander VI lifted this burden from the shoulders of Castilian rulers. The Christian princes who had conflicting claims against Castile had now to prove their entitlements over portions of the exclusive Castilian sphere of influence. This proof became an implicit requirement to maintain the dominion, '*qui actualiter possederit*'. Otherwise, wide-ranging rights over the whole Indies west of the line were automatically assigned to Castile. In other words, while Nicholas V had made a kind of *ex ante* recogni-

113 Ibidem. Cf. Coelho, *Alguns documentos*, 65–8.

114 Davenport, *European Treaties*, vol. 1, doc. 7, 77.

115 García-Gallo, *Las bulas*, 461–829.

116 Hébié, *Souveraineté territoriale*, 58–9.

tion of the actual discovery and occupation later to be made by Portugal, Alexander VI assigned instead to Castile *hic et nunc*, with immediate effect, all seas and territories to the West of the line, regardless of any effective possession and control.[117] Significantly, the Alexandrine bulls did not envisage the clause '*postquam acquisita fuerint*', which was contained in the *Romanus pontifex*.[118]

Isabel and Ferdinand certainly interpreted the bulls as granting them exclusive rights west of the line. Their correspondence with Columbus reinforces this interpretation. For example, in May 1493, they wrote to him reaffirming his substantial privileges as governor, viceroy, and admiral (*el dicho oficio de nuestro Almirante del dicho mar Océano*), while explicitly referring to the demarcation line established by the *Inter caetera*. They further asserted their dominion over 'the said Sea Ocean' (*el dicho Mar Oceano*):

> that belongs to us, which begins with a line that we have requested to be drawn extending from the islands of the Azores to the islands of Cape Verde, from north to south, from pole to pole; in such a way that everything beyond that line to the west is ours and belongs to us; and thus we make and appoint you our Admiral, and your heirs or successors, one after the other, of all this forevermore; and likewise, we appoint you our Viceroy and Governor...[119]

The use of verbs indicating possession and ownership is revealing. It might suggest a different understanding of the legal status of the ocean compared to the Portuguese kings, who were more focused on the concept of *ius excludendi alios*. In any case, the Spanish monarchs clearly believed they had the rightful authority to exclude others from the newly discovered regions and to restrict access to the seas west of the Alexandrine line. This conviction is evi-

117 Cassi, *Ius commune*, 111.

118 Vander Linden, 'Alexander VI and the Demarcation', 16.

119 My translation from Fernández de Navarrete: 'Confirmación del título dado á D. Cristóbal Colon de Almirante, Visorey y Gobernador de las islas y tierra firme que había descubierto y descubriese, 28 May 1493', in *Colección de los viajes*, II, 67–73, at 70: '*que es nuestro, que comienza por una raya ó linea que Nos habernos fecho marcar que pasa desde las islas de los Azores á las islas de Cabo Verde, de Septentrion en Austro, de polo á polo; por manera, que todo lo que es allende de la dicha línea al Occidente, es nuestro é nos pertenece; ó así vos facemos é creamos nuestro Almirante, é á vuestros hijos ó subcesores, uno en pos de otro de todo ello para siempre jamás; é asimismo vos facemos nuestro Visorey é Gobernador*'. See also Ricardo Cerezo Martínez, 'El meridiano y el antimeridiano de Tordesillas en la geografía, la náutica y la cartografía', *Revista de Indias*, 54 (1994), 509–42.

dent in a letter dated 23 May 1493, sent by the royal couple to Columbus: 'We forbid and command that no one dares to go towards the said islands and mainlands of the Indies without our licence and mandate, under those penalties contained in our letters'.[120] At the same time, the 'Catholic Monarchs' reaffirmed the prohibition against their subjects sailing towards Mina (and Guinea in general), thereby respecting the exclusivity of Portuguese rights in that region.[121]

In conclusion, although the Alexandrine bulls did not explicitly mention the seas as their primary object, the prohibition on discovering and settling new lands clearly implied a significant limitation on the freedom of navigation. As previously noted, the Atlantic constituted the necessary antecedent to the Americas, West Africa, and India. Control of its corridors would grant the best opportunities to colonise and dominate lands and trade. Moreover, the boundary outlined in the second *Inter caetera* was fundamentally a maritime demarcation. Additionally, the *Romanus pontifex*, the Treaty of Alcaçovas, and various documents issued by Isabella and Ferdinand all explicitly referred to the seas in their provisions.

The instructions given by the Catholic Monarchs to their envoys at the Portuguese court on 3 November 1493 provide further evidence. The monarchs insisted on the need to delineate two separate spheres of influence in the Atlantic, explicitly employing the term 'partition' (… *quel mar Oçéano se partiese entre Nos*). They also referred to the seas west of the line as their solitary possession, 'all the seas, islands, and remaining lands that are found from the said line straight to the west and to the north, shall be ours'.[122] In the same document, Isabella and Ferdinand reiterated their interpretation of the treaty of 1479 as being limited to the eastern Atlantic and Guinea, rejecting John II's broader interpretation.[123] Therefore, from their point of view, Columbus' voy-

120 The letter is reported in Fernández de Navarrete: 'Carta patente, prohibiendo que vaya á las Indias ningún navio ni persona, ni se lleven mercaderías sin permiso Real ó del Almirante…, 23 May 1493', in *Colección de los viajes*, II, 61–3, my translation. They repeated similar instructions in another letter, dated 4 August 1493. Ibid., 102–4.

121 'Carta Patente nombrando a D. Cristobal Colon por Capitan General de la Armada que iba a las Indias, 28 May 1493', ibid., 73–4: '*Ni vosotros, ni alguno de vos non vayades á la Mina, ni al trato de ella que tiene el Serenísimo Rey de Portogal, nuestro Hermano, porque nuestra voluntad es de guardar é que se guarde por nuestros súbditos é naturales lo que cerca de la dicha Mina tenemos capitulado é asentado con el dicho Rey de Portogal*'.

122 'Instrucciones dadas a los embajadores castellanos que se envían a Juan II de Portugal, 3 November 1493', in García-Gallo, *Las bulas*, appx. 20, 817–9: '*e que todos los mares, islas, tierras restantes que se hallaren desde la dicha línea derecha al poniente hasta el norte, sean nuestros*'.

123 Ibid., 817.

age had not violated any Portuguese right since he had taken a route far away from Guinea and the south-eastern Atlantic, (*tanto que no pasase de las dichas islas de Canaria contra Guinea*).[124] What emerges from the reading of this document is the persisting difficulty to distinguish from a legal point of view title over land and seas.[125]

4 The Treaty of Tordesillas

4.1 *Contents*

Alexander VI's bulls utterly displeased King John II of Portugal, who feared they could jeopardise Portuguese interests. The provisions allowed Castile not only to claim Columbus's discoveries but also to assert rights over any undiscovered lands not covered by the Treaty of Alcaçovas (1479). This posed a significant threat to further Portuguese explorations.[126] However, the Portuguese government did not openly challenge the legitimacy of the papal intervention, as pontifical acts formed the foundation of their own pretensions.[127] Instead, they requested that their Spanish counterparts open direct negotiations to resolve the issue. This diplomatic initiative culminated in the signing of the famous Treaty of Tordesillas on 2 July 1494. In this agreement, John II of Portugal and the Spanish monarchs, Isabella of Castile, and Ferdinand of Aragon, sought to coordinate their maritime expansion and permanently resolve disputes over Atlantic navigation. The treaty superseded the provisions of the Treaty of Alcaçovas and earlier papal bulls regarding territorial partitions.[128]

124 Ibidem.

125 Grewe, *Epochs*, 257.

126 Duve, 'Spatial perceptions', 428; Vander Linden, 'Alexander VI and the Demarcation', 18–21; Tedeschi, 'Le bolle alessandrine', 139; On the treaty, see Luis A. Ribot García, Adolfo Carrasco Martínez and Luis Adao da Fonseca (eds.), *El Tratado de Tordesillas y su época: Congreso internacional de historia* (Valladolid: Junta de Castilla y León, 1995); Jesús Varela and Juan Vernet (eds.), *El Tratado de Tordesillas en la cartografía histórica* (Valladolid: Junta de Castilla y León, 1994); Agustín Remesal, *1494. La raya de Tordesillas* (Salamanca: Junta de Castilla y León, 1994); Thomaz O. Marcondes de Souza, 'O descobrimento da América: O tratado de Tordesillas e as Molucas', *Revista de História*, 25(51) (1962), 125–38.

127 Hébié, *Souveraineté territoriale*, 64.

128 For the text and its English translation, see Davenport, *European Treaties*, doc. 9, 84. For the original text, see García-Gallo, *Las bulas*, appx. 21, 818–23; Fernández de Navarrete, *Colección de los viajes y descubrimientos*, II, 147–61. See also Antonio Rumeu de Armas, *El Tratado de Tordesillas: rivalidad hispano-lusa por el dominio de océanos y continentes* (Madrid: Mapfre, 1992), doc IV.

In fact, two treaties were concluded: the first focused on the division of the Atlantic Ocean, while the second addressed West African fisheries and the boundaries of the Kingdom of Fez.[129]

A new demarcation line (*raya*) was established, running from north to south in the Atlantic Ocean, set 370 leagues west of the Cape Verde islands, far more westward than the initial line proposed by Spanish negotiators or the one defined in Alexander VI's bull *Inter caetera*. All lands and islands, *inventae et inveniendae* (discovered or to be discovered), west of the line were designated to the Spanish Crown, while those to the east fell under Portuguese control.[130] Portuguese negotiators insisted on a more westward line primarily because their mariners had already understood the importance of the Atlantic wind circulation system. Additionally, there is speculation that Portuguese ships might have already sighted the coast of modern-day Brazil, which would officially be 'discovered' only in 1500.[131]

The treaty also stipulated a joint scientific expedition to be undertaken 'within the ten months immediately following the date of this treaty'. This expedition was to consist of two caravels – one from each signatory –, accompanied by a team of 'pilots, astrologers, and sailors', tasked with precisely determining the demarcation line.[132] This endeavour posed significant challenges, as the line traversed largely uncharted waters, and no accurate method for measuring longitude existed at the time.[133] The two vessels were instructed to meet at Grand Canary Island and proceed together toward the Cape Verde Islands:

> from whence they shall lay a direct course to the west, to the distance of the said three hundred and seventy degrees, measured as the said persons shall agree, and measured without prejudice to the said parties. When this point is reached, such point will constitute the place and mark for measuring degrees of the sun or of north latitude by daily runs measured in leagues [...]. This said line shall be drawn north and south as aforesaid, from the said Arctic pole to the said Antarctic pole.[134]

129 Coelho, *Alguns documentos*, 80–90.
130 Therefore, the line previously set by Pope Alexander VI in the bull *Inter caetera* was moved 170 leagues to the West. See Vander Linden, 'Alexander VI and the Demarcation', 18–21; Parry, *The Spanish Seaborne Empire*, 46.
131 For the initial Spanish negotiating position, see García-Gallo, *Las bulas*, appx. 20, 817–9.
132 Davenport, *European Treaties*, I, doc. 9, 96.
133 Duve, 'Spatial perceptions', 430.
134 Davenport, *European Treaties*, I, doc. 9, 96.

A traditional interpretation of both the fifteenth-century papal bulls and the treaty of Tordesillas has held that these documents were mostly concerned with territorial rights over lands and islands, leaving the seas in a sort of legal vacuum.[135] However, a closer reading of the treaty and its context reveals the remarkable connection between the legal status of the oceans and the broader discourse on overseas expansion.[136] The agreement sought to the partition of the Atlantic, and only indirectly of the lands found across its immensities. Both the Portuguese and the Spanish recognised the ocean as the indispensable conduit connecting what they conceived as the Old and the New Worlds. Consequently, they mutually agreed to restrict their respective freedoms of navigation, swearing not to send ships into one another's spheres of influence 'for the purpose of discovering and seeking any mainlands or islands, or for the purpose of trade, barter or conquest of any kind'.[137] Furthermore, if by chance a Spanish ship discovered an island within the Portuguese sphere, or vice versa, possession of the land was to be immediately transferred to its 'legitimate' owner.[138]

In keeping with prior Hispano-Portuguese practices, the treaty effectively excluded all other European powers from this duopolistic division of the oceans, new territories, and associated commerce. No vessel was permitted to sail to the Indies without a written authorisation from the respective authorities of Castile or Portugal, depending on the sphere of influence.[139] As an additional provision, Portugal allowed Spanish ships free passage through its waters, 'in either direction, freely, securely, and peacefully', as the Spanish needed to traverse Portuguese-controlled waters in the eastern Atlantic to reach their own designated territories west of the demarcation line.[140] In exchange, Spanish ships were required to refrain from exploration or occupation in Portuguese-controlled areas, adhere to the most direct route possible, and avoid deviation unless forced by adverse weather conditions.[141]

Lastly, both parties solemnly pledged not to seek absolution from the pope concerning the treaty's provisions (*de no pedir absoluçion ni rrelaxa-*

135 Fenn, *The Origin of the Right of Fishery*, 222.

136 A view supported by Grewe and Gidel. See Grewe, *Epochs*, 257; Gidel, *Le droit international public de la mer*, I, 202.

137 Davenport, *European Treaties*, doc. 9, 89; García-Gallo, *Las bulas*, appx. 21, 821: '*de oy en adelante no embiaran navios algunos* [...] *a descubrir e buscar tierras ni yslas algunas, ni a contratar, ni rescatar, ni conquistar en manera alguna*'.

138 Ibidem.

139 Duve, 'Treaty of Tordesillas'.

140 Davenport, *European Treaties*, I, doc. 9, 97.

141 Ibidem. See also Grewe, *Epochs*, 258; Duve, 'Spatial perceptions', 430.

çion de a nuestro muy santo Padre) and not to exploit any absolution eventually granted by the Holy Father by his own will.[142] However, the treaty did allow for the possibility that either or both parties might later request papal confirmation and approval of its terms (*confirmer e aprobar esta dicha capitulaçion*).[143]

4.2 *Aftermath*

4.2.1 Hispano-Portuguese Balance of Power

The implementation of the Treaty of Tordesillas proved far from straightforward. Longitude remained at the time impossible to determine with exactitude, while the joint scientific expedition envisioned in the treaty never materialised. Hence, the demarcation line remained imprecisely defined as the two parties disagreed on the exact length of a 'league' and faced difficulties determining which specific island formed the starting point to calculate the *raya*.[144] Understandably, the Portuguese favoured the westernmost Cape Verde islands, while the Castilians preferred the easternmost ones. These differences sparked intense diplomatic negotiations throughout the early sixteenth century. For example, in 1495, another round of talks focused on the Atlantic demarcation line and the proposed joint expedition to delineate it. While the Portuguese gradually expanded their Brazilian territories beyond the demarcation line into the Amazon region, the Spanish did not entirely refrain from venturing into Portuguese-controlled waters.[145] Nonetheless, it is widely acknowledged that the 1494 treaty succeeded in stabilising relations between the two kingdoms for the following decades.

The majestic and exotic entrance in Rome by Tristão da Cunha (1514), newly appointed Portuguese ambassador at the papal court, well symbolised the prestige his kingdom had reached at the beginning of the sixteenth cen-

142 Davenport, *European Treaties*, I, doc. 9, 97.

143 Ibidem; Hébié, *Souveraineté territoriale*, 65.

144 Barrado Navascués, *Cosmography in the Age of Discovery*, 42–6.

145 Luís Mendoça de Albuquerque, 'El Tratado de Tordesillas e as dificuldades técnicas da sua aplicacão rigorosa', in *El Tratado de Tordesillas y su proyección*, vol. 1, Seminario de Historia de América (Valladolid: Universidad de Valladolid, 1973), 119–36. See also Germán Santana Pérez, 'Spanish Maritime Experience in Southern Africa during the Early Modern Period', *International Journal of Maritime History*, 30(4) (2018), 621–33; Peter E. Russell, 'Some Portuguese Paradigms for the Discovery and Conquest of Spanish America', *Renaissance Studies*, 6(3-4) (1992), 377–90; Paulo J. de Sousa Pinto, *No extremo da redonda esfera: relaçoes luso-castelhanas na Ásia, 1565–1640 – um ensaio sobre os impérios ibéricos* (Ph.D. dissertation, Lisboa: Universidade Católica Portuguesa, 2010).

tury.[146] Meanwhile, Spain was rising to the centre of European international relations, a position that solidified with the accession of Charles of Habsburg (1500–1558) to the throne following the death of his grandfather, Ferdinand II, in 1516.[147] Seaborne expansion played a pivotal role in this ascent. At the time, the Iberian kingdoms were the only European nations deeply engaged in overseas exploration. From their perspective, the 1494 treaty had resolved all disputes in the Atlantic. The grounds upon which their seaborne expansion rested appeared solid: naval predominance, title of prior discovery, occupation, as well as papal donation and endorsement.

By 1501, the Spanish crown formally prohibited the passage of foreigners to the Americas without explicit government authorisation. However, this ban was not always strictly enforced, and a degree of flexibility proved necessary. For instance, in 1534, due to a shortage of skilled Spanish pilots, Charles V issued a *cédula* authorising the recruitment of foreign pilots residing in Spain.[148] In 1503, the Spanish government established in Seville the first organ of colonial administration, the *Casa de la Contratación de las Indias*. Its purpose was to regulate and promote trade under the framework of a Crown monopoly. For decades, all ships bound for the Indies were required

---

146 'Carta do doutor J. de Faria a El-Rei D. Manuel, descrevendo a entrada solemne do embaixador de Portugal, Tristão da Cunha, em Roma, encarregado de prestar obediência a Sua Santitade, e de lhe offerecer alguns presentes das conquistas da Asia, 18 May 1514', in Coelho, *Alguns documentos*, 353–6. For an overview, see Anthony R. Disney, *A History of Portugal and the Portuguese Empire: From Beginnings to 1807* (Cambridge: University Press, 2009), 143–71; Kirti N. Chaudhuri, 'The Portuguese Maritime Empire, Trade, and Society in the Indian Ocean during the Sixteenth Century', *Portuguese Studies*, 8 (1992), 57–70.

147 For further details, see Geoffrey Parker, *Emperor: A New Life of Charles V* (New Haven, CT: Yale University Press, 2019); Paul Kennedy, *The Rise and Fall of the Great Powers* (London: Unwin Hyman Limited, 1988), 31–72; Thomas J. Mandelet, *The Renaissance of Empire in Early Modern Europe* (Cambridge: University Press, 2014); Randall Lesaffer, 'Charles V, Monarchia Universalis and the Law of Nations', *Legal History Review*, 71(1–2) (2003), 79–123; John M. Headley, 'The Habsburg World Empire and the Revival of Ghibellinism', *Medieval and Renaissance Studies*, 7 (1978), 93–127; Escamilla, *Le siècle d'or de l'Espagne*, 153–88; Franz Bosbach, *Monarchia universalis. Storia di un concetto cardine della politica europea (secoli XVI–XVIII)* (Milano: Vita e Pensiero, 1998).

148 'Provisión para que ninguna persona pueda ir á descubrir ni á lo descubierto, sin licencia de sus Altezas, 3 September 1501', in Fernández de Navarrete, *Colección de los viajes y descubrimientos*, II, 286–9. See also Salvador de Madariaga, *The Rise of the Spanish American Empire* (Westport: Greenwood Press, 1975), 307–9. For a critical overview, see María B. Villar García and Pilar Pezzi Cristóbal (eds.), *Los extranjeros en la España moderna: actas del I Coloquio Internacional. Celebrado en Málaga del 28 al 30 de noviembre de 2002*, vol. 1 (Málaga: Portadilla, 2003), 73–99.

to depart from Seville, and the same applied to returning vessels, albeit with some carefully controlled exceptions.[149] Meanwhile, the Portuguese focused on solidifying their position in the Indian Ocean.

An analysis of how the Iberian monarchs styled themselves in official documents sheds light on their maritime ambitions.[150] For instance, in the treaty of Vitoria (1524), King John III of Portugal (r. 1521–1557) was referred to as: 'Dom Joao, by the grace of God King of Portugal, of the Algarves on this side of and beyond the sea in Africa, Lord of Guinea and of conquest, navigation, and commerce of Ethiopia, Arabia, Persia, India, etc'.[151] Interestingly, the king described himself as the lord of distant lands, such as 'Ethiopia', which were not under his control – a common practice among monarchs of the time. He is mentioned as king, and therefore fully sovereign, only in relation to the Algarves and Portugal. Instead, concerning navigation, he was defined more generally as 'lord'. He claimed full sovereignty (as 'king') only over Portugal and the Algarves, while the title of 'lord' indicated a more limited claim, encompassing navigation (*ius navigationis*) and trading rights, rather than full sovereignty over the eastern Atlantic and Indian oceans. Nevertheless, the concept of excluding others from certain privileges (*ius excludendi omnes alios*) had long been considered an attribute of property rights.

On the Spanish side, the advisors of Charles V – who in addition to King of Spain was elected Holy Roman Emperor in 1519 – referred to his dominion over the Ocean Sea and the New World to foster a revival of the idea of empire.[152] The so-called 'columnar device' created after his accession to the throne as his personal emblem constituted a powerful symbol of this aspiration. The device contains the two columns of Hercules rising from the sea, as well as the motto 'Further beyond' (*Plus ultra*). This imagery symbolised that now Charles V's empire extended beyond the known world's traditional

149 Parry, *The Spanish Seaborne Empire*, 54; Elliott, *Imperial Spain*, 182–3. See also Manuel Bustos-Rodriguez, 'Le commerce colonial et le développement des ports et des flottes commerciales espagnoles', in *The Sea in History*, vol. III, 40–3; Nieto Olarte, *Exploration, Religion and Empire*, 58–64.

150 Hébié, *Souveraineté territoriale*, 53.

151 'Treaty between Spain and Portugal concluded at Vitoria, 19 February 1524', in Davenport, *European Treaties*, I, doc. 13, 126.

152 Hébié, *Souveraineté territoriale*, 53; Mandelet, *The Renaissance of Empire*, 83–4; Anthony Pagden, *Lords of All the World: Ideologies of Empire in Spain, Britain and France, 1492–1830* (New Haven, CT: Yale University Press, 1998), 31–3, 40–1; Peter Burke, 'L'image de Charles Quint: construction et interprétations', in Hugo Soly (dir.), *Charles V 1500–1558. L'empereur et son temps* (Arles: Actes sud, 1999), 393–475; Fernando Checa Cremades, *Carlos V. La imagen del poder en el Renacimiento* (Madrid: El Viso, 1999).

boundaries, surpassing even the Roman Empire.[153] In the Treaty of Vitoria (1524), Charles V was styled as:

> Don Charles, by the grace of God King of the Romans and Emperor ever august, Dona Joana, his mother, and the said Don Charles, by the said grace, King and Queen of Castile, Leon, Aragon, the Two Sicilies, Jerusalem, Navarre, Granada, Toledo, Valencia, Galicia, the Majorcas, Seville, Sardinia, Cordova, Corsica, Murcia, Jaen, the Algarves, Algeciras, Gibraltar, the Canary Islands, the Indies, the islands and mainland of the ocean sea.[154]

One enduring legacy of the Treaty of Tordesillas was the division of Central and South America into two distinct cultural spheres: Portuguese-speaking Brazil and Spanish-speaking Hispanic viceroyalties. More relevant to our discussion, however, is its role as the starting point for the partition of the Pacific Ocean between Spain and Portugal. This partition became necessary as new tensions arose concerning the Moluccas, a group of islands (now part of Indonesia) renowned for their spices. While the Portuguese had reached the Moluccas via India, a Castilian expedition led by Ferdinand Magellan, a Portuguese-born mariner, arrived there by crossing the Pacific.[155] As observed by Gasparo Contarini, Venetian ambassador to Charles V's court (1521–1525), both parties recognised the need to define their respective areas of influences in the

153 On the so-called columnar device, see Earl Rosenthal, 'Plus Ultra, Non Plus Ultra, and the Columnar Device of Emperor Charles V', *Journal of the Warburg and Courtauld Institutes*, 34 (1971), 204–28; idem, 'The Invention of the Columnar Device of Emperor Charles V at the Court of Burgundy in Flanders in 1516', *Journal of the Warburg and Courtauld Institutes* 36 (1973), 198–230; Marcel Bataillon, *'Plus Oultre: la cour découvre le Nouveau Monde', Les fêtes de la Renaissance: II. Fêtes et cérémonies au temps de Charles V* (Paris: Éditions du CNRS, 1960), 23–7. See also Carlos Martinez Shaw and Marina Alfonso-Mola, 'Les formes complexes de la prédominance de l'Espagne, première puissance mondiale de l'histoire', in Buchet and Le Bouëdec (eds.), *The Sea in History*, III, 446–7.

154 Davenport, *European Treaties*, I, doc. 13, 125.

155 The 'Magellan-Elcano expedition' completed the first circumnavigation of the globe (1519–1522). Magellan, however, died during a military encounter with natives in the Philippines on 27 April 1521. See David Salomoni, *Magellano: Il primo viaggio intorno al mondo* (Bari: Laterza, 2021); Guadalupe Fernández Morente and Ignacio Fernández Vial, *Fernando de Magallanes: Expediciones marítimas* (Sevilla: Ayuntamiento de Sevilla, 2021); Joyce E. Chaplin, *Round about the Earth: Circumnavigation from Magellan to Orbit* (New York: Simon & Schuster, 2012), 38–9; Matteo Salonia, 'Encompassing the Earth: Magellan's Voyage from Its Political Context to its Expansion of Knowledge', *International Journal of Maritime History*, 34(4) (2022), 543–60; Oskar H. K. Spate, *The Spanish Lake. The Pacific since Magellan, vol. 1* (Camberra: ANU E-press, 2004), 25–57.

Pacific, especially regarding the Moluccas whose legendary wealth was the most serious bone of contention.[156]

Building on previous negotiations that had proved unconclusive,[157] Spain and Portugal eventually reached a new compromise with the treaty of Zaragoza, signed in 1529 respectively by Charles V and John III.[158] The original manuscript signed by the Portuguese king clearly stated the object of the treaty: '... there was doubt and dispute in respect to the ownership and possession (or quasi possession), title, navigation, and commerce of the Moluccas and other islands and seas, each of us saying that they belonged to him and that he was in the possession of all the aforesaid...'.[159]

The 1529 treaty established an anti-meridian dividing the Pacific from north to south, effectively creating two distinct spheres of influence for Portugal and Spain. Article one decided the controversy concerning the Moluccas in favour of the Lusitanian kingdom.[160] In compensation, Spain retained control over the Philippines and received 350,000 gold ducats. In articles five, six and seven, the emperor prohibited his subjects from sailing beyond the line, notably towards the Moluccas for purpose of trade (*entrar, navegar, tratar ny comerciar ny cargar cosa alguna que en las dichas yslas, tieras, y mares*).[161] The trespassers could be captured by the Portuguese and punished as 'violators of the peace' (*quebrantadores de fee y de paz*). If such trespassers managed to return to Spanish ports, local authorities were required to detain them until Portugal provided evidence of their transgressions. Once again, the Iberian

156 'Relazione di Gasparo Contarini ritornato ambasciatore da Carlo V, letta in Senato, 16 novembre 1525', in Alberi (ed.), *Relazioni*, Serie I, vol. 2, 48–9. The ambassador also relayed precise information on the Spanish conquest of modern-day Mexico, ibid., 50–1.

157 See 'Compact between Spain and Portugal signed by the Catholic Sovereigns at Madrid, 7 May 1495' and 'Draft of an unconcluded treaty between Spain and Portugal, 1526'. For the texts, see Davenport, *European Treaties*, I, doc. 10, 101–6; doc. 14, 131–45; Fernández de Navarrete, *Colección de los viajes*, II, 192–5.

158 Davenport, *European Treaties*, I, doc. 16, 169–98. See also Vila-Santa, *Knowledge Exchanges*, 31–42.

159 Davenport, *European Treaties*, I, doc. 16, 171: '... *avia duvida e debate sobre a propriedade e pose, ou quasy pose, e dereito, naveguancam, e comercio de Maluquo e outras ilhas e mares, por cada huum de nos dizer lhe pertencer e estar em pose de todo o sobredito...*'.

160 For a detailed and critical discussion on the relationship between the Tordesillas and Zaragoza meridians, see Duve, 'Spatial perceptions', 431–6. See also Leoncio Cabrero, 'El empeño de las Molucas y los tratados de Zaragoza: cambios, modificaciones y coincidencias entre el no ratificado y el ratificado', in Ribot García, Carrasco Martínez and Adao da Fonseca (eds.), *El Tratado de Tordesillas y su época*, 1091–132.

161 Ibid., doc. 16, 190.

rulers were disposing of the oceans without taking into consideration the aspirations of other nations.

4.2.2 Influence on the Evolution of International Law

The Treaty of Tordesillas is often regarded as a significant step in the evolution of the law of nations.[162] As previously noted, it served as a prototype for subsequent agreements based on demarcation lines, marking a turning point in the practice of formalising agreements grounded in mutual recognition of spheres of influence and establishing a balance of power between polities.[163] During the nineteenth and twentieth centuries, the treaty continued to be referenced, particularly in the context of South American decolonisation and the emergence of the *uti possidetis* doctrine. This agreement exemplified the excessive importance attributed to discovery and symbolic annexation in the early stages of European exploration.[164]

Additionally, the treaty signalled a transition from the late medieval practice of seeking papal approval in relation to territorial expansion. The Iberian monarchs agreed on moving the Alexandrine *raya* to the west autonomously, without any mediation of the Holy See. Papal confirmation came only in 1506 with the bull *Ea Quae*. By the time Spain and Portugal signed the Treaty of Zaragoza two decades later, neither party sought papal confirmation. As Thomas Duve observed: 'the days of Pope Alexander VI's hierocratic ambitions, basis for the concession of the papal bulls of 1493, were over'.[165]

On the one hand, it is important to emphasise that the treaty adhered to several medieval customs regarding treaty-making.[166] The agreement was concluded on behalf of the Iberian rulers as individuals, 'who happened to be rulers' rather than as representatives of two states conceived as monolithic political entities. More broadly, all the treaties examined in this chapter re-

162 Tatiana Waisberg, 'The Treaty of Tordesillas and the (re)Invention of International Law in the Age of Discovery', *Meridiano. Journal of Global Studies*, 47 (2017), 1–12.

163 Detlev Vagts, 'Balance of power', in *Max Planck Encyclopedia of Public International Law*, vol. I, 786.

164 Duve, 'Spatial perceptions', 431–2; Hanspeter Neuhold, 'Spheres of influence', in *Max Planck Encyclopedia of Public International Law*, vol. VII, 431.

165 Duve, 'Treaty of Tordesillas'.

166 Randall Lesaffer, 'The Medieval Canon Law of Contract and Early Modern Treaty Law', *Journal of the History of International Law*, 2(2) (2000), 178–98; Dominique Bauer, 'The importance of medieval canon law and the scholastic tradition for the emergence of the early modern international legal order', in Randall Lesaffer (ed.), *Peace Treaties and International Law in European History: From the Late Middle Ages to World War One* (Cambridge: University Press, 2004), 198–221.

tained a form that closely resembled contracts. Their drafting and implementation followed the general principles of private contract law.[167] On the other hand, it is undeniable that the treaty heralded a shift towards a more modern conception of inter-polity relations, based on agreements between princes enjoying full external sovereignty. As discussed in Chapter 1, this process originated in the Late Middle Ages but had now become a key driver in the development of what we today term international law. The treaty also marked the emergence of Spain – the dynastic union between the Crowns of Castile and Aragon – as a dominant actor for the two following century and half, a period that Wilhelm Grewe famously termed as the 'Spanish age of international law'.[168]

Lastly, the Treaty of Tordesillas perfectly illustrates how temptations of solitary possession shaped the first legal approach to the oceans. Exclusive rights over territories were intrinsically intertwined with the *ius navigationis* over the ocean corridors connecting them. At this stage, no specific legal status for the seas had been developed. Spanish and Portuguese jurists did not elaborate a comprehensive theory of the 'claimed seas'. Nevertheless, from the outset, Spain and Portugal pursued the practical goal of monopolising oceanic

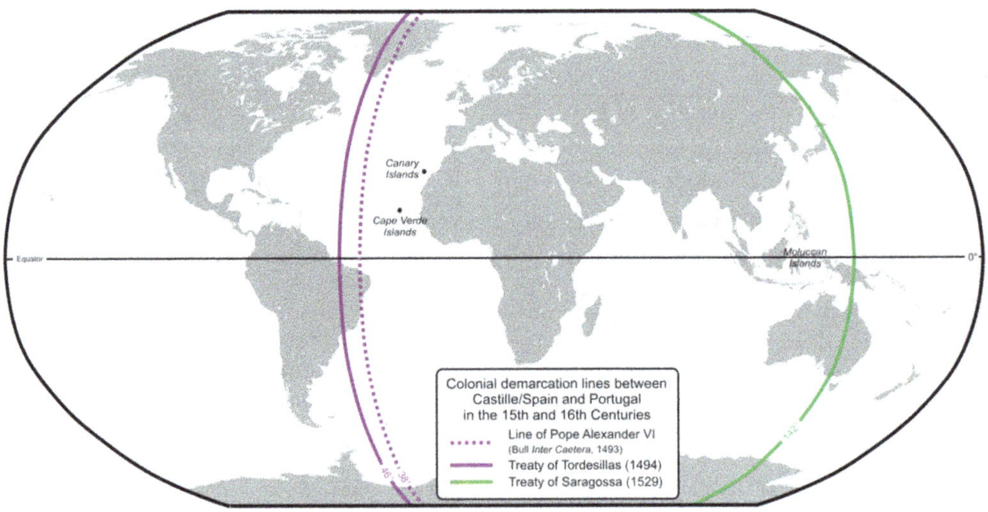

FIGURE 2.1 Castilian/Portuguese demarcation lines as defined by the papal bull *Inter caetera* (1493), the Treaty of Tordesillas (1494) and Zaragoza (1529)
SOURCE: WIKIMEDIA COMMONS

167 Lesaffer, 'Charles V…', 98; Grewe, *Epochs*, 421.
168 Grewe, *Epochs*, 23.

navigation and excluding all potential competitors. Once the Tordesillas-Zaragoza compromise was reached, both powers shifted their focus towards consolidating control over their respective spheres of influence.

4.2.3 Early Reactions to the Partition

From a strictly legal standpoint, the Tordesillas agreement could only bind the two signatories under the principle *res inter alios acta, aliis nec nocet nec prodest* (an agreement between others neither harms nor benefits third parties). Nonetheless, for nearly half a century, other European nations appeared to acquiesce to the Iberian duopoly. Spain and Portugal strictly enforced their exclusive rights, with unauthorised navigation to their newly claimed territories or unlicensed trade punishable by death and confiscation of goods.[169] Iberian authorities regarded acts of violence committed against interlopers as mere law enforcement, not as acts of war. Portuguese authorities treated harshly the crews of French vessels that dared to sail towards Brazil in the late 1520s, despite protests from the French court.[170] For example, at the end of 1531, the Portuguese hanged the entire garrison of the small commercial outpost that the French had established the previous year near Pernambuco.[171]

No systematic diplomatic actions aimed at refuting and openly challenging the Hispano-Portuguese closed sea policies were put forward in the immediate aftermath of the partition. As Mamadou Hébié reports, the letters of license granted by Henry VII of England (r. 1485–1509) to the explorer Giovanni Caboto (John Cabot) testify the will of the English king to respect Spanish discoveries and sovereignty in the Caribbean Sea.[172] The king authorised the explorer to sail to the West to: 'find, discover, investigate whatsoever islands, countries, regions or provinces of heathens and infidels, in whatsoever part of the world placed, which before this time were unknown to all Christians'.[173]

---

169 Theutenberg, 'Mare Liberum et Mare Clausum', 490; Preiser, 'History of international law', 889.

170 See 'Relazione di Francia del clarissimo Marino Giustiniano, 1535', in Alberi (ed.), *Relazioni*, Serie I, vol. I, 182; Charles de la Roncière, *Histoire de la marine française – III, Les guerres d'Italie, liberté de mers* (Paris: Libraire Plon, 1906), 269–71, 279.

171 de La Roncière, *Histoire de la marine française*, III, 281–2.

172 Hébié, *Souveraineté territoriale*, 67–71.

173 'First letters patent granted by Henry VII to John Cabot and his sons, 5 March 1496', in Henry P. Biggar, *The Precursors of Jacques Cartier, 1497–1534* (London: Forgotten Books, 2016), doc IV, 9. Another letter granted to Cabot, dated 5 March 1498, is included in the online collection of the *Avalon Project, Documents in Law, History and Diplomacy*: http://avalon.law.yale.edu/15th_century/cabot01.asp.

Spanish authorities, for their part, often displayed a flexible attitude towards expeditions by other European nations in North America, acknowledging the existence of *ratione loci* limits to their sphere of influence in the western Atlantic. The Spanish were primarily focused on defending their positions in the Caribbean Sea rather than fending off all crossing of the *raya*. Moreover, Spanish seafarers had shown little interest for the American Atlantic coast north of Florida and in any case lacked the resources to extend their control in that region too. For instance, the ambassador of the Duke of Milan in London reported on Cabot's voyages to North America without mentioning any breach of Spanish privileges.[174] Indeed, early English expeditions into the North Atlantic posed little threat to Spanish dominance.

On his part, the French King Francis I (r. 1515–1547) protested the *raya* set out in the Treaty of Tordesillas, issuing statements on the natural commonality of the sea and asserting his subjects' freedom of navigation, as '*le fait de traffic et échange de marchandises est de tous les droits un des plus naturels et des plus autorisés*'.[175] In 1541, the French monarch allegedly declared in front of the Spanish ambassador: '*Le soleil luit pour moi comme pour les autres. Je voudrais bien voir la clause du testament d'Adam qui m'exclut du partage du monde*'.[176] Francis I had already backed a few oceanic expeditions, such as those lead by Jacques Cartier in the northern Atlantic (1534, 1535–1536, 1541–1542), whose declared aim was to discover an alternative route to China and Japan through a hypothetical North-West passage, thus bypassing Spanish and Portuguese possessions.

At the time, the French court's attention was largely focused on Italy and on countering Habsburg encirclement in Europe, reflecting a pronounced 'continental bias'.[177] The resources of Francis I were heavily strained by constant

174 Hébié, *Souveraineté territoriale*, 67–71.

175 'Lettre de François i du 6 septembre 1528', in de la Roncière, *Histoire de la marine française*, III, 280. My translation: 'The fact of trading and exchanging goods is one of the most natural and permitted of all rights'.

176 The phrase is reported in ibid., 300 and Jack Lang, *François Ier, ou le rêve italien* (Paris: Perrin, 1997), 77. My translation: 'The sun shines for me as for the others. I would like to see the clause in Adam's will that excludes me from the partition of the world'.

177 Martine Acerra, 'Le modèle français: la recherche par l'État de la prédominance maritime, réussites et échecs', in Buchet and Le Bouëdec (eds.), *The Sea in History*, III, 482–3; Raymonde Litalien, 'Les Français en Amérique du Nord au XVIe siècle: partenaires at concurrents', in Mickaël Augeron et Dominique Guillemet (eds.), *Champlain ou les portes du Nouveau Monde. Cinq siècles d'échanges entre le Centre-Ouest français et l'Amérique du Nord* (La Crèche: Geste Edition, 2004), 51–6; Maurice de Brossard, 'La France de la Renaissance et ses rois Face aux problèmes océaniques', *Revista da Universidade de Coimbra*, 32 (1986), 299–328.

conflicts with the armies of Charles V. Consequently, no coherent oceanic strategy was developed at the central government level. However, it was in provincial centres such as Dieppe that wealthy private ship owners like Jean d'Ango (1480–1551) took the initiative. They financed expeditions that ventured deep into Portuguese and Spanish spheres of influence, reaching as far as Sumatra during the voyage led by the brothers Jean and Raoul Parmentier in 1529–1530.[178]

As early as 1544, the Franco-Spanish treaty of Crépy-en-Laonnais included a colonial compromise formulated with remarkable diplomatic skills.[179] Without explicitly recognising the Tordesillas demarcation line, the king of France promised to respect the Iberian spheres of influence in the Indies: '... *doresnavant luy et ses successeurs, roys ed France, et ses subgectz, laisseront paisibles lesdits sieurs Empereur et Roy de Portugal en tout ce qui concerne lesdictes Yndes, descouvertes et a descouvrir, sans directement ou indirectement y faire emprises quelconques...*'.[180] However, a clause allowed French trade with Iberian overseas possessions under certain conditions, such as avoiding violence and refraining from engaging in discovery or settlement activities: '...*que en cas que soubz cqulleur de ceste navigacion ilz font aucune violances, soit esdictes Yndes en allant ou retournant, quilz soient chastiez selon et où ilz seront trouvez coulpables*'.[181] The Spanish Council of the Indies objected to the provision fearing that the French, if admitted in the western Atlantic, would not respect trade regulations. The Portuguese ambassador in Madrid shared these fears.

One year later, Francis I was compelled to ban his subjects from sailing in the western Atlantic, effectively conceding to the Spanish closed sea policy. However, this agreement lapsed with Francis I's death in 1547. His successor, Henry II (r. 1547–1559), once again authorised navigation towards the Indies.[182] Marino Cavalli, Venetian ambassador to Francis I's court between

178 de la Roncière, *Histoire de la Marine Française*, III, 243–90; John Nothnagle, 'Two Early French Voyages to Sumatra', *The Sixteenth Century Journal*, 19(1) (1988), 97–107.

179 For the text, see Davenport, *European Treaties*, I, doc. 18, 206. See also Grewe, *Epochs*, 154.

180 Davenport, *European Treaties*, I, doc. 18, 209, '... from now on, he and his successors, kings of France, and his subjects, will leave in peace the said Emperor and King of Portugal, in all matters concerning the said territories, discovered and discovered, without directly or indirectly attempting any enterprise there...'.

181 Ibidem, '... that in case they were to commit violences during these navigations, both going or returning from the said Indies, they shall be punished if found to be guilty'.

182 Paul E. Hoffman, *The Spanish Crown and the Defense of the Caribbean, 1535–1585: Precedent, Patrimonialism, and Royal Parsimony* (Baton Rouge: Louisiana State University Press, 1980), 65.

1544 and 1546, reported to his government that relations between France and Portugal remained execrable, characterised by a state of 'secret and continuous war' (*una secreta e continua Guerra*).[183] He added that the French presumed to sail freely across Lusitanian closed sea areas, and that the Portuguese 'sent them to the abysses' whenever they could, prompting the French to retaliate with reprisals. Moreover, Cavalli observed that if once the French and the Portuguese had fostered good relations in an anti-Castilian perspective, the king of Portugal had now 'thrown himself into the emperor's arms' due to his growing disdain for French incursions and depredations.[184]

In 1556, following yet another renewal of hostilities between Spain and France, a five-year truce was agreed. Intense negotiations were held regarding access to the Indies, with the French asserting their right to navigate and trade freely. However, the French ultimately conceded in order to bring an end to the conflict. As a result, the Armistice Treaty of Vaucelles generally prohibited French subjects from sailing to the Indies without express permission (*expres conge et licence*) from Philip II of Spain.[185] Spanish authorities retained the right to punish trespassers without compromising the validity of the truce: '*sera licite user contre eulx dhostilite, demeurant toutte ffois ladite tresve en sa force et vigeur*'.[186]

The discussions leading to the truce are poorly documented, leaving the exact meaning of the term 'Indies' unclear. It appears, however, that Spain was primarily concerned with defending the Caribbean Sea and the critical sea lanes connecting it to Europe, rather than adhering strictly to the demarcation line established by the Treaty of Tordesillas.[187] In comparison with the treaty of Crepy, only a dozen years older, the truce concluded at Vaucelles turned towards a more pragmatic approach. Cartier's expeditions had been viewed as a danger only if they were directed to the Caribbean area, and not if they explored the north-western Atlantic. Paolo Tiepolo, the Venetian ambassador at the court of Philip II between 1558 and 1562, sheds light on these diplomatic developments.[188] Once back in Venice, he submitted a detailed

183 'Relazione di Francia dell'ambasciatore Marino Cavalli, 1546', in Alberi (ed.), *Relazioni*, Serie I, vol. I, 249, '*pretendendo Francesi poter navigare alla Guinea e terra di Brasile, ad ogni suo piacere*'.

184 Ibidem. '*Ora quel re si ha gettato nelle braccia dell'imperatore, e sta malissimo contento del cristianissimo* [i.e. Francis I]'.

185 Grewe, *Epochs*, 154–5.

186 Davenport, *European Treaties*, I, doc. 20, 217: 'it will be rightful to use force against them, and the said truce shall stay in force and operate nonetheless'.

187 Hoffman, *The Spanish Crown and the Defense of the Caribbean*, 104.

188 'Relazione di Paolo Tiepolo, letta in Senato il 19 gennaio 1563', in *Relazioni degli ambasciatori Veneti al Senato*, Serie I, vol. V, 1–76. On the birth of modern diplomacy, see Dante

rapport of his tenure as an ambassador to the Venetian Senate where he also addressed the question of navigation towards the Indies. He summed up Iberian expansion, Alexander VI's bulls, as well as the treaties of Tordesillas and Zaragoza. He also informed the Senate that the French and other nations were still sailing towards the North Atlantic, without creating much concern at the Spanish court, since those places were remote and lacking either gold or silver:

> But despite all this, some nations have not refrained from venturing into those areas to try their luck, such as the English, Danes, Norwegians, and especially the French, who continue to frequent the routes and trade of the land of Labrador and de los Bacallaos. The Spaniards, partly because they were engaged in other ventures and partly because the areas frequented by the French were not very favourable – neither rich in gold nor silver, and far from their own territories – did not take much care to drive them out.[189]

In conclusion, Spanish diplomacy prioritised preserving the core of its overseas empire – the Caribbean Sea and Central America – rather than the entire sphere of influence established by the treaty of Tordesillas. Overall, English and French expeditions were tolerated as long as they sailed enough to the North. This stance implicitly acknowledged some *ratione loci* limits on the claims that could be advanced by Spain following the treaty of Tordesillas. As for the eastern Pacific Ocean and the eastern coasts of South America, Spanish settlements, ships, and claims were, for the time being, safeguarded more by the region's remoteness from Europe than by any substantial Spanish military presence.[190]

5 Discoveries, Legal Claims, and Cartography

Even as late as 1489, the 'World Map' by German cartographer Henricus Martellus Germanus depicted the coasts of West Africa with relative accuracy, yet it still portrayed the *Oceanus Occidetal* surrounding Europe and Africa as an

---

Fedele, *Naissance de la diplomatie moderne (XIIIe–XVIIe siècles): l'ambassadeur au croisement du droit, de l'éthique et de la politique* (Baden-Baden: Nomos Verlagsgesellschaft, 2017); Lucien Bely, *L'art de la paix en Europe: Naissance de la diplomatie moderne, XVIe–XVIIIe siècle* (Paris: Presses universitaires de France, 2007).

189 'Relazione di Paolo Tiepolo, letta in Senato il 19 gennaio 1563', 31. My translation.

190 Spate, *The Spanish Lake*, 229–31.

undefined frontier.[191] As European seafarers pushed further into the Atlantic, the urgency to visualise and make sense of these expanding geographic horizons grew. As Francesca Fiorani observed: 'Fundamentally human is the need to know the places that we inhabit and to dominate them through mapping. In the process of mastering the geography of our world, we define our place within it and our relations to others'.[192]

A new generation of cartographers began incorporating the new discoveries into their maps, taking on the colossal task of synthetising extensive oral and written sources into single images that captured and rationalised a rapidly expanding world. This effort brought about a veritable revolution in the science (and art) of cartography.[193] Cartographers built on sedimented medieval know-how, developed having as its reference limited geographic boundaries. Medieval nautical charts, known as portolan charts (*portolani*), formed the basis for the design of early modern world maps. Portolans focused mainly on navigation at sea and paid little attention to the interiors of landmasses, instead emphasising coasts, shoals, rivers, harbours, winds, and sailing directions. These charts were initially developed for close-to-shore navigation over relatively short distances in the Mediterranean.[194]

The process of mapping new regions also served a legal function, helping to delineate areas of influence and justify claims, as the 'geometric division of space [...] made it possible for as yet unknown places to be claimed, so long as they fall within the geometric division proposed by the map'.[195] Nautical charts are therefore of critical importance for our purposes since we can ana-

191 Ralph E. Ehrenberg, *Mapping the World: An Illustrated History of Cartography* (Washington: National Geographic, 2005), 60–1; Anthony Pagden, *The Burdens of Empire: 1539 to the Present* (Cambridge: University Press, 2015), 155. The map in question is conserved at the British Library.

192 Francesca Fiorani, 'Mapping and voyages', in Michael Wyatt (ed.), *The Cambridge Companion to the Italian Renaissance* (Cambridge: University Press, 2014), 59.

193 Fernández- Armesto, 'Maps and exploration', 738–70; Alison Sandman, 'Spanish nautical cartography in the Renaissance', in David Woodward (ed.), *The History of Cartography, Vol. III: Cartography in the European Renaissance*, part 1 (Chicago: University Press, 2007), 1095–142; David Woodward, 'Maps and the rationalization of geographic space', in Jay A. Levenson (ed.), *Circa 1492: Art in the Age of Exploration* (New Haven, CT: Yale University Press, 1991), 83–8.

194 Ehrenberg, *Mapping the World*, 41; Leo Bagrow, *History of Cartography: Enlarged Second Ed.* (Chicago: Precedent Publishing, 2009), 105; Jim Siebold, *Juan de la Cosa Portolan World Chart*, on the webpage: http://www.myoldmaps.com/renaissance-maps-1490-1800/305-juan-de-la-cosa-portola/305-la-cosa.pdf; Torelló, 'The "Cantino Planisphere"', 15.

195 Branch, Jordan, *The Cartographic State: Maps, Territory and the Origins of Sovereignty* (Cambridge: University Press, 2014), 59. For a critique, see Lauren Benton, *A Search for*

lyse them in tandem with 'traditional' legal sources, forging a more complete understanding of early modern explorations and ensuing 'claimed seas' pretensions. From the outset, maps functioned as symbols of power and as tools for the further appropriation of land and maritime spaces.[196] Portuguese and Castilian authorities jealously guarded all knowledge related to their newly established oceanic routes. In Castile, it was the *Casa de Contratación* that was tasked with centralising the cosmographical, nautical, and cartographic knowledge generated throughout the Castilian/Spanish Empire. It hosted the 'Padrón Real', a master map that integrated the most up-to-date geographical information.[197] In this context, maps rapidly became prized targets of espionage for other nations with seaborne aspirations.[198]

Two maps from this period are especially relevant since they provide the earliest known depictions of the Americas.[199] The first is the world map (*mappa mundi*) attributed to the Basque cartographer Juan de la Cosa in 1500, who had reportedly accompanied Columbus on his first two voyages. The second is the anonymous 'Cantino planisphere', dated 1502. More specifically, the De la Cosa map still refers the Atlantic as 'Mare Oceanus' and offers a partial depiction of the American coasts, while underestimating the distance between Europe and the Americas. Commissioned by Castilian officials, it

---

Sovereignty, Law and Geography in European Empires, 1400–1900 (Cambridge: University Press, 2012), 10–2.

196 Luisa Martín-Meras Verdejo, 'The exploration and geopolitical stakes of Iberian cartography, 15th and 16th centuries', in Catherine Hofmann, Hélène Richard, and Emmanuelle Vagnon (eds.), *The Golden Age of Maritime Maps: When Europe Discovered the World* (New York: Firefly Books, 2013), 108–35; David Turnbull, 'Cartography and Science in Early Modern Europe: Mapping the Construction of Knowledge Spaces', *Imago Mundi*, 48(1) (1996), 5–24.

197 Duve, 'Spatial perceptions', 433–4; Nieto Olarte, *Exploration, Religion and Empire*, 217–44. For further details, see Antonio Sánchez Martínez, *La espada, la cruz y el Padrón (Soberanía, fe y representación cartográfica en el mundo ibérico bajo la Monarquía Hispánica), 1503–1598* (Madrid: CSIC, 2013); José M. García Redondo, *Cartografía e imperio. El Padrón Real y la representación del Nuevo Mundo* (Madrid: Ediciones Doce Calles, 2018); Ricardo Padrón, 'Mapping Plus Ultra: Cartography, Space, and Hispanic Modernity', *Representations* 79 (2002), 28–60; Ricardo Cerezo Martínez, *La cartografía náutica española en los siglos XIV, XV y XVI* (Madrid: Editorial CSIC, 1994).

198 Alison Sandman, 'Controlling knowledge: navigation, cartography, and secrecy in the early modern Spanish Atlantic', in James Delbourgo and Nicholas Dew (eds.), *Beyond the New Atlantis: Science and Empire in the Atlantic World, 1500–1800* (London: Routledge, 2008), 31–51; María M. Portuondo, *Secret Science: Spanish Cosmography and the New World* (Chicago: University Press, 2009); Joan C. Oliver Torelló, 'The "Cantino Planisphere": Transition to a New Age', *National Geographic History*, March-April Issue (2017), 14.

199 Arthur Dürst, 'Brasilien im frühen Kartenbild', *Cartographica Helvetica*, 6 (1992), 8–16.

marked the shores of the Americas and Caribbean islands as Castilian territories, using small flags to denote sovereignty.[200] Portuguese possessions were indicated by blue rectangles with five *quinas* (shields), the emblem of the Aviz dynasty. Castilian territories were represented by flags bearing the castles of Castile and the red and yellow stripes of Aragon. Notably, the map includes a vertical green line representing the demarcation established by the Treaty of Tordesillas for the first time (see Figure 2.2 below).[201] Reflecting a distinctly Castilian perspective, the map allocated only a small portion of Brazilian territory to Portugal, leaving most of the western Atlantic and the Americas to Castile. Interestingly, English coats of arms appear in northern America, indicating awareness of Cabot's expeditions to Newfoundland.

In Portugal, it was the cartographers of the *Casa da Mina e Índia* who summed up and elaborated the new geographical information added by each expedition.[202] King John II of Portugal in particular imposed a policy of total secrecy, under the penalty of death, regarding the sailing routes pioneered by his mariners. This policy likely explains why almost no official Portuguese charts from this period have survived. However, sooner or later information inevitably leaked.[203] For instance, Alberto Cantino, an agent of the Duke of Ferrara in Lisbon, obtained the Cantino Planisphere, a map based on secret Portuguese travel reports and nautical charts. While retaining some medieval elements, such as a red-coloured Red Sea and the prominence of Jerusalem, this map included the Tordesillas demarcation line, drawn in a bright blue and explicitly labelled: 'This is the boundary between Castile and Portugal' (*Este he o marco dantre Castella i Portuguall*) (see Figure 2.3 below).

200 Jesús Varela Marcos (ed.), *Juan de la Cosa: la Cartografía Histórica de los Descubrimientos Españoles* (Sevilla: Universidad Internacional de Andalucía, 2011); Pagden, *The Burdens of Empire*, 157; Jerry Brotton, *Great Maps: The World's Masterpieces Explored and Explained* (London: DK, 2014), 76–9; Sánchez Martínez, *La espada*, 62–3. Regarding the doubts on its date, see Arthur Davies, 'The Date of Juan de La Cosa's World Map and its Implications for American Discovery', *The Geographical Journal*, 142(1) (1976), 111–6; Nieto Olarte, *Exploration, Religion and Empire*, 234–5.

201 Hugo O'Donnell and Duque de Estrada, 'La Carta de Juan de la Cosa, primera presentación cartográfica del Tratado de Tordesillas', in Ribot García, Carrasco Martínez and Adao da Fonseca (eds.), *El Tratado de Tordesillas y su época*, 1231–44.

202 Maria F. Alegria et al. (eds.), *História da Cartografia Portuguesa, séculos XV a XVII* (Porto: Fia de Palavra, 2012); idem et al. 'Portuguese cartography in the Renaissance', in *The History of Cartography*, Vol. III, part 1, 975–1068.

203 See Armando Cortesão, *History of Portuguese Cartography* (Lisboa: Junta de Investigações do Ultramar, 1969); Anand, *Origin and Development*, 81; Brotton, *A History*, 190–1.

The planisphere depicts American coasts as known in the aftermath of Columbus' expeditions, omitting most part of mainland Americas.[204] Portuguese possessions are marked more generously than on the De la Cosa map, reflecting Portugal's claims across the Americas, Africa, the Indian Ocean, and even Newfoundland, described as '*Terra del rey de Portuguall*'. Interestingly, the flags are depicted on the sea and not on land, perhaps alluding to the extensive maritime claims of Portugal. Furthermore, we may link the fact that mostly Portuguese possessions are depicted with the monopoly of navigation claimed by the Aviz kings. Indeed, looking at the map, it is natural to deduce that the Portuguese would be the only ones having business in sailing towards their overseas possessions; the only exception being the Castilian sphere of influence to the west of the *raya* (significantly reduced in area compared to De la Cosa's map). Be as it may, in this planisphere, the link between discoveries, oceans, and cartography appears particularly strong, and the Portuguese perspective becomes visually compelling.

As the years passed, new maps appeared, becoming increasingly accurate thanks to technical innovations and continued exploration.[205] For instance, with the 'Miller Atlas' (1519) the Brazilian coastline became better delineated.[206] Interestingly, in the sea area between the Gulf of Guinea and Brazil, the author sketched many large Portuguese vessels and Aviz coats of arms. The Portuguese vessels are of the *naus* type, with forecastles and square sails bearing the cross of Christ, and visually occupy the southern Atlantic, asserting Portuguese dominance and legal claims in the region. Similarly, in 1454 the Castilian cartographer Pedro de Medina created another notable map that reflected a better knowledge of the Atlantic and Indian Oceans, though the Pacific remained largely unexplored and uncharted.[207]

6 Concluding Observations: A New 'Claimed Seas' Tradition?

The maps briefly discussed above illustrate how cartographers sought to domesticate the new horizons created by European overseas expansion. At the

204 Fiorani, *Mapping and Voyages*, 78; Pagden, *The Burdens of Empire*, 157.

205 E.g., see Joaquim Alves Gaspar, 'From the Portolan Chart to the Latitude Chart: The Silent Cartographic Revolution', *Comité Français de Cartographie*, 216 (2013), 67–77.

206 Mappemonde circulaire représentant l'hémisphère portugais – Atlas Miller: [Pedro et Jorge Reinel, António de Holanda, Portugal], 1519. Manuscrit enluminé sur vélin, 41.5 × 59 cm et 61 × 118 cm. BnF, département des Cartes et Plans, CPL GE D-26179 (RES), f. 1 © Bibliothèque nationale de France, online.

207 Benton, *A Search for Sovereignty*, 104–6.

same time, they were visualising claims over newly encountered lands and pelagic spaces. The Castilians and Portuguese, while delineating the Atlantic and Pacific demarcation lines (*rayas*), had little understanding of the actual extent of the oceans. In this process, both jurists and cartographers ventured into previously unexplored intellectual and geographical territory. The sheer vastness of the oceans likely explains why Iberian governments and jurists avoided invoking late medieval concepts to justify their 'claimed seas' policies. For instance, ideas such as Bartolus' one-hundred-mile maritime jurisdiction, developed in late medieval Italy, appeared wholly inadequate for regulating intercontinental sea routes stretching thousands of kilometres. More broadly, as David Armitage observed, 'arguments developed to justify rights of sovereignty and property over land could not readily be transferred to the different medium of the sea'.[208]

In this respect, Portugal and Spain initiated a third 'claimed seas' tradition, centred on oceangoing navigation and clearly distinguished from the older Nordic and Mediterranean ones. However, some similarities can be observed between Iberian bans on navigation beyond imaginary lines drawn across the oceans and the Norwegian practice of restricting foreign navigation north of Bergen. Both traditions involved banning navigation and commerce outright and employed demarcation lines to define the areas affected. In this sense, we can refer to both Norwegian and Iberian pretensions not only as 'claimed seas' but also more specifically as 'closed seas'. That said, no direct connection can be established between the Norwegian and Iberian traditions.

In the next chapter, we will continue to explore how in the second half of the sixteenth century the vastness of the oceans and Iberian closed seas claims contributed to the emergence of the freedom of the sea in legal discourse. We will also examine how the various 'claimed seas' traditions eventually converged and dialogued at the turn of the sixteenth century, as they all faced pressure from the rise of new international actors and legal arguments.

---

208 Armitage, 'The elephant and the whale', 52.

FIGURE 2.2 'Universal Map' by Juan de la Cosa, 1500
SOURCE: MUSEO NAVAL, MADRID. 117 × 95,5 CM. SOURCE: WIKIMEDIA COMMONS.

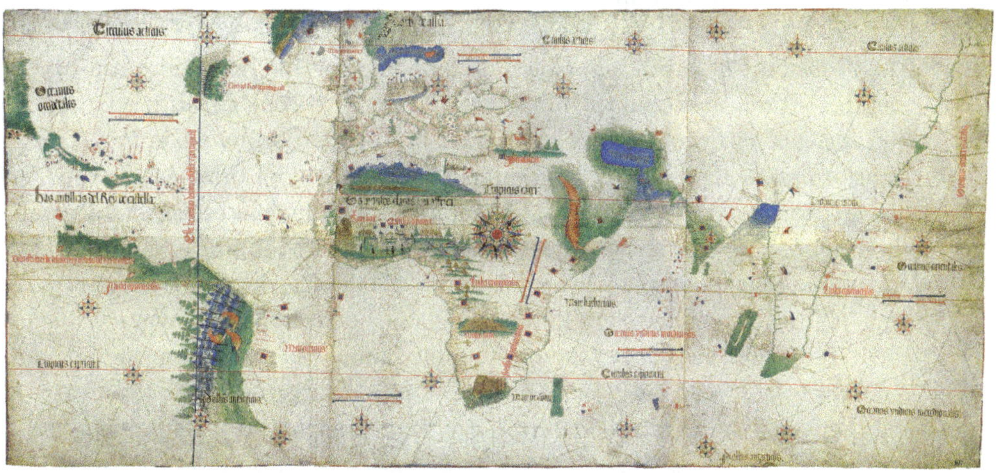

FIGURE 2.3 'Cantino Planisphere' by anonymous Portuguese cartographer, ca. 1502. Map on parchment, 220 × 105 cm. Conserved at the Biblioteca Estense Universitaria, Modena, Italy
SOURCE: WIKIMEDIA COMMONS

CHAPTER 3

The Emergence of the Freedom of the Sea, Grotius' *Mare liberum*

> Quid phohibetis acquas, communis usus acquarum.[1]
>
> •••
>
> Why do you stop me from drinking these waters,
> if nature intended their use to be common?

•••

1 Rise of New Actors

The Protestant Reformation, which unfolded during the first half of the sixteenth century, shattered the ideal that (Western) Europe constituted a unified *societas christiana* under the leadership of the *romanus pontifex*. This transformation significantly undermined the authority of titles to new lands and territories derived from papal donation, and diminished the influence of the Holy See in international relations.[2] Concurrently, the balance of naval and commercial power slowly began to shift from Portugal and the Mediterranean polities to northwestern Europe. England, under the Tudor dynasty, fully recovered from the scars of the civil conflict known as the War of the Roses (ca. 1455–1487), and the oceans became a new battleground for the rivalry between Spain and France. Meanwhile, observers such as the Venetian diplo-

1 Ovid, *Metamorphoses*, VI, quoted in Fernando Vázquez y Menchaca, *Controversiarum illustrium aliarumque usi frequentium libri tres* (Venice: apud Franciscum Rampazetum, 1564), II, 89, § 34.

2 Randall Lesaffer, 'The Grotian Tradition Revisited: Change and Continuity in the History of International Law', *British Yearbook of International Law*, 73 (2002), 103–39, at 113; idem, 'Charles V…', 98; idem, *The Classical Law of Nations (1500–1800)*, 412; Preiser, 'History of International Law', 889. For further details, see Harold J. Berman, *Law and Revolution, II. The Impact of the Protestant Reformations on the Western Legal Tradition* (Cambridge, MA: Harvard University Press, 2006).

 | DOI:10.1163/9789004741409_005

mat Gasparo Contarini noted the first signs of weakness within the Iberian maritime empires, particularly in the *Estado da Índia*. The Portuguese overseas empire was indeed spread thinly across four continents and its operation imposed considerable costs on the Crown.[3]

The revolt in the Low Countries against Spanish rule in the 1570s became another transformative event in the history of oceangoing navigation and long-range trade. The Low Countries, which had long enjoyed autonomy under Habsburg rulers, witnessed increasing hostility towards Philip II of Spain due to high taxation and the spread of the Reformation.[4] The Union of Utrecht in 1579 marked the creation of a republican and federal entity among the seven northern provinces: Holland, Utrecht, Guelders, Zeeland, Overijssel, Frisia, and Groningen. A prolonged conflict ensued, during which the rebels fought for survival against Spanish forces that retained control over the southern Low Countries. The United Provinces often received support from France and England.[5] In the process, Antwerp was sacked in 1585 and gradually lost its status as world emporium in favour of Amsterdam, the economic centre of the leading rebellious province, Holland.[6] The conflict spanned roughly eighty years and ultimately resulted in the establishment of the Republic of the

3 'Relazione di Gasparo Contarini ritornato ambasciatore da Carlo V, letta in Senato, 16 novembre 1525', in Alberi (ed.), *Relazioni*, Serie I, vol. 2, 49. On human and material resources, see de Madariaga, *The Rise of the Spanish American Empire*, 309–11; John T. Wing, 'Keeping Spain Afloat: State Forestry and Imperial Defense in the Sixteenth Century, *Environmental History*, 17(1) (2012), 116–45.

4 In the sixteenth century, the term 'Low Countries' referred roughly to the area of present-day Benelux. It consisted of several polities of different nature, most of them lying within the Holy Roman Empire. During the fourteenth century, most of the Low Countries came under the rule of the House of Burgundy. Subsequently, through matrimonial and dynastic accidents, the Low Countries entered the Habsburg orbit. See Escamilla, *Le siècle d'or de l'Espagne*, 481; Charles R. Boxer, *The Dutch Seaborne Empire, 1600–1800* (London: Hutchinson, 1965), 2. See also Graham Darby (ed.), *The Origins and Development of the Dutch Revolt* (London: Routledge, 2001).

5 See, among others 'Traité de confédération entre Henri IV, Roi de France, & Jaques I, Roi d'Angleterre principalement pour la défense des Provinces-Unies des Païs-Bas, contre le Roi d'Espagne, fait à Hamptoncourt, 30 juillet 1604', in *CUD*, V.2, 30–1; 'Traité de Ligue défensive entre Henri IV, Roi de France, & les Etats des Provinces-Unies des Pays-Bas, fait à La Haye, 23 janvier 1608', ibid., 89–91.

6 Jonathan I. Israel, *Dutch Primacy in World Trade, 1585–1740* (Oxford: Clarendon Press, 1989), 5–7; François Bellec, 'Quand les persécutions religieuses préparaient la fortune d'Amsterdam', in Martine Acerra and Guy Martinière (eds.), *Coligny, les protestants et la mer* (Paris: Presses de l'Université Paris Sorbonne, 1997), 15–23.

United Provinces as a new maritime power and staunch opponent of Iberian closed sea claims.[7]

The Dutch had been faster in developing new technological and organisational solutions for optimising seaborne trade, enabling them to challenge both their former business partner, Portugal, and their former overlord, Spain. Meanwhile, the crowns of Spain and Portugal had been united under Philip II in 1580, forming the 'Iberian Union'. Yet, this union ultimately harmed Portuguese commercial interests, as they became subordinate to Spain's priorities and increasingly exposed to Philip II's numerous enemies.[8]

Traditionally, merchants from the Low Countries had relied on the Portuguese to deliver Asian and African goods to Lisbon or Antwerp. However, after being excluded from Philip II's ports, they were forced to procure those goods independently. Over previous decades, the Dutch had acquired substantial knowledge of Portugal's secret sea routes and Indian trade. The Portuguese, often short-staffed, had employed many sailors from the Low Countries. Individuals like the Dutch explorer Jan Huyghen van Linschoten (1563–1611), the author of the famous *Itinerario*, carefully documented what they observed in Asia and brought intelligence back home.[9] More broadly, despite efforts to maintain secrecy, Iberian maritime knowledge inevitably spread across sea-

---

7 See Geoffrey Parker, 'War and economic change: the costs of the Dutch Revolt', in Jay M. Winter (ed.), *War and Economic Development, Essays in Memory of David Joslin* (Cambridge: University Press, 1975), 60; Louis Sicking, 'Le maritime, fondement de la prédominance commerciale et économique des Provinces-Unies', in Buchet and Le Bouëdec (eds.), *The Sea in History*, III, 456; Eco O. G. Haitsma Mulier, *The Myth of Venice and Dutch Republican Thought in the Seventeenth Century* (Assen: Van Gorcum, 1980); Boxer, *The Dutch Seaborne Empire*, 10–3.

8 John H. Elliott, 'The Spanish Monarchy and the Kingdom of Portugal, 1580–1640', in Mark Greengrass (ed.), *Conquest and Coalescence: The Shaping of the State in Early Modern Europe* (London: Edward Arnold, 1991), 45–67; Ronald Cueto, '1580 and All That ...: Philip II and the Politics of the Portuguese Succession', *Portuguese Studies*, 8 (1992), 150–69; James C. Boyajian, *Portuguese Trade in Asia under the Habsburgs, 1580–1640* (Baltimore and London: The Johns Hopkins University Press, 1993).

9 Arun Saldanha, 'The Itineraries of Geography: Jan Huygen van Linschoten's Itinerario and Dutch Expeditions to the Indian Ocean, 1594–1602', *Annals of the Association of American Geographers*, 101(1) (2011), 149–77; Cornelis Koeman, 'Jan Huygen Van Linschoten', *Revista da Universidade de Coimbra*, 32 (1985), 27–47; Nuno Vila-Santa, 'Jan Huygen van Linschoten and the Reys-gheschrift: Updating Iberian Science for the Dutch Expansion', *Historical Research*, 95(265) (2021), 1–22; idem, 'Jan Huygen van Linschoten's Itinerario: a decaying commercial portrait of Portuguese Asia?', in Pablo Sánchez León, Carla Vieira and Nina Vieira (eds.), *Espelhos de Mercúrio. A representação do comércio nas Monarquias Ibéricas, 1500–1800* (Coimbra: Imprensa da Universidade, 2024), 261–88.

faring Europe.[10] By the 1590s, the Dutch were determined to assert themselves as competitors in the East and West Indies. They now had the resources to do so, including a vast fleet of merchant vessels – easily convertible into warships, when needed – and advanced trading techniques that enabled them to transport goods at lower costs than their rivals.[11]

In essence, as the sixteenth century progressed, Iberian 'closed sea' claims faced increased challenges. Other nations began to recognise the potential benefits of oceanic navigation and entertained ambitions of supplanting Spanish and Portuguese dominance, and the freedom of the seas gained prominence as a tool to dismantle Iberian 'closed sea' pretensions. This opposition unfolded on three main fronts. First, various forms of maritime predation challenged closed (or claimed) sea policies. Second, the idea of the freedom of the sea gained traction in the diplomatic arena. Finally, jurists began debating the legal status of the seas in the doctrinal realm, further eroding Iberian maritime claims.

2 Maritime Raiding and Private Naval Warfare

Overall, Spain and Portugal maintained their position as leading actors in oceangoing navigation throughout most of the sixteenth century. However, from an early stage, other European nations acted in an 'informal' way to undermine the duopoly claimed by the Iberian powers.[12] Illegal trade was the first method employed, as merchants from various nations started violating Iberian sea laws – initially sailing towards West Africa and the Caribbean. In the Caribbean, these merchants often benefited from the cooperation of Spanish overseas settlements, whose inhabitants were dissatisfied with the

---

10 Nuno Vila-Santa, *Knowledge Exchanges*, 75–120 (England), 267–322 (Dutch Republic).

11 Catia Antunes, 'Portugal and the United Provinces: two innovative countries: common factors, related developments', in Buchet and Le Bouëdec (eds.), *The Sea in History*, III, 343–4. For further details, see Israel, *Dutch Primacy in World Trade*, 12–38; idem, *The Dutch Republic, its Rise, Greatness, and Fall, 1477–1806* (Oxford: University Press, 1997), 307–27; Boxer, *The Dutch Seaborne Empire*, 6–7. The cargo vessel known as *fluyt* – designed to optimise space for merchandise and crew efficiency – well represented Dutch leadership in the carrying trade.

12 An early version of this paragraph appeared in Stefano Cattelan, 'Challenging empires: pirates, privateers and the europeanisation of ocean Spaces (c.1500–1650)', in Giuseppina de Giudici, Dante Fedele and Elisabetta Fiocchi Malaspina (eds.), *Soggettività contestate e diritto internazionale in età moderna* (Roma: Historia et ius, 2023), 125–51.

quality, price, and limited supply of goods received through official trade channels, i.e. from Seville.[13]

An even more effective strategy to undermine Iberian pretensions involved unleashing various forms of maritime predation against the Iberian 'lords of the ocean'. In Chapter 1, we observed that maritime predation played a decisive role in the speculations concerning the legal status of the Mediterranean Sea – anti-piracy campaigns being at the origin of the Roman concept of *mare nostrum* – as well as seas in northern Europe. In dealing with the oceans, it is appropriate to reverse the perspective. It was the partition of the oceans, and the consequent *ius excludendi alios* put forward by Iberian authorities that created the very conditions that facilitated the global expansion of maritime predation.[14] In this regard, Aldo Andrea Cassi suggested that the race across the ocean had a double soul, an official and an unofficial one, a saint and a damned one. The 'apostolic mission' bestowed upon the emissaries of the Iberian countries, blessed by the pope, and the challenge launched by pirates and other raiders, 'cursed by the Holy See, as *hostes humani generi*'.[15]

In the pre-modern world, maritime trade was closely intertwined with violence and pillaging at sea, as the clear-cut distinction between 'the peaceful trader and the aggressive pirate' was largely non-existent.[16] In addition, throughout the early modern period, maritime warfare remained shaped by the scarcity of resources available to governments to wage it. Central authorities – with few exceptions such as the Republic of Venice – were in no position to monopolise the use of force at sea by their subjects. With this in mind, John D. Ford and Nicholas A. M. Rodger have argued that the dichotomy established by previous scholarship between piracy and privateering – i.e.

13 Hoffman, *The Spanish Crown and the Defense of the Caribbean*, 69; Milton Zambrano Pérez, 'Piratas, piratería y comercio ilícito en el Caribe: la visión del otro (1550–1650)', *Historia Caribe*, 12 (2007), 23–56.

14 Cassi, *Ius commune*, 101; Anne Perotin-Dumon, 'The pirate and the emperor: power and the law on the seas, 1450–1850', in James D. Tracy (ed.), *The Political Economy of Merchant Empires* (Cambridge: University Press, 1991), 196–227; Michael Kempe, *Fluch der Weltmeere: Piraterie, Volkerrecht und internationale Beziehungen, 1500–1900* (Frankfurt: Campus Verlag, 2010).

15 Cassi, *Ius commune*, 101.

16 Nicholas A. M. Rodger, 'The new Atlantic: naval warfare in the sixteenth century', in Hattendorf and Unger (eds.), *War at Sea*, 233–47, at 233–6. For example, Rodger notes that piracy was not recognised as a crime in English law until 1536. See also Cassi, *Ius commune*, 85; Richard W. Unger, 'Channelling Violence at Sea: States, International Trade and the Transformation of Naval Forces from the High Middle Ages to the Age of Steam', *International Journal of Maritime History*, 31(2) (2019), 202–31, at 215; Amirell, Hägerdal and Buchan, 'Introduction', in idem (eds.), *Piracy in World History*, 21.

clearly distinct unlicensed/unlawful vs state-sanctioned forms of predation during a publicly declared war – constitutes an anachronism when applied to the period covered by the present volume.[17] The term privateering only began to appear in primary sources from around the 1660s. That said, earlier practices, such as Dutch or Flemish issuance of *kaperbrief* resembled privateering to some extent.[18] Ultimately, the distinction between public and private naval warfare made little sense until the mid-seventeenth century, when states began maintaining publicly owned fleets of warships and the accompanying administrative structures.[19]

Nevertheless, governments did not wait until the seventeenth century to begin, albeit tentatively, distinguishing between lawful and unlawful forms of maritime violence. First, no jurist questioned the right of a private captain and crew to attack the ships of an enemy of their sovereign during a publicly declared war (*occupatio* of *res hostium*). Limitations on this practice were only gradually introduced, starting from the fifteenth century.[20] Ford refers to this as 'licit plunder', denoting instances where maritime raiding was deemed legitimate by contemporary standards – distinct from piracy.[21] Second, even during peacetime, the legal institute of reprisals – of medieval, rather than Roman, origin – provided a framework for legalised acts of maritime preda-

17 John D. Ford, *The Emergence of Privateering* (Leiden: Brill, 2023), 2. On the persisting confusion and misuse regarding terminologies such as pirate, corsair, privateer, and freebooter, see Nicholas A. M. Rodger, 'The Law and Language of Private Naval Warfare', *The Mariner's Mirror*, 100(1) (2014), 5–16. See also David J. Bederman, 'Privateering', in *The Max Planck Encyclopedia of Public International Law*, vol. VIII (Oxford: University Press, 2012), 475–7.

18 Louis Sicking, *Zeemacht en Onmacht: Maritieme politiek in de Nederlanden, 1488–1558* (Amsterdam: De Bataafsche Leeuw, 1988), 214–21.

19 Stefano Cattelan, 'Maritime warfare in Old Regime Europe' in Randall Lesaffer (ed.), *The Cambridge History of International Law, Vol. 6. Part 2: International Law in Ancien Regime Europe, 1660–1776* (Cambridge: University Press, 2025), 551–87; Richard Harding, *Seapower and Naval Warfare, 1650–1830* (London: UCL Press, 1999), 37–120.

20 Ford, *The Emergence of Privateering*, 102–20, 137.

21 Ibid., 3, 51. See also Louis Sicking, *Neptune and the Netherlands. State, Economy and War at Sea in the Renaissance* (Leiden: Brill, 2004), 420–1; David J. Starkey, 'Voluntaries and sea Robbers: A Review of the Academic Literature on Privateering, Corsairing, Bucaneering and Piracy', *The Mariner's Mirror*, 97(1) (2011), 127–47; Dorothy A. Gardiner, 'The History of Belligerent Rights on the High Seas in the Fourteenth Century', *The Law Quarterly Review*, 48 (1932), 521–46; Jurriaan Wink and Louis Sicking, 'Reprisal and Diplomacy: Conflict Resolution within the Context of Anglo-Dutch Commercial Relations, c1300–c1415', *Comparative Legal History*, 5(1) (2017), 1–19.

tion.[22] Specifically, an individual who had suffered losses on the high seas could petition his government for a letter of reprisal (known in French as a *lettre de merk*). This legal document authorised the individual to seize goods equivalent to the value of their losses. Importantly, this authorisation did not require targeting the specific party responsible for the original harm; instead, the holder of the letter could seize goods from any compatriot of the offending party, reflecting the principle of collective responsibility.[23]

The issuance of a letter of reprisal typically depended on fulfilling certain conditions. The victim was first required to seek redress for their losses through the legal system of the offender's nation. Only if justice was 'neglected, denied, or unduly delayed' (*neglecta, denegata vel retardata iustitia* in legal terminology), could the reprisal procedure progress. The issuing authority usually took steps to verify the extent of the claimed losses, assess the value of any goods seized, and ensure that the reprisal did not exceed the authorised amount.[24] In other words, the issuing authority normally sought to oversee the entire reprisal process (*adiudicatio*). Ships seized under a letter of reprisal had to be brought to port, where officials reviewed and accounted for their value and cargo. As a result, provided the legal procedures were respected and deemed fair, the issuance of a letter of reprisal initiated a private war, rather than a public one, while the two polities involved officially remained at peace.[25]

Maritime raiding, or 'licit plunder', during publicly declared wars was often the preferred strategy of weaker naval powers, as it allowed smaller forces or individual ships to inflict significant damage to their enemies' commercial interests. This approach was exemplified by Francis I of France, who lacked a royal fleet capable of challenging Charles V's naval dominance. Instead,

22 René de Mas Latrie, 'Du droit de marque ou droit de représailles au Moyen Âge', *Bibliothèque de l'École des chartes*, 27 (1866), 529–77; Pierre Prétou, *L'invention de la piraterie en France au Moyen Age* (Paris: Presses universitaires de France, 2021), 9–78. For an analysis of the legal differences between 'licit plunder' and reprisals, see Ford, *The Emergence of Privateering*, 51–4.

23 Rodger, 'The Law and Language', 6–7; idem, 'The New Atlantic', 238; Ford, *The Emergence of Privateering*, 39–54. For examples of letters of reprisal, see 'Letter of reprisal granted by James IV, King of Scotland, 1560', in Marsden, *Documents*, vol. 1, 170–2; 'Letters of marque to William and George Winter, 1569', ibid., 184–9; 'Letters of reprisal to John Kitchin against Spain, 1585', ibid., 237–41.

24 Ford, *The Emergence of Privateering*, 51.

25 Rodger, 'The New Atlantic', 244; Florence E. Dyer, 'Reprisals in the Sixteenth Century', *The Mariner's Mirror*, 21(2) (1935), 187–97; Philip C. Jessup and Francis Deák, *Neutrality: its History, Economics and Law: The Origins Vol. 1* (New York: Columbia University Press, 1935), 12.

Francis I relied on private ship owners from coastal regions such as Brittany and Normandy, with the already mentioned Jean d'Ango of Dieppe being the most notable figure.[26] French admiralty regulations and royal edicts issued in 1373, 1517, 1544, and 1584 offered a coherent – at least on paper – legal framework for prize-taking against the enemies of the King of France.[27]

Maritime raiding often blended varying degrees of patriotism with the promise of substantial private profit. While, in theory, it was distinct from piracy – which involved the unauthorised plundering of ships regardless of nationality – in practice, the line between piracy and state-sanctioned maritime predation was often blurred.[28] Furthermore, belligerent powers sometimes encouraged outright piracy by their subjects as a strategy to disrupt enemy trade and communication lines while simultaneously providing economic benefits to coastal communities.

After Hernán Cortés's conquest of Mexico in 1519–1520, huge quantities of gold and silver began to flow across Atlantic watery highways. By the 1520s, French corsairs such as François le Clerc, 'Jambe de Bois', were targeting Spanish treasure ships in the Atlantic. In 1523, one of Jean d'Ango's captains, Jean Fleury, intercepted and captured three Spanish vessels near the Azores that were transporting some of Cortés's leading lieutenants and the treasure of the last Aztec emperor, Cuauhtémoc.[29] French raiders also plundered Spanish settlements in the Caribbean, all within the broader context of the prolonged

---

26 Patrick Villiers, 'Développement naval et développement commercial: les leçons de l'Histoire, 1500–1815', in Buchet and Le Bouëdec (eds.), *The Sea in History*, III, 787; David S. Berry, 'The Caribbean', in Fassbender and Peters (eds.), *The Oxford Handbook of the History of International Law*, 594.

27 See 'Édit sur l'amirauté, fevrier 1544', in François-André Isambert et al. (eds.), *Recueil général des anciennes lois françaises, depuis l'an 420 jusqu'à la Révolution de 1789…* (Paris: Belin-Leprieur, Verdière, 1828), vol. 12, n. 380, 854–67; 'Édit sur l'amirauté, du mois de mars 1584', in Jean-Marie Pardessus, *Collection de lois maritimes antérieures au XVIII*[e] *siècle*, vol. 4 (Paris: Imprimerie Royale, 1837), 302. For a detailed analysis, see Ford, *The Emergence of Privateering*, 140–4.

28 Louis Sicking, 'God's Friend, the Whole World's Enemy. Reconsidering the Role of Piracy in the Development of Universal Jurisdiction', *Netherlands Journal of Legal Philosophy*, 47(2) (2018), 176–7; idem, 'The Pirate and the Admiral: Europeanisation and Globalisation of Maritime Conflict Management', *Journal of the History of International Law*, 20(4) (2018), 429–70; idem, *Neptune and the Netherlands*, 421; Donald A. Petrie, *The Prize Game: Lawful Looting on the High Seas in the Days of Fighting Sail* (Annapolis: Naval Institute Press, 1999); Kris E. Lane, *Pillaging the Empire: Global Piracy on the High Seas, 1500–1750* (London: Routledge, 2016), 18–9; Christopher Rossi, *Sovereignty and Territorial Temptation: The Grotian Tendency* (Cambridge: University Press, 2017), 37; Benton, *A Search for Sovereignty*, 113.

29 de la Roncière, *Histoire de la marine française*, III, 249–51.

Valois-Habsburg struggle for hegemony in Western Europe.[30] Periods of undeclared war alternated with peace, truces, and officially sanctioned hostilities, further obscuring the legal nature of acts of maritime violence occurring in distant waters.

Meanwhile, Portuguese crackdowns on French interlopers in Brazil and Guinea prompted French authorities to issue letters of reprisal against Lusitanian ships, igniting new cycles of violence.[31] In letters of reprisals issued in 1533, Francis I again reaffirmed the freedom for all peoples 'to navigate the common sea' (*de naviguer sur la mer commune*).[32] In July 1536, Portugal agreed to allow French corsairs to use its strategic harbours in the Azores and Madeira as stopover points during their anti-Spanish operations. In return, Portuguese diplomats likely hoped to redirect French activities away from Brazilian and Guinean waters, which fell within Portugal's sphere of influence, and sought a formal commitment to this effect from Francis I. However, by granting access to French vessels, Portugal effectively permitted them into the Lusitanian 'closed sea' zone, established under the Treaty of Tordesillas.[33] This provoked strong protests from Charles V's diplomats. In response, the Portuguese government argued that only French merchant ships – not corsairs – were allowed to use its Atlantic islands as stopovers. Portuguese officials also suggested that Spain should improve the organisation and protection of its transatlantic routes. As it was to be expected, this argumentation failed to convince the emperor's envoys, who highlighted the difficulty of distinguishing in practice between merchants and raiders. They insisted that Lusitanian authorities deny shelter to all French vessels.[34]

In 1555, the French Protestant Jacques de Sores looted and burnt down the city of Havana, one of the most important Spanish bases in the Caribbeans.[35]

30 Jeremy Black, *European Warfare, 1494–1660* (London: Routledge, 2002), 71–87.

31 Ibid., 281–7.

32 Bibliothèque Nationale de France, 5503, fol. 65, quoted in ibid., 291.

33 'Articles concluded between France and Portugal at Lyons, 14 July 1536', in Davenport, *European Treaties*, I, doc. 17, 199–204.

34 'Spain, February 1537', in *Calendar of State Papers, Spain*, vol. 5, part 2, 1536–1538, edited by P. de Gayangos (London: Her Majesty's Stationery Office, 1888), 310–27. British History Online: http://www.british-history.ac.uk/cal-state-papers/spain/vol5/no2/pp310-327; 'Spain, March 1537', ibid., 328–48. British History Online: http://www.british-history.ac.uk/cal-state-papers/spain/vol5/no2/pp328-348.

35 De La Roncière, *Histoire de la marine française*, III, 579–84; Mickaël Augeron, 'Pour "la défense et l'advencement de la vraye religion": Jacques de Sores, un corsaire au service de la Cause protestante', in idem, Didier Poton and Bertrand van Ruymbeke (eds.), *Les huguenots et l'Atlantique: vol. 1, Pour dieu, la cause ou les affaires* (Paris: Presses de l'Université Paris-Sorbonne, 2009), 189–205.

Temporary moments of peace, such as those established by the treaties of Crépy and Vaucelles, only partially curtailed the activity of French corsairs. The Venetian ambassador Federico Badoero reported to the Senate that King Philip II was enraged by continued presence of French vessels in the West Indies, which violated the terms of the 1556 truce.[36] Captains who had operated under royal commissions or during publicly declared wars often chose to continue their activities without the blessing of their sovereign once peace was declared, effectively becoming pirates.

In response, Spanish authorities introduced minimum requirements for vessels sailing to the Indies, mandating specific standards for crew sizes, armament, and tonnage. These regulations, first issued in 1522, were renewed multiple times.[37] The legal titles discussed in the previous chapter were evidently insufficient to guarantee safe navigation within what were supposed to be the 'Iberian seas'. To enhance security, the Spanish Crown implemented a twice-yearly convoy system, requiring merchant vessels to travel together under armed escort at pre-determined times of the year. Despite significant logistical and technological challenges, the Crown also established a system of naval patrols to deter intruders.[38]

Meanwhile, Portuguese merchant ships were not spared from French attacks. As a result, Spain and Portugal grew closer again and agreed to collaborate.[39] In a set of articles dating back to 1552, they planned the reorganisation

---

36 'Relazione delle persone, governo e stati di Carlo V e di Filippo II, letta in Senato da Federico Badoero, 1557', in *Relazioni degli ambasciatori Veneti al Senato*, 1861, Serie I, vol. III, 304: '*la cagione del nuovo odio nasce, perché avendo fatto tregua per cinque anni insieme, il re di Francia, innanzi la conclusione di essa, abbia segretamente formata la lega col Pontefice, dalla quale procede la presente guerra* [...] *e che fino all'Indie abbia mandato navi per occupare alcun luogo ed impedire la navigazione* ...'. My translation: 'The cause of the new hatred arises, because having made a truce together for five years, the king of France, before its signature, has secretly formed the league with the Pontiff, from which the present war derives [...] and that he sent ships as far as the Indies to occupy some places and to impede navigation ...'.

37 See Esteban Mira Caballos, *El sistema naval del imperio español. Armadas, flotas y galeones en el siglo XVI* (Madrid: Punto de Vista Editores, 2015); idem, *Las armadas del imperio. Poder y hegemonía en tiempo de los Austrias* (Madrid: La Esfera de los Libros, 2019); Oscar Cruz Barney, *El combate a la piratería en Indias: 1555–1700* (Ciudad de México: Oxford University Press, 1999); Carlo M. Cipolla, *La odisea de la plata española: conquistadores, piratas y mercaderes* (Barcelona: Critica, 1999), 37–40.

38 Hoffman, *The Spanish Crown and the Defense of the Caribbean*, 88; Jan Glete, *Warfare at Sea, 1500–1650. Maritime Conflicts and the Transformation of Europe* (London: Routledge, 2000), 150–1.

39 '*Paresce que para buscar los corsarios, unos por una parte y otros por otra, se devria conformar, syn embargo del respecto que el señor Rey de Portugal quiere tener a no romper*

of coastguards along the Iberian coasts. They also agreed to bolster patrols and defences in the Atlantic, especially in the strategic waters surrounding the Azores. Lusitanian diplomats believed they could punish French *corsairos* without breaching peace with France, reasoning that these raiders were not part of the French royal fleet but mere criminals (*ladrones*).[40]

In the 1560s, the English navigator John Hawkins (1532–1595) organised three voyages that defied both Portuguese and Spanish closed sea policies.[41] Backed by influential members of the royal court, Hawkins employed a mix of commerce and violence (*trade-cum-plunder*) to enter the West African slave trade, later selling enslaved individuals to Spanish settlements in the Americas.[42] In the following years, as the tension between the protestant Queen Elizabeth I of England and Philip II escalated, English raiders began striking the Caribbean, often joining forces with French Huguenots based in La Rochelle – and later Dutch rebels – who shared their hate towards the Catholic might of Spain and taught them the secrets of long-range oceanic raiding.[43]

---

por el presente con Francia, pues que estos corsarios no son armada que anda a sueldo del rey, syno ladrones, que andan a robar a toda ropa, como paresce por el daño que Portugueses han recibido dellos, y justamente el señor Rey de Portugal los puede mandar buscar y seguir para castigallos', Archives of Simancas, Secretaria de Estado, leg. 375, f. 120.

40 Davenport, *European Treaties*, I, doc. 19, 210–4.

41 For Hawkins' biography, see Harry Kelsey, *Sir John Hawkins: Queen Elizabeth's Slave Trader* (New Haven, CT: Yale University Press, 2003).

42 Clements R. Markham (ed.), *The Hawkins Voyages during the Reigns of Henry VIII, Queen Elizabeth, and James I* (London: Hakluyt Society, 1878). English and Spanish sources referring to English raiding voyages have been published in Irene A. Wright, *Spanish Documents Concerning English Voyages to the Caribbean, 1527–1568* (London: Hakluyt Society, 1929), and idem, *Documents Concerning English Voyages to the Spanish Main, 1569–1580* (London: Hakluyt Society, 1932) and in Kenneth R. Andrews, *English Privateering Voyages to the West Indies, 1588–1595* (Cambridge: Hakluyt Society, 1959). Andrews studied English piracy extensively in *The Spanish Caribbean: Trade and Plunder, 1530–1630* (New Haven, CT: Yale University Press, 1978); idem, *Trade, Plunder, and Settlement: Maritime Enterprise and the Genesis of the British Empire, 1480–1630* (Cambridge: University Press, 1984). Cf. Antonio Rumeu de Armas, *Los viajes de John Hawkins a America, 1562–1595* (Seville: Escuela de Estudios Hispano Americanos, 1947); John C. Appleby, *Under the Bloody Flag: Pirates of the Tudor Age* (Stroud: The History Press, 2009), 104; Vila-Santa, *Knowledge Exchanges*, 75–120.

43 Rodger, 'The New Atlantic', 244; idem, *The Safeguard of the Sea*, 238–53; Policante, *The Pirate Myth*, 37–8; Berry, 'The Caribbean', 593–6; Kenneth R. Andrews, *Elizabethan Privateering: English Privateering during the Spanish War, 1585–1603* (Cambridge: University Press, 1965); idem, *Drake's Voyages: A Reassessment of their Place in Elizabethan Maritime Expansion* (London: Weidenfeld & Nicolson), 1967; Brian Dietz, 'The Huguenot and English Corsairs during Third Civil War in France, 1568 to 1570', *Proceedings of the Huguenot Society*, 19 (1952–1958), 278–94; Marcel Delafosse, 'Les corsaires protestants à

Francis Drake (1540–1596) became one of the most celebrated English captains of the time. His exploits exemplify how long-range raiding cruises challenged Iberian sea power. Drake's 1577–1580 circumnavigation of the globe was particularly significant. He departed Plymouth in November 1577 with five ships, capturing a Portuguese merchantman near the Cape Verde Islands before reaching Brazil. Sailing south, he crossed the Strait of Magellan into the eastern Pacific Ocean – known at the time as the 'Southern Sea', which Spain regarded as a vast 'Spanish lake', shielded by its remoteness.[44] Drake's crew pillaged several ports along the Chilean coast, including Callao, and captured rich prizes, most notably the Spanish treasure ship *Nuestra Señora de la Concepción*, which carried bullion from Peru to Panama.[45] After crossing the Pacific, Drake returned to England nearly three years later, laden with considerable booty.[46] Remarkably, Spain and England were still officially at peace throughout this expedition.

La Rochelle (1570–1577)', *Bibliothèque de l'école des chartes*, 121 (1963), 187–217; David Trim, 'The Secret War of Elizabeth I: England and the Huguenots during the Early Wars of Religion, 1562–77', *Proceedings of the Huguenot Society*, 27(2) (1999), 189–99; idem, 'Transnational Calvinist co-operation and "mastery of the sea" in the late sixteenth century', in Rommelse, Davies and James (eds.), *Ideologies of Western Naval Power*, 153–87; Mickaël Augeron, 'Les élites calvinistes et la course anti-catholique à La Rochelle: attitudes, justifications et contestations dans les années 1570', *Anglophonia*, 17 (2005), 123–34; Frank Lestringant, 'Les protestants et la liberté des mers, d'Urbain Chauveton à Grotius', in Acerra and Martinière (eds.), *Coligny, les protestants et la mer*, 25–33.

44 Elizabeth Montañez-Sanabria, 'The Spanish Lake: Pirates, Privateers, and the Contest for the Pacific Ocean', in *Oxford Research Encyclopedia of Latin American History*, (2023), 1–21, accessed online: https://oxfordre.com/latinamericanhistory/display/10.1093/acrefore/9780199366439.001.0001/acrefore-9780199366439-e-948?rskey=sG6Cek&result=1; Spate, *The Spanish Lake*, 229–64; Peter T. Bradley, *The Lure of Peru: Maritime Intrusion into the South Sea, 1598–1701* (London: Palgrave McMillan, 1989).

45 For a contemporary account, see Richard Hakluyt, *The Famous Voyage of Sir Francis Drake into the South Sea, and there hence about the Whole Globe of the Earth, Begun in the Year of our Lord 1577* [1589], in *The Voyage of Sir Francis Drake around the Whole Globe* (London: Penguin, 2015). See also Harry Kelsey, *Sir Francis Drake: The Queen's Pirate* (New Haven, CT: Yale University Press, 1998), 17–21.

46 For an almost contemporary account, see William Camden, *The history of the most renowned and victorious Princess Elizabeth, late queen of England: containing all the most important and remarkable passages of state, both at home and abroad* [...], II (London: printed by M. Flesher, for C. Harper, 1675), 248–54. See also Sheryllynne Haggerthy, 'Actors of maritime trade in the British Atlantic: from the "Sea Dogs" to a trading empire', in Buchet and Le Bouëdec (eds.), *The Sea in History*, III, 351–2; Nicholas A. M. Rodger, 'Social structure and naval power: Britain and the Netherlands', ibid., 679–81; Escamilla, *Le siècle d'or de l'Espagne*, 614; David Salomoni, *Francis Drake: Il corsaro che sfidò un impero* (Bari: Editori Laterza, 2023).

Generalised hostilities between Spain and England erupted in 1585, though war was never formally declared by either side. Before this, the English Privy Council had attempted to avoid a full diplomatic rupture with Philip II. However, as tensions escalated and Elizabeth I continued to permit trade-cum-plunder expeditions, Philip ordered the seizure of all English ships in Spanish and Portuguese ports in the summer of 1585, imprisoning their crews.[47] In retaliation, Elizabeth authorised the Lord Admiral, Lord Howard of Effingham (1536–1624) – assisted by the jurist and admiralty judge Julius Caesar (1557–1636) – to issue letters of reprisals against the Spaniards more liberally than before.[48] That same year, the Privy Council issued an eight-article regulation to formalise the issuance of reprisals from a legal standpoint.[49]

It should be noted that Hawkins's voyages in the 1560s and Drake's in the 1570s were likely not provided with commissions for reprisals and thus whenever they captured Portuguese and Spanish vessels in the Atlantic they were technically acting as pirates.[50] Drake's circumnavigation, in particular, was privately supported by Elizabeth I, the Earl of Leicester, and Francis Walsingham, but no formal agreement was put on paper. Hence, the blurred legal nature of the expedition allowed the English government to deny any involvement, if necessary, what Janice Thomson refers to as 'plausible deniability'.[51]

In other words, the lightning and elusive raids of the marauders of the sea – who employed ship designs better adapted 'to disrupting command of the sea

47 Ford, *The Emergence of Privateering*, 127; Geoffrey Parker, *The Grand Strategy of Philip II* (New Haven, CT: Yale University Press, 1998), 173–6.

48 'Letters patent to the Lord Admiral, authorizing him to issue letters of reprisals, 1585', in George W. Prothero (ed.), *Select Statutes and Other Constitutional Documents Illustrative of the Reign of Elizabeth and James I* (Oxford: Clarendon Press, 1913), 464. On the legal aspects, see Ford, *The Emergence of Privateering*, 127–8; for the broader context, see Paul E. J. Hammer, *Elizabeth's Wars: War, Government and Society in Tudor England, 1544–1604* (Basingstoke: Red Globe Press, 2003), 119–220; Bruce Lenman, *England's Colonial Wars, 1550–1688: Conflicts, Empire, and National Identity* (Harlow: Longman, 2001), 34–5.

49 'Regulation as to letters of marque', in Julian S. Corbett (ed.), *Papers Relating to the Navy during the Spanish War, 1585–1587* (London: Printed for the Navy Records Society, 1898), 36–8. See also 'Letter from the Lord Admiral to the judge of the Admiralty, directing him to issue letters of reprisals against Spain to John Foxall, 28 November 1585', in Marsden, *Documents*, vol. 1, 241–2.

50 John Sugden, *Sir Francis Drake* (London: Pimlico, 2006), 47; Cattelan, 'Challenging empires', 145; Mark Chadwick, *Piracy and the Origins of Universal Jurisdiction: On Stranger Tides?* (Leiden: Brill, 2019), 59.

51 Janice E. Thomson, *Mercenaries, Pirates, and Sovereigns, State Building and Extraterritorial Violence in Early Modern Europe* (Princeton: University Press, 1994), 21; Costas M. Constantinou, *States of Political Discourse: Words, Regimes, Seditions* (London: Taylor & Francis, 2004), 57.

than to gaining or keeping it'[52] – showcased for the first time the weaknesses of Iberian 'closed sea' claims over the oceans, in fact, if not in law. As discussed in Chapter 1, the ability to suppress piracy and impose order at sea formed the foundation of jurisdictional claims over the oceans. The fact that Iberian authorities failed to enforce such control undermined their claims. Spanish authorities cyclically lost control (e.g. in 1552–1556) over their most vital sea lanes, creating a stark contrast between their formal claims over the oceans and the harsh reality where they enemies roamed freely, except for the main fortified colonial towns and the armed naval convoys.[53]

This tension reflects two contrasting images of the sea: one as a vast, lawless expanse, difficult to govern due to the unique nature of the marine environment; the other as a *res* that could be controlled by polities, akin to a portion of their territory. These competing perceptions repeatedly shaped the history of human interaction with the seas, gaining new relevance in the global and oceanic context.[54] From this perspective, piracy and maritime raiding provided to the enemies of the Iberian powers the first means to question Iberian closed seas claims and 'shocked the self-assurance of Spain's imperial subjects'.[55] The sheer vastness of the oceans worked against Hispano-Portuguese pretensions as there were 'no physical barrier(s) that could prevent foreigners penetrating into the waters, from which they were excluded by Spanish and Portuguese laws'.[56]

In a context of transition for both naval warfare and geographical knowledge, northern Europeans adapted their 'private, commercial style of war' – which dated back to the Middle Ages – to long-range, trans-continental raiding cruises against the Iberian powers.[57] While France and England often de facto encouraged maritime predation of dubious legality, their governments officially condemned outright piracy. The distinction between licit and illicit

52 Rodger, 'The New Atlantic', 246. Rodger refers in particular to the nimble galleons designs adopted by the Huguenots and the English to suit their style of private, commercial warfare.

53 In the Caribbean, pirates and raiders started to use swift oared vessels, e.g. the *patache*, hard to intercept for Spanish vessels. See Hoffman, *The Spanish Crown and the Defense of the Caribbean*, 69.

54 Benton, *A Search for Sovereignty*, 104–6.

55 Policante, *The Pirate Myth*, 45.

56 Rodger, 'The New Atlantic', 242; Michael Kempe, '"Even in the Remotest Corners of the World": Globalized Piracy and International Law, 1500–1900', *Journal of Global History*, 5(3) (2010), 353–72.

57 Rodger, 'The New Atlantic', 242. See also Louis Sicking, 'Naval warfare in Europe, c.1330–c.1680', in Frank Tallet and David J. B. Trim (eds.), *European Warfare, 1350–1750* (Cambridge: University Press, 2010), 236–63.

plunder, however, largely remained a matter of perspective. The English 'Sea Dogs', for example, were hailed as heroes in England but viewed as criminals and heretics by Spanish colonial authorities, who executed them without ceremony, if captured.[58] From the Spanish perspective, all foreigners crossing the Tordesillas *raya* without formal approval from Spain were deemed excommunicated heretics (often referred to as *corsarios luteranos*), who jeopardised Spanish missionary efforts in the Americas and undermined the Catholic Church's authority.[59]

Spanish envoys in London complained bitterly about English depredations, particularly as Spain and England remained officially at peace until the mid-1580s. Throughout her reign, Elizabeth I issued proclamations requiring her subjects to obtain licenses from the Admiralty Court before putting a ship at sea 'either on warfare, merchandise, or otherwise' – for example, immediately after acceding to the throne in 1558 and in 1564–, however, such provisions were cyclically relaxed or not enforced.[60] Royal proclamations condemning piracy continued to be issued until the end of her reign, with notable examples in 1578, 1599, and 1602.[61]

Once Spain and England eventually signed a peace in 1604, some English crews turned pirates continued their depredations without official or unofficial backing. These masterless crews at times joined forces with pirates based in Morocco and the Barbary Coast and when they operated close to the British Islands they severely undermined the crown's authority in its own

58 Cattelan, 'Challenging empires', 144–5; Kris E. Lane, 'Punishing the Sea Wolf: Corsairs and Cannibals in the Early Modern Caribbean', *New West Indian Guide*, 77(3–4) (2003), 201–20, at 211.

59 Policante, *The Pirate Myth*, 45.

60 Paul L. Hughes and James F. Larkin (eds.), *Tudor Royal Proclamations: Vol. 2, the Later Tudors (1553–1587)* (New Haven, CT: Yale University Press, 1969), 100–1 (1558) and 253–5 (1564).

61 See 'Articles extracted out of the order made by her Majestic for to remedie and meet with the depredations daily committed by the subjects of this Realme upon Frenchmen and other nations, […] which are in amitie and good correspondence with her said Majestic, 1578', in Marsden, *Documents*, vol. 1, 221–2; 'Proclamatio Regia specialis pro causis maritimis, February 8, 1599', in Rymer, *Foedera*, VII.1, 211 and ibid., 'De proclamatione regia, ad reprimenda deprædationes super mare, March 19, 1602', VII.2, 31. See also 'Commission from the Queen to the Lord High Admiral to issue commissions to capture pirates, 5 February 1572', in Marsden, *Documents*, vol. 1, 191–2; 'Instructions given by the Lords…, 19 May 1576', in idem, 210. In 1577, the Wardens of the Cinque Ports were instructed to license privateers to hunt pirates, see idem, 216.

waters.[62] Finally, it is worth noting that the Spanish Habsburgs were not merely victims of maritime predation. They too resorted to maritime raiding, pirate hunters (*contra-corsarios*), and piracy against their enemies. At the height of the Dutch revolt, pro-Spanish corsairs were installed in the strategically located Flemish ports still under Spanish rule, Dunkirk, Ostend, and Nieuwpoort. From there, they began launching unrelenting and rather effective assaults on enemy shipping.[63]

3 Diplomatic Arena

3.1 *Premises*

While maritime raiding succeeded in undermining the closed-sea claims of Spain and Portugal, it was not sufficient on its own to end their predominance over oceangoing navigation. Consequently, France, the Dutch Republic, and England began to challenge the Iberian duopoly both diplomatically and militarily, contesting the legal foundations upon which it rested. Over time, the prospect of securing exclusive rights over the oceans was decisively rejected. During the negotiations of 1558–1559 that led to the peace of Cateau-Cambrésis, Spanish envoys insisted on gaining recognition of their closed sea policy in the West Indies. The initial Spanish proposal still sought to uphold the *raya* established by the Treaty of Tordesillas, but the French now deemed this line impracticable. The Spanish then attempted to negotiate a revised agreement that would delimit a reduced maritime area – defined by specific longitude and latitude lines – under exclusive Spanish rule.[64]

However, a compromise on this point could not be reached and was therefore excluded from the treaty signed on April 3, 1559.[65] Instead, the two lead negotiators, Sebastien de l'Aubespine (1518–1582), bishop of Limoges (for

62 Barbara Fuchs, *Mimesis and Empire: The New World, Islam, and European Identities* (Cambridge: University Press, 2004), 125; Rodger, *The Safeguard of the Sea*, 348–51; Christopher Lloyd, *English Corsairs on the Barbary Coast* (London: Collins, 1981).

63 For further details, see Robert A. Stradling, *The Armada of Flanders: Spanish Maritime Policy and European War, 1568–1668* (Cambridge: University Press 2009); Patrick Villiers, *Les corsaires du littoral: Dunkerque, Calais, Boulogne, de Philippe II à Louis XIV (1568–1713)* (Villeneuve d'Ascq: Presses universitaires du Septentrion, 2020), 45–96; David Goodman, *Spanish Naval Power, 1589–1665: Reconstruction and Defeat* (Cambridge: University Press, 1997), 4; Henry Malo, *Les corsaires dunkerquois et Jean Bart, des origins à 1662* (Paris: Le Mercure de France, 1913).

64 Fuchs, *Mimesis and Empire*, 105.

65 For the treaty, see Davenport, *European Treaties*, I, doc. 21, 219–22; *CUD*, V.1, 34–46; Grewe, *Fontes*, II, 19–38.

France), and Antoine Perrenot de Granvelle (1517–1586), bishop of Arras (for Spain), came to an oral agreement that established that the peace treaty would not apply beyond 'lines of amity', i.e. south of the Tropic of Capricorn and west of the Azores Islands – a policy later referred to as 'no peace beyond the line(s)'.[66] As a result, even after peace was formally restored in Europe between France and Spain, maritime encounters in extra-European waters remained hostile and ships captured in these regions constituted legitimate prizes.[67] The constant private-commercial naval warfare therefore persisted, especially in regions like the Caribbean, where Spanish and French warships could attack each other without breaching the official state of peace in Europe.[68] In essence, it became increasingly difficult for Spanish negotiators to include clauses in international agreements that restricted the *ius navigandi* of other powers.[69]

3.2 *Elizabeth I and Iberian Claims*

During the sixteenth century, Tudor England gradually altered its posture vis-à-vis foreign 'claimed seas' pretensions. As early as the 1550s, diplomatic exchanges were ongoing between England and Portugal concerning English navigation to Brazil and Guinea (West Africa). In 1555, the Portuguese ambassador in London lodged a complaint with Queen Mary I of England (r. 1553–1558), alleging that English vessels had sailed to San Jorge da Mina in Guinea. According to the envoy, these ships had violated Portugal's maritime monopoly in the region and, under the pretext of trade, brought havoc to Portuguese settlements and vessels.[70] The Portuguese ambassador demanded

---

66 Rodger, 'The New Atlantic', 242; James A. Williamson, *Hawkins of Plymouth* (London: Adam and Charles Black, 1949), 46; Blake, *European Beginnings*, 160; Pearce Higgins, 'International law and the outer world, 1450–1648', 186–7. If the parallel is relatively certain to have been the Tropic of Cancer, in relation to the meridian things are much less certain (also given the oral nature of the agreement), see Garrett Mattingly, 'No Peace beyond what Line?', *Transactions of the Royal Society*, 13 (1963), 145–62. Grewe curiously attributed the formula to Francis Drake, in *Epochs*, 155.

67 Cialdea, *La formazione dell'ordinamento marittimo*, 32–3; Sicking, '*Mare Liberum, Mare Clausum*', 194; Jörg Fisch, *Die Europäische Expansion und das Völkerrechts. Die Auseinandersetzungen um den Status der überseeischen Gebiete vom 15. Jahrhundert bis zur Gegenwart* (Stuttgart: Steiner, 1984), 114.

68 Rodger, 'The New Atlantic', 242.

69 Bernard Barbiche, 'Henri IV et l'outre-mer: un moment décisif', in Raymonde Litalien and Denis Vaugeois (dir.), *Champlain. La naissance de l'Amérique française* (Quebec City: Septentrion, 2004), 30–8.

70 'Reclamação que dirigio o Embaixador de Portugal em Londres, Diogo Lopes de Souza contra alguns Inglezes que tinhão ido á Costa da Mina, 1555' in Barros y Sousa, *Quadro*

reparations and requested that the offending English sailors be extradited to Portugal. Additionally, he insisted that English subjects refrain from venturing into Lusitanian overseas domains in the future.[71]

In response, Queen Mary I issued a ban on English navigation to Guinea. Her staunch Catholicism likely facilitated her acceptance of Portugal's claims, as they were grounded in papal donation.[72] Furthermore, her marriage to Prince Philip of Spain (soon to become Philip II) probably reinforced her support for Lusitanian 'claimed seas' policies, which aligned with Spain's own closed-sea doctrine.[73] Similar prohibitions were included in subsequent decrees issued in 1556 and 1557.[74] In essence, Mary I acknowledged Portuguese closed sea policies throughout her reign, prohibiting her subjects from sailing to Guinea and Brazil. The East Indies, still far beyond England's maritime ambitions, were not even considered at the time. Nonetheless, many English sailors clandestinely continued their ventures, prompting renewed Anglo-Portuguese diplomatic exchanges.[75] Moreover, at the time, England was engaged in a war against France, and Mary I and Philip jointly issued letters of reprisals, authorising attacks on French shipping 'for the anoyaunce of their Majesties' enemies, the Frenchmen'.[76]

Everything changed – albeit only gradually – when Mary's younger Protestant sister, Elizabeth I (r. 1558–1603), ascended the throne.[77] If initially English diplomacy continued to focus on Scotland and France and securing her throne, with time, the queen adopted a more assertive stance towards Portu-

elementar, vol. XV, 94–6. For an analysis of Anglo-Portuguese relations in the 1550s, see Vila-Santa, *Knowledge Exchanges*, 75–120.

71 Barros y Sousa, *Quadro elementar*, vol. XV, 95.

72 'Carta da Rainha Maria d'Inglaterra…, December 18, 1555', ibid., 96; Frei Luis de Sousa, *Annaes de D. João III* (Lisboa: Typ. da Sociedade Propagadora…, 1844), 446–7.

73 Edgar Prestage, 'The Anglo-Portuguese Alliance', *Transactions of the Royal Historical Society*, 17 (1934), 69–100, at 81; Alexander Samson, *Mary and Philip: The Marriage of Tudor England and Habsburg Spain* (Manchester: University Press, 2020); Hilda F. M. Prescott, *Mary Tudor: The Spanish Tudor* (London: Phoenix, 2003).

74 Frei Luis de Sousa, *Annaes de D. João III*, 446–7.

75 'Ordem da Rainha Maria d'Inglaterra, dada em Conselho, prohibindo aos vassallos Inglezes irem á Guiné e ã Mina por serem estes paizes da Coroa de Portugal, July 1556', in Barros y Sousa, *Quadro elementar*, 99–100.

76 'Proclamation licensing all subjects of the King and Queen to set forth ships against their enemies, 1557', in Marsden, *Documents*, vol. 1, 162–3.

77 The queen did not show any haste of breaking the strong economic ties between England and the Iberian Peninsula, see Escamilla, *Le siècle d'or de l'Espagne*, 601; Wendy R. Childs, 'Anglo-Portuguese Trade in the Fifteenth Century', *Transactions of the Royal Historical Society*, 2 (1992), 195–219; Susan Doran, *Elizabeth I and Foreign Policy, 1558–1603* (London: Routledge, 2000).

guese complaints and became a vocal proponent of the freedom of the seas.[78] In April 1561, a Portuguese envoy once again protested against widespread English depredations on Portuguese shipping. He asked the queen to stop these ventures in order to restore 'the friendship between the two kingdoms', and to punish her subjects who violated the peace. The envoy focused especially on English attempts to trade and depredations along the West African coasts. In the process, he recapitulated the legal grounds of Portugal's closed sea policies. He argued that navigation and trade in the region had been initiated (i.e. discovery) and rightfully acquired by Lusitanian kings through expenses and sacrifices (i.e. labour-occupation). Moreover, he asserted that the other Christian princes had not disputed ancient Portuguese possession, or *antiga posse* (i.e. pontifical donation-prescription-acquiescence):

> And among the various harms caused by the English to the Portuguese, one of the most significant was that English ships had sailed to the ports of Mina and Malagueta, as well as to other maritime provinces belonging to the Crown of Portugal, despite the fact that their navigation and trade were the legitimate property of the said Crown, acquired by the predecessors of the aforementioned King at great expense, and at the cost of the blood and toil of the Portuguese, who had discovered them. Moreover, no Prince of Christendom had ever disputed the longstanding possession of these lands. In light of this, the King of Portugal requested that the said Queen of England strictly prohibit her subjects from daring to venture into those regions.[79]

78 Richard Tuck, *The Rights of War and Peace: Political Thought and the International Order from Grotius to Kant* (Oxford: University Press, 2001), 111; Escamilla, *Le siècle d'or de l'Espagne*, 613. For further details, see Antonio-Miguel Bernal, *Monarquía e imperio*, vol. III, *Historia de España* (Madrid: Editorial Crítica, 2007), 470. On Elizabeth I, see Bernard Cottret, *La royauté au féminin: Élisabeth Ire d'Angleterre* (Paris: Fayard, 2009); Wallace T. MacCaffrey, *Queen Elizabeth and the Making of Policy, 1572–88* (Princeton: University Press, 1981); idem, *Elizabeth I* (London: Edward Arnold, 1991).

79 My translation from 'Mensagem d'ElRei de Portugal, á Rainha d'Inglaterra contra os Inglezes que ião á Guiné…, April 1561', in Barros y Sousa, *Quadro elementar*, vol. XV, 104–6: '*E como entre outros prejuizos causados pelos Inglezes aos Portuguezes, um dos mais consideráveis era o de terem ido navios Inglezes aos portos da Mina e da Malagueta, e a outras Províncias marítimas da Coroa de Portugal, sendo a navegação e commercio dellas legitima propriedade da mesma Coroa adquirida pelos predecessores do dito Rei, á custa de grandes despezas, e do sangue e fadigas dos Portuguezes, e por elles descobertas, e que nenhum Príncipe da Christandade havia disputado a antiga posse das mesmas terras; á vista do que el Rei de Portugal pedia á dita Rainha d'Inglaterra que prohibisse positivamente aos seus vassallos de terem a audácia de ir áquellas regiões*'. See also

The English government responded that the queen had not authorised the seizure of Portuguese property and assured that she would address the matter. However, the English side expressed concerns over the poor treatment of their traders and questioned Portugal's assertion that it could exclude them from trade.[80] Lusitanian envoys pressed their demands, asking the queen to issue a decree – to be announced in all English ports – banning her subjects from sailing across Portuguese closed seas under penalty of death and confiscation of goods. Special emphasis was placed on Guinea and Brazil.[81] Shortly after, Elizabeth I issued a decree instructing coastal authorities and her subjects to respect Portuguese properties.[82] She also urged her captains not to sail towards Portuguese overseas possessions. However, for the first time, she argued it was unfair for her subjects to be forbidden to sail across the seas claimed by the king of Portugal, Sebastian I (r. 1557–1578). Overall, she adopted an ambiguous stance, mindful that England was not yet prepared for an escalation.[83] On 1 May 1561, Elizabeth I ordered the 'High Admyrall of England' to ensure that English captains stayed clear of Portuguese overseas possessions.[84] In a subsequent letter, she assured Sebastian I that she had taken steps to that end. However, she expressed hope that her goodwill might encourage the Portuguese king to allow English merchants to trade peacefully, as prescribed by 'the law of nations (*Direito das Gentes*) for merchants of all nations'.[85]

Calendar of State Papers Foreign: Elizabeth, vol. 3, 8 April 1561, n. 97–8, 54–5; Nuno Vila-Santa, 'Fighting for a *Mare Clausum* and Secret Science: France, England and Spain in the Strategies of Ambassador Dantas (1557–1568)', *Vegueta. Anuario de la Facultad de Geografía e Historia*, 23(2) (2023), 1115–51.

80 'Resposta do governo Inglez ás reclamações do enviado Portuguez, dada em 8 d'Abril', in Barros y Sousa, *Quadro elementar*, vol. XV, 106–10; *Calendar of State Papers Foreign: Elizabeth*, vol. 3, 8 April 1561, n. 99, 55.

81 Barros y Sousa, *Quadro elementar*, vol. XV, 110.

82 'Salvo-conducto da Rainha Isabel, ordenando aos Inglezes que não perturbassem os Portuguezes no seu Commercio com a Africa, prohibindo que fossem á Guiné ..., 24 April 1561', ibid., 112; *Calendar of State Papers Foreign: Elizabeth*, vol. 3, 24 April 1561, n. 138, 78.

83 Ibidem. Sebastian I acceded to the throne when he was three years old, therefore a regency was established during his minority. See Disney, *A History of Portugal*, 172–97.

84 'Ordem da Rainha Isabel expedida ao Lord Almirante d'Inglaterra, 1 May 1561', in Barros y Sousa, *Quadro elementar*, vol. XV, 114. '*para que não ignorassem a resolução que havia tomado de prohibir que se navegasse para es partes d'Africa, ou da Ethiopia, bem como para a Mina...*'.

85 'Carta da Rainha Isabel a ElRei D. Sebastião..., 22 November 1561', ibid., 115, '*afim de que os vassallos Britanicos podessem gozar pacificamente da mesma liberdade estabelecida pelo Direito das Gentes em favor dos mercadores de todas as Nações*'.

Diplomatic exchanges continued in the following years, with Portuguese envoys deploying their arsenal of legal titles and arguments. They continued to refer to discovery, the fight against the 'Saracens', missionary efforts, and the longstanding, uncontested monopoly over navigation as justifications for Portugal's claims.[86] On her part, Elizabeth I noted that the Portuguese had always been welcomed to trade across her dominions, so it seemed logical to expect the same from Portugal. It goes without saying that such an argument was seen as unfair by the Portuguese, since at the time, only them, and not the English, possessed colonies and oceanic commercial interests. Lusitanian diplomats maintained that while English traders were welcomed to trade in mainland Portugal and the Atlantic Islands, they could not sail farther south than the Azores.

The correspondence frequently referenced the sea and navigation; the Portuguese envoys for example stating that: 'it was demonstrated that the Kings of Portugal enjoy peacefully and publicly and without opposition not only the benefits and advantages of these countries, but also the navigation of the seas that they bathe'.[87] Portuguese diplomacy also referred to the title used in official documents by Lusitanian kings as further proof of the wide acceptance of their exclusive titles by other princes.[88] Portuguese ambassadors specified that their kings had long acquired the right under the

86 *Calendar of State Papers Foreign: Elizabeth*, vol. 5, 20 May 1562, n. 28, 41–2.

87 My translation from 'Exposição do Embaixador de Portugal em Londres, dirigida á Rainha Isabel, para mostrar que os Inglezes não devião ir commerciar á Guiné, 22 May 1562', in Barros y Sousa, *Quadro elementar*, vol. XV, 123: '*Era demonstrado que os Reis de Portugal gozarão pacificamente e publicamente e sem opposição nâo só dos proveitos e vantagens dos ditos paizes, mas tambem da navegação dos mares que os banhão*'.

88 Ibidem: '...*de cuja posse e direitos erão provas os dictados de que usavão os mesmos Soberanos de Portugal, a saber de Senhor de Guiné, da conquista y navegação e commercio da Elhiopia, da Arabia, da Persia, e da India, tilulos que não forão jámais disputados, nem contestados por nenhum Principe Christão, por terem sido justamente alcançados com grandissimos trabalhos, tendo os Principes da Christandade antes louvado os Portuguezes de terem emprehendido uma cousa, que não só se julgava duvidosa e incerta, mas também impossível segundo a opinião dos mais famosos historiadores, mathematicos e cosmographos que havião existido*'. My translation: '...of the said possession and rights were proof the titles that the said Sovereigns of Portugal employed, namely Lord of Guinea, of the conquest and navigation and trade of Ethiopia, Arabia, Persia, and India, of titles that were never contested, nor disputed, by any Christian Prince; because they had been justly achieved with great efforts, the Princes of Christendom having previously praised the Portuguese for undertaking something which was not only considered doubtful and uncertain, but even impossible, by the most famous historians, mathematicians, and cosmographers that ever existed'.

law of nations (*ius gentium*) to exclude others from navigation towards their possessions.[89]

The English Privy Council eventually revised its official position. On the one hand, it acknowledged that English traders had to respect Portuguese properties and vessels, as well as to stay clear of Portuguese overseas bases. On the other hand, it began to question the legitimacy of Portugal's ban on navigation to Guinea and Brazil. In particular, the English government grew increasingly resistant to restrictions on oceanic navigation, especially when English ships sailed to areas with little or no Portuguese presence.[90] In any case, the Portuguese government remained distrustful of English commitments to halt voyages to Guinea. Portuguese agents in London were instructed to monitor English vessels, noting their numbers, armament, and intended destinations to alert officials in West Africa or Brazil. The instructions given to Ambassador Ayres Cardoso in 1564 illustrate this vigilance.[91] Upon his arrival in London, Cardoso quickly lodged fresh complaints with the English government.[92]

Meanwhile, the Privy Council complained that peaceful English merchants were often apprehended and treated as pirates by Portuguese authorities. The Portuguese countered by reiterating the validity of their exclusive claims and the unopposed nature of their maritime expansion that allowed them to pun-

89 'Replica do Embaixador de Portugal em Londres á resposta dada pelo Conselho Privado da Rainha…, 7 June 1562', ibid., 130; *Calendar of State Papers Foreign: Elizabeth,* vol. 5, 7 June 1562, n. 158, 76.

90 'Resposta do Conselho Privado á Memoria apresentada pelo Embaixador de Portugal", 15 June 1562', in Barros y Sousa, *Quadro elementar*, vol. XV, 135: '*Que a mesma Rainha não tinha visto tudo quanto se linha escripto acerca das ditas navegações. Que os autores que ella tinha lido não sanccionavão, nem combatiào os pontos que tratavão da possessão d'EIRei de Portugal, e não contestavão nenhuma parte do que elle então possuia, nem que elle possuia mais do que podia desejar. Conclue, que a Rainha estava determinada a impedir que seus súbditos fossem commerciar onde El Rei de Portugal exercia a Soberania, e lhe pagavão tributo, e onde tinha Fortalezas; mas não nos outros logares em que o dito Rei nào tinha Soberania*'. My translation: 'That the Queen had not seen all that is written about these navigations. That the authors that she had read did not sanction nor fight the points that dealt with the possession of the King of Portugal, and did not contest any part of what he then possessed, nor that he possessed more than he could have wished. In conclusion, the Queen was determined to prevent her subjects from trading where the King of Portugal exercised sovereignty, received tribute as well as where he held strongholds; but not in other places where the said King did not have sovereignty'.

91 'Instrucções passadas por ElRei D. Sebastião enviando á Corte de Londres Ayres Cardoso, September 1564', ibid., 156.

92 *Calendar of State Papers Foreign: Elizabeth,* vol. 7, 19 November 1562, n. 804, 246.

ish interlopers.[93] They also referred to Portuguese-Castilian treaties dividing the oceans and to pontifical donation.[94] Moreover, Sebastian I's envoys boasted that earlier Portuguese kings had conquered, or received allegiance from, all regions such as 'Ethiopia, Arabia, etc.', leaving no 'non-Portuguese' destinations for the English to trade within the southern Atlantic and beyond. They stressed that Portuguese laws required even Lusitanian subjects to obtain royal consent before engaging in oceanic navigation towards Brazil or West Africa.[95]

In 1564, Elizabeth I finally stated that her subjects had the right to sail to all regions not under direct Portuguese control. She agreed only to exclude her subjects from Lusitanian settlements, rejecting Sebastian I's claim to dominion over vast regions based on control of a few coastal strongholds.[96] This marked a growing influence in Elizabethan diplomatic circles of the idea that the oceans constituted free highways and lay outside the control of the Iberian powers. Spain and Portugal could exercise authority only over their immediate overseas possessions. In this context, English captains began lodging new complaints whenever Portuguese squadrons attacked them on the high seas, particularly when it happened in areas far from Portuguese bases.[97]

Although peace officially continued between England and Portugal, Lisbon and London viewed maritime incidents through opposing lenses. From Portugal's perspective, their actions defended established rights against trespassers and pirates. Conversely, the Privy Council considered these attacks unwarranted acts of war in peacetime, targeting legitimate traders. For instance, in 1568, Elizabeth I demanded reparations for the capture of an English ship, whose crew was detained in Mina. The Portuguese ambassador rejected these demands, stating that foreigners caught in Guinean waters faced capital punishment. Moreover, he demanded 60,000 ducats to compensate for English piratical acts.[98] In retaliation, the queen issued letters of reprisals to the

93 'Replica á resposta dada em nome da Rainha d'Inglaterra ao Embaixador de Portugal em 15 junho deste anuo de 1562, 19 June 1562', in Barros y Sousa, *Quadro Elementar*, 137–50; *Calendar of State Papers Foreign: Elizabeth*, vol. 5, 19 June 1562, n. 222, 107.

94 Barros y Sousa, *Quadro elementar*, vol. XV, 142.

95 Ibid., 141–2.

96 'Resposta do Conselho da Rainha d'Inglaterra á representação do Enviado de Portugal Ayres Cardoso, 24 November 1564', ibid., 161–2; *Calendar of State Papers Foreign: Elizabeth*, vol. 7, 24 November 1564, n. 820, 250.

97 For instance in 1567, see Barros y Sousa, *Quadro elementar*, vol. XV, 163.

98 *Calendar of State Papers Foreign: Elizabeth*, vol. 8, 24 November 1564, n. 2224, 466.

traders who had suffered losses, who could seize Portuguese ships and goods to recover their losses.[99]

In the instructions given to her envoy Thomas Wilson, Elizabeth I rejected the accusation of piracy, insisting that the English sailing towards Guinea were simple traders. In addition, Wilson was instructed to stand against any Portuguese argument based on the authority of the Pope, 'that she the Queen does not recognise'.[100] Anglo-Portuguese diplomacy remained tense throughout the 1570s. Despite efforts to resolve disputes, disagreements over the scope of English navigation persisted. That said, the parties managed to preserve the official state of peace, though constellated by mutual acts of violence on the high seas. Trade embargoes and projects of treaties of amity alternated in rapid succession in the 1560s.[101] These discussions were largely put aside in the 1570s and negotiations re-centred on the recuperation of goods, reparations, and attempts to curb maritime violence.[102] For instance, a draft treaty was signed by the envoys Francisco Giraldes and Francis Walsingham in October 1576, but it was never ratified. Article 7 envisaged freedom of navigation for the English to Portugal, Madeira, the Azores, and vice versa. Nothing was said on navigation beyond the Azores since the issue remained contentious.[103] English traders were thus left to navigate those waters at their own risk.

The diplomatic deadlock ended abruptly in 1580 when Philip II of Spain succeeded the last Portuguese king of the House of Aviz, Henry II (r. 1578–1580).[104] In April 1581, the Portuguese Cortes convened in Tomar officially recognised Philip as their lawful monarch, in exchange for his solemn oath to preserve the laws, customs, and maritime sphere of influence of the Lusitanian kingdom. Thus, the 'Iberian Union' between Spain and Portugal was formed, providing both new resources and challenges to Philip II's diplomacy.[105]

---

99 'Letters of marque ..., 11 February 1569', in Marsden, *Documents*, vol. I, 184–8.

100 'Instrucções dadas pela Rainha Isabel d'Inglaterra a Thomaz Wilson, mandado a Portugal como Enviado d'Inglaterra, June 1567', in Barros y Sousa, *Quadro elementar*, vol. XV, 169: '*que ella Rainha a não reconhencia*'.

101 For instance, see the articles of agreement in *Calendar of State Papers Foreign: Elizabeth*, vol. 9, 27 December 1571, n. 2191, 579; ibid., vol. 10, 1 January 1572, n. 1, 1.

102 *Calendar of State Papers Foreign: Elizabeth*, vol. 12, 1577–78, 417.

103 'Tratado original entre Portugal e Inglaterra ..., 29 October 1576', in Barros y Sousa, *Quadro elementar*, vol. XV, 302.

104 See Fernando Bouza Álvarez, *Portugal en la monarquía Hispánica (1580–1640), Felipe II, las cortes de Tomar y la génesis del Portugal Católico* (Ph.D. dissertation, Universidad Complutense de Madrid, 1987); Elliott, *Imperial Spain*, 268–74; Escamilla, *Le siècle d'or de l'Espagne*, 581–96; Disney, *A History of Portugal*, 176, 198–200.

105 John Elliott, for instance, estimated that the combined Portuguese and Spanish merchant fleets – with 250.000–300.000 tons available – still outnumbered those of other

Immediately, Anglo-Portuguese relations were subsumed into the broader, intermittent struggle between Elizabeth I and Philip II, leading to outright English opposition to Portuguese closed sea policies.[106]

One of Philip II's councillors, Cardinal de Granvelle, urged the king to permanently relocate his capital from Madrid to Lisbon to improve communication across the components of his empire and to better oversee the Atlantic, which Granvelle and others regarded as the strategic battleground of the future. However, the king remained in Lisbon only until March 1583 before returning to Madrid, deep in the heart of Castile. Due to the sustained increase in the flow of precious metals from the Americas, the 1580s and the 1590s probably represented the last historical juncture in which the Iberian fleets still had the necessary resources to impose the respect of their 'claimed seas', at least in certain regions.[107]

Since the 1560s, Spanish envoys in London had consistently raised objections to English expeditions such as those led by John Hawkins, which they viewed as outright piracy. Nevertheless, when Francis Drake returned from his circumnavigation of the globe in 1580, Queen Elizabeth I received him 'graciously', as the chronicler William Camden noted, and even knighted him.[108] Drake's exploits in the Atlantic and Pacific oceans on the constituted a flagrant violation of King Philip II's closed sea pretensions, which now the queen stoutly refused to recognise.[109] Bernardino de Mendoza, the Spanish resident ambassador in London (1578–1584), repeatedly complained about the depredations of the Sea Dogs. In 1580, Elizabeth I rebutted that the Spaniards had violated the 'Law of the Nations' by attempting to prevent other nations from sailing to the Americas and trading there. In her view, the Span-

nations, compared e.g. the c.230.000 tons of the Low Countries and c.45.000 tons of England. See Elliott, *Imperial Spain*, 276–7.

106 From the mid-1580s the English government liberally issued letters of reprisals against Philip II's subjects. See Marsden, *Documents*, vol. I, 236–80; 'Commission to Sir John Hawkins and Sir Francis Drake against the Spaniards, 29 January 1576', idem., 284; Prestage, 'The Anglo-Portuguese Alliance', 80; Escamilla, *Le siècle d'or de l'Espagne*, 615; Disney, *A History of Portugal*, 198–220; Rodger, *The Safeguard of the Sea*, 238–53.

107 Elliott, *Imperial Spain*, 275. However, vast resources were dissipated in expensive endeavours such as the attempt to invade England in 1588, or the war against the rebellious provinces in the Low Countries.

108 Camden, *The history of the most renowned and victorious Princess Elizabeth*, II, 254.

109 Theutenberg, 'Mare Liberum et Mare Clausum', 490. For an interesting account of Elizabethan court at the time, see Retha Warnicke, 'Diplomatic rumor-mongering: an analysis of Mendoza's report on Elizabeth I's audience with Scottish ambassadors in 1583', in Robert S. Sturges (ed.), *Law and Sovereignty in the Middle Ages and the Renaissance* (Turnhout: Brepols, 2011), 115–31.

iards had drawn the mischief on themselves by doing so.[110] The queen declared that she could not comprehend the basis on which her subjects were excluded from the 'Indies', rejecting Iberian titles of possession, especially pontifical donation:

> The queen does not acknowledge that her subjects and those of other nations may be excluded from the Indies on the claim that these have been donated to the king of Spain by the pope, whose authority to invest the Spanish king with the New World as a fief she does not recognise. The Spaniards have no claim to property there except that they have established a few settlements and named rivers and capes. This donation of what does not belong to the donor and his imaginary right of property ought not to prevent other princes from carrying their commerce in those regions or establishing colonies there in places not inhabited by the Spaniards. Such action would in no way violate the law of nations, since prescription without possession is not valid.[111]

William Camden reported that, after refusing to accept Spanish titles over the Indies, Queen Elizabeth I shifted her attention to the ocean. She asserted that her subjects had the right to sail the vast oceans freely, 'seeing that the use of the Sea and Air is common to all'.[112] In her view, neither nations nor individuals could acquire exclusive titles of possession or ownership over the ocean, 'forasmuch as neither Nature, nor publick use and custome permitteth any possession thereof'.[113] By invoking the law of nature, Elizabeth I alluded to the principle of freedom of the seas, notably referencing the Roman concept of *res communis omnium*. As previously mentioned, Elizabeth I had already developed these arguments in her controversies with the kings of Portugal. It is less known that she developed similar arguments in her dealings with the kings of Denmark-Norway – a matter to which we will now turn our attention.[114]

---

110 Ibidem.

111 'Queen Elizabeth of England to the Spanish Envoy in London, Mendoza in 1580', in Grewe, *Fontes*, II, 151.

112 Camden, *The history of the most renowned and victorious Princess Elizabeth*, II, 254.

113 Ibidem. She was referring to the Roman law distinction between private and public property. See *supra* ch. 1, 3.

114 Theutenberg, 'Mare Liberum et Mare Clausum', 490.

3.3 *Elizabeth I and Dano-Norwegian Claims*

The 'Indian' oceans were not the only issue at stake. While questioning Iberian maritime policies, Elizabeth I also had to contend with the long-standing Dano-Norwegian claims over what are now the Norwegian Sea and the North Atlantic, or *dominium maris septentrionalis*.[115] To some extent, these claims had weakened, following the pawning of Orkney and Shetland to Scotland in 1468.[116] Furthermore, as the centre of power of the Dano-Norwegian monarchy – ruled by the Oldenburg dynasty – was Copenhagen, the *mare sptentrionalis* was not the foremost concern of the royal court. Civil wars and dynastic struggles in the 1520s and 1530s further hampered the dual monarchy's ability to effectively govern the northern periphery of the Oldenburg conglomerate. In this context, English sailors ceased paying the navigation licences stipulated in fifteenth-century treaties.[117] Nonetheless, Dano-Norwegian royal decrees, such as those of 1524 and 1536, continued to reaffirm the prohibition on foreign navigation, north of Bergen.[118]

In the 1550s, the English discovered a maritime route to the White Sea and established a new trading link with northwestern Russia, culminating in the creation of the Muscovy Company in 1555.[119] Frederick II of Denmark-Norway (r. 1559–1588) objected to this English trade, viewing it as an infringement of Norway's traditional closed sea policies in the North Atlantic. In July 1577,

115 I treated in more detail the issue at hand in: Stefano Cattelan, 'Claims of Dominion and the Freedom of the Sea: Diplomatic Tensions between England and Denmark-Norway in the Late Tudor Period', *Journal on European History of Law*, 12(2) (2021), 29–42. See also Fulton, *The Sovereignty of the Sea*, 108–12.

116 Barbara E. Crawford, 'The Pawning of Orkney and Shetland: A Reconsideration of the Events of 1460–9', *The Scottish Historical Review*, 48(145) (1969), 35–53.

117 See *supra* ch. 1, 3.

118 For the texts in question, *Diplomatarium Norvegicum*, VII, 606 and 749. See also 'Traité fait entre Frederic II. Roi de Danemarc &c., & les Villes Anseatiques, 25 juillet 1560', in Dumont, *CUD*, V.1, 67–76. In 1523, King Christian II was deposed in the wake of domestic rebellions and international tensions that led his uncle Frederick I (r. 1523–1533) to the Dano-Norwegian throne. Then, in 1534–1536, the Counts' Feud saw different factions within the Oldenburg state fighting for the succession to the late king. In the same period, Sweden, under the newly established Vasa dynasty, permanently seceded from the Nordic Union. See Lockart, *Denmark*, 11–28.

119 See Felicity J. Stout, *Exploring Russia in the Elizabethan Commonwealth: The Muscovy Company and Giles Fletcher, the Elder (1546–1611)* (Manchester: University Press, 2015); Maria Salomon Arel, *English Trade and Adventure to Russia in the Early Modern Era: The Muscovy Company, 1603–1649* (Lahnam: Lexington Books, 2019); Louis Sicking and Remco (C. H.) van Rhee, 'The English Search for a Northeast Passage to Asia Reconsidered: How 'Flemish' fishermen put the Edward Bonaventure in jeopardy on its return journey in 1554', *The Mariner's Mirror*, 105(4) (2019), 388–406.

Elizabeth I requested Frederick II to appoint commissioners and initiate direct negotiations on the matter. Instructions provided to her envoys asserted that no records of treaties limiting English navigation had been found in English archives.[120] The envoys were also instructed to emphasise that these voyages to Russia had been ongoing since the reigns of Edward VI and Mary I (r. 1547–1553; 1553–1558) without significant objections, thus constituting a 'trade of long continuance'.[121] In August 1577, commissioners from both sides convened in Hamburg. While the Dano-Norwegian representatives acknowledged the general principle that the sea was free and common to all, they argued that this principle could be modified or extinguished by treaties, longstanding practices, or prescription.[122]

Two years later, Frederick II raised concerns about alleged English 'piratical activities', in what he considered 'his' waters. On two occasions, some Lubeckers and Norwegians had been attacked while en route to Iceland. These merchants had paid navigation licences to Danish authorities and therefore Frederick II considered them under his protection, particularly since the attacks occurred within waters he claimed as exclusively Dano-Norwegian.[123] In the summer of 1582, the English envoy Peregrine Bertie travelled to Denmark to invest Frederick II with the Order of the Garter. However, the mission's underlying objective was to improve the treatment of English merchants. In 1583, new negotiations were held in the Danish town of Haderslev.[124] During these discussions, the Dano-Norwegian delegation reiterated their claim that Norway had long exercised dominion over the shores of the 'Northern Sea' and, by extension, the interjacent waters between Greenland, Iceland, and Norway. They contended that any rule of natural law asserting the commonality of the sea had, in this case, been overridden by established practices under the law of nations.[125] Nevertheless, an agreement was reached: English ships en-

120 The queen asked the Lord Keeper to find the 'old treaties' which were relevant to the dispute, see *Calendar of State Papers Foreign: Elizabeth*, vol. 12, 9 July 1577, 4.

121 Ibid., 20 July 1577, n. 28, 18–9.

122 Ibid., August 1577, n. 171, 126. See also Raestad, *La mer territoriale*, 77–8. The Danes were still referring to the conception of the Northern Sea as an interior sea.

123 *Calendar of State Papers Foreign: Elizabeth*, vol. 12, 5 February and 22 February 1579, n. 577–8, 428–9. The king lamented that these pirates were well-connected to members of her court.

124 Camden, *The history of the most renowned and victorious Princess Elizabeth*, III, 274; Raestad, *La mer territoriale*, 78; Cattelan, 'Claims of Dominium', 37–8. For background information, see Lars Laursen, *Danmark-Norges Traktater 1523–1750. Med dertil hørende Aktstykker*, II (København: Gad 1912), n. 31, 612–27.

125 Raestad, *La mer territoriale*, 78.

gaged in the Muscovy trade would be permitted to sail through 'Norwegian waters':

> The Company of English merchants trading to Muscovy shall lawfully pass through the North seas to the port of St. Nicolas; and if they be compelled by tempest or other violent means, they may safely enter into any port of Norway or Iceland, even those that by former conventions between the Kings of England and Denmark were prohibited, and may there stay and depart at convenient times for their commodity, so as they do not traffic in any of the prohibited parts of Norway or Iceland without the king's special licence nor offer any injury to the inhabitants and abstain from all manner of evil-doing.[126]

In exchange for this concession, English merchants accepted to pay an annual fee to the Dano-Norwegian Crown: '100 rose-nobles (*nobiles rosatos*) during the continuance of this grant, the first payment to begin in the spring, 1584 [...]. This award shall be duly observed during the lives of both princes, but after the decease of either of them it shall be lawful to leave it, without breach of any former league'.[127] Hence, even though Elizabeth I still acknowledged Dano-Norwegian pretensions, English merchants obtained the right of passage that they coveted.[128] The agreement was understood to last as long as the respective rulers, Elizabeth I and Frederick II, lived. However, the Nordic ruler died soon after in 1588.

Dano-Norwegian claims found new vigour with the accession to the throne of Christian IV (r. 1588–1648), especially after he began his personal rule in 1596. For a time, he was widely regarded as the most powerful ruler in northern Europe and a standard-bearer of the Protestant cause.[129] He enlarged and

126 *Calendar of State Papers Foreign: Elizabeth*, vol. 17, 22 June 1583, n. 382, 411–2. For the whole text of the agreement, see Laursen, *Traktater*, 632–8, at 637.

127 Ibidem. See also *Fisheries* case, ICJ 1951, Counter-Memorial submitted by the Government of the Kingdom of Norway, 240.

128 The terms of the agreement were rather general. Queen Elizabeth issued a new document interpreting it. See *Calendar of State Papers Foreign: Elizabeth*, vol. 18, 12 October 1583, n. 162, 139–40; Laursen, *Traktater*, 642–4. See also Frank N. Stagg, *North Norway. A History* (London: George Allen & Unwin Ltd., 1952), 83.

129 Stefano Cattelan, 'Cristiano IV di Danimarca-Norvegia (r. 1588–1648): potere navale e diplomazia nell'Europa del Nord', *Nuova antologia militare*, 3(11) (2022), 195–228; Birger Mikkelsen, *Christian IV: A Pictorial Biography* (København: Nordisk forlag for videnskab og teknik, 1988); Bodil Wamberg, *Christian IV – en mand under indflydelse* (København: G.E.C. Gad, 1993); Iben Tandgaard and Gregers Dirckinck-Holmfeld, *Christian 4.s København* (København; Politikens Forlag, 2006); Lockart, *Denmark*, 127–47.

embellished its capital, Copenhagen, equipping it with modern fortifications and a state-of-the-art arsenal. He also strengthened the Dano-Norwegian fleet, a lifelong interest of his, thereby reinforcing Denmark's control over the Øresund.[130] A significant portion of his wealth came from the Sound Toll, which he raised multiple times to exert influence and conduct economic warfare against his adversaries. In the early decades of his reign, Christian IV successfully maintained Danish pre-dominance in the Baltic Sea (*dominium maris baltici*) against regional rivals such as Sweden.[131]

In the 1590s, he reaffirmed Norwegian closed sea policies in the pelagic zone between Iceland and Norway, as 'lord of both shores' and 'master of the sea'. In 1597, he dispatched ambassadors to London to protest English violations of Norwegian 'claimed seas' policies, particularly regarding fisheries near Iceland and northern Norway. He insisted that 'the fishing should be lawfully and regularly managed according to the ancient Leagues', citing fifteenth-century treaties in which England had acknowledged Dano-Norwegian 'claimed seas' as the legal basis for regulating navigation and fishing in the North Atlantic.[132] In 1599, Christian IV personally commanded a royal fleet to northern Norway, during which several English ships were captured. These included Muscovy traders as well as fishing vessels operating near Norwegian coasts without royal licences.[133] Not by chance then, Christian IV enjoyed being represented as the god of the sea Neptune by court artists and during public festivities (see Figure 3.3 below).

In 1600, Norwegian authorities continued to detain a group of fishermen from the English port of Hull. Elizabeth I wrote to Christian IV, protesting this action and asserting that seagoing fishing (*maris piscatione*) was free under the law of nations and the customs of all nations (*jure gentium omniumque nationum moribus libera*). She also argued for her subjects' right to access Norwegian harbours for trade and shelter during storms.[134] In the same year, Dano-Norwegian and English commissioners convened in Embden to discuss

---

130 Martin Bellamy, *Christian IV and his Navy* (Leiden: Brill, 2006), 9–25.

131 Ibid., 25–34.

132 Camden, *The history of the most renowned and victorious Princess Elizabeth*, IV, 539; see *supra* ch. 1, 3.

133 Fulton, *The Sovereignty of the Sea*, 108–9.

134 'A Regina ad Regem Daniæ, super piscatione in alto mare, 1600', in *Foedera*, VII, 2–3: '*Cum igitur maris usus ad piscationem littorum vero ac portuum ad negotationem exercendam, ac tempestatum vim declinandam, amicorum principum subditis negari plerumque non solent*'.

the disputed issue of navigation, without results.[135] On the one hand, the English contended that earlier Dano-Norwegian monarchs had ceased collecting licence fees, claiming that 'fault of the omission was not in the English, but in the Danes'.[136] Moreover, they stated that 'the famousest lawyers have given their opinion' in favour of the idea that the sea 'is free and common by the Law of Nations, and cannot be engrossed by any prince whatsoever'.[137] On the other hand, Dano-Norwegian commissioners reaffirmed their traditional position. The English chronicler William Camden remarked that Elizabeth's envoys complained that the Danes had left in haste the negotiations because they aimed at:

> the continuation of things in the same state they then were, that they might every day at their pleasure exact new customs on the English in the straight called *Oresund*, confiscate their ships and goods by new orders and decrees, and wholly prohibited their fishing in the open Northern Ocean, and their navigation by that sea into *Moscovia*.[138]

Therefore, two seemingly distinct maritime issues – the crossing of the Oresund and navigation across the 'Northern Ocean' – became the primary bones of contention between the two Protestant crowns. However, Arnold Raestad identified a deeper connection between the two disputes. In his view, governmental circles in Copenhagen feared that the new route to Russia around northern Norway might compete with the Oresund, diverting trade and diminishing the payment of tolls to Danish officials in Elsinore.[139] The Dano-Norwegian court was certainly aware that it was far more difficult to exact payments at the remote fortress of Vardøhus in northern Norway than in the Sound, close to the Oldenburg seat of power.

The parties reconvened in the northern German city of Bremen during the winter of 1602.[140] The detailed instructions prepared by Secretary of State Robert Cecil (1563–1612) for the English envoys underscore the signifi-

135 Camden, *The history of the most renowned and victorious Princess Elizabeth*, IV, 594–5. Camden suggests that Elizabeth I asked for an arbitration and Christian IV refused.

136 Ibidem.

137 Ibidem.

138 Ibid., IV, 595–6.

139 Raestad, *La mer territoriale*, 77.

140 Camden, *The history of the most renowned and victorious Princess Elizabeth*, IV, 649. Cf. Cattelan, 'Claims of Dominium', 38–41.

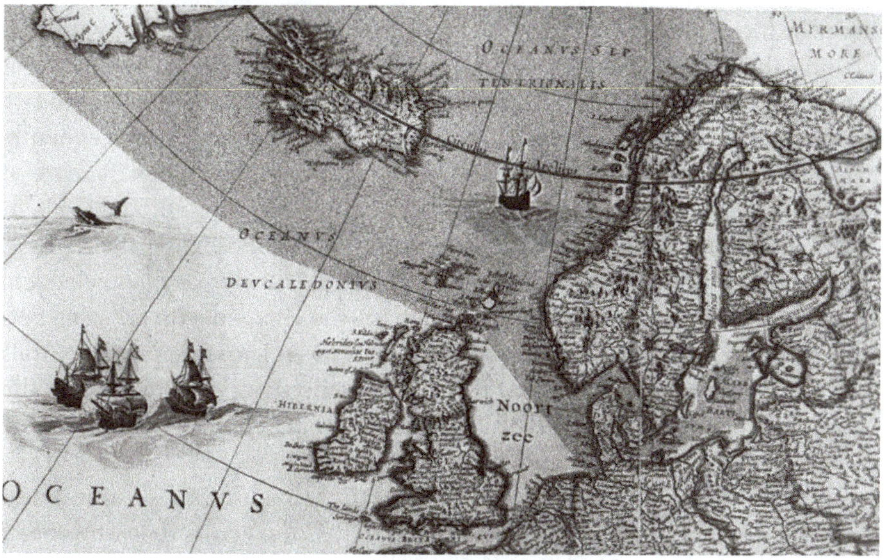

FIGURE 3.1 Detail from Willelm Janszoon Bleau's map of Europe, 1617. The shaded sea area roughly shows Dano-Norwegian maritime claims in the 'Oceanus Septentrionalis'.
SOURCE: BELLAMY, *CHRISTIAN IV AND HIS NAVY*

FIGURE 3.2 Kronborg castle, Elsinore and the Oresund from the 1580s geography treatise *Civitates Orbis Terrarum*, vol. IV, map 26

cance of the discussions.[141] Firstly, the commissioners were tasked with persuading the Danes to avoid placing undue emphasis on older treaties that were unfavourable to England. Secondly, they were instructed to advocate for the interests of English merchants traversing the Sound, who frequently complained of being 'verie much abused there, as well by a daily increase of exactions, as also by the uncertainties of the duties required, with taking light occasions to stay them, searching their ships, and confiscating their goods, punishing the innocent for the fault of another'.[142] Thus, while acknowledging Danish authority over the Sound, the envoys were charged with securing better treatment for English merchants and ensuring a clearer definition of tolls and their amounts. Thirdly, the English representatives were to address the issue of navigation in the Northern Sea, arguing that 'it is a very unreasonable servility to which our merchants (i.e. the Muscovy Company) are tied'.[143] They were also instructed to emphasize that certain ancient treaties – not better specified – had guaranteed the English free navigation across the 'King's Seas' (of Norway) and to highlight how other nations:

> In the Straights of England, Spaine and the Adriatique Gulf, esteem the Sea as common for passage, it being a high strained Soverantie to loke for such a Power over another Monarch in a Sea of such dimension as is between his Countries and Island, when it is well known that none of our ships do ever come within the sight of land.[144]

Therefore, the 1602 instructions underlined how vast the area claimed by Denmark-Norway was, framing it as an open ocean rather than an inland sea. The document also emphasised that English vessels typically navigated beyond the sight of land, thereby subtly linking legitimate maritime claims to the visual limit from the coast. The English envoys were directed to argue that it would be excessive for one sovereign to claim 'sovereignty' in a manner that restricted another sovereign's powers at sea under such circumstances.[145] Furthermore, the envoys were authorised to threaten reciprocal measures, including the imposition of similar tolls and navigational restrictions 'upon all

141 'Instructions aux Ambassadeurs pour traiter avec ceux du Roi de Danemarc, 1602', in Rymer, *Foedera*, VII, 2, 25–31.

142 Ibid., 26.

143 Ibid., 27.

144 Ibidem.

145 This point is particularly interesting as it seems to underline that only under certain special conditions, a monarch could limit the rights of another ruler (or peer) on the sea.

ships of his country [i.e. Christian IV's] that shall pass throw anie of our channels, or about our Kingdoms Dominions and Islands'.[146]

The instructions referenced the dynastic turmoil faced by the Danish Crown in the sixteenth century, which the English considered a key reason for the cessation of seven-year license payments. Additionally, the English claimed that previous diplomatic correspondence had permitted fishing in northern waters, suggesting that Christian IV's predecessors had, to some extent, relinquished their rights.[147] The English envoys criticised the Dano-Norwegian authorities for attempting to reassert control over the northern seas through brute force. Once again, the law of nations was invoked as the foundation for England's legal arguments:

> And you shall further declare that the Lawe of Nations alloweth of fishing in the sea every where, as also of using ports and coasts of Princes in amitie for commerce, and avoiding danger of tempests; so that if our men be barred therof, it should be by some contract: We acknowledge none of that nature, but rather of conformity with the Lawe of Nations in these respects, as declaring the same for the removing of all clayme and doubt; so that it is manifest by denying of this fishing and much more, for spoyling our Subjects for this respect, We have been injured against the Lawe of Nations, expreslie declared by contract, as in the aforesaid Treaties, and the King's oun Letters of 85.[148]

Concerning the issue of payment of licences, where it was difficult to deny that previous English sovereigns had yielded on the matter, the instructions stated that:

> If our Predecessors yelded thereunto, it was more than by Law of Nations was due, yelded perhaps upon some special consideration, yet growing out of use it remained due by the Law of Nations, what was otherwise due before all contract; wherefore by omitting licence, it cannot be concluded in any case, that the right of fishing, due by the Lawe of Nations, faileth.[149]

---

146 Rymer, *Foedera*, VII, 2, 28.

147 Ibidem: 'In this King's Great Grandfather and Grandfather's time there was never made anie mention thereof'.

148 Ibidem.

149 Ibidem.

Hence, even if past treaties had limited English rights, they contravened the prescribed legal status of the sea under the law of nations. The instructions further noted that 'sometimes in speech' Denmark-Norway claimed dominion over the pelagic area between Norway and Iceland, based on its control of the opposing shores. However, the English government argued that such legal right could not be held over such a vast area.[150] Only oversight (*protectio*) and jurisdiction (*iurisdictio*) could legitimately be exercised over the immediate coastal seas. In any case, navigation (passage) and fishing had to remain permissible. The logical conclusion of the English argument was that Dano-Norwegian authorities should protect English sailors rather than harass them. The English government drew upon its own policies in the seas surrounding the British Isles as a counterexample. Interestingly, they also referred to Venetian practices in the Adriatic Sea. The English contended that even the Venetians, who held dominion over the Adriatic, permitted fishing and merchant navigation.[151] The intention was to underline the exceptional and unreasonable nature of the restrictions imposed by Christian IV on other nations' freedom of navigation.

By this time, the English government regarded claims of dominion over marine spaces extending far beyond the shores as excessive, as they effectively undermined the common nature of the oceans. Consequently, the English delegation was instructed not to yield on principle, being directed to assert in Elizabeth I's name: 'We cannot with our Dignitie yeld that our subjects absolutelie be forbidden those seas ports or coasts for the use of fishing, negotiation and safetie', especially as the queen had already rejected similar closed sea claims from the Iberian countries: 'neither did We ever yeld anie such right to Spaine and Portugall for the Indian Seas'.[152] Nevertheless, the envoys were still granted discretion to reach an agreement with the Danes on more limited restrictions if they deemed it unavoidable:

> Yet yf our good Brother the King upon speciall reason maie desire diat we yeild to some renuinge of licence, or that some speciall place upon some speciall occasion, be reserved to his particular use in yours discretion, for Amitie sake, you may yeld thereunto; but then to define the

150 Ibidem. In this passage the legal status of the sea was opposed to that of rivers. The latter under Roman law could be owned under certain conditions as *res publicae*, especially if both their banks were controlled by the same state. This argument was later restated by both Vázquez y Menchaca and Grotius.

151 Though, in reality with a number of limitations, as we noted in ch. 1.

152 Rymer, *Foedera*, VII, 2, 29.

manner of seking licence in such sort as it be not prejudiciall to our subjects.[153]

It is worth noting how during the reign of Elizabeth I the three different 'claimed seas' traditions identified in the previous chapters began to converge and interact. Notably, Elizabeth I's 1602 instructions to her envoys included references to both Venetian state practice and Iberian claims, in this case used to reinforce English legal arguments in favour of the freedom of the seas. At the same time, Elizabethan diplomacy saw a revival of Roman law arguments and concepts such as the *res communis omnium*. This was not coincidental, as England's geographic position had long fostered interactions with the Iberian Peninsula, Nordic countries, and Mediterranean polities such as Venice and Genoa. Conversely, geography and distance hindered sustained and direct diplomatic and trade interactions between Venice and Denmark-Norway.

The 1602 instructions exemplify the English line of argumentation in relation to the legal status of the sea at the end of the Tudor dynasty. They also highlight the flexibility with which certain limitations on the freedom of navigation were still considered acceptable to secure a compromise with Christian IV. Indeed, England was not in a position to risk a full-scale conflict with another prominent Protestant – and traditionally friendly – kingdom while the Anglo-Spanish naval conflict endured.[154] Nevertheless, the Bremen conference of 1602 failed to yield tangible results, and diplomatic manoeuvring continued in subsequent months.[155] However, the death of Elizabeth I in March 1603 brought these negotiations to a temporary halt. Chapter 4 will examine how the new Stuart dynasty ascending to the English throne redefined English policies regarding the opposing doctrines of the freedom of the seas and the 'claimed seas'.

3.4 *Shifting Equilibria*

Under Elizabeth I, sea power and freedom of the sea arguments became instrumental in advancing English maritime trade, also in view of the establishment of overseas settlements, and improving England's international stand-

153 Ibidem.

154 For the report (dated 1 December 1602) sent by the English envoys to the Privy Council on the negotiation with the Danish counterpart, see Rymer, *Foedera*, VII, 2, 53.

155 'Regina ad Regem Dania', ibid., 33.

FIGURE 3.3 'Allegory of the Sound' by Isaacs Isaaczs, 1622. King Christian IV commissioned this highly symbolic painting to represent Danish sovereignty over the Sound and showcase his maritime power. The castle of Kronborg and Danish warships occupy the background. In the foreground, the lion refers to the heraldic symbol of the Kingdom of Denmark. Neptune embodies the king himself, who enjoyed being represented as the god of the sea. He leans on a vessel dispensing water, which likely symbolises the Sound as the 'Danish Stream'. A female figure adorned with a castle-shaped hat, traditionally a symbol of a city, likely alludes to either Elsinore, the site where the Sound tolls were collected, or Copenhagen, the Danish capital. Beside her, a cornucopia symbolises prosperity while the shells at the feet of the figures reflect the abundant riches of the sea. Together, these elements combine to convey to the observer Denmark's wealth, naval power and maritime claims.
SOURCE: STATENS MUSEUM FOR KUNST IN COPENHAGEN

ing.[156] Such ambitious objectives could be pursued only if closed sea policies, whether in the Northern Atlantic or the 'Indian' seas, were set aside, allowing

156 Alan James, 'Commanding the world itself: Sir Walter Raleigh, La Popelinière, and the Huguenot influence on early English sea power', in Richard Blakemore and James Davey (eds.), *The Maritime World of Early Modern Britain* (Amsterdam: University Press, 2020), 67–80; David M. Loades, *The Making of the Elizabethan Navy, 1540–1590: From the Solent*

the oceans to serve as highways shared by all nations. Long before Hugo Grotius' *Mare liberum*, Elizabeth I's ministers and diplomats employed legal arguments such as the denial of pontifical donation and the natural law commonality of pelagic spaces to outline the idea of the freedom of the sea.[157] However, this concept remained underdeveloped in legal doctrine and was still mostly confined to the realms of politics and diplomacy.

In the broader context of Elizabethan rejection of closed sea policies should also be read the 'letters patent' granted by the queen from the 1570s onwards.[158] For instance, in 1578, she instructed Sir Humfrey Jilberte to explore the North Atlantic to 'discover, finde, search out, and view such remote, heathen and barbarous lands, countries and territories not actually possessed of any Christian prince or people'.[159] Even though Jilberte was required to avoid territories already possessed by other Christian princes (notably Spain), he was also instructed to defend himself 'as well by sea as by land' against any interference.[160] This represented a significant shift with the earlier letters patent granted by Henry VII to John Cabot and his sons. Now, Spain and Portugal were as entitled to govern only those lands they had actively occupied; they could no longer impede navigation or exclude other nations from establishing new colonies. A similar provision was included in the 1584 charter granted to Sir Walter Raleigh.[161]

---

to the Armada (Woodbridge: Boydell Press, 2009); Nicholas A. M. Rodger, 'Queen Elizabeth and the Myth of Seapower in English History', *Transactions of the Royal Historical Society*, 14 (2004), 153–74. See also James Davey (ed.), *Tudor and Stuart Seafarers. The Emergence of a Maritime Nation, 1485–1707* (London: Adlard Coles, 2018).

157 Fulton, *The Sovereignty of the Sea*, 105. However, Fulton notes that starting from the 1570s, some English jurists and pamphleteers started to defend the English crown's own exclusive rights over the surrounding seas. For instance, in 1577, John Dee published *General and rare memorials pertayning to the perfect arte of nauigation annexed to the paradoxal cumpas* (London: John Daye, 1577), where he argued that even though navigation was free, coastal fisheries pertained to England. See Glyn Parry, 'John Dee and the Elizabethan British Empire in its European Context', *The Historical Journal*, 49(3) (2006), 643–75.

158 See, for instance, 'Commission to Thomas Stucley to command and discipline the crews of five ships upon a voyage of discovery to Terra Florida, 1563', in Marsden, *Documents*, vol. I, 175–6. Cf. Louis B. Wright, *English Explorers' Debt to the Iberians* (Coimbra: Junta de Investigaçoes Científicas do Ultramar, 1980).

159 'Letters patent to Sir Humfrey Gylberte June 11, 1578', the text is included in the collection of the *Avalon Project, Documents in Law, History and Diplomacy*, available online: http://avalon.law.yale.edu/16th_century/humfrey.asp; Marsden, *Documents*, vol. I, 222.

160 Ibidem.

161 'Charter to Sir Walter Raleigh, 25 March 1584', Ibid. The document is accessible online: http://avalon.law.yale.edu/16th_century/raleigh.asp.

Philip II of Spain and his successors, however, continued to defend their unenforceable regime of 'closed seas' in the diplomatic arena, striving to exclude foreigners from their 'Indian Seas'. It was not until the Anglo-Spanish Treaty of 1670 that the court in Madrid explicitly acknowledged that peace treaties applied south of the Tropic of Cancer and west of the Azores, formally abandoning the 'no peace beyond the line(s)' policy.[162] In any case, by the late sixteenth century, clauses limiting oceanic navigation in international treaties had become obsolete. For instance, the Hispano-French Treaty of Vervins (1598), which ended hostilities in Europe, made no mention of whether French navigation towards the Indies was to be considered free or restricted.[163] As no compromise had been reached on this point, it was tacitly understood that peace would not apply 'beyond the line'.[164] A similar arrangement was reached in the 1604 peace treaty between Philip III of Spain and James I of England.[165] In a letter to his envoy in London, Maximiliane de Béthune, Henry IV of France referred to the above-mentioned treaty in these terms: 'As much as the said Treaty with England did not say anything about voyages to the Indies, it is nevertheless certain that the Spaniards promised to the English they would never search nor molest those who travelled there, provided they went for trade and not in course'.[166] However, the king believed that:

> they (the English and the Spanish) will proceed on both sides as my subjects and the Spanish have done since the peace of 1559: the French

---

162 Rodger, 'The New Atlantic', 242; Mattingly, 'No Peace beyond what Line?', 145–62.

163 'To whose advantage was this long-drawn out war? Beyond question the only ones to benefit were the Protestant powers, whose ships were ravaging the oceans. [...] While France and Spain were fighting over townships, forts, and hillocks of ground, the Dutch and the English were conquering the world. This fact seems to have been grasped by the papacy by 1595. Clement VIII offered to act as mediator and was vigorous in his efforts to obtain peace between France and Spain'. In Fernand Braudel, *The Mediterranean and the Mediterranean World in the Age of Philip II* (New York: Harper, 1976), vol. II, 1218–21. See also Randall Lesaffer, 'La paix de Vervins (2 mai 1598): souveraineté, territorialité en développement du droit public européen', in Jean-Marie Cauchies and Serge Dauchy (dir.), *Personnalité, territorialité et droit: Actes des journées internationales de la Société d'Histoire du Droit tenues à Bruxelles 28–31 mai 1998* (Bruxelles: Facultés universitaires Saint-Louis, 1999), 131–52.

164 For the text: CUD, V.1, 561–4; For the English and German translations, see Grewe, *Fontes*, II, 39–48.

165 For the text: CUD, V.2, 32–6. For the original text of the treaty: *Archivo General de Simancas*, Signatura: Ptr, Leg, 55, doc. 38. Available online: http://pares.mcu.es/ParesBusquedas/servlets/Control_servlet?accion=3&txt_id_desc_ud=2208218&fromagenda=N.

166 Grewe, *Fontes*, II, 136.

> have continued their said voyages although the said peace treaty does not mention anything thereof; but just as the Spanish have treated them as enemies if they met them beyond the line, the French have done the same on their part, and so they were in agreement, that the peace treaty had not been violated.[167]

In other words, the only limitation the English would accept was to refrain from sailing to places effectively held by the Iberian powers. Navigation to the Indies could no longer be forbidden as a general principle.[168] However, the freedom of navigation had to be asserted by force, as the Iberians were unwilling to openly renounce their claims of exclusive access to their oceanic routes.

4 Doctrinal Arena

4.1 *Premises*

Elizabeth I's diplomatic efforts notwithstanding, the first scholars to address Hispano-Portuguese closed-sea claims from a doctrinal standpoint were not English but instead Spanish. Far from surprising, this reflected the flourishing Spanish intellectual and cultural milieu of the sixteenth century – *el siglo de oro*. One of the first figures to revisit the concept of the freedom of the seas was the relatively obscure Rodrigo Suárez, who likely passed away in the early 1520s. His major work, *Allegationes et consilia*, was not published until 1550.[169] In this text, Suárez argued that, under natural law, the sea was common to all humanity, and any human attempts to claim ownership of it amounted to usurpation.[170] Suárez's reflections on the legal status of the sea drew largely on well-known passages from the *Digest*, the *Institutes*, and certain provisions of Spanish domestic law.[171]

The theologian Francisco de Vitoria (1483–1546), a seminal figure of the School of Salamanca, certainly played a far more influential role in shaping

167 Ibidem.

168 Davenport, *European Treaties*, I, 245.

169 Rodericus Suarez, *Allegationes et consilia quaedam ... Eiusdem exactissima in aliquas fori leges lectura ...* (Lugduni: apud haeredes Iacobi Iuntae, 1559).

170 Ibidem, fol. 48.

171 Perruso, 'The Development of the Doctrine of the Res Communes', 88; Luis García Arias, 'La libertad de los mares según Rodrigo Suárez', *Anuario de la Asociación Francisco de Vitoria*, 17 (1969–1970), 49.

the law of nations.[172] Arthur Nussbaum regarded him as one of the first thinkers to revive the concept of freedom of the seas.[173] However, Vitoria's contribution to the subject was more indirect, as he did not expound the validity of maritime claims as such. Two of his *relectiones* are particularly relevant for our purposes: *On the American Indians* (*Relectio de indis*) and *On the Law of War* (*Relectio de jure belli*), both based on lectures delivered by Vitoria to his students in 1539.[174]

In the *Relectio de indis*, Vitoria engaged with the contentious issue of the legitimacy of Spain's colonisation of the Americas. He began by assessing whether the indigenous peoples of the Americas held dominion over their lands prior to the arrival of the *conquistadores*.[175] He then identified the unjust titles invoked to subjugate the Indigenous population and seize their lands,[176] including pontifical donation (i.e. the Alexandrine Bulls). Drawing on arguments developed in the reflection *On the Power of the Church*, Vitoria argued that the pope possessed no temporal authority over the American natives and the other non-Christians peoples.[177] Finally, he delineated the titles of conquest that could instead be considered legitimate.[178] Although he did not directly address maritime claims, his discussions of land dominion and the rights of the indigenous peoples have bearing on broader debates surrounding legal claims over the sea. In article 1 of the third question within *De indis*, Vitoria outlined the 'first just title, of natural partnership and communication', under which 'the Spaniards have the right to travel and dwell in those countries, so long as they do no harm to the barbarians, and cannot be prevented by them

172 Rafael Ramis Barceló, *La Segunda Escolástica. Una propuesta de síntesis histórica* (Madrid: Dykinson, 2024).

173 Nussbaum, *A Concise History of the Law of Nations*, 62. See also Kristin Bunge, 'Francisco de Vitoria: a redesign of global order on the threshold of the Middle Ages to modern times' in Kadelbach et al. (eds.), *System, Order, and International Law*, 38–55.

174 The *relectiones*, or re-readings, constituted investigations of a particular problem, as opposed to lectures commenting a text, e.g. Thomas Aquinas' *Summa theologica*. They survived from the notes taken by Vitoria's pupils, since he did not publish anything during his lifetime. See Anthony Pagden and Jeremy Lawrance (eds.), *Vitoria. Political Writings* (Cambridge: University Press, 2010), xvii–xviii.

175 Francisco de Vitoria, 'On the American Indians', 1.1–6, ibid., 239–51. See also Anthony Anghie, *Imperialism, Sovereignty and the Making of International Law* (Cambridge: University Press, 2004), 13–31; David M. Lantigua, *Infidels and Empires in a New World Order. Early Modern Spanish Contributions to International Legal Thought* (Cambridge: University Press, 2020); Emiliano Paolini, *Filosofia politica e diritto internazionale in Francisco de Vitoria* (Rome: Curcio, 2011).

176 Francisco de Vitoria, 'On the American Indians', 2. 1–7, 251–77.

177 Ibid., 2.2, 258–64; Idem, 'On the Power of the Church', 5.1–5, 82–90.

178 Idem, 'On the American Indians', 3.1–8, 277–91.

from doing so'.[179] Offering fourteen justifications for this claim, Vitoria drew on the *ius gentium* (law of nations), which condemned unwarranted restrictions on peaceful travel and commerce, since 'amongst all nations it is considered inhuman to treat strangers and travellers badly without some special cause, humane and dutiful to behave hospitably to strangers'.[180] He further posited that, even after the division of property (*divisio rerum*), the right to travel persisted, having originated in the time when all things were held in common.[181]

Vitoria's tenth argument on the right of communication touched briefly on the sea, stating: 'The jurist's determination that by natural law running water and the open sea, rivers, and ports are the common property of all, and by the law of nations (*ius gentium*) ships from any country may lawfully put in anywhere (*Institutions*, II.1.1–4)'.[182] This concise yet clear assertion – grounded on the Roman law tradition – was made in the 1530s, during a period when Spain still effectively defended its closed sea policies despite growing challenges posed by French raiders. At this time, the systematic diplomatic and doctrinal attacks on Iberian maritime claims were yet to unfold. Hence, in his writings, Vitoria focused exclusively on the relations between native Americans and Spanish and did not elaborate on Spanish attempts to deny the *ius communicationis* to other European nations. If Vitoria placed emphasis on the 'right of communication', he also derived from it a set of more specific *ius gentium* rights, including the *ius peregrinandi et degendi* (right to travel and reside), the *ius commercii* (right to trade), and the *ius migrandi* (right to migrate).[183] He went so far as to suggest that unjust restrictions on movement and commerce

179 Ibid., 3.1, 278. See also Isabel Trujillo Pérez, *Francisco de Vitoria. Il diritto alla comunicazione e i confini della socialità umana* (Giappichelli: Torino, 1997); Benedict Kingsbury and Adam Roberts, 'Introduction: Grotian thought in international relations', in Hedley Bull, Benedict Kingsbury and Adam Roberts (eds.), *Hugo Grotius in International Relations* (Oxford: Clarendon Press, 2002), 45; Pagden, 'Dispossessing the barbarian', 79–98; John H. Elliott, 'The seizure of overseas territories by the European powers', in Hans Pohl (ed.), *The European Discovery of the World and its Economic Effects on Pre-industrial Society, 1500–1800* (Stuttgart: Franz Steiner, 1990), 43–61.

180 Vitoria, 'On the American Indians', 3.1, 278.

181 Ibidem.

182 Ibid., 3.1, 279.

183 Francisco Carpintero, *Del derecho natural medieval al derecho natural moderno* (Salamanca: Universidad de Salamanca, 1977), 270; María C. Añaños Meza, 'El título de "sociedad y comunicación natural" de Francisco de Vitoria. Tras las huellas de su concepto a la luz de la teoría del dominio', *Anuario Mexicano de Derecho Internacional*, 12 (2012), 525–96; Nicolás Salom-Franco, 'Vitoria y Grocio frente al mar', *Estudios Socio-Jurídicos*, 3(1) (2010), 93–141, at 106–7.

by native Americans could justify a 'just war'. However, he underscored that, if missionaries retained the right to preach freely, they could not impose conversion by force.[184]

Overall, Vitoria's writings suggest a general opposition to broad restrictions on the rights of other peoples to navigate and trade across the oceans. While he ultimately legitimised certain Spanish titles justifying the brutal conquest and colonisation of American lands, his arguments inadvertently opened a Pandora's box with respect to the exclusion of other European powers from Spain's claimed sphere of influence and seaways.[185] In subsequent decades, many authors would expand and reinterpret Vitoria's work, often citing him as an authority to challenge closed sea policies.

4.2 *Fernando Vázquez y Menchaca*

It is not by chance then that in 1564, an author named Fernando Vázquez y Menchaca (1512–1569) frontally questioned Iberian oceanic claims. A student of Francisco de Vitoria and generally associated with the School of Salamanca, Vázquez de Menchaca distinguished himself as more of a legist than a theologian or canonist.[186] He is an important transitional figure, bridging medieval natural law traditions and modern ius-naturalism.[187] His views on maritime claims are articulated in his major work, *Controversiarum illustrium aliarumque usu frequentium libri tres* ('Three Books of Famous and Other Controversies Frequently Occurring in Practice').[188] Vázquez de Menchaca's contribution is remarkable not only for referencing the familiar passages of the *Corpus*

---

184 Vitoria, 'On the American Indians', 3.2, 278–81. See also Joseph Hoffner, *Kolonialismus und Evangelium* (Trier: Paulinus-Verlag, 1969), 342.

185 García Arias, *Historia del principio de la libertad de los mares*, 44; Nieves San Emeterio Martín, 'El debate sobre el dominio de los mares en el imperio español durante los siglos XVI y XVII', *Iberian Journal of the History of Economic Thought*, 7(2), 133–42, at 134–5.

186 Gustaaf van Nifterik, 'Controversiarum illustrium…', in Serge Dauchy et al. (eds.), *The Formation and Transmission of Western Legal Culture, 150 Books that Made the Law in the Age of Printing* (New York: Springer, 2016), n. 32, 118–20; for the cultural and temporal context of the author's life, see Salvador Rus Rufino, 'Fernando Vázquez y Menchaca', in Raphael Domingo and Javier Martínez-Torrón (eds.), *Great Christian Jurists in Spanish History* (Cambridge: University Press, 2018), 157–62.

187 Carpintero, *Del derecho natural*, 27; Patrick Capps, 'Natural law and the law of nations', in Orakhelashvili (ed.), *Research Handbook on the Theory and History of International Law*, 58–89.

188 Fernando Vázquez y Menchaca, *Controversiarum illustrium aliarumque usu frequentium libri tres* (Valladolid: Cuesta, 1931–34). This edition, and Spanish translation, by Fidel Rodríguez Alcalde reproduces the original Latin edition from 1564, published in Venice (apud Franciscum Rampazetum).

Iuris Civilis but also for incorporating classical authors such as Ovid, Seneca, and Cicero. This reflects his pronounced humanistic leanings, contrasting with medieval commentators, who confined their analyses to Justinian's codification.[189]

To understand Vázquez de Menchaca's views on the legal status of the sea, it is necessary to examine the broader framework of his legal thought, as it profoundly shaped his arguments. He divided the *ius gentium* (law of nations), which he viewed as originating from natural law, into two categories. The first, *ius gentium primaevum*, was closer to natural law and the primordial state where private property did not exist. This form of *ius gentium* was considered immutable and coeval with the creation of humanity.[190] The second, *ius gentium secundarium*, was a later development, originating not from natural law but from the positive-civil law adopted by most nations, and as such, it was mutable and contingent upon human institutions.[191] In Vázquez de Menchaca's view, only natural law and *ius gentium primaevum* could legitimately govern relations between polities and princes. Positive laws and customs inconsistent with these higher laws were invalid.

Bearing these notions in mind, it is interesting to examine chapter 89, book II, of *Controversiarum illustrium*. Even though it is a rather heteronomous section, being primarily devoted to prescription and custom, it also offers a

189 That said, it is still debated whether he was already part of the so-called legal humanism. See van Nifterik, *Controversiarum illustrium*, 118–20; Perruso, 'The Development of the Doctrine of the Res Communes', 88; Carpintero, *Del derecho natural*, 270. For further details, see Camilo Barcia Trelles, 'Fernando Vázquez de Menchaca (1512–1569): l'école espagnole du droit international du XVIe siècle', *Collected Courses of the Hague Academy of International Law*, 67 (1939), 430–534; Annabel S. Brett, *Liberty, Right and Nature: Individual Rights in Later Scholastic Thought* (Cambridge: University Press, 1997), 165–204; Adolfo Miaja de la Muela, *Internacionalistas españoles del siglo XVI: Fernando Vázquez de Menchaca (1512–1569)* (Valladolid: Cuesta, 1932); Sebastián Contreras, 'Derecho natural, derecho de gentes y libertad de los mares en Fernando Vásquez de Menchaca', *International Law: Revista Colombiana de Derecho Internacional*, 24 (2014), 169–91; San Emeterio Martín, 'El debate sobre el dominio de los mares', 135–6.

190 Vázquez y Menchaca, *Controversiarum illustrium*, II, 53, § 2; 89 § 24. The author considers that the *ius gentium primaevum* constitutes a subspecie of natural law. However, the first category applied only to men. The second one was wider, applying also to other animals, *tam brutis, quam ratione utentibus*. The relationship between them was *ut genus a sua specie*.

191 Ibid., II, 89, § 25: '*sicque id jus gentium secundarium non tam naturale, quam positivum dicitur esse, sicque non fixum, et immobile, sed commutabile esse dicitur non secus, quam ius civile…*'. My translation: 'Thus, this secondary law of nations is not said to be natural, but rather positive; it follows it is not fixed, immutable, but instead changeable, similarly to the civil law…'.

substantial discussion on the legal status of the sea and related legal claims.[192] In section 12, Vázquez de Menchaca immediately dismissed the possibility of acquiring ownership over public or common spaces – such as the sea – through prescription. He presented this principle as undisputed, citing medieval jurists like Johannes Faber, Bartolus, Paulus de Castro, Caepolla, and Franciscus Balbus to bolster his position.[193]

He then outlined the arguments used in the past to justify state control over the sea, only to subsequently refute them. He acknowledged that medieval jurists had identified mechanisms other than prescription to justify such claims. These included three key arguments. The first was custom (*consuetudo*), distinguished from prescription by its application to things that had never been owned, as opposed to the transfer of rights from one party to another.[194] The second was privilege, typically granted by the Holy Roman Emperor, or possession from time immemorial. Here, he challenged the long-standing claims of Venice and Genoa to limit navigation in the Mediterranean, describing their assertion as *jus interdicendi et vetandi reliquis mortalibus potentia navigandi* – the right to forbid and prevent others from navigating.[195] Vázquez y Menchaca acknowledged that several influential authors had considered Venetian and Genoese claims as legally sound, especially based on immemorial possession.[196] The third argument proposed that, while prescription could not apply to public and common things (*res publicae* and *res communes*), polities could still acquire over time, a limited *ius excipiendi* (*derecho de excepción* in the Spanish translation), derived from occupation (until the latter lasted). Such right was instrumental in order not to be thrown out of an established possession, and it had two consequences: if 'we are disturbed in possession we can act against those who disturb us' and before such possession is challenged, 'we can prohibit the entrance in such place to those who want to do so against our will'.[197]

After presenting the arguments traditionally used to justify sea claims, Vázquez de Menchaca pivoted to his central thesis, arguing that the solution to the question of whether the sea could be owned or not lay in a proper under-

192 Ibid., II, 89, § 12–41.

193 Ibid., II, 89, § 12.

194 Ibid., II, 89, § 13.

195 Ibid., II, 89, § 16.

196 Ibid., II, 89, § 17: '*Jus enim navigandi secundum eos regale est,* [...] *sicque acquire potest vel privilegio, vel tanto tempore cujus initii memoria non sit, secundum eos*'.

197 My translation, ibid., II, 89, § 21: '*Tertio limita ut quae sunt publica, aut jure gentium communia licet non praescribantur, tamen sempre acquiri potest jus excipiendi, ut de tali possessione non expellatur, eritque duplex effectum, primus...*'.

standing of natural law and the *ius gentium*.[198] The distinction outlined above between different 'laws' became the fulcrum of his argumentation. He proceeded to confute Venetian and Genoese claims over portions of the Mediterranean Sea, sketching the principle of the freedom of the seas. He maintained that any attempt to restrict navigation violated Roman law, as enshrined in the *Corpus Iuris*, as well as immutable natural law and the fundamental principles of *ius gentium*, which deemed the sea a shared resource for all humanity. He categorically rejected prescription as a valid basis for maritime claims, asserting that it was merely an institution of civil law.[199]

Expanding his critique, Vázquez de Menchaca turned to Portuguese and Spanish claims over oceanic corridors.[200] This is proof of bold intellectual independence, given his position as a Spanish subject with significant administrative responsibilities, a career shared by many members of his family.[201] In contrast to Vitoria, Vázquez de Menchaca explicitly argued that neither the Portuguese nor the Spanish monarchs could lawfully close the expansive pelagic spaces leading to the Indies, based on prescription, which he considered an inadequate legal basis derived solely from civil law:

> Even among our own Spaniards, the common people seem to be almost entirely of the opinion that no one but the Spaniards has the right to navigate across the vast and immense ocean to the regions of the Indies, which our most powerful kings of Spain have conquered, as if that right had been exclusively prescribed by them. However, all these opinions are no less absurd than those of people who are accustomed to harbouring a similar delusion regarding the Genoese and the Venetians.[202]

198 Ibid., II, 89, § 23: '*Istarum rerum veritas pendet a vera juris tam naturae, quam gentium cognitione…*'.

199 Ibid., II, 89, § 30–1.

200 Ibid., II, 89, § 32: '*Quamvis ex Lusitanis magnam turnam saepe audiverim, in hac esse opinione, ut eorum rex ita praescripserit navigationem Indici occidentalis ejusdem vastissimi mari, ita ut reliquis gentibus aequora illa transfetare*'. My translation: 'And even though I have often heard that a large number of Portuguese defend the opinion that their king has so prescribed the navigation of the vast sea of the West Indies, that it is not lawful for the other peoples to cross those immense seas…'. See also Grewe, *Epochs*, 259; Miaja de la Muela, *Internacionalistas españoles*, 59.

201 Carpintero, *Del derecho natural*, 270. Grotius will refer to him in *Mare liberum* as 'Glory of Spain' also for this reason.

202 Vázquez y Menchaca, *Controversiarum illustrium*, II, 89, § 32, my translation from the Latin original: '*… ex nostrismet Hispanis vulgus in eadem opinione fere esse videatur, ut per vastissimum immensumque pontum ad Indorum regiones, quas potentissimi reges nostri Hispaniorum subegerunt, reliquis mortalium navigare, praeterquam Hispanis jus*

Thus, the Spanish jurist equated the closed-sea pretensions of Venice, Genoa, Portugal, and Spain. He further asserted that the sea could not be acquired through custom (*consuetudo*) either. In his view, the distinction between prescription and custom was largely artificial, as the rationale underpinning both legal concepts was fundamentally the same. Consequently, he did not hesitate to contradict the prevailing opinions of *ius commune* authorities, firmly declaring that custom could not be invoked to override the immutable principles of natural law:

> The opinion of Faber, Angelus, Baldus, Franciscus Balbus, whom we mentioned above, also appears to be suspect when they consider that the places that by the law of nations are common – although they cannot be acquired by virtue of prescription – can nevertheless be acquired through custom. This is entirely false, and such a doctrine is blind and obscure, completely lacking any light of reason. [...]. Indeed, in the cases concerning the seas of the Spaniards, Portuguese, Venetians, Genoese, and others, it is clear that the right to navigate and the right to prohibit others from navigating cannot be acquired by custom any more than by prescription, since, as is evident, the same rationale applies in both cases.[203]

Vázquez y Menchaca, as both a humanist and Roman law expert, supported his thesis with references to the Roman definition of the sea as a *res communis omnium*. He restated that the original commonality prescribed by the primary law of nations (*ius gentium primaevum*) remained applicable to the sea, which had never been partitioned, unlike lands and rivers.[204] The Spanish jurist rhetorically asked: 'why does the secondary law of nations (*ius gentium secundar-*

---

minime sit, quasi ab eis id jus praescriptum fuerit, tamen istorum omnium non minus insanae sunt opiniones, quam eorum qui quoad Genuenses & Venetos in eodem fere somnio esse adsolent...'.

203 My translation from ibid., II, 89, § 36: '*Apparet suspectam esse sententiam Joannis Fabri, Angeli, Baldi, & Francisci Balbi quos supra retulimus, existimantium loca iuris gentium communia, & si acquiri non possint praescriptione posse tamen acquiri consuetudine, quod omnino falsum est, eaque traditio caeca & nubila est, omnique rationis lumine carens* [...]. *In exemplis enim de mari Hispanorum, Lusitanorum, Venetorum, Genuensium et reliquorum constat consuetudine ius tale navigandi, & alios navigare prohibendi non magis acquiri, quam praescriptione, utroque enim casu ut patet par ratio est*'. See also Cavanagh, 'Prescription and Empire', 284–6.

204 Ibid., II, 89, § 39: '*Ratio differentiae inter mare ex una parte et terram vel flumina ex altera, quia illo casu, ut olim, ita et hodie et semper, tam quoad piscandum quam quoad navigandum, mansit integrum ius gentium primaevum, neque numquam fuit a communio*

ium) that introduced the division of property with regard to lands and rivers not apply to the sea?'.[205] He answered that in the first case, it was convenient to do so, but not in the latter one, proceeding with a twofold explanation.[206] Firstly, he argued that marine resources, such as fisheries, were inexhaustible, unlike the finite resources of rivers or forests. He explained, 'it is evident that if many hunt or fish on land or in a river, the forest is quickly emptied of game, and the river of fish, which is not the case in the sea'.[207] Secondly, he emphasised that the sea offered ample space for all to navigate without conflict, unlike crowded rivers where navigation could easily be obstructed: 'similarly, river navigation easily deteriorates and is hindered by constructions, which does not occur across the vast sea'.[208]

Vázquez y Menchaca thus reaffirmed the fundamental distinction between land and rivers, on the one hand, and seas on the other. As far as the sea was concerned, its original status as common property persisted, both for navigation and fishing purposes. From this, he deduced the impossibility of occupying pelagic spaces, which nature had destined to remain common to all humankind. Hence, humans could acquire no legal rights over marine areas beyond their original communal use. To substantiate this, he drew upon the Digest, the Gospel of Saint John, Bartolus, Cicero's *De Officiis*, and even the Roman playwright Terence.[209]

Conversely, Vázquez y Menchaca acknowledged that humans had, over time, legitimately acquired exclusive rights over rivers and terrestrial territories through occupation.[210] In his opinion, occupation constituted the only valid legal basis for territorial claims. However, he deemed the occupation of the sea impossible, as the sea was a *res communis*, not a *res nullius*. Such an act would contravene natural law, amounting to an illegitimate usurpation. Furthermore, occupation required the exercise of effective governmental power and a continuous physical presence, conditions he deemed unattainable with

hominum separatum, et alicui vel aliquibus applicatum, posterior autem casu, nempe in terra vel fluminibus, aliud fuit, ut jam disseruimus'.

205 My translation from ibidem, '*Sed quare ius gentium secundarium ut eam separationem quoad terras et flumina fecit, eandem quoad mare facere desiit?*'.

206 Ibidem, '*Responde, quia illo casu expediebat ita fieri, hoc autem casu non expediebat*'.

207 Ibidem, '*Constat enim quod si multi venentur, aut piscentur in terra, vel flumine, facile nemus feris, et flumen piscibus evacuatum redditur, id quod in mari non est ita*'.

208 Ibidem, '*Item fluminum navigatio facile deterior fit, et impeditur per aedificia, quod in mari non est per totum*'.

209 Ibid., II, 89, § 36: '*Ergo in aequoribus et aquis nullum jus est aut esse potest humano generi, praeterquam quoad usum commune*'.

210 Ibid., II, 89, § 39. See also Miaja de la Muela, *Internacionalistas españoles*, 63.

respect to the sea. For the Spanish jurist, the marine element was ontologically distinct from land. Hugo Grotius would later adopt many of these ideas, often citing the Spanish jurist as an authoritative source.[211] Interestingly, in chapter 89 of his *Controversiarum illustrium*, Vázquez y Menchaca did not explicitly address papal grants as a basis for maritime monopolies. However, elsewhere in the same work, he denied the pope's claim to universal temporal jurisdiction.[212] Thus, his stance on the matter was already evident. On this point too, Grotius, as a Protestant, would be more forthright in *Mare Liberum*.[213]

Although Vázquez y Menchaca was among the earliest critics of Iberian oceanic claims, his treatment of the sea as object of study was somewhat generic. In *Controversiarum illustrium*, he made no distinction between seas and oceans, nor did he reference northern Europe or what we termed the Nordic 'claimed seas' tradition.[214] Linguistically, he used terms such as *mare* and *pontus* (albeit *vastissimi*), rather than *oceanus*. On this front, Grotius would provide a further contribution to the evolution of the law of the sea. Nevertheless, it seems clear that Vázquez y Menchaca played a historical significant – though often overlooked – role in reviving the idea of the sea as a *res communis* and in shaping early discussions on its legal status, clearly anticipating Grotius. He strongly reaffirmed the natural commonality of the sea, unequivocally rejecting the exceptions to this principle formulated by medieval jurists.

In this context, and given the sheer scope of Iberian claims, the relative lack of doctrinal support for them is striking.[215] During the fifteenth and sixteenth centuries, Spanish and Portuguese rulers largely sought to enforce their oceanic duopoly through international state practice and diplomacy rather than developing a comprehensive 'claimed seas' theory. For the Catholic monarchs of Spain and Portugal, the legitimacy derived from papal donation remained paramount. However, as explored in Chapter 2, Spain and Portugal also invoked titles of 'private law' origin such as discovery (*inventio*), occupation (*occupatio*), and prescription (*praescriptio*) to support their claims. For example, during the Franco-Spanish negotiations that culminated in the already mentioned Treaty of Cateau-Cambrésis (1559), Spanish commissioners justified Spain's monopoly over the western Atlantic on the

211 Grotius in *Mare liberum* quoted Vázquez y Menchaca approximately fifteen times.

212 Ibid., I, 20, § 1–4.

213 Carpintero, *Del derecho natural*, 275.

214 Potter judged the Spanish author did not go 'very far beyond Roman law', in *The Freedom of the Sea in History, Law and Politics*, 51.

215 Grewe, *Epochs*, 258; Neff, *Justice among Nations*, 55.

grounds that Spain alone had borne the labour and expense of discovery.[216] In comparison, the Portuguese more frequently invoked conquest and just war as bases for their claims, particularly in relation to West Africa and the Indian Ocean.

4.3 *Grotius'* Mare liberum

4.3.1 The Dutch Encroachment on the Oceans

This chapter has thus far examined the initial emergence of the principle of the freedom of the seas within late sixteenth-century political and legal discourse. Attention will now shift to the Dutch contribution to this development. As a nascent and expanding maritime power, the Dutch Republic naturally championed the freedom of the seas as a means to challenge the established Iberian powers. This principle even became a cornerstone of Dutch maritime policy around the turn of the sixteenth century. However, this commitment was not immutable and often fluctuated in response to the shifting political priorities of the newly formed republic. That said, it was during this precise historical moment that the seminal legal treatise advocating the freedom of the seas, Hugo Grotius' *Mare liberum*, was published. The immediate context leading to its publication can only be briefly summarised here; for a detailed examination, reference should be made to the comprehensive studies of Martine J. van Ittersum and Peter Borschberg, among others.[217]

The 1590s marked a turning point for the Dutch Republic in geopolitical terms. Philip II of Spain, preoccupied with military campaigns in France, eased the naval embargo against the Dutch, allowing them to adopt a more assertive stance both on land and at sea.[218] By the early seventeenth century, the Dutch had successfully challenged Portuguese control in Guinea and had begun exploratory visits to the Caribbean and Brazil, although initially avoiding direct confrontation with Iberian strongholds in these regions. Simultaneously, the Dutch launched privately financed expeditions to the East Indies,

216 Davenport, *European Treaties*, doc. 21, 219–22.

217 Martine J. van Ittersum, *Profit and Principle: Hugo Grotius, Natural Rights Theories and the Rise of Dutch Power in the East Indies 1595–1615* (Leiden/Boston: Brill, 2006); idem, 'Hugo Grotius in Context: Van Heemskerck's Capture of the Santa Catarina and its Justification in *De jure praedae* (1604–1606)', *Asian Journal of Social Science*, 31 (2003), 511–48; Peter Borschberg, 'The Seizure of the Sta. Catarina Revisited: The Portuguese Empire in Asia, VOC Politics and the Origins of the Dutch-Johor Alliance (1602–1616)', *Journal of Southeast Asian Studies*, 33(1) (2002), 31–62; idem, *Hugo Grotius, the Portuguese and Free Trade in the East Indies* (Singapore: NUS Press, 2011).

218 Israel, *Dutch Primacy in World Trade*, 40.

aiming to bypass Portuguese middlemen and maximise profits. Despite opposition from Portugal, these ventures largely succeeded, yielding considerable returns on investment.[219] However, these small trade companies (*voorcompagnieën*) lacked the capacity to mount a serious challenge to the Portuguese *Estado da Índia*.

In response, the States General of the United Provinces established the United Dutch East India Company (*Verenigde Oostindische Compagnie*, or VOC) in 1602. This new entity absorbed the existing Dutch trading companies, reducing intra-Dutch competition and optimising profits. The VOC was an unprecedented commercial-political organisation for its time, granted extensive military and political powers by the States General. Additionally, it held a monopoly over Dutch trade and navigation east of the Cape of Good Hope, an area that overlapped with the pelagic area still claimed by Portugal as its exclusive sphere of influence.[220] In the broader struggle against Habsburg hegemony, the VOC's charter specified that the company's purpose extended beyond economic profit, aiming also to undermine Hispano-Portuguese 'claimed seas' pretensions.[221] In this sense, the VOC functioned as an extension of the Dutch state.

In the Far East, tensions between Portuguese and Dutch seafarers escalated rapidly. On 25 February 1603, with a small fleet of VOC ships under his command, Dutch admiral and explorer Jacob van Heemskerk (1567–1607) captured the richly laden Portuguese carrack Santa Catarina in the Singapore Straits. While the captured prize was undeniably valuable, the incident became le-

219 C. G. Roelofsen, 'Grotius and the law of the sea', in L. E. van Holk and C. G. Roelofsen (eds.), *Grotius Reader* (The Hague: Asser Instituut, 1983), 8. The initiative was taken by consortia of businessmen such as the Hollander Reinier Pauw, with a variable degree of support by the authorities. See Israel, *Dutch Primacy in World Trade*, 67; Philippe Haudrère, 'Les compagnies de commerce, instruments de la puissance maritime', in *The Sea in History*, III, 763–5; Boyajian, *Portuguese Trade in Asia*, 86–105. The English on their part continued to be active interlopers in the Caribbean, see Elliott, *Imperial Spain*, 291–2.

220 Boxer, *The Dutch Seaborne Empire*, 23–5; Harris, *Going the Distance*, 272–90; Arthur Weststeijn, 'The VOC as a Company-State: Debating Seventeenth-Century Dutch Colonial Expansion', *Itinerario*, 38(1) (2014), 13–34.

221 Koen Stapelbroek, 'Trade, chartered companies, and mercantile associations', in Fassbender and Peters (eds.), *The Oxford Handbook of the History of International Law*, 338–58; Israel, *Dutch Primacy in World Trade*, 68; Claudio Tommasi, 'La "Libertà dei Mari". Ugo Grozio e gli sviluppi della talassocrazia olandese nel primo seicento', *Scienza & Politica*, 9(16) (1997), 42–3.

gendary, primarily because of its repercussions.[222] Confronted with domestic and international criticism of van Heemskerk's actions, the VOC directors enlisted the services of the young and talented jurist Hugo Grotius (1583–1645) to defend the legality of the seizure.[223] Between 1604 and 1606, Grotius composed *De jure praedae commentarius* (*Commentary on the Law of Prize and Booty*), a treatise that justified Dutch actions within the framework of traditional just war theory.[224]

The Portuguese typically regarded Dutch interlopers encountered within their sphere of influence as criminals, while the Dutch increasingly adopted aggressive tactics in their expeditions. Both sides sought to delegitimise their rivals, frequently branding them as pirates, particularly in communications with Asian rulers and trading partners.[225] In *De jure praedae*, Grotius detailed the Portuguese atrocities against Dutch traders and the indigenous populations who engaged with them. These violations of natural law, he argued,

222 van Ittersum, 'Hugo Grotius in Context', 523; idem, *Profit and Principle*, 1–52; Roelofsen, 'Grotius and the Law of the Sea', 9; Peter Borschberg, 'The Seizure of the Sta. Catarina Revisited: The Portuguese Empire in Asia, VOC Politics and the Origins of the Dutch-Johor Alliance (1602–1616)', *Journal of Southeast Asian Studies*, 33(1) (2002), 31–62; Guido Acquaviva, 'Libertà o dominio dei mari: il caso della Santa Catarina', *Anuario de Derecho Internacional*, 17 (2001), 239–68; Edward Keene, *Beyond the Anarchical Society: Grotius, Colonialism and Order in World Politics* (Cambridge: University Press, 2002), 42–52.

223 On Grotius' figure, see L. E. van Holk, 'Hugo Grotius, 1583–1645, a Biographical Sketch', in *Grotius Reader*, 23–44. For a more substantial work, see Henk Nellen, *Hugo Grotius. A Lifelong Struggle for Peace in Church and State 1583–1645* (Leiden/Boston: Brill, 2007); William S. M. Knight, *The Life and Works of Hugo Grotius* (London: Sweet & Maxwell, 1925); Tuck, *The Rights of War and Peace*, 78–108. For a comprehensive overview, see Randall Lesaffer and Janne E. Nijman (eds.), *The Cambridge Companion to Hugo Grotius* (Cambridge: University Press, 2021); Janwillem Oosterhuis, 'Hugo Grotius', in Wim Decock and idem (eds.), *Great Christian Jurists in the Low Countries* (Cambridge: University Press, 2021), 97–122.

224 Peter Borschberg, 'Grotius, Maritime Intra-Asian Trade and the Portuguese Estado da India: Problems, Perspectives and Insights from *De Iure Praedae*', *Grotiana*, 26–28 (2005–2007), 31–60; Ford, *The Emergence of Privateering*, 243–52; Robert Fruin, 'An Unpublished Work of Hugo Grotius', *Bibliotheca Visseriana*, 5 (1925), 1–100; Ileana M. Porras, 'Constructing International Law in the East Indian Seas: Property, Sovereignty, Commerce and War in Hugo Grotius' *De Iure Praedae – The Law of Prize and Booty*, or "On How to Distinguish Merchants from Pirates"', *Brooklyn Journal of International Law*, 31 (2006), 742–804.

225 Michael Kempe, 'Beyond the Law. The Image of Piracy in the Legal Writings of Hugo Grotius', *Grotiana*, 26–28 (2005–2007), 379–95. Both Dutch and the Portuguese actions were often perceived as outright piracy by non-Europeans, see Adam Clulow, 'European Maritime Violence and Territorial Sates in Early Modern Asia, 1600–1650', *Itinerario*, 33(3) (2009), 72–94; Hans Blom (ed.), *Property, Piracy and Punishment: Hugo Grotius on War and Booty in De Jure Praedae. Concepts and Contexts* (Leiden: Brill, 2009).

justified the defensive and retaliatory actions – notably prize taking on the high seas – carried out by van Heemskerk and his compatriots.[226] In September 1604, the Amsterdam Admiralty Court ruled that the capture of the *Santa Catarina* constituted a legitimate prize.[227] However, due to prevailing circumstances, the manuscript of *De jure praedae* was never published during Grotius' lifetime and remained largely unknown until its rediscovery in the nineteenth century. It has since become a subject of significant scholarly interest.[228] However, since the present work focuses on Grotius' actual influence on the debate on the legal status of pelagic spaces and the 'claimed seas', the analysis will focus on *Mare liberum*.

4.3.2 Contents

A few years later, Grotius adapted chapter XII of *De jure praedae*, publishing it anonymously in 1609 under the title *Mare liberum, sive de iure quod Batavis competit ad indicana commercia* ('The Free Sea or a Disputation Concerning the Right which the Hollanders ought to have to the Indian Trade').[229] By 1607, Spain and the United Provinces were engaged in truce negotiations, with one

226 Grotius, *Commentary on the Law of Prize and Booty*, vol. I, 168–282; Peter Borschberg, *Hugo Grotius, the Portuguese and Free Trade in the East Indies* (Singapore: NUS Press, 2011), 20–40; Ford, *The Emergence of Privateering*, 243–52, 258–63.

227 van Ittersum, *Profit and Principle*, 21; Frans de Pauw, *Grotius and the Law of the Sea* (Bruxelles: Editions de l'Institut de Sociologie, 1965), 16.

228 The manuscript remained in the possession of Grotius' descendants until 1864, when his personal papers were sold at auction and subsequently acquired by Leiden University. The Latin text was first published in 1868, followed by an English translation in 1950. A comprehensive edition, including additional materials, is available in Hugo Grotius, *Commentary on the Law of Prize and Booty*, edited by Martine Julia van Ittersum (Indianapolis: Liberty Fund, 2006).

229 The analysis will be based on the edition and translation by Robert Feenstra (ed.), *Hugo Grotius Mare Liberum, 1609–2009: Original Latin Text and English Translation* (Leiden: Brill, 2009). It is the most recent edition of Grotius' booklet; it refers to the 1609 version of the Latin text. Another edition is the seventeenth-century translation by Richard Hakluyt of *Mare Liberum* edited by David Armitage (Indianapolis: Liberty Fund, 2004). A further English translation is dated 1916, by Ralph Van Deman Magoffin: Hugo Grotius, *The Freedom of the Seas: or, The Right Which Belongs to the Dutch to Take Part in the East Indian Trade* (New York: Oxford University Press, 1916). Magoffin's version refers to Elzevier's 1633 edition but contained several imprecisions. For example, he translated *dominium* as sovereignty. The first Latin edition to unveil Grotius as the author of *Mare liberum* was published in 1618 by Elzevier. See also Martine J. van Ittersum, 'Preparing *Mare liberum* for the press: Hugo Grotius' rewriting of chapter 12 of *De jure praedae* in November-December 1608', in Blom (ed.), *Property, Piracy and Punishment*, 246–80; Eric Wilson, 'Erasing the Corporate Sovereign, Inter-Textuality and an Alternative Explanation for the Publication of Hugo Grotius' *Mare Liberum* (1609)', *Itinerario*, 30(2)

of the most contentious issues being Dutch access to the Indies. VOC officials feared that Dutch negotiators might concede on this point, in exchange for peace on the continent.[230] Once again, Grotius was called upon to defend the VOC's commercial interests and to persuade public opinion of the critical importance of maintaining Dutch access to Asian waters in the face of Hispano-Portuguese opposition. In this regard, Arnold Raestad aptly remarked that *Mare liberum* constituted 'an eloquent plea, unscrupulously employing legal doctrine for political purposes'.[231] Grotius condensed his arguments in a short and passionate treatise, which opened with a preface directly addressing the audience he intended to persuade: 'the rulers and the free nations of the Christian world'.[232] Its declared aim was to demonstrate the legitimacy of Dutch actions while highlighting the singularity of the case at hand:

> It is in very truth no petty case such as private citizens are wont to bring against their neighbours about dripping eaves or inserting a beam in a wall; nor is it a case such as nations frequently bring against one another about boundary lines or the possession of a river or an island. No! It is a case which concerns practically the entire expanse of the high seas, the right of navigation, the freedom of trade![233]

Then Grotius identified his opponents as the 'Spaniards':[234]

> Between us and the Spaniards the following points are in dispute: Can the vast, the boundless sea be the accessory of one kingdom alone, and that not the greatest? Can any one nation have the right to prevent

(2006), 78–103; Antonio del Vecchio, *La legge nell'Oceano. Ugo Grozio e le origini dello spazio politico moderno* (Bologna: Il Mulino, 2021).

230 Pagden, *The Burdens of Empire*, 158–9; Roelofsen, *Grotius and the Law of the Sea*, 13; Jeroen Vervliet, 'General Introduction' to Feenstra (ed.), *Hugo Grotius Mare Liberum*, x; Helen Thornton, 'Hugo Grotius and the Freedom of the Seas', *International Journal of Maritime History*, 16(2) (2004), 17–38.

231 My translation from Raestad, *La mer territoriale*, 89, '*un plaidoyer éloquent, employant sans scrupules la doctrine juridique dans un but politique*'.

232 Grotius, *Mare liberum*, preface, 5. See Scobbie, 'Rhetoric, persuasion, and interpretation in international law', in Bianchi, Peat and Windsor (eds.), *Interpretation in International* Law, 61–77.

233 Ibid., preface, 15 [Fol. 4 verso].

234 With the term Spaniards, Grotius refers to the both Portuguese and the Spanish, at the time still associated in the Iberian Union. Throughout the text, he uses the term *Batavi* (Batavians) to refer to the Dutch. The Batavians were an ancient people, contemporary of the Romans, who early modern Dutch scholars identified as the forefathers of their nation.

> other nations which so desire, from selling to one another, from bartering with one another, actually from communicating with one another? Can any nation give away what it never owned, or discover what already belonged to someone else? Does a manifest injury of long time create a specific right?[235]

Grotius declared that he would rely on Spanish scholars of divine and human law – namely, second scholastics such as de Vitoria and Vázquez y Menchaca – and on the laws of Spain itself. This was a tactically astute move, highlighting that even Spanish thinkers had nurtured doubts on the legitimacy of Hispano-Portuguese maritime claims. It was also a necessary strategy, given the limited guidance provided by Roman legal sources on this matter. Throughout the text, Grotius compensated for the lack of relevant legal precedents by incorporating erudite references to classical Greek and Latin literary works, as well as biblical texts – a method often described as being 'more literary than scientific'.[236] This approach drew inspiration from Vázquez y Menchaca and diverged from the methodology of late medieval authors, who typically confined their analyses to the *Corpus Iuris*.[237] As a final recourse, Grotius appealed to the conscience of nations and the moral sensibilities of his readers.[238] He proclaimed natural law as the principal foundation of his arguments, once again following the intellectual path laid out by Vázquez y Menchaca. Grotius emphasised that he was not grappling with an intricate legal dilemma or a divisive religious controversy, 'which seems to possess much obscurity'.[239] Instead, he asserted that the law determining the case between the Dutch and the Spanish was clear and straightforward to discern:

> ...seeing that it is the same among all nations; and it is easy to understand, seeing that it is innate in every individual and implanted in his mind. Moreover the law to which we appeal is one such as no king ought to deny to his subjects, nor a Christian to non-Christians. For it is a law

235 Grotius, *Mare liberum*, preface, 15 [Fol. 4 verso].

236 Philip Allott, 'Language, Method and the Nature of International Law', *British Year Book of International Law*, 45 (1971), 79–135; Martin J. Schermaier, 'Res Communes Omnium: The History of an Idea from Greek Philosophy to Grotian Jurisprudence', *Grotiana*, 30(1) (2009), 20–48; Jonathan Ziskind, 'International Law and Ancient Sources: Grotius and Selden', *The Review of Politics*, 35(4) (1973), 537–59.

237 Perruso, 'The Development of the Doctrine of Res Communes', 86–90; Benton, *A Search for Sovereignty*, 123.

238 Grotius, *Mare liberum*, preface, 19 [Fol. 4 verso].

239 Ibidem.

> derived from nature, which is an equal parent to us all, whose bounty falls on all, and whose sway extends over those who rule nations.[240]

Mare liberum comprises sixty-six pages and thirteen chapters, which advance three interconnected lines of argument. Grotius systematically refuted Iberian claims, respectively, over the Indies, the sea (navigation), and trade, deploying similar reasoning against each of these assertions. One by one, he dismantled the titles of possession claimed by the Portuguese, namely possession-occupation, discovery, war title/conquest, pontifical donation, prescription, and custom.[241] The intrinsic link between navigation and trade is emphasised in chapter I, titled 'That by the law of nations navigation is free for everybody to whomsoever'. From the outset, Grotius stated his intention to demonstrate that the Dutch had the right to navigate to the Indies to conduct trade. He asserted this right as stemming from the irrefutable principle of the primary law of nations (*ius gentium primarium*), which endowed all peoples with the right to travel and trade freely with others.[242] Navigation, in Grotius' view, was a fundamental human activity born of the necessity to exchange resources. He argued that God, through the intermediation of nature, had made nations interdependent and compelled them to engage in commerce and sociability. To act contrary to this natural order would be, in his view, an affront to nature itself. The sea, in this framework, served a crucial purpose:

> Consider the ocean, with which God has encircled the different lands, and which is navigable from boundary to boundary; consider the breath of the winds in their regular courses and in their special deviations, blowing not always from one and the same region but from every region at one time or another: are these things not sufficient indications that nature has granted every nation access to every other nation?[243]

Grotius cited the Stoic philosopher Seneca to illustrate how the sea and its winds fostered connections between distant peoples, thereby enabling com-

---

240 Ibidem.

241 For an overview, see Hedley Bull, 'The importance of Hugo Grotius in the study of international relations', in Hedley Bull, Benedict Kingsbury and Adam Roberts (eds.), *Hugo Grotius and International Relations* (Oxford: University Press, 1990), 65–94.

242 De Pauw, *Grotius and the Law of the Sea*, 33. Therefore, Grotius divided the law of nations (*ius gentium*) into two categories, of which the *ius gentium primarium* covered the core principles elaborated by nature for mankind. In this respect, Grotius appears close to Vázquez y Menchaca.

243 Grotius, *Mare liberum*, ch. 1, 27 [2].

merce that benefited all of humanity. He asserted that 'jurisconsults of the greatest renown' had extended this principle to reject the idea that polities or princes could lawfully prohibit travel and trade.[244] To support his claim, the jurist from Delft drew on historical and biblical examples of wars fought to uphold the right of innocent passage through foreign lands.[245] Even transit through one's own land must be allowed under the *ius humanae societatis*, 'law of human fellowship'. Next, Grotius affirmed that even if the Portuguese had legitimately owned the Indies, denying the Dutch access to those territories would violate natural law. However, the Lusitanians could not even claim the Indies at all. He dismissed the Portuguese as acting like 'robbers and pirates' (*latrones et piratas*) whenever they sought to block access to the Indies.[246]

Grotius' more specific rebuttal of Iberian claims began with the argument that the Portuguese did not hold *dominium* over the 'Indians' (or the East Indies). Firstly, Grotius rejected the title deriving from discovery (*inventio*), both in law and in fact (Chapter 2). Secondly, he challenged the title deriving from pontifical donation, *donatio ponificiae* (Chapter 3). Thirdly, he dismissed conquest and the title of war (*titulus belli*) as a valid legal ground (Chapter 4). To this end, Grotius argued that the Portuguese were merely tolerated as visitors in the East Indies, where local polities had not provided grounds for a just war, such as refusing peaceful trade. Furthermore, Portuguese territorial control was minimal, limited to a few coastal outposts.[247] He also reminded his readers that the Romans and the Venetians had engaged in trade with India, long before the Portuguese, demonstrating the implausibility of the claim to 'discovery'.[248] Grotius argued that discovery could not confer property rights over lands already inhabited by complex societies, which, although non-Christian ('in part idolaters, in part Mohammedans'), could not be dispossessed without a just cause, since they enjoyed public and private ownership over their lands.[249] Concerning the technical definition of discovery, he noted that the Portuguese lacked the conditions required under Roman law and

244 Ibidem. Reference to Alberico Gentili, *De iure belli*, I, 19.

245 For instance, the war between the Megarians and the Athenians, the conflict between Bologna and Venice or between the Israelites and the Amorites.

246 Grotius, *Mare liberum*, ch. 1, 31, [4]. Cf. Kempe, 'Beyond the Law. The Image of Piracy in the Legal Writings of Hugo Grotius', 385.

247 Grotius, *Mare liberum*, ch. 4, 41–9 [9–13].

248 Ibid, ch. 2, 35 [6].

249 Ibidem.

natural law, notably due to the lack of possession: 'for discovery consists, not in perceiving a thing with the eye, but in actual seizure'.[250]

Regarding pontifical donation, Grotius asserted that papal bulls were valid only as a means of arbitration between Portugal and Spain. Even if their validity were granted for the sake of argument, they would still require actual possession to establish rightful ownership; as he argued, 'it was necessary to add the title of actual possession to the title of donation', since 'it is not the act of donation but the subsequent delivery that creates ownership'.[251] Furthermore, in Grotius' view, the pope only held a spiritual jurisdiction, applicable only to the adherents to Catholicism. He was not the temporal lord of the entire world and could not donate something that was 'the property of others'.[252] Besides, the pope could not dispossess Asian polities based on their faith, as 'even the Saracens were never despoiled on such grounds'.[253]

Believing he had demonstrated that the Indies did not constitute Portuguese possessions, in chapter v Grotius went back to discuss the issues of navigation and the legal status of the sea.[254] The oceans, he argued, were indispensable routes to the Indies, making it pointless to question Iberian rights over land territories if the seaways connecting them remained barred to the Dutch. Consequently, Grotius gave the sea new prominence as an independent object of legal analysis. This chapter, spanning twenty-three of the booklet's sixty-six pages, constitutes its theoretical core. Grotius examined the Roman law classification of things (*res*) to underline the distinctiveness of the legal status of the sea.[255] Drawing on multiple classical sources, he traced the historical evolution of ownership (*dominium*) starting from the mythical

---

250 Ibid, ch. 2, 33 [5]. Grotius refers to the Roman grammarian Nonius Marcellus, *De compendiosa doctrina*, IV, on the word *occupare*.

251 Ibid, ch. 3, 39 [8].

252 Ibid, ch. 3, 40–1 [8–9].

253 Ibid, ch. 3, 41 [9]. Here, Grotius builds on the medieval debate within the Church on whether non-Christian could hold a lawful right to govern their territories. The most influential opinion, sponsored among others by Pope Innocent IV, had long been the affirmative one. See Neff, *Justice among Nations*, 101–2; James Muldoon, *Popes, Lawyers, and Infidels: The Church and the Non-Christian World, 1250–1550* (Liverpool: University Press, 1970), 29–48.

254 Ibid, ch. 5, 50–1 [13–4].

255 Grotius classified the sea as one of the *res communes omnium*, consciously overlooking the fact that this category was not universally agreed upon among Roman jurists. (Gaius for example did not mention it). Perhaps the category was more of a literary-philosophical origin rather than purely legal. The *res communes omnium* are treated in a fragment of the classical jurist Marcian included both in the *Digest* (D., 1.8.2) and in the *Institutiones* (I., 2.1.1). See *supra* ch. I, 2.1.

'golden age' described by Hesiod, Ovid, and others when all things were held in common.[256]

The Dutch jurist explained that in origin, all things were held in common and private property did not exist. Only gradually, 'under the guidance of nature', private property emerged gradually as humans appropriated consumable goods and, subsequently, immovable property through acts of occupation (*occupatio*). By definition, private property was exclusive, precluding shared ownership or simultaneous use of the same *res*.[257] Over time, the emergence of organised polities introduced laws that regulated ownership, usually requiring acts of use and physical attachment (*per applicationem corporalem*).[258] This established *occupatio* as the fundamental mechanism for creating property rights. For movable goods, this process required *apprehensio* (physical seizure), while for immovable property it entailed actions such as constructing buildings or delineating boundaries.[259] Grotius further argued that both *res privatae* (privately owned things) and *res publicae* (community-owned things) – albeit distinct from a theoretical standpoint – could be acquired through occupation.[260]

Grotius inferred two conclusions from this overview. First, he argued that items incapable of being occupied could not be transformed into private property, as all property rights ultimately derived from the act of occupation. Second, he asserted that objects that, even after use, remained available for use by others retained their original status as common property.[261] To support this, Grotius reaffirmed the Roman legal distinction between *res publicae*, which belonged to a specific nation, and *res communes omnium*, which were held in common by the 'whole society of mankind'. In Grotius view, again supported by classical quotes, air was the quintessential *res communis* since it could not be occupied.[262] The same applied to the sea (and the seashores): 'since it is so vast that no one could possibly take possession of it, and since it is fitted for use by all, with reference to purposes of navigation and to purposes of fishing, as well'.[263] The sea, Grotius maintained, was simply too vast to be

256 For instance, he quoted Ovid, Quintilian, Cicero, Seneca, and Virgil. See also Fulton, *The Sovereignty of the Sea*, 345.

257 Grotius, *Mare liberum*, ch. 5, 55 [16].

258 Ibid, ch. 5, 57 [17]; reference to Seneca, *De beneficiis*, VII, 12.

259 Ibidem.

260 Ibid, ch. 5, 59 [18]. See also ibid, 75 [26].

261 Ibid, ch. 5, 61 [19].

262 Ibid, ch. 5, 63 [20].

263 Ibidem. This is one of the few references to fishing in *Mare liberum*. The booklet is more concerned with the role of pelagic spaces as trade highways, which indeed was the

the object of possession, it could not be enclosed and occupied. Following Vázquez y Menchaca, he emphasised the Roman jurists' classification of the air and the sea as fundamentally distinct from land.[264]

Next, Grotius elaborated on the distinction between *res nullius* and *res communes omnium*. The former, which included things like fish and wild animals, were not owned by anyone but could become private property through possession. By contrast, the latter were also unowned, but inherently incapable of being possessed or appropriated. According to Grotius, nature itself had intentionally exempted these items – such as the sea – from private ownership, commanding that they remain common to all.[265] At this juncture, Grotius leaned more heavily on references to the *Corpus Iuris Civilis*. He also cited Hugo Donellus to characterise the sea as *extra commercium* (i.e. a thing outside commerce) and Placentinus and Johannes Faber to reassert that the sea remained in its primaeval state of commonality.[266] Grotius then went back to the distinction between *res publicae* and *res communes*, emphasising that the latter category differed from the former because it could not be the object of 'public' occupation by any one nation. This, he argued, marked a fundamental difference between seas and rivers.[267]

Following this, Grotius turned his attention to medieval claims over the sea, examining the arguments of jurists such as Baldus and Angelus de Ubaldis. He posited that polities could divide maritime areas into distinct jurisdictions for the purpose of combating piracy.[268] However, such agreements were only binding upon the parties who consented to them: 'Such an arrangement is binding, to be sure, upon the parties who have imposed a legal agreement of this kind upon themselves; but it is not binding in like manner upon other peoples'.[269] Furthermore, Grotius maintained that these agreements did not confer *dominium*: 'Nor does it convert an area thus delimited into the private

---

primary object of Iberian claims. Instead, the successive disputes between the Dutch and the English will concern also fisheries, see *infra* Chapter 4, 1.3.

264 Cf. Vázquez y Menchaca, *Controversiarum illustrium*, II, 89, § 2 and Marcian's passages in *Digest* (D., 1.8.2); *Institutiones* (I., 2.1.1). Cf. Schermaier, 'Res Communes Omnium', 20–48.

265 Grotius extended this principle, in general, to seashores, though he appeared to acknowledge the possibility of limited occupation in their case.

266 Grotius, *Mare liberum*, ch. 5, 75 [26]. Grotius references are to Donellus, *Commentarii de iure civili*, ed. I, 241; Johannes Faber on Inst., 2.1.5, ed. fol. 29 v. Doctores on D., 14.2.9 (references from Feenstra).

267 Grotius, *Mare liberum*, ch. 5, 75 [26]. Cf. Vázquez y Menchaca, *Controversiarum illustrium*, II, 89, § 12–41.

268 Elizabeth I's envoys had developed similar arguments during the 1602 negotiations with their Dano-Norwegian counterparts. See *supra*, ch. II, 3.3.

269 Grotius, *Mare liberum*, ch. 5, 77, [27].

property of any possessor, for it merely establishes rights between the contracting parties'.[270] Grotius also engaged with the question of whether the Romans had exercised ownership over the Mediterranean Sea. He contended that the Romans had acquired jurisdiction over the sea solely to protect seafarers from piracy, with the goal of safeguarding the *ius navigandi* (the right of navigation) for all peoples, rather than asserting exclusive dominion over maritime territories.[271]

Up to this point, Grotius had persuasively argued his case by selectively drawing upon sources from antiquity, Roman law, and the *ius commune* tradition. He asserted that the sea constituted a *res communis* and, as such, could neither be occupied nor owned. *Mare liberum* marked the first instance in which the status of the oceans was explicitly distinguished from that of more confined seas.[272] Indeed, this distinction represented a significant milestone in the evolution of the law of the sea, particularly when compared to Vázquez y Menchaca's writings. The jurist from Delft, clarified that his primary focus was on 'that part of the sea, which one traverses while sailing to the Indies' (*mare quo ad Indos navigatur*):[273]

> We are not treating here of an inner sea which washes against the land on all sides and is in some places no wider than a mere river; [...] The subject of our discussion is the Ocean, which was described in older times as immense, infinite, the father of created things, and bounded only by the heavens; the Ocean, whose never-failing waters fed not only upon the springs and rivers and seas, according to the ancient belief, but upon the clouds, also, and in a certain measure upon the stars themselves; in fine, that Ocean which encompasses the terrestrial home of mankind with the ebb and flow of its tides.[274]

Grotius emphasised that the ocean could neither be owned nor enclosed, as it functioned as the possessor rather than something to be possessed. Consequently, the author underscored the absurdity of the Portuguese claims:

270 Ibidem. On this passage, see Johanna K. Oudendijk, *Status and Extent of Adjacent Waters. A Historical Orientation* (Leiden: Sijthoff, 1970), 27–9.

271 Grotius, *Mare liberum*, ch. 5, 75 [26].

272 Ibid., ch. 5, 79 [28].

273 Ibidem. Feenstra's translation.

274 Ibid., ch. 5, 81 [29].

> In this Ocean, the question at issue is not limited to some bay or strait, nor even to the entire expanse of its waters visible from the shore. On the contrary, the Portuguese claim for themselves the whole tract lying between two parts of the world, which are separated by spaces so vast that in the course of many centuries, those two regions were not able to make themselves known to each other. Indeed, if the share of the Spaniards (who join in the same claim) is added to the share demanded by the Portuguese, very nearly the entire Ocean will have been delivered into the hands of two peoples, while all the remaining nations will find themselves restricted to the narrow waters of the north.[275]

In Grotius' view, nature intentionally encircled all peoples with the oceans to provide essential resources and facilitate long-range human interaction. As such, nature would be profoundly displeased by any attempt to exclude others from accessing these oceanic spaces. Such efforts would inevitably attract the reproach of 'monstrous cupidity'.[276] Navigation by one group did not obstruct the use of the sea by others, and as a result, it could not be legitimately restricted. Grotius likened the use of the ocean to that of fire, an indispensable element for human existence that must remain universally accessible.[277]

The Portuguese had not enclosed the ocean with fortifications or barriers, as might be done with land. Oceans lacked natural or artificial boundaries, making their occupation impossible. Grotius pointed to the Alexandrine and Tordesillas lines, highlighting that the Portuguese and Spanish claims rested solely on imaginary demarcations. These lines, he argued, were arbitrary and binding only upon the signatory parties, not universally (*erga omnes*).[278] He provocatively asked: 'Where, then, in the present case, do we encounter that factor of corporeal attachment without which ownership has never been established?'.[279] Such attachment could not exist, as the sea was no more capable of being seized or possessed than the air we breathe.[280] Moreover, Gro-

275 Ibidem. On this passage, see Oudendijk, *Status and Extent of Adjacent Waters*, 25–6.

276 Ibid., ch. 5, 83 [30].

277 For a similar argument, see Vázquez y Menchaca, *Controversiarum illustrium*, II, 89, § 39.

278 'If this claim is to be recognized, and if such a method of measurement suffices to constitute valid possession, the geometers must have taken the earth from us long since, just as the astronomers must also have taken the heavens'. Grotius, *Mare liberum*, ch. 5, 85 [31].

279 Ibidem.

280 Ibidem, '*Ubi hic igitur est ista, sine qua nulla dominie coeperunt, corporis ad corpus adjunctio?*'.

tius dismissed the notion that simple navigation constituted occupation. Given the vastness of the ocean, a ship would invariably be the first to traverse a specific route, leaving no enduring trace.[281]

He further noted that the Portuguese were not the first to sail the western Atlantic. According to Grotius, the western coasts of Africa and the Arabian Sea were known in antiquity, and at the time of the Roman Empire, voyages to Arabia and India were routine. He even speculated that the Carthaginian admiral Hanno (fifth century BCE) might have pioneered the Cape route. In this light, the Portuguese had merely rediscovered a long-forgotten maritime route, for which they undoubtedly deserved recognition (*gratia, laude & gloria*).[282] For a time, they had rightly reaped the benefits of their endeavours alone. However, it was now time for them to share the wealth derived from seaborne trade with other nations – namely, the Dutch! In essence, neither equity nor historical precedent supported Portuguese claims. Nevertheless, he recognised that past authorities had sometimes acknowledged that: 'the sea can be made subject to individual sovereignty, attributes such sovereignty to him who has dominion over the closest ports and neighbouring shores';[283] however, even this argument, he asserted, was inapplicable to the Portuguese:

> But on all the vast extent of coast to which we have referred, the Portuguese can point to no possession aside from a few fortified posts, which they may call their own. Furthermore, even if a given person did possess sovereignty over the sea, he would still lack authority to diminish its common usefulness, just as the Roman People lacked authority to prevent the commission, on shores belonging to the Roman Empire, of any act whatsoever that was permissible under the law of nations.[284]

Even if it were possible to prohibit certain activities, such as fishing, it would be impossible to restrict navigation, as it did not interfere in any way with others' use of the sea.[285] In conclusion, Grotius argued that nature itself had ordained the sea to be held and used in common by all peoples. Consequently,

---

281 Ibidem, 'For there is no part of the sea upon which someone has not been the first to enter, so that it would necessarily follow from such a contention that every navigable region had been "occupied" by some voyager'.

282 Grotius, *Mare liberum*, ch. 5, 91 [34].

283 Ibid., ch. 5, 93 [35]. Grotius refers to the Gloss 'territorio' on VI, 1, 6, 3, 2 and Gloss 'ecclesiis' on X. 2, 9, 3. Feenstra argues that he took over the two references from Rodrigo Suárez (Zuarius), *Consilium* I 'de usu maris' (see below p. 36 note c), num. 1 and 2.

284 Ibidem.

285 Ibidem.

the Dutch, along with all other nations, possessed the natural law right to navigate freely, and the Portuguese were in no position to obstruct them.[286]

The following chapter (VI) follows the path laid down in the preceding one. Its title is 'That the sea or the right of navigation thereon does not belong to the Portuguese by title of papal donation'. Grotius observed that Pope Alexander VI could not donate something that could neither be privately owned nor traded (*res extra commercium*), and the Portuguese could not lawfully receive it.[287] Expanding on his arguments from chapter III – where he had dismissed the validity of pontifical donation concerning the Indies – Grotius demonstrated that the Pope was not the temporal lord of the entire earth. *A fortiori*, he could not claim dominion over the seas.[288] In a European context marked by religious conflicts, Grotius emphasised that the Pope's authority was confined to spiritual matters and only extended to Catholics. The Holy See had no legitimate right to govern temporal affairs. Moreover, Grotius noted that Portuguese activities in Asia were driven more by profit and material gain than by faith, providing little justification for papal interference. Finally, Grotius argued that the Pope lacked the power to contravene the laws of nature, and any attempt to donate parts of the sea would represent a blatant violation of these laws.[289]

The following chapter (VII), the second longest in *Mare liberum* (spanning fourteen out of sixty-six pages), focuses on refuting prescription and custom as potential Portuguese titles of possession over the sea and oceanic routes.[290] As previously discussed, medieval jurists had explored this topic extensively, and Vázquez y Menchaca had devoted considerable thought to it. Following Vázquez y Menchaca's lead, Grotius argued that these legal institutes were often invoked 'as a last resort to justify injustice', but they certainly did not provide valid titles in the case at hand, as 'prescription is rooted in civil law [positive law]. Therefore, it is not applicable between kings or between free peoples, and far less can it have force in opposition to the law of nature, or [primary] law of nations'.[291] In his view, natural law always prevailed over civil law and, in any case, even civil law did not allow prescription as pelagic spaces were concerned:

---

286 Ibid., ch. 6, 95 [36], '… *omnes igitur vident eum qui alterum navigare prohibeat nullo iure defendi*'.

287 Ibid., ch. 6, 97 [37], '… *sequitur neque dari a Pontifice, neque a Lusitanis accipi potuisse*'.

288 Ibidem, '… *non esse dominum temporalem totius orbis*'.

289 Ibidem. See also Frank Lestringant, 'Les protestants et la liberté des mers', 25–33.

290 Ibid., ch. 7, 99 [38].

291 Ibidem. Cf. Vázquez y Menchaca, *Controversiarum illustrium*, II, 89.

> For it prohibits acquisition by usucapion or by prescription in regard to those things which cannot be included under the head of property, and also in regard to those which are not susceptible of possession nor of quasi possession, or which cannot be alienated; and all of these characteristics are correctly ascribed to the sea and to the use thereof.[292]

Grotius argued that claiming ownership of a *res communis* through prescription or custom amounted to blatant usurpation. He criticised the jurists who had endorsed Venetian and Genoese claims in the past – explicitly referencing Angelus de Ubaldis – as being either 'deceived or guilty of deceit', maliciously suggesting that their conclusions were shaped by a desire to please their patrons. Furthermore, he pointed out that earlier jurists had focused on the Mediterranean Sea, rather than the oceans.[293] In Grotius' view, the two maritime areas in question differed significantly in terms of occupation. For instance, Venice and Genoa exercised control over considerable stretches of the shores of the Adriatic and Ligurian seas, which were naturally enclosed and relatively small in size. By contrast, the Portuguese could make no such claim regarding the vast expanses of the oceans, where they held only a limited number of outposts, scattered across great distances.[294] Throughout this chapter, the comparison between Mediterranean polities' and Portugal's 'claimed seas' assertions hovers around. In Grotius view, if Venetian claims were theoretically questionable as a matter of principle, Portuguese claims appeared significantly weaker and legally indefensible, both in law and in practice – or 'reality on the waters'.

Even if the principle of acquisition of title through the passage of time were considered valid, Grotius contended that Portugal would still fail to meet the requisite legal criteria. First, the Portuguese relied on acts of navigation towards the Indies that they had not practised for a sufficiently long period. Second, during the formative period of prescription, no other party should have engaged in the same activities, except with the claimant's permission or clandestinely. Additionally, the claimant was required to actively prevent all others from using the disputed possession, securing the acquiescence of all parties concerned.[295] Grotius observed that past legal authorities

292 Grotius, *Mare liberum*, ch. 7, 99 [38]. See also Calafat, *Une mer jalousée*, 70–2; Cavanagh, 'Prescription and Empire', 290–1.

293 Grotius, *Mare liberum*, ch. 7, 121 [49], '*Illi enim de Mediterraneo loquuntur, nos de Oceano, de immenso mari*'.

294 Ibid., ch. 7, 123 [50].

295 Ibidem.

consistently upheld the necessity of satisfying these two conditions simultaneously.[296]

He then summarised the timeline of Portuguese maritime expansion to demonstrate the absence of the aforementioned criteria. According to Grotius, the Lusitanians only began serious efforts to reach India under King John II in the 1470s. It was not until two decades later that they eventually reached the Indian Ocean, with the conquest of Malacca occurring even later.[297] Thus, approximately one hundred years had elapsed between the discovery of the Cape route and the arrival of the Dutch in the 1590s. Furthermore, as early as 1519, the Castilians had contested Portuguese control of the Moluccas. During this period, English and French vessels entered the Indian Ocean and beyond, without seeking permission and in full view. Therefore, the Portuguese lacked both the temporal consistency and the effective control required to justify their claims through either prescription or custom.[298]

The following chapters addressed the issue of trade, which Grotius viewed as intrinsically linked to navigation. Believing it essential for the survival and prosperity of humankind, Grotius argued that trade must remain free for all nations under the laws of nature.[299] Consequently, he rejected the arguments supporting a Portuguese trade monopoly. Many of his points echoed those he had made regarding the sea, with particular emphasis on the 'incorporeal' nature of trade. In chapter XII, he turned to the principle of equity to refute any Portuguese claims to justify their monopolies on this basis.

After systematically dismissing Iberian titles of possession – both from a law and equity perspective –, over the Indies, seas, and trade, Grotius concluded *Mare liberum* with chapter XIII. Here, he boldly asserted that natural law entitled the Dutch to maintain their right to access Asian waters 'by peace, truce or war'. He argued that peace, whether temporary or long-lasting, should be pursued as a priority. However, the Dutch could not renounce their rights to navigation and trade; if all else failed, they were justified in waging war to defend these rights – not only in the interest of Dutch liberty but for the bene-

296 Ibidem.

297 Ibid., ch. 7, 125 [51].

298 Ibidem.

299 For a critical examination of Grotius as a proponent of free trade and liberalism in service of the empire, see Mark Somos, 'Open and closed seas: the Grotius-Selden dialogue at the heart of liberal imperialism', in Edward Cavanagh (ed.), *Empire and Legal Thought. Ideas and Institutions from Antiquity to Modernity* (Leiden/Boston: Brill/Nijhoff, 2020), 322–61; Andrea Weindl, 'Grotius's *Mare Liberum* in the Political Practice of Early Modern Europe', *Grotiana*, 30(1) (2009), 131–51.

fit of humanity as a whole.[300] In this chapter, Grotius' references to the medieval doctrine of just war are especially pronounced.[301] To strengthen his case, he concluded the booklet with a series of concise and compelling quotations from authoritative sources, affirming that any fair judge (*vir bonus iudicans*) would inevitably rule in favour of the young Dutch Republic in its dispute with Portugal.[302]

However, Grotius conceded that if such a judgement could not be achieved – particularly since the Pope was no longer recognised as an impartial arbiter – a just war could be declared. He cited Saint Augustine: 'The injustice of an adversary brings a just war' and Cicero: 'There are two ways of settling a dispute; first, by discussion; second, by physical force; we must resort to force in case we may not avail ourselves of discussion'.[303] Grotius also referred to the Roman jurist Pomponius, who asserted that a person attempting to seize common property must be resisted.[304] Drawing on the authority of 'theologians,' he further argued that if a just war could be waged to defend private property, it was even more permissible (*a fortiori*) to defend the sea and its legal status as *res communis omnium*.[305]

5 Concluding Observations: Grotius' *Mare liberum*, a Turning Point?

Grotius has traditionally been regarded as a towering figure in the historiography of international law, often hailed as the founding father of 'modern' international law. Among his many contributions, he has been particularly associated with the principle of the freedom of the seas. In this vein, Christian Meuner likened the principle to Sleeping Beauty, slumbering in obscurity until Grotius, the valiant knight from Holland, 'kissed her awake once

300 Grotius, *Mare liberum*, ch. 13, 149 [63]: '*Si ita necesse esse, perge gens mari invictissima, nec tuam tantum, sed humani generis libertatem*'.

301 For further details, see Frederick H. Russell, *The Just War in the Middle Ages* (Cambridge: University Press, 1975); Peter Haggenmacher, *Grotius et la doctrine de la guerre juste* (Paris: Presses universitaires de France, 1983); Randall Lesaffer, 'The laws of war and peace making', in idem and Nijman (eds.), *The Cambridge Companion to Hugo Grotius*, 433–56; Stephen C. Neff, *War and the Law of Nations. A General History* (Cambridge: University Press, 2005), 54–62.

302 Grotius, *Mare liberum*, ch. 13, 153 [65].

303 Ibid., ch. 13, 155 [66].

304 Ibidem. References to Augustinus, *De civitate Dei*, IV; Cicero, *De officiis*, I [34]; D., 41.1.50.

305 Ibidem.

more'.[306] This interpretation suggests that Grotius rediscovered the principle of the freedom of the seas, which had supposedly been lost or forgotten. However, recent scholarship has placed Grotius in a broader intellectual context, highlighting his debts to Alberico Gentili and the second scholastics.[307]

This is particularly evident in relation to the law of the sea, where Grotius' ideas built substantially on those of Vázquez y Menchaca and were anticipated by Elizabethan diplomacy. This chapter has aimed to demonstrate that the emergence of the freedom of the seas as a legal and political principle was a gradual process beginning in the sixteenth century, with *Mare liberum* serving as its resounding culmination. Contemporary scholars have also emphasised the apologetic and hypocritical nature of Grotius' defence of Dutch seaborne imperialism,[308] Peter Borschberg has gone so far as to question the juridical nature of both *De jure praedae* and *Mare liberum*.[309] Furthermore, it is worth noting that Grotius wrote *Mare liberum* in his youth, and his views evolved in his later works. For instance, in his 1625 masterpiece, *De iure belli ac pacis* (*On the Laws of War and Peace*), he conceded that, under certain circumstances, states could exercise control over portions of the coastal seas.[310] More broadly, as Hedley Bull observed, Grotius was: 'seldom strikingly original and it is in the vast range of his knowledge, together with his capacity to synthesise

306 Christian Meurer, *The Program of the Freedom of the Seas. A Political Study in International Law* (Washington: Nabu Press, 1919), 7. See also Alison Reppy, 'The Grotian Doctrine of the Freedom of the Seas Reappraised', *Fordham Law Review*, 19 (1950), 260–70; Ivan Shearer, 'Grotius and the Law of the Sea', ASLP Bulletin, 26 (1983), 46–65.

307 William E. Butler, 'The freedom of the seas', in Lesaffer and Nijman (eds.), *The Cambridge Companion to Hugo Grotius*, 477; Roelofsen, *Grotius and the Law of the Sea*, 15–6; Bull, 'The importance of Grotius', in idem, Kingsbury and Roberts (eds.), *Hugo Grotius and International Relations*, 73; Anand, *Origin and Development*, 2–3; León M. Gómez Rivas, 'Influencia de Diego de Covarrubias en la obra de Hugo Grotius (*Mare Liberum*, 1609)', *Procesos de mercado: revista europea de economía política*, 10(2) (2013), 321–42; Salom Franco, 'Vitoria y Grocio frente al mar', 107–11.

308 See Bernard V. A. Röling, '*Jus ad Bellum* and the Grotian Heritage', in *International Law and the Grotian Heritage* (The Hague: T.M.C. Asser Instituut, 1985), 122; Fulton, *The Sovereignty of the Sea*, 340; Martine J. van Ittersum, 'The Long Goodbye: Hugo Grotius and the Justification of Dutch Expansion Overseas (1604–1645)', *History of European Ideas*, 36 (2010), 386–411; John T. Parry, 'What Is the Grotian Tradition in International Law?', *University of Pennsylvania Journal of International Law*, 35(2) (2014), 299–377, at 340.

309 Peter Borschberg, 'Hugo Grotius' Theory of Trans-Oceanic Trade Regulation: Revisiting *Mare Liberum* (1609)', (Aug. 2006), IILJ Working Paper No. 2005/14, 9.

310 Karl Zemanek, 'Was Hugo Grotius Really in Favour of the Freedom of the Seas?', *Journal of the History of International Law*, 2(1) (1999), 48–60; Brüel, *International Straits* (vol. 1), 48–9; Scovazzi, 'Libertà o dominio', 19.

this knowledge and focus it upon the issues at hand that he commands our attention'.[311] This statement, I believe, is particularly apt when assessing Grotius' contributions to the law of the sea. It was the concise and compelling nature of *Mare liberum*'s arguments that secured its enduring influence – and the intense animosity it immediately provoked. While it is now clear that Grotius did not 'invent' the principle of the freedom of the seas, the significance of *Mare liberum* in the historical development of the law of the sea and ocean governance remains undeniable, particularly in two key respects.

Firstly, prior to 1609, the principle of the freedom of the seas had never been so explicitly articulated in legal doctrine. While Roman and medieval jurists had outlined the idea, they had refrained from developing a coherent theory. Vázquez y Menchaca had advanced clear-minded views on the legal status of the sea, but his influence was largely confined to scholarly circles, as his reflections were buried in the meanders of a large and ponderous treatise. In contrast, Grotius brought the issues of navigation and the legal status of the sea to the forefront of early modern legal discourse. The boldness and clarity of his arguments amplified the resonance of the principle of the freedom of the seas.[312]

Secondly, and perhaps even more significantly for our present purposes, *Mare liberum*'s publication triggered an unprecedented conceptualisation of the opposing principle, that we termed the 'claimed seas'. As explored in chapters 1 and 2, the notion of preferential/exclusive rights over the sea had long preoccupied European policymakers and jurists. Three distinct 'claimed seas' traditions had emerged in the Mediterranean, the seas of northern Europe, and the world oceans. However, these traditions had not yet been developed into a coherent theoretical framework. The publication of *Mare liberum* marked a pivotal moment, creating a clear 'before' and 'after' in the intellectual and diplomatic history of the law of the sea – especially in relation to the oceans. Grotius himself emphasised that medieval jurists had primarily concerned themselves with the seas bordering the European continent. In contrast, he explicitly differentiated the legal status of the oceans from that of more confined pelagic spaces like the Mediterranean or the Baltic. This dis-

---

311 Bull, 'The importance of Grotius', in idem, Kingsbury and Roberts (eds.), *Hugo Grotius and International Relations*, 73; Gary Edmond, 'The Freedom of Histories: Reassessing Grotius on the Sea', *Law Text Culture*, 2 (1995), 179–217.

312 Roelofsen, *Grotius and the Law of the Sea*, 10–1; Anand, *Origin and Development*, 2–3; Scovazzi, 'Libertà o dominio', 16; Reppy, 'The Grotian Doctrine', 276. Cf. Ernest Nys, 'La liberté des mers', in idem, *Les origines du droit international* (Bruxelles: A. Castaigne, 1894), 379–87.

tinction was swiftly adopted by both his supporters and opponents in the 1610s and 1620s.

Chapter 4 will now delve deep into the vigorous revival of the 'claimed seas' principle that followed the publication of *Mare liberum*. This examination will include an analysis of relevant state practice and the works of the most prominent advocates of the right of polities to claim exclusive control over the sea. Many of these works were written in direct opposition to Grotius, as their authors sought to adapt the concept of claimed-closed seas to the evolving realities of the seventeenth century. This chapter will once again explore the Mediterranean, the seas of northern Europe, and the oceans, while also highlighting the growing interconnections between these three maritime macro-regions.

CHAPTER 4

Replies to *Mare liberum*, the (Re)Emergence of *Mare clausum*

> But as Popelinire well observeth, the forces of princes by sea are *marques de grandeur d'estat*, 'are marks of the greatness of an estate', for whosoever commands the sea commands the trade; whosoever commands the trade of the world commands the riches of the world, and consequently the world itself.[1]

1 Premises

1.1 *The Twilight of Iberian Claims*

While Grotius was working on *Mare liberum*, negotiations were underway for a truce between the Iberian Union and the Dutch Republic. The Treaty of Antwerp, signed on 9 April 1609, formalised the agreement. Initially, it was concluded by Dutch envoys and representatives of the Archdukes Albert and Isabella, who governed the southern Low Countries on behalf of King Philip III of Spain (r. 1598–1621), who later ratified the treaty.[2] This marked the beginning of the so-called Twelve Years' Truce, granting both Spain and the Dutch Republic a respite from the burdens of war.[3]

---

1 Passage from Sir Walter Raleigh, *A Discourse of the Invention of Ships*, in *Works*, VIII (written in the 1610s, first published in 1650) (Oxford: University Press, 1829), 325. Raleigh here references the Huguenot historiographer and thinker Henri Lancelot Voisin de La Popelinière (1541–1608).

2 Randall Lesaffer, 'Introduction' to idem (ed.), *The Twelve Years Truce (1609)* (Leiden: Brill-Nijhoff, 2014), 1; Jonathan I. Israel, *The Dutch Republic and the Hispanic World* (Oxford: Clarendon Press, 1986), 3–4; idem, *The Dutch Republic: Its Rise, Greatness, and Fall, 1477–1806* (Oxford: Clarendon Press, 1995), 408–10.

3 Peter Brightwell, 'The Spanish System and the Twelve Years' Truce', *The English Historical Review*, 89(351) (1974), 270–92; Paul C. Allen, *Philip III and the Pax Hispanica, 1598–1621: The Failure of Grand Strategy* (New Haven, CT: Yale University Press, 2000), 172–244; Miguel A. Echevarría Bacigalupe, *La diplomacia secreta en Flandes, 1598–1643* (Bilbao: Servicio Editorial: Universidad del Pais Vasco, 1984); Robert A. Stradling, *Europe and the Decline of Spain*

 | DOI:10.1163/9789004741409_006

During the negotiations the leading Dutch negotiator, Johan van Oldenbarnevelt (1547–1619), sought to secure Spain's de facto recognition of the Republic as a free and independent state.[4] The issue of Dutch navigation towards the West and East Indies was another matter of contention. Habsburg envoys attempted to extract concessions on this matter in exchange for partial recognition of Dutch sovereignty.[5] Yet, Oldenbarnevelt understood that neither the Dutch East India Company (VOC) nor its influential shareholders would tolerate the dissolution of the company or the continuation of Iberian *mare clausum* policies. As a result, the final agreement contained no explicit provisions restricting Dutch navigation to the Indies, nor did the term 'Indies' appear as a geographical reference.[6] The most relevant clause, number four, addressed trade relations between the United Provinces and Spain. It referred to navigation only in general and ambiguous terms, stipulating:

> The subjects and inhabitants of the countries of the said King, Archdukes and States, will have peaceful intercourse between them during the said Truce, without grief for past offences and damages: they will also be able to visit and sojourn in the countries of each other and to trade unhindered by sea and by land.[7]

Spanish diplomats, however, continued to refuse explicit concessions regarding navigation in the 'Indian seas'. The clause permitted Dutch trade only with

(London: Allen & Unwin, 1981); Bernardo García (ed.), *Tiempo de paces. La Pax Hispanica y la Tregua de los Doce Años (1609–2009)* (Madrid: Fundación Carlos de Amberes, 2009); Bernardo J. García, M. Herrero Sánchez and Alain Hugon (eds.), *El arte de la prudencia. La tregua de los Doce años en la Europa de los Pacificadores* (Madrid: Fundación Carlos de Amberes, 2012).

4 'Déclaration Préliminaire des Seigneurs Etats Generaux des Provinces Unies des Païs-Bas touchant la qualité d'Etats Libres, qui devra leur être donnée…, Fait à la Haye le 11 janvier 1609', in CUD, V.2, 97–8.

5 Israel, *The Dutch Republic and the Hispanic World*, 4–5; León M. Gómez Rivas, 'Comercio y diplomacia: la Tregua de los Doce Años en el marco de las disputas sobre la libertad de los mares', in José Martínez Millán and Rubén González Cuerva (eds.), *La Dinastía de los Austria. Las relaciones entre la Monarquía Católica y el Imperio*, vol. II (Madrid: Ediciones Polifemo, 2011), 1245–62.

6 For the text, see CUD, V.2, 99–102.

7 My translation. Ibid., 100: '*Les Sujets & Habitants és Païs desdits Sieurs Roi, Archiducs, & Etats, auront toute bonne correspondance & amitié par ensemble durant ladite Tréve, sans se rassentir des offences & dommages qu'ils ont reçu par le passé: pourront aussi fréquenter & séjourner és Païs l'un de l'autre, & y exercer leur trafic & commerce en toute seureté tant par Mer & autres Eaux, que par Terre*'.

Philip III's domains 'which he has in Europe and other places and seas'.[8] The negotiators deliberately left these provisions vague, as no consensus could be reached. From the Dutch perspective, the reference to 'other places and seas' could be interpreted to include the Indies, but the Spanish rejected such a reading. This interpretive deadlock represented a diplomatic setback for Philip III, who had long regarded the cessation of Dutch expeditions into Iberian-controlled seas as a prerequisite for any agreement. Nevertheless, the truce was designed to halt the immediate conflict on the European continent, leaving the more divisive issues to be resolved later, either through diplomacy or war.

During the truce (1609–1621), both sides continued to engage in hostilities in the Indian Ocean, much to the dismay of Philip III's Portuguese subjects.[9] In retrospect, the truce proved more advantageous for the Dutch who were coming on top from naval engagements. They steadily advanced their positions in the Indian Ocean while achieving less success in the western Atlantic. Despite this, the Dutch remained cautious of a potential resurgence of Spanish power.[10] By this time, the prospect of the Dutch renouncing their freedom of navigation had become entirely unrealistic. As early as the 1600s, they already possessed the world's largest merchant fleet, with ships often superior in design to their Iberian counterparts.[11]

In 1605, Dutch forces seized Amboina in the Moluccas, and by the late 1610s, they began to emulate the monopolistic policies once implemented by the Portuguese at the height of their influence. While the Portuguese had focused their power on the northern shores of the Indian Ocean, the Dutch established

---

8 Ibidem. My translation: 'However, the said king understands this to be restrained and limited to the kingdoms, countries, lands, and lordships which he has in Europe and other places and seas in which the subjects of other princes who are his friends and allies have the said trade by mutual consent; as regards the places, towns, ports, and harbours that he holds beyond the said limits, that the lords' estates and their subjects may not carry on any trade without the express permission of the said lord king; but they shall be allowed to carry on the said trade, if it seems good to them, in the countries of all other princes, potentates, and peoples who may wish to grant them to do so, even outside the said limits, without the said lord king, his officers and subjects making any impediment in this event to the said princes, [...] who may have permitted it to them, nor equally to them or to the persons with whom they have carried out or will carry out the said trade'.

9 Israel, *The Dutch Republic and the Hispanic World*, 25–7; Brightwell, 'The Spanish System', 281; George N. Clark, 'Grotius's East India Mission to England', *Transactions of the Grotius Society*, (20) (1934), 45–84, at 50; Elliott, *Imperial Spain*, 321–3.

10 Clark, 'Grotius's East India Mission to England', 50; Elliott, *Imperial Spain*, 326.

11 Leften S. Stavrianos, *The World Since 1500: A Global History* (Englewood: Prentice Hall, 1966), 128; Boxer, *The Dutch Seaborne Empire*, 69; Villiers, *The Indian Ocean*, 149.

their primary power base in the Indonesian islands.[12] In the Moluccas, the archetypal Spice Islands, the Dutch began treating European rivals harshly, restricting native Asian shipping, and imposing onerous conditions on local rulers. From the perspective of the native islanders, the monopolistic policies of the VOC were far stricter than those of the Portuguese.[13] However, as with their Lusitanian predecessors, the Dutch were only able to establish effective monopolies in certain regions of the East Indies. In essence, as they became the leading European naval power in the East Indies, the Dutch gradually abandoned their advocacy of *mare liberum* in favour of a closed-sea stance, consolidating control over the highly profitable spice trade.[14]

1.2 *England and the Dutch Republic: Valuable Allies, Dangerous Rivals*

English seafarers were the first to observe the shift in Dutch attitudes. Formerly steadfast allies against the Iberian empires, the English and Dutch had even entertained joint plans to divide the East Indian trade. However, the Dutch began restricting the freedom of navigation and trade for their erstwhile allies as English competition intensified. This growing hostility led to a series of Anglo-Dutch colonial conferences: in London (1613), The Hague (1615), and London again (1618).[15] Among the Dutch delegates was Grotius, the author of *Mare liberum*, who found himself in the awkward position of defending the recent monopolistic policies of the VOC in the East Indies. English delegates lamented the mistreatment of English merchants and their exclusion from certain Indonesian ports through violent means. The discussions shifted focus from the legal status of the sea to the right of trade. Dutch envoys sought to avoid openly contradicting the principles laid out in *Mare liberum*.

On the one hand, the Dutch argued that the English, as latecomers, were attempting to reap the harvest of Dutch efforts against the Hispano-

12 Boxer, *The Dutch Seaborne Empire*, 96–7; Anand, *Origin and Development*, 91.

13 Boxer, *The Dutch Seaborne Empire*, 96–8. Marie A. Petronella Meilink-Roelofsz, *Asian Trade and European Influence in the Indonesian Archipelago between 1500 and about 1630* (The Hague: M. Nijhoff, 1962), 196; Kavalam M. Panikkar, *Asia and Western Dominance: A Survey of the Vasco da Gama Epoch of Asian History, 1498–1945* (London: Allen & Unwin, 1953), 58–9; Alexander Bick, *Governing the Free Sea: The Dutch West India Company and Commercial Politics, 1618–1645* (Ph.D. dissertation, Princeton University, 2012).

14 Anand, *Origin and Development*, 89.

15 See George N. Clark and Willem J. M Van Eysinga, *The Colonial Conferences between England and the Netherlands in 1613 and 1615*, II (Leiden: Brill, 1951); Van Ittersum, *Profit and Principle*, 359–411; Nellen, *Hugo Grotius*, 243–5; Andrew Ruoss, *Competitive Collaboration: The Dutch and English East India Companies & The Forging of Global Corporate Political Economy (1650–1700)* (Ph.D. Dissertation, Durham, NC: Duke University, 2017), 56–66.

Portuguese without bearing the associated costs.[16] They advanced an argument rooted in the financial and human toll of oceanic expeditions, similar to earlier Portuguese justifications. Additionally, the Dutch commissioners placed great emphasis on treaties concluded between the VOC and native polities, many of which had granted the Dutch a monopoly over the spice trade in return for 'protection against the Portuguese and the Spanish'.[17] The Dutch characterised these *do ut facias* agreements as fully valid under the law of nations and natural equity, asserting that they also served the best interests of the native rulers who had previously suffered under Lusitanian oppression.[18] Grotius and his fellow delegates argued that native princes held the natural right to bind themselves through treaties. By extension, these rulers were free to limit their own trade and exclude the English in favour of the Dutch. In certain circumstances, the Dutch argued, 'contract extinguished the liberty of the law of nations', as the ability to form treaties itself arose from natural freedom.[19]

On the other hand, the English defended the principles of freedom of travel and trade as primitive rights under the law of nations.[20] They even cited passages from *Mare liberum* against its author, referring to Grotius as the *assertor maris liberi* (champion of free seas). English officials decried the illegality of Dutch monopolies, pointing out that the English had known of these islands before the Dutch and had concluded their own treaties of commerce with certain native rulers.[21] The English commissioners, representing the newly crowned James I, went so far as to compare Dutch practices to those of the Portuguese. This comparison offended the Dutch, who argued that Iberian claims to monopolies were based on papal donation and extended over entire oceans, while the VOC claimed only a few specific strongholds and limited local trade monopolies.[22] If the Portuguese had sought to close vast swathes

16 'Rapport des délégués anglais au Conseil Privé du mai 1613…', annexe 39, reported in George N. Clark and Willem J. M Van Eysinga, *The Colonial Conferences between England and the Netherlands in 1613 and 1615*, I (Leiden: Brill, 1940), 117–23. See also Jan H. W. Verzijl, *International Law in Historical Perspective*, VII (Leiden: A. W. Sijthoff, 1971), 35.

17 'Troisième mémoire néerlandais du 13 mars 1615, British Museum, MSS. Harleian 147', annexe 77, in Clark and Van Eysinga, *The Colonial Conferences*, I, 207.

18 Annexe 35. Ibid.

19 Ibid., 71. See also annexe 40.

20 Annexe 34. Ibid.

21 Annexe 77. Ibid., 201–11. Special reference was made to Drake's circumnavigation of the globe.

22 'Rapport des délégués anglais au Conseil Privé du 10 mai 1613', annexe 39, ibid., 102.

of the ocean, the Dutch insisted they were merely defending their hard-won agreements with local rulers. King James VI–I himself weighed in, declaring to Grotius and his fellow envoys that he would not allow for his subjects to be excluded from the Indies. Grotius countered that the Dutch had no intention of imposing such restrictions. The king further asserted that 'where neither is in possession neither should impede the other's free commerce', proposing that VOC monopolies should be confined to Dutch settlements while the ocean remained open as a common trade route to the East.[23]

In conclusion, the 1613–1615 conferences ended in a stalemate. The Dutch employed dilatory diplomatic tactics to maintain the VOC's dominance in the spice trade. Both parties, however, agreed on the common threat posed by Philip III, recognising that Anglo-Dutch disputes could enable a resurgence of Iberian power in the East Indies.[24] Nonetheless, tensions in the Indian Ocean continued to accumulate in the following years, ultimately contributing to the eruption of the Anglo-Dutch conflicts of the second half of the

FIGURE 4.1 The Arms of the Dutch East India Company (VOC) and of the Town of Batavia, by Jeronimus Becx (active c.1649–658), oil on panel, 1651
SOURCE: RIJKSMUSEUM AMSTERDAM

23 Clark, 'Grotius's East India Mission to England', 64; Pagden, *The Burdens of Empire*, 157.

24 'Caron to the States General, 24 March 1613; annexe 28', in Clark and Van Eysinga, *The Colonial Conferences*, I, 60.

seventeenth century. Later, the English ambassador in The Hague, Sir George Downing, would summarise the Dutch stance with this remark: 'It is a *mare liberum* in the British seas but *mare clausum* on the coast of Africa and in the East-Indies.'[25]

1.3 *Spatio-temporal Relativism and Opportunism*

International politics and the law of the sea have always been closely interwoven. The early modern debates on the 'claimed seas' were no exception, as governments and jurists often displayed a notable lack of consistency – at best – in their positions on the legal status of the sea. The same polity might easily advocate divergent ideas depending on the geographical context. Furthermore, reversals were commonplace, spurred by geopolitical shifts, the passage of time, or the personal ambitions of the rulers involved. In the preceding section, we highlighted how swiftly Dutch behaviour in the Indian Ocean evolved following changes in the balance of power. The Dutch were by no means unique in adjusting their stance on the 'claimed seas'; England provides another compelling example.

In the 1610s, as we have seen, the English invoked the principle of freedom of the seas to assert their right of access to the East Indies. Meanwhile, King James VI of Scotland (r. 1566–1625), who inherited the English throne from Elizabeth I as James I (r. 1603–1625),[26] made peace with Spain and gradually abandoned the Tudor-era tradition of championing free movement and fisheries exploitation in the waters surrounding the British Isles – a practice we discussed in Chapter 1.[27] As Thomas W. Fulton notes, James VI–I was merely extending to England the longstanding Scottish attitude towards foreign fishermen, observing that 'the Scottish people had always been very jealous of foreigners sharing in their fisheries, and never

25 'Sir George Downing to Lord Clarendon, 20 November 1663', quoted in Boxer, *The Dutch Seaborne Empire*, 92. For more details, see Roger Downing and Gijs Rommelse, *A Fearful Gentleman: Sir George Downing in The Hague, 1658–1672* (Hilversum: Verloren, 2011).

26 James supported a 'perfect union' between Scotland and England, declaring himself 'King of Great Britain and Ireland' in 1604. See Jenny Wormald, 'James VI, James I and the identity of Britain', in Brendan Bradshaw and John Morrill (eds.), *The British Problem, c.1534–1707: State Formation in the Atlantic Archipelago* (London: Macmillan Education, 1996), 148–71, at 154–5. On King James VI–I, see Pauline Croft, *King James* (New York: Palgrave Macmillan, 2003); Rosalind Mitchison, *A History of Scotland* (New York: Routledge, 2003), 107–36. On the new dynasty, see Barry Coward, *The Stuart Age – England, 1603–1714* (London: Routledge, 2011); Godfrey Davies, *The Early Stuarts 1603–1660* (Oxford: Clarendon Press, 1959).

27 Rodger, *The Safeguard of the Sea*, 347–8; Fulton, *The Sovereignty of the Sea*, 338–42. See *supra*, chapter 1, 3.2.

consented to give them the liberty to fish, so freely accorded by England'.[28] The new Stuart policies soon eclipsed Dano-Norwegian claims as the principal catalyst for diplomatic and doctrinal debates in the northern European waters.[29] Indeed, as Christian IV of Denmark-Norway became increasingly embroiled in conflicts with Sweden and in imperial politics – culminating in a disastrous intervention in the Thirty Years' War, – his assertions of maritime dominion significantly weakened.[30]

As early as 1604, James VI–I and his Privy Council established the concept of the 'King's Chambers', which comprised sea areas defined by straight baselines drawn between coastal promontories (see Figure 4.2 below). From that point onwards, several bays along the English coastline were considered under the king's jurisdiction, with access prohibited to foreign belligerents. James VI–I even issued a proclamation detailing the geographical extent of these chambers.[31] This measure should be understood in the context of ongoing Dutch-Spanish naval engagements around the British Isles, often perilously close to English shores. As the Dutch gained the upper hand in their conflict with Spain, Spanish vessels increasingly sought refuge in English neutral waters.

> We haue thought it convenient to make an open declaration how our said Officers and subjects shall demeane themselves towards the Subjects as well as the King of Spaine and Archdukes, as also of the States united in the cases following [...] That within our Portes, Hauens, Rodes, Creekes, or other places of our dominion, or so neere to any of our sayd portes or hauens as may bee reasonablie construed to bee within that tytle, limitt, or precinct, there shall be no force, violence, surprise, or

28 Fulton, *The Sovereignty of the Sea*, 123–5.

29 Ibidem.

30 Brüel, *International Straits*, II, 20–1. See also Paul D. Lockart, *Denmark in the Thirty Years' War, 1618–1648: King Christian IV and the Decline of the Oldenburg State* (Selinsgrove: Susquehanna University Press, 1996); idem, 'Denmark and the Empire: A Reassessment of Danish Foreign Policy under King Christian IV', *Scandinavian Studies*, 64(3) (1992), 390–416; Steve Murdoch, *Britain, Denmark-Norway and the House of Stuart, 1603–1660* (East Linton: Tuckwell Press, 2000); idem, 'Diplomacy in transition. Stuart-British diplomacy in northern Europe, 1603–1618', in Allan I. Macinnes, Thomas Riis and Frederik G. Pedersen (eds.), *Ships, Guns and Bibles in the North Sea and Baltic States* (East Linton: Tuckwell Press, 2000), 93–138; Robert I. Frost, *The Northern Wars. War, State and Society in Northeastern Europe, 1558–1721* (London: Longman, 2000), 135–40.

31 'Declaration of jury of the Trinity House as to the limits of the King's Chambers', Appendix E (State Papers, Domestic, James I, vol. 13, n. 11, 1605), reported in Fulton, *The Sovereignty of the Sea*, 754.

> offence suffered to be done, either from Man of warre to Man of warre, or Man of warre to Merchant, or Merchant to Merchant of either partie, but that all of what Nation soever, so long as they shall bee within those our ports and places of our jurisdiction, or where our Officers may prohibite violence, shall be understood to be under our protection to be ordered by course of justice, and be at peace with each other.[32]

With the establishment of the 'King's Chambers', all vessels sailing within these designated areas were placed under royal protection, hostilities were prohibited, and prizes taken by belligerents were declared invalid.[33] This measure represented a clear extension of royal authority over adjacent seas, assimilating their legal regime to that of harbours. However, the chambers did not imply sovereignty or ownership but rather sought to ensure respect for English neutrality and curb licensed and unlicensed maritime predation. In essence, the concepts underpinning these policies were jurisdiction, protection, and the creation of a neutrality zone.

Furthermore, James VI–I soon declared his intention to assert control over 'British' fisheries, a move that predominantly targeted Dutch fishermen. At the time, the Dutch dominated the lucrative herring fisheries of the North Sea, particularly along the eastern coasts of England and Scotland, referred to as the 'great fishery' (*Groote Visscherye*).[34] Dutch predominance was well-recognised by contemporaries and provoked resentment among English fishermen and governmental circles alike.[35] Dutch officials, including the ambas-

32 'Proclamation for revocation of mariners from forreine services', Appendix D (A Booke of Proclamations, published since the beginning of his Majesties most happy Reigne over England…, 1602–1612), reported in Fulton, *The Sovereignty of the Sea*, 750–3. Fulton gave 1604 as the date of the document. Marsden erroneously reported 1605 in *Documents*, vol. I, pp. 353–8. The closing formula of the text – 'Given at Thetford the firste day of March in the second yeere of our Raigne of Great Britaine' – confirms 1604 as the correct date.

33 Raestad, *La mer territoriale*, 84; Feakes, *Formative Influences*, 137–8.

34 Fulton, *The Sovereignty of the Sea*, 132; Cialdea, *La formazione dell'ordinamento marittimo*, 64–71. On the geoeconomic importance on North Sea fisheries, see Jan de Vries and Ad van der Woude, *The First Modern Economy: Success, Failure, and Perseverance of the Dutch Economy (1500–1815)* (Cambridge: University Press, 1997), 235–69; Hendrik A. H. Kranenburg, *De zeevisscherij van Holland in den tijd der Republiek* (Amsterdam: H.J. Paris, 1946). See also Kenneth H. D. Haley, *The British and the Dutch: Political and Cultural Relations through the Ages* (London: George Philip, 1988); George Edmundson, *Anglo-Dutch Rivalry during the First Half of the Seventeenth Century* (Oxford: Clarendon Press, 1911), 34–57.

35 Raestad, *La mer territoriale*, 70, 85.

sador Noël de Caron, closely monitored James's growing interest in claiming the surrounding seas, as it threatened a maritime area of immense geostrategic and economic importance to the Dutch Republic. On one hand, James VI–I viewed the fledgling Dutch Republic as dependent on his patronage and support for its political survival. On the other hand, the increasingly wealthy and militarily secured Republic was becoming ever less inclined to tolerate English interference in its affairs.

Moreover, following the Anglo-Spanish peace of 1604, James appeared suspiciously well disposed towards Madrid.[36] In this regard, the Venetian ambassador in London, Nicolò Molin (1603–1606), reported to the Venetian Senate that Spanish envoys were pressuring James to persuade the Dutch to make peace with Spain – a truce that would soon become the Twelve Years' Truce. The Spanish argued that continued hostilities allowed the Dutch to 'seize those seas (i.e. the British seas), ordinarily having at their disposal more than one hundred ships, well deployed in various areas; thus, they could say they already were in possession of the said seas, for whose possession the ancient kings of England waged very long and costly wars against the princes of Europe'.[37]

Molin further noted that the king had affirmed he was aware of the situation, but also that: 'Just with one nod from him, the Dutch would surrender to him all the dominion they had gained'.[38] The keen-eyed ambassador observed that this was plausible as long as the Dutch were at war with Spain, as they could not afford to confront both Spain and England simultaneously. However, should peace with Spain be achieved, it was far from certain that the Dutch would relinquish any portion of the maritime power they had acquired. To this end, Molin reported that Spanish envoys urged James to target Dutch herring fisheries, which were among the Republic's primary sources of

36 Simon Adams, 'Spain or the Netherlands? The dilemmas of early Stuart foreign policy', in Howard Tomlinson (ed.), *Before the English Civil War: Essays on Early Stuart Politics and Government* (Palgrave: London, 1983), 79–101.

37 My translation. 'Relazione d'Inghilterra di Nicolò Molin, ambasciatore ordinario appresso Giacomo I, 1607', in Nicolò Barozzi Guglielmo and Berchet (eds.), *Relazioni degli Stati Europei lette al Senato*, Serie IV – Inghilterra, volume unico (Venezia: P. Naratovich, 1863), 73–4: '*Gli Spagnuoli però non cessano di mettere in considerazione al re che per interesse proprio doverebbe premer grandemente in questo negozio affine che se si venga a qualche conclusione, poiché continuando la guerra, gli Olandesi vengono ad impadronirsi di quelli mari, tenendo loro armate ordinariamente cento e più navi, le quali se ben sono sparse in diversi luoghi, possono però dire e con verità di esser padroni di detti mari, per il possesso dei quali li re antichi dell'Inghilterra hanno fatte lunghissime e dispendiosissime guerre contro li principi d'Europa*'.

38 Ibid., 73.

wealth.[39] Molin, impressed by Dutch maritime capabilities, estimated their commercial and fishing fleet at 3,000 ships and 40,000 sailors[40] – figures that contrasted starkly with his negative assessment of the Royal Navy, which he judged to have been severely neglected in comparison to Elizabeth I's times.[41] Subsequent Venetian ambassadors, such as Marcantonio Correr and Girolamo Lando, corroborated this critical view of English naval strength.[42]

In this charged context, on 15 March 1608, the State Council of Holland passed a secret resolution declaring that the Dutch would never 'in whole or in part, directly or indirectly, withdraw, surrender or renounce the freedom of the seas, everywhere and in all regions of the world'.[43] Despite this, momentum for English assertiveness continued to grow in the ensuing years. English mercantile and governmental circles were increasingly dismayed by the number of Dutch fishing vessels depleting the 'British seas' of their halieutic resources. English and Scottish fishermen, lagging far behind their Dutch counterparts in both efficiency and numbers, complained of being driven out of their own waters. For instance, the Dutch were the first to implement curing and barrelling techniques directly on board of their herring busses, which

39 Ibid., 73–4: '*Conosce il re tutto ciò esser vero, ma ha anco opinione che ad un solo suo cenno sieno gli Olandesi per cedergli tutto quel dominio che potessero aversi guadagnato; il che senza dubbio seguirla mentre durasse la guerra co' Spagnuoli, non potendo loro in uno stesso tempo contrastare con due dei maggiori principi di Cristianità. Ma se con il tempo che matura le cose, succedesse la pace tra loro e la corona di Spagna, non so se fossero così pronti a cedere come il re d'Inghilterra si promette; poiché così come questa professione da mare va manifestamente ogni di più inclinando in Inghilterra, così ogni dì più si aumenta e prende forza e vigore tra gli Olandesi:* [...] *Hanno gli Spagnuoli tentata un'altra via che senza dubbio porterebbe gran danno agli Olandesi, quando la cosa riuscisse, ed è con aver fatto raccordar al re non esser servigio suo nè de' suoi sudditi il permetter libera ed immune ad Olandesi la pesca delle aringhe, la quale si fa nella parte settentrionale dell'isola verso la Scozia, e di questa ne cavano profitto più di due milioni d'oro all'anno*'.

40 Ibidem.

41 Ibid., 31.

42 'Relazione d'Inghilterra di Marcantonio Correr, ambasciatore ordinario appresso Giacomo I, 1611', ibid., 96; 'Relazione d'Inghilterra di Girolamo Lando, ambasciatore ordinario appresso Giacomo I, 1622', ibid., 235. See also Rodger, *The Safeguard of the Sea*, 364–70; Christopher D. Penn, *The Navy under the Early Stuarts and its Influence on English History* (Manchester: The Faith Press, 1913), 1–53.

43 Later in 1645, the States General of the United Provinces restated: 'The existence, welfare and reputation of the State consists in navigation and maritime trade'. Quoted in Boxer, *The Dutch Seaborne Empire*, 90–91. Cf. Anand, *Origin and Development*, 96.

prevented the early decomposition of fish and resulted in a better taste for the final product.[44]

In response, English pamphleteers and polemicists called for the exclusion of Dutch fishermen from the seas around the British Isles or, at the very least, for strict limitations on their activities. Admittedly, a 'claimed seas' approach to fisheries would not only revitalise the British fishing industry but also expand the kingdom's maritime economy and bolster the Royal Navy, as fishermen were the primary source of skilled manpower for naval service.[45] Hence, in May 1609, James VI–I went a step further by issuing the 'Proclamation for the restraint of foreigners fishing on the British coasts'. The king justified this measure as necessary to preserve his royal prerogatives:

> Whereas wee haue bene contented since our comming to the Crowne, to tolerate an indifferent and promiscuous kinde of libertie to all our friends whatsoeuer, to fish within our streames, and vpon any of our coasts of Great Britaine, Ireland, and other adiacent Islands, so farre foorth as the permission or use thereof might not redound to the empeachment of our Prerogative Royall, nor to the hurt and damage of our louing Subiects, whose preseruation and flourishing estate we hold our selfe principally bound to aduance before all worldly respects: So finding that our conniuence therein, hath not onely giuen occasion of ouer great encrochments upon our Regalities, or rather questioning for our Right, but hath bene a meanes of much dayly wrongs to our owne people that exercise the trade of Fishing as (either by the multitude of Strangers, which doe preoccupy those places, or by the iniuries which they receiue most comonly at their hands) our Subiects are constrained to abandon their Fishing, or at the least are become so discouraged in the same, as they hold it better for them, to betake themselues to some other course of liuing, whereby not onely diuers of our Coast-townes are much decayed, but the number of Mariners dayly diminished, which is a matter of great consequence to our Estate, considering how much the strength thereof consisteth in the power of Shipping, and use of Nauigation.[46]

44 Martine J. van Ittersum, '*Mare Liberum* Versus the Propriety of the Seas? The Debate between Hugo Grotius (1583–1645) and William Welwood (1552–1624) and its Impact on Anglo-Scotto-Dutch Fishery Disputes in the Second Decade of the Seventeenth Century', *Edinburgh Law Review*, 10(2) (2008), 239–76; Anand, *Origin and Development*, 100–1.

45 Fulton, *The Sovereignty of the Sea*, 58.

46 'Proclamation of James I for the restraint of foreigners fishing on the British coasts, issued on 6th May 1609', Appendix F, reported in Fulton, *The Sovereignty of the Sea*, 756.

The king continued that it was both just and necessary to adopt lawful measures to increase his control over the surrounding seas and to put an end to the abuses perpetrated by foreign fishermen. Nevertheless, he emphasised that he had no desire to deprive his neighbours of 'those fruits and benefits of peace and friendship', that were deemed just under the 'principles of honour and reason'.[47] In his proclamation, James VI–I sought to strike a balance between the expectations of his subjects and the legitimate interests of foreign powers. To this end, he declared that, effective from 1 August 1609:

> No person of what Nation or qualitie soeuer, being not our naturall borne Subiect, be permitted to fish upon any of our Coasts and Seas of Great Britaine, Ireland, and the rest of the Isles adiacent, where most usually heretofore any fishing hath bene, untill they haue orderly demanded and obtained licenses from vs, or such our Commissioners, as we haue authorised in that behalfe, viz. at London for our Realmes of England and Ireland, and at Edenborough for our Realme of Scotland: Which Licenses, our intention is, shall be yeerely demanded, for so many Vessels and ships, and the Tonnage thereof, as shall intend to fish for that whole yeere, or any part thereof, vpon any of our Coastes and Seas as aforesaid, upon paine of such chastisement, as shalbe fit to bee inflicted upon such wilfull offendors.[48]

Therefore, foreigners were still permitted to fish along the coasts of England, but they were required to obtain yearly licences from the king's officials. However, James VI–I, cautious by nature, did not press the matter further and acquiesced to the Dutch request to defer the issue of fishing licences for the time being.[49] It was instead agreed to prioritise discussions on the East Indies during the 1613–1615 conferences, as mentioned in the previous section. In other words, from the 1610s onwards the Dutch and English became embroiled in a series of interconnected disputes over commerce and navigation.[50] While the Dutch were leaning towards monopolising access to spice

47 Ibidem.

48 Ibidem.

49 John C. Grayson, *From Protectorate to Partnership. Anglo-Dutch Relations 1598–1625* (Ph.D. Thesis, University College London, 1978), 245–7. See also 'Relazione d'Inghilterra di Marcantonio Correr, ambasciatore ordinario appresso Giacomo I, 1611', in Berchet and Barozzi, *Relazioni degli Stati Europei lette al Senato*, Serie IV - Inghilterra, 128–9.

50 Jack S. Levy, 'The rise and decline of the Anglo-Dutch rivalry, 1609–1689', in Thompson (ed.), *Great Power Rivalries*, 172–200.

FIGURE 4.2 Map showing the extent of the King's Chambers claimed by James VI–I in 1604
SOURCE: FULTON, *THE SOVEREIGNTY OF THE SEA*, 123

production centres in the East Indies, they claimed the freedom of the sea in the pelagic spaces surrounding the British Isles. Conversely, James VI–I reversed traditional English foreign policy by asserting exclusive rights over the 'British seas' while demanding access to the seas of the East based on Grotian arguments. In the final section of this chapter, we will examine the further developments of the Stuart pretensions over the 'British seas'. In conclusion, to fully appreciate the doctrinal development of 'claimed seas' argumentation in the first half of the seventeenth century, it is crucial to consider the geopolitical context in which diplomats operated and scholars wrote. As Thomas W. Fulton aptly observed, the defenders of both *mare liberum* and *mare clausum*: 'including some of the most learned men of their age, were in large measure inspired by patriotic motives. National interests as much as lofty ethics or legal principles were at its root'.[51]

1.4 *Reactions to Grotius'* Mare liberum

In the rapidly changing world briefly outlined above, the international significance of Grotius' *Mare liberum* proved profound. It became a focal point for polemics and controversies, provoking vibrant reactions from polities whose interests were directly or indirectly threatened by Grotius' ideas, which were far from universally accepted at the time.[52] The principle of the freedom of the seas found in Grotius a formidable champion, whose clarity and intellectual prowess set a new standard for the debate. In response, numerous jurists rose to defend the opposing principle of the 'claimed seas'. The papacy's reaction was unequivocal: as early as January 1610, *Mare liberum* was included in the Index of Forbidden Books. As David Armitage observed, 'Grotius' arguments could still justify the VOC's encroachment on the Portuguese colonial empire, despite the armistice in Europe', and 'their applicability to other contemporary disputes regarding the freedom of navigation, trade, and fishing made *Mare liberum* a shot heard around the world'.[53]

As Grotius officially targeted Portuguese claims in the Indian Ocean, the geographical and temporal scope of his arguments was ostensibly limited. Yet, *Mare liberum* carried vast and universal implications, prompting many sovereigns and jurists to perceive it as a direct threat to their national interests. Grotius' reasoning could indeed undermine a range of different maritime claims, whether in the Mediterranean, northern Europe or distant oceans, bearing implications for both smaller seas and the oceanic expanses.[54] In this regard, Luis García Arias noted that: 'The *Free Sea* had been written against Portugal, published against Spain, and used against England'.[55]

51 Fulton, *The Sovereignty of the Sea*, 338–42.
52 Bederman, 'The Sea', 366–9.
53 David Armitage, 'Introduction' to *H. Grotius, The Free Sea*, xi.
54 Ibidem; Grewe, *Epochs*, 257–75.
55 'Introduction' to Hugo Grocio, *De la libertad de los mares* (Instituto de Estudios Políticos: Madrid, 1956), 14, my translation. See also José A. Martínez Torres, '«Gobernar el Mundo». La polémica *Mare Liberum versus Mare Clausum* en las Indias Orientales (1603–1625)', *Anuario de Estudios Americanos*, 74(1) (2017), 71–96.

The publication of *Mare liberum* played a pivotal role in forcing its opponents to restructure their legal arguments in favour of the 'claimed seas' principle. Reactions emerged from a wide range of authors with diverse backgrounds and motives. Among the most notable were the Scottish jurist William Welwod, who authored *An Abridgement of All Sea-Lawes* (1613) and *De dominio maris* (1615); the English scholars John Borough, who wrote *The Sovereignty of the British Seas* (1651),[56] and John Selden, whose *Mare Clausum seu de dominio maris libri duo* (1635) remains the most prominent response. From the Iberian Peninsula came the Portuguese monk and jurist Justo Seraphim de Freitas with *De justo imperio Lusitanorum Asiatico* (1625), and the Spanish jurist and colonial official Juan Solórzano Pereira, who addressed Iberian maritime claims in *De indiarum jure* (1629).[57] However, the earliest known reply to *Mare liberum* came from a relatively obscure Flemish Jesuit based in Spain, Nicolas Bonaert (1564–?), who penned the unpublished and long-forgotten manuscript *Minos seu mare tutum* in 1610.[58] In this work, Bonaert advanced the concept of *mare tutum*, or 'the secure sea', arguing that the open sea was characterised by anarchy and piracy and required strong authority to impose order. In his view, rulers who 'pacified' the sea – such as Minos in antiquity or the Iberian monarchs of his own time – were entitled to reap the profits and taxes generated by maritime trade.[59]

56 The original title of the work was: *Dominium maris Britannici assertum ex archivis historiis et municipalibus regni legibus*. Even though Borough completed it in 1633, the treatise was published only posthumously in 1651, destined to remain in the shadow of Selden's work.

57 Juan de Solórzano Pereira, *Disputationem de Indiarum iure* (Madrid: Tipografía Francisco Martínez, 1629).

58 For the text, see Nicolaes Bonaert, 'Textus Ineditі: Minos seu mare tutum', edited by Primitivo Mariño Gomes. *Archivum Historicum Societatis Iesu*, 61 (1992), 309–38. The surviving portion of the Latin manuscript was only rediscovered in 1989 by Primitivo Mariño Gomes. Crucial to Bonaert's idea was Thucydides' account of the mythological Cretan-Minoan King Minos, who had allegedly established the first thalassocracy.

59 Of course, Bonaert also referred to the traditional titles claimed by the Portuguese and the Spanish, i.e. discovery, occupation, papal donation, just war, and custom. See Salom-Franco, 'Vitoria y Grocio frente al mar', 113–4, the author also includes a Spanish translation as an appendix; Giuseppe Marcocci, 'Machiavelli, la religione dei romani e l'impero portoghese', *Storica*, 41–2 (2008), 35–68, at 43–4; San Emeterio Martín, 'El debate sobre el dominio de los mares', 137–9; Alexander Batson, 'Mare Tutum: Thucydides, King Minos, and the Concept of the "Secure Sea" in Seventeenth-Century Maritime Law', *Grotiana*, 4 (15) (2024), 1–31.

In addition, pro-Venetian works were published in reaction, even though not in direct contraposition, to Grotius' *Mare liberum*. The most notable ones were Paolo Sarpi's *Dominio del Mare Adriatico della Serenissima Repubblica di Venezia* (1612), and Giulio Pace da Beriga's *De dominio maris Hadriatici disceptatio* (1619). Later, Pietro Battista Borgo defended Genoese claims in the Ligurian Sea with *De dominio Serenissimae Genuensis Repubblicae in mari Ligustico libri duo* (1641).[60] Dutch authors, including Dirk Graswinckel and Johan Van de Brug, often commissioned by the States General, conversely took on the task of defending Grotius' arguments against the growing number of critics.[61] This ongoing debate between the advocates of the freedom of the sea and the 'claimed seas' (*mare clausum*) continued well into the mid-seventeenth century, earning the moniker '*la bataille des livres*' (the battle of the books) from the Belgian scholar Ernest Nys, one of the first professional historians of international law.[62]

Guido Acquaviva has noted a connection between the development of 'claimed seas' arguments in the seventeenth century and the contemporaneous rise of the concept of sovereignty.[63] Jean Bodin's *Les six livres de la république* (1576) played a key role in this process, offering a systematic exposition of sovereignty; as Acquaviva explains: 'To cope with a new composite reality, made up of autonomous sovereigns who governed over more or less large territories, the idea of institutionalised relations between different political entities arose, based on the concept of absolute, indivisible, and inalienable sovereignty developed by Bodin'.[64] During the seventeenth century, the

60 Pietro Battista Burgus, *De dominio Serenissimae Genuensis Reipublicae in Mari Ligustico libri II* (Romae: D. Marcianus, 1641).

61 For instance, see Graswinckel's replies to Welwod: *Maris liberi vindiciae adversus Guilielmum Welwodum britannici maritimi dominii assertorem* (1653) and Borgo: *Maris liberi vindiciae adversus Petrum Baptistam Burgum Ligustici maritimi dominii assertorem* (1652).

62 Ernest Nys, 'Une Bataille de Livres, an Episode in the Literary History of International Law', *Juridical Review*, 3(1–2) (1891), 131–7; idem, 'La liberté des mers', 379–87.

63 Acquaviva, 'Giulio Pace: la giurisdizione di Venezia sul Mare Adriatico', in Acquaviva and Scovazzi, *Il dominio di Venezia*, 41. My translation.

64 Ibidem. For the most relevant of Bodin's passages, see Jean Bodin, *On Sovereignty. Four Chapters from the Six Books of the Commonwealth*, edited by Julian H. Franklin (Cambridge: University Press, 2004). See also Diego Quaglioni, *La sovranità* (Bari: Laterza, 2004); Merio Scattola, 'Jean Bodin on international law' in Kadelbach et al. (eds.), *System, Order, and International Law*, 78–91; Daniel Lee, *The Right of Sovereignty: Jean Bodin on the Sovereign State and the Law of Nations* (Oxford: University Press, 2021); Philippe Denis, 'Edmond Richer, Jean Bodin and the idea of sovereignty', in Cornel Zwierlein, Corncl and Daniel Lee (eds.), *Sovereignty. European and Global Histories, 1400–1800* (Leiden/Boston: Martinus Nijhoff/Brill, 2024), 88–107.

term sovereignty became politically and philosophically entrenched, initially referring primarily to land territories before gradually extending to maritime spaces as a 'reasonable corollary'.[65] This conceptual shift facilitated the interplay between emerging notions of sovereignty and longstanding legal categories – such as property, protection, and jurisdiction – that had previously shaped debates on the legal status of the sea.

The following sections will explore the development of the 'claimed seas' principle in the aftermath of *Mare liberum's* publication. The analysis will focus on the same geographical macro-areas examined in previous chapters: first, the Mediterranean Sea, with particular attention to Venetian claims in the Adriatic as an example of a smaller, naturally enclosed sea; second, Iberian claims over the open oceans; and third, the seas of Northern Europe, where British claims gradually replaced those of Denmark–Norway as sources of regional tensions and diplomacy.

2 The Mediterranean: Pro-Venetian Defence of Adriatic Predominance

2.1 *Ancient Claims, Renewed Threats*

As we have seen, the Dutch Republic emerged at the forefront of European geopolitics in the early decades of the seventeenth century. It was successfully fighting for survival and global maritime expansion in an international system dominated by larger monarchies. Meanwhile, another, more ancient republic faced challenges to its maritime power and even its existence as an independent state.[66] Once again, our focus will shift to the Mediterra-

65 Acquaviva, 'Giulio Pace: la giurisdizione di Venezia sul Mare Adriatico', in Acquaviva and Scovazzi, *Il dominio di Venezia*, 41. My translation.

66 Paragraphs 2.1 and 2.2 formed the basis of: Stefano Cattelan, 'The Defence of Venetian Dominion over the Adriatic Sea: Situating Paolo Sarpi, c.1600–1625', *Comparative Legal History*, 9(2) (2021), 177–207, https://doi.org/10.1080/2049677X.2021.2001968. On the similarities and differences between the Venetian and Dutch republics, see Eco O. G. Haitsma Mulier, *The Myth of Venice and Dutch Republican Thought in the Seventeenth Century* (Assen: Van Gorcum, 1980), 64–70. Influential Dutch authors of the time, such as Grotius, Althusius, Heinsius, and Busius often referred to Venice as an example to follow for their own young republic. They praised its stability, republicanism, and role in to maintaining the balance of power. By November 1609, the first Dutch ambassador arrived in the lagoon and was received with great honours. See 'Wotton to Earl of Salisbury', 14 November 1609, *Life and Letters*, vol. 1, 476, quoted in Webster G. Tarpley, *Paolo Sarpi, His Networks, Venice and the Coming of the Thirty Years' War* (Ph.D. dissertation, Washington D.C.: The Catholic University of America, 2009), 432.

nean Sea, notably to the Republic of Venice. The success of Portuguese and Dutch East-West commercial routes had destabilised the Mediterranean trading network that Venice had carefully constructed over the centuries. Additionally, northern European shipping had begun to penetrate the Mediterranean in force, successfully competing for regional markets and the carrying trade.[67]

At the same time, Ottoman expansion in the Levant stripped Venice of key possessions, notably Cyprus in 1571, while imposing crippling military expenses on the Venetian treasury. However, during periods of peace – such as between 1573 and 1645 – Venice and the Ottoman Empire maintained strong commercial ties, and Venetian diplomats worked to prevent renewed military conflicts.[68] However, attacks by Christian corsairs on Ottoman vessels or towns in the Adriatic frequently threatened to entangle Venice in new hostilities. The Sublime Porte usually held Venice accountable for acts of maritime predation committed against Ottoman subjects in waters ostensibly under Venetian jurisdiction, including the Adriatic and the seas adjacent to Crete.[69]

On the Italian peninsula, Venice managed to preserve its independence during the protracted conflicts between France and Spain for dominance in

67 Cialdea, *La formazione dell'ordinamento marittimo*, 28–9; Gino Luzzatto, 'La decadenza di Venezia dopo le scoperte geografiche nella tradizione e nella realtà', *Archivio Veneto*, serie V, 54–5 (1954), 162–81; Angela Caracciolo-Aricò (cur.), *L'impatto della scoperta dell'America nella cultura veneziana* (Roma: Bulzoni, 1990); Andrea Zannini, 'Economic and social aspects of the crisis of Venetian diplomacy in the seventeenth and eighteenth centuries' in Daniela Frigo (ed.), *Politics and Diplomacy in Early Modern Italy: The Structure of Diplomatic Practice, 1450–1800* (Cambridge: University Press, 2000), 109–46; idem, 'L'economia veneta nel Seicento. Oltre il paradigma della "crisi generale"', in *Società Italiana di Demografia Storica, La popolazione nel Seicento, relazione presentata al convegno di Firenze*, 28–30 novembre 1996 (Bologna: CLUEB, 1999), 473–502; Alberto Bin, *La Repubblica di Venezia e la questione adriatica, 1600–1620* (Roma: Il Veltro, 1992), 33–40; Frederic C. Lane, *I mercanti di Venezia* (Torino: Einaudi, 1982), 195–203; Teofilo F. Ruiz, 'The Mediterranean and the Atlantic', in Peregrine Horden and Sharon Kinoshita (eds.), *A Companion to Mediterranean History* (New York: Wiley Blackwell, 2014), 411–24, at 411; Molly Greene, 'Beyond the Northern Invasion: The Mediterranean in the Seventeenth Century', *Past & Present*, 174(1) (2002), 42–71.

68 Corrado Vivanti, *Quattro lezioni su Paolo Sarpi* (Napoli: Bibliopolis, 2005), 11–21; Geraud Poumarède, *L'empire de Venise et les turcs, XVIe–XVIIe* (Paris: Garnier, 2020); Arbel, 'Venice's Maritime Empire in the Early Modern Period', 143–4; Piero Del Negro, 'La politica militare di Venezia e lo stato da mar nel Sei-Settecento', *Studi veneziani*, 39 (2000), 113–21.

69 Nani Mocenigo, *Storia della marina veneziana*, 85–105.

the region – an achievement of considerable significance.[70] In the early seventeenth century, Venice, always vigilant in defending its jurisdiction and sovereign prerogatives, repeatedly clashed with Counter-Reformation popes, who were often politically aligned with Spain.[71] The apples of discord consisted of matters of ecclesiastical jurisdiction and privileges, as well as the Roman Curia's general disdain for Venetian particularism. Despite its unwavering Catholic identity, Venice maintained a suspicious degree of autonomy from Rome, engaging in diplomatic relations with Protestant polities while continuing to trade with Muslim powers. However, in 1596, when the Apostolic Nuncio Anton Maria Graziani (1537–1611) arrived in Venice, he was also demanding concessions concerning the freedom of navigation in the Adriatic Sea. He argued that Venetian sea laws suffocated the ports of the Papal States such as Ancona, forcing merchant ships to stopover in Venice.[72] The Venetian government refused to yield, and by April 1606, mounting tensions culminated in Pope Paul V (r. 1605–1621) issuing an interdict against Venice.[73]

By the late sixteenth century, most Italian states had fallen under the control of the Spanish Habsburgs, notably the Kingdom of Naples and the Duchy of Milan. The Austrian Habsburg domains further encircled Venice to the north and east. Militarily, Venice was no longer perceived as a great power and pursued a policy of neutrality whenever possible.[74] However, the republic continued to maintain a sizeable navy and remained a significant player

---

70 Ugo Tucci (cur.), *Venezia nel cinquecento* (Roma: Istituto della Enciclopedia Italiana, 1974), 23–4; Aurelio Musi, *L'Italia dei viceré. Integrazione e resistenza nel sistema imperiale spagnolo* (Napoli: Avagliano Editore 2000).

71 Géraud Poumarède, 'L'Europe de Paolo Sarpi' in Marie Viallon (dir.), *Paolo Sarpi: Politique et religion en Europe* (Paris: Garnier, 2010), 333–42.

72 Tucci, *Venezia nel cinquecento*, 62–3.

73 William J. Bouwsma, *Venice and the Defense of Republican Liberty: Renaissance Values in the Age of the Counter Reformation* (Berkeley: University of California Press, 1984); A. D. Wright, 'Why the Venetian Interdict?', *The English Historical Review*, 89(352) (1974), 534–50; Walter Recht, 'International law as a political language, 1600–1859', in Giulio Bartolini (ed.), *A History of International Law in Italy* (Oxford: University Press, 2020), 48–55; Romanin, *Storia documentata di Venezia*, VII, 36–49; Sylvio Hermann De Franceschi, 'Venetian republicanism against the Roman ambitions of pontifical theocracy – Sovereignty according to Paolo Sarpi: political theory and the challenge of the Venetian interdict crisis (1606–1607) and its aftermath', in Zwierlein and Lee (eds.), *Sovereignty*, 108–30.

74 Éric Schnakenbourg, *Entre la guerre et la paix: Neutralité et relations internationales, XVIIe–XVIIIe Siècles* (Rennes: Presses universitaires de Rennes, 2013), 23; Mario Nani Mocenigo, *Storia della marina veneziana, da Lepanto alla caduta della Repubblica* (Venezia: Filippi Editore, 1935), 6–7.

in diplomacy, intelligence, and counterintelligence.[75] In the 1610s, tensions appeared to be escalating in the Adriatic Sea. Spanish officials in the Kingdom of Naples, which possessed an extensive Adriatic coastline, developed a conflict of jurisdiction with Venetian authorities, questioning the traditional dominance of Venice over its 'Gulf', from whose governance they felt unjustly excluded.[76] The ambitious viceroy of Naples, Pedro Téllez-Girón, Duke of Osuna (1574–1624), took the lead in asserting Spanish-Neapolitan claims, often acting with a degree of independence from the distant court in Madrid.[77] Spanish-Neapolitan naval squadrons entered the 'Gulf of Venice' in open defiance. Simultaneously, the Austrian Habsburg, who nurtured expansionist designs in the Balkans, supported Uskok piracy in Dalmatia to damage Venetian commerce and undermine Venetian rule, possibly provoking a new Ottoman–Venetian military confrontation. In other words, the major threats to Venetian dominion over the Adriatic came from the Archduke of Austria (and future emperor) Ferdinand II of Habsburg (1578–1637) and the Spanish viceroy of Naples.[78]

Tensions escalated in open warfare during the War of Gradisca (1615–1618), as Venetian and (Austrian) Habsburg forces clashed along their borders. The Habsburgs employed Uskok pirates as irregular forces against Venetian shipping, while Venetian and Spanish-Neapolitan squadrons manoeuvred in the Adriatic, albeit avoiding large scale and decisive engagements.[79] Venetian diplomacy secured support from the Dutch and the English and recruited thousands of Protestant mercenaries.[80] In 1618, Alfonso de la Cueva, Marqués de

75 Romanin, *Storia documentata di Venezia*, VII, 7–20; Tarpley, *Paolo Sarpi*, 15, 179–82; Paolo Preto, *I servizi segreti di Venezia. Spionaggio e controspionaggio ai tempi della Serenissima* (Milano: Il Saggiatore, 2010).

76 Raestad, *La mer territoriale*, 65–6.

77 The Duke of Osuna belonged to the imperialist-bellicist faction of the Spanish establishment who despised the 'pacifist' policies of the *valido* the Duke of Lerma. See Bohdan Chudoba, *Spain and the Empire, 1519–1643* (New York: Octagon Books, 1969), 211; Elliott, *Imperial Spain*, 325.

78 Simone Paliaga, 'Il dominio dell'Adriatico. Sarpi, Giannone e la sovranità contesa tra Venezia, Napoli e Vienna', *Naval History, Quaderno SISM 2014*, online version: http://www.societaitalianastoriamilitare.org; Romanin, *Storia documentata di Venezia*, VII, 82–3.

79 Luis García Arias, 'Una pugna hispano-veneciana sobre el dominio del Mar Adriático', *Revista General de la Marina*, 132 (1947), 233–305; Antonio Battistella, 'Una campagna navale veneto-spagnola in Adriatico poco conosciuta', *Archivio veneto-trìdentino*, 2 (1922), 58–119; 3 (1923), 1–78.

80 Gunther E. Rothenberg, 'Venice and the Uskoks of Senj: 1537–1618', *The Journal of Modern History*, 33(2) (1961), 148–56. For further details, see Catherine W. Bracewell, *The Uskoks of Senj: Piracy, Banditry, and Holy War in the Sixteenth-Century Adriatic* (Ithaca: Cornell

Bedmar and Spanish ambassador to Venice, was expelled after being implicated in a suspected coup d'état against Venice's republican institutions, the so-called 'Spanish or Bedmar conjure'.[81] Thus, Spain, which was still clinging to its crumbling closed sea claims over the oceans, was indirectly challenging another polity's maritime claims in a different geographical context.[82]

The Venetian government was deeply alarmed by these developments. The bellicose faction of the Venetian oligarchy, known as the *giovani* ('young'), advocated a resolute defence of Venetian interests against Papal and Habsburg encroachments.[83] The denial of Venetian control over the Adriatic Sea appeared especially concerning, as it could easily be the first step towards undermining Venetian independence, which was fundamentally linked to its relationship with the Adriatic. For centuries, cartographers had consistently referred to the Adriatic as the *Gulfum Veneciarum* (Gulf of Venice, see below figure n. 12). Yet, all of this was now being called into question.

During the 1610s, numerous pamphleteers and authors, whether pro-Papal or pro-Habsburg, attacked Venetian claims to the Adriatic. They invoked the principle of freedom of navigation, argued for limiting Venetian jurisdiction to the northern Adriatic, or even asserted that the Adriatic rightfully belonged to other coastal powers, such as the Kingdom of Naples (and, by extension, Spain). For instance, Cardinal Cesare Baronio (1538–1607) questioned the historical basis of Venetian claims in volume XII of his *Annales Ecclesiastici* (1612), including the supposed twelfth-century donation of Adri-

University Press, 2011); Gaetano Cozzi, *Il doge Nicolo Contarini: Ricerche sul patriziato veneziano agli inizi del seicento* (Venezia: Istituto per la Collaborazione Culturale, 1958), 149–50; Gaetano Cozzi, Michael Knapton and Giovanni Scarabello, *La Repubblica di Venezia nell'età moderna: dal 1517 alla fine della Repubblica* (Torino: UTET, 1992), vol. 2, 100–102; Romolo Quazza, *Storia Politica d'Italia: Preponderanza Spagnuola (1559–1700)* (Milano: Vallardi, 1950), 425; Romanin, *Storia documentata di Venezia*, VII, 74–81.

81 An episode that remains partially covered in mystery. See Paolo Preto, 'La "congiura di Bedmar" a Venezia nel 1618: colpo di Stato o provocazione?', in *Complots et conjurations dans l'Europe moderne. Actes du colloque international organisé à Rome, 30 septembre-2 octobre 1993* (Rome: École Française de Rome, 1996), 289–315; Maria P. Pedani, *Venezia porta d'Oriente* (Bologna: Il Mulino, 2010), 231–2; Zorzi, *La Repubblica del Leone*, 385–9; John J. Norwich, *Storia di Venezia*, II. *Dal 1400 alla caduta della Repubblica* (Milano: Mursia Editore, 1989), 310–24.

82 Yet another clear example of how political-geographical relativism impacted on the conceptualisation of the law of the sea and the *mare liberum* vs *mare clausum* debate.

83 Rothenberg, 'Venice and the Uskoks of Senj: 1537–1618', 152–3; on the *giovani* party, see Tarpley, *Paolo Sarpi*, 165–70; Gino Benzoni *Venezia nell'età della controriforma* (Milano: Mursia, 1973), 50–5.

atic dominion by Pope Alexander III to Venice.[84] In the same year, the Venetian ambassador in Rome, Gerolamo Soranzo, reported the appearance of a particularly aggressive pamphlet, *Squitinio della liberta veneta nel quale si adducono anche le raggioni dell'Imperio sopra la città et signoria di Venetia.* Its anonymous author sought to demolish the idea itself of Venice as an independent state, asserting its subjection to the Holy Roman Empire (and thus the Austrian Habsburgs).[85]

It is therefore unsurprising that when Grotius' *Mare liberum* began circulating in Venice in 1611, the patrician government sought to strengthen and renew the arguments in defence of Venetian maritime claims.[86] As Giulio Acquaviva noted, Venice, while seeking to halt its decline, could not rely solely on military expeditions to Dalmatia or the use of naval force to maintain its dominion over the Adriatic. Instead, it needed to re-establish the legitimacy of its exclusive jurisdiction, drawing on tradition while adapting to the changing times.[87] Medieval legal arguments and the hagiographical 'myth of Venice' no longer sufficed to protect its independence and Adriatic predominance. In Acquaviva's words: 'If the myth of the ring was no longer taken for granted, it was necessary not only to show its truthfulness [...], but also to create new foundations for the dominion over the sea itself. At a time when everything seemed to be questioned, it was not only a matter of controlling the Adriatic, but also of the freedom of Venice as a whole'.[88]

2.2 *Paolo Sarpi*

2.2.1 *Consultore in Jure*

The activity of the Servite friar Paolo Sarpi (1552–1623) must be understood within the context of this turbulent period in Venetian history. An accomplished scholar and polymath, Sarpi cultivated an extensive epistolary net-

84 Giuseppe A. Guazzelli, Raimondo Michetti and Francesco Scorza Barcellona, *Cesare Baronio tra santità e scrittura storica* (Roma: Viella, 2012).

85 *Squitinio della libertà veneta nel quale si adducono anche le raggioni dell'Imperio sopra la città et signoria di Venetia,* (anonymous) (Mirandola: Giouanni Benincasa, 1612). See also Cozzi, Knapton and Scarabello, *La Repubblica di Venezia nell'età moderna*, 99; De Vivo, 'Historical Justifications', 166–7. For further information, see idem, *Information and Communication in Venice. Rethinking Early Modern Politics* (Oxford: University Press, 2019).

86 Paliaga, 'Il dominio dell'Adriatico', 5; De Vivo, 'La publication comme enjeu polémique: Venise au début du XVIIe siècle', in Christian Jouhaud and Alain Viala (dir.), *De la publication: entre Renaissance at Lumières* (Paris: Fayard, 2012), 161–75.

87 Acquaviva, 'Giulio Pace', 70–1.

88 Ibidem, my translation. See also Tarpley, *Paolo Sarpi*, 5; De Vivo, 'Historical Justifications', 172.

work across Europe, engaging with both Catholic and Protestant correspondents. At the beginning of the seventeenth century, he was appointed by the Doge as an adviser on legal and theological matters for the Republic (*consultore in iure*). Sarpi became highly influential within governing circles; his legal opinions often served as the foundation for Senate policies, and his reputation extended well beyond Venice.[89] Of particular interest are Sarpi's *consulti* – formal memoranda and legal opinions requested by the Doge, the cabinet, and Venetian senators on specific matters. These documents followed the medieval tradition of the *consilia*.[90] During the 1606–1607 interdict, Sarpi provided a legal defence of Venetian prerogatives and jurisdiction, championing a clear distinction between temporal and spiritual domains.[91]

A few years later, he applied the same expertise to defend Venetian claims in the Adriatic. Among the proponents of the 'claimed seas', Sarpi's position is

89 Cattelan, 'The Defence of Venetian Dominion', 177–207; Romanin, *Storia documentata di Venezia*, VII, 29–30; Vivanti, *Quattro lezioni su Paolo Sarpi*, 39–63; Norwich, *Storia di Venezia*, II, 296–310; David Wootton, *Paolo Sarpi. Between Renaissance and Enlightenment* (Cambridge: University Press, 1983), 46–54. Regarding the institution of the *Consultore in iure*, see Gaetano Cozzi, *Repubblica di Venezia e Stati italiani. Politica e giustizia dal secolo XVI al secolo XVIII* (Torino: Einaudi, 1982), 355. On Sarpi, see also Corrado Vivanti, *Paolo Sarpi* (Roma: Istituto poligrafico e Zecca dello Stato, 2000); Gaetano Cozzi, *Paolo Sarpi tra Venezia e l'Europa* (Torino: Einaudi, 1978); Ivone Cacciavillani, *Paolo Sarpi: la guerra delle scritture del 1606 e la nascita della nuova Europa* (Venezia: Corbo e Fiore, 2005); Jaska Kainulainen, *Paolo Sarpi: A Servant of God and State* (Leiden: Brill, 2014); Romain Descendre. 'Quand la mer est territoire: Paolo Sarpi et le «Dominio del mare Adriatico»', *Studi Veneziani* (2008), 55–73; Corrado Pin (cur.), *Ripensando Paolo Sarpi: Atti del convegno internazionale di studi nel 450° anniversario della nascita di Paolo Sarpi* (Venezia: Ateneo Veneto, 2006); Vittorio Frajese, *Sarpi scettico. Stato e chiesa a Venezia tra Cinque e Seicento* (Bologna: Il Mulino, 1994); Antonella Barzazi, 'Paolo Sarpi', in *Dizionario biografico degli italiani*, vol. 90, 2017, online version: http://www.treccani.it/enciclopedia/paolo-sarpi_%28Dizionario-Biografico%29; idem, 'Paolo Sarpi', in Marco Sgarbi (ed.), *Encyclopedia of Renaissance Philosophy* (Cham: Springer International Publishing, 2015), online version: https://doi.org/10.1007/978-3-319-02848-4_359-2. Paul van Heck, 'La fortuna di Paolo Sarpi in Olanda', in Viallon (dir.), *Paolo Sarpi*, 369–405.

90 The *consilia* consisted of legal opinions requested by public authorities from jurists in order to clarify specific legal issues. See Tarpley, *Paolo Sarpi*, 5; Descendre, 'Quand la mer est territoire', 58.

91 Corrado Pin, 'Paolo Sarpi senza maschera: l'avvio della lotta politica dopo l'Interdetto del 1606', in Viallon (dir.), *Paolo Sarpi*, 55–104; Antonella Barzazi, 'Tra Venezia e Roma: l'interdetto, Sarpi, i serviti', in Massimo Firpo (ed.), *Nunc alia tempora alii mores. Storici e storia in età postridentina. Atti del convegno, Torino, 24–27 settembre 2003* (Olschki: Firenze, 2005), 233–61. John J. Norwich noted that: 'The leadership of Venice during the Interdict had passed, in fact, if not in theory, to Sarpi', 859, in *Storia di Venezia*, II, 311.

notable for its originality. In the second decade of the seventeenth century, he authored five writings, or *scritture*, collectively known as *Dominio del Mare Adriatico della Serenissima Repubblica di Venezia*.[92] These works formed an extended *consulto* in which Sarpi addressed the Republic's traditional dominance in the Adriatic and the challenges it faced at the time. Although these writings were published only posthumously, they circulated widely among the senior officials of the Republic, making their direct audience the patrician ruling class. Since Venetian ambassadors were members of this elite, Sarpi's arguments could ultimately reach influential foreign audiences as well.[93] The following pages will examine the first four of these writings. The fifth focuses on more specific issues concerning the regulation of river traffic along the Po River and its delta, which are of lesser relevance for our purposes. In Sarpi's own words:

> The first will deal with the true title (*testimonio*) and possession upon which this Dominion (*Dominio*) rests, demonstrating that it was not acquired but rather preserved together with the Republic, strengthened by the virtue of arms, and established through custom that exceeds all memory. The second will show that it is neither true nor useful to claim that the Most Serene Republic holds Dominion over the Sea by privilege of the Pope or the Emperor, nor even by prescription. The third will examine whether the dominion over the sea includes bays, ports, and other inlets, as well as the shores within, and whether such jurisdiction extends to enacting and imposing laws upon seafarers, issuing ordinances as required by public utility, punishing crimes committed at sea,

92 In 1750, an important edition of Sarpi's writings on the Adriatic issue was published in Helmstat (fictitious location, likely published in Venice): *Dominio del Mare Adriatico della Serenissima Repubblica di Venezia*, in *Opere Varie del molto reverendo padre Paolo Sarpi dell'Ordine dei Servi di Maria teologo consultore della Serenissima Repubblica di Venezia divise in due tomi* (Helmstat: per i tipi di Jacopo Mulleri, 1750), tomo II. In this chapter the analysis is based on the 1750 edition, recently re-edited in Acquaviva and Scovazzi, *Il Dominio di Venezia*. Sarpi writings had already been printed in 1685: Paolo Sarpi, *Dominio del Mare Adriatico e sue Raggioni per il ius belli della Serenissima Republica di Venetia* (Venetia: per i tipi di Roberto Meietti, 1685). In 1945, Roberto Cessi proposed a further re-edition: Paolo Sarpi, *Dominio del Mare Adriatico* (Padova: Tolomei, 1945).

93 Corrado Pin, 'Recensione di: *Fra' Paolo Sarpi, Dominio del Mare Adriatico della Serenissima Repubblica di Venezia*, introduzione di Tullio Scovazzi, Torino: Giappichelli, 2005,' *Studi veneziani*, 50 (2005), 392–6, at 395; Calafat, *Une mer jalousée*, 79; Descendre. 'Quand la mer est territoire', 59.

and levying charges on those who make use of it. The fourth will explain and refute the opinions of some who argue otherwise.[94]

2.2.2 The True Source of Venetian Maritime Dominion

In the first of these writings, drafted in the spring of 1612, Sarpi addressed the nature of the title (*testimonio*) claimed by Venice over the Adriatic. In his view, the historical origins of Venice in the fifth century and its dominion over the Adriatic were inextricably linked. The acquisition of the Adriatic coincided with the city's foundation: 'City, born in the Sea, of which it was no Master, and therefore born free, and for the same reason Master of the water where it had its beginning; therefore, to look for the origins of Venetian maritime *imperio* is the same of investigating the origins of its liberty – that is to say, its foundation'.[95] This statement reflects the legal doctrine of *fundatio in mari*, which dates back at least to Baldus de Ubaldis, who, in his commentary on *Digest* 1.8.1 (*lex Summa*), asserted that 'according to the law of nations, cities [and Venice in particular] built on the sea belong to those who built them' since they were not build on somebody else's territory'.[96]

To substantiate his argument, Sarpi provided a historical overview of Venice's gradual expansion across the Adriatic, emphasising that its title to the sea was intrinsically tied to its liberty. The first embryo of the Republic was founded during the barbaric invasions and the collapse of the Western Roman

94 My translation from Sarpi, *Dominio del Mare Adriatico*, 327–8: '*La prima tratterà il vero testimonio, e possessione, dè quali questo Dominio costa, mostrandolo non acquistato, ma anche insieme con la Repubblica conservato, ed aumentato con la virtù delle armi, e stabilito con la consuetudine ch'eccede ogni memoria. La seconda farà in mostrare non esser vero, né utile il dire, che la Serenissima Repubblica abbia il Dominio del Mare per privilegio del Papa, o dell'Imperatore, né meno per prescrizione. La terza considerazione farà valere se il dominio del Mare comprenda i Seni, i porti e altri ridotti, ed inclusi i Lidi ancora, e se questa giurisdizione s'estenda a statuire, ed imponer leggi à naviganti, facendo quell'ordinazioni, che ricerca la pubblica utilità, ed a punire i delitti commessi in Mare, e ad imporre gravezze a quelli, che si vaglino dell'uso di esso. La quarta farà in esplicare, e risolvere l'opinioni d'alcuni che vengono fatte in contrario*'.

95 Ibid., 328: '*Così questa inclita Città nata nel Mare, del quale non era alcun padrone, è nata libera, e per l'istessa ragione Padrona dell'acqua dove ebbe il suo principio; per lo che tanto è il ricercare l'Imperio Marittimo di Venezia, quanto ricercare l'origine della libertà sua, ovvero la sua fondazione*'.

96 Baldus de Ubaldis, *Commentaria in primam Digesti veteris partem* (Venezia: Giunti, 1572), 48r. See also Fredona, 'Angelo degli Ubaldi and the Gulf of the Venetians', in idem and Reinert (eds.), *New Perspectives*, 45; Ugo Petronio, 'Civitas Venetiarum est edificata in mari', in Gino Benzoni et al. (cur.), *Studi veneti offerti a Gaetano Cozzi* (Venezia: Cardo, 1992), 171–85; Christian Mathieu, *Inselstadt Venedig: Umweltgeschichte eines Mythos in der Frühen Neuzeit* (Cologne: Böhlau, 2007), 212–3.

Empire, and Venice had been established on a portion of the sea – the lagoon – unclaimed by any other power.[97] At the time of its founding, Venetian dominion was limited to the waters immediately surrounding the city, which the Venetians could effectively guard and protect.[98] The barbarian invaders, lacking war fleets, left maritime sovereignty 'vacant' until Byzantine warships (dromons) temporarily regained control of the Adriatic during Justinian's Gothic War (535–554). However, as the Eastern Roman Empire weakened, its influence over the Adriatic faded, creating a new power vacuum that was eventually filled by the rising power of Venice. The absence of a supreme authority capable of policing the sea prompted Venice to extend its jurisdiction beyond the lagoon to restore law and order. Over centuries, Venetian control of the Adriatic became established as an 'immemorial custom' (*consuetudine immemorabile*).[99]

Sarpi then outlined the conditions required by legal doctrine for the establishment of jurisdiction through irrevocable custom: first, jurisdictional acts must be performed consistently over a prolonged period; second, no other party may exercise the same authority without the possessor's consent; and third, the creation of the custom must be explicit, not secret, and must be acquiesced to by others.[100] In the following pages, Sarpi documented dozens of examples of Venetian jurisdictional acts, as well as instances of acquiescence by third parties. For example, Venice had long maintained the office of the Captain of the Gulf, whose primary role was to patrol the Adriatic, suppress piracy, and enforce Venetian maritime laws – chief among them the prohibition on other Adriatic polities maintaining military fleets.[101] Sarpi also emphasised acknowledgements of Venetian jurisdiction by popes and emperors, noting that challenges to Venetian dominion had repeatedly failed. Opponents included Hungary, Pisa, Bologna, Genoa, Papal subjects such as the Anconetans, and the Kingdom of Naples. Additionally, the ceremony of the 'wedding of the sea', conducted in the presence of foreign diplomats, served as a symbol of international recognition of Venetian sovereignty over the Adriatic.[102]

97 Sarpi, *Dominio del Mare Adriatico*, 328.

98 Ibid., 329.

99 Ibid., 330. Sarpi referred to 'more than six hundred years'.

100 Ibidem.

101 Or *Capitano del Golfo*. In the early modern period, he would be based on the island of Corfu, strategically located at the entrance of the Adriatic Sea. Ibidem.

102 Ibid., 333–6.

Sarpi identified two essential components of 'sovereignty' (*dominio*): title (*titolo, testimonio*) and possession (*possesso*).[103] In his view, Venice held both. Regarding title, Sarpi noted four key characteristics: first, its origin was original, not derivative, and rooted in abandonment by others (*pro derelicto*); second, it had expanded gradually over the centuries; third, it had been maintained through military means, sacrifices, and expenses to ensure safe navigation; and fourth, it was confirmed by immemorial custom, 'whose origin was far older than any human memory'.[104] Additional evidence of Venice's title included the assent of other princes, the testimony of historians and the approval of jurists.[105] Sarpi went on to cite twenty-three renowned jurists who had affirmed the validity of Venetian maritime dominion, basing their arguments on privilege (either papal or imperial), prescription, or immemorial custom.[106]

Turning to the second element of 'sovereignty', possession (*possesso*), Sarpi argued it was evidenced by: first, the continuous appointment of officials such as the Captain of the Gulf and his subordinates, tasked with overseeing navigation; second, the military custody of the sea, which included excluding foreign warships from the Gulf; third, the promulgation of maritime laws and the punishment of violators; and fourth, the universally accepted payment of Venetian tolls in the 'Gulf'. Sarpi asserted that these demonstrations of Venetian possession had been well-known and widely accepted, rendering them indisputable.[107] However, Sarpi emphasised that Venice needed to sustain its possession through the continuous exercise of jurisdictional acts and, if necessary, defend its rights by military means. He cautioned that possession not only needed to be grounded in the past but also to be preserved in the present and continued in the future. Sarpi grimly compared any right not backed by actual force to a 'dead body without a soul'. This added an element of precariousness to the notion of maritime dominion.[108] Nevertheless, Sarpi maintained that Venice's repeated jurisdictional acts in the Adriatic had established its title through immemorial custom.

103 Ibid., 336.

104 Ibidem: '*Confermato per una lunghissima consuetudine, il principio della quale supera ogni memoria*'.

105 Ibidem.

106 Ibid., 343.

107 Ibid., 336–7.

108 Scovazzi, 'Libertà o dominio', 29; Calafat, *Une mer jalousée*, 93–5. This aspect of Sarpi's argumentation could backfire as soon as Venice was no more in the position to impose militarily its dominion over its 'Gulf'.

Throughout his writings, Sarpi invoked the concept of *fatica* (labour, effort, expense), underscoring the human and material costs of exercising maritime jurisdiction and maintaining control of the sea. This concept closely aligns with that of *occupatio* (occupation) but also served to justify Venice's imposition of tolls and other navigational restrictions.[109] Notably, although Sarpi employed the term *dominio* – derived from the Roman concept of *dominium* – he explicitly rejected its equivalence to the Roman category of *dominium iuris civilis*. Instead, he equated *dominio* with possession, understood as continuous, permanent, recognised, and effective control over a *res*. The Republic's governance structure, with its largely ceremonial head of the state (the Doge), likely facilitated the conceptualisation of dominion as belonging not to a monarch or an individual, but to the Venetians as a political community. Thus, although Sarpi did not use the term 'sovereignty', his concept of *dominio* was inherently publicist and not far removed from a modern understanding of sovereignty.[110]

2.2.3 Not All Titles Are Good Titles…

In the second writing (*scrittura*), Sarpi refuted the notion that Venetian dominion over the Adriatic derived from privilege – whether granted by the pope or the emperor – or from prescription. First, Sarpi observed that a prince who received a privilege from another authority could not truly be 'absolute', as the object granted would never be entirely their own. Second, he pointed out that privileges or donations could always be revoked by the original grantor or their successors.[111] Third, while third parties might be easily excluded from the use of the granted object, the same could not be said of the grantor, who might assert their own rights. Not by chance, papal diplomats argued that since the popes had conceded the Adriatic to Venice papal subjects should not be excluded from using it. In Sarpi's view, however, the Popes had never exercised control over the Adriatic and therefore could

---

109 Sarpi, *Dominio del Mare Adriatico*, 337: '*Siccome la ragioni, ed i titoli de' privati sono cadaveri senz'anima, quando non siano vivificati dalla forza della legge e del giudizio, che danno il vigore; così la ragione, ed il titolo del principe sono cadaveri, quando non siano animati dalla forza, ed uso di quella, dalla quale ricevono la vita*'. My translation: 'Because the rights, and the titles of private people are dead bodies without soul, when they are not fortified by the strength of the law and judgement; similarly, the right and the title of the prince are dead bodies, whenever they are not animated by strength and its use, from whom they receive life'.

110 Federico Chabod, *La politica di Paolo Sarpi* (Roma-Venezia: Istituto per la collaborazione culturale, 1962), 60–1 and 71–3; Calafat, *Une mer jalousée*, 87–9.

111 Sarpi, *Dominio del Mare Adriatico*, 338.

not have granted privileges over something that had never been theirs to give. This argument applied equally to the papacy and the Holy Roman Empire:

> No one can grant dominion over an object to somebody else if he does not own the object in question; and it is equally certain that neither the pope nor the emperor, from Charlemagne onward, from whom the present empire originates, ever held dominion or custody over this sea, and they never kept a fleet there; hence, they could never have granted it to others.[112]

Therefore, Sarpi also dismissed the idea that Venetian dominion over the Adriatic was rooted in imperial concession, a theory supported by some medieval jurists who regarded the Holy Roman Emperors as successors to the Ancient Roman Empire. Sarpi rejected the concept of *continuatio imperii* – the continuity of the empire – between the Roman emperors and their German epigones. While the Romans had undoubtedly been lords (*domini*) of the Mediterranean, they left the sea vacant (*senza padrone*) after their empire's collapse.[113] Centuries later, the German emperors entered the historical stage, but they never exercised control over the sea and therefore lacked the authority to grant it to others. In this light, Sarpi regarded the celebrated peace of Venice in 1177 – an agreement between the Pope and the Emperor – as merely a symbolic recognition by powerful international actors of an already-established Venetian maritime dominion. Although this episode had been mythologised by Venetian propaganda, Sarpi did not consider it the source of Venetian rights through donation or privilege.[114]

Sarpi's argument also neutralised critiques such as those by Cardinal Baronio, who questioned the historical accuracy of the events surrounding

---

112 My translation from ibid., 339: '... *niuno può concedere Dominio ad altri di cosa, che non sia sua; ed insieme è certo, che nè il papa, nè l'Imperadore da Carlo Magno in qua, dal quale viene l'origine di quest'Imperio, mai hanno avuto Dominio, nè custodia di questo Mare, nè mai hanno tenuto Armata in esso; adunque non hanno mai potuto concederlo ad altri*'. Cf. Roberto Cessi, *La Repubblica di Venezia e il problema adriatico* (Napoli: Edizioni Scientifiche Italiane, 1953), 224.

113 Grotius gave a different interpretation of Roman *mare nostrum,* excluding the Romans that were really aspiring to *dominium.* See Grotius, *Mare liberum*, ch. 5, 75, [26]. In Sarpi's view, even the Romans had been masters of the Mediterranean only until they could control it with their fleets. He identified once more effectiveness as a necessary corollary to support legal claims.

114 Sarpi, *Dominio del Mare Adriatico*, 338, 332. Cf. supra, ch. 1, 2.3.

the peace of Venice and the alleged papal donation of the golden ring to the Doge, symbolising maritime dominion.[115] While these narratives had been central to pro-Venetian propaganda and myth-making, Sarpi departed from traditional pro-Venetian authors by asserting that these events were not decisive for the legitimacy of Venetian maritime rights. Building on this reasoning, Sarpi also rejected prescription as a potential basis for Venice's claims over the Adriatic.[116] He argued that one could not prescribe rights over something that had never been previously owned by another party.[117]

2.2.4 The Nature and Content of Venetian Prerogatives

In the third *scrittura*, the legal adviser of the Republic began by acknowledging that Venice controlled only a portion of the Adriatic coastline. Why, then, could it claim such extensive dominion over the sea? Sarpi admitted that jurisdictional frictions were inevitable with other Adriatic polities, as Venice's dominion over the entire Adriatic – encompassing the high seas, bays, shallow waters, and natural harbours – would limit their freedom to use their coastal waters and related resources.[118] He conceded that coastal cities, whether subject to Venice or not, could hold specific rights over the use of their immediate waters and resources. The extent of such areas depended on the size and nature of each city. That said, only Venice exercised 'supreme' dominion and jurisdiction across the entire Adriatic, including its ports and bays, for two main reasons.

First, it was impractical to divide the sea into precise territorial zones. Second, shallow waters, bays, and harbours were particularly vulnerable to piratical attacks, necessitating the protection of the only power capable of providing it: Venice. For Sarpi, dominion and 'protection and custody for the security of seafarers' were inseparable.[119] In other words, Sarpi identified two coexisting levels of legal rights in the Adriatic: a superior one comprising Venetian dominion and jurisdiction over the entire sea and a subordinate

115 De Vivo, 'Historical Justifications', 171–2; Descendre. 'Quand la mer est territoire', 61.

116 Sarpi, *Dominio del Mare Adriatico*, 342–3. In Chapter 1 we saw that medieval jurists dealt with prescription as the potential source of maritime rights. Vázquez y Menchaca as well as Grotius denied the validity of prescription in such cases.

117 Ibid., 342–3.

118 Sarpi instead admitted that artificially built and closed harbours (*porti serrati*) were under exclusive sovereignty of the coastal city.

119 Ibid., 345: '*Ma la formal ragione, per la quale tutte le acque marine debbono essere sottoposte a chi signoreggia il Mare, è perchè il Dominio del Mare si dice protezione, e custodia per sicurezza de' Naviganti*'.

one under which coastal cities could exploit resources in their adjacent waters, notably fisheries.

Sarpi advanced his argument further by asserting that the ruler of a territory held the jurisdictional right to impose laws on all individuals within it. The same principle, he argued, applied to Venice's maritime territory in the Adriatic. Indeed, Sarpi used the term *territorio* (territory), to refer to both land and sea as the spatial framework for jurisdiction: 'The Adriatic Sea is the territory of Venice, where it has the same power that any prince has over their own territory, and so it must exercise at sea the same actions that are exercised by princes in the lands under their rule'.[120] Thus, Sarpi argued for the extension of the legal principles governing land to the Adriatic. He contended that Venice's dominion (*dominio*) over its mainland territories in northern Italy (*Domini di Terraferma*, or *Stato da Tera*), its Mediterranean colonies, and its Adriatic maritime territory (*Domini da Mar*, or *Stato da Mar*) were equivalent.[121] This dominion manifested in three key ways: first, Venice could 'enact laws for seafarers'; second, it held the right and duty to punish crimes committed at sea; and third, it could demand the payment of duties and customs.[122] Examples included prohibiting foreign military vessels from entering the Adriatic and requiring merchant ships to dock in Venice to pay taxes.

Sarpi's vision thus centred on extending the legal regime of land to the surrounding sea, or the 'territorialisation' of marine areas. He argued that a 'tight and limited' sea, such as the Adriatic, could be subject to sovereignty, allowing states to extend their territorial boundaries beyond their coasts. This maritime territory, according to Sarpi, would correspond to the radius of a state's naval power and practical needs. It was a modern concept rooted in the 'reality on the water' rather than abstract theory or general principles.[123]

Sarpi next addressed the arguments advanced by earlier jurists who questioned the 'just and lawful' dominion of the Most Serene Republic.[124] Chief among these was the idea that the sea, by its nature and by the law of nations (*diritto delle genti*), was free and common – impossible to occupy or possess

120 My translation. Ibid., 346: '*Il mar Adriatico è il territorio di Venezia, dove ha quella istessa potestà che ciascun principe ha nel territorio suo, per il che ha da esercitar in mare quelle azioni che sono esercitate dalli principi nelle terre di loro soggezione*'.

121 Descendre. 'Quand la mer est territoire', 61. Descendre underlines the specific meaning of the term *dominio* in Venetian political and legal vocabulary.

122 Sarpi, *Dominio del Mare Adriatico*, 346.

123 Scovazzi, 'Libertà o dominio', 30.

124 Sarpi, *Dominio del Mare Adriatico*, 349.

because it could not be enclosed or divided.[125] In Sarpi's view, these jurists had likened the sea to air and light, which could be freely used by one person without depriving others of their use, contending that navigation did not render the sea unusable to others. Additionally, they had rejected the validity of immemorial or long-standing prescription.[126] Sarpi acknowledged that certain Dutch authors – undoubtedly referring to Grotius – had employed similar arguments against the Iberians regarding navigation to the Indies.[127]

At this juncture, Sarpi directly challenged the ideas of Vázquez de Menchaca, who had launched 'launched great invectives against those jurists who asserted that the Venetians and the Genoese were lords of their respective seas, being entitled to prohibit navigation to others, considering their opinions against nature; saying that the use of the sea could only be common'.[128] Sarpi countered that these critics failed to consider what the original commonality of the sea truly entailed. While both land and sea were initially common under natural law, God and nature had allowed peoples to divide and occupy them over time. Polities thus acquired exclusive rights through occupation and by restricting others' use of the territory in question:

> ... likewise, whoever found a sea unguarded by anyone [...] could take custody of it for their benefit with the consent of God and men; indeed, just as it is in the public interest of humanity that lands are divided and guarded to protect them from violence, and those who assume dominion use their power for custody [...] so too is it in the public interest that seas are made secure; nor can anyone find a reason for this chimerical distinction they wish to draw between land and water; indeed, the same principles of occupation, possession, prescription, and custom, which hold true on land, apply equally to water.[129]

125 Ibidem.

126 Ibidem.

127 Ibidem.

128 Ibid., 349–50. Cf. Vázquez y Menchaca, *Controversiarum illustrium*, II, 89, § 30–2.

129 Ibidem, my translation: '... *così parimenti chi ha trovato un Mare non custodito da alcuno* [...] *ha potuto per sua utilità pigliarne la custodia con consentimento di Dio, e degli Uomini; anzi come in Terra a pubblico servizio del genere umano compie, che le regioni sieno divise, e custodite, perché così si rendono sicure dalle violenze; e quelli che ne hanno assunto il Dominio usano le forze nella custodia* [...] *così torna a pubblico servizio di tutti che i Mari siano resi sicuri; né mai alcuno potrà trovar ragione di questa chimerica differenza, che vogliono mettere fra la terra, e l'acqua; anzi le stesse ragioni d'occupazioni, possessioni, prescrizioni e consuetudini, le quali danno ragione in terra, la danno parimente in acqua*'.

On the one hand Sarpi agreed with Grotius and Vázquez y Menchaca on the original commonality of the sea. On the other, he frontally opposed them by arguing that both seas and lands had been rightfully divided through time, losing that original status 'without offence to God or Nature' (*senza offesa di Dio e della Natura*).[130] Sarpi also rejected the claim that the sea was indivisible, pointing out that geographers had long given distinct names to specific maritime regions. He cited the Adriatic as a clear example of such a distinct part of the Mediterranean, delimited to the south by the Strait of Otranto. Furthermore, he noted that since medieval times, most cartographers had referred to the Adriatic as the 'Gulf of Venice'.[131] This remained the case decades later, as shown by the works of the famous Venetian cartographer and cosmographer Vincenzo Maria Coronelli (1650–1718). For example, Coronelli's 1688 map (see Figure 4.3 below) indicated the Adriatic Sea as *Golfo di Venezia, olim Adriaticum Mare*, 'Gulf of Venice, once known as the Adriatic Sea'. More broadly, as Venice was a major hub of early modern printing and mapmaking, it significantly influenced the topographic and cartographic representation of its region.[132]

In opposing Vázquez de Menchaca and Grotius, Sarpi identified more similarities between land and sea than between sea and air. He argued that 'bad men cannot impede the use of the air', and hence, there was no need to guard it against their mischief.[133] By contrast, without proper authority armed with jurisdiction the sea could not be adequately safeguarded, leaving seafarers vulnerable to piratical attacks.[134] Consequently, Sarpi viewed the payment of tolls to sustain the expenses of guarding the sea as justified. In his opinion, no 'chimeric distinction' could reasonably be made between the legal status of

130 Cf. Vázquez y Menchaca, *Controversiarum illustrium*, II, 89, § 36; Grotius, *Mare liberum*, ch. 5, 55 [16].

131 Sarpi, *Dominio del Mare Adriatico*, 350. See also Faričić, Selva and Umek, 'Geographical names of the Adriatic Sea', 68–80.

132 Calafat, *Une mer jalousée*, 119–49; Quazza, *Storia Politica d'Italia: Preponderanza Spagnuola*, 354. Coronelli was also granted the official title of 'geographer of the Venetian Republic'.

133 Sarpi, *Dominio del Mare Adriatico*, 350.

134 On the struggles between Venice and pirates, see Alberto Tenenti, *Venezia e i Corsari, 1580–1615* (Laterza: Bari, 1961); idem, *Piracy and the Decline of Venice* (London: Longmans, 1967); Sergio Anselmi, *Pirati e corsari in Adriatico* (Pesaro: Silvana, 1998); Silvino Gigante, *Venezia e i pirati del mare Adriatico. Venezia contro gli uscocchi* (Vittorio Veneto: De Bastiani Editore, 2010). Sarpi authored a partisan account of the war against the Uskoks: 'Storia degli Uscocchi', in *Opere Varie del molto reverendo padre Paolo Sarpi dell'Ordine dei Servi di Maria teologo consultore della Serenissima Repubblica di Venezia divise in due tomi*, II (Helmstat: per i tipi di Jacopo Mulleri, 1750).

land and sea. It logically followed that states possessing the capability to protect seafarers could divide the seas and regulate their use.[135]

In any case, Sarpi clarified that his analysis was limited to seas that were 'possessed and guarded with great expenses since time immemorial, limited by extension, naturally enclosed by lands'.[136] Unsurprisingly, he viewed the Adriatic as the archetype of such a category. Sarpi's position has often been misunderstood, with his writings being interpreted as a reply to Grotius' *Mare liberum* or a precursor to Selden's theses. However, Grotius explicitly distinguished between oceans and smaller seas like the Mediterranean. He did not treat Genoese and Venetian claims on par with Spanish and Portuguese assertions, but rather highlighted their differences to better refute Iberian efforts to monopolise oceangoing navigation.[137]

Sarpi himself emphasised that 'the cause of the Most Serene Republic' could not be equated with the 'controversy between the Spaniards and the Dutch'.[138] He made this distinction to avoid conflating Venetian claims with Iberian ones and to prevent the Venetian position from being undermined alongside the Spanish cause. Moreover, the Venetian ruling class harboured little sympathy for Spain, and during the 1610s, a growing diplomatic coziness between the Dutch and Venetians emerged due to their shared anti-Spanish inclination.[139] Sarpi explicitly stated that he considered claims of dominion over the oceans to be untenable. The ocean, 'due to its immensity, cannot be guarded in its entirety by any human power', and the level of effectiveness required to establish dominion could neither be achieved nor maintained.[140] Furthermore, Sarpi criticised the brevity of Spain's (and Portugal's) alleged dominion – less than a century – a small parenthesis in world history compared to Venetian claims, which dated back to the High Middle Ages.[141] He concluded by reaffirming that no valid comparison could be drawn between Iberian and Venetian 'claimed seas' policies.

The historian Roberto Cessi observed that in *Dominio del Mare Adriatico* Sarpi adopted a political-philosophical approach rather than a strictly legal-

135 Sarpi, *Dominio del Mare Adriatico*, 350.

136 Ibidem.

137 Cf. Grotius, *Mare liberum*, ch. 7, 121 [49] and 123 [50]. See also Paliaga, 'Il dominio dell'Adriatico', 2; Calafat, *Une mer jalousée*, 91–2; Cessi, *La Repubblica di Venezia e il problema adriatico*, 210–2; Descendre. 'Quand la mer est territoire', 56–8.

138 Sarpi, *Dominio del Mare Adriatico* 350.

139 Calafat, *Une mer jalousée*, 91–2; Tarpley, *Paolo Sarpi*, 683.

140 Sarpi, *Dominio del Mare Adriatico*, 351.

141 Ibidem.

dogmatic one.[142] He subordinated his theoretical framework to political considerations, grounding it in historical context rather than abstract principles.[143] Sarpi focused on the tangible aspects of Adriatic history and geopolitics as the primary basis for Venetian *dominium maris*. This perspective was reflected in his concise and effective writing style, which avoided unnecessary doctrinal references. Tullio Scovazzi noted that Sarpi's arguments appeared 'legally slender as a scientific contribution to the theoretical construction of modern *ius gentium*'.[144] Indeed, Sarpi did not aim to establish general or absolute principles. Unlike Grotius, he showed no ambition to create a comprehensive legal framework. Instead, Sarpi concentrated on defending the Venetian Republic's maritime claims in the Adriatic and their immediate implications.[145] The intersection of law and politics, a central element in Grotius' *Mare liberum*, was also a defining aspect of Sarpi's discussions on the law of the sea. All of his *consulti* were designed as both political and legal documents.

In 1619, a short epistle titled *De iurisdictione Serenissimae Reipublicae Venetae in Mare Adriaticum epistola Francisci de Ingenuis germani* was published under the pseudonym Franciscus de Ingenuis. The work defended Venetian maritime dominion while refuting criticisms by the Spanish-Neapolitan writer Valenzuela and the Roman Lorenzo Mutino.[146] It is well known that Sarpi often used pseudonyms to express his views more freely, and the arguments presented in the epistle align closely with Sarpi's own. As a result, the pseudonymous author is widely identified as Sarpi himself. A few years later, Selden's *Mare clausum* cited De Ingenuis as one of the authorities supporting Venetian claims.

142 Cessi, *La Repubblica di Venezia e il problema adriatico*, 205. On Sarpi's uneasy relationship with Venetian law, see Claudio Povolo, 'Un rapporto difficile e controverso. Paolo Sarpi e il diritto veneto', in Corrado Pin (ed.), *Ripensando Paolo Sarpi* (Venezia: Ateneo Veneto, 2006), 395–416.

143 Cessi, *La Repubblica di Venezia e il problema adriatico*, 205.

144 Scovazzi, 'Libertà o dominio', 12.

145 Ibidem; Paliaga, 'Il dominio dell'Adriatico', 220.

146 Franciscus de Ingenuis, *De iurisdictione Serenissimae Reipublicae Venetae in mare Adriaticum Epistola Francisci de Ingenuis Germani,* [...] *ad Liberium Vicentium Hollandum adversus Johannem Baptistam Valenzolam Hispanum et Laurentium Motinum Romanum qui iurisdictionem illam non pridem impugnare ausi sunt*, Eleutheropoli [fictious location], 1619. See Ingrid A. R de Smet, *Menippean Satire and the Republic of Letters, 1581–1655* (Genève: Librairie Droz, 1996), 204–8.

2.3 *Giulio Pace da Beriga*

2.3.1 Premises

In 1619, within the same political and international context, Giulio Pace da Beriga (1550–1635) published *De dominio maris Hadriatici Disceptatio*.[147] Originally from Vicenza, Pace had studied law and philosophy at the University of Padua, the Republic of Venice's leading educational institution. During his studies, he joined Protestant circles, and in 1574, he emigrated to avoid conflict with the authorities. Over the following years, he taught in various cities, including Geneva, Heidelberg, Sedan, Montpellier, Nîmes, Aix, and Valence in southern France, establishing himself as an itinerant scholar with a long and varied academic career.[148] Thus, unlike Sarpi, Pace was a university-trained jurist, which likely explains his decision to write *De dominio* in Latin, whereas Sarpi opted for Italian. In 1619, Pace formally recanted his Protestant faith to facilitate his return to the University of Padua. His publication of *De dominio* was probably an attempt to gain favour with Venetian authorities as part of his efforts to resettle within the Republic's territory. Sarpi participated in the panel that evaluated Pace's work and, in a letter to the Doge, praised Pace's erudition and legal reasoning:

> 'Most Serene Prince, the treatise on the dominion of the Adriatic Sea by Giulio Pace has been examined diligently by us in all its parts [...] I must report that in this brief treatise, the author demonstrates great learning and sound judgment, as he does in all his other works in print, where he has shown excellent erudition [...]. In this work on the 'Dominion of the Adriatic Sea,' he has presented the title and possession of the Most Serene Republic with proper and solid reasoning and foundations, [...]

147 In the following pages, reference is made to the 1619 edition. The Latin text is reproduced in Acquaviva and Scovazzi (eds.), *Il dominio di Venezia sul Mare Adriatico nelle opere di Paolo Sarpi e Giulio Pace*, 119–213. A concise late seventeenth century French translation, made by Achille III de Harlay (1639–1712), is available in Gallica BNF: ms. Français, 16733, 'Traités sur la marine et le droit maritime', more specifically: f. 218–133v: https://gallica.bnf.fr/ark:/12148/btv1b9060972j/f1.image.r=achille%20III%20de%20harlay.

148 On Pace da Beriga, see Sara Parini, 'Giulio Pace', in Italo Birocchi et al. (cur.), *Dizionario biografico dei giuristi italiani* (*secc. XII–XX*), II (Bologna: Il Mulino, 2013), 1477–8; Alfred Dufour, 'Un adepte italien de l'humanisme juridique à Genève. Jules Pacius de Beriga (1550–1635)', in Luc Monnier (dir.), *Genève et l'Italie* (Genève: Libraire Droz, 1969), 113–47; Louise Guiraud, 'Julius Pacius en Languedoc (1597–1616). Avec documents inédits' (Montpellier: Valat, 1910), 1–36; Antonio Franceschini, 'Giulio Pace da Beriga e la giurisprudenza dei suoi tempi', in *Memorie del Regio istituto veneto* (Venezia: Istituto Veneto di Scienze, Lettere e Arti, 1903); Joshua Freed, 'Jurisdiction, territory, sovereignty: Giulio Pace and the dominion of the sea', in Zwierlein and Lee (eds.), *Sovereignty*, 131–66.

> further confirming and defending them with strong arguments, precise legal terms, and well-crafted responses to the Neapolitan objections.[149]

Pace was probably familiar with Sarpi's writings on the Adriatic question, yet he did not explicitly refer to him in his work. In *De dominio*, Pace frequently cited the authoritative opinions of Bartolus and Baldus, often aligning himself with their perspectives. However, he did not hesitate to contradict them when necessary, reflecting his engagement with Sarpi's 'more modern' arguments. Pace's essay is structured into three parts. First, he outlined the premises he deemed essential. Second, he addressed the core issue, examining the sources and content of Venetian *dominium* over the Adriatic. Third, he responded to those who had recently challenged Venetian jurisdiction.[150]

Pace began by establishing certain terminological and juridical foundations. He first narrowed the focus of his analysis, asserting that while many seas existed, his attention would be confined to the Adriatic, 'called in the vernacular language *Golfo di Venetia*'.[151] Next, he explored the Roman concept of *dominium*. He noted that the term was used in two contexts: (1) in public law, to signify jurisdiction, a component of state sovereignty (*dominium ratione jurisdictionis, dominium universale, superioritas*); and (2) in private law, as a synonym for private property (*dominium ratione particularis, dominium particulare*).[152]

Pace drew a clear distinction between ownership and jurisdiction, specifying that his focus was solely on *dominium* in the public sense (i.e. *dominium universale ratione iurisdictionis et protectionis*).[153] Moreover, he argued that dominion-jurisdiction possessed a dual nature (*dominium jurisdictionis du-*

---

149 My translation, the original text is reported in Franceschini, 'Giulio Pace da Beriga e la giurisprudenza dei suoi tempi', 50: '*Serenissimo Principe, il trattato del dominio del Mare Adriatico di Giulio Pacio è stato veduto da noi con diligenza et havendolo esaminato in tutte le parti* [...] *dobbiamo riferire l'auttore in questa breve trattatione mostra molta dottrina et giudicio siccome in tutte le altre opere sue che sono in stampa, s'è mostrato di eccellente erudizione e* [...]. *In questo del "Dominio del Mare Adriatico" egli ha portato il titolo et la possessione della Serenissima Repubblica con quel modo et con quelle raggioni et fondamenti propri et sodi,* [...] *le ha di più confermate et diffese con buone allegationi et termini legali et risolute obiettioni dei Napoletani in buona forma*'.

150 Acquaviva, 'Giulio Pace', 50; Fulton, *The Sovereignty of the Sea*, 374.

151 Pace da Beriga, *De dominio*, 9: '*Cum multa sint maria, non esse de universe, nec de quocumque mari quaestionem, sed de mari Hadriatico dumtaxat, quod sermone vernaculo vocatur Golfo di Venetia*'.

152 Ibidem.

153 Ibid., 4–5.

plex esse).[154] He distinguished between inferior-secondary authority (*inferior potestas*), held by polities like his native Vicenza, which depended on a superior (in Vicenza's case, the Republic of Venice), and primary-absolute authority (*dominium principale*), held by sovereign entities like Venice or France, which recognised no superior (*superiorem non recognoscens*). Pace thus identified three types of *dominium*: one private and two public (inferior and superior). He clarified that his analysis would concern only 'primary-absolute' dominion, as the Republic of Venice recognised no superior.[155]

Guido Acquaviva noted that Pace's legal framework marked a departure from feudal theories, which often conflated the lord's personal property with the sovereign's jurisdiction. As in Sarpi's case, Pace's arguments moved closer to the modern concept of state sovereignty.[156] Pace emphasised that no one – not even a prince or a republic – could 'own' the sea in a private sense. Regarding the sea's legal status, Pace cited Baldus, who famously argued that the sea's ownership was *nullius* (belonging to no one), its use was common, and its jurisdiction belonged to the prince: 'On the sea and its shores, three things are to be observed: ownership, use, and jurisdiction. Ownership belongs to no one; use is common to all; jurisdiction belongs to the prince [...]. Regarding use and ownership, there is no controversy; the question is jurisdiction'.[157]

Hence, Pace subtly argued that the sea constituted a *res nullius*, and should remain so as ownership was concerned. However, at the same time it could – and it should – be subjected to jurisdiction (*iurisdictio*). Indeed, the scholar started from the assumption of an international community of polities not acknowledging a superior in temporal affairs, wherein the Venice and the Empire were formally on equal footing. Pace explicitly rejected the notion of the emperor as *dominus totius orbis*.[158] He further noted that Venice was founded on water and *terra nullius*, and had never been subject to the Holy

154 Ibid., 7.

155 Ibid., 8.

156 Acquaviva, 'Giulio Pace', 50.

157 Pace da Beriga, *De dominio*, 9: '*In mari, et littoribus maris tria spectari: proprietatem, usum, iurisdictionem. Proprietas est nullius; usus est communis omnium hominum; iurisdictio est principis* [...]. *Ac de usu quidem, et proprietate nulla est controversia: sed de iurisdictione quaestio est*'. Cf. *supra* ch. 1, 2.3.

158 Ibid., 13: '... *tum etiam quia omnes in eo consentiunt, Remplublicam Venetam, ut alias quasdam respublicas, et alios quosdam principes a potestate Imperatoris exemptos esse: quamquam alij hoc esse dicant, quia aedificata est in mari, alij privilegio, alij consuetudine, vel praescriptione*'.

Roman Empire.[159] According to Pace, Venice's independence from both the German and Byzantine Empires had been formally recognised in the ninth-century treaty between the Byzantine Emperor Nicephorus and Charlemagne. Venice, he argued, had developed freely in the Adriatic, situated at the interstice of two empires that were incapable of extending their jurisdiction there. Consequently, Venice had been a free city (*libera civitas*) from its inception – not by privilege or prescription (*non privilegio aut praescriptione*), but because it was built on the sea, beyond the jurisdiction of any other authority (*quia aedificata est in mari nullius iurisdictioni tunc temporis subiecto*).[160]

Pace identified the law of nations, *ius gentium,* as the relevant body of law for determining whether Venice held *dominium jurisdictionis* over the Adriatic Sea. In his view, Roman law, Venetian law, and natural law were less pertinent. Venetian law applied only to its citizens, while Roman law applied in Venetian territory only if it had been incorporated into the Venetian legal system.[161] By contrast, the law of nations applied to all peoples by natural reason; among other things, it regulated the division of territories between political entities – territories that were initially common under natural law.[162]

---

159 Ibid., 14: '*Praemitto septimo, cum eorum, qui non sunt Imperatori subiecti, alij nec sint, nec fuerint umquam subiecti, ut Parthi, Persae, Poloni; alij aliquando fuerint sed esse desierint, ut Gallia et Hispania; inclytam Venetiarum civitatem in illarum numero esse, quae numquam imperio subditae fuerunt*'. Cf. Sarpi, *Dominio del Mare Adriatico*, 328.

160 Pace da Beriga, *De dominio*, 15–6: '*Ut Veneti inter utrumque imperium positi, liberi atque immunes, et ab utroque securi viverent, ac sine molestia res suas in agro Italico possiderent*'. My translation: 'So the Venetians being placed between the two empires, free and exempted from taxes, and they lived safe from both (empires), and without annoyance they possessed their things in Italy'. Cf. Petronio, 'Civitas Venetiarum…', in Benzoni et al. (cur.), *Studi veneti*, 171–85; Mathieu, *Inselstadt Venedig*, 212–23.

161 Since the Middle Ages, Venetian institutions had developed a certain wariness of Roman law and *ius commune*, perceived as too filo-Imperial. For further information on the Venetian legal system, see Laura Ikins Stern, 'Politics and Law in Renaissance Florence and Venice', *American Journal of Legal History*, 46(2) (2004), 209–34; Lamberto Pansolli, *La gerarchia delle fonti di diritto nella legislazione medievale Veneziana* (Milano: Giuffrè, 1970), 13–22; Pier S. Leicht, 'Lo stato veneziano e il diritto comune', in *Miscellanea in onore di Roberto Cessi*, I (Roma: Edizioni di Storia e Letteratura, 1958), 203–11; Gaetano Cozzi, 'Authority and law in Renaissance Venice', in John Hale (ed.), *Renaissance Venice* (London: Faber and Faber, 1973), 193–345; idem (cur.), *Stato, società e giustizia nella repubblica Veneta (sec. XV–XVIII)*, 2 vols. (Milano: Jouvence, 1980); Silvia Gasperini, *Pax tibi Marce. Venice: Government, Law, Jurisprudence. Venezia: istituzioni, diritto, giurisprudenza* (Firenze: Register Italia, 2014).

162 Ibid., 18: '*Restat igitur, ut decidantur ex iure gentium, quod naturali ratione apud omnes gentes valet*'. My translation: 'Therefore, it remains to be decided by the law of nations that applies among all peoples by natural reason'.

2.3.2 Is Venice *Domina Maris Hadriatici*?

After these preliminary considerations, Pace turned to the central question of the dispute: 'Whether the Most Serene Republic of Venice is the master of the Adriatic Sea, by which law and to which degree' (*An Serenissima Respublica Veneta sit domina maris Hadriatici, et quo iure, et in quantum*).[163] He observed that since the Middle Ages, most jurists had regarded Venetian dominion as legitimate and valid. However, Pace did not merely rely on past *auctoritates* but developed his own reasoning in support of Venetian claims.[164] While he frequently cited Bartolus, Baldus, and other commentators, he did not shy away from contradicting certain of their assertions. For example, he rejected Bartolus' claim, shared by other commentators, that the emperor was *dominus totius orbis* (de jure, at least) and that Venice had acquired the Adriatic either by imperial concession or through prescription.[165]

Pace noted that medieval jurists had often considered prescription (sometimes referred to as 'custom', he added), and privilege as the sources of Venetian maritime rights. Similarly to Sarpi, he considered both privilege and prescription as problematic because of their derivative, and not original, nature. Instead, he focused on the process of occupation of the Adriatic by the Venetians, which, over the centuries, had evolved into the immemorial custom already evoked by Sarpi. Pace argued that this process, originating in the early Middle Ages, reflected the acquisition of a *res nullius*, *communis*, and *derelicta*:[166]

> Having established this, I say that the Most Serene Republic of Venice is the master of the Adriatic Sea through its occupation. This can be proven. Since the sea belongs to no one, by natural reason it is therefore granted by the law of nations to those who occupy it, just as it applies to other things that are considered common.[167]

In other words, Venice, as a free and independent city not subject to the emperor, had acquired the Adriatic through occupation in accordance with nat-

163 Pace da Beriga, *De dominio*, 18–9.

164 Ibid., 19; Acquaviva, 'Giulio Pace', 51.

165 Ibid., 32: '*Non obstat, quod Bartolus et eius sectatores dicunt, Imperatore esse dominum totius Orbis* …'.

166 Ibid., 31.

167 My translation from ibidem: '*Hoc posito, dico, Serenissimam Rempublicam Venetam esse dominam maris Hadriatici per eius occupationem. Probatur hoc fieri posse. Quia mare cum sit nullius, naturali ratione, proinde iure gentium conceditur occupant, ut cetera, quae communia dicuntur*'.

ural reason and the law of nations. At the time, the sea was abandoned (*res derelicta*) and unowned (*res nullius*). Thus, Venice could not acquire the Adriatic through prescription since it already held it by occupation.[168] In this perspective, the title derived from prescription, criticised both by Vázquez y Menchaca and by Grotius, lost importance as a source of Venetian dominion over the 'Gulf'. Pace relied on historical evidence to demonstrate the effectiveness of Venetian *dominium*. He cited the annual ceremony of the Marriage of the Sea as a symbolic yet practical representation of Venice's unique bond with the Adriatic. He pointed out that the numerous diplomats who attended it had never contested this symbolic ritual, which was nevertheless charged with practical meanings.[169]

In any case, Pace argued that dominion-jurisdiction was ultimately legitimised by the effectiveness of occupation and the continuous exercise of jurisdictional acts, rather than by the original basis of the title, which he considered secondary to its practical implementation over the centuries.[170] Due to their long-standing possession (*longissima possessione*), the Venetians were not even obliged to prove their original title of acquisition. However, Pace suggested that prescription could still serve as a legal exemption (*non ut modus adquirendi dominij, sed tamquam exceptio*), rather than a means of acquiring dominion, before a hypothetical tribunal to counter challenges to Venetian maritime rights.[171]

Finally, Pace defined the scope of Venetian maritime dominion and jurisdiction, outlining five main functions: 1) the protection of Venetian citizens and subjects; 2) the suppression of piracy and the preservation of maritime safety; 3) the regulation of navigation, including its restriction when necessary; 4) the exercise of criminal jurisdiction; 5) the imposition of taxes and tolls to seafarers.[172] This enumeration makes it clear that Pace conceived of *dominium* as fundamentally public in nature, avoiding any association with the private law concept of ownership. Criminal jurisdiction emerged as the central component of his understanding of maritime dominion, although it

168 Ibid., 33: '*Non potuit igitur Serenissima Respublica dominium acquirere praescriptione, quod iam occupatione acquisierat: quia non possumus res nostras praescribere*'. My translation: 'Therefore, the Most Serene Republic could not acquire ownership by prescription of that which it had already acquired by occupation, since we cannot prescribe what already belongs to us.' '*Quod nostrum est, amplius nostrum fieri non potest*'. My translation: What is ours cannot become more securely ours.

169 Ibid., 18–9, 32–3. See also Pezzolo, 'The Groom of the Sea', 23–7.

170 Pace da Beriga, *De dominio*, 34.

171 Ibidem.

172 Ibid., 35–8.

was by no means the only one. Pace saw no distinction between the exercise of jurisdiction on land and at sea. He argued that the Romans had introduced the concept of *mare nostrum* to protect seafarers, and that this necessity persisted even after the fall of the Roman Empire. In the Adriatic, Venetian fleets eventually filled the resulting power vacuum, restoring security and prosperity. Thus, the right and duty to safeguard the sea became both the foundation and the substance of Venetian maritime dominion over the Adriatic.[173]

2.4 *The Adriatic Sea as a Unique Typology of 'Claimed Sea'?*

In the early seventeenth century, despite its somewhat diminished geopolitical importance, Venice remained a paradigmatic example of a polity that had succeeded in establishing exclusive rights over marine territory. Indeed, the 'Queen of the Sea' (*Regina maris*) continued to be frequently referenced in works addressing the legal status of the sea. As explored in the preceding chapter, Elizabethan diplomacy, Vázquez y Menchaca, and Grotius all made reference to Venice. Later, Seraphim de Freitas would cite Venetian practice, while John Selden dedicated an entire chapter of the first book of *Mare clausum* to the lagoon city, portraying it as a model for Great Britain to emulate.[174] The dominion claimed by Venice could slowly start to be identified as 'maritime sovereignty'. Guillaume Calafat succinctly summarised the legal position in question as comprising the continuous exercise of jurisdiction (*iurisdictio*) and full authority (*imperium*) over a delimited and specific maritime area (*dominium maris*).[175]

In the preceding discussion, we focused on two of the most significant pro-Venetian authors of the early seventeenth century: Paolo Sarpi and Giulio Pace da Beriga. Despite their differing backgrounds, educational paths, and public roles, both rooted their arguments in the unique characteristics of the Adriatic Sea and Venice's related 'claimed seas' policies.[176] Pace, for his part, avoided any reference to the oceans or northern Europe, explicitly stating on the first page of his work that he would address only the Adriatic Sea – the Gulf of Venice. Sarpi, by contrast, sought to emphasise the differences between Venetian claims and Iberian oceanic claims. He argued that smaller seas could not be compared to the vast oceans, fully acknowledging the impracticability of dominating the latter and the necessity for a distinct set of rules to

173 Acquaviva, 'Giulio Pace', 57.

174 See *infra*, ch. IV, 3.2.4 (Freitas), 4.3.2 (Selden).

175 Calafat, *Une mer jalousée*, 113–4.

176 Ibidem.

govern them. In this respect, Sarpi aligned with Grotius more closely than is often assumed.

In addition, both Sarpi and Pace underscored that 'claimed seas' pretensions could only be justified if substantiated through the vigorous and sustained exercise of jurisdictional acts over time. While both authors were attuned to the venerable tradition of the *ius commune* – Pace probably more so due to his legal training – their writings reflect a conviction that medieval and traditional arguments had become insufficient. For instance, both rejected Bartolus' 100-mile limit for maritime jurisdiction, a notion that had been pervasive in earlier treatises. They also dismissed the idea of the papacy playing a dominant role in international relations, as well as the notion of a fictitious imperial jurisdiction beyond the Holy Roman Empire's borders.[177] Both authors aimed to reposition Venetian arguments on firmer, more modern foundations better suited to the realities of the seventeenth century.

Sarpi's approach, in particular, prioritised the real and experienced dimensions of law over abstract theory and general principles.[178] For him, law and empirical realities could coexist and reinforce one another. In the context of international relations, Sarpi conceived a vision of law that was inseparable from geopolitical realities. He defended a right of jurisdiction rooted neither in inherited/derivative titles nor in abstract principles derived from natural law. Pace, for his part, highlighted the autonomous existence of *dominium jurisdictionis* within the public and international law sphere, taking a significant step towards modern conceptions of sovereignty. In essence, the emergence of the principle of freedom of the sea prompted Venetians to adapt their defence of their claims over the Adriatic to meet these new challenges.

Ultimately, the controversy between Venice and its Adriatic rivals was decided more by the Republic's naval build-up during the 1610s and 1620s rather than by doctrinal arguments.[179] However, the intellectual support and propaganda materials provided by scholars like Sarpi and Pace undoubtedly bolstered the resolve of the Venetian patriciate.[180] This highlights one of the central themes of this volume: the ongoing interplay between doctrine and state practice. Indeed, debates over Venetian maritime dominion gradually faded in the following years, silenced for as long as Venetian

177 Acquaviva, 'Giulio Pace', 55–7.

178 Descendre, 'Quand la mer est territoire', 56–8.

179 Nani Mocenigo, *Storia della marina veneziana*, 101–21. Philip III of Spain finally recalled a disgraced Duke of Osuna in 1620, also to deescalate the confrontation with Venice.

180 Calafat, *Une mer jalousée*, 135; Lane, *Venice*, 400.

warships maintained effective control over the Adriatic.[181] In 1621, following the election of Pope Gregory XV (r. 1621–1623), the Venetian Senate dispatched ambassadors to Rome. These envoys defended Venetian maritime dominion using the arguments developed by Sarpi and Pace while also seeking to restore cordial relations with the Holy See and counterbalance Spanish influence in Rome. They presented the Pope with a justification of Venice's claims, or: 'The most rightful and undoubted rights of the Republic' (*giustissime e indubitate ragioni*), concerning 'this our just, ancient and undoubted possession over the Gulf' (*questo nostro giusto, antico et indubitato possesso sopra il Golfo*).[182]

> … (possession) which has never been interrupted, violated, or contested by any Prince, as it is the rightful and inherent property of the Most Serene Republic, born, one might say, with the Republic itself. It has been safeguarded for so many centuries through the great shedding of its citizens' blood, defended and kept intact from corsairs and the fiercest enemies of the Catholic faith, having driven away every kind of armed vessel that illegitimately attempted to navigate there. And should anyone presume to unjustly attempt such an act, the Republic would find itself compelled to make every effort and undertake every serious endeavour for its rightful and necessary defence.[183]

181 During the Cretan War (1645–1669), the Venetian navy – employing both galleys and sailing warships in synergy – was able to repeatedly bombard Constantinople and blockade the Dardanelles, while consistently keeping Ottoman fleets outside the Adriatic. See Roger C. Anderson, *Naval Wars in the Levant, 1559–1853* (Princeton: University Press), 121–84. However, already during the War of the Spanish Succession (1701–1714), the Venetian government, which opted for armed neutrality throughout the war, appeared utterly incapable of enforcing its Adriatic claims against the powerful squadrons of the belligerents. See Norwich, *A History of Venice*, 576; Nani Mocenigo, *Storia della marina veneziana*, 131–232, 255–306.

182 'Relazione di Roma di Girolamo Giustinian *et alii*, 1621' in Berchet and Barozzi (eds.), *Relazioni degli Stati Europei lette al Senato dagli ambasciatori veneti nel secolo decimosettimo*, Serie III - Italia, vol. I, 127.

183 My translation from ibidem.: '… (*possesso*) *che non ci era mai stato da alcun Principe nè interrotto, nè violato, nè preteso di alterarcelo, poichè debito et proprio della Serenissima Repubblica, nato si può dir con lei medesima, havendolo per tanti secoli custodito col spargimento di gran sangue dei suoi Cittadini, et tenutolo difeso et illeso da Corsari et da acerrimi nemici della Cattolica Religione, havendo da esso fugato ogni qualità di legni armati, che indebitamente han preteso di navigarvi, et sempre che si pretendesse da qualsivogli di dar di mano a tentativo si ingiusto, si costituirebbe la Repubblica in necessità di far ogni sforzo, et ogni grave tentativo per la sua giusta et necessaria difesa*'.

In their appeal, the envoys emphasised Venetian deference towards the Catholic Church while highlighting the Republic's role in securing the Adriatic against pirates and infidels. However, they also alluded to the possibility of seeking alliances with the heretical Dutch and English, or even the Turks, as a last resort to defend Venetian dominion from Habsburg and papal interference.[184] Upon their return, the envoys reported that their arguments had moved the Pope.[185] A few years later, in 1630, when Maria Anna of Spain (1606–1646), sister to King Philip IV, was en route to Hungary to marry the future Holy-Roman Emperor Ferdinand III (r. 1637–1657), the Spanish court in Madrid sought to escort her across the Adriatic with a squadron of galleys. This manoeuvre aimed to challenge yet again Venetian Adriatic pretensions and to show that the freedom of navigation applied to all flags.[186] In response, the Venetian Senate firmly reasserted its exclusive rights by deploying its fleet and insisting that Venetian warships alone would escort the princess. Confronted with this determined stance, Madrid relented, allowing Maria Anna to travel aboard a Venetian galley commanded by the senior naval official Antonio Pisani.[187]

Alvise Contarini, Venetian ambassador in Rome between 1632 and 1635, made very straightforward observations on the Adriatic 'issue' upon his return to the lagoon.[188] In his report to the senate, he urged against unnecessary doctrinal disputes with the Pope, instead warning that the reinforcement of Venetian military presence in the Gulf was the only way for Venice to maintain its *dominium maris*, based as it was on 'sword and possession'.[189] In his words, the 'cure for all the ills' lay in maintaining a ready fleet – which had

184 Ibidem, '*(La Repubblica) ricorrerebbe ad aiuti stranieri, si valerebbe di Inglesi, Olandesi et dei Turchi medesimi per la sua indennità, et se Sua Santità havesse fomentato le ingiuste et indebite pretensioni dei Spagnuoli, havrebbe posto tutta la Cristianità in grandissimo scompiglio*'. My translation: '(The Republic) would have recourse to foreign aid, it would avail itself of the British, the Dutch and even the Turks for his safety, and if His Holiness was to foment the unjust and undue pretensions of the Spaniards, he would have placed all of Christianity in great disarray'.

185 Ibidem. For an overview on diplomacy in Rome, see Gianvittorio Signorotto and Maria A. Visceglia (eds.), *Court and Politics in Papal Rome, 1492–1700* (Cambridge: University Press, 2002).

186 Nani Mocenigo, *Storia della marina veneziana*, 122.

187 Ibidem.

188 Alvise Contarini, 'Relazione di Roma, 1632–1635', in Berchet and Barozzi (eds.), *Relazioni degli Stati Europei lette al Senato dagli ambasciatori veneti nel secolo decimosettimo*, Serie III – Italia, vol. I 402. Cf. Anton M. Bettanini, 'Alvise Contarini Ambasciatore Veneto (1597–1651)', *Rivista di Studi Politici Internazionali*, 9(3) (1942), 371–416.

189 Ibid., 398.

FIGURE 4.3 'Golfo di Venezia, descritto dal Padre Minorita Coronelli Cosmografo della Serenissima Repubblica', printed in Venice (1688). Technique: copper engraving, 45 × 61 cm
SOURCE: NATIONAL AND UNIVERSITY LIBRARY IN ZAGREB

always proved the safeguard of the Republic in times of peril.[190] He continued, 'with warships and nothing else we can defend the sea upon which our liberty rests – a liberty as perpetual as the flow of tides'. In Contarini's opinion, only with a powerful navy could Venice also hope to 'keep the popes in their place'.[191] Contarini's assertive realism appears in line with Sarpi's vision, showing the enduring influence of the friar on Venetian political and legal thinking.

3 The Oceans: Seraphim de Freitas and the Defence of Iberian Claims

3.1 *Decline and Stubbornness*

Many Spanish and Portuguese observers criticised the Twelve Years' Truce, especially the aforementioned fourth clause, believing it had made it easier

190 Ibid., 403.
191 Ibidem.

for the Dutch to consolidate and expand their colonial gains.[192] By 1621, Dutch naval power was undoubtedly ascendant in the seas of northern Europe and the Mediterranean.[193] However, as Jonathan Israel notes, Dutch expansion in the East Indies slowed with the scaling down of hostilities. Naval engagements between the Iberians and the Dutch still occurred but on a reduced scale compared to earlier years. While the Spanish and Portuguese maintained control over important bases in Southeast Asia, the VOC continued to strengthen its position in the region.[194] In 1619, the Dutch established the strategically located Batavia (modern day Jakarta) as the centre of their trading network in Asia.[195] The precarious coexistence between the Dutch and the English persisted, even though incidents continued to occur between the two competing allies.[196]

When the Twelve Years' Truce expired in 1621, both the Duke of Lerma and the Grand Pensionary Oldenbarnevelt – the two principal statesmen involved in its signing – had fallen from power in disgrace. The new King of Spain, Philip IV (r. 1621–1665), and his government resumed hostilities with the Dutch, reintroduced an embargo on Dutch shipping across the Iberian Peninsula, and initiated an ambitious campaign of maritime raids from the ports of the Spanish Low Countries. The Dutch retaliated, and the conflict resumed across the oceans. Guinea, the original cradle of Portuguese seaborne expansion, was soon overwhelmed by European competitors. In the East Indies, Portuguese and Spanish naval capabilities continued to deteriorate; they were no longer the strongest European actors in the region. Nevertheless, it was in this context that a comprehensive doctrinal defence of the fading Iberian 'claimed seas' pretensions finally appeared in 1625.[197]

---

192 Brightwell, 'The Spanish System', 279.

193 Israel, *Dutch Primacy in World Trade*, 96–101.

194 Sanjay Subrahmanyam, *The Portuguese Empire in Asia, 1500–1700: A Political and Economic History* (London-New York: Longman, 1993), 153–89; Leonor Freire Costa, 'Portuguese resilience in global war: military motivation and institutional adaptation in the sixteenth- and seventeenth-century Cape route', in Coppolaro and McKenzie (eds.), *A Global History of Trade and Conflict since 1500*, 38–61; Boyajian, *Portuguese Trade in Asia*, 128–65.

195 Israel, *Dutch Primacy in World Trade*, 101–6; Boxer, *The Portuguese Seaborne Empire*, 106–16. Remco Raben, 'The Asian foundations of the Dutch thalassocracy: creative absorption and the company empire in Asia', in Strootman, van den Eijnde and van Wijk (eds.), *Empires of the Sea*, 312–37.

196 Anand, *Origin and Development*, 102–3. The English conquered Ormuz from the Portuguese, and in 1612, they successfully established themselves in the Indian port of Surat.

197 Grewe, *Epochs*, 259; António H. de Oliveira Marques, *History of Portugal* (New York: Columbia University Press, 1976), 277–9; Anthony R. Disney, *A decadencia do império da pimenta. Comercio portugués na Índia no início do séc. XVII* (Lisboa: Edições 70, 1981).

3.2 De Iusto Imperio Lusitanorum Asiatico

3.2.1 Modernity and Tradition

Seraphim de Freitas (c. 1570–1633), a Portuguese friar and jurist, offered a markedly different reaction to *Mare liberum* compared to the Venetian authors discussed in the previous section. Although of Portuguese origin, Freitas taught canon law at the Spanish University of Valladolid.[198] Little is known about his life, and William Knight observed: 'his only claim to fame is that he was a critic of the *Mare liberum*'.[199] From the late 1610s, Freitas had been working on a ponderous treaty, *De iusto imperio Lusitanorum Asiatico* (*Do justo império Asiático dos Portugueses*), comprising eighteen chapters. This work aimed to refute, point by point, the arguments developed by Grotius in *Mare liberum*. However, Spanish authorities delayed its publication until 1625, likely because Philip III had sought to preserve the truce with the Dutch.[200]

Freitas imbued his work with intense patriotic fervour, no less than Grotius or Sarpi. In addition, Freitas displayed an intense *vis polemica* against *Mare liberum*'s author, referred throughout the book as *Incognitus*, 'unknown author' – even though by 1625 it was well-known who the author was. Scholars have often considered that the treatise in question failed as a confutation to *Mare liberum*. Indeed, it is generally assumed that *De iusto imperio* had little impact on the further development of the law of the sea, as it remained largely unknown outside the Iberian Peninsula. Knight remarked that the work

198 Cassi, *Ius commune*, 156–66; Anand, *Origin and Development*, 102–3; Acquaviva, 'Libertà o dominio dei mari', 256.

199 William S. M. Knight, *Seraphim de Freitas: Critic of Mare Liberum* (Cambridge: University Press, 1925), 4; Charles H. Alexandrowicz, 'Freitas versus Grotius', *The British Yearbook of International Law*, 35 (1959), 162–82; Monica Brito Vieira, 'Mare Liberum vs. Mare Clausum: Grotius, Freitas, and Selden's Debate on Dominion over the Seas', *Journal of the History of Ideas*, 64(3) (2003), 361–77; Pagden, *The Burdens of Empire*, 153–70; Neff, *Justice among Nations*, 134; Martínez Torres, '«Gobernar el Mundo». La polémica *Mare Liberum versus Mare Clausum* ', 75–7; Camilo Barcia Trelles, 'Fray Serafín de Freitas y el problema de la libertad oceánica', *Revista General de la Marina*, 130 (1946), 331–48; Moses Bensabat Amzalak, *Trois précurseurs portugais: Santarém et les assurances. Freitas et la liberté des mers. Veiga et les opérations de bourse* (Paris: Librairie du Recueil Sirey, 1935); Marcello Caetano, 'Introduçao', en Serafin de Freitas, *Do Justo imperio asiático dos portugueses*, traducción de Miguel Pinto Meneses (Lisboa: Instituto Nacional de Investigação Científica, 1983), 7–86; Gumersindo Placer López, *Fray Serafín de Freitas, mercedario jurisconsulto portugués* (Madrid: Artes Gráficas, 1956).

200 Seraphin De Freitas, *De iusto imperio Lusitanorum Asiatico* (Valladolid: H. Morillo, [1625]), French translation: Alfred G. de Grandpont, *Freitas contre Grotius sur la liberté des mers, justification de la domination portugaise* (Paris: Aillaud, Gaillard & Cie, 1893). In the following references to Freitas' work the page number refers to the French translation, the folio numbers to the Latin original.

lacked 'the ardent rhetoric of Grotius' generous passion of a youthful genius', further describing it as 'a work of the cloister, and of a man whose passions have long been subordinate to rules and routine. [...] there is little or nothing in it of the advocate. From first to last it is a grave record of the research of a patient and profound erudition'.[201] Consequently, Freitas' treatise failed to resonate with the wider public and proved ineffective as a tool of persuasion and propaganda.[202]

Freitas' background as a canon lawyer profoundly influenced his arguments. The significant space he devoted to issues such as papal authority and the war against infidels rendered *De iusto imperio* somewhat anachronistic when compared to the evolving conceptions of the law of nations outside the Iberian Peninsula. Nevertheless, Freitas was more than just a relic of the past. Contemporary scholars now regard him as a more complex figure, whose dense and convoluted scholastic style obscured the modernity of some of his arguments. For example, Anthony Pagden and Monica Brito Vieira note that certain reflections in Freitas' work seem to anticipate Selden's ideas, and in some respects, even surpass them in incisiveness.[203]

Adolfo Miaja de la Muela viewed Freitas' defence of the closed seas principle as a departure from the dominant Vázquezian tradition among Spanish scholars, who generally supported the freedom of the sea.[204] As noted in chapter 3, both Iberian nations, following the establishment of their exclusive spheres of influence, did not defend their claims over ocean corridors through comprehensive doctrinal frameworks. Instead, they relied on a combination of diplomacy and naval power to enforce their positions. Freitas' work, therefore, offers valuable insights into Iberian legal justifications for the establishment of exclusive maritime rights – arguments that had largely gone unwritten (at least in the doctrinal/theoretical sphere) in prior decades. Notably, his reasoning closely align with those employed by Portuguese envoys at the court of Elizabeth I in 1560–1570s.[205] The fact that Freitas was a Portuguese working in Spain and the period in which he was active (i.e. the Iberian Union) make his work relevant in relation to both Spain and Portugal.

201 Knight, *Seraphim de Freitas*, 4.

202 Ibidem.

203 Pagden, *The Burdens of Empire*, 153–70; Brito Vieira, 'Mare Liberum vs. Mare Clausum', 377.

204 Miaja de la Muela, *Internacionalistas españoles*, 59; San Emeterio Martín, 'El debate sobre el dominio de los mares', 139–41.

205 Cf. *supra*, ch. III, 3.2.

In a way, *De iusto imperio* can be seen as the culmination – or swansong – of the Iberian-oceanic 'claimed seas tradition'. The treatise represents an ambitious attempt to demonstrate that exclusive rights could extend not only to enclosed seas but also to the oceans. Ironically, however, Freitas' work was published at a time when Iberian maritime dominance was already waning. From this perspective, *De iusto imperio* appeared too late to serve as anything more than a scholarly exercise in erudition. One might speculate that its impact could have been significantly greater had it been published some fifty years earlier.

3.2.2 Prior Discovery, Blood, and Expenses

Considering the depth and complexity of Freitas' arguments, this section focuses on those parts of *De iusto imperio* most relevant to the discussion of the 'claimed seas'. Freitas began the treatise with a dedication to Philip IV of Spain, exhorting him to fight all his enemies, defend the true faith, and safeguard the Portuguese empire in the East.[206] He followed this with an appeal to the 'Sovereign princes of the Christian world', akin to Grotius' preface in *Mare liberum*.[207] Freitas declared his intent to defend the rights of his king against the Dutch, whom he accused of seeking to impose the freedom of navigation to the Indies through violence. From the outset, Freitas stated that his refutation would target *Mare liberum*'s unknown author (*Incognitus*). Freitas immediately accused Grotius of cherry-picking literary and legal sources favourable to his argument while omitting or distorting less convenient passages. As an example, Freitas cited two excerpts from the *Corpus Iuris* by the jurists Ulpian and Paulus, which he alleged Grotius had manipulated.[208]

In chapter 1, Freitas recounted Portuguese discoveries, beginning with the voyages of Henry the Navigator. He enumerated the exclusive privileges granted to the Lusitanian kings by successive popes in exchange for spreading the true faith. Freitas reiterated that his principal aim was to demonstrate that the right to navigate and trade in the Indies belonged solely to the king of

---

206 Freitas, *De iusto imperio*, 1–3. The author writes that many of his relatives served the king as soldiers. He states that he would not serve him with arms, but with the quill and the law (*calamo et iure*).

207 Ibid., 4–7.

208 Ibid., 5–7. Grotius' name appeared from the second edition onwards as *Mare liberum*'s author. Curiously, Freitas decided to refer to him as *Incognitus* throughout the book, perhaps as a metaphor of his arguments' obscurity. '*Solum doctores, qui, ut ipse interpretatur, aliquot modo sibi patrocinatur, admittit, alios ut adulatores reculat*'. My translation: 'Among the scholars, he admits only those he interprets to fit in his argumentation, he refuses the others for being adulators'.

Spain–Portugal.[209] In his words, 'we shall succinctly demonstrate that the Dutch have no right to navigate to or trade with the Indies'.[210]

Freitas rejected the distinction between primary, immutable laws of nations and secondary, mutable ones – proposed by both Vázquez y Menchaca and Grotius.[211] The latter had argued that, under the primary law of nations, all peoples possessed the right to travel and engage in trade, and that the Portuguese, by excluding the Dutch from the East Indies, were in violation of this principle. This idea derived from Vitoria's concept of the 'right of natural partnership and communication'.[212]

Freitas countered that the law of nations had a single source – natural reason (*ratio naturalis*) – and a singular purpose: the prosperity of humankind (*bonum naturae humanae*).[213] Thus, he posited, the law of nations constituted a unified category (*consequens est dicamus unicum esse ius gentium*). To support this claim, Freitas referenced several passages from the *Corpus Iuris*.[214] He argued that the right to travel and trade did not supersede a ruler's authority to exclude foreigners from his domain.[215] Freitas acknowledged Francisco Suárez's distinction between an original state of innocence and the corrupted state following original sin. In this framework, certain laws (e.g., religion, parental obedience, self-defence) originated in the former, while others (e.g., property division, servitudes) arose in the latter. Freitas placed navigation and trade in the latter category, considering them mechanisms to address scarcity of resources in a fallen world. To substantiate this view, he cited ancient authors and poets, including Virgil, Ovid, Horace, Claudian, and Boethius, whose authority he believed Grotius had invoked selectively.[216]

209 Ibid., ch. 1, 12–3 [ff. 3–4].

210 My translation from ibidem, '*ac succinte ostendemus Batavis ad Indos navigandi, aut cum illis commercia exercendi ius non esse*'.

211 Brito Vieira, 'Mare Liberum vs. Mare Clausum', 365.

212 Freitas, *De iusto imperio*, 1–3. Cf. Grotius, *Mare liberum*, ch. I, 27 [2].

213 Ibid., ch. 1, 15–6 [ff. 5].

214 Ibid., ch. 1, 15 [ff. 3–4]. '*Sed ut hinc incipiamus diviso iuris gentium in primatium et secundarium Iuris Consultis incognita fuit at contraria, qui ius gentium unicum esse docuerunt*'. My translation: 'However, this distinction of the law of nations between primary and secondary was ignored by jurisconsults who, to the contrary, taught that the law of nations is unitary'.

215 Ibid., ch. 1, 19–20. Francisco Suarez, *De legibus*, II, ch. 17–9.

216 Respectively: *Georgics*, *Metamorphoses*, *Carmina*, *De raptu Proserpinae*. Ibid., 15–7 [ff. 3–4]. See also Brito Vieira, 'Mare Liberum vs. Mare Clausum', 365; Alexandrowicz, 'Freitas versus Grotius', 165; Cassi, *Ius commune*, 160–1; Martínez Torres, '«Gobernar el Mundo». La polémica *Mare Liberum versus Mare Clausum*', 85.

In chapter II, Freitas addressed the right of passage through foreign territories, accusing Grotius of oversimplifying the issue. Freitas distinguished three scenarios: first, simple transit; second, passage in situations of extreme necessity; and third, unqualified freedom to traverse foreign lands. He argued that while access could not be denied in the first two cases, it could be restricted in the third.[217] Drawing an analogy, Freitas reasoned that just as a private landowner could exclude others from using his property, a polity could deny foreigners access to communal resources or trade within its territory.[218] This right, he contended, was even more critical when dealing with powerful foreign entities, whose presence might threaten the sovereignty of the host polity. Thus, even if the law of nations recognised a general right to passage, this right could be conditional upon the consent of the receiving state.[219]

In chapters III and IV, Freitas tackled the question of Portuguese title over the Indies and the oceans based on discovery (*inventio*), a claim Grotius had dismissed in chapter II of *Mare liberum*. Freitas fully acknowledged that Asian polities possessed statehood and sovereignty over their territories, regardless of their religious beliefs.[220] He agreed with Grotius that the Indies were not *res nullius* prior to Portuguese arrival and thus could not be acquired by discovery. However, he engaged in an extensive semantic and legal analysis of the Latin verb *invenire* ('to discover'), exploring its implications in both legal and geographical contexts. Freitas conceded that Europeans had known of India since antiquity but emphasised that Portuguese seafarers were the first to chart a sea route to India via the Cape of Good Hope. He attached significant legal weight to this achievement, asserting that it granted the Portuguese exclusive rights (*ius privativum*) over the route.[221] To bolster this argument, Freitas cited numerous literary and historical sources but placed particular emphasis on the principle of *prior in tempore, potior in iure* – priority in time grants priority in law. For Freitas, the sea route to the Indies, rather than the

217 Freitas, ch. 2, *De iusto imperio*, 24–5.

218 Ibid., ch. 2, 28 [ff. 12], '*Sic etiam respublicae aut Princeps licite prohibere potest omnibus extraneis …*'.

219 Ibid., ch. 2, 29–30 [ff. 12–13].

220 A prevailing opinion dating back to the Middle Ages, supported among others by Vitoria and Grotius. Ibid., ch. 3, 34 [ff. 14–5]. '*Fides namque non tollit ius naturale, aut humanum ex quo dominia profecta sunt*'. My translation: 'Faith does not erase the natural or human law from which the division of property derives'. Cf. Grotius, *Mare liberum*, ch. 3, 40–1 [8–9].

221 Ibid., ch. 3, 38–41 [ff. 16–8].

abstract ocean or the Indies themselves, constituted the primary object of contention.[222]

Concerning the title based on war, addressed in chapter IX, Freitas admitted that infidels could not be attacked or dispossessed solely on the basis of their faith.[223] However, he argued that the Pope and his appointed envoys – the Portuguese – could compel non-Christian rulers to permit the free preaching of the Gospel. Furthermore, just wars could be waged to protect converts from persecution. In Africa, Freitas asserted that the Portuguese had a legitimate basis for war in territories previously Christian but subsequently conquered by Muslims.[224] In Asia, this rationale did not apply, but Freitas maintained that the Portuguese often acted in self-defence against unprovoked attacks by local rulers. Through these conflicts, they came to control certain sea lanes and port cities, either by legitimate conquest or through alliances with local princes.[225]

3.2.3 Pontifical Donation and *Mare clausum*

In chapter 3 of *Mare liberum*, Grotius had dismissed the validity of Alexander VI's division of the Atlantic between the Iberian powers, regarding it at best as an arbitration between two parties over something that could not be granted as a gift. In response, Freitas addressed the question of whether the Portuguese held title over the Indies by pontifical donation in chapter VII of *De iusto imperio*, directly opposing Grotius. As a prelude to this discussion, Freitas dedicated a lengthy chapter VI to exploring the pope's authority over temporal affairs. However, the impression arises that the author became carried away; instead of offering a concise premise, he delved deeply into the issue of pontifical power, devoting more space to it than to topics such as occupation or discovery. His reflection began with the notion of a *respublica Christiana*, united under the spiritual leadership of the papacy. As a devout Catholic cleric, Freitas refused to acknowledge that nearly half of Europe was Protestant by the time of his writing.[226] Indeed, he polemicised extensively with the Scottish jurist and theologian William Barclay (1546–1608), whose treatise *De*

222 Ibid., ch. 4, 43–6 [ff. 19–21]. Cf. Alexandrowicz, 'Freitas versus Grotius', 167; Cassi, *Ius commune*, 163–4.

223 Freitas, *De iusto imperio*, ch. 9, 171–2.

224 Ibid., ch. 9, 175.

225 Ibid., ch. 9, 175–7.

226 Knight, *Seraphim de Freitas*, 6. Freitas also tended to see the spiritual sphere as ultimately superior to the temporal one. See for instance, ibid., 85, 91 and 122.

potestate papae had provided a sharp critique of Roman interference in secular matters.[227]

In essence, he regarded the pope's power as primarily spiritual, though capable of extending indirectly into the temporal realm when serving spiritual purposes.[228] Among the pope's prerogatives, Freitas listed the right to send missionaries for the propagation of the faith (chapter VII).[229] Although the pope could not grant dominion over the 'Indians' because he was not their temporal lord, he could authorise the sending of preachers. These missionaries could only reach distant continents by sea, an endeavour requiring extraordinary expense. Thus, Freitas argued, it was reasonable for those charged with missionary work to receive special privileges to offset these costs. Accordingly, the pope could grant 'temporal' exclusive rights of navigation and commerce to those entrusted with 'spiritual' missionary efforts.[230]

But why had successive popes assigned this mission and the associated privileges to Portugal? In chapter VIII, Freitas enumerated eight reasons. First, the Portuguese had discovered the sea route to the East Indies. Second, they possessed superior navigational expertise. Third, while trade was generally open to all nations under the law of nations, this rule applied only in the absence of prior lawful appropriation by a prince. The Portuguese, having

227 William Barclay, *De potestate papae, an et quatenus in reges et principes seculares ius et imperium habeat* (Mussiponti: Iacobum Garnich, 1610). Freitas referenced the theologian and catholic cardinal Robert Bellarmine (1542–1610)'s reply to Barclay. The cardinal had also defended the papal position during the 1606–1607 interdict crisis with Venice, opposing Sarpi's arguments. See Robert Bellarmine, *On Temporal and Spiritual Authority: On Laymen or Secular People on the Temporal Power of the Pope. Against William Barclay on the Primary Duty of the Supreme Pontiff* (Indianapolis: Liberty Fund, 2012).

228 Freitas, *De iusto imperio*, ch. 6, 65–139. The Portuguese friar explained that Catholic theologians and jurists were divided in two principal camps. Some maintained that Christ neither possessed nor wished to possess secular dominion, and therefore had not entrusted such authority to Saint Peter or his successors, not even *in potentia*. Others, however, defended the view that Christ did exercise temporal dominion, which the popes inherited through Peter. While popes ordinarily allowed princes and emperors to govern secular affairs – thus retaining such powers only *in potentia* – they could, on occasion, exercise them directly, *in actu*, without recourse to secular intermediaries. See also Brito Vieira, 'Mare Liberum vs. Mare Clausum', 368; Knight, *Seraphim de Freitas*, 6.

229 Ibid., ch. 7, 140–1 [ff. 75]: '*Amplificare et propagare ecclesiam* [...] *mittere in regiones infidelium predicatores*'.

230 Ibid., ch. 7, 144–6 [ff. 77–8]: '*Atque ita ius navigandi et commerciandi Pontifices Romani Lusitanis non concesserunt, sed potius et principaliter ius mittendi praedicatores et convertendi infideles*'. My translation: 'Thus, it is not the right of navigation and commerce that popes granted exclusively to the Lusitanians, but more specifically and primarily the right of sending missionaries and converting the infidels'.

pioneered the route to the Indies through considerable sacrifice and expense, were entitled to exclude latecomers. Fourth, there was a fear that other Europeans would engage in trade with infidels. Fifth, in the fifteenth century, popes had invited other princes to join Portugal's missionary efforts, but they had declined. Sixth, the Alexandrine bulls dividing the oceans had been published in Rome in the presence of state representatives, implying their acquiescence. Seventh, Freitas cited the *cartaz* system, established by the Portuguese in the Indian Ocean, as evidence of their mastery over the sea. This licensing system had evolved into a widely accepted legal regime, with the Portuguese successfully repelling attacks from Muslims and pirates while policing the ocean.[231]

Finally, Freitas argued that the Hispano-Portuguese division of the oceans, formalised in papal bulls and bilateral treaties, was binding under the natural law principle of *pacta sunt servanda*. This obligation extended not only to the signatory princes but also to their subjects. Since Philip the Fair (1478–1506), ruler of the Burgundian Low Countries and Count of Flanders, had succeeded (as Philip I) to the throne of Castille, Alexander VI's donation also bound the 'people of Flanders'.[232] Therefore, the Dutch Republic, being a portion of the Habsburg Low Countries who had rebelled against their rightful sovereign Philip II of Spain (Philip I's nephew), was still bound by the agreements signed by their past rulers. These included treaties and papal arbitrations defining the spheres of influence of Spain and Portugal over the oceans.[233] Thus, Freitas believed he had successfully countered Grotius' argument that papal arbitrations and bilateral agreements could not impinge upon third-party rights under the principle *res inter alios acta, aliis nec nocet nec prodest*.

In chapter XII, Freitas concluded his argument on pontifical donation. Like Grotius, he reiterated that the pope, while the Vicar of Christ on Earth, did not possess temporal jurisdiction over the entire world. Consequently, the pope was not lord of the ocean and could not donate it.[234] However, Freitas emphasised that the papacy, by virtue of its spiritual jurisdiction, could authorise temporal princes to undertake missionary efforts. To facilitate these spiritual objectives, the pope could grant exclusive navigation rights to help finance the costly oceangoing missions essential for spreading

231 Ibid., ch. 8, 150–66 [ff. 82–90].

232 Ibidem. Philip was Charles V's father.

233 Ibidem.

234 Ibid., ch. 12, 225–6.

the faith.[235] In conclusion, the exclusion of other Europeans from the Indian Ocean was rooted in the papacy's indirect temporal power, exercised in view of spiritual ends.[236]

3.2.4 Occupation and Quasi-occupation

Freitas believed he could also refute Grotius' arguments based on occupation and possession (chapter x). The Dutch author, especially in chapter v of *Mare liberum*, had asserted the impossibility of occupying the sea. Freitas observed that Grotius' reasoning relied heavily on the works of ancient poets, whom he considered authorities on natural law. Employing a similar strategy, Freitas invoked the Roman legal maxim: 'no one can refuse the application of a law that he applied to others'.[237] To strengthen his critique, he extensively cited passages from *Mare Liberum* – notably from chapters v, vi, and vii – where Grotius characterised the ocean as a *res communis omnium*, by natural law common, indivisible, and incapable of any occupation.[238] Freitas set out to disprove Grotius' assertion that navigation to the Indies was universally free, arguing instead that sovereign rulers could acquire exclusive rights over the sea. To support his case, he drew on passages from Virgil, the 'prince of poets,' particularly where Roman dominion over the ocean is prophesied in the *Aeneid* and *Georgics*.[239]

Additionally, Freitas appealed to Roman law, the Rhodian Sea Laws, and the *ius commune* doctrine, citing scholars such as Baldus, as evidence of a broad and long-standing acceptance of 'claimed seas' policies.[240] For example, he argued that the *Incognitus* had misinterpreted a passage from the Roman jurist Paulus. Grotius had cited Paulus' passage on the *uti possidetis* action regarding rights over coastal seas, treating it as applicable only to private law matters. Instead, Freitas believed that Grotius had made an artificial distinction and that the passage also applied to inter-polity relations. He insisted there was no justification for denying a prince rights that were recognised

235 Ibid., ch. 12, 229.
236 Ibid., ch. 12, 230.
237 Ibid., ch. 10, 179.
238 Ibid., ch. 10, 181–3.
239 Ibid., ch. 10, 184–5 [ff. 102].
Aeneid, I: '*Nascetur pulchra Trojanus origine Cesar*
Imperium Oceano, famam qui terminet astris'.
Georgics, I: '*Tua nautae*
Numina sola colant; tibi serviat ultima Thule
Teque sibi generum Thetis emat omnibus undis'.
240 Ibid., ch. 10, 184–8 [ff. 102–4].

for private individuals. Moreover, Freitas argued that exclusive rights could be derived from natural law over resources previously held in common. He substantiated this claim with an extended quotation from the French jurist Donellus (Hugues Doneau).[241]

Freitas agreed with Baldus' position that ownership of the sea was unattainable: 'The starting point of my reasoning is accepting that ownership of the sea is *nullius*; however, it is subjected to the emperor or to the king regarding jurisdiction and protection'.[242] He was referring to the fact that certain European polities had succeeded in achieving recognition of their maritime jurisdiction. As we saw in Chapter 1, the *ius commune* doctrine generally admitted the validity of such jurisdictional claims, often as a means of combating piracy or levying tolls on navigation. As an illustrative example, Freitas cited Venice and its symbolic 'marriage to the sea'. However, unlike Sarpi and Pace, he identified papal donation as the veritable source of Venetian dominion over the Adriatic.[243] At this point, Freitas dismissed Grotius' argument that the ocean's vastness precluded the acquisition of exclusive rights. He rejected the ontological distinction between the sea and the ocean posited by Grotius and Sarpi, asserting:

> Neither the immensity of the sea nor its nature and qualities preclude jurisdiction and occupation, as suggested by the *Incognitus*. The argument that the entire expanse of the ocean cannot be occupied due to human incapacity does not imply that parts of it cannot be subject to occupation.[244]

In this regard, Freitas interestingly compared the ocean to the desert: sparsely populated and difficult to occupy, yet still capable of being included within state boundaries. Similarly, he considered it self-evident that coastal states

241 Ibid., ch. 10, 188–9 [ff. 104–5].

242 Ibid., ch. 10, 190 [ff. 105]: '*Quartum nostre assertionis fundamentum sit, quod quamuis maris proprietate nullius esse concedamus; attamen quo ad protectionem et iurisdictione Caesaris vel Regis*'.

243 Ibid., ch. 10, 191 [ff. 105]: '*Veneti qui potissimum in maritimis prevalent dum eligunt Ducem, eumque initiant solemni modo coronatum, lubent mare sibi disponsare iniecto annulo in symbolo veri et perpetui imperii*'. My translation: 'The Venetians, who excel in maritime affairs, whenever they elect a doge and solemnly crown him, command to the sea to marry him, throwing a ring into it as symbol of true and perpetual domination'.

244 My translation. Ibid., ch. 10, 193 [ff. 107]: '*Nec huic iurisdictioni et occupationi repugnant vel maris immensitas, vel natura et qualitas, ut pungit Incognitus. Nam quoad immensitatem, argumentum concludit non posse omnem Oceani tractum occupari, idque propter nostram impotentiam, non tamen inde sequitur, nec partem occupationis capacem esse*'.

could extend control over neighbouring seas, even if jurists differed on the precise extent of such maritime zones (*maris districta*).[245] In Freitas' view, natural law did not prescribe any specific rule in this regard. The only solution was to determine the area subjected to a prince based on their strength and naval capabilities. You would not have expected a Sarpian-pragmatic argument from Freitas at this point, and a slippery one indeed considering the failing naval power of the Portuguese.[246] Freitas further argued that the sea's unpossessable nature, comparable to air, did not preclude jurisdiction. Drawing an analogy with rivers, he noted that while Roman law regarded flowing water (*aqua perfluens*) as unownable, the riverbed itself could be owned. Similarly, sovereigns could exercise control over maritime areas based on jurisdictional rights over the seabed.[247]

In chapter XI, Freitas continued his assault on Grotius by inundating the reader with citations from poets and jurists, aiming to demonstrate not only his erudition but also Grotius' alleged errors.[248] For instance, he underlined another example of misquote by Grotius, which concerned a passage by the Roman jurisconsult Ulpian. Freitas considered the right wording to be: 'No servitude can be imposed on the sea by private law because it is by nature open to all persons'. Hence, he accused Grotius of cutting part of the text, namely the words *privata lege,* 'by private law'. Grotius' omission was aimed to suggest that neither a private person nor a prince could impose a servitude on the sea. Instead, Freitas argued that Ulpian never said that, since he specified that he was referring only to private law easements.[249]

Freitas pressed his case further, claiming that most past authors acknowledged the feasibility of exclusive maritime rights.[250] While he concurred with Grotius that the sea could not be occupied or possessed in the same way as land, he diverged sharply in affirming that the sea could still be subject to 'quasi-occupation' through activities like fishing and navigation, thus respect-

245 Ibid., ch. 10, 194 [ff. 107]. Bonaert in *Minos seu mare tutum* (ch. V, 139) had also compared the legal status of the sea to that of sea to that of the desert, text in Salom Franco, 'Vitoria y Grocio frente al mar'.

246 Ibid., ch. 10, 195 [ff. 107]. Cf. Scovazzi, 'Libertà o dominio', 30.

247 References are made to Gaius, Ulpian, Bartolus, Donellus, *et alii.* Ibid., ch. 10, 195 [ff. 107].

248 However, already Knight underlined that Freitas operated in a similar way, selecting the sources and quoting them as he saw fit for his aims. In *Seraphim de Freitas*, 7.

249 '*Quamvis mari quod natura omnibus patet, servitus imponi* PRIVATA LEGE *non potest*'. Freitas, *De iusto imperio*, ch. 11, 198 [ff. 111]. On this passage, see also Alexandrowicz, 'Freitas versus Grotius', 172.

250 Freitas, *De iusto imperio*, ch. 11, 198–205 [ff. 111–5].

ing its natural status.[251] Freitas contended that Grotius had framed the issue incorrectly, focusing on veritable occupation and possession, rather than rights over the sea consisting of navigation and fisheries' exploitation.[252] After another meticulous exegesis of Roman law and *ius commune*, Freitas concluded that princes could, under specific circumstances, alter the legal status of the sea. While *ius gentium* and *ius naturale* treated the sea as free and common, sovereigns could justifiably carve out exclusive rights to fishing and navigation:

> It is evident from the above that fishing rights can be occupied and granted by a prince. While under the law of nations, and as long as it persists, the use of the sea or a public river – like hunting and similar activities – remains public and accessible to all, [...] nonetheless, for a just cause, a prince can alter these rights, transforming the public use of the sea or river into private rights.[253]

Finally, Freitas clarified that Portugal was not claiming exclusive dominion over the entire ocean. The Dutch, he asserted, were free to navigate the European seas and the North Atlantic, establishing their own routes to the Indies if desired. However, they could not usurp the Cape of Good Hope route, which the Portuguese had opened at great cost and effort. Once again, Freitas identified specific ocean corridors, rather than the oceanic expanses, as the real object of Portuguese exclusive rights.[254]

3.2.5 Prescription

Lastly, Freitas defended Portuguese claims based on prescription (chapters XIII and XIV). Vázquez de Menchaca had already rejected the validity of such titles in relation to the sea, and Grotius had similarly dismissed them in

251 Ibidem, '*maris occupatione et possessione vere et proprie dari non posse, quemadmodum in terra datur, haec enim pedibus possidetur*'.

252 Ibid., ch. 11, 206–7 [ff. 115]: '*Agit enim de vera occupatione et apprehensione, nos vero de iure maris, quod consistit in navigando aut piscando et ideo impropríssime confundit terminos et quaestione*'. My translation: 'Indeed, he refers to true occupation and possession, while we speak of maritime rights, consisting in navigation and fishing, and he improperly confuses the terms and the issue at hand'.

253 Ibid., ch. 10, 211–2 [ff. 117], my translation. '*Constat igitur ex dictis ius piscandi occupari et donari posse a Principe, licet enim attento iure gentium et interim dum illud perdurat, usus piscandi in mari, vel flumine publico, sicut et venandi et similium, publicus sit et omnibus competat; [...] tamen ex iusta causa potest Princeps, [...], ista haec omnia immutare et efficere, ut usus maris, fluminis et similium publicus esse destinat et fiat iuris privati*'.

254 Ibid., ch. 11, 224 [ff. 123–4].

chapter VII of *Mare liberum*. In their view, prescription was a construct of civil law and therefore could not alter the original *res communis* status of the sea, as defined by natural law.[255] Moreover, they argued that prescription could not apply to relations between sovereign princes or to a *res extra commercium* (i.e., not subject to private commerce) such as the sea.[256] Freitas, however, contended that if the sea could be subject to quasi-occupation, it could also be subject to prescription. Once again, he supported his argument with an extensive array of scholarly citations to demonstrate his ability to refute the opposing position. For instance, while he agreed with Grotius' assertion that prescription emerged as a legal concept under Roman civil law, Freitas argued that similar mechanisms existed elsewhere, such as in Ancient Athens, as described by Plato. Therefore, he concluded, prescription should be considered an institution of *ius gentium* (the law of nations), which would allow its application to relations between sovereign princes.[257]

Freitas further emphasised that 128 years had passed since Vasco da Gama's arrival in India and his initial occupation of the new sea route to the Indies on behalf of the Portuguese Crown in 1498. Such a lengthy period of quasi-possession, he argued, constituted valid prescription or even immemorial custom. While Freitas admitted that jurists disagreed on the exact duration required to establish prescription, he pointed out that, for a significant portion of this time, other European nations had not seriously challenged Portuguese *bona fide* possession over the route leading to the Indian Ocean.[258] He maintained that only if the Portuguese ceased their expeditions could rival nations, such as the Dutch, claim a prescriptive right to navigate the sea routes to the Indies.[259] Otherwise, the *ius privativum* (arising from prior quasi-occupation) would remain with the Spanish-Portuguese Crown, legitimising their exclusion of all other Europeans from the ocean corridors leading to the Indies.

3.3 *The Oceans as 'Claimed Seas', a Lost Battle?*

Freitas skilfully highlighted the inconsistencies and exegetical errors made by Grotius. Writing in a dense and intricate style, the friar addressed all the vari-

---

255 Vázquez y Menchaca, *Controversiarum illustrium*, II, 89; Grotius, *Mare liberum*, ch. 7, 99 [38–51], '*Mare aut ius navigandi proprium non esse Lusitanorum titulo praescriptionis aut consuetudinis*'. See also Miaja de la Muela, *Internacionalistas españoles*, 64.

256 Freitas, *De iusto imperio*, ch. 11, 224 [ff. 152]. See also Cavanagh, 'Prescription and Empire', 291.

257 Ibidem.

258 Ibid., ch. 13, 259 [ff. 145].

259 Ibid., ch. 14, 294 [ff. 168].

ous titles claimed by the Portuguese as well as the counterarguments in *Mare liberum*.[260] In some respects, his reasoning appears somewhat outdated. As previously discussed, he devoted considerable energy to defending papal authority, attributing continued validity to pontifical bulls as a source of rights in international relations. Moreover, he argued that the primary justification for the Portuguese monopoly on navigation was not economic profit but the propagation of Catholicism, coupled with the fight against infidels. These arguments reflect little progression from those advanced by Henry the Navigator and others during the first wave of oceanic expeditions two centuries earlier.[261]

That being said, Freitas often aligned with contemporary authors like Grotius. For instance, he described the King of Spain as a ruler *superiorem non recognoscens* (recognising no superior) in temporal affairs, as sovereign in his territories as the Emperor was in his.[262] Furthermore, he suggested that the distinction between Portuguese jurisdiction and ownership over the sea routes leading to the Indies was not the crux of the debate. In his view, both legal positions ultimately conferred a *ius privativum* (exclusive right) in favour of Spain and Portugal. As we have seen, Freitas readily conceded that the sea was fundamentally different from land, developing the concepts of quasi-occupation and quasi-possession to address the unique nature of the ocean. This enabled him, in discussing prescription, to assert: 'Thus, from all this we conclude the *Incognitus* gave himself a pointless task in refusing prescription in relation to public things. This issue is superfluous, as the matter at hand is concerned', he continued, 'even if his denial was grounded in the law, that would not change much, because it suffices us to be in that quasi-possession of the navigation towards the Indies, to the exclusion of others; this being acknowledged by everybody…'.[263]

Freitas repeatedly invoked the glory and naval prowess of the Portuguese, accusing the Dutch of enlisting the *Incognitus* to maliciously attack and vilify the Lusitanians because they had been defeated and repelled numerous times. Yet, by the time *De iusto imperio* was published, the Portuguese position was

---

260 Knight, *Seraphin de Freitas*, 9.

261 Freitas, *De iusto imperio*, ch. 17, 311.

262 Ibid., ch. 12, 229.

263 Ibid., 294, my translation. '*Hinc deduces frustra de fatigatum Incognitum totus est in neganda rerum publicarum praescriptione. Ea enim quaestio quoad propositu inutilis est; esto namque quod vera esset pars negativa, nihil officeret, cum nobis sufficiat esse in ea quasi possessione navigandi in Indos privative quoad alios; qua data concors est omnium sententia…*'.

increasingly defensive. References to the effectiveness of Portuguese control over sea routes became a double-edged sword, as the practical impossibility of controlling vast oceanic expanses and their innumerable routes was becoming apparent. The *Estado da Índia* and Portuguese closed sea pretensions were crumbling under relentless competition. By the 1620s, Portuguese ships were consistently outnumbered along the sea routes they ostensibly 'possessed' and sought to deny to others. From this perspective, the combative friar was waging a battle with his quill that had already been lost on the seas, where cannons and ships determined outcomes.[264]

In the years that followed, the Dutch continued to dismantle the defence system established by the viceroy Afonso de Albuquerque over a century earlier. They captured the strategic Portuguese base of Malacca in 1641, drove the Portuguese out of Ceylon in 1654, and seized Cochin – the first Lusitanian settlement in the East – in 1660. By then, only a handful of bases, such as Goa, remained in Portuguese hands.[265] Nonetheless, the true and often overlooked historical significance of Freitas' work lies elsewhere. In *De iusto imperio*, Freitas successfully wove together the legal arguments underpinning the ambitious 'claimed seas' tradition concerning the oceans. As discussed in Chapter 2, the first two colonial empires – Spain and Portugal – began forging this tradition as early as the fifteenth century.[266]

Coincidentally, in 1625, the same year that Freitas' *De iusto imperio* appeared, Grotius published his magnum opus, *De iure belli ac pacis* (*On the Law of War and Peace*). In the second book of this treatise, Grotius revisited the legal status of the sea, demonstrating a significant evolution from the arguments he had presented in his earlier legal brief of 1609. Grotius' more mature reflections sought to reconcile his legal philosophy with a more nuanced understanding of state practice, shaped by his experiences as a diplo-

---

264 It is important to note that the decline of the Portuguese empire in Asia was not solely the result of Dutch competition. For a detailed analysis of this issue, see Ernst van Veen, *An Inquiry into the Portuguese Decline in Asia, 1580–1645. Decay or Defeat?* (Leiden: CNWS Publications, 2000). For a different perspective and a historiographical survey, see Geovani Dias Pereira, 'Dilemas historiográficos sobre a decadência de um Império: O "ocaso" do Estado da Índia (séc. XVI e XVII)', *Aedos*, 10(22) (2018), 285–309.

265 Anand, *Origin and Development*, 92; Meilink-Roelofsz, *Asian Trade and European Influence in the Indonesian Archipelago*, 175–81; Panikkar, *Asia and Western Dominance*, 58–9; Disney, *A History of Portugal*, 198–220; Boxer, *The Portuguese Seaborne Empire*, 106–27. The failure of the Habsburg monarchy to protect Portuguese colonial interests contributed to Portugal's secession from the Iberian Union in 1640. See Elliott, *Imperial Spain*, 346–7; Martínez Torres, '«Gobernar el Mundo». La polémica *Mare Liberum versus Mare Clausum*', 80–1.

266 Cf. *supra* ch. II, 3; Cattelan, 'Iberian Expansion', 1–28.

mat.[267] He now conceded that, under certain conditions, states could legitimately acquire exclusive rights – more easily jurisdiction than ownership – over limited portions of coastal seas without contravening natural law.[268] Grotius referred specifically to waters closely bordered by land, such as inland seas, bays, and straits.[269] Hence, in *De iure belli ac pacis* Grotius' views on the legal status of the sea became more balanced. However, he still maintained that the general rule remained the impossibility of acquiring ownership over vast marine spaces, or the high seas, to the exclusion of others. In other words, Grotius continued to conceptualise the oceans in fundamentally different terms from Freitas.

4 Northern Europe: John Selden and the British Replies to *Mare liberum*

4.1 *The 'British Seas', Fisheries, and Royal Prerogatives*

4.1.1 William Welwod

When the Scottish king James VI Stuart inherited the English throne in 1603 as James I, he gradually steered British policies towards the 'claimed seas' principle, albeit only as the waters surrounding his kingdoms were concerned. A peace-loving monarch by nature, yet fiercely protective of his royal prerogatives, he established the King's Chambers – jurisdictional zones designed to safeguard British neutrality at sea. Furthermore, he asserted a preferential claim over coastal fisheries, requiring foreign fishermen to purchase licences. However, James VI–I never clearly defined which fisheries he considered to be within 'British' waters. At the same time, Great Britain continued to challenge Iberian and Dano-Norwegian closed-sea claims, though James VI–I managed to maintain a degree of understanding with these nations. His strong personal ties with Christian IV, his brother-in-law, helped ease ongoing tensions in the northern seas with Denmark–Norway.[270] In the meanwhile, English and Scot-

267 De Pauw, *Grotius and the Law of the Sea*, 65–6; Butler, 'The law of the sea', in Bull, Kingsbury and Roberts (eds.), *Hugo Grotius and International Relations*, 214; Zemanek, 'Was Hugo Grotius Really in Favour of the Freedom of the Seas?', 58.

268 Hugo Grotius, *The Rights of War and Peace* [*De iure belli ac pacis*, 1625], edited and with an introduction by Richard Tuck (Indianapolis: Liberty Fund, 2005), II, ch. 3, § 8–15, 34–7.

269 Ibid., ch. 3, § 8, 34.

270 Murdoch, *Britain, Denmark-Norway and the House of Stuart*, 22–43; Calvin F. Senning, 'The Visit of Christian IV to England in 1614', *The Historian*, 31(4) (1969), 555–72. In 1589 James VI had married Christian IV's sister, Anne of Denmark.

tish mercantile and governmental circles continued to voice their frustration over Dutch exploitation of the halieutic resources in the 'British seas'.[271] Pamphleteers loudly advocated for the exclusion of Dutch fishermen from the waters surrounding the British Isles, or at least for the limitation of their activities. More broadly, the commercial dominance of the Dutch sparked growing envy and resentment among James VI–I's subjects.[272]

Against this backdrop, it is not surprising that one of the first British responses to *Mare liberum* emerged from Scotland, the birthplace of the Stuart dynasty. Unlike England, Scotland had a long-standing tradition of restricting foreign fishing in its coastal waters. William Welwod (or Welwood) (1578–1622), a professor of civil law at the University of St Andrews (from 1590 to 1611), published the treatise *An Abridgement of All Sea-Lawes* in 1613.[273] This work built upon an earlier maritime law publication of 1590 entitled *The Sea-Law of Scotland, Shortly Gathered and Plainly Dressit for the Reddy Use of All Sea-Fairingmen*.[274] This earlier work, a concise treatise of twenty-nine pages, focused on Scottish coastal shipping and related legal issues. In 1615, Welwod released *De dominio maris iuribusque ad dominium praecipue spectantibus assertio brevis ac methodica*, an expanded and refined Latin version of *An Abridgement*, aimed at a broader readership.[275] Significantly, Welwod dedi-

271 van Ittersum, '*Mare Liberum* Versus the Propriety of the Seas?', 240–3; Fulton, *The Sovereignty of the Sea*, 352; Anand, *Origin and Development*, 100–1; Tommasi, *La libertà dei mari*, 48–53; de Vries and Van der Woude, *The First Modern Economy*, 235–69.

272 Simon Schama, *La cultura olandese dell'epoca d'oro* (Milano: Il Saggiatore, 1988), 263–4; Godfrey Davies, *The Early Stuarts, 1603–1660* (Oxford: Clarendon Press, 1959), 51–2.

273 William Welwod, *An Abridgement of All Sea-Lawes, Gathered Forth of All Writings and Monuments which are to be Found among Any People or Nation, upon the Coasts of the Great Ocean and Mediterranean Sea, and Specially Ordered and Disposed for the Use and Benefit of All Benevolent Sea-Farers within His Majesties Dominions of Great Britanne, Ireland and the Adjacent Isles Thereof* (London: Printed for Humfrey Lownes, for Thomas Man, 1613). A digital version of the 1613 edition is available at: http://maritimelawdigital.com/uploads/PDFs/Welwod-Sea_Laws.pdf. In 1636, a second edition was 'printed by the Assignes of Ioane Man and Benjamin Fisher', also in London. Copies of the 1613 treatise have survived in greater numbers than copies of the 1590 work, partly because it was more successful commercially. In 1636, a new edition was printed by Thomas Harper of London, and in 1686 the treatise reappeared as an appendix to a new edition of Gerard Malynes' *Consuetudo vel lex mercatoria*. For a discussion on Welwod's treatises, the relationship between them and their historical context, see John D. Ford, 'William Welwod's Treatises on Maritime Law', *The Journal of Legal History*, 34(2) (2013), 172–210.

274 William Welwod, *The Sea-Law of Scotland: Shortly Gathered and Plainly Dressed for the Reddy Use of All Sea-Fairingmen* (Edinburgh: Robert Waldegraue, 1590).

275 William Welwod, *De dominio Maris iuribusque ad dominium praecipae spectantibus assertio brevis ac methodica* (London: excudebat G. Fonti, 1615).

cated *An Abridgment* to King James VI–I and to the 'Lords Admiralls of England, and Ireland, of Scotland and the Isles, and of the Cinque Ports', the naval officials charged with ensuring the security of the seas 'for all loyall subjects, traders on Sea specially, for Fishers and others, happily disposed to adventure and exercise the trade of fishing; to the end, that not onely a peaceable, but also a full and plentifull fishing may be enjoyed by his M(ajesty) kingdoms'.[276] Thus, Welwod sought to provide doctrinal support for James VI–I's efforts to preserve and expand his royal prerogatives at sea.

In *An Abridgment*, Welwod concentrated on the issue of coastal fishing, deliberately avoiding the broader matter of oceangoing navigation.[277] Although Grotius in *Mare liberum* had only touched briefly on fisheries, Welwod believed that his arguments could easily be misused to justify further encroachments on British coastal fisheries – a concern shared by many within Britain's merchant and political elite.[278] The Scottish jurist devoted chapter (or title) XXVII, entitled 'Of the Community and Propriety of the Sea', to refuting the fifth chapter of the anonymous *Mare liberum*. This chapter, by far the longest in the treatise, suggests that Welwod was prompted to draft *An Abridgment* after stumbling upon a copy of *Mare liberum*:

> Having of late seen and perused a very learned, but a subtle treatise (incerto Authore) intituled *Mare Liberum*, conteyning in effect a plain Proclamation of a libertie common for all of all Nations to fish indifferently on all kind of Seas, and consequently, a turning of undoubted proprieties to a community; as the fifth chapter thereof at large discovers, and the discourse being covered with the maintenance of a liberty to sail to the Indians, I thought always expedient by occasion of this argument of fishing contained in my former Title, by God's Grace, to occur thereunto, as manifestly direct, at least tending to the prejudice of my most worthy Prince and his subject; and that not only by argu-

276 Welwod, *An Abridgement*, iii.

277 Van Ittersum, '*Mare Liberum* Versus the Propriety of the Seas?', 243–9; Fulton, *The Sovereignty of the Sea*, 352–4; William Senior, 'Early Writers on Maritime Law', *Law Quarterly Review*, 37 (1921), 323–36; A. R. G. McMillan, 'Admiralty and maritime law', in Hector McKechnie (ed.), *An Introductory Survey of the Sources and Literature of Scots Law* (Edinburgh: Printed for the Stair Society by R. Maclehose & Co., 1936), 325, 329–30; David Armitage, *The Ideological Origins of the British Empire* (Cambridge: University Press, 2000), 110–1; Anand, *Origin and Development*, 100–1.

278 Reppy, *The Grotian Doctrine*, 262–4; Theutenberg, 'Mare Liberum et Mare Clausum', 487.

> ments derived from the first verity of the nature of things, but also from his own proofs, warrants, and their authors.[279]

Welwod agreed with Grotius that navigation as such could not be forbidden, being 'a thing far off from all controversies, at least upon the Ocean'.[280] However, he vehemently disagreed with him in relation to fisheries exploitation in the coastal seas. To counter the arguments developed in *Mare liberum*, Welwod relied heavily on interpretations of ancient authors and Roman law, much like Grotius and Freitas. Additionally, he referenced the legislation of several northern European nations.[281] In contrast, Grotius in *Mare liberum* had largely dismissed contemporary state practices as sources for the law of nations.

In Welwod's view, the anonymous author of *Mare liberum* sought to demonstrate 'by the opinions and sayings of some old poets, orators, philosophers, and jurisconsults, that land and sea, by the first condition of nature, hath been, and should be common to all, and proper to none'.[282] The Scottish jurist, however, pointed out that the fragments from the *Codex* referenced by Grotius consisted of edicts issued by Roman emperors to their subjects. Moreover, Welwod argued that Grotius had 'creatively' interpreted passages from Roman jurists compiled in the *Digest*.[283] To bolster his argument, Welwod cited the supreme *auctoritas* for all Christians, the Bible, notably a passage from the *Genesis* in which God encouraged humankind to subjugate the earth and to reign over fishes (*Genesis*, 1, 28). From this, Welwod derived the possibility of appropriating the waters in which marine creatures lived. In other words, the Scottish jurist did not hesitate to place the Divine Providence at James VI–I's side, against the insatiable greed of the Dutch:[284]

> ... against this I mind to use no other reason, but a simple and orderly reciting of the words of the holy spirit, concerning that first condition natural of land and sea from the very beginning; at which time, God having made, and so carefully toward man disposed the four elements, two to swim above his head, and two to lye under his feet: that is to say, the earth and water, both wonderfully for that effect ordered to the up-

279 Welwod, *An Abridgement*, 61.
280 Ibid., 61–2.
281 Ford, 'William Welwod's Treatises on Maritime Law', 181–2; Bederman, 'The Sea', 367–8.
282 Welwod, *An Abridgement*, 62.
283 Ibid., 62–8.
284 Fulton, *The Sovereignty of the Sea*, 353; Shearer, 'Grotius and the Law of the Sea', 52.

> making of one and a perfite globe, for their more mutual service to mans use: according to this, immediately after the creation, God saith to man, *Subdue the earth, and rule over the fish* (*Genesis*, 1, 28) which could not be, but by a subduing of the waters also.[285]

Welwod did not dispute the theory of property developed by Grotius in *Mare liberum*. He conceded that, in the beginning, all land and seas were held in common, and that private property, trade, and navigation were later human constructs.[286] As already mentioned, he even agreed that, as a general rule, navigation remained free, particularly for trade and communication across oceans. However, he disagreed on whether the sea could – or had – been divided and appropriated like land territories.[287] Grotius had argued that the sea never lost its original status of commonality, being incapable of occupation or possession, indivisible by boundaries, and physically distinct from land.[288] In response, Welwod countered that the 'lack of solidity' of the sea did not preclude occupation, as 'a mind to possess' was sufficient:

> For answer, first concerning the nature of the sea, as supposed impossibly occupiable or acquirable; is this so thought, because the sea is not so solid, as is the land, that men, may trade thereon, as upon land? Or that it is continually flowing to and from? Surely, that lack of solidity for man his trading thereon by foot, shall not hinder the solid possession of it, far less the occupation and acquiring, if we will give to the sea, that which the jurisconsults indulgently grant to the land, which also cannot be denied. Paulus the jurisconsult saith, [...]: That is, it is not needful for him who would possess himself in any part of the land, to go about and tread over the same; but it is sufficient to enter in upon any thereof; with a mind to possess all the rest thereof, even to the due marches. And what can stay this to be done on sea, as well as on Land? And thus far concerning the solidity.[289]

Even though the sea was undeniably 'liquid, fluid and unstable', Welwod argued that it nevertheless maintained 'the prescribed bounds strictly enough' in certain geographical subdivisions such as the North Sea, where natural

285 Welwod, *An Abridgement*, 62.
286 Ibid., 63.
287 van Ittersum, '*Mare Liberum* Versus the Propriety of the Seas?', 246.
288 Grotius, *Mare liberum*, 31 [85].
289 Welwod, *An Abridgement*, 67.

limits and landscape marks existed.[290] Such marks made it possible to divide the sea with an acceptable degree of precision. However, Welwod admitted that: 'There are not, in every part of the sea, isles sensible, (as Guernsey is to England in the narrow seas) or sands (as the washes at the west seas of England) nor rocks, or other eminent and visible marks above water, for the designation of the bounds (or laying out limits) of the divisible parts thereof'.[291] Nevertheless, Welwod considered that God, 'who is both the distributer and first author of the division and distinction of both land and sea', provided men with intelligence to solve complex issues, and also had 'diversly informed men by the helps of the compasse, counting of courses, sounding, and other ways, to find forth, and to design *finitum in infinito*; so farre as is expedient for the certain reach and bounds of Seas, properly pertaining to any prince or people'.[292] Welwod referred to Bartolus' 100-mile jurisdictional limit as a potential framework for state control over the sea.[293]

Welwod kept his central argument, 'the chief point of our purpose', for the conclusion of chapter XVII. Vázquez y Menchaca had openly described fisheries as inexhaustible, with the logical consequence that there would always be plenty of fishes for all nations. Hence, limiting such activity would be pointless and contrary to natural law.[294] Grotius in his turn had stated: 'The principle applicable in regard to navigation – namely, that the activity in question shall remain open to all – should also be applied in connection with fishing'.[295] Welwod, however disputed this, arguing that fish stocks could become exhausted by overfishing. As a Scotsman, he cited first-hand experiences of severe fishing stocks' depletion of in Scottish coastal waters.[296] He attributed the excesses of overfishing to the hundreds of Dutch herring busses operating annually along Britain's eastern coast:

290 Ibid., 68.

291 Ibidem.

292 Ibidem.

293 Ibid., 69: 'Which bounds Bartolus hardily extends and allows for Princes and People at the sea-side, an hundred miles of sea forth from their coasts, at least; and justly, it they exercise a protection and conservancie so far: And this reach is called by the Doctors, *Districtas maris, & territorium.* It is true, Baldus esteemeth *potestatem, jurisdictionem & districtum,* to be all one'.

294 Vázquez y Menchaca, *Controversiarum illustrium,* II, 89, § 39.

295 Grotius, *Mare liberum,* 23 [69]. It is also true that in another passage Grotius had been more nuanced, stating that: 'Even if it were possible to prohibit some particular act of this kind, such as fishing (for it may be maintained that the supply of fishes is, in a sense, exhaustible), it would in any case be impossible to prohibit navigation, through which the sea loses nothing'. Ibid., 35 [93].

296 Fulton, *The Sovereignty of the Sea,* 354.

> … for whereas aforetime the white fishes dayly abounded, even into all the shoars on the eastern coast of Scotland; now (forsooth) by the near and dayly approaching of the buses fishers the sholes of fishes are broken, and so far scattered away from our shoars and coasts, that no fish now can be found worthy of any pains and travels; to the impoverishing of all the sort of our home-fishers, and to the great damage of all the nation.[297]

For Welwod, it was only fair that fisheries should belong to the closest coastal state, which could exclude foreigners or grant fishing rights in exchange for the payment of licences. Recognising that fisheries could become exhausted, he argued that coastal states should have the authority to close and guard adjacent waters for this limited purpose.[298] Hence, Welwod did not advocate for a comprehensive maritime dominion or an *ius excludendi alios* in relation to all maritime activities. Instead, he promoted a preferential claim limited to fishing in adjacent waters. *An Abridgment* thus marked a preliminary step towards constructing a British 'claimed seas' theory aligned with James VI–I's aspirations.

In conclusion, while Welwod lacked Grotius' dogmatic and literary sophistication, he made a significant contribution by unequivocally linking the 'claimed seas' principle to the exploitation of marine resources, addressing overfishing in a manner that resonates with contemporary concerns about ocean governance. He was one of the first to reject the ancient conception of the sea as an inexhaustible reservoir of resources and strongly asserted the preferential rights of coastal states to adjacent fisheries.[299] Grotius himself took notice of *An Abridgment* while he was in London for one of the Anglo-Dutch diplomatic conferences. In 1615, he wrote a point-by-point defence of chapter V of *Mare liberum* against Welwod's critiques, *Defensio capitis quinti Maris Liberi* (*Defence of Chapter V of Mare Liberum*).[300] This marked the only instance of Grotius responding directly to one of his critics. However, it remained unfinished and was never published as Grotius' vicissitudes and political exile diverted his focus from these polemics.

297 Welwod, *An Abridgement*, 72.

298 Ibidem.

299 Fulton, *The Sovereignty of the Sea*, 355.

300 Vervliet, 'General Introduction' to Feenstra, *Hugo Grotius Mare Liberum*, xx; van Ittersum, '*Mare Liberum* Versus the Propriety of the Seas?', 246.

4.1.2 The Diplomatic Standoff Continued

In 1611, Welwod left the University of St. Andrews and moved to England in search of a patron. He found one in Anne of Denmark (1574–1619), wife of James VI–I.[301] Both his 1613 and 1615 works were published in London. British diplomats and Privy Councillors, including Sir Julius Caesar, read these works and sought to use Welwod's arguments in subsequent discussions with the Dutch. During the later years of James VI–I's reign, British and Dutch diplomats continued to negotiate. While Dutch envoys employed delaying tactics regarding fishing licences, the king was unwilling to jeopardise his longstanding alliance with them.[302] In 1616, Dutch fishermen paid a small number of licences to John Brown, deputy to the High Admiral of Scotland, the Duke of Lennox. James VI and I later cited these payments as evidence that the Dutch recognised his rights over the fisheries. However, this compliance was short-lived; the Dutch consistently refused to acquiesce, and in the following year, John Brown was captured and detained by the Dutch after attempting to enforce similar payments. This affront to his authority greatly enraged James.[303]

Meanwhile, Anglo-Dutch tensions were further exacerbated by competition for the lucrative whaling and fishing grounds between Greenland and Spitsbergen. James VI and I laid claim to the area as part of a British closed sea, citing prior discovery and occupation supposedly achieved through navigation and fishing. In 1613, the English king granted the Muscovy Company a monopoly on whaling around Spitsbergen, excluding all foreign competitors.[304] The States General refused to accept James' claim, opposing any interference with their fishermen operating in the far north.[305] They denied that Hugh Willoughby had sighted Spitsbergen already in 1553 and instead asserted that the Dutch captain Jacob van Heemskerk had discovered the island in 1596, naming it Spitsbergen and planting the Dutch flag there. If any nation

---

301 Murdoch, *Britain, Denmark-Norway and the House of Stuart*, 22–5; James D. Alsop, 'William Welwood, Anne of Denmark and the Sovereignty of the Sea', *The Scottish Historical Review*, 59(168) (1980), 171–4.

302 Raestad, *La mer territoriale*, 85–6.

303 Fulton, *The Sovereignty of the Sea*, 171–3; van Ittersum, '*Mare Liberum* Versus the Propriety of the Seas?', 263; Scovazzi, 'Libertà o dominio', 21.

304 Fulton, *The Sovereignty of the Sea*, 181–5.

305 Edmundson noted that due to the geographic ignorance at that time, the two terms, Greenland and Spitzbergen, were used almost interchangeably at that time. In *Anglo-Dutch Rivalry*, 43–7. See also Davies, *The Early Stuarts, 1603–1660*, 51; Louwrens Hacquebord, Frits Steenhuisen and Huib Waterbolk, 'English and Dutch Whaling Trade and Whaling Stations in Spitsbergen (Svalbard) before 1660', *International Journal of Maritime History*, 15(2) (2003), 117–34.

had preferential rights to the surrounding waters, they argued, it was the Dutch. However, the States General refrained from asserting any exclusive claims. Reciprocal acts of aggression soon followed in these distant waters, with both sides lodging loud complaints against one another.[306]

In 1618, the Stadtholder Maurice of Nassau (1567–1625), supreme commander of the Dutch navy and army, made his final move against Oldenbarnevelt's political faction. Among those whose careers were abruptly ended in the ensuing coup was Grotius himself. James VI–I, who sympathised with Maurice, immediately sought to take advantage of the temporary chaos afflicting Dutch institutions. He pressured the Dutch States General to send envoys entrusted with the full powers to resolve, once and for all, the various disputes causing Anglo-Dutch tensions, including the North Sea fisheries.[307] However, when the Dutch envoys arrived in London, they revealed that their mandate only extended to discussions concerning the East Indies. During their meeting with the Privy Council in December 1618, they continued to employ Grotian arguments to counter British claims.

The States General issued proclamations instructing their nationals to avoid mistreating English and Scottish fishermen but stopped short of banning them from fishing or acknowledging in principle British claims. The Dutch envoys argued that the freedom of navigation and fishing was theirs by virtue of: 'the liberty due to them by the law of nations', but also based on past treaties, prescription, and immemorial possession.[308] The English side was quick to highlight the contradictions in this dual argument. First, they noted that the relatively young Dutch polity lacked the historical depth to claim prescription, which had also been rejected as a valid title in *Mare liberum*. Second, they questioned why, if the law of nations enshrined the freedom of fishing as a general principle, the Dutch repeatedly referred to fifteenth-century treaties between England and the Burgundian Low Countries. While the English had a valid point, the negotiations reached another impasse and were postponed, as both sides sought a fragile compromise regarding the East Indies.

306 See Clements R. Markham, 'Dutch and English whaling voyages in the Spitzbergen Seas', in idem, *The Threshold of the Unknown Region* (Cambridge: University Press, 2014), 46–74; idem, *The Lands of Silence: A History of Arctic and Antarctic Exploration*, edited by Francis H. H. Guillemard (Cambridge: University Press, 2015), 117–28.

307 The other issues at stake concerned trade and navigation in the East Indies, the cloth trade, and the import to the United Provinces of British coin. See Fulton, *The Sovereignty of the Sea*, 171–3; van Ittersum, '*Mare Liberum* Versus the Propriety of the Seas?', 263; Grayson, *From Protectorate to Partnership*, 210–59.

308 van Ittersum, '*Mare Liberum* Versus the Propriety of the Seas?', 263.

In early 1618, the King of Denmark–Norway protested against Scottish fishermen operating near the Faroe Islands, where Dano-Norwegian authorities strictly prohibited foreign fishing. In response, the affected Scottish burghs presented their case before the Scottish Council of the Realm, asserting that increasing Dutch aggression had displaced them from their customary fishing grounds, compelling them to venture further north.[309] The Council, however, ruled that Dutch wrongdoing did not justify encroaching on the rights of another monarch. Consequently, it issued a proclamation banning Scottish fishermen from operating near Dano-Norwegian domains while urging James VI–I to apply diplomatic pressure on The Hague over Dutch behaviour.[310] In 1619, both the British and the Dutch sides opted for a more conciliatory attitude, at least for the time being. In the same year, the States Generals ordered that Dutch herring busses not come closer than the limit of sight to Scottish coasts.[311]

4.2 *Charles I Stuart, Personal Ambitions, and* Mare clausum

Throughout James VI–I's reign the Dutch managed to avoid the payment of fishing licences and any open recognition of James VI–I's pretensions over the 'British Seas'.[312] In this regard, Thomas W. Fulton considered James VI–I's policies a substantial failure as the issue of fisheries was concerned.[313] Nevertheless, the king did succeed in expanding the English arsenal of legal-political arguments on the matter, and the idea that royal prerogatives extended to the adjacent sea gained momentum. Once he succeeded his father, Charles I (r. 1625–1649) first opted for opening hostilities against Spain in alliance with the Dutch Republic (1625–1630)[314] but soon adopted a more confrontational stance towards the Dutch.[315] The new Stuart monarch al-

309 12 March 1618. *Reg. Privy Counc. Scot.*, xi. 329. Quoted in Fulton, *The Sovereignty of the Sea*, 175.

310 Reg. Privy Counc. Scot., xi. 328, 330. Quoted in Fulton, *The Sovereignty of the Sea*, 176.

311 Initially, James VI–I had demanded an interdiction zone of fourteen nautical miles. See Fulton, *The Sovereignty of the Sea*, 192–3.

312 Feakes, *Formative Influences*, 165, 195.

313 Fulton, *The Sovereignty of the Sea*, 203, 361.

314 For the agreement on a joint Anglo-Dutch naval expedition against Cadiz, see Dumont, *CUD*, V.2, 478. For the Anglo-Dutch Treaty of alliance of Southampton (17 September 1625), see ibid., 478–81. On the issuing of 'letters of reprisal' against the King of Spain's subjects, see the Privy Council's instructions reported in Marsden, *Documents*, vol. 1, 410–3 and the special commission granted to the High Admiral the Duke of Buckingham, in Rymer, *Foedera*, vol. 8, part 2, 9.

315 Samuel Muller, *Mare clausum: Bijdrage tot de geschiedenis der rivaliteit van Engeland en Nederland in de zeventiende eeuw* (Amsterdam: F. Muller, 1872); Feakes, *Formative Influ-*

tered the nature of British maritime claims, reasserting British pretensions over coastal fisheries and developing a more expansive notion of 'claimed seas'. Efforts were made to revive a national British fishing industry capable of competing with the Dutch. However, these plans quickly ran into obstacles, including the difficulty of balancing English and Scottish interests and the inability of project promoters to make the venture economically viable.[316]

Charles I's ambitions extended beyond fisheries, as he sought to restore the naval reputation of his kingdoms and renew English claims to the 'sovereignty of the seas' – a title he intended to 'sparkle like a diamond in his crown'.[317] His vision included establishing an area around the British Isles where only British warships held jurisdiction, combating piracy and preventing hostilities between foreign powers within 'his Majesty's seas'.[318] To support these aspirations, Charles I ordered the royal archives to be thoroughly searched for evidence of medieval Plantagenet claims over the sea.[319] At the same time, English naval officers became more assertive, demanding flag salutes wherever possible, particularly in the Narrow Seas, as reflected in instructions issued to English admirals during the 1630s.[320] Unlike James VI–I, his son sought to enforce his claims with formidable summer fleets. Due to financial constraints and his inability to secure parliamentary approval for new taxes, he revived the unpopular medieval 'Ship Money' levy

---

ences, 181. On Charles I, see Mitchison, *A History of Scotland*, 137–52; Richard Cust, *Charles I: A Political Life* (London: Pearson Longman, 2005); Charles Carlton, *Charles I. The Personal Monarch* (London: Routledge, 1995). On Charles I's intercourse with the Dutch Republic, see Anton Poot, *Anglo-Dutch Relations. A Political and Diplomatic Analysis of the years 1625–1642* (Ph.D. dissertation, Royal Holloway, University of London, 2013).

316 For example, the Scottish did not want English fishermen in 'Scottish waters'. For an account of the Anglo-Scottish negotiations, see Fulton, *The Sovereignty of the Sea*, 224–45.

317 Brian Quintrell, 'Charles I and his Navy in the 1630s', *The Seventeenth Century*, 3 (1988), 159–79, at 160.

318 Rodger, *The Safeguard of the Sea*, 383; Fulton, *The Sovereignty of the Sea*, 259–75; Quintrell, 'Charles I and his Navy', 164–9.

319 See supra, ch. 1, 3.2.

320 One of the principal English naval appointments of the period was that of Admiral of the Narrow Seas, whose primary responsibilities included patrolling the fisheries, enforcing the flag salute, and upholding English neutrality regulations. See Rodger, *The Safeguard of the Sea*, 380. The French were always little inclined to perform the flag salute, see Charles de la Roncière, *Histoire de la marine française – IV, En quête d'un empire colonial* (Paris: Libraire Plon, 1910), 626–8.

from 1634 onward, a measure previously employed by Elizabeth I to fund naval operations.[321]

To many British observers the international situation of the early 1630s underscored the necessity of strengthening the Royal Navy. The Dutch merchant and fishing fleets remained as numerous as ever, while the French navy rapidly expanded under the leadership of Cardinal Richelieu (1585–1642) and Spanish naval power began to recover.[322] Barbary and Moroccan pirates wreaked havoc as far as the Irish Sea, enslaving entire villages, while Dutch and Dunkirker raiders operated across the North Sea, undermining Charles I's authority in his own coastal waters. Charles' neutrality policy during the 1630s, much like his father's, effectively favoured Spain.[323] In response, Dutch warships repeatedly violated the 'King's Chambers', pursuing fleeing Dunkirker and Spanish vessels. On occasion, they even landed armed parties on the English coast to apprehend privateers and pirates attempting to escape with stolen goods.[324]

It was no coincidence, then, that a new edition of *Mare liberum* was published in the Dutch Republic in 1633, reaffirming the States General's official

321 Fulton, *The Sovereignty of the Sea*, 246–51. See also Henrik Langelüddecke, '"I Finde All Men & My Officers All Soe Unwilling": The Collection of Ship Money, 1635–1640', *Journal of British Studies*, 46(3) (2007), 509–42; M. D. Gordon, 'The Collection of Ship-Money in the Reign of Charles I', *Transactions of the Royal Historical Society*, 4 (1910), 141–62; Alison Gill, *Ship Money during the Personal Rule of Charles I: Politics, Ideology and the Law, 1634 to 1640* (Ph.D. dissertation, Sheffield University, 1990); Kevin Sharpe, *The Personal Rule of Charles I* (New Haven, CT: Yale University Press, 1992), 545–95; idem, 'The personal rule of Charles I', in Tomlinson (ed.), *Before the English Civil War*, 69–74; Penn, *The Navy under the Early Stuarts*, 205–264; Rodger, *The Safeguard of the Sea*, 379–84; Derek A. Thrush, *The Navy under Charles I*, Ph.D. Dissertation (London: University College, 1990); Rebecca A. Bailey, '"Thy sceptre to a trident change / and straight, unruly seas thou canst command": contemporary representations of King Charles I and the ship money fleets within the cultural imagination of Caroline England', in James Davey and Richard Blakemore (eds.), *The Maritime World of Early Modern Britain* (Amsterdam: University Press, 2020), 193–228.

322 Rémi Monaque, *Une histoire de la marine de guerre française* (Paris: Perrin, 2016), 37–56.

323 Harding, *Warfare at Sea*, 181; Rodger, *The Safeguard of the Sea*, 383–4. On Anglo-Spanish secret diplomacy, see Harland Taylor, 'Trade, Neutrality, and the "English Road", 1630–1648', *The Economic History Review*, 25(2) (1972), 236–60; Albert J. Loomie, 'The Spanish Faction at the Court of Charles I, 1630–8', *Historical Research*, 59(139) (1986), 37–49; Patrick I. O'Neill, *Charles I and the Spanish Plot: Anglo-Habsburg Relations and the Outbreak of the War of Three Kingdoms, 1630–1641* (Ph.D. dissertation, University of California, Riverside, 2014).

324 Fulton, *The Sovereignty of the Sea*, 249–50.

position.[325] Charles I responded by stiffening his resolve to control the surrounding seas. In 1633, he instructed Sir Henry Marten, judge of the High Court of Admiralty, to draft regulations aimed at preserving 'his Majesty's ancient rights, honours and sovereignty in the Narrow Seas and in the chambers and ports' amidst the ongoing Hispano-Dutch naval conflict.[326] The resulting document lamented the increasing lawlessness in 'his seas (the King's), commonly called the Four English Seas, are more infested nowadays than heretofore, by men of Warre and such others, who living by spoile haunt those seas'. The document made a direct reference to:

> that sovereignty and special and peculiar interest and property which he and his predecessors, time out of mind, have had and enjoyed in the said seas, and so approved not only by fundamental laws of this his kingdom, but by the acknowledgement and assent of the bordering princes and nations, as appareth by undoubted records.[327]

Admiralty judges and royal counsellors continued to issue legal opinions in support of the king's maritime rights and prerogatives. However, in 1635, the first Ship Money fleet, commanded by the Earl of Lindsey, failed in its ambitious attempt to compel the Franco-Dutch fleet blockading the coast of the Spanish Low Countries to strike their flags in recognition of Charles I's 'lordship of the sea'. It later proved equally ineffective in locating the Dutch herring busses in the North Sea, accomplishing little despite the considerable expenses incurred in assembling it.[328] The following year, a second Ship Money fleet, under the command of the Earl of Northumberland, sailed into the Channel with orders to force the Franco-Dutch fleet to strike their flags. Again, the fleet could not be found. The earl then requested permission to move north in pursuit of the Dutch herring busses to demand payment of licences in exchange for the king's protection. He was instructed to enforce payments at a rate of twelve pence per ton of herrings or compel the Dutch to leave British waters. Those who refused to comply were to be apprehended

325 Mattew Cleary et al., 'A printer's view of Hugo Grotius' Mare liberum (1633)', in Gaby Mahlberg and Thomas Munck (eds.), *Ideas Across Borders. Translating Visions of Authority and Civil Society in Europe c.1600–1840* (London: Routledge, 2024), 211–44.

326 Ibid., 250.

327 'Règlement for preventing abuses in and about the narrow seas and ports', (*State Papers Domestic, James I*, vol. 11, n. 40, 1604; Charles I, vol. 279, n. 18, 1634). Reported as appendix H, ibid., 759–61.

328 Ibid., 775.

and detained. Unlike his father, who had relied on a lightly armed pinnace and legal arguments, Charles I sent a powerful fleet to enforce his claims.[329] On 10 May 1636, after consulting the Lords of the Admiralty and their legal advisers, Charles issued a proclamation explicitly renewing his father's 1609 directive to restrict unlicensed foreign fishing:

> … since which time, albeit neither our said Father, nor our self have made any considerable evacuation of the same proclamation, but have with much patience expected a voluntary conformity of our neighbours and Allies, to so just and reasonable Prohibitions and Directions, as are contained in the same.[330]

Charles declared that the circumstances motivating his father's proclamation had worsened and reaffirmed his commitment to maintaining British maritime rights:

> We being very sensible of the premises, and well knowing how far we are obliged in honour to maintain the Rights of our Crown, especially of so great consequence, have thought it necessary, by Advise of our Privy Council, to renew the aforesaid Restraint of Fishing upon our aforesaid Coasts and Seas, without Licences first obtained from Us, by these presents to make publick declaration that our resolution is […] to keep such a competent Strength of Shipping upon our Seas, as may (by God's blessing) hinder such further Encroachments upon our Regalities and assist and protect those our good Friends and Allies, who shall henceforth by virtue of our Licences (to be first obtained) endeavour to take the benefit of Fishing upon our Coasts and Seas in the Places accustomed.[331]

During the Earl of Northumberland's 1636 cruise, Dutch herring boats attempted to avoid contact with English ships, only paying for licences when compelled by force. Dutch naval escorts refrained from challenging the superior English fleet, and a Dutch squadron dispatched to prevent any pay-

329 Ibid., 293.

330 'A Proclamation for restraint of Fishing upon His Majesty's Seas and Coasts without Licence', in Rymer, *Foedera*, XX, 15.

331 Ibidem.

ment arrived too late.[332] While Dutch authorities had previously exercised restraint, Charles I's increasingly assertive policies began to alarm them. His actions no longer appeared as mere vanity projects but as a coordinated state policy threatening Dutch interests in maintaining the freedom of the seas across northern Europe. While the Dutch were willing to tolerate symbolic gestures, such as flag salutes, to appease English sensibilities, they firmly resisted any attempt to impose a 'claimed seas' doctrine that jeopardised their fishing industry, trade networks, and the broader security of their seaborne economy.[333]

In March 1636, a special Dutch envoy joined the resident ambassador in London, Albert Joachimi, to investigate Charles I's intentions. The Privy Council informed them that the king intended to use his fleet to enforce his sovereignty and hereditary rights over the sea, protect convoys, and maritime traffic, and ensure that no one fished in British waters without paying for licences. When the Dutch requested a written statement of these claims, they were referred to John Selden's recently published treatise *Mare clausum* as the definitive expression of the king's position. In the following years, Dutch diplomats sought to divert Charles I's attention to other matters, urging further negotiations. However, the king and his Privy Council refused, asserting that James VI–I's claims had already been made clear and acknowledged through past actions, including the payment of licences by Dutch fishermen.[334] Soon after, however, the prospect of a new alliance with the Dutch and the French prevented Charles I from using his third ship-money fleet to chase the fishermen.

Meanwhile, growing discontent over the ship-money tax, Charles I's autocratic style of governance, and his religious policies was spreading across his kingdoms, destabilising both his rule and his foreign policy. Somewhat ironically, in 1637, the massive warship *Sovereign of the Seas* was launched – the first

332 Hugh Dunthorne, *Britain and the Dutch Revolt, 1560–1700* (Cambridge: University Press, 2013), 116.

333 Jack S. Levy, 'The rise and decline of the Anglo-Dutch rivalry, 1609–1689', 172–200; Charles H. Wilson, *Profit and Power: A Study of England and the Dutch Wars* (The Hague/Boston/London: M. Nijhoff, 1978), 25–47.

334 Indeed, the few payments of licences occurred in 1636 were instrumentalised by the English to argue that the Dutch had acknowledged their claims. Fulton, *The Sovereignty of the Sea*, 304–5: 'The same attitude was maintained in a formal paper handed to Joachimi a little later, […]. In this Charles announced his firm intention to control the fisheries in his own seas. He would only permit foreigners to fish there if they accepted his license and acknowledged his right, that is, paid tribute. The request for a conference of commissioners to consider the question was rejected'.

three-decker and the largest English warship built to that date (see Figure 4.4 below).[335] The king closely oversaw its construction, viewing it as a symbol of his maritime ambitions and royal prestige, with its very name serving as an unambiguous political and ideological statement.[336] The vessel's lavish gilded decorations and elaborate carvings – featuring allusions to imperial Rome and mythological figures such as Jupiter, Mars, and Neptune – further reinforced its ideological significance.[337] Inscribed on its stern were the words: 'May He whom the seas and tides obey and the winds that blow and the ships Guard this, Great Charles, thy man-of-war with sustenance Divine'.[338] Each of its 102 bronze cannons bore the motto 'Charles has established Edgar's sceptre on the waters' (*Carolus Edgari sceptrum aquarium*), referring to the supposed dominion over the sea enjoyed by the Anglo-Saxon King of England Edgar (r. 959–975). In essence, the *Sovereign of the Seas* was conceived as a floating symbol of naval supremacy and royal prestige, intended to overawe potential enemies with its sheer magnificence.

However, by 1638–1639, revolts in Scotland, precarious finances, and mounting parliamentary opposition had begun to seriously undermine Charles I's authority and consequently his capacity to project 'claimed seas' policies. The *Sovereign of the Seas* remained idle throughout the English Civil War, a costly emblem of unfulfilled ambitions.[339] In 1639, the Dutch Admiral Marteen Tromp (1598–1653) annihilated the Spanish fleet that had sought refuge in the Downs, a roadstead (i.e. an area of sheltered, favourable sea) off the East Kent coast in southern England. The small English squadron tasked with

335 Fulton, *The Sovereignty of the Sea*, 326; Brian Quintrell, 'Charles I and his Navy in the 1630s', 172; Rodger, *The Safeguard of the Sea*, 388–9; Rif Winfield, *British Warships in the Age of Sail, 1603–1714. Design, Construction, Careers and Fates* (Barnsley: Seaforth Publishing, 2009), 10, 59.

336 J. D. Davies, '"Great Neptunes of the Main": Myths, mangled histories, and "maritime monarchy" in the Stuart navy, 1603–1714', in Davies, James, and Rommelse (eds.), *Ideologies of Western Naval Power*, 106–21; Stefano Cattelan, 'Review article of: Ideologies of Western Naval Power, c.1500–1815', *The Mariner's Mirror*, 109(1) (2023), 104–7, https://doi.org/10.1177/00253359.2023.2159959a. See also Armitage, *The Ideological Origins*, 100–24.

337 Davies, '"Great Neptunes of the Main"', 109; Hendrik Busmann, *Sovereign of the Seas: die skulpturen des Britischen königsschiffes von 1637* (Hamburg: Convent, 2002), 66–75.

338 '*Qui mare, qui fluetus, ventos, navesque gubernat, Sospitet hanc arcem, Carole Magne, tuam*', English translation from Davies, '"Great Neptunes of the Main"', 109.

339 John G. A. Pocock, 'The Atlantic Archipelago and the War of the Three Kingdoms', in Bradshaw and Morrill (eds.), *The British Problem, c.1534–1707*, 172–91; Richard Cust, 'The collapse of royal power in England, 1637–1642', in Michael J. Braddick (ed.), *The Oxford Handbook of the English Revolution* (Oxford: University Press, 2015), 60–76.

FIGURE 4.4 John Payne's engraving of the *Sovereign of the Seas* (1637). Engraving on paper, 67.2 cm × 93 cm
SOURCE: THE BRITISH MUSEUM, LONDON

ensuring the respect of English neutrality and sovereignty could do little against Tromp's overwhelming show of force.[340]

4.3 *John Selden*

4.3.1 A Polymath at the Service of the Stuarts

As early as 1618, the prominent English lawyer and polymath John Selden (1584–1654) had a treatise on the 'claimed seas' ready for publication.[341] How-

340 The Dutch sank forty out of fifty-three Spanish ships, mostly galleons and merchant vessels. Glete, *Warfare at Sea*, 181–2; Robert A. Stradling, 'Catastrophe and Recovery: The Defeat of Spain, 1639–43', *History*, 64(11) (1979), 205–19; Luc Panhuysen, *Het monsterschip. Maarten Tromp en de armada van 1639* (Amsterdam: Atlas Contact, 2021); Harding, *Seapower and Naval Warfare*, 61; Sicking, 'Naval warfare in Europe, c.1330–c.1680', in Tallet and Trim (eds.), *European Warfare*, 258.

341 Mark Somos, 'Selden's *Mare Clausum*. The Secularisation of International Law and the Rise of Soft Imperialism', *Journal of the History of International Law*, 14 (2012), 287–330, at 292. Selden was a lawyer, scholar, antiquary, orientalist, legal historian, historian and politician. For an overview on Selden, see Gerald J. Toomer, *John Selden, a Life in Scholarship*, I (Oxford: University Press, 2009); Eric G. M. Fletcher, 'John Selden (Author of

ever, due to the prevailing international situation, King James V–I ordered its publication to be delayed. The king, like Elizabeth I before him, sought to avoid a diplomatic confrontation with his brother-in-law, the king of Denmark–Norway, who held conflicting closed sea claims of its own in the North. Furthermore, James VI–I was attempting to secure a loan from the Nordic monarch at the time. During James VI–I's reign, several British authors and pamphleteers had asserted and defended his 'claimed seas' ambitions, yet none of their works were sufficiently rigorous or authoritative to counter the Grotian concept of the freedom of the seas.

Under Charles I, the task of uncovering historical evidence to support English maritime claims was assigned to the Keeper of Records, John Borough.[342] This effort culminated in the treatise *The Soveraignty of the British Seas*, completed in 1633 but only published in 1651, likely due to the appearance of Selden's superior work.[343] Selden, however, made extensive use of the materials unearthed by Borough, such as the fourteenth-century handwritten roll *De superioritate Mari Angliae et jure officii Admirallatus in eodem*. This document compiled proclamations and records concerning maritime dominion dating back to the Plantagenet kings.[344] For example, Charles I referred to a commission issued by Edward III in 1336 to Admiral Geoffrey de Say as a precedent when drafting his first Ship Money writ in October 1634. The com-

Mare Clausum) and His Contribution to International Law', *Transactions of the Grotius Society*, 19 (1933), 1–12; David S. Berkowitz, *John Selden's Formative Years: Politics and Society Early Seventeenth Century England* (Washington D.C.: Folger Shakespeare Library, 1988); Paul Christianson, *Discourse on History, Law, and Governance in the Public Career of John Selden, 1610–1635* (Toronto: University Press, 1996); Harold D. Hazeltine, 'Selden as Legal Historian', *Harvard Law Review*, 24(2) (1910–11), 105–18; Harold Berman and John Witte, 'The integrative Christian jurisprudence of John Selden', in Mark Hill and Richard Helmholz (eds.), *Great Christian Jurists in English History* (Cambridge: University Press, 2017), 139–62; John Baker, 'John Selden and English legal history' in idem, *Collected Papers on English Legal History*, 3 vols. (Cambridge: University Press, 2013), II, 765–77; Johann P. Sommerville, 'John Selden, the Law of Nature, and the Origins of Government', *The Historical Journal*, 27(2) (1984), 437–47.

342 Wade, 'The Roll *de Superioritate Maris Angliae*', 100.

343 John Borough, *Soveraignty of the British Sea* [1651] (Edinburgh: W. Green & Son Ltd., 1920). The original Latin version of 1633 is entitled *Dominium Maris Britannici assertum ex archivis historiis et municipalibus regni legibus, per D. Johannem de Burgo*, and is conserved at the British Museum.

344 Fulton noted: 'Borough's work was the first successful attempt to bring together a great array of historical facts in favour of the English claims to the dominion of the seas' such as 'the ordinance of John, the rolls of Edward I and Edward III, the charter of Edgar, the Laws of Oleron, the commissions to the admirals, safe-conducts, and extracts from the Burgundy treaties'. Fulton, *The Sovereignty of the Sea*, 338–42.

mission declared: 'Forasmuch as We and our Progenitors, Kings of England, have been always heretofore masters of the aforesaid sea, and it would be very irksome to us if that princely honour in our time be lost or in anything diminished'.[345] However, Borough and the others found little concrete evidence from the Lancastrian, Yorkist, or Tudor periods, as the maritime claims of medieval English monarchs had been largely symbolic, as noted in Chapter 1.[346]

Ultimately, it was John Selden who emerged as the ideal figure to substantiate Stuart claims in the doctrinal arena, possessing both the intellectual rigour and legal acumen to utilise the available sources and materials effectively. By the 1620s, Selden had become actively involved in parliamentary politics, co-authoring the Petition of Right (1628) and generally opposing the autocratic tendencies of both James VI–I and Charles I. This resistance led to his imprisonment on two occasions. Upon his release, Selden increasingly devoted himself to scholarly pursuits and sought to repair his relationship with the Crown. When his treatise, *Mare clausum, seu de dominio maris libri duo*, was finally published in 1635, it was dedicated to Charles I and evidently had the king's approval.[347]

As noted in the previous section, Charles I was at the time deploying Ship Money fleets and exerting diplomatic pressure on the Dutch Republic to se-

345 'First Ship-money writ, 20 October 1334' in John Rushworth, *Historical Collections of Private Passages of State, Weighty Matters in Law, Remarkable Proceedings in Five Parliaments: Beginning the Sixteenth Year of King James. Anno 1618, And Ending the Fifth Year of King Charles* [*sic*], *Anno 1629* (London: Printed by Tho. Newcomb for George Thomason, 1659–1701), vol. II, 257

346 See *supra* ch. 1, 3.2.

347 John Selden, *Mare clausum seu de dominio maris libri duo* (London: excudebat Will. Stanesbeius, pro Ricardo Meighen, 1635). An English translation by Marchamont Nedham appeared in 1652: John Selden, *Of the Dominion, or Ownership of the Sea. Two Books. Translated into English and set forth with some Additional Evidences and Discourses* (London: William du Gard, 1652). For a discussion of Nedham's translation, see David J. Padwa, 'On the English Translation of John Selden's *Mare Clausum*', *American Journal of International Law*, 54 (1960), 156–9. Nedham replaced Selden's dedication to the deposed Charles I with one to Parliament. He also introduced some changes and additions to Selden's text to better fit the new political environment. His translation appeared during the First Dutch War between the Commonwealth and the United Provinces. Later in 1663, a new edition appeared in London through the endeavours of the court historiographer, James Howell (Printed for Andrew Kembe and Edward Thomas). Howell deleted Nedham's modifications and restored Selden's original dedication to Charles I. This time, the publication occurred in support of Charles II's anti-Dutch policies following the Restoration of 1660. The analysis in this section is based on the 1652 English translation in conjunction with the Latin original.

cure recognition of his maritime claims. Selden's work appeared in print at the perfect moment.[348] Shortly thereafter, Charles explicitly referred to *Mare clausum* as having been published 'by our express command', to assert 'the right and Dominion of us and our Royal Progenitors in the Seas which encompass these our Realm and Dominions of Great Britain and Ireland'.[349] Hence, Charles I unequivocally signalled that *Mare clausum* matched his own views on the matter and was more than the work of a private person. It is reported that on 26 March 1636, he brought the treatise in the Privy Council, requiring for the future: 'One of the said Books to be kept in the Council Chest, another in the Court of Exchequer, and a third in the Court of Admiralty, as faithful and strong evidences to the Dominion of the British Seas'.[350] The Dutch ambassador, Albert Joachimi, promptly reported the publication of *Mare Clausum* to the States General, and the treatise was taken seriously in Dutch governmental circles.[351] By 1636, three unauthorised editions of the book had appeared in the United Provinces, prompting Charles to ban these pirated versions across his kingdoms.[352]

In *Mare clausum,* Selden immediately clarified that his objective was to: 'Treat of the Dominion or Ownership of the Sea, encompassing the Isle of Great Britain, as belonging to the Empire of the same; two main particulars are chiefly to be considered. The one concerns matter of *Law*, the other of *Fact*'.[353] To achieve this, Selden divided his work into two books. The first,

---

348 Helen Thornton, 'John Selden's Response to Hugo Grotius: The Argument for Closed Seas', *International Journal of Maritime History*, 18(2) (2006), 105–27; Randall Lesaffer, 'Mare Clausum (The Closure of the Sea or The Ownership of the Sea) 1635, John Selden (1584–1654)', in Wijffels et al. (eds.), *The Formation and Transmission of Western Legal Culture*, n. 32, 190–4; Brian Tierney, *John Selden* in *Liberty and Law* (Washington, D.C.: Catholic University of America Press, 2014), 251–72; D. M. Barratt, 'The Publication of John Selden's *Mare Clausum*', *The Bodleian Library Record*, 7 (1964), 204–5; Bederman, 'The Sea', 367; Ofir Haivry, 'John Selden and the Jewish religious fountainhead of the international law of the sea', in Martti Koskenniemi, Mónica García-Salmones Rovira, and Paolo Amorosa (eds.), *International Law and Religion: Historical and Contemporary Perspectives* (Oxford: University Press, 2017), 113–30.

349 'A proclamation concerning [...] *Mare Clausum*, 15 April 1636', in Rymer, *Foedera*, XX, 12.

350 Rushworth, *Historical Collections*, II, 320.

351 The reception of *Mare clausum* in the Dutch Republic is analysed in Martine J. van Ittersum, 'Debating the Free Sea in London, Paris, The Hague and Venice: The Publication of John Selden's *Mare Clausum* (1635) and its Diplomatic Repercussions in Western Europe', *History of European Ideas*, 47(8) (2021), 1193–210. Cf. Fulton, *Sovereignty of the Sea*, 367.

352 Peter J. Lucas, 'Printing Anglo-Saxon in Holland and John Selden's *Mare Clausum seu de Dominio Maris*', *Quaerendo*, 31(2) (2001), 120–36.

353 Selden, *Mare clausum*, I, ch. 1, 1–2.

more general and theoretical, refuted Grotius' claim that the high seas, by their nature, could not be subject to occupation or dominion. As a 'matter of law', Selden framed the central question as: 'Whether by law the sea be capable of private dominion or propriety?'. He argued that the sea was in no way incompatible with ownership or dominion and was fully capable of being subject to such claims. The second book instead sought to demonstrate as 'matter of *Fact*' that English monarchs had exercised uninterrupted control over the adjacent seas since ancient times, or 'the long and continued conjunction with the British Empire, of enjoiment and possession, or lawful prescription; whereupon as on a most strong Title, the dominion or ownership of the same Empire herein may bee funded'.[354] Selden employed an array of historical references to prove that the maritime dominion claimed by the inhabitants of the British Islands constituted a historic right.[355]

Selden deemed the first book the necessary starting point 'for, except manifest proof bee made of the first point, it will bee utterly in vain to discours about the second'.[356] The first book comprised twenty-six chapters, while the second extended to thirty-two. The size and articulation of Selden's work and its explicit aim of countering *Mare liberum* reveal similarities with Freitas' *De iusto imperio*.[357] However, Richard Tuck has observed that *Mare clausum* is, in essence, a deeply Grotian work, highlighting the points of contact with the Dutch author, e.g. their shared understanding of the gradual emergence of private/public property on land.[358] Interestingly, Selden was a self-declared admirer of Grotius as early as 1613.[359] The critical divergence between the two authors lay in their views on whether the sea could be appropriated as private or public property – and whether it already had been.

---

354 Ibidem.

355 Lesaffer, 'Mare Clausum', 192.

356 However, Toomer notes: 'After stating that book I deals with law and book II with fact, Selden notes that each book contains a mixture of both laws and facts', in *John Selden*, 395.

357 Neff, *Justice among Nations*, 134–5.

358 Richard Tuck, *Natural Rights Theories: Their Origin and Development* (Cambridge: University Press, 1979), 87–91; idem, *Philosophy and Government, 1572–1651* (Cambridge: University Press, 1993), 212–7; Somos, 'Selden's *Mare Clausum*', 299. See also Hans J. Klee, *Hugo Grotius und Johannes Selden, von den geistigen ursprüngen des kampfes um die meeresfreiheit* (Bern: P. Haupt, 1946).

359 Toomer, *John Selden*, 330–2.

4.3.2 Book I

4.3.2.1 *Setting the Premises*

Selden opened the first book of *Mare clausum* by outlining the three main arguments used in the past to deny the possibility of acquiring maritime dominion: 1) the supposed universal freedom of trade, passage, and travel; 2) the natural characteristics of the sea – its fluidity, vastness, and the perceived impossibility of marking boundaries on its ever-changing surface; and 3) the writings and testimonies of ancient learned men, whether 'poets, divines, lawyers'.[360] Selden then included several quotes from the *Corpus Iuris* and authors such as Plautus, Ovid, and Virgil,[361] acknowledging that these quotes had often been interpreted as implying 'that the sea is common to all men, by the Law of Nature and Nations; which if it were truly proved, either from the nature of the sea itself, or from either of those laws, then it could not possibly be admitted, that the sea might become the peculiar possession of any one', unless 'a change were made of the law of nature, which is commonly said to bee altogether unchangeable [...] and therefore from thence they seem to hold, that a Dominion over the Sea cannot be attained by any ancient usage, custom or prescription, nor under any other pretence or title whatsover'.[362] Among 'our modern Lawyers', Selden noted that especially two authors opposed the idea of the dominion of the sea, openly referring to Vázquez y Menchaca (Vasquius) and Grotius, whom he described as 'a man of acute judgement, and for his excellencie in all kinds of learning incomparable'.[363]

Secondly, Selden clarified that with the term 'sea' he meant 'the whole Sea, as well the main Ocean or out-land Seas, as those which are within-land, such as the Mediterranean, Adriatic, Aegean or Levant, British, and Baltic Seas, or any other of that kind'.[364] Thirdly, he addressed the more complicated issue of defining the different categories of 'Law, (as it is the rule, measure, and pointing out of things lawful or unlawful)' relevant for the discussion.[365] According to Selden, there were two types of law: 1) *obligatorie-perceptive law*, by which things are 'commanded or forbidden', and 2) *permissive-concessive law*, which 'is set forward by things whose use is neither commanded nor forbidden, but permitted'. Both types of law could apply universally to all peoples or

360 Selden, *Mare clausum*, I, ch. 2, 3.
361 Ibid., 5–7. See also Ziskind, 'International Law and Ancient Sources', 537–59.
362 Ibid, I, ch. 2, 8.
363 Ibid., 11.
364 Ibid., I, ch. 3, 12.
365 Ibidem.

specifically to individual 'nations'.[366] The law that related to all men or nations, being 'either *Natural* or *Divine*. That is either manifested by the light of nature or the use of right reason [...] or else it is declared and set down in those Divine Oracles that have been committed to writing'.[367] Divine and natural law together constituted 'the *universal Law of Nations*, or *the Common Law of mankind*. And whatever is *obligatorie* in either of these, either out of the nature of the thing itself, or rather from the authority of the father of nature, is reputed by men to be unchangeable; according to that saying so often used by philosophers, divines and lawyers, *That the rights and laws of nature are immutable*'.[368]

Thus, Selden posited that while the *obligatorie law* (of whatever sub-kind) was immutable, it could be expanded or clarified to ensure its practical application. In contrast, the *permissive law* by its very nature was flexible, subject to change, and could be altered by 'those in power'. In other words, Selden's scheme meant that even the *obligatorie* laws deriving from God and nature required human interpretation in their application to specific circumstances. Thus, these so-called unchangeable laws could be amended when they became incorporated in the laws of particular polities.[369]

Positive-civil law constituted a further category composed by the alterations to permissive law and additions to obligatory law 'which is of a more narrow sense and acceptation, and relates not to all Nations or the Universalitie of mankind, but onely to som particulars thereof'.[370] Positive-civil law could be subdivided into two: 1) law that is 'singular and peculiar to any one particular nation or Societie of mankinde', or *Law purely Civil*; 2) law that 'is received by divers Nations'. The latter one was further divided into two categories, the first being 'that which binds divers Nations jointly, equally, and indifferently, by som common obligation' (or *Common Law of divers Nations*), the second being 'that which binds divers Nations or people, not jointly, and equally, or by any common obligation, but singly and by accident' (or *Law of som or divers Nations*).[371]

The 'Common Law of diverse nations' was divided into two further subtypes: *Imperative* and *Intervenient*. The imperative law of nations referred to those laws which bound several independent nations through shared obliga-

366 Ibidem.

367 Ibidem. Cf. Thornton, 'John Selden's Response to Hugo Grotius', 110.

368 Ibid., I, ch. 3, 13.

369 Thornton, 'John Selden's Response to Hugo Grotius', 110.

370 Selden, *Mare clausum*, I, ch. 3, 14.

371 Ibidem.

tions (e.g., Catholic states subjected to papal authority). Instead, the intervenient law of nations arose 'not from any command imposed upon several Nations in common, but through the intervention either of some compact, or custom', and comprised the addition to obligatory law and the alteration to permissive law.[372] It was usually styled as secondary law of nations and concerned things such as 'proclaiming war, ambassies, prisoners of war, hostages, leagues and covenants, commerce etc. …'. Lastly, the remaining natural or divine law could be termed 'Universal or Primitive Law of Nations'.[373]

Throughout the original Latin version of *Mare clausum*, Selden consistently used terms such as *imperium, occupatio, dominium privatum – proprietas* (dominion) to refer to the legal position whose validity he was determined to prove. The English author largely set aside the term *iurisdictio* (jurisdiction), which had proved so popular among medieval and early modern commentators. It may be suggested that the legal rights enshrined in the term 'jurisdiction' appeared to Selden as just one facet of the more absolute legal position claimed by the Stuarts over the 'British seas'. The term denoting property in ancient Rome, *dominium*, in his opinion better reflected Charles I's pervasive pretensions.[374] A legal position that also may appear to the modern reader not so dissimilar from full-fletched sovereignty.

Selden defined 'dominion' as the right to 'use, enjoy, alienate, and free dispose' of property,[375] specifying that it could be either could be common (shared equally among all people) or private (reserved for specific states, princes, or individuals, thereby excluding others).[376] He traced the origins of property to the mythical Golden Age, when common ownership prevailed, and argued that private property arose later with the development of societies. Drawing from biblical texts, Selden contended that God had granted both land and sea to Noah's descendants, who established boundaries and private dominion through agreements, customs, and effective occupation.[377] Selden declared that neither the 'Law Natural nor Divine which was universal hath expressly commanded or forbidden, but permitted both; that is to say, a common enjoiment, as well as private dominion or possession of the things of this life'.[378]

372 Ibidem.
373 Ibid., 15.
374 Raestad, *La mer territoriale*, 101.
375 Selden, *Mare clausum*, I, ch. 4, 16.
376 Ibidem.
377 Ibidem.
378 Ibid., 20. See also Somos, 'Selden's *Mare Clausum*', 298.

As highlighted by Richard Tuck, Selden's theory of the gradual emergence of property is very similar to Grotius'.[379] Moreover, he specified that the division of property had occurred either expressly with a compact or implicitly by custom, as Grotius himself had written in the *De iure belli ac pacis*, while eventual leftovers had then been acquired through occupation.[380] The private or public owner could: 'lawfully hinder such a communitie of use and enjoyment, nor might any other man use it lawfully without permission'.[381] Selden recapitulated that all these things derived from 'an alteration of that Universal or Natural Law of nations which is permissive', which later was incorporated in civil-positive law. However, private dominion was also established by the universal obligatory law rule *pacta sunt servanda*.[382]

4.3.2.2 *Can the Sea Become Private or Public Property?*

Having laid out these premises, Selden reiterated his central thesis: that the sea was capable of occupation and dominion in the same way as land. The English author acknowledged that no express reference to the sea was included in the initial 'distributions and to Noah's sons, and that in the beginning the sea was perhaps conceived more as boundary than as a territory in itself. In that eventuality, 'it remains next to be considered whether they [the seas] might not lawfully bee acquired afterwards by title of occupation, as things vacant and derelict'. To this end, it was essential to assess whether the *Natural or Divine universal Law which is Permissive* somehow prevented it and if under the *Law of divers Nations, Common or Civil*, or positive law (which was also the best interpreter of the permissive law) dominion over the sea could be introduced.[383]

First, he devoted a long chapter VI to arguing for the positive answer based on passages from the holy scripts, 'law divine', in a much more articulated way than Welwod. He took into consideration several passages from the Old Testament concerning property, which he considered in close relation to their interpretation by the Talmudic scholars.[384] Second, he dealt with the law of

379 Tuck, *Natural Rights Theories*, 87–91. However, Selden relied on the Bible and Jewish texts more than Grotius. See Somos, 'Selden's *Mare Clausum*', 314–8.

380 Selden, *Mare clausum*, I, ch. 4, 20. Selden's reference is to Grotius, *De iure belli ac pacis*, II, ch. 2, § 2.

381 Ibid., I, ch. 5, 24.

382 Ibid., 25.

383 Ibid., 24–7.

384 Ibid., I, ch. 6, 27–42. Cf. Welwod, *An Abridgement of All Sea-Lawes*, 62. For further details, see Jonathan Zizkind, 'International Law and Ancient Sources: Grotius and Selden', *The*

nature 'derived from a right and discreet use of reason'.[385] Selden believed that the rules of nature could be discerned through an analysis of the laws and customs of actual polities (*positive Law of Nations of every kind, which is humane*), because alterations to permissive-concessive law and additions to obligatory-perceptive law had over time been incorporated into the laws of existing polities, especially 'the more civilised and more eminent Nations of the past and present age'.[386] If these customs and laws allowed a dominion of the sea, it had to be assumed that it was not against nature. Reasoning this way, history and customs became the primary source of the law of nations. However, according to Selden, the customs of different nations could not tell us anything about 'things Divine or such as relate unto Divine worship', since different peoples worshipped diverse gods in various ways.[387] Thus, the English scholar stated that in the following chapters, he would employ two types of evidence to show that the *Civil Law of Nations*, the *Common Law of Diverse Nations* and the *Natural Permissive Law*, 'which in this case is to be drawn out of the Customs of Nations', all admitted the possibility of acquiring maritime dominion:

> Some are those which show that a Soveraigntie and private Dominion of the Sea hath been by historians and other writers, almost in all ages, acknowledged and granted to princes, peoples and others. Other testimonies there are which demonstrate out of lawyers, also by Leagues and Treaties, and other particulars of that nature, that such a Dominion of the Sea, is in like manner agreeable unto Law.[388]

4.3.2.3 *Historical and Modern Examples of* Mare clausum

It is therefore unsurprising that, in the following eleven chapters of the first book, Selden presented a wide array of historical examples to support the concept of maritime dominion. He began with the ancient cases of Greece, Carthage, and Rome, considering both the dominion held by individual Romans under civil law and the dominion exercised collectively by the Roman state. He then examined examples from more modern nations, includ-

---

Review of Politics, 35 (1973), 537–59; Berman and Witte, 'The Integrative Christian Jurisprudence of John Selden', 139–62; Grewe, *Epochs*, 268.

385 Ibid., I, ch. 7, 42–3.

386 Ibid., 45.

387 Ibid., 42–3.

388 Ibid., 45–6. See also Somos, 'Selden's *Mare Clausum*', 311; Thornton, 'John Selden's Response to Hugo Grotius', 111.

ing Venice, Portugal, Spain, France, the Ottoman Empire, Denmark, Sweden, and Norway. In Selden's view, all these polities had claimed sovereignty over their adjoining seas, thereby demonstrating a long-established practice grounded in the law of nations.[389] Interestingly, Freitas had also referred to examples such as Venice in his *De iusto imperio* when defending Portuguese claims.[390] Significantly, Selden included references to all three major 'claimed seas' traditions discussed in the preceding chapters, weaving them into his legal argument to illustrate the widespread acceptance of *dominium maris*. These traditions were: 1) the Mediterranean one, notably Venetian claims; 2) the Nordic tradition; and 3) the Iberian-oceanic tradition. Regarding Venice, Selden observed:

> There is nothing that can more clearly illustrate the point in hand than the Dominion of the Adriatick Sea, which the most noble Commonwealth of Venice hath enjoyed for so many ages. The truth of this is everywhere attested and acknowledged, not onely by historians and chorographers, but by very many lawyers.[391]

Selden cited Franciscus de Ingenuis' *Epistula*, which had defended Venetian maritime rights and referenced more than thirty legal authorities, including Bartolus and Baldus.[392] Selden demonstrated that he was aware that Venetian dominion over the Adriatic Sea had been challenged in the 1610s and 1620s by Neapolitan-Spanish, pro-imperial, and pro-papal authors, but chose to take for demonstrated the arguments in favour of Venetian dominion. Since Franciscus de Ingenuis was likely a pseudonym of Sarpi, we can affirm that some of the Venetian scholar's ideas reached Selden, even though he could not directly reference Sarpi's unpublished *Dominio del Mare Adriatico*.

389 Selden, *Mare clausum*, I, ch. 9–19 survey these historical examples. In *Discourse on History, Law, and Governance*, 259, Christianson noted that Selden gave very little historical evidence for his claims, except for Book I, ch. 19, concerning the Nordic countries, where he referred to several treaties. Potter and Fulton on their part underlined that in most cases the evidence adduced by Selden merely showed that naval power was exercised for a certain time in a determined pelagic area, respectively in *The Freedom of the Seas*, 19; *Sovereignty of the Sea*, 371. Cf. Thornton, 'John Selden's Response to Hugo Grotius', 112; Toomer, *John Selden*, 405–6; Raestad, *La mer territoriale*, 98.

390 Freitas, *De iusto imperio*, 191 ff. [105]; see also Brito Vieira, 'Mare Liberum vs. Mare Clausum', 373.

391 Selden, *Mare clausum*, I, ch. 16, 99.

392 Ibidem. Cf. *supra*, ch. IV, 2.2.3.

Concerning the Iberian 'claimed seas' tradition related to the oceans, Selden paid particular attention to Portuguese claims. He highlighted the titles used to style Portuguese monarchs in official documents, such as: 'Lord of Guinea, and by conquest of the navigation and commerce of Ethiopia, Arabia, Persia etc.', which in his view implied the dominion over the sea.[393] He also quoted extensively from the *Ordenações Manuelinas* – the compilation of Portuguese laws completed during the reign of Manuel I (1495–1521) – which reiterated a prohibition, originally introduced in the fifteenth century, against foreigners and Portuguese subjects sailing to Lusitanian discoveries without royal authorisation, under penalty of death and confiscation of goods.[394]

Selden suggested that even claims to the open ocean could, in theory, be justified: 'Wee see the Nation of Portugal also made no question, but that Dominion might bee justly acquired over the ocean itself. And this Law, in the extent of it, reached as well to forraigners, as to the King's subjects. Although forraigners do not acknowledge that Portugal hath acquired any such right'.[395] Selden further added that: 'In the Law of Nature which is obligatory, there is nothing to hinder, but that such a right may bee acquired, if (I suppose) acknowledged by all nations in Europe'.[396] The English scholar was aware of the diplomatic intercourse which had been going on between the courts of Elizabeth I and Sebastian I: 'touching the Dominion of the Atlantick and South Sea that open the way to the East Indies, which was claimed by the Portugals'.[397] However, in Selden's view, the heart of question was not whether Sebastian I could claim to be 'Lord of Navigation or Sea', but whether 'hee had made any lawful acquisition of such Dominion'.[398] This, Elizabeth I had denied, and the dispute centred not on the theoretical possibility of claiming the ocean, but on whether the Portuguese had met the requirements of effective occupation. Lastly, Selden referenced the claims of Denmark in the Baltic and of Norway in the *Oceanus Septentrionalis* as further examples of maritime dominion established in the past.[399]

393 Ibid., I, ch. 17, 107.

394 See *Ordenações Manuelinas*, V, title 112. The full text is available online, http://www.ci.uc.pt/ihti/proj/manuelinas//l5p324.htm.

395 Selden, *Mare clausum*, I, ch. 17, 108.

396 Ibidem.

397 Ibidem. Cf. *supra* ch. III, 3.2.

398 Ibid., 108–9.

399 Ibid., I, ch. 19, 118–9. Cf. *supra* ch. III, 3.3. Selden briefly mentioned the treaties signed between Elizabeth I of England and Frederick II of Denmark–Norway.

4.3.2.4 *Objections to* Mare clausum *and Selden's Answers*

In the final six chapters of book 1, Selden systematically countered various arguments used in the past to deny maritime dominion, namely by Grotius.[400] First, Selden addressed the argument based on the idea that 'the freedom of commerce, travel and passage' are common to all. While he acknowledged that such activities were generally permitted, he argued that sovereign polities with dominion over specific land or sea territories could restrict access to protect their interests.[401]

To illustrate this, Selden referenced the Spanish conquest of the Indies. He observed that Vitoria had claimed that 'The Spaniards had a lawful Right to subdue the Indians because they denied Commerce and Entertainment'.[402] Selden rejected this reasoning outright, stating: 'Wee do as easily deny as any other man can affirm', as no nation, in his view, was obliged to allow commerce or travel if it threatened their security or well-being.[403] The English scholar noted with irony that it was illogical that: 'The Spaniards should have a Right to acquire the Indies, upon a denial of commerce, since it is very well known that both they and the Portugals do openly profess, that they may lawfully prohibit Commerce in both the Indies', i.e. the main reason for which Grotius had written *Mare liberum*.[404]

Second, Selden addressed the objection concerning the fluid and ever-changing nature of the sea, which Grotius argued rendered it incapable of being owned or occupied. Selden provocatively asked: 'Are not Rivers and Fountains much more in perpetual Flux or Motion? Rivers always run forward, wherewith the Sea being compared, it seems to stand immovable'.[405] He argued that even if we 'grant it be so fluid, as is usually said of the most Northernly Seas and Channels; yet certainly the Channels and places out of which the waters flow, remain ever the same, though the waters themselves do shift and change continually'.[406] Citing Roman law and *ius commune* doctrine, Selden asserted that the fluid nature of rivers had never precluded their ownership or dominion, so there was no logical reason to treat the sea differently.[407] Selden also pointed to laws from Spain, Italy, France, Poland, and Venice, that

400 Thornton, 'John Selden's Response to Hugo Grotius', 117.

401 Selden, *Mare clausum*, 1, ch. 20, 125. Freitas had developed a similar argument in *De iusto imperio*, ch. 2, 22–30 [ff. 12–3].

402 Vitoria, *On the American Indians*, 3, 1–8, 277–91.

403 Selden, *Mare clausum*, 1, ch. 20, 125.

404 Ibid., 126. It was an inconsistency Freitas had opportunely avoided to confront.

405 Ibid., 1, ch. 20, 127.

406 Ibidem.

407 Ibidem.

recognised 'the private Dominion of Rivers as well as their Banks' as evidence.[408] In essence, Selden refused the distinction between the legal status of seas and rivers, used as an argument in the past by Vázquez y Menchaca and Grotius.[409] He affirmed that the only thing that changed between the various bodies of water was their 'largeness or narrowness' and not their intrinsic nature. Drawing on the Greek philosopher Heraclitus, Selden highlighted that, rivers being more dynamic than seas, changed constantly, yet were still widely accepted as subject to ownership. Thus, if rivers could be owned, *a fortiori*, the sea could too.[410]

Third, Selden countered the argument that the sea's vastness and lack of fixed boundaries rendered it impossible to divide or occupy. Grotius, in *Mare liberum*, had argued that lines of latitude and longitude were unsuitable for delimiting maritime boundaries.[411] Selden disagreed, stating that he could not understand: 'why Shores should not be called and reputed lawful Bounds, whereon to ground a distinction of Dominion in the Sea, as well as Ditches, Hedges, Meers, rows of Trees, Mounds, and other things used by Surveyors in the bounding of Lands'.[412] He pointed out that the ancients often described land as bounded by the sea, asking rhetorically why then not argue the reverse, that the land created boundaries for the sea?[413]

Selden emphasised that every sea had specific names and identifiable boundaries. He pointed to shores, promontories, islands, and even geometric tools like the compass and celestial degrees of latitude and longitude as sufficient means to define maritime borders.[414] He cited the 1609 truce between the Dutch and the Spanish, which used such methods to delineate boundaries, as evidence that maritime space could indeed be divided.[415] Furthermore, the English jurist noted that even the supporters of the 'Community of every Sea' often employed geographical delimitations for the coastal jurisdiction of

---

408 Ibid., 128.

409 Vázquez y Menchaca, *Controversiarum illustrium*, II, 89, § 32; Grotius, *Mare liberum*, ch. V, 75 [26].

410 Ibid., 130, 'Yea, the Rivers themselves are onely lesser Seas, as also the Fenns and Lakes; even as the sea itself is no other than a River, fen or Lake'.

411 Grotius, *Mare liberum*, ch. V, 84–5, [30–1].

412 Selden, *Mare clausum*, I, ch. 22, 135.

413 Ibidem, 'the Land is contained and bounded by the water or Sea; as if the whole Earth made as it were one Island, being surrounded by the Sea'.

414 Ibid., 137–8, 'the useful invention of the sea-man's Compass, and the help of Celestial degrees either of Longitude or Latitude, together with the doctrine of Triangles arising therefrom'. Welwod had argued something similar Cf. Welwod, *An Abridgement of All Sea-Lawes*, 67.

415 As a further example, Selden also cited the Alexandrine line of 1493. Ibid., 139.

states, for example one hundred nautical miles. Selden saw this as proof that even they accepted that both sea and land could be 'measured according to the Rules of Geometry'.[416] Selden also rejected the claim that the sea's vastness or the inexhaustibility of its resources precluded dominion.[417] Following Welwod, he argued that the sea, like land, could become depleted – especially concerning fish stocks, coral, and pearls.[418] Thus, Selden concluded that the same principles of acquisition of private and public applied to both land and sea.

Fourth, Selden tackled the works of ancient writers and jurists, who, he argued, had often been misinterpreted or decontextualised to support the notion of the sea's universal commonality.[419] For instance, the passage from Ovid, '*Quid prohibetis aquas*?', which was usually quoted (e.g. by Vázquez y Menchaca) was not 'so much an assertion of the communitie of waters, as a vehement and hyperbolical reproof of the inhumanitie of that rustic Rout in Lycia. Latona being thirstie and wearie, asked for a draught of water; and that out of a lake. The barbarous people denie her; and therefore shee most deservedly reproves them'.[420] Regarding ancient jurists, Selden admitted that some supported the idea of the sea as a common resource under natural law. However, he contended that the opposite conclusion emerged from historical records, legal practices, customs across ages and nations, and the *Common law of diverse Nations intervenient*.[421] From this, it became apparent what the 'Natural Permissive Law' really prescribed in the matter. Selden especially referred to Justinian's *Corpus Iuris*:

> … and here, especial care must bee taken to avoid that which som have presumed to affirm, touching those most excellent Books of Justinian, which make up an entire Bodie of the ancient Law; *that the Law prescribed in those Books is not the Law onely of a Citie, but even of Nations and nature; and that the whole is so fitted unto nature, that after the*

416 Ibid., 139–40.

417 Cf. Grotius, *Mare liberum*, ch. v, 93 [35].

418 Selden, *Mare clausum*, i, ch. 22, 141, 'We often see that the Sea itself, by reason of other men's Fishing, Navigation, and Commerce, becomes the worse for him that owns it, and others that enjoie it in his right; So that less profit ariseh, than might otherwise bee received thereby'. Cf. Welwod, *An Abridgement of All Sea-Lawes*, 72.

419 Ibid., i, ch. 23–5, 145–68.

420 Ibid., i, ch. 23, 146.

421 The law also styled as secondary law of nations, being the category of the law that developed in different nations and rose through the intervention of some either compact or custom.

> *empire was extinct, though the Law was a long time buried; yet it rose again, and spread it self through the world. And therefore that it concerns even Princes, although it was framed by Justinian for private persons.*[422]

Selden criticised those who treated the *Corpus Iuris* as the sole source of natural or universal law, arguing that its principles had often been modified or outright contradicted by the practices of nations, for example concerning shipwreck and the enslavement of prisoners of war.[423] He cited examples such as the laws of Spain and France, which limited the application of Justinian law, and the Germanic customs codified within the Holy Roman Empire. These divergences, Selden argued, demonstrated that the *Corpus Iuris* was merely one among many legal sources, albeit a venerable one.[424] Therefore, even though the *Corpus Iuris* included passages suggesting the commonality of the sea, that did not 'in any wise diminish the Autoritie of the received customs of so many Ages and Nations'.[425]

Turning to more recent commentators, Selden criticised Vázquez y Menchaca and Grotius for their opposition to maritime dominion. The Spanish jurist in particular 'would have prescription to cease betwixt Foreigners in relation to each other, and not to take place in the Law of Nations, but in Civil Law; so that by his opinion prescription should bee of no force between those (as between two supreme states or princes) who are not indifferently subject to the Civil Law, which admits prescription'.[426] Grotius similarly maintained that prescription lacked legal force in matters of the law of nations.[427] Selden, however, strongly opposed this view, arguing that most rules of the *Intervenient Law of Nations* were established over time by the consent of the peoples who adhered to them. Given the weight he placed on historical precedent, Selden concluded that prescription could serve as a legitimate basis for acquiring maritime dominion.[428]

While Selden acknowledged Grotius as 'a man of great learning, and extraordinarie knowledge in things both Divine and Humane',[429] he also accused him of writing *Mare liberum* to serve specific Dutch economic and

422 Ibid., I, ch. 24, 152. Italics from the original text signalling Selden's quote from Gentili, *De iure belli*, I, ch. 3.

423 Ibidem.

424 Ibid., 153.

425 Ibid., 155.

426 Ibid., I, ch. 26, 170. Cf. Vázquez y Menchaca, *Controversiarum illustrium*, II, 89, § 12.

427 Grotius, *Mare liberum*, ch. VII, 99, [38].

428 Selden, *Mare clausum*, I, ch. 26, 170.

429 Ibid., 171.

political interests. He also pointed out the inconsistencies between his 1609 brief and his mature work *De iure belli ac pacis*.[430] In Selden's opinion, *Mare liberum* also mixed in a confusing way issues such as discovery and pontifical donation with the core matter of the dominion of the sea. The English jurist was aware that Grotius had focused his critics on oceanic closed sea claims. Ultimately, Selden conceded that it would be 'very difficult' to occupy the entire ocean but maintained that effective occupation could theoretically justify even oceanic claims. By this standard, he argued, the Spanish and Portuguese had nevertheless failed to maintain effective control over the vast ocean spaces they had claimed.[431]

4.3.3 Book II

4.3.3.1 *The British Dominion of the Seas*

In the first book of *Mare clausum*, Selden established the theoretical framework of his discussion on *mare clausum* and included several chapters surveying ancient and modern practices of maritime dominion. From this, he derived the broad acceptance of maritime dominion under the *Common or Intervenient Law of most Nations* (the secondary law of nations), which he argued did not breach *Law either Natural and Divine* (the universal law of nations).[432] Selden dedicated the entire second book to a more detailed collection of historical evidence supporting British dominion over the *Oceanus Britannicus*. It was this second book that endowed the treatise with resounding political relevance, particularly in the context of escalating Anglo-Dutch tensions.[433]

In the first chapter, he broadly defined the British Seas as extending to the North, South, East, and West of the British archipelago. Especially to the South and to the East, the British seas extended as far as the coasts of the continent.[434] In the subsequent chapters, he crafted a narrative asserting that the inhabitants of the British Isles had exercised sovereign *imperium* over the sea since ancient times, continuously benefiting from its privileges.[435] Raestad referred to as sort of 'primitive occupation' to refer to Selden's way of think-

430 Ibidem.

431 Ibid., 173.

432 Ibid., 179.

433 Fulton, *The Sovereignty of the Sea*, 372; van Ittersum, 'Debating the Free Sea', 1193–5.

434 Selden, *Mare clausum*, II, ch. 1, 181–7.

435 'Such a private or peculiar use or enjoiment of the Sea, as consists in a setting forth of Ships to Sea, either to defend or make good the Dominion; in prescribing Rules of Navigation to such as pass through it; in receiving such Profits and Commodities as are peculiar to every kinde of Sea-Dominion whatsoever; and, which is the principal,

ing.[436] Selden claimed this dominion had been successively inherited by the Romans, Anglo-Saxons, Danes, and Normans, who all 'enjoyed the Dominion of that Sea by perpetual occupation; that is to say, by using and enjoying it as their own after a peculiar manner, as an undoubted portion either of the whole bodie of the estate of the British Empire, [...] or as an inseparable appendant of this Land'.[437]

As Mark Somos has observed, Selden's argument linked maritime dominion to the geography of the British Isles rather than to a specific dynasty, ethnic group, language, or political continuity.[438] Selden's narrative wove together a long-term historical justification for British exceptionalism, framing contemporary British sovereignty as the culmination of a legacy dating back to antiquity. Even regimes like the Normans, which had historically emphasised their break with their predecessors, were seamlessly integrated into this lineage of dominion.

4.3.3.2 *To the South and to the East…*

In his historical narrative, Selden placed the Angevine-Plantagenet kings of England at the centre of his argument. In the twelfth century, these rulers had inherited dominion over the sea from their Norman predecessors while simultaneously holding extensive territories in mainland France. He described them as 'kings of both shores', whose authority as 'Lords of the Sea' had been widely acknowledged by other European princes.[439] Hence, Selden initially focused on the 'Narrow Seas' – the English Channel, the Strait of Dover, and the southern North Sea – among the most heavily trafficked and strategically significant waterways in Europe. His arguments took on particular urgency against the backdrop of French naval expansion under Cardinal Richelieu, who in 1626 was appointed *grand maître, chef et surintendant général de la navigation et commerce de France*. Following the advice of naval expert Isaac de Razilly, Richelieu appeared to adhere to the principle that 'he who commands the sea holds great power over land'.[440] This surge in

either in admitting or excluding others at pleasure'. Ibid., II, ch. 2, 188; Toomer, *John Selden*, 412–5.

436 Raestad, *La mer territoriale*, 101.

437 Selden, *Mare Clausum*, II, ch. 1, 182.

438 Somos, 'Open and closed seas', 341; idem, 'Selden's *Mare Clausum*', 313

439 Selden, *Mare clausum*, II, ch. 2–12, 188–282.

440 '*Quiconque est maistre de la mer, a ung grand pouvoyr sur la terre*', in 'Mémoire du chevalier Isaac de Razilly au Cardinal Richelieu, 16 novembre 1626', cited in de la Roncière, *Histoire de la marine française*, IV, 490–1. See also Monaque, *Une histoire de la marine*, 37–56; Léon Deschamps, 'Un colonisateur du temps de Richelieu: Isaac de

French maritime activity alarmed the English government, which feared it could be aimed at the 'usurping of an absolute or equal dominion with his Majesty upon the British Ocean, to the great prejudice of his majesty's regality and the ancient inheritance of his imperial crown'.[441]

Selden countered these fears by asserting that French kings had never enjoyed dominion in the waters lying between England and the continent. English possession-occupation of the surrounding seas was both 'civil' (compliant with the law) and 'corporal', effectively recognised by long consent.[442] According to Selden, English monarchs exercised absolute and far-reaching maritime sovereignty, encompassing: 1) the custody (i.e. *protectio*), governance and admiralty of the English Sea, as if it was a territory or province of the kingdom; 2) sovereignty over all islands within the Channel; 3) the right to grant or deny passage to foreign vessels; 4) authority over fishing rights and the protection of foreign fishermen; 5) the power to impose laws and restrictions to belligerents who were at war with one another, but in peace with Great Britain, as to acts of hostility and the taking of prizes.[443]

As evidence of the established and recognised control of the sea enjoyed by past English kings, Selden referred to a multitude of documents and records. For instance: a) the appointment of admirals and guardians for the sea dating back to the Norman period; b) the equipment of ships of war, the imposition of taxes to finance the said custody, e.g., the *Danegeld*; c) documents granting leave of passages through the British seas; d) documents granting the license to fish in the British seas; e) commissions to the admirals to be found in the public records; and f) the custom of foreigners performing the flag salute when encountering an English warships in the British seas.[444] Selden viewed King James VI–I's proclamation of the King's Chambers as a continuation of this

---

Razilly', *Revue de géographie*, 19 (1886), 273–84; Pierre Castagnos, *Richelieu face à la mer* (Rennes: Éditions Ouest-France, 1989); Alan James, *The Navy and Government in Early Modern France, 1572–1661* (Woodbridge: Boydell Press, 2004), 55–75; Benjamin W. D. Redding, *The English and French Navies, 1500–1650: Expansion, Organization and State-Building* (Martlesham: Boydell & Brewer, 2022).

441 '1626 naval commission', quoted in Roger Lockyer, *Buckingham. The Life and Political Career of George Villiers, First Duke of Buckingham, 1592–1628* (Routledge: London, 1981), 345–6. See also Poot, *Anglo-Dutch Relations*, 66–7.

442 Selden, *Mare clausum*, II, ch. 13, 284.

443 Ibid., 285. Cf. Fulton, *The Sovereignty of the Sea*, 373; Grewe, *Epochs*, 268.

444 Selden, *Mare clausum*, II, ch. 14, 287. In relation to the documents granting leave of passage, see ibid., II, ch. 20, 344–54. Regarding the licenses to fish, see ibid., ch. 21, 355–62. Concerning the flag salute, see ch. 26, 398–402.

maritime tradition, acting as the 'lawful sovereign and moderator of the Seas'.[445]

Selden highlighted the role of the *custodes maris* (guardians of the sea), medieval officials responsible for protecting coastal waters, whom he considered the precursors of England's admirals, formally established during Edward I's reign (r. 1272–1302). Selden quoted many of the royal commissions to the admirals as proof of the long-established claims of maritime dominion of the English monarchs.[446] The number of medieval diplomatic acts, rolls, and royal edicts referenced by the English scholar, who was drawing on John Borough's research, is considerable.[447] While the sheer quantity of documentation is impressive, Selden's tendency to extrapolate broad conclusions from isolated or decontextualised records may appear less convincing to modern readers. For instance, Selden referred to a few documents scattered through the centuries to argue that foreign princes had consistently asked leave of passage for their vessels while crossing the British kings' seas, which they clearly did not.[448]

4.3.3.3 *To the West and to the North…*

Selden argued that the Irish Sea, bordered by Ireland, Great Britain, and the Isle of Man, had long been an integral part of the dominion of English kings. He likened it to a river bounded by two banks under the same sovereign authority.[449] Selden criticised Elizabeth I's commissioners for statements made during the 1602 Bremen conference, where they had mentioned the long standing tradition of freedom of navigation and fishing in the Irish Sea in their arguments against Dano-Norwegian closed sea claims.[450] In Selden's view, this argument, which implied a necessary communal ownership of the sea, was both inaccurate and detrimental to English claims. He supported his critique by citing parliamentary acts, treaties with Spain, and royal proclamations that required foreign vessels to obtain licences for fishing in the Irish

445 Ibid., II, ch. 22, 363–75.

446 Ibid., II, ch. 16–17, 305–20.

447 Ibid., II, ch. 20, 24, 27, 28. For example ch. 27, 406 references as proof of English maritime sovereignty to the already mentioned 'Petition presented by the proctors of the King of England …' dated 1306, in Chaplais, *English Medieval Diplomatic Practice*, part I, vol. I, n. 206, 367 (see *supra* ch. I, 3.2). See also Fulton, *The Sovereignty of the Sea*, 43–56.

448 Selden, *Mare clausum*, II, ch. 20, 344–54.

449 Ibid., ch. 30, 433–40.

450 On the 1602 Bremen conference between English and Dano-Norwegian commissioners, see *supra* ch. III, 3.2; Cattelan, 'Claims of Dominion', 38–41.

Sea.[451] Selden further suggested that English claims might in fact extend westward to the waters surrounding British colonies in North America. Although he admitted his research on this matter was incomplete, Selden considered the discovery and occupation of these territories – starting from the voyages of Sebastian Cabot under Henry VII – as a basis for extending English dominion to the surrounding seas and fisheries.[452]

In the two final chapters of *Mare clausum*, Selden dealt with the seas lying to the North of the British Isles. It was likely this portion of the treatise that caused the delay in its publication since it clearly was incompatible with Dano-Norwegian closed sea claims.[453] Selden considered well-established the right of the kings of Scotland (now united with England and Ireland under the Stuarts) to the Scottish seas, as proved by many proclamations and acts of the parliament of Edinburgh banning foreigners from fishing in the coastal seas without a royal license. Selden acknowledged that in the Middle Ages, the Vikings, and later the Norwegians, had acquired control of all the islands to the North of Great Britain, such as the Shetlands, Orkneys, and Iceland. In the process, they had also gained dominion over the surrounding seas, 'those Sea-Appendants of the Dominion of Britain, in the Northern parts, were invaded by foreigners'.[454]

That said, Selden argued that through wars, marriages, and treaties, the kings of Scotland had gradually recovered the sovereignty over the Hebrides, Orkneys, and Shetland in addition to dominion over the sea areas surrounding these islands. Selden traced the beginning of this trend from the times of King Alexander III of Scotland (r. 1249–1286) who had signed with Norway the Treaty of Perth of 1266 under which the Hebrides and the Isle of Man became Scottish.[455] Another decisive step had been the marriage between

451 Selden, *Mare clausum*, II, ch. 30, 436, 'let fall those words too unadvisedly in the Treatie, with the Danish commissioners, about free Navigation and Fishing in the Norwegian Sea; that the Kings of England never had prohibited Navigation and Fishing in the Irish Sea between England and Ireland; as if they would have had it proved from thence, that the Dane ought not to bee prohibited Fishing or Navigation between Island and Norway, because neither were Lords of the Sea, but had possessed the Shores onely on both sides by an equal rights'.

452 Ibid., 441–3, 'I have as yet made but little enquiries…'.

453 Van Ittersum, 'Debating the free Sea', 1196; idem, '*Mare Liberum* versus the Propriety of the Seas?'; Toomer, *John Selden*, 388–9.

454 Selden, *Mare clausum*, II, ch. 31, 443–5. Selden here quoted Welwod's *De dominio maris*, ch. 3.

455 Ibid., 445. See also Erik Opsahl, 'The treaty of Perth: Union of the realm and the king's law', in Andrew R. C. Simpson and Jørn Øyrehagen Sunde (eds.), *Comparative Perspectives in Scottish and Norwegian Legal History, Trade and Seafaring, 1200–1800* (Edinburgh:

James III of Scotland (r. 1460–1488) and Margaret of Denmark, who brought as dowry the Orkney and Shetland Islands.[456] In Selden's mind the maritime dominion of the kings of Norway, later Denmark–Norway, had receded in front of a corresponding and gradual expansion of the Scottish, later British, counterpart. To him, this process appeared justified since those islands and seas constituted the natural appendage of the British Islands.

In the last chapter of the treatise, Selden questioned in particular the ancient Dano-Norwegian pretension of prohibiting foreign navigation in the waters between Iceland and Norway.[457] The English scholar accepted that early treaties between England and Denmark–Norway had imposed a ban on English seafarers, while later agreements required English fishermen to pay licences to go to Iceland and the Norwegian Sea to trade and catch fish. However, during the sixteenth century, such payments had been discontinued and forgotten by Dano-Norwegian authorities. On this point, Selden was following the argumentation of the English envoys in Bremen who he had previously criticised.

In essence, Selden did not question the existence of a maritime dominion belonging to the Dano-Norwegian monarchy, but he argued that it was limited to the portions of the *Oceanus Septentrionalis* immediately adjacent to the coasts of Norway and Iceland. More surprisingly, he declared that: 'It appears the King of Great Britain hath Empire and Dominion also in the Sea which lies far more northerly than Iceland'.[458] The English scholar claimed that the sea area to the North of Iceland and between it and Greenland 'having never been entered by occupation, nor used in the art and exercise of fisherie, was first in the memory of our fathers rendred very gainful', especially concerning whaling, which, in 1613, had been granted in monopoly to the Muscovy Company by James VI–I.[459] The pelagic area in question, whose use was never: 'entered by Occupation and such a kinde of profit being first discovered doth according to the manner of the claim, give a Dominion to the discoverer who claims it in the name of another', namely the king of Great Britain, who had displayed a corporal, as well as intentional possession.[460]

University Press, 2023), 35–62; Dauvit Broun, 'The treaty of Perth: Union of the realm and the laws of the kingdom', ibid, 63–94.

456 Selden, *Mare clausum*, ch. 31, 445. Cf. Steve Murdoch, 'War and peace: Scottish-Norwegian relations in the early modern period (ca. 1520–1707)', in Simpson and Øyrehagen Sunde (eds.), *Comparative Perspectives*, 211–31.

457 Ibid., II, ch. 32, 448–56.

458 Ibid., 456–7.

459 Ibidem.

460 Ibid., 457.

Thus, Selden argued that his compatriots had discovered, occupied, and 'made gainful' those seas, acquiring a preferential title by which they could exclude others, namely the Dutch. This was a direct reference to the ongoing Anglo-Dutch dispute concerning Greenland and Spitzbergen whaling and fishing grounds.[461] Both the Dutch and the English claimed prior discovery in the area; if the Muscovy Company sought to exclude all interlopers, whether English or foreign, the Dutch States General repeatedly refused to recognise British claims, creating in 1614 its own Greenland Company, or *Noordsche Compagnie*.[462] Hence, Selden incorporated in his survey of British *mare clausum* these relatively new and extensive claims in the far North, fiercely contested by the Dutch and the Dano-Norwegians.

After addressing British claims extending across all cardinal directions, Selden concluded *Mare clausum* convinced he had demonstrated beyond doubt, in law and in history, 'that the very Shores or Ports of the Neighbour-Princes beyond-Sea, are Bounds of the Sea-Territorie of the British Empire to the Southward and Eastward', but also that 'in the open and vast Ocean of the North and West, they are to bee placed at the utmost extent of those most spacious Seas, which are possest by the English, Scots and Irish'.[463] For Selden, the seas adjoining Britain were an inseparable part of Charles I's kingdom. More broadly, British dominion over the seas exemplified the broader acceptance of *dominium maris* throughout history, grounded in legal precedent, historical practice, and compliance with the laws of nations and nature.

---

461 See *supra* ch. IV, 4.1.2. As already noted, due to the geographic ignorance of the time the two terms, Greenland and Spitzbergen, were used almost interchangeably in the documents of the time to refer to the fishing and whaling grounds in the far North. See Edmundson, *Anglo-Dutch Rivalry*, 43–5.

462 Fulton, *The Sovereignty of the Sea*, 181–5; Samuel Muller, *Geschiedenis der Noordsche Compagnie* (Utrecht: Gebr. van der Post, 1874); Hacquebord, Steenhuisen and Waterbolk, 'English and Dutch Whaling ...', 117–34; Louwrens Hacquebord, *De Noordse Compagnie: Opkomst, bloei en ondergang* (1614–1642) (Zutphen: Walburg Pers, 2014).

463 Selden, *Mare clausum*, II, ch. 32, 459.

CHAPTER 5

Conclusions

1 Apogee and Decline of the 'Claimed Seas' in Legal Argumentation?

If Elizabeth I of England played a significant role in bringing the freedom of the sea to the forefront of politics and diplomacy, Selden's treatise reflected the Stuart monarchs' shift towards claimed seas policies in the 'British seas'. More broadly, *Mare clausum* represents the peak of the early seventeenth-century resurgence of the closed seas principle in legal and political discourse. Selden was the first to develop a comprehensive *mare clausum* legal theory, aligning with Sarpi in advocating for the assimilation of pelagic legal regimes with those governing terrestrial territories. Under this framework, the Stuart monarchs could extend their dominion over surrounding waters, effectively advancing a legal position akin to modern notions of sovereignty. To support his argument, Selden cited Venetian, Dano-Norwegian, and Iberian precedents, demonstrating that the law of nations had long recognized the possibility of acquiring maritime dominion. He argued that various polities had exercised control over marine spaces in the past and continued to do so in his own time. Thus, by the 1630s, the three 'claimed seas' traditions traced in previous chapters had become fully aware of each other, engaging in direct interaction, particularly in relation to the strategically positioned British Isles.

In the preceding chapters, we explored the role of the 'claimed sea' principle in legal and political discourse. Chapter 1 examined the development of these tendencies across the Mediterranean and northern European seas in the Late Middle Ages. While both northern and southern Europe saw increasing political control over maritime spaces, jurists generally avoided framing such control in terms of outright dominion or ownership. Instead, they developed concepts of jurisdiction and protection, compatible with the Roman law tradition that classified the sea as *res communis omnium*. This approach allowed polities such as Venice, Genoa, and Denmark to impose restrictions on the use of certain maritime areas. Norway (later Dano-Norway) went further, banning navigation and fishing north of Bergen and towards Iceland in an effort to impose a strictly closed sea regime.

Chapter 2 explored how Portugal and Spain, as pioneers of oceanic exploration in the fifteenth century, applied their own version of the closed sea principle to the oceanic routes leading to the East and West Indies. Like Norway, the Iberian powers sought to exclude other European nations entirely,

 | DOI:10.1163/9789004741409_007

asserting a strict *ius excludendi alios*. However, from the outset, the vastness of the oceans presented significant challenges to these ambitions. By the latter half of the sixteenth century, it was evident that the Iberians lacked the capacity to enforce control over extensive ocean corridors or to curb piracy and hostile maritime incursions.

Chapter 3 traced the gradual emergence of the principle of the freedom of the sea in the sixteenth century, a process shaped by the transformative effects of the Age of Exploration and the Protestant Reformation. Initially, Iberian claims faced scrutiny, but the challenge soon extended to older 'claimed seas' practices across European waters. Elizabeth I of England and Vázquez de Menchaca revitalized the concept of the freedom of the sea in state practice and legal doctrine, respectively. The Dutch incursions into the Indian Ocean culminated in Grotius' *Mare liberum* (1609), which provoked strong opposition from governments and jurists with competing interests.

Chapter 4 examined the early seventeenth-century resurgence of the 'claimed seas' principle, marked by an intensified interplay between politics and law. The discussion began with developments in the Mediterranean, then moved to the oceans, and finally to northern European seas. Despite its waning power, the Republic of Venice fiercely defended its dominance in the Adriatic through military, diplomatic, and legal means. In the 1610s, Paolo Sarpi and Giulio Pace da Beriga provided scholarly support for Venice's claims, emphasizing the Adriatic's geographical and historical distinctiveness. However, Sarpi sided with Grotius in rejecting the possibility of dominion over the open ocean. This distinction between enclosed seas and the open ocean marked a turning point in the early development of the law of the sea. Nevertheless, Seraphin de Freitas, in *De iusto imperio* (1625), rejected this conclusion, producing the first systematic defence of Iberian closed sea claims over the oceans. He focused on the *ius excludendi alios* concerning Portuguese sea routes and introduced the concept of quasi-occupation. However, by this time, Portugal and Spain had already entered a period of relative naval decline. The final section of chapter 4 examined northern Europe, where Dano-Norwegian closed sea claims were swiftly overshadowed by the ambitious maritime assertions of James VI–I and Charles I. Encouraged by economic and political factions in London envious of Dutch commercial success, the Stuarts pursued assertive maritime policies. While Welwod offered a limited defence of Stuart claims focused on fisheries, Selden's *Mare clausum* provided a fully developed 'claimed seas' theory.[1]

1 van Ittersum, 'Debating the Free Sea', 1193–210.

2 High Seas and Territorial Seas

In the decades following *Mare liberum* and *Mare clausum*'s publication, further doctrinal works emerged in defence of the 'claimed seas' principle, as the geopolitical landscape remained unfavourable to any compromise between the ideals of maritime freedom and dominion.[2] Venetian, Genoese, and Dano-Norwegian claims slowly continued to wane due to the relative naval-geopolitical resizing of the three polities in question. Between 1652 and 1674, the Dutch and the English – by then the leading European sea powers – engaged in three bloody naval wars for maritime and commercial supremacy, a direct outcome of the increasing tensions outlined in Chapter 4.[3] In the long term, Great Britain emerged victorious, steadily consolidating its maritime primacy throughout the eighteenth century, though this dominance was repeatedly challenged, particularly by France, as late as the Napoleonic era. Interestingly, after Great Britain imposed its naval supremacy in the aftermath of the Battle of Trafalgar (1805), references to the 'flag salute' and the dominion of the seas – so coveted by the Stuart kings and Oliver Cromwell alike – were abandoned.[4] Admittedly, the British government recognised that the freedom of the seas was of greater value in facilitating the interconnectivity of its expanding colonial empire. Other nations subsequently followed suit.

Over time, discussions on the legal status of the seas receded into the background. The focus of jurists and diplomats shifted to issues such as the treatment of neutrals by belligerents during wartime and the fierce mercantilist competition between European seafaring nations.[5] It was in this context

2 For instance, Borgo, *De dominio Serenissimae Genuensis Reipublicae in mari Ligustico* (1641); Francesco Zamboni, *Del dominio del mare Adriatico, overo golfo di Venetia* (Vicenza: F. Grossi, 1620); Francesco De' Silvii Zamboni, *Del dominio del mare Adriatico, ovvero golfo di Venetia* (Venice: G. Zattoni, 1676); Charles Molloy, *De iure maritimo et navali* (London: printed for J. Bellinger, G. Dawes & R. Boulter, 1676).

3 David Ormrod and Gijs Rommelse (eds.), *War, Trade and the State: Anglo-Dutch Conflict, 1652–89* (Woodbridge: Boydell Press, 2020); Roger Hainsworth and Christine Churches, *The Anglo-Dutch Naval Wars, 1652–1674* (Phoenix Mill: Sutton Pub Ltd, 1998); James R. Jones, *The Anglo-Dutch Wars of the Seventeenth Century* (London: Longman, 1996); Izidor Janžekovič, 'The Balance of Sea Power in the Early Modern Era: The Anglo-Dutch Wars (1652–1674)', *International Journal of Maritime History*, 36(4) (2024), 1–26.

4 Fulton, *The Sovereignty of the Sea*, 523.

5 Stefano Cattelan and Frederik Dhondt (eds.), *Small Power Neutrality and the Law of the Sea in the Long Eighteenth Century (1650–1800). Law as Argument in the Pelagic Arena* (Leiden/Boston: Brill, 2025); Stefano Cattelan, 'In the Shadow of the Great Powers: Freedom of the Sea and Neutrality in the Long Eighteenth Century', research note in *Grotiana*, 44(1) (2023), 145–53, https://doi.org/10.1163/18760759-20230005; idem, 'Maritime warfare in Old Regime

that the Dutch jurist and judge Cornelius van Bynkershoek (1673–1743) proposed a lasting compromise between the doctrines of *mare liberum* and *mare clausum* in his treatise *De dominio maris dissertatio*, first published in 1703.[6] Drawing on contemporary developments in state practice, he argued that coastal states should be entitled to hold sovereign rights (*dominium, imperium*) over a strip of coastal waters – only later termed the 'territorial sea' – whose breadth was determined by the range of coastal artillery, the so-called 'cannon-shot rule'.[7] Beyond the outer edge of the territorial sea, marine spaces would lie outside state jurisdiction, with the freedom of the sea constituting the cardinal principle. Hence, Bynkershoek saw the concept of effectiveness as the deciding factor for determining the extension of state jurisdiction over the sea. However, he did not conceive it as control exercised by warships – that could not continuously offer protection and 'occupy' marine spaces, – but as the protection offered by coastal batteries.[8]

The underlying principle, which continues to inform modern international law of the sea, is that legal claims over coastal waters are ancillary to sovereign rights established on land.[9] State practice gradually coalesced around a fixed limit of three nautical miles, a standard proposed by the Neapolitan economist Ferdinando Galiani (1728–1787) in a treatise addressing issues of neutral-

Europe', 551–87; Stephen C. Neff, *The Rights and Duties of Neutrals: A General History* (Manchester: University Press, 2000), 27–108; Leos Müller, *Neutrality in World History* (New York: Routledge, 2019), 43–81; Koen Stapelbroek (ed.), *Trade and War: The Neutrality of Commerce in the Inter-State System* (Helsinki: Collegium for Advanced Studies 2011); Schnakenbourg, *Entre la guerre et la paix.*

6 Cornelius van Bynkershoek, *De dominio maris dissertatio* (Lugduni Batavorum: apud Joannem van Kerckhem, 1744) (first published in 1702). For an English translation, see Cornelius van Bynkershoek, *De dominio maris dissertatio* [1744], translated by Ralph Van Deman Magoffin (Carnegie Endowment for International Peace, New York: Oxford University Press, 1923), especially ch. II, 41–5 and ch. III. For an overview, see Kinji Akashi, *Cornelius van Bynkershoek: His Role in the History of International Law* (The Hague: Kluwer Law International, 1998).

7 van Bynkershoek, *De dominio maris dissertatio*, ch. II, 44–5.

8 Ibid., ch. VII, 81.

9 Tullio Scovazzi, 'The Evolution of International Law of the Sea: New Issues, New Challenges', *Recueil des Cours – Collected Courses of the Hague Academy of International Law (Vol. 286, 2000)* (The Hague/Boston/London: M. Nijhoff, 2001), 69; idem, 'The origin of the theory of sovereignty of the sea', in Lilian del Castillo (ed.), *From Grotius to the International Tribunal for the Law of the Sea: Liber Amicorum Judge Hugo Caminos* (Leiden: Brill, 2015), 61–2; Douglas M. Johnston, *The International Law of Fisheries: A Framework for Policy-Oriented Inquiries* (New Haven/Dordrecht: New Haven Press/M. Nijhoff, 1987), 174–80; Philip C. Jessup, *The Law of Territorial Waters and Maritime Jurisdiction* (New York: G. A. Jennings Co., 1927), 73.

ity.[10] While this three-nautical-mile limit was endorsed by leading naval powers such as Great Britain, France, and the United States, some states continued to assert claims over broader territorial waters. For example, the Nordic states claimed four nautical miles, Spain and Portugal six nautical miles, and some Latin American countries put forward claims to territorial seas up to two hundred nautical miles.[11] Thus, although the right of coastal states to exercise sovereignty over adjacent maritime zones was broadly accepted, differences persisted regarding the extent of such zones.

In the context of British maritime predominance, the era of expansive claims over vast stretches of seas and oceans came to an end and *mare clausum* pretensions 'vanished not in obedience to any abstract theory, nor in the twinkling of an eye, but gradually, as a nation after nation estimated the effort necessary for the maintenance of each particular claim and, openly or tacitly, threw up the sponge', and eventually 'the claim to an exclusive lordship of the seas became meaningless'.[12] Law consistently develops to meet the needs of society, and Ram Prakash Anand observed that, in the case of the law of the sea, it was the interest of European colonial empires – dominating the oceans by the late eighteenth century – in maintaining freedom of movement between continents that served as the driving force behind its evolution up to the mid-twentieth century.[13] It is worth noting, however, that aside from a few codification attempts, the law of the sea remained largely customary and usage-based well into the last century. While this arrangement provided relative stability, it also gave rise to ambiguities and uncertainties.

3 Significance of the Concept of 'Claimed Seas' in the Contemporary Law of the Sea Discourse

It is often argued that the eighteenth-century compromise between the principles *mare liberum* and *mare clausum* sanctioned the predominance of the

10 Ferdinando Galiani, *De' doveri dei principi neutrali verso i principi guerreggianti, e di questi verso i neutrali, libri due* (Napoli, 1782), 422.

11 Joel G. Verner, 'Changes in the Law of the Sea: Latin American Contributions and Rationales', *Social and Economic Studies*, 30(2) (1981), 18–44.

12 Geoffrey Butler and Simon Maccoby, *The Development of International Law* (London: Longman, 1928), 53; William McFee, *The Law of the Sea* (New York: J. B. Lippincott Co., 1950), 142; Anand, *Origin and Development*, 124–53.

13 Anand, *Origin and Development*, 124–53. On the interconnectedness between imperial and maritime history see Armitage, 'The elephant and the whale', 46–56. See also Mawani, 'The law of the sea', 121.

freedom of the sea.[14] Outside the territorial seas no state could claim preferential titles, and the use of the marine spaces was supposed to remain free and common to all, at least in times of peace.[15] However, the evolution of the law of the sea in the twentieth century demonstrates that the seeds of the 'claimed seas' principle survived under the surface of the supposed dominance of the freedom of the sea paradigm. The balance between the two principles began to shift with the advent of new technologies that enabled the exploitation of previously inaccessible marine resources, such as underwater minerals, gas, and oil fields.

Furthermore, the finite nature and exhaustibility of fisheries had long become apparent with the introduction of steam-powered trawlers and increasingly capable fishing boats, and tensions over fishing rights persisted. In response, coastal states sought to extend their maritime jurisdiction, securing exclusive access to living and non-living resources in their coastal waters and protecting them from unregulated exploitation by foreign entities.[16] The twentieth-century phenomenon of decolonisation further accelerated this trend, as newly independent states were particularly eager to assert control over their coastal waters and resources, albeit often hindered by the persistent economic dominance of the former colonial powers and western corporations.

On the one hand, this shift in the balance of interests within the international community heralded a new era for coastal states' rights to the exclusive exploitation of marine resources. On the other hand, the freedom of the seas remained the cardinal principle for navigation beyond territorial waters. From the 1950s onwards, the progressive codification of the law of the sea sought to consolidate and expand upon existing customary rules, incorporating new developments in the field. After earlier efforts marked

---

14 E.g. see Laurence Boisson de Chazournes et Guillaume Gros, 'La frontière en droit international: centrale ou périphérique?', in Jorge Viñuales et al. (eds.), *The International Legal Order in the XXIst Century. Essays in Honour of Professor Marcelo Gustavo Kohen* (Leiden/Boston: Brill/Nijhoff, 2023), 17–34, at 28; Michèle Battesti, 'La haute mer: une «chose commune»', *Stratégique*, 123(3) (2019), 67–86; Michaela Young, 'Then and Now: Reappraising Freedom of the Seas in Modern Law of the Sea', *Ocean Development & International Law*, 47(2) (2016), 165–85.

15 Cattelan, 'In the Shadow of the Great Powers', 147–8.

16 A famous example of this are the Icelandic policies that led to the so-called 'Cod Wars' between Iceland and the United Kingdom in the 1950s–1970s. See Guðni T. Jóhannesson, *Troubled Waters: Cod War, Fishing Disputes, and Britain's Fight for the Freedom of the High Seas, 1948–1964* (Reykjavík: North Atlantic Fisheries History Association, 2007); Sverrir Steinsson, 'The Cod Wars: A Re-Analysis', *European Security*, 25(2) (2016), 256–75.

by mixed success,[17] extensive negotiations culminated in the adoption of the United Nations Convention on the Law of the Sea (UNCLOS III) in 1982, which came into force in 1994.[18] This landmark agreement established key provisions, including the extension of territorial waters to twelve nautical miles, a special status for archipelagic states, the creation of 200-nautical-mile Exclusive Economic Zones (EEZs), and exclusive rights over continental shelf resources.[19] With more than 160 signatories, the convention is widely regarded as a success of multilateralism, and even a 'constitution for the oceans'. UNCLOS III might be conceived as both the culmination of the twentieth-century trend towards the territorialisation and appropriation of the sea and an attempt to regulate and temper this movement, e.g. by reaffirming the freedom of navigation on the high seas and different rights of passage through waters under state jurisdiction.

In recent years, expansive maritime claims – such as those by China in the South China Sea – have raised concerns not only about resource grabbing but also about potential interference with the freedom of navigation in international waters.[20] At this historical juncture, several trends can be observed. First, coastal states continue to expand their jurisdiction through broad interpretations of legal institutes like the EEZ and the continental shelf. Second, strategic maritime areas are increasingly being leveraged – sometimes in vio-

17 The First United Nations Conference on the Law of the Sea (UNCLOS I) in 1958 resulted in four treaties, collectively known as the 1958 Geneva Conventions: (a) the Convention on the Territorial Sea and Contiguous Zone, (b) the Convention on the High Seas, (c) the Convention on Fishing and Conservation of Living Resources of the High Seas, and (d) the Convention on the Continental Shelf. While a step forward, they failed, for instance, to establish a uniform maximum breadth for territorial seas. Instead, the Second United Nations Conference on the Law of the Sea (UNCLOS II) of 1960 ended without an agreement.

18 See Kirsten Sellars, *A 'Constitution for the Oceans'. The Long Hard Road to the UN Convention on the Law of the Sea* (Cambridge: University Press, 2025).

19 United Nations, *United Nations Convention on the Law of the Sea* (UNCLOS), UNTS vol. 1833 (10 December 1982), see Part V, arts. 55–75 on the legal regime of the EEZ, granting coastal states exclusive rights over marine resources' exploration and exploitation in both the water column and the seabed; and Part VI, arts. 76–85, on the continental shelf regime, which applies solely to the seabed.

20 The Arctic Ocean provides a further example. Arctic states are trying to secure the largest share of the remote but increasingly ice-free region, where new possibilities of exploitation and navigation are arising. See Margaret Blunden, 'Geopolitics and the Northern Sea Route', *International Affairs*, 88(1) (2012), 115–29. For an overview, see Rudiger Wolfrum, 'The freedom of navigation: modern challenges seen from a historical perspective', in del Castillo (ed.), *From Grotius to the International Tribunal for the Law of the Sea*, 89–103.

lation of existing rules – for geopolitical advantage. Third, there is growing recognition that current ocean governance frameworks, such as Regional Fishery Management Organisations (RFMOs), inadequately protect areas beyond national jurisdiction from the so-called 'tragedy of the commons', particularly in relation to marine biodiversity.[21] However, the 2023 adoption of the UN Biodiversity Beyond National Jurisdiction Treaty (BBNJ Agreement) offers a glimmer of hope for improved international cooperation.[22] Fourth, the influence of western nations, which shaped a eurocentric law of the sea over the past five centuries, appears to be seriously weakening.

In conclusion, the law of the sea and ocean governance remain as intertwined with geopolitics and economics today as they were in the times of Grotius and Selden. The most significant difference between the seventeenth and twenty-first centuries is the existence of a more structured international legal framework which – though imperfect – provides platforms for debate, policymaking, legislation, and adjudication. One could argue that the management of continental shelf and EEZ resources by coastal states can, when exercised rationally and judiciously, offer significant benefits – ensuring public oversight, accountability, and sustainable resource exploitation.[23] However, 'closing the seas' can by no means be the solution regarding the pelagic areas extending beyond already expanded national jurisdictions or in relation to peaceful navigation and seaborne trade. Ultimately, the sustainable and equitable management of the world's oceans will depend on the ability of states and international institutions to balance sovereign rights with the collective responsibility to preserve marine spaces as a shared global heritage, ensuring they continue to sustain life, economic prosperity, and ecological balance on this blue planet we inhabit.

---

21 See, for instance, Richard Schiffman, 'A Global Ban on Fishing on the High Seas? The Time is Now. Interview with Marine Biologist Daniel Pauly', in *YaleEnvironment360*, September 27, 2018.

22 United Nations, *Agreement under the United Nations Convention on the Law of the Sea on the Conservation and Sustainable Use of Marine Biological Diversity of Areas beyond National Jurisdiction* (BBNJ Agreement), adopted 19 June 2023, not yet in force, UN Doc. A/CONF.232/2023/4. See also Todd Berry, *Sovereignty and the Limits of International Law: Regulating Areas beyond National Jurisdiction* (London: Routledge, 2024).

23 Although this can lead to severe issues in developing countries with limited resources and institutional resilience vis-à-vis corruption and foreign influences. For further details, see Alfonso Daniels et al., *Western Africa's Missing Fish: The Impacts of Illegal, Unreported and Unregulated Fishing and Under-Reported Catches by Foreign Fleets* (London: Overseas Development Institute, 2016).

Bibliography

Historical Sources

Doctrine

Barclay, William, *De Potestate Papae, an et quatenus in Reges et Principes seculares ius et imperium habeat* (Mussiponti: Iacobum Garnich, 1610).

Bellarmine, Robert, *On Temporal and Spiritual Authority: On Laymen or Secular People on the Temporal Power of the Pope. Against William Barclay on the Primary Duty of the Supreme Pontiff* (Indianapolis: Liberty Fund, 2012).

Bodin, Jean, *On Sovereignty. Four Chapters from the Six Books of the Commonwealth* [1576], edited by Julian H. Franklin (Cambridge: University Press, 2004).

Bonaert, Nicolaes, 'Textus inediti: Minos seu mare tutum', edited by Primitivo Mariño Gomes. *Archivum Historicum Societatis Iesu*, 61 (1992), 309–38.

Borough, John, *Sovereignty of the British Sea* [1651] (Edinburgh: W. Green & Son Ltd., 1920).

Burgus, Pietro B., *De dominio Serenissimae Genuensis Reipublicae in mari Ligustico* (Romae: D. Marcianus, 1641).

Caepolla, Bartholomaeus, *Tractatus de servitutibus: tam urbanorum, quam rusticorum praediorum* (Coloniæ Agrippinæ: apud Ioannem Gymnicum, 1616).

Cicero, *De officiis*, translated by Walter Miller (London/New York: William Heinemann Ltd./G. P. Putman's Sons, 1913).

Corpus Iuris Civilis, vol. I (*Institutiones – Digesta*), edited by Theodor Mommsen and Paul Krueger (Berolini: apud Weidmannos, 1872).

da Sassoferrato, Bartolo, *Tractatus de fluminibus*, or *Tyberiadis D. Bartoli De Saxoferrato, iurisconsultorum omnium facile principis, tractatus de fluminibus: tripertitus ab Hercyle Buttrigario sacrae* [...] *restitutus in lucem prodit* (London: Forgotten Books, 2018).

de Bracton, Henry, *De legibus et consuetudinibus Angliae*, edited by George E. Woodbine, vol. II (Oxford: University Press, 1922).

de Freitas, Serafin, *Do justo imperio asiático dos portugueses*, traducción de Miguel Pinto Meneses [1625] (Lisboa: Instituto Nacional de Investigação Científica, 1983).

de Freitas, Seraphin, *De iusto imperio Lusitanorum Asiatico*, Valladolid, H. Morillo, [1625], French translation in Alfred G. de Grandpont, *Freitas contre Grotius sur la liberté des mers, justification de la domination portugaise* (Paris: Aillaud, Gaillard & Cie, 1893).

de Ingenuis, Franciscus, *De iurisdictione Serenissimae Reispublicae Venetae in mare Adriaticum epistola Francisci de Ingenuis Germani, [...] ad Liberium Vicentium Hollandum adversus Johannem Baptistam Valenzolam Hispanum et Laurentium Moti-*

num Romanum qui iurisdictionem illam non pridem impugnare ausi sunt (Eleutheropoli [fictious location], 1619).

de Solórzano Pereira, Juan, *Disputationem de Indiarum iure* (Madrid: Tipografía Francisco Martínez, 1629).

de Ubaldis, Angelus, *Consilia D. Angeli de Ubaldis perusini...* (Francofurti: Typis Andrea Wecheli, 1575).

de Ubaldis, Baldus, *Commentaria in primam Digesti veteris partem* (Venezia: Giunti, 1572).

de Vitoria, Francisco, *On Civil Power* [1528], in *Political Writings*, edited by Anthony Pagden and Jeremy Lawrance (Cambridge: University Press, 1991).

de Vitoria, Francisco, *On the American Indians* (*De indis*) [1539], in *Political Writings*, edited by Anthony Pagden and Jeremy Lawrance (Cambridge: University Press, 1991).

de Vitoria, Francisco, *On the Law of War* (*De indis relectio posterior, sivi de iure belli*) [1539], in idem, *Political Writings*, edited by Anthony Pagden and Jeremy Lawrance (Cambridge: University Press, 2010).

Dee, John, *General and rare memorials pertayning to the perfect arte of nauigation annexed to the paradoxal cumpas...* (London: John Day, 1577).

Galiani, Ferdinando, *De' doveri dei principi neutrali verso i principi guerreggianti, e di questi verso i neutrali, libri due* (Napoli, 1782).

Gentili, Alberico, *De jure belli libri tres* [1588], translated by J. C. Rolfe (Oxford: Clarendon Press, 1933).

Gentili, Alberico, *Hispanicis advocationis libri dvo* [1613], trans. Frank Frost Abbott (Oxford: University Press, 1921).

Graswinckel, Dirk, *Maris liberi vindiciae adversus Gulielmum Welwodum britannici maritimi dominii assertorem* (The Hague: Adriani Vlag, 1652).

Graswinckel, Dirk, *Maris liberi vindiciae adversus Petrum Baptistam Burgum Ligustici maritimi dominii assertorem* (The Hague: Adriani Vlag, 1653).

Grocio, Hugo, *De la libertad de los mares* (Madrid: Instituto de Estudios Políticos, 1956).

Grotius, Hugo, *Commentary on the Law of Prize and Booty* [1604], edited by Martine J. van Ittersum (Indianapolis: Liberty Fund, 2006).

Grotius, Hugo, *De iure praedae commentarius* [1604], in James B. Scott (ed.), *The Classics of International Law* (Oxford: Clarendon Press, 1950).

Grotius, Hugo, *Mare Liberum* 1609–2009, original Latin text and English translation, edited by Robert Feenstra (Leiden: Brill, 2009).

Grotius, Hugo, *On the Law of War and Peace* [*De Iure Belli ac Pacis*, 1625], student edition, edited and annotated by Stephen C. Neff (Cambridge: University Press, 2012).

Grotius, Hugo, *The Freedom of the Seas: or, The Right Which Belongs to the Dutch to Take Part in the East Indian Trade*, ed. by R. Van Deman Magoffin (New York: Oxford: University Press, 1916).

Grotius, Hugo, *The Rights of War and Peace* [*De Iure Belli ac Pacis*, 1625], edited and with an introduction by Richard Tuck, 3 vols. (Indianapolis: Liberty Fund, 2005).

Liber iurium reipublicae genuensis [=Monumenta historiae patriae 7], vol. 2 (Torino: Officina regia, 1857).

Molloy, Charles, *De iure maritimo et navali* (London: printed for J. Bellinger, G. Dawes & R. Boulter, 1676).

Pace da Beriga, Giulio, *De dominio maris Hadriatici disceptatio*, [1619], original text reproduced in Guido Acquaviva e Tullio Scovazzi (cur.), *Il Dominio di Venezia sul Mare Adriatico nelle opere di Paolo Sarpi e Giulio Pace* (Milano: Giuffrè, 2007).

Releigh, Walter, *A Discourse of the Invention of Ships*, in *Works*, VIII [1650] (Oxford: University Press, 1829).

Sarpi, Paolo, *Dominio del Mare Adriatico della Serenissima Repubblica di Venezia*, in *Opere Varie del molto reverendo padre Paolo Sarpi dell'Ordine dei Servi di Maria teologo consultore della Serenissima Repubblica di Venezia divise in due tomi*, Helmstat, Jacopo Mulleri, 1750. The text of the 1750 edition is reported in Guido Acquaviva e Tullio Scovazzi (cur.), *Il Dominio di Venezia sul Mare Adriatico nelle opere di Paolo Sarpi e Giulio Pace* (Milano: Giuffrè, 2007).

Selden, John, *Mare clausum seu de dominio maris, libri duo* (London: W. Stanesbeius pro R. Meighen, 1635).

Selden, John, *Of the Dominion, or Ownership of the Sea. Two books. Translated into English and set forth with some Additional Evidences and Discourses* (London: William du Gard, 1652).

Squitinio della libertà veneta nel quale si adducono anche le raggioni dell'Imperio sopra la città et signoria di Venetia (anonymous work) (Mirandola: Giouanni Benincasa, 1612).

Suarez, Rodericus, *Allegationes et consilia quaedam ... Eiusdem exactissima in aliquas fori leges lectura ...* (Lugduni: apud haeredes Iacobi Iuntae, 1559).

The Digest of Justinian, English translation edited by Alan Watson, 4 vols. (Philadelphia: Pennsylvania University Press, 1985).

van Bynkershoek, Cornelius, *De dominio maris dissertatio* (Lugduni Batavorum: apud Joannem van Kerckhem, 1744).

van Bynkershoek, Cornelius, *De dominio maris dissertatio* [1744], translated by R. Van Deman Magoffin, Carnegie Endowment for International Peace (New York: Oxford University Press, 1923).

Vázquez y Menchaca, Fernando, *Controversiarum illustrium aliarumque usi frequentium libri tres*, Valladolid, Cuesta, 1931–1934. Edition by D. F. Rodríguez Alcalde; it reproduces the original Latin edition (Venice: apud Franciscum Rampazetum, 1564).

Warner, George (ed.), *The Libelle of Englyshe Polycye. A Poem on the Use of Sea Power, 1436* (Oxford: Clarendon Press, 1926).

Welwod, William, *An Abridgement of All Sea-Lawes, Gathered Forth of All Writings and Monuments Which Are to be Found among Any People or Nation, upon the Coasts of the Great Ocean and the Mediterranean Sea, and Specially Ordered and Disposed for the Use and Benefit of All Benevolent Sea-Farers within His Majesties Dominions of Great Britanne, Ireland and the Adjacent Isles Thereof* (London: Printed for Humfrey Lownes, for Thomas Man, 1613).

Welwod, William, *An Abridgement of All Sea-Lawes, Gathered Forth of All Writings and Monuments Which Are to be Found among Any People or Nation, upon the Coasts of the Great Ocean and the Mediterranean Sea, and Specially Ordered and Disposed for the Use and Benefit of All Benevolent Sea-Farers within His Majesties Dominions of Great Britanne, Ireland and the Adjacent Isles Thereof* (London: Printed by the Assignes of Ioane Man and Benjamin Fisher, 1636).

Welwod, William, *De dominio maris iuribusque ad dominium praecipae spectantibus assertio brevis ac methodical* (London: excudebat G. Fonti, 1615).

Welwod, William, *The Sea-Law of Scotland: Shortly Gathered and Plainly Dressed for the Reddy Use of All Sea-Fairingmen* (Edinburgh: Robert Waldegraue, 1590).

Zamboni de' Silvii, Francesco, *Del dominio del mare Adriatico, overo golfo di Venetia* (Venice: G. Zattoni, 1676).

Zamboni, Francesco, *Del dominio del mare Adriatico, overo golfo di Venetia* (Vicenza: F. Grossi, 1620).

State Practice and Diplomacy

Alberi, Eugenio (ed.), *Relazioni degli ambasciatori veneti al Senato durante il secolo decimosesto* (Firenze: Società editrice fiorentina [etc.], 1839–1863).

Barozzi, Nicolò and Berchet, Guglielmo (eds.), *Relazioni degli Stati Europei lette al Senato dagli ambasciatori veneti nel secolo decimosettimo* (Venezia: P. Naratovich, 1856–1877).

Calendar of State Papers Foreign: Elizabeth 1578–1583, vols. 12–17, edited A. J. Butler (London, 1901–1913), *British History Online*, http://www.british-history.ac.uk/cal-state-papers/foreign/vol13 [accessed 14 October 2019].

Calendar of State Papers Foreign: Elizabeth, 1559–1565, vols. 1–7, edited by J. Stevenson (London, 1865–1870), *British History Online*, http://www.british-history.ac.uk/cal-state-papers/foreign/vol2 [accessed 14 October 2019].

Calendar of State Papers Foreign: Elizabeth, 1566–1577, vols. 8–11, edited by A. J. Crosby (London, 1871–1880), *British History Online*, http://www.british-history.ac.uk/cal-state-papers/foreign/vol8 [accessed 14 October 2019].

Calendar of State Papers Foreign: Mary 1553–1558, edited by W. B. Turnbull (London, 1861), *British History Online*, http://www.british-history.ac.uk/cal-state-papers/foreign/mary [accessed 14 October 2019].

Calendar of State Papers, Spain, vol. 5, part 2, 1536–1538, edited by Pascual de Gayangos (London, 1888), British History Online, http://www.british-history.ac.uk/cal-state-papers/spain/vol5/no2 [accessed 5 May 2020].

Camden, William, *The history of the most renowned and victorious Princess Elizabeth, late queen of England: containing all the most important and remarkable passages of state, both at home and abroad (so far as they are linked with English affairs) during her long and prosperous reign*. Third edition (London: printed by M. Flesher for C. Harper [etc.], 1675).

Chaplais, Pierre, *English Medieval Diplomatic Practice*, part I, vol. I (London: Her Majesty's Stationery Office, 1982).

Coelho, José R., *Alguns documentos do Archivo Nacional da Torre do Tombo ácerca das navegações e conquistas portuguezas publicados por ordem do governo de sua majestade fidelissima ao celebrarse a commemoração quadricentenaria do descobrimento da America* (Lisboa: Imprensa Nacional, 1892).

Corbett, Julian S. (ed.), *Papers Relating to the Navy during the Spanish War, 1585–1587* (London: Printed for the Navy Records Society, 1898).

Davenport, Frances G., *European Treaties Bearing on the History of the United States and its Dependencies to 1648* (Washington: The Carnegie Institution, 1917).

de Barros y Sousa, Manuel F., Visconde de de Santarem, *Quadro elementar das relações políticas e diplomáticas de Portugal com as diversas potencias do mundo, desde o principio da monarchia Portugueza até aos nossos dias*, vol. XV (Lisboa: Tipographia da Academia Real das Sciencas, 1865).

de Sousa, Frei Luis, *Annaes de D. João III* (publicados por A. Herculano, Lisboa: Typ. da Sociedade Propagadora…, 1844).

Dias Dinis, António J. (ed.), *Monumenta Henricina, colectânea documental relativa ao Infante D. Henrique*, 15 vols (Coimbra: Oficinas Gráficas de Atlântida, 1960–1974).

Diplomatarium Danicum, online version: https://diplomatarium.dk/english.

Diplomatarium Norvegicum, online version where it is possible to search in the volumes I–XXIII of the printed edition of the collection; available at: https://www.dokpro.uio.no/dipl_norv/diplom_field_eng.html.

du Mont de Carels-Kroon, Jean, *Corps universel diplomatique du droit des gens; contenant vn recueil des traitez d'alliance, de paix, de trêve, de neutralité, de commerce, d'échange … & autres contrats, qui ont été faits en Europe, depuis le regne de l'empereur Charlemagne jusques à présent* (Amsterdam, chez P. Brunel, etc., 1726–31).

Fernández de Navarrete, Martín, *Colección de los viajes y descubrimientos que hicieron por mar los españoles desde fines del siglo XV: con varios documentos …*, II (*Documentos de Colon y de las primeras poblaciones*) (Madrid: Imprimeria Nacional, 1859).

García-Gallo, Alfonso, *Las bulas de Alejandro VI y el ordenamiento jurídico de la expansión portuguesa y castellana en África e Indias* (Madrid: Instituto Nacional de Estudios Jurídicos, 1958).

García-Gallo, Alfonso, *Las bulas de Alejandro VI y el ordenamiento jurídico de la expansión portuguesa y castellana en África e Indias* (Madrid: Instituto Nacional de Estudios Jurídicos, 1958).

Godinho, Vitorino M., *Documentos sôbre a expansão portuguesa* (Lisboa: Edições Cosmos, 1956).

Godinho, Vitorino M., *Documentos sôbre a expansão portuguesa*, Vols. I–II (Lisboa: Editorial Gleba, 1943–1944).

Grewe, Wilhelm G., *Fontes historiae iuris gentium*, I (1380 v. Chr./ B. C.-1493) (Berlin -New York: De Gruyter, 1992).

Grewe, Wilhelm G., *Fontes historiae iuris gentium*, II (1493–1815) (Berlin-New York: De Gruyter, 1992).

Hakluyt, Richard, *The Famous Voyage of Sir Francis Drake into the South Sea, and there hence about the Whole Globe of the Earth, Begun in the Year of our Lord 1577*, [1589], in *The Voyage of Sir Francis Drake around the Whole Globe* (London: Penguin, 2015).

Henderson, Ernest F., *Select Historical Documents of the Middle Ages* (London: George Bell & Sons, 1896).

Hughes, Paul L. and Larkin, James F. (eds.), *Tudor Royal Proclamations*, 3 vols. (New Haven, CT: Yale University Press, 1964–9).

Institutes of Justinian, translated by J. B. Moyle, Oxford, 1911 (Some emendations by CD.), made available online by the Ames Foundation: https://amesfoundation.law.harvard.edu/digital/CJCiv/JInst.pdf.

Isambert, François-André et al. (eds.), *Recueil général des anciennes lois françaises, depuis l'an 420 jusqu'à la Révolution de 1789*... (Paris: Belin-Leprieur, Verdière, 1822–133), 29 vols.

Laursen, Lars, *Danmark-Norges Traktater 1523–1750. Med dertil hørende Aktstykker*, 11 dele i 12 bind (København: Gad, 1905–1949).

Marsden, Reginald G., *Documents Relating to the Law and Custom of the Sea, 1205–1767*, 2 vols. (London: Printed for the Navy Records Society, 1915–1916). *Norges Gamle Love*, 'Recueil des anciennes Lois de Norvège', online version.

Ordenações Manuelinas, online version: http://www1.ci.uc.pt/ihti/proj/manuelinas/.

Pardessus, Jean-Marie, *Collection de lois maritimes antérieures au XVIIIe siècle*, 6 vols (Paris: Imprimerie Royale, 1828–45).

Polo, Marco, *The Description of the World* [*Il Milione*, 1298] (Indianapolis/Cambridge: Hackett Publishing Co., 2016).

Prothero, George W. (ed.), *Select Statutes and Other Constitutional Documents Illustrative of the Reign of Elizabeth and James I* (Oxford: Clarendon Press, 1913).

Rushworth, John, *Historical Collections of Private Passages of State, Weighty Matters in Law, Remarkable Proceedings in Five Parliaments: Beginning the Sixteenth Year of King James. Anno 1618, And Ending the Fifth Year of King Charles* [*sic*], *Anno 1629* (London: Printed by T. Newcomb for G. Thomason, 1659–1701).

Rymer, Thomas (ed.), *Foedera, conventiones, literæ, et cujuscunque generis acta publica, inter reges Angliæ et alios quosvis imperatores, reges, pontifices, principes, vel communitates, ab ineunte sæculo duodecimo, viz. ab anno 1101, ad nostra usque tempora habita aut tractate ...* (Hagæ éis: Apud Joannem Neaulme, 1742).

Rymer, Thomas (ed.), *Foedera, conventiones, literæ, et cujuscunque generis acta publica, inter reges Angliæ et alios* [...], 4 vols., revised ed. by Adam F. Clarke and Fred Hoolbroke (London, 1816–1869).

Suma Oriental of Tomé Pires, An Account of the East, from the Red Sea to Japan Written in Malacca and India 1512–1515, translated by Armando Cortesão (London: The Hakluyt Society, 1944).

Twiss, Travers (ed.), *The Black Book of the Admiralty*, vols. 4 (London: Longman & Co. et al., 1871–1876).

Modern Sources

Abulafia, David (ed.), *The New Cambridge Medieval History*, v, *1198–1300* (Cambridge: University Press, 1999).

Abulafia, David and Berend, Nora (eds.), *Medieval Frontiers: Concepts and Practices* (London: Routledge, 2002).

Abulafia, David, *The Boundless Sea. A Human History of the Oceans* (Oxford: University Press 2019).

Abulafia, David, *The Great Sea: A Human History of the Mediterranean* (Oxford: University Press, 2013).

Acerra, Martine and Martinière, Guy (eds.), *Coligny, les protestants et la mer* (Paris: Presses de l'Université Paris Sorbonne, 1997).

Acquaviva, Guido, 'Libertà o dominio dei mari: il caso della Santa Catarina', *Anuario de Derecho Internacional*, 17 (2001), 239–68.

Akashi, Kinji, *Cornelius van Bynkershoek: His Role in the History of International Law* (The Hague: Kluwer Law International, 1998).

Akerman, James R., *The Imperial Map: Cartography and the Mastery of Empire* (Chicago: University Press, 2009).

Alegria, Maria F., et al. (eds.), *História da Cartografia Portuguesa, séculos XV a XVII* (Porto: Fia de Palavra, 2012).

Alexandrowicz, Charles H., 'Freitas versus Grotius', *The British Yearbook of International Law*, 35 (1959), 162–82.

Alexandrowicz, Charles H., *An Introduction to the History of the Law of Nations in the East Indies (16th, 17th and 18th Centuries)* (Oxford: Clarendon Press, 1967).

Alexandrowicz, Charles H., *The Law of Nations in Global History*, edited by David Armitage and Jennifer Pitts (Oxford: University Press, 2017).

Allen, Paul C., *Philip III and the Pax Hispanica, 1598–1621: The Failure of Grand Strategy* (New Haven, CT: Yale University Press, 2000).

Allmand, Christopher (ed.), *The New Cambridge Medieval History, VII, 1415–1500* (Cambridge: University Press, 1998).

Allott, Philip, 'International Law and the Idea of History', *Journal of the History of International Law*, 1(1) (1999), 1–21.

Allott, Philip, 'Language, Method and the Nature of International Law', *British Yearbook of International Law*, 45 (1971), 79–135.

Alsop, James D.,'William Welwood, Anne of Denmark and the Sovereignty of the Sea', *The Scottish Historical Review*, 59(168) (1980), 171–4.

Alves Gaspar, Joaquim, 'From the Portolan Chart to the Latitude Chart: The Silent Cartographic Revolution', *Comité Français de Cartographie*, 216 (2013), 67–77.

Anand, Ram P., 'Maritime Practice in South-East Asia until 1600 A. D. and the Modern Law of the Sea', *The International and Comparative Law Quarterly*, 30(2) (1981), 440–54.

Anand, Ram P., 'The influence of history on the literature of international law', in Ronald St. John Macdonald and Douglas M. Johnston (eds.), *The Structure and Process of International Law: Essays in Legal Philosophy, Doctrine, and Theory* (The Hague: Martinus Nijhoff, 1983), 341–80.

Anand, Ram P., *Law of the Sea in Historical Perspective*, in *Changing Dimensions of International Law: An Asian Perspective* (Leiden/Boston: M. Nijhoff, 2006), 12–5.

Anand, Ram P., *Origin and Development of the Law of the Sea. History of International Law Revisited* (The Hague/Boston/London: M. Nijhoff, 1983).

Anand, Ram P., *Studies in International Law and History. An Asian Perspective* (Leiden/Boston: M. Nijhoff, 2004).

Añaños Meza, María C., 'El título de "sociedad y comunicación natural" de Francisco de Vitoria. Tras las huellas de su concepto a la luz de la teoría del dominio', *Anuario Mexicano de Derecho Internacional*, 12 (2012), 525–96.

Andersen, Per, *Legal Procedure and Practice in Medieval Denmark* (Leiden: Brill, 2011).

Anderson, John L., 'Piracy and World History: An Economic Perspective on Maritime Predation', *Journal of World History*, 6(2) (1995), 175–99.

Anderson, Roger C., *Naval Wars in the Levant, 1559–1853* (Princeton: University Press).

Andrews, Kenneth R., *Drake's Voyages: A re-assessment of their place in Elizabethan maritime expansion* (London: Weidenfeld & Nicolson, 1967).

Andrews, Kenneth R., *Elizabethan Privateering: English Privateering during the Spanish War, 1585–1603* (Cambridge: University Press, 1965).

Andrews, Kenneth R., *The Spanish Caribbean: Trade and Plunder, 1530–1630* (New Haven, CT: Yale University Press, 1978).

Angermann, Norbert and Friedland, Klaus (eds.), *Novgorod. Markt und Kontor der Hanse* (Cologne: Böhlau Verlag, 2002).

Anghie, Anthony, *Imperialism, Sovereignty and the Making of International Law* (Cambridge: University Press, 2004).

Anselmi, Silvana, *Pirati e corsari in Adriatico* (Silvana: Pesaro 1998).

Anthony Pagden (ed.), *The Languages of Political Theory in Early Modern Europe* (Cambridge: University Press, 1986).

Appleby, John C., *Under the Bloody Flag: Pirates of the Tudor Age* (Stroud: The History Press, 2009).

Armitage, David (ed.), *Theories of Empire, 1450–1800* (London: Routledge, 2016).

Armitage, David, *Foundations of Modern International Thought* (Cambridge: University Press, 2013).

Armitage, David, *The Ideological Origins of the British Empire* (Cambridge: University Press, 2000).

Arvidsson, Matilda and Bak McKenna, Miriam, 'The Turn to History in International Law and the Sources Doctrine: Critical Approaches and Methodological Imaginaries', *Leiden Journal of International Law*, 33(1) (2020), 37–56.

Ashburner, Walter, *Nomos Rhodion Nautikos. The Rodian Sea-Law* (Oxford: Clarendon Press, 1909).

Ashtor, Eliyahu, *Levant Trade in the Later Middle Ages* (Princeton: University Press, 1983).

Augeron, Mickaël and Guillemet, Dominique (dir.), *Champlain ou les portes du Nouveau Monde. Cinq siècles d'échanges entre le Centre-Ouest français et l'Amérique du Nord* (La Crèche: Geste Edition, 2004).

Augeron, Mickaël, 'Les élites calvinistes et la course anti-catholique à La Rochelle: attitudes, justifications et contestations dans les années 1570', *Anglophonia*, 17 (2005), 123–34.

Augeron, Mickaël, 'Pour "la défense et l'advencement de la vraye religion": Jacques de Sores, un corsaire au service de la Cause protestante', in idem, Didier Poton and Bertrand van Ruymbeke (eds.), *Les Huguenots et l'Atlantique: vol. I, Pour Dieu, la Cause ou les Affaires* (Paris: Presses de l'Université Paris-Sorbonne, 2009), 189–205.

Aymard, Maurice (cur.), *Storia d'Europa, IV, L'Età Moderna, Secoli XVI–XVIII* (Torino: Einaudi, 1995).

Backhaus, Gary and Murungi, John (eds.), *Colonial and Global Interfacings: Imperial Hegemonies and Democratizing Resistances* (Newcastle: Cambridge Scholars Press, 2007).

Baker, John, 'John Selden and English Legal History' in idem, *Collected Papers on English Legal History*, 3 vols. (Cambridge: University Press, 2013), II, 765–77.

Ball, Warwick, *Rome in the East: Transformation of an Empire* (London-New York: Routledge, 2016).

Ballard, George A., *Rulers of the Indian Ocean* (London: Duckworth, 1927).

Barcia Trelles, Camilo, 'Fernando Vázquez de Menchaca (1512–1569): l'école espagnole du droit international du XVIe siècle', *Collected Courses of the Hague Academy of International Law*, 67 (1939).

Barcia Trelles, Camilo, 'Fray Serafín de Freitas y el problema de la libertad oceánica', *Revista General de la Marina*, 130 (1946), 331–48.

Barrado Navascués, David. *Cosmography in the Age of Discovery and the Scientific Revolution* (Cham: Springer, 2023).

Barratt, D. M., 'The Publication of John Selden's *Mare Clausum*', *The Bodleian Library Record*, 7 (1964), 204–5.

Barzazi, Antonella, 'Paolo Sarpi', in *Dizionario biografico degli italiani*, vol. 90, 2017, Online Version: http://www.treccani.it/enciclopedia/paolo-sarpi_%28Dizionario-Biografico%29/.

Barzazi, Antonella, 'Paolo Sarpi', in Marco Sgarbi (ed.), *Encyclopedia of Renaissance Philosophy* (Cham: Springer International Publishing, 2015), online version: https://doi.org/10.1007/978-3-319-02848-4_359-2.

Bataillon, Marcel, *'Plus Oultre: la cour découvre le Nouveau Monde', Les fêtes de la Renaissance: II. Fêtes et cérémonies au temps de Charles V* (Paris: Éditions du CNRS, 1960).

Batson, Alexander, 'Mare Tutum: Thucydides, King Minos, and the Concept of the "Secure Sea" in Seventeenth-Century Maritime Law', *Grotiana*, 4 (15) (2024), 1–31.

Battesti, Michèle, 'La haute mer: une «chose commune»', *Stratégique*, 123(3) (2019), 67–86.

Battistella, Antonio, 'Una campagna navale veneto-spagnola in Adriatico poco conosciuta', *Archivio veneto-trìdentino*, 2 (1922), 58–119; 3 (1923), 1–78.

Beaujard, Philippe, 'The Indian Ocean in Eurasian and African World-Systems before the Sixteenth Century', *Journal of World History*, 16(4) (2005), 411–65.

Beazley, Raymond C., 'Prince Henry of Portugal and the African Crusade of the Fifteenth Century', *The American Historical Review*, 16(1) (1910), 11–23.

Begley, Vimala and de Puma, Richard D. (eds.), *Rome and India. The Ancient Sea Trade* (Madison: The University of Wisconsin Press, 1991).

Bellamy, Martin, *Christian IV and his Navy* (Leiden: Brill, 2006).

Bely, Lucien, *L'art de la paix en Europe: Naissance de la diplomatie moderne, XVIe–XVIIIe siècle* (Paris: Presses universitaires de France, 2007).

Benedict, Robert D., 'The Historical Position of The Rhodian Law', *Yale Law Journal*, 18(4) (1909), 223–42.

Bensabat Amzalak, Moses, *Trois précurseurs portugais: Santarém et les assurances. Freitas et la liberté des mers. Veiga et les opérations de bourse* (Paris: Librairie du Recueil Sirey, 1935).

Benson, Joel D., 'England, Holland, and the Fishing Wars', *Philosophy Study*, 5(9) (2015), 447–52.

Bentley, Jerry H., 'Sea and Ocean Basins as Frameworks of Historical Analysis', *Geographical Review*, 89(2) (1999), 215–24.

Benton, Lauren and Perl-Rosenthal, Nathan (eds.), *A World at Sea: Maritime Practices and Global History* (Philadelphia: University of Pennsylvania Press, 2020).

Benton, Lauren, 'Beyond Anachronism: Histories of International Law and Global Legal Politics', *Journal of the History of International Law*, 21(1) (2019), 7–40.

Benton, Lauren, 'Legal Spaces of Empire: Piracy and the Origins of Oceanic Regionalism', *Comparative Studies in Society and History*, 47 (2005), 700–24.

Benton, Lauren, *A Search for Sovereignty, Law and Geography in European Empires, 1400–1900* (Cambridge: University Press, 2012).

Benton, Lauren, *Law and Colonial Cultures: Legal Regimes in World History, 1400–1900* (Cambridge: University Press, 2002).

Benzoni, Gino, *Venezia nell'età della controriforma* (Milano: Mursia, 1973).

Berkowitz, David S., *John Selden's Formative Years: Politics and Society Early Seventeenth Century England* (Washington D.C.: Folger Shakespeare Library, 1988).

Berman, Harold J., *Law and Revolution, I: The Formation of the Western Legal Tradition* (Cambridge, MA: Harvard University Press, 1983).

Berman, Harold J., *Law and Revolution, II: The Impact of the Protestant Reformations on the Western Legal Tradition* (Cambridge, MA: Harvard University Press, 2006).

Bernal, Antonio-Miguel, *Monarquía e imperio*, vol. III de *Historia de España* (Madrid: Editorial Crítica, 2007).

Berry, Todd, *Sovereignty and the Limits of International Law: Regulating Areas beyond National Jurisdiction* (London: Routledge, 2024).

Besson, Samantha and d'Aspremont, Jean (eds.), *The Oxford Handbook of the Sources of International Law* (Oxford: University Press, 2017).

Bethencourt, Francisco and Curto, Diogo R. (eds.), *A Expansão Marítima Portuguesa, 1400–1800* (Lisbon: Edições 70, 2010).

Bettanini, Anton M., 'Alvise Contarini Ambasciatore Veneto (1597–1651)', *Rivista di Studi Politici Internazionali*, 9(3) (1942), 371–416.

Bianchi, Andrea, Peat, Daniel and Windsor, Matthew (eds.), *Interpretation in International* Law (Oxford: University Press, 2015).

Biarnès, Pierre, *La Route de la Soie, une histoire géopolitique* (Paris: Ellipses Marketing, 2014).

Bick, Alexander, *Governing the Free Sea: The Dutch West India Company and Commercial Politics, 1618–1645* (Ph.D. dissertation, Princeton University, 2012).

Biggar, Henry P., *The Precursors of Jacques Cartier, 1497–1534* (London: Forgotten Books, 2016).

Billé, Franck, Mehendale, Sanjyot and Lankton, James (eds.), *The Maritime Silk Road. Global Connectivities, Regional Nodes, Localities* (Amsterdam: University Press, 2022).

Billion, Didier and Ventura, Christophe, *Désoccidentalisation. Repenser l'ordre du monde* (Agone: Marseille, 2023).

Bin, Alberto, *La Repubblica di Venezia e la questione adriatica, 1600–1620* (Il Veltro: Roma, 1992).

Birks, Peter, 'The Roman Concept of *Dominium* and the Idea of Absolute Ownership', *Acta Juridica*, 31 (1985), 1–38,

Birocchi, Italo et al. (cur.), *Dizionario biografico dei giuristi italiani (secc. XII–XX)*, vol. II (Bologna: Il Mulino, 2013).

Bjork, David K., 'Piracy in the Baltic, 1375–1398', *Speculum, a Journal of Mediaeval History*, 18(1) (1943), 39–68.

Bjork, David K., 'The Peace of Stralsund, 1370', *Speculum, a Journal of Mediaeval History*, 7(4) (1932), 447–76.

Black, Jeremy, *European Warfare, 1494–1660* (London: Routledge, 2002).

Black, Jeremy, *The British Seaborne Empire* (New Haven, CT: Yale University Press, 2004).

Blake, John W., *European Beginnings in West Africa, 1454–1478* (Westport: Greenwood Press, 1969).

Blakemore, Richard and Davey, James (eds.), *The Maritime World of Early Modern Britain* (Amsterdam: University Press, 2020).

Blockmans, Wim, Krom, Mikhail and Wubs-Mrozewicz, Justyna (eds.), *The Routledge Handbook of Maritime Trade around Europe, 1300–1600* (London: Routledge, 2017).

Blom, Hans (ed.), *Property, Piracy and Punishment: Hugo Grotius on War and Booty in De Jure Praedae. Concepts and Contexts* (Leiden: Brill, 2009).

Blunden, Margaret, 'Geopolitics and the Northern Sea Route', *International Affairs*, 88(1) (2012), 115–29.

Booth, Ken, *Law, Force and Diplomacy at Sea* (London: George Allen & Unwin, 1985).

Borschberg, Peter, 'Hugo Grotius' Theory of Trans-Oceanic Trade Regulation: Revisiting *Mare Liberum* (1609)', (Aug. 2006), IILJ Working Paper No. 2005/14.

Borschberg, Peter, 'The Seizure of the Sta. Catarina Revisited: The Portuguese Empire in Asia, VOC Politics and the Origins of the Dutch-Johor Alliance (1602–1616)', *Journal of Southeast Asian Studies*, 33(1) (2002), 31–62.

Borschberg, Peter, *Hugo Grotius, the Portuguese and Free Trade in the East Indies* (Singapore: NUS Press, 2011).

Bosbach, Franz, *Monarchia universalis. Storia di un concetto cardine della politica europea (secoli XVI–XVIII)* (Milano: Vita e Pensiero, 1998).

Bottin, Michel, 'Droit romain et jus commune. Considérations sur les fondements juridiques de la liberté des mers', in *Droit International et coopération internationale. Hommage à Jean André Touscoz* (Nice: France Europe Éditions, 2007), 1225–38.

Bottin, Michel, 'Grotius et la liberté du commerce maritime. Itinéraire d'une contradiction', in *Actes de la journée d'études sur le commerce maritime*, organisée par le

LexFEIM, Université du Havre, 13 novembre 2014, *Annuaire de droit maritime et océanique*, 33 (2015).

Boulnois, Luce, *La Route de la Soie* (Paris: Olizane 2010).

Bouwsma, William J., *Venice and the Defense of Republican Liberty: Renaissance Values in the Age of the Counter Reformation* (Berkeley: University of California Press, 1984).

Bouza Álvarez, Fernando, *Portugal en la monarquía Hispánica (1580–1640), Felipe II, las cortes de Tomar y la génesis del Portugal Católico* (Ph.D. dissertation, Madrid: Universidad Complutense de Madrid, 1987).

Boxer, Charles R., *The Dutch Seaborne Empire, 1600–1800* (London: Hutchinson, 1965).

Boxer, Charles R., *The Portuguese Seaborne Empire, 1415–1825* (London: Hutchinson, 1969).

Boyajian, James C., *Portuguese Trade in Asia under the Habsburgs, 1580–1640* (Baltimore and London: The Johns Hopkins University Press, 1993).

Braddick, Michael J. (ed.), *The Oxford Handbook of the English Revolution* (Oxford: University Press, 2015).

Bradley, Peter T., *The Lure of Peru: Maritime Intrusion into the South Sea, 1598–1701* (London: Palgrave McMillan, 1989).

Branch, Jordan, *The Cartographic State: Maps, Territory and the Origins of Sovereignty* (Cambridge: University Press, 2014).

Brand, Hanno and Knol, Egge (red.), *Koggen, kooplieden en kantoren: de Hanze, een praktisch netwerk* (Hilversum/Groningen: Uitgeverij Verloren/ Groninger Museum, 2009).

Braudel, Fernand and Duby, George (eds.), *La Méditerranée. II: Les hommes et l'héritage* (Paris: Flamarrion, 1986).

Braudel, Fernand, *Civilization and Capitalism, 15th–18th Century, Vol. I: The Structure of Everyday Life: The Limits of the Possible* (Berkeley: University of California Press, 1981).

Braudel, Fernand, *The Mediterranean and the Mediterranean World in the Age of Philip II* (New York: Harper, 1976), vol. II.

Brendan Bradshaw and John Morrill (eds.), *The British Problem, c.1534–1707: State Formation in the Atlantic Archipelago* (London: Macmillan Education, 1996).

Brett, Annabel, Donaldson, Megan and Koskenniemi, Martti (eds.), *History, Politics, Law* (Cambridge: University Press, 2021).

Brett, Annabel, *Liberty, Right and Nature: Individual Rights in Later Scholastic Thought* (Cambridge: University Press, 1997).

Brightwell, Peter, 'The Spanish System and the Twelve Years' Truce', *The English Historical Review*, 89(351) (1974), 270–92.

Briquel, Dominique, 'The Punishment of the Hellespont by Xerxes: Perception of Religious Behaviour of the Enemy in Conflict Situations', *Graeco-Latina Brunensia*, 21(2) (2016), 51–60.

Brito Vieira, Monica, 'Mare Liberum vs. Mare Clausum: Grotius, Freitas, and Selden's Debate on Dominion over the Seas', *Journal of the History of Ideas*, 64(3) (2003), 361–77.

Brook, Timothy, *Mr. Selden's Map of China: Decoding the Secrets of a Vanished Cartographer* (New York: Bloomsbury Press, 2013).

Brotton, Jerry, *A History of the World in Twelve Maps* (London: Allen Lane, 2012).

Brotton, Jerry, *Great Maps: The World's Masterpieces Explored and Explained* (London: DK, 2014).

Brown, Stephen R., *Merchant Kings, when Companies Ruled the World, 1600–1900* (New York: Thomas Dunne Books, 2010).

Brüel, Erik, *International Straits. A Treatise on International Law: The General Legal Position of International Straits* (vol. I) (London: Sweet & Maxwell, 1947).

Brüel, Erik, *International Straits. Straits Comprised by Positive Regulations* (vol. II) (London: Sweet & Maxwell, 1947).

Brummett, Palmira, *Ottoman Seapower and Levantine Diplomacy in the Age of Discovery* (Albany: State of New York University Press, 1994).

Brundage, James A., *Medieval Canon Law* (London: Longman, 1995).

Buchet, Christian (ed.), *The Sea in History* (4 vols.) (Woodbridge: Boydell Press, 2017).

Buchet, Christian, *La grande histoire vue de la mer* (Paris: Cherche-Midi, 2017).

Buisseret, David (ed.), *The Oxford Companion to World Exploration*, Vols. I (A–L) and II (M–Z) (Oxford: University Press, 2007).

Bull, Hedley and Watson, Adam (eds.), *The Expansion of International Society* (Oxford: University Press, 1984).

Bull, Hedley, Benedict Kingsbury and Adam Roberts (eds.), *Hugo Grotius and International Relations* (Oxford: University Press, 1990).

Burdon, Peter D. and Martel, James (eds.), *The Routledge Handbook of Law and the Anthropocene* (London: Routledge, 2023).

Burns, J. H. (ed.), *The Cambridge History of Political Thought 1450–1700* (Cambridge: University Press, 1991).

Busmann, Hendrik, *Sovereign of the Seas: die skulpturen des Britischen königsschiffes von 1637* (Hamburg: Convent, 2002).

Butler, Geoffrey and Maccoby, Simon, *The Development of International Law* (London: Longman, 1928).

Cacciavillani, Ivone, *Paolo Sarpi: la guerra delle scritture del 1606 e la nascita della nuova Europa* (Venezia: Corbo e Fiore, 2005).

Caetano, Marcello, 'Introduçao', en Serafin de Freitas, *Do Justo imperio asiático dos portugueses*, traducción de Miguel Pinto Meneses (Lisboa: Instituto Nacional de Investigação Científica, 1983), 7–86.

Caffio, Fabio, Carnimeo, Nicolò and Leandro, Antonio, *Elementi di diritto e geopolitica degli spazi marittimi* (Bari: Caciucchi Editore, 2013).

Cahen, Raphael, Dhondt, Frederik and Fiocchi Malaspina, Elisabetta, 'L'essor récent de l'histoire du droit international', *Clio@Thémis*, 18 (2020), 1–7.

Calafat, Guillaume et Grenet, Mathieu, *Méditerranées. Une histoire des mobilités humaines (1492–1750)* (Paris: Éditions du Seuil, 2019).

Calafat, Guillaume, 'The "battle of the books" in the Mediterranean: sovereignty, jurisdiction and free ports during the seventeenth century', in Peter Burschel and Sünne Juterczenka (eds.), *Das Meer. Maritime Welten in der Frühen Neuzeit – The Sea. Maritime Worlds in the early Modern Period* (Cologne: Böhlau, 2021), 635–52.

Calafat, Guillaume, *Une mer jalousée, Contribution à l'histoire de la souveraineté (Méditerranée,* XVIIe *siècle)* (Paris: Points, 2023).

Calasso, Francesco, 'Iurisdictio del diritto comune classico', in *Studi in onore di Vincenzo Arangio-Ruiz nel* XLV *anno del suo insegnamento* (Napoli: Jovene, 1953), 423–43.

Calasso, Francesco, *I glossatori e la teoria della sovranità. Studio di diritto comune pubblico* (Milano: Giuffrè, 1957).

Camarda, Guido, Corrieri, Salvatore and Scovazzi, Tullio, *La formazione del diritto marittimo nella prospettiva storica* (Milano: Giuffrè Editore, 2010).

Canning, Joseph, *A History of Medieval Political Thought: 300–1450* (London: Routledge, 1996).

Canning, Joseph, *The Political Thought of Baldus de Ubaldis* (Cambridge: University Press, 1987).

Caracciolo-Aricò, Angela (cur.), *L'impatto della scoperta dell'America nella cultura veneziana* (Roma: Bulzoni, 1990).

Cardim, Pedro, et al. (eds.), *Polycentric Monarchies: How did Early Modern Spain and Portugal Achieve and Maintain a Global Hegemony?* (Eastbourne: Sussex Academic Press, 2012).

Cardini, Franco, *Europa e Islam, storia di un malinteso* (Bari: Laterza, 2006).

Carlton, Charles, *Charles I. The Personal Monarch* (London: Routledge, 1995).

Carter, Charles H., 'Gondomar: Ambassador to James I', *The Historical Journal*, 7(2) (1964), 189–208.

Casati, Luigi A., *La guerra di Chioggia e la pace di Torino: Saggio storico con documenti inediti* (Firenze: Le Monnier, 1866), 248–54.

Cassi, Aldo A. and Sciumè, Alberto (cur.), *Dalla civitas Maxima al totus Orbis: diritto comune europeo e ordo iuris "globale" tra età moderna e contemporanea* (Soveria Mannelli: Rubbettino, 2007).

Cassi, Aldo A., *Ius Commune tra vecchio e nuovo mondo. Mari, terre, oro nel diritto della Conquista* (Milano: Giuffrè Editore, 2004).

Castagnos, Pierre, *Richelieu face à la mer* (Rennes: Éditions Ouest-France, 1989).

Castañeda Delgado, Paulino, 'La interpretación teocrática de las bulas alejandrinas', *Anuario Mexicano de Historia del Derecho*, 5 (1993), 20–59.

Castañeda Delgado, Paulino, *La teocracia pontifical en las controversias sobre el Nuevo Mundo* (México: UNAM, Instituto de Investigaciones Jurídicas, 1996).

Cattelan, Stefano and Dhondt, Frederik (eds.), *Small Power Neutrality and the Law of the Sea in the Long Eighteenth Century (1650–1800). Law as Argument in the Pelagic Arena* (Leiden/Boston: Brill, 2025).

Cattelan, Stefano, 'Challenging empires: pirates, privateers and the europeanisation of ocean spaces (c.1500–1650)', in Giuseppina de Giudici, Dante Fedele and Elisabetta Fiocchi Malaspina (cur.), *Soggettività contestate e diritto internazionale in età moderna* (Roma: Historia et ius, 2023), 125–51.

Cattelan, Stefano, 'Claims of Dominion and the Freedom of the Sea: Diplomatic Tensions between England and Denmark-Norway in the Late Tudor Period', *Journal on European History of Law*, 12(2) (2021), 29–42.

Cattelan, Stefano, 'Cristiano IV di Danimarca-Norvegia (r. 1588–1648): potere navale e diplomazia nell'Europa del Nord', *Nuova antologia militare*, 3(11) (2022), 195–228.

Cattelan, Stefano, 'Iberian Expansion over the Oceans: Law and Politics of Mare Clausum on the Threshold of Modernity (XV–XVI centuries)', *Historia et ius*, 18 (2020), 1–28.

Cattelan, Stefano, 'In the Shadow of the Great Powers: Freedom of the Sea and Neutrality in the Long Eighteenth Century', *Grotiana*, 44(1) (2023), 145–53.

Cattelan, Stefano, 'Maritime warfare in Old Regime Europe' in R. Lesaffer (ed.), *The Cambridge History of International Law, Vol. 6. Part 2: International Law in Ancien Regime Europe, 1660–1776* (Cambridge: University Press, 2025), 551–87.

Cattelan, Stefano, 'Review article of: Ideologies of Western Naval Power, c.1500–1815', *The Mariner's Mirror*, 109(1) (2023), 104–7.

Cattelan, Stefano, 'The Defence of Venetian Dominion over the Adriatic Sea: Situating Paolo Sarpi c 1600–1625', *Comparative Legal History*, 9(2) (2021), 177–207.

Cattelan, Stefano, 'Warfare on land in Old Regime Europe', in Randall Lesaffer (ed.), *The Cambridge History of International Law, Vol. 6. Part 2: International Law in Ancien Regime Europe, 1660–1776* (Cambridge: University Press, 2025), 517–50.

Cavaller, Georg, 'Vitoria, Grotius, Pufendorf, Wolff and Vattel: Accomplices of European Colonialism and Exploitation or True Cosmopolitans?', *The Journal of the History of International Law*, 10(2) (2008), 181–209.

Cavanagh, Edward (ed.), *Empire and Legal Thought. Ideas and Institutions from Antiquity to Modernity* (Leiden/Boston: Brill/Nijhoff, 2020).

Cavanagh, Edward, 'Prescription and Empire from Justinian to Grotius', *The Historical Journal*, 60(2) (2017), 273–99.

Cerezo Martínez, Ricardo, *La cartografía náutica española en los siglos XIV, XV y XVI* (Madrid: Editorial CSIC, 1994).

Cessi, Roberto, *La Repubblica di Venezia e il problema adriatico* (Padova: Cedam, 1953).

Cessi, Roberto, *Politica ed economia di Venezia nel Trecento* (Roma: Edizioni di Storia e Letteratura, 1952).

Chabod, Federico, *La politica di Paolo Sarpi* (Roma-Venezia: Istituto per la collaborazione culturale, 1962).

Chadwick, Mark, *Piracy and the Origins of Universal Jurisdiction: On Stranger Tides?* (Leiden: Brill, 2019).

Chambers, David S, *The Imperial Age of Venice, 1380–1580* (London: Thames & Hudson, 1970).

Chambers, David S. and Pullan, Brian S. (eds.), *Venice, A Documentary History, 1450–1630* (Toronto: University Press, 1992).

Chang, Kuei-Sheng, 'The Maritime Scene in China at the Dawn of Great European Discoveries', *Journal of the American Oriental Society*, 94(3) (1974), 347–59.

Chaplin, Joyce E., *Round about the Earth: Circumnavigation from Magellan to Orbit* (New York: Simon & Schuster, 2012).

Chaudhuri, Kirti N., 'European trade with India', in Tapan Raychaudhuri and Irfan Habib (eds.), *The Cambridge Economic History of India, vol. I: c.1200–c.1750* (Cambridge: University Press, 1982), 382–407.

Chaudhuri, Kirti N., 'The Portuguese Maritime Empire, Trade, and Society in the Indian Ocean during the Sixteenth Century', *Portuguese Studies*, 8 (1992), 57–70.

Checa Cremades, Fernando, *Carlos V. La imagen del poder en el Renacimiento* (Madrid: El Viso, 1999).

Cheyette, Frederic L., 'The Sovereign and the Pirates, 1332', *Speculum*, 45(1) (1970), 40–68.

Cheynet, Jean-Claude (dir.), *Le monde byzantin: Tome 2, L'Empire byzantin 641–1204* (Paris: Presses universitaires de France, 2006).

Childs, Wendy R., 'Anglo-Portuguese Trade in the Fifteenth Century', *Transactions of the Royal Historical Society*, 2 (1992), 195–219.

Christian, David, 'Silk Roads or Steppe Roads? The Silk Roads in World History', *Journal of World History*, 11(1) (2000), 1–26.

Chudoba, Bohdan, *Spain and the Empire, 1519–1643* (New York: Octagon Books, 1969).

Cialdea, Basilio, *La formazione dell'ordinamento marittimo nelle relazioni internazionali (secoli XIV–XVIII)*, 2 vols. (Milano: Giuffrè, 1959).

Cipolla, Carlo M., *La odisea de la plata española: conquistadores, piratas y mercaderes* (Barcelona: Critica, 1999).

Cipolla, Carlo M., *Vele e cannoni* (Bologna: Il Mulino, 2011).

Clark, George N. and Van Eysinga, Willem J. M., *The Colonial Conferences between England and the Netherlands in 1613 and 1615*, part I (Leiden: Brill, 1940).

Clark, George N. and Van Eysinga, Willem J. M., *The Colonial Conferences between England and the Netherlands in 1613 and 1615*, part II (Leiden: Brill, 1951).

Clark, George N., 'Grotius's East India Mission to England', *Transactions of the Grotius Society*, 20 (1934), 45–84.

Clendinnen, Inga, *Ambivalent Conquests: Maya and Spaniard in Yucatan, 1517–1570* (Cambridge: University Press, 1987).

Clulow, Adam, 'European Maritime Violence and Territorial Sates in Early Modern Asia, 1600–1650', *Itinerario*, 33(3) (2009), 72–94.

Constantinou, Costas M., *States of Political Discourse: Words, Regimes, Seditions* (London: Taylor & Francis, 2004).

Contreras, Sebastián, 'Derecho natural, derecho de gentes y libertad de los mares en Fernando Vásquez de Menchaca', *International Law, Revista Colombiana de Derecho Internacional* 24 (2014), 169–91.

Coppolaro, Lucia and McKenzie, Francine (eds.), *A Global History of Trade and Conflict since 1500* (London: Palgrave Macmillan, 2013).

Cordingly, David, *Storia della pirateria* (Milano: Mondadori, 2003).

Cortesão, Armando, *History of Portuguese Cartography* (Lisboa: Junta de Investigações do Ultramar, 1969).

Costa, Pietro, *Iurisdictio. Semantica del potere politico nella pubblicistica medievale* (Roma: Bulzoni, 2002).

Cottret, Bernard, *La royauté au féminin: Élisabeth Ire d'Angleterre* (Paris: Fayard, 2009).

Coward, Barry, *The Stuart Age – England, 1603–1714* (London: Routledge, 2011).

Cozzi, Gaetano (cur.), *Stato, società e giustizia nella repubblica Veneta* (sec. XV–XVIII), 2 vols. (Milano: Jouvence, 1980).

Cozzi, Gaetano, *Il doge Nicolo Contarini: Ricerche sul patriziato veneziano agli inizi del seicento* (Venezia: Istituto per la Collaborazione Culturale, 1958).

Cozzi, Gaetano, Knapton, Michael and Scarabello, Giovanni, *La Repubblica di Venezia nell'età moderna: dal 1517 alla fine della Repubblica*, vol. 2 (Torino: UTET, 1992).

Cozzi, Gaetano, *Paolo Sarpi tra Venezia e l'Europa* (Torino: Einaudi, 1978).

Cozzi, Gaetano, *Repubblica di Venezia e stati italiani. Politica e giustizia dal secolo XVI al secolo XVIII* (Torino: Einaudi, 1982).

Craven, Matthew, Fitzmaurice, Malgosia and Vogiatzi, Maria (eds.), *Time, History and International Law* (Leiden: Brill, 2007).

Crawford, Barbara E., 'The Pawning of Orkney and Shetland: A Reconsideration of the Events of 1460-9', *The Scottish Historical Review*, 48(145) (1969), 35–53.

Croft, Pauline, *King James* (New York: Palgrave Macmillan, 2003).

Crouzet-Pavan, Élisabeth, *Venise triomphante, les horizons d'un mythe* (Paris: Éditions Albin Michel, 1999).

Crouzet-Pavan, Élisabeth, *Venise, VIe–XXIe siècle* (Paris: Belin, 2021).

Crowley, Roger, *City of Fortune, How Venice Won and Lost a Naval Empire* (London: Faber & Faber, 2011).

Cruz Barney, Oscar, *El combate a la piratería en Indias: 1555–1700* (Ciudad de México: Oxford University Press, 1999).

Cueto, Ronald, '1580 and All That ...: Philip II and the Politics of the Portuguese Succession', *Portuguese Studies*, 8 (1992), 150–69.

Cust, Richard, *Charles I: A Political Life* (London: Pearson Longman, 2005).

Daniels, Alfonso, et al., *Western Africa's Missing Fish: The Impacts of Illegal, Unreported and Unregulated Fishing and Under-Reported Catches by Foreign Fleets* (London: Overseas Development Institute, 2016).

Daru, Pierre, *Histoire de la République de Venise, des origines à la Bataille de Lépant* (Paris: Robert Laffont, 2004).

Dauchy, Serge et al. (eds.), *The Formation and Transmission of Western Legal Culture, 150 Books that Made the Law in the Age of Printing* (New York: Springer, 2016).

Davey, James (ed.), *Tudor and Stuart Seafarers. The Emergence of a Maritime Nation, 1485–1707* (London: Adlard Coles, 2018).

Davey, James and Blakemore, Richard (eds.), *The Maritime World of Early Modern Britain* (Amsterdam: University Press, 2020).

Davies, Arthur, 'The Date of Juan de La Cosa's World Map and its Implications for American Discovery', *The Geographical Journal*, 142(1) (1976), 111–6.

Davies, Godfrey, *The Early Stuarts, 1603–1660* (Oxford: Clarendon Press, 1959).

Davies, J. D., James, Alan and Rommelse, Gijs (eds.), *Ideologies of Western Naval Power, c.1500–1815* (London: Routledge, 2021).

Davis, Ralph, *English Overseas Trade, 1500–1700* (London: Macmillan, 1985).

de Azevedo, Luiz C., 'O reinado de D. Manuel e as Ordenações Manuelinas', *Revista Da Faculdade De Direito, Universidade De São Paulo*, 95 (2000), 19–32.

de Bom, Erik et al. (eds.), *Early Modern Sovereignties. Theory and Practice of a Burgeoning Concept in the Netherlands* (Leiden: Brill-Nijhoff, 2020).

de Brossard, Maurice, 'La France de la Renaissance et ses rois face aux problèmes océaniques', *Revista da Universidade de Coimbra*, 32 (1986), 299–328.

de Córdova Miralles, Alvaro F., *Alejandro VI y los Reyes Católicos: Relaciones político-eclesiásticas (1492–1503)* (Roma: Edizioni della Santa Croce, 2005).

de Cortázar Fernando G. and Gonzàlez Vesga, José M., *Storia della Spagna* (Milano: Bompiani, 2001).

de la Rasilla del Moral, Ignacio, 'The Problem of Periodization in the History of International Law', *Law and History Review*, 37(1) (2019), 275–308.

de la Rasilla del Moral, Ignacio, 'The Shifting Origins of International Law', *Leiden Journal of International Law*, 28(3) (2015), 419–40.

de la Rasilla del Moral, Ignacio, *International Law and History: Modern Interfaces* (Cambridge: University Press, 2021).

de la Roncière, Charles, *Histoire de la marine française – III, Les guerres d'Italie, liberté de mers* (Paris: Libraire Plon, 1906).

de la Roncière, Charles, *Histoire de la marine française – IV, En quête d'un empire colonial* (Paris: Libraire Plon 1910).

de Madariaga, Salvador, *The Rise of the Spanish American Empire* (Westport: Greenwood Press, 1975).

del Vecchio, Antonio, *La legge nell'Oceano. Ugo Grozio e le origini dello spazio politico moderno* (Bologna: Il Mulino, 2021).

de Mas Latrie, René, 'Du Droit de marque ou droit de représailles au Moyen Âge', *Bibliothèque de l'École des chartes*, 27 (1866), 529–77.

de Oliveira Marques, Antonio H., *History of Portugal* (New York: Columbia University Press, 1976).

de Pauw, Frans, *Grotius and the Law of the Sea* (Bruxelles: Editions de l'Institut de Sociologie, 1965).

De ruysscher, Dave et al. (eds.), *The Company in Law and Practice: Did Size Matter? (Middle Ages–Nineteenth Century)* (Leiden/Boston: Brill-Nijhoff, 2017).

de Smet, Ingrid A. R., *Menippean Satire and the Republic of Letters, 1581–1655* (Genève: Librairie Droz, 1996).

de Sousa Pinto, Paulo J., *No extremo da redonda esfera: relaçoes luso-castelhanas na Ásia, 1565–1640 – um ensaio sobre os impérios ibéricos* (Ph.D. dissertation, Lisboa: Universidade Católica Portuguesa, 2010).

de Souza, Philip, 'Rome's Contribution to the Development of Piracy', *Memoirs of the American Academy in Rome*, 6 (2008), 71–96.

de Souza, Philip, *Piracy in the Graeco-Roman World* (Cambridge: University Press, 1999).

de Vivo, Filippo, 'Archives of Speech: Recording Diplomatic Negotiation in Late Medieval and Early Modern Italy', *European History Quarterly*, 46 (2016), 519–44.

de Vivo, Filippo, 'Historical justifications of Venetian Power in the Adriatic', *Journal of the History of Ideas*, 64(2) (2003), 159–76.

de Vivo, Filippo, 'La publication comme enjeu polémique: Venise au début du XVIIe siècle', in Jouhaud, Christian and Viala, Alain (dir.), *De la publication: entre Renaissance at Lumières* (Paris: Fayard, 2012), 161–75.

de Vivo, Filippo, *Information and Communication in Venice. Rethinking Early Modern Politics* (Oxford: University Press, 2019).

de Vries, Jan and Van der Woude, Ad, *The First Modern Economy: Success, Failure, and Perseverance of the Dutch Economy (1500–1815)* (Cambridge: University Press, 1997).

de Witte, Charles-Martial, 'Les bulles pontificales et l'expansion portugaise au XVe siècle', *Revue d'histoire ecclésiastique*, 48 (1958), 683–718.

Decock, Wim and Oosterhuis, Janwillem (eds.), *Great Christian Jurists in the Low Countries* (Cambridge: University Press, 2021).

Degn, Ole (ed.), *The Sound Toll at Elsinore, Politics, shipping and the Collection of Duties 1429–1857* (Chicago: University Press, 2018).

del Castillo, Lilian (ed.), *Law of the Sea, from Grotius to the International Tribunal for the Law of the Sea: Liber Amicorum Judge Hugo Caminos* (Leiden: Brill, 2015).

del Negro, Piero, 'La politica militare di Venezia e lo stato da mar nel Sei-Settecento', *Studi veneziani*, 39 (2000), 113–21.

Delafosse, Marcel, 'Les corsaires protestants à La Rochelle (1570–1577)', *Bibliothèque de l'école des chartes*, 121 (1963), 187–217.

Derry, Thomas K., *A History of Scandinavia* (London: George Allen & Unwin, 1979).

Descendre, Romain, 'Quand la mer est territoire: 'Paolo Sarpi et le «Dominio del mare Adriatico»', *Studi Veneziani* (Pisa: Istituti Editoriali e Poligrafici Internazionali, 2008), 55–73.

Deschamps, Léon, 'Un colonisateur du temps de Richelieu: Isaac de Razilly', *Revue de géographie*, 19 (1886), 273–84.

Dhondt, Frederik 'The historiography of international law on the European continent', in Lesaffer, Randall and Peters, Anne (eds.), *The Historiography of International Law, vol. I of The Cambridge History of International* Law (Cambridge: University Press, 2024), 244–72.

Dhondt, Frederik, '*Delenda est haec Carthago*. The Ostend Company as a Problem of European Great Power Politics (1722–1727)', *Revue Belge de Philologie et d'Histoire*, 93 (2015), 397–437.

Dhondt, Frederik, 'Looking beyond the Tip of the Iceberg: Diplomatic Praxis and Legal Culture in the History of Public International Law', *Rechtskultur* 2 (2013), 31–42.

Dias Pereira, Geovani, 'Dilemas historiográficos sobre a decadência de um Império: O "ocaso" do Estado da Índia (séc. XVI e XVII)', *Aedos*, 10(22) (2018), 285–309.

Dietz, Brian, 'The Huguenot and English Corsairs during Third Civil War in France, 1568 to 1570', *Proceedings of the Huguenot Society*, 19 (1952–1958), 278–94

Diffie, Bailey W. and Winius, George D., *Foundations of the Portuguese Empire, 1415–1580* (*Europe and the World in the Age of Expansion, vol. I*) (Minneapolis: University of Minnesota Press, 1977).

Disney, Anthony R., *A decadencia do império da pimenta. Comercio portugués na Índia no início do séc. XVII* (Lisboa: Edições 70, 1981).

Disney, Anthony R., *A History of Portugal and the Portuguese Empire: From Beginnings to 1807: Vol. I:Portugal* (Cambridge: University Press, 2009).

Distefano, Giovanni, *Atlante storico della Serenissima Repubblica di Venezia* (Venezia: Supernova, 2010).

Distefano, Giovanni, *L'ordre international entre légalité et effectivité: le titre juridique dans le contentieux territorial* (Paris: Pedone, 2002).

Domingo, Rafael and Martínez-Torrón, Janvier (eds.), *Great Christian Jurists in Spanish History* (Cambridge: University Press, 2018).

Domingo, Rafael, *Roman law: an Introduction* (London: Routledge, 2018).

Domínguez Ortiz, Antonio, *La España de los Reyes Católicos*, in *España, tres milenios de Historia* (Madrid: Marcial Pons Ediciones de Historia, 2007).

Doran, Susan, *Elizabeth I and Foreign Policy, 1558–1603* (London: Routledge, 2000).

Doumerc, Bernard, *L'Adriatique du XIIIe au XVIIe siècle*, in Pierre Cabanes (dir.), *Histoire de l'Adriatique* (Paris: Seuil, 2001).

Downing, Roger and Rommelse, Gijs, *A Fearful Gentleman: Sir George Downing in The Hague, 1658–1672* (Hilversum: Verloren, 2011).

Dreyer, Edward L., *Zheng He: China and the Oceans in the Early Ming Dynasty, 1405–1433* (New York: Pearson Longman, 2006).

Drocourt, Nicolas and Schnakenbourg, Éric (eds.), *Thémis en diplomatie. Droits et arguments juridiques dans les relations internationales de l'Antiquité tardive à la fin du XVIIIe siècle* (Rennes: Presses universitaires de Rennes, 2016).

Dunthorne, Hugh, *Britain and the Dutch Revolt, 1560–1700* (Cambridge: University Press, 2013).

Dupuy, Pierre-Marie and Chetail, Vincent (eds.), *The Roots of International Law/Les fondements du droit international. Liber Amicorum Peter Haggenmacher* (Leiden: Brill, 2013).

Dupuy, René-Jean and Vignes, Daniel (dir.), *Traité du nouveau droit de la mer* (Paris: Bruylant, 1985).

Dursi, Domenico, *Res communes omnium. Dalle necessità economiche alla disciplina giuridica* (Napoli: Jovene, 2017).

Dürst, Arthur, 'Brasilien im frühen Kartenbild', *Cartographica Helvetica*, 6 (1992), 8–16.

Dursteler, Eric (ed.), *A Companion to Venetian History, 1400–1797* (Leiden: Brill, 2014).

Duve, Thomas (ed.), *Entanglements in Legal History: Conceptual Approaches* (Frankfurt am Main: Max Planck Institute for European Legal History, 2019).

Duve, Thomas and Pihlajamäki, Heikki (eds.), *New Horizons in Spanish Colonial Law: Contributions to Transnational Early Modern Legal History* (Frankfurt Am Main: Max Planck Institute for European Legal History, 2015).

Duve, Thomas, *Global Legal History: A Methodological Approach* (Oxford Handbooks Online, 2017).

Dyer, Florence E., 'Reprisals in the Sixteenth Century', *The Mariner's Mirror*, 21(2) (1935), 187–97.

Echevarría Bacigalupe, Minguel A., *La diplomacia secreta en Flandes, 1598–1643* (Bilbao: Servicio Editorial Universidad del Pais Vasco, 1984).

Edmond, Gary, 'The Freedom of Histories: Reassessing Grotius on the Sea', *Law Text Culture*, 2 (1995), 179–217.

Edmundson, George, *Anglo-Dutch Rivalry during the First Half of the Seventeenth Century* (Oxford: Clarendon Press, 1911).

Ehrenberg, Ralph E., *Mapping the World: An Illustrated History of Cartography* (Washington: National Geographic, 2005).

Eklöf Amirell, Stefan, Hägerdal, Hans and Buchan, Bruce (eds.), *Piracy in World History* (Amsterdam: University Press, 2021).

Elliott, John H., 'The Spanish Monarchy and the Kingdom of Portugal, 1580-1640', in Mark Greengrass (ed.), *Conquest and Coalescence: The Shaping of the State in Early Modern Europe* (London: Edward Arnold, 1991), 45–67.

Elliott, John H., *Empires of the Atlantic World: Britain and Spain in America, 1492–1830* (New Haven, CT: Yale University Press, 2006).

Elliott, John H., *Imperial Spain, 1469–1716* (London: Penguin Books, 2002).

Epstein, Steven A., *Genoa & the Genoese, 958–1528* (Chapel Hill: The University of North Carolina Press, 1996).

Escamilla, Michèle, *Le siècle d'or de l'Espagne, apogée et déclin, 1492–1598* (Paris: Tallandier, 2015).

Etting, Vivian, *Queen Margrete I (1353–1412) and the Founding of the Nordic Union* (Leiden: Brill, 2004).

Fagan, Brian, *Beyond the Blue Horizon. How the Earliest Mariners Unlocked the Secrets of the Oceans* (London: Bloomsbury Press, 2012).

Fahl, Gundolf, *El principio de la libertad de los mares. Práctica de los Estados de 1493 a 1648* (Madrid: Instituto de Estudios Políticos, 1974).

Fang, Liaw Y., *Undang-Undang Melaka. The Laws of Melaka* (The Hague: M. Nijhoff, 1976).

Faričić, Josip, Selva, Orietta and Umek, Dragan, 'Geographical Names of the Adriatic Sea on Medieval and Early-Modern Maps and Nautical Charts', *Journal of Historical Geography*, 82 (2023), 68–80.

Fassbender, Bardo and Peters, Anne (eds.), *The Oxford Handbook of the History of International Law* (Oxford: University Press, 2012).

Feakes, Michael J., *Formative Influences on the Evolution of International Law: A Case Study of Territorial Waters (1550–1650)* (Ph.D. dissertation, Hull: University of Hull, 1994).

Fedele, Dante and Druwé, Wouter, 'Introduction. Dossier: Le *ius commune* à la fin du Moyen Âge et au début de l'époque moderne. Notions, méthodes, (dis)continuités', *Clio@Themis*, 27 (2024), 1–15.

Fedele, Dante, *Naissance de la diplomatie moderne (XIIIe–XVIIe siècles): l'ambassadeur au croisement du droit, de l'éthique et de la politique* (Baden-Baden: Nomos Verlagsgesellschaft, 2017).

Fedele, Dante, Randall Lesaffer and Pierre Savy (dir.), *Avant l'Etat. Droit international et pluralisme politico-juridique en Europe, XIIIe–XVIIe siècle* (Rome: Historia et ius, 2024).

Fedele, Dante, *The Medieval Foundations of International Law: Baldus de Ubaldis (1327–1400). Doctrine and Practice of the Ius Gentium* (Leiden/Boston: Brill/Nijhoff 2021).

Feenstra, Robert (ed.), *Hugo Grotius's Mare Liberum: 1609–2009* (Leiden/Boston: M. Nijhoff, 2009).

Fenn, Percy T., 'Justinian and the Freedom of the Sea', *American Journal of International Law*, 19(4) (1925), 716–27.

Fenn, Percy T., 'Origins of the Theory of Territorial Waters', *American Journal of International Law*, 20(3) (1926), 465–82.

Fenn, Percy T., *The Origin of the Right of Fishery in Territorial Waters* (Cambridge, MA: Harvard University Press, 1926).

Fernández Morente, Guadalupe and Fernández Vial, Ignacio, *Fernando de Magallanes: Expediciones marítimas* (Sevilla: Ayuntamiento de Sevilla, 2021)

Fernández, Rafael D., 'Proceso jurídico del descubrimiento de América (bulas, tratados y capitulaciones)', *Anuario Mexicano de Historia del Derecho*, 2 (1990), 81–114.

Fink, Alexander, 'The Hanseatic League and the Concept of Functional Overlapping Competing Jurisdictions', *Kyklos*, 65(2) (2012), 194–217.

Finlay, Robert, 'The Voyages of Zheng He: Ideology, State Power, and Maritime Trade in Ming China', *Journal of The Historical Society*, 8(3) (2008), 327–47.

Fiorentini, Mario, 'L'acqua da bene economico a "res communis omnium" a bene collettivo', *Analisi Giuridica dell'Economia*, 1 (2010), 39–78.

Fiorentini, Mario, *Fiumi e mari nell'esperienza giuridica romana* (Milano: Giuffré, 2003).

Firpo, Massimo (ed.), *Nunc alia tempora alii mores. Storici e storia in età postridentina. Atti del convegno, Torino, 24–27 settembre 2003* (Leo S. Olschki: Firenze, 2005).

Fisch, Jörg, *Die Europäische Expansion und das Völkerrechts. Die Auseinandersetzungen um den Status der überseeischen Gebiete vom 15. Jahrhundert bis zur Gegenwart* (Stuttgart: Steiner, 1984).

Fitzmaurice, Andrew, 'Context in the History of International Law', *Journal of the History of International Law*, 20(1) (2018), 5–30.

Fitzmaurice, Andrew, *Sovereignty, Property and Empire, 1500–2000* (Cambridge: University Press, 2014).

Flamigni, Antonio, *Il potere marittimo in Roma Antica. Dalle origini alla guerra siriaca* (Roma: Rivista Marittima, 1995).

Fletcher, Eric G. M., 'John Selden (Author of *Mare Clausum*) and his Contribution to International Law', *Transactions of the Grotius Society*, 19 (1933), 1–12.

Flynn, Gerard, 'Padre Las Casas, Literature, and the Just War', *Revista de Historia de América*, 61/62 (1966), 57–72.

Focarelli, Carlo, *Lezioni di storia di diritto internazionale* (Perugia: Morlacchi Editore, 2007).

Ford, John D., 'William Welwod's Treatises on Maritime Law', *The Journal of Legal History*, 34(2) (2013), 172–210.

Ford, John D., *The Emergence of Privateering* (Leiden: Brill, 2023).

Forteau, Mathias and Thouvenin, Jean-Marc (dir.), *Traité de droit international de la mer* (Paris: Editions A. Pedone, 2017).

Frajese, Vittorio, *Sarpi scettico. Stato e chiesa a Venezia tra Cinque e Seicento* (Bologna: II Mulino, 1994).

Frankot, Edda, 'Medieval maritime law from Oléron to Wisby: jurisdictions in the law of the sea', in Juan Pan-Montojo and Frederik Pedersen (eds.), *Communities in European History: Representations, Jurisdictions, Conflicts* (Pisa: Edizioni Plus – Pisa University Press, 2007), 151–72.

Frankot, Edda, *'Of Laws of Ships and Shipmen': Medieval Maritime Law and its Practice in Urban Northern Europe* (Edinburgh: University Press, 2012).

Fredona, Robert and Reinert, Sophus A. (eds.), *New Perspectives on the History of Political Economy* (London: Palgrave Macmillan, 2018).

Freund, Eleanor, *Freedom of Navigation in the South China Sea: A Practical Guide*, Belfer Center for Science and International Affairs, Harvard Kennedy School, Special Report (June 2017).

Friel, Ian, *Henry V's Navy: The Sea-Road to Agincourt and Conquest, 1413–1422* (Cheltenham: History Press, 2015).

Frost, Robert I., *The Northern Wars, 1558–1721* (London: Longman, 2000).

Frova, Carla, 'Le traité de fluminibus de Bartolo da Sassoferrato (1355)', *Médiévales*, 36 (1999), 81–9.

Fruin, Robert, 'An Unpublished Work of Hugo Grotius', *Bibliotheca Visseriana*, 5 (1925), 1–100.

Fulton, Thomas W., *The Sovereignty of the Sea* (London-Edinburgh: William Blackwood & Sons, 1911).

Gade, John A., *The Hanseatic Control of Norwegian Commerce during the Late Middle Ages* (Leiden: Brill, 1951).

Galasso, Giuseppe, *Storia d'Europa, I, l'antichità e il medioevo* (Torino: UTET, 2013).

Galasso, Giuseppe, *Storia d'Europa, II, l'età moderna dal XV al XVIII secolo* (Torino: UTET, 2013).

García Arias, Luis, 'La libertad de los mares según Rodrigo Suárez', *Anuario de la Asociación Francisco de Vitoria*, 17 (1969–1970), 49.

García Arias, Luis, 'Una pugna hispano-veneciana sobre el dominio del Mar Adriático', *Revista General de la Marina*, 132 (1947), 233–305.

García Arias, Luis, *Historia del principio de la libertad de los mares* (Santiago: Editora Universitaria Compostelana, 1946).

García Redondo, José M., *Cartografía e imperio. El Padrón Real y la representación del Nuevo Mundo* (Madrid: Ediciones Doce Calles, 2018).

García y García, Antonio, *La donación pontificia de las Indias* (Salamanca: Universidad Pontificia, 1992).

García, Bernardo J. (ed.), *Tiempo de paces. La Pax Hispanica y la Tregua de los Doce Años (1609–2009)* (Madrid: Fundación Carlos de Amberes, 2009).

García, Bernardo J., Herrero Sánchez, Manuel and Hugon, Alain (eds.), *El arte de la prudencia. La tregua de los Doce años en la Europa de los Pacificadores* (Madrid: Fundación Carlos de Amberes, 2012).

Gardiner, Dorothy A., 'The History of Belligerent Rights on the High Seas in the Fourteenth Century', *The Law Quarterly Review*, 48 (1932), 521–46.

Gardiner, Robert (ed.), *The Age of the Galley: Mediterranean Oared Vessels Since Pre-Classical Times* (New York: Book Sales, 2000).

Garofalo, Luigi (cur.), *I beni di interesse pubblico nell'esperienza giuridica romana* (Napoli: Jovene, 2016).

Gasperini, Silvia, *Pax tibi Marce. Venice: Government, Law, Jurisprudence. Venezia: istituzioni, diritto, giurisprudenza* (Firenze: Register Italia, 2014).

Gaurier, Dominique, *Droit maritime romain* (Rennes: Presses universitaires de Rennes, 2004).

Gaurier, Dominique, *Histoire du droit international* (Rennes: Presses universitaires de Rennes, 2014).

Gidel, Gilbert, *Le droit international public de la mer*, 3 Vols. (Paris: Établissements Mellottee Chateauroux, 1932–1934).

Gigante, Silvino, *Venezia e i pirati del mare Adriatico. Venezia contro gli uscocchi* (Vittorio Veneto: De Bastiani Editore, 2010).

Gill, Alison A., *Ship Money during the Personal Rule of Charles I: Politics, Ideology and the Law, 1634 to1640* (Ph.D. dissertation, Sheffield University, 1990).

Glete, Jan, *Warfare at Sea, 1500–1650. Maritime Conflicts and the Transformation of Europe* (London: Routledge, 2000).

Goldstone, Jack A., *Why Europe? The Rise of the West in World History, 1500–1850* (New York: McGraw-Hill, 2009).

Gómez Rivas, León M., 'Comercio y diplomacia: la Tregua de los Doce Años en el marco de las disputas sobre la libertad de los mares', in José Martínez Millán and Rubén González Cuerva (eds.), *La Dinastía de los Austria. Las relaciones entre la Monarquía Católica y el Imperio*, vol. II (Madrid: Ediciones Polifemo, 2011), 1245–62.

Gómez Rivas, León M., 'Influencia de Diego de Covarrubias en la obra de Hugo Grotius (*Mare Liberum*, 1609)', *Procesos de mercado: revista europea de economía política*, 10(2) (2013), 321–42.

Goodman, David, *Spanish Naval Power, 1589–1665: Reconstruction and Defeat* (Cambridge: University Press, 1997).

Gordon, M. D., 'The Collection of Ship-Money in the Reign of Charles I', *Transactions of the Royal Historical Society*, 4 (1910), 141–62.

Gordon, Robert W., *Taming the Past: Essays on Law in History and History in Law* (Cambridge: University Press, 2018).

Gormley, W. Paul, 'Development and Subsequent Influence of the Roman Legal Norm of Freedom of the Seas', *The University of Detroit Law Journal*, 40(1) (1963), 561–84.

Gozzi, Gustavo, *Diritti e civiltà, Storia e filosofia del diritto internazionale* (Bologna: Il Mulino, 2010).

Grasman, Edward, 'A Salute to You: Expansion under the Wings of Saint Mark', *Artibus et Historiae*, 33(66) (2012), 121–31.

Grayson, John C., *From Protectorate to Partnership – Anglo-Dutch relations 1598–1625* (Ph.D. Thesis, London: University College London, 1978).

Greenblatt, Stephen, *Marvelous Possessions: The Wonder of the New World* (Oxford: Clarendon Press, 1991).

Greene, Molly, 'Beyond the Northern Invasion: The Mediterranean in the Seventeenth Century', *Past & Present*, 174(1) (2002), 42–71.

Grewe, Wilhelm G., *The Epochs of International Law*, translated and revised by M. Byers (Berlin-New York: De Gruyter, 2000).

Grimal, Pierre (ed.), *L'Ellenismo e l'ascesa di Roma. Il mondo mediterraneo nell'antichità*, II. Vol. 6 *Storia Universale Feltrinelli* (Milano: Feltrinelli, 1968).

Grohse, Ian P., 'Medieval Maritime Diplomacy: the Case of Norwegian-Scottish Relations, ca. 1266-1468/69', *International Journal of Maritime History*, 26 (2014), 512–28.

Grossi, Paolo, *Il dominio e le cose. Percezioni medievali e moderne dei diritti reali* (Milano: Giuffré, 1992).

Guarino, Antonio, *Storia del diritto romano* (Napoli: Jovene, 1998).

Guazzelli, Giuseppe A., Michetti, Raimondo and Scorza Barcellona, Francesco, *Cesare Baronio tra santità e scrittura storica* (Roma: Viella, 2012).

Guidoni, Enrico and Soragni, Ugo (eds.), *Lo spazio nelle città venete (1348–1509)* (Rome: Edizioni Kappa, 1997).

Guiraud, Louise,'Julius Pacius en Languedoc (1597–1616). Avec documents inédits' (Montpellier: Valat, 1910), 1–36.

Gullino, Giuseppe, *Storia della Repubblica Veneta* (Brescia: Editrice la Scuola, 2010).

Hacquebord, Louwrens, *De Noordse Compagnie: Opkomst, bloei en ondergang* (1614–1642) (Zutphen: Walburg Pers, 2014).

Hacquebord, Louwrens, Steenhuisen, Frits and Waterbolk, Huib, 'English and Dutch Whaling Trade and Whaling Stations in Spitsbergen (Svalbard) before 1660', *International Journal of Maritime History*, 15(2) (2003), 117–34.

Haggenmacher, Peter, *Grotius et la doctrine de la guerre juste* (Paris: Presses universitaires de France, 1983).

Hainsworth, Roger and Churches, Christine, *The Anglo-Dutch Naval Wars, 1652–1674* (Phoenix Mill: Sutton Pub Ltd, 1998).

Haitsma Mulier, Eco O. G., *The Myth of Venice and Dutch Republican Thought in the Seventeenth Century* (Assen: Van Gorcum, 1980).

Hale, John (ed.), *Renaissance Venice* (London: Faber and Faber, 1973).

Haley, Kenneth H. D., *The British and the Dutch: Political and Cultural Relations through the Ages* (London: George Philip, 1988).

Hamilton, Earl J., *American Treasure and the Price Revolution in Spain, 1501–1650* (Cambridge, MA: Harvard University Press, 1934).

Hammer, Paul E. J., *Elizabeth's Wars: War, Government and Society in Tudor England, 1544–1604* (Basingstoke: Red Globe Press, 2003).

Harding, Richard, *Seapower and Naval Warfare, 1650–1830* (London: UCL Press, 1999).

Harley, John B. and Woodward, David (eds.), *The History of Cartography* (Chicago: University Press, 1987).

Harreld, Donald J. (ed.), *A Companion to the Hanseatic League* (Leiden: Brill, 2015).

Harris, Ron, *Going the Distance: Eurasian Trade and the Rise of the Business Corporation, 1400–1700* (Princeton: University Press, 2020).

Harrison, James, *Making the Law of the Sea: A Study in the Development of International Law* (Cambridge: University Press, 2011).

Hart, Henry H., *Sea Road to the Indies* (New York: The Macmillan Company, 1950).

Hattendorf, John B. and Unger, Richard W. (eds.), *War at Sea in the Middle Ages and the Renaissance* (Woodbridge: Boydell Press, 2003).

Hay, Denys, *Europe: the Emergence of an Idea* (Edinburgh: University Press, 1957).

Hazeltine, Harold D., 'Selden as Legal Historian', *Harvard Law Review*, 24(2) (1910–1911), 105–118.

Headley, John M., 'The Habsburg World Empire and the Revival of Ghibellinism', *Medieval and Renaissance Studies*, 7 (1978), 93–127.

Headley, John M., *The Emperor and His Chancellor: A Study of the Imperial Chancellery under Gattinara* (Cambridge: University Press, 1983).

Headley, John M., *The Europeanization of the World: On the Origins of Human Rights and Democracy* (Princeton: University Press, 2008).

Headrick, Daniel R., *The Tools of Empire: Technology and European Imperialism in the Nineteenth Century* (Oxford: University Press, 1981).

Hébié, Mamadou, *Souveraineté territoriale par traité, une étude des accords entre puissances coloniales et entités politiques locales* (Paris: Presses universitaires de France, 2015).

Heebøll-Holm, Thomas, *Ports, Piracy and Maritime War. Piracy in the English Channel and the Atlantic, c.1280–c.1330* (Leiden: Brill, 2013).

Heers, Jacques, *Gênes au XVe siècle: Activité économique et problèmes sociaux* (Paris: Sevpen, 1961).

Helle, Knut (ed.), *The Cambridge History of Scandinavia, vol. I: Prehistory to 1520* (Cambridge: University Press, 2003).

Heller-Roazen, Daniel *The Enemy of All. Piracy and the Law of Nations* (New York: Zone Books, 2009).

Hemming, John, *The Conquest of the Incas* (New York: Harcourt Brace Jovanovich, 1970).

Hill, Mark and Helmholz, Richard H. (eds.), *Great Christian Jurists in English History* (Cambridge: University Press, 2017).

Hilsdale, Cecily J., *Byzantine Art and Diplomacy in an Age of Decline* (Cambridge: University Press, 2014).

Hocquet, Jean-Claude, *Venise et la mer, XIIe–XVIIIe siècle* (Paris: Fayard, 2006).

Hocquet, Jean-Claude, *Venise et le monopole du sel. Production, commerce et finance d'une République marchande*, 2 vols. (Paris: Les Belles Lettres, 2012).

Hoffman, Paul E., *The Spanish Crown and the Defence of the Caribbean, 1535–1585: Precedent, Patrimonialism, and Royal Parsimony* (Baton Rouge: Louisiana State University Press, 1980).

Hoffner, Joseph, *Kolonialismus und Evangelium* (Trier: Paulinus-Verlag, 1969).

Hofmann, Catherine, Richard, Hiélène and Vagnon, Emmanuelle (eds.), *The Golden Age of Maritime Maps: When Europe Discovered the World* (New York: Firefly Books, 2013).

Höhn, Philipp, 'La "lutte contre les pirates" comme paradigme. Conflit, concurrence et criminalisation à Lübeck et dans le commerce nord-européen aux XVe et XVIe siècles', *Annales. Histoire, Sciences Sociales*, 77(2) (2022), 293–327.

Holland Rose, John et al. (eds.), *The Cambridge History of the British Empire. Vol 1: The Old Empire. From the Beginnings to 1783* (New York/Cambridge: Macmillan/University Press, 1929).

Horden, Peregrine and Kinoshita, Sharon (eds.), *A Companion to Mediterranean History* (New York: John Wiley & Sons, 2014).

Hueck, Ingo J., 'The Discipline of the History of International Law – New Trends and Methods on the History of International Law', *Journal of the History of International Law*, 3(2) (2001), 194–217.

Hunyadi, Zsolt and Laszlovszky, József (eds.), *The Crusades and the Military Orders: Expanding the Frontiers of Medieval Latin Christianity* (Budapest: Central European University Press, 2001).

Hwang, Yih-Jye and Frettingham, Edmund (eds.), *Maritime and Territorial Disputes in the South China Sea. Faces of power and law in the Age of China's Rise* (London-New York: Routledge, 2021).

Ikins Stern, Laura, 'Politics and Law in Renaissance Florence and Venice', *American Journal of Legal History*, 46(2) (2004), 209–34.

Ilari, Virgilio, *L'interpretazione storica del diritto di guerra romano fra tradizione romanistica e giusnaturalismo* (Milano: Giuffrè, 1981).

Innes Miller, James, *The Spice Trade of the Roman Empire: 29 b.c. to 641 a.c.* (Oxford: Clarendon Press, 1969).

Israel, Jonathan I., *Dutch Primacy in World Trade, 1585–1740* (Oxford: Clarendon Press, 1989).

Israel, Jonathan I., *Empires and Entrepots. The Dutch, the Spanish Monarchy and the Jews 1585–1713* (London-Ronceverte: The Hambledon Press, 1990).

Israel, Jonathan I., *The Dutch Republic and the Hispanic World* (Oxford: Clarendon Press, 1986).

Israel, Jonathan I., *The Dutch Republic, its Rise, Greatness, and Fall, 1477–1806* (Oxford: University Press, 1997).

Jackson, Anna, and Jaffer, Amin, *Encounters: The Meeting of Asia and Europe 1500–1800* (London: Victoria & Albert Museum, 2004).

Jahnke, Carsten, *Die Hanse* (Stuttgart: Reclam Verlag, 2014).

James, Alan, *The Navy and Government in Early Modern France, 1572–1661* (Woodbridge: Boydell Press, 2004).

Janžekovič, Izidor, 'The Balance of Sea Power in the Early Modern Era: The Anglo-Dutch Wars (1652–1674)', *International Journal of Maritime History*, 36(4) (2024), 1–26.

Jaritz, Gerhard and Kreem, Juhan (eds.), *Edges of the Medieval World* (Budapest: Central European University Press, 2008).

Jessup, Philip C. and Deák, Francis, *Neutrality: its History, Economics and Law: The Origins Vol. 1* (New York: Columbia University Press, 1935).

Jessup, Philip C., *The Law of Territorial Waters and Maritime Jurisdiction* (New York: G. A. Jennings Co., 1927).

Jóhannesson, Guðni T., *Troubled Waters: Cod War, Fishing Disputes, and Britain's Fight for the Freedom of the High Seas, 1948–1964* (Reykjavík: North Atlantic Fisheries History Association, 2007).

Johnson, Donald S., *Phantom Islands of the Atlantic* (Fredericton: Goose Lane Editions, 1994).

Johnston, Douglas M., *The International Law of Fisheries: A Framework for Policy-Oriented Inquiries* (New Haven/Dordrecht: New Haven Press/M. Nijhoff, 1987).

Johnston, Douglas M., *The Theory and History of Ocean Boundary-Making* (Kingston & Montreal: McGill-Queen's University Press, 1988).

Jones, Dan, *The Wars of the Roses, The Fall of the Plantagenets and the Rise of the Tudors* (London: Penguin Books, 2015).

Jones, Henry, 'Lines in the Ocean: Thinking with the Sea about Territory and International Law', *London Review of International Law*, 4(2) (2016), 307–43.

Jones, James R., *The Anglo-Dutch Wars of the Seventeenth Century* (London: Longman, 1996).

Jones, Michael (ed.), *The New Cambridge Medieval History, VI, 1300–1415* (Cambridge: University Press, 2000).

Kadelbach, Stefan, et al. (eds.) *System, Order, and International Law. The Early History of International Legal Thought from Machiavelli to Hegel* (Cambridge: University Press, 2017).

Kagan, Robert, *Of Paradise and Power* (New York: Alfred Knopf, 2004).

Kainulainen, Jaska, *Paolo Sarpi: A Servant of God and State* (Leiden: Brill, 2014).

Kamen, Henry, *Spain's Road to Empire* (London: Penguin Books, 2009).

Keene, Edward, *Beyond the Anarchical Society: Grotius, Colonialism and Order in World Politics* (Cambridge: University Press, 2002).

Kelly, John N. D., *The Oxford Dictionary of Popes* (Oxford: University Press, 1987).

Kelsey, Harry, *Sir Francis Drake: The Queen's Pirate* (New Haven, CT: Yale University Press, 1998).

Kelsey, Harry, *Sir John Hawkins: Queen Elizabeth's Slave Trader* (New Haven, CT: Yale University Press, 2003).

Kemmerer, Alexandra, '"We do not need to always look to Westphalia…" A Conversation with Martti Koskenniemi and Anne Orford', *Journal of the History of International Law*, 17 (2005), 1–14.

Kempe, Michael, '"Even in the Remotest Corners of the World": Globalized Piracy and International Law, 1500–1900', *Journal of Global History*, 5(3) (2010), 353–72.

Kempe, Michael, 'Beyond the Law. The Image of Piracy in the Legal Writings of Hugo Grotius', *Grotiana*, 26–28 (2005–2007), 379–95.

Kempe, Michael, *Fluch der Weltmeere: Piraterie, Volkerrecht und internationale Beziehungen, 1500–1900* (Frankfurt: Campus Verlag, 2010).

Kennedy, Paul, *The Rise and Fall of the Great Powers* (London: Unwin Hyman Ltd., 1988).

Khalilieh, Hassan S., *Admiralty and Maritime Laws in the Mediterranean Sea (ca. 800–1050): The Kitāb Akriyat Al-Sufun Vis-à-Vis the Nomos Rhodion Nautikos* (Leiden/Boston: Brill, 2006).

Khalilieh, Hassan S., *Islamic Law of the Sea: Freedom of Navigation and Passage Rights in Islamic Thought* (Cambridge: University Press, 2019).

Kieniewicz, Jan, 'The Portuguese Factory and Trade in Pepper in Malabar during the Sixteenth Century', *The Indian Economic and Social History Review*, 6(1) (1969), 61–84.

Kingsbury, Benedict and Straumann, Benjamin (eds.), *The Roman Foundation of the Law of Nations. Alberico Gentili and the Justice of Empire* (Oxford: University Press, 2010).

Kirby, David G. and Hinkkanen, Merja-Liisa, *The Baltic and the North Seas* (London: Routledge, 2000).

Kirk, Thomas A., *Genoa and the Sea, Policy and Power in an Early Modern Maritime Power* (Baltimore: The John Hopkins University Press, 2013).

Klee, Hans J., *Hugo Grotius und Johannes Selden, von den geistigen ursprüngen des kampfes um die meeresfreiheit* (Bern: P. Haupt, 1946).

Kleen, Richard, *Lois et usages de la neutralité d'après le droit international conventionnel et coutumier des états civilisés* (Paris: Chevalier-Maresq, 1898).

Knight, William S. M., *Seraphim de Freitas: Critic of Mare Liberum* (Cambridge: University Press, 1925).

Knight, William S. M., *The Life and Works of Hugo Grotius* (London: Sweet & Maxwell, 1925).

Koeman, Cornelis, 'Jan Huygen Van Linschoten', *Revista da Universidade de Coimbra*, 32 (1985), 27–47.

Koskenniemi, Martti, 'Histories of International Law: Dealing with Eurocentrism', in *Rechtsgeschichte. Zeitschrift des Max-Planck-Instituts für europäische Rechtsgeschichte*, 19 (2011), 152–76.

Koskenniemi, Martti, 'Vitoria and Us. Thoughts on critical Histories of International Law', *Rechtsgeschichte. Journal of the Max Planck Institute for European Legal History*, 22 (2014), 119–38.

Koskenniemi, Martti, *From Apology to Utopia. The Structure of International Legal Argument. Reissue with a New Epilogue* (Cambridge: University Press, 2006).

Koskenniemi, Martti, Mónica García-Salmones Rovira, and Paolo Amorosa (eds.), *International Law and Religion: Historical and Contemporary Perspectives* (Oxford: University Press, 2017).

Koskenniemi, Martti, Recht, Walter, and Jiménez Fonseca, Manuel (eds.), *International Law and Empire. Historical Explorations* (Oxford: University Press, 2017).

Koskenniemi, Martti, *The Gentle Civilizer of Nations: The Rise and Fall of International Law 1870–1960* (Cambridge: University Press, 2001).

Koskenniemi, Martti, *To the Uttermost Parts of the Earth: Legal Imagination and International Power 1300–1870* (Cambridge: University Press, 2021).

Kranenburg, Hendrik A. H., *De zeevisscherij van Holland in den tijd der Republiek* (Amsterdam: H.J. Paris, 1946).

Krever, Tor, *The Ideological Origins of Piracy in International Legal Thought* (Ph.D. dissertation, London: The London School of Economics and Political Science, 2018).

Kulsrud, Carl J., *Maritime Neutrality to 1780: A History of the Main Principles Governing Neutrality and Belligerency to 1780* (Boston: Little, Brown, and Co., 1936).

Ladero Quesada, Miguel Á., 'Los debates sobre el Mare Clausum', *Cuadernos de Historia de España*, 74 (1997), 233–54.

Laghmani, Slim, *Histoire du droit des gens. Du jus gentium imperial au jus publicum europaeum* (Paris: Pedone, 2004).

Lane, Frederic C., 'Pepper Prices before Da Gama', *Journal of Economic History*, 28(4) (1968), 590–97.

Lane, Frederic C., *I mercanti di Venezia* (Torino: Einaudi, 1982).

Lane, Frederic C., *Venice, a Maritime Republic* (Baltimore-London: The John Hopkins University Press, 1973).

Lane, Kris E., 'Punishing the Sea Wolf: Corsairs and Cannibals in the Early Modern Caribbean', *New West Indian Guide*, 77(3–4) (2003), 201–20.

Lane, Kris E., *Pillaging the Empire: Global Piracy on the High Seas, 1500–1750* (London: Routledge, 2016).

Lane, Kris E., *Pillaging the Empire: Piracy in the Americas, 1500–1750* (New York: M.E. Sharpe, 1998).

Lang, Jack, *François 1er, ou le rêve italien* (Paris: Perrin, 1997).

Langelüddecke, Henrik, '"I Finde All Men & My Officers All Soe Unwilling": The Collection of Ship Money, 1635–1640', *Journal of British Studies*, 46(3) (2007), 509–42.

Lantigua, David M., *Infidels and Empires in a New World Order. Early Modern Spanish Contributions to International Legal Thought* (Cambridge: University Press, 2020).

Lauring, Palle, *A History of the Kingdom of Denmark* (Copenhagen: Høst, 1960).

le Goff, Jacques, *Il re nell'Occidente medievale* (Roma-Bari: Laterza, 2006).

le Goff, Jacques, *La civilization de l'occident médiéval* (Paris: Flammarion, 1964).

Lebeau, Christine (dir.), *L'espace du Saint-Empire: Du Moyen Âge à l'époque moderne* (Strasbourg: Presses universitaires de Strasbourg, 2004).

Lee, Daniel, *The Right of Sovereignty: Jean Bodin on the Sovereign State and the Law of Nations* (Oxford: University Press, 2021).

Leicht, Pier S., 'Lo stato veneziano e il diritto comune', in *Miscellanea in onore di Roberto Cessi*, I (Roma: Edizioni di Storia e Letteratura, 1958), 203–11.

Lenman, Bruce, *England's Colonial Wars, 1550–1688: Conflicts, Empire, and National Identity* (Harlow: Longman, 2001).

Lesaffer, Randall (ed.), *Peace Treaties and International Law in European History: From the Late Middle Ages to World War One* (Cambridge: University Press, 2004).

Lesaffer, Randall and Nijman, Janne E. (eds.), *The Cambridge Companion to Hugo Grotius* (Cambridge: University Press, 2021).

Lesaffer, Randall and Peters, Anne (eds.), *The Historiography of International Law*, vol. I of *The Cambridge History of International Law* (Cambridge: University Press, 2024).

Lesaffer, Randall, 'Charles V, Monarchia Universalis and the Law of Nations', *Legal History Review*, 71(1–2) (2003), 79–123.

Lesaffer, Randall, 'La paix de Vervins (2 mai 1598): Souveraineté, territorialité en développement du droit public européen', in Jean-Marie Cauchies, and Serge Dauchy (dir.), *Personnalité, territorialité et droit: Actes des journées internationales de la Société d'Histoire du Droit tenues à Bruxelles 28–31 mai 1998* (Bruxelles: Facultés universitaires Saint-Louis, 1999), 131–52.

Lesaffer, Randall, 'Law and history: law between past and present', in Bart van Klink and Sanne Taekema (eds.), *Law and Method: Interdisciplinary Research into Law* (Tübingen: Mohr Siebeck, 2011), 133–52.

Lesaffer, Randall, 'The Grotian Tradition Revisited: Change and Continuity in the History of International Law', *British Yearbook of International Law*, 73 (2002), 103–39.

Lesaffer, Randall, 'The Medieval Canon Law of Contract and Early Modern Treaty Law', *Journal of the History of International Law*, 2(2) (2000), 178–98.

Lesaffer, Randall, 'The Westphalia Peace Treaties and the Development of Great European Peace Treaties prior to 1648', *Grotiana*, 18 (1997), 1–25.

Lesaffer, Randall, *European Legal History: A Cultural and Political Perspective* (Cambridge: University Press, 2009).

Lesaffer, Randall, *The Twelve Years Truce (1609): Peace, Truce, War and Law in the Low Countries at the Turn of the 17th Century* (Leiden/Boston: Brill/Nijhoff, 2014).

Levathes, Louise, *When China Ruled the Seas: The Treasure Fleet of the Dragon Throne 1405–1433* (New York: Simon & Schuster, 1994).

Levenson, Jay A. (ed.), *Circa 1492: Art in the Age of Exploration* (New Haven, CT: Yale University Press, 1991).

Lewis, Andrew and Lobban, Michael (eds.), *Law and Legal History* (Oxford: University Press, 2004).

Lewis, Archibald R. and Runyan, Timothy J., *European Naval and Maritime History, 300–1500* (Bloomington: Indiana University Press, 1985).

Liggio, Leonard P., 'The Hanseatic League and Freedom of Trade', *Journal of Private Enterprise*, 23(1) (2007), 134–41.

Lindsay, William S., *History of Merchant Shipping and Ancient Commerce*, II (Cambridge: University Press, 2013).

Liu, Ying, Chen, Zhongping and Blue, Gregory (eds.), *Zheng He's Maritime Voyages (1405–1433) and China's Relations with the Indian Ocean World: A Multilingual Bibliography* (Leiden: Brill, 2014).

Livet, Georges, *L'équilibre européen de la fin du XVe à la fin du XVIIIe siècle* (Paris: Presses universitaires de France, 1976).

Lloyd, Cristhopher, *English Corsairs on the Barbary Coast* (London: Collins, 1981).

Lloyd, Terrence H., 'A Reconsideration of Two Anglo-Hanseatic Treaties of the Fifteenth Century', *The English Historical Review*, 102(405) (1987), 916–33.

Lloyd, Terrence H., *England and the German Hanse, 1157–1611. A Study of their Trade and Commercial Diplomacy* (Cambridge: University Press, 1991).

Loades, David M., *The Making of the Elizabethan Navy, 1540–1590: From the Solent to the Armada* (Woodbridge: Boydell Press, 2009).

Lockard, Craig A., '"The Sea Common to All"; Maritime Frontiers, Port Cities, and Chinese Traders in the Southeast Asian Age of Commerce, ca. 1400–1750', *Journal of World History*, 21(2) (2010), 219–47.

Lockart, Paul, 'Denmark and the Empire: A Reassessment of Danish Foreign Policy under King Christian IV', *Scandinavian Studies*, 64(3) (1992), 390–416.

Lockart, Paul, *Denmark in the Thirty Years' War, 1618–1648: King Christian IV and the Decline of the Oldenburg State* (Selinsgrove: Susquehanna University Press, 1996).

Lockart, Paul, *Denmark, 1513–1660, The Rise and Decline of a Renaissance Monarchy* (Oxford: University Press, 2007).

Loomie, Albert J., 'The Spanish Faction at the Court of Charles I, 1630–8', *Historical Research*, 59(139) (1986), 37–49.

Lopez, Roberto S., *Storia delle colonie genovesi nel Mediterraneo* (Torino: Marietti1820, 1996).

Louis, Florian, *Atlas historique de la Méditerranée: de l'Antiquité à nos jours* (Paris: Autrement, 2022).

Lozzi, Antonio, *Codici e consuetudini nella storia del commercio marittimo. Dal Codice di Hammurabi alle repubbliche marinare* (Milano: Mursia, 2010).

Lucas, Peter J., *Mare Clausum seu de Dominio MarisMare Clausum seu de Dominio Mariso* Maris', *Quaerendo*, 31(2) (2001), 120–36.

Luzzatto, Gino, 'La decadenza di Venezia dopo le scoperte geografiche nella tradizione e nella realtà', *Archivio Veneto*, serie V, 54–55 (1954), 162–81.

MacCaffrey, Wallace T., *Elizabeth I* (London: Edward Arnold, 1991).

MacCaffrey, Wallace T., *Queen Elizabeth and the Making of Policy, 1572–88* (Princeton: University Press, 1981).

Maccarrone, Michele, *Studi su Innocenzo III* (Padova: Editrice Antenore, 1972).

Macinnes, Allan I., Riis, Thomas and Pedersen, Frederik G. (eds.), *Ships, Guns and Bibles in the North Sea and Baltic States* (East Linton: Tuckwell Press, 2000).

Maffei, Domenico, 'Lectura super Digesto veteri di Cino da Pistoia', *Quaderni di studio senesi* (Milano: Giuffrè Editore, 1963).

Mahlberg, Gaby and Munck, Thomas (eds.), *Ideas Across Borders. Translating Visions of Authority and Civil Society in Europe c.1600–1840* (London: Routledge, 2024).

Maiolo, Francesco, *Medieval Sovereignty: Marsilius of Padua and Bartolus of Saxoferrato* (Delft: Eburon, 2007).

Malo, Henry, *Les corsaires dunkerquois et Jean Bart, des origins à 1662* (Paris: Le Mercure de France, 1913).

Maloni, Ruby, 'Control of the Seas: the Historical Exegesis of the Portuguese "Cartaz"', *Proceedings of the Indian History Congress*, 72(1) (2011), 476–84.

Mancke, Elizabeth, 'Early Modern Expansion and the Politicization of Oceanic Space', *Geographical Review*, 89(2), 225–36.

Mancke, Elizabeth, 'Oceanic Space and the Creation of a Global International System, 1450-1800', in Daniel Finamore (ed.), *Maritime History as World History* (Gainesville: University Press of Florida, 2004).

Mandelet, Thomas J., *The Renaissance of Empire in Early Modern Europe* (Cambridge: University Press, 2014).

Mantran, Robert, *Histoire de l'Empire Ottoman* (Paris: Fayard, 2003).

Manzano, Juan, 'El derecho de la Corona de Castilla al descubrimiento y conquista de las Indias de Poniente', *Revista de India*, 3(9) (1942), 397–427.

Marcocci, Giuseppe, 'Machiavelli, la religione dei romani e l'impero portoghese', *Storica*, 41–42 (2008), 35–68

Marcocci, Giuseppe, *L'invenzione di un impero: Politica e cultura nel mondo portoghese* (1450–1600) (Roma: Carocci, 2011).

Marcondes de Souza, Thomaz O., 'O descobrimento da América: O tratado de Tordesillas e as Molucas', *Revista de História*, 25(51) (1962), 125–38.

Markham, Clements R., 'Early Spitzbergen voyages', in Francis H. H. Guillemard (ed.), *The Lands of Silence: A History of Arctic and Antarctic Exploration* (Cambridge: University Press, 2015), 117–28.

Markham, Clements R., *The Threshold of the Unknown Region* (Cambridge: University Press, 2014).

Martínez Torres, José A., '«Gobernar el Mundo». La polémica *Mare Liberum versus Mare Clausum* en las Indias Orientales (1603-1625)', *Anuario de Estudios Americanos*, 74(1) (2017), 71–96.

Martínez, Ricardo Cerezo, 'El meridiano y el antimeridiano de Tordesillas en la geografía, la náutica y la cartografía', *Revista de Indias*, 54 (1994), 509–42.

Mathew, Kuzhippalli S., 'Trade in the Indian Ocean and the Portuguese System of Cartazes', in Malyn Newitt (ed.), *The First Portuguese Colonial Empire* (Exeter: University Press, 1986).

Mathieu, Christian, *Inselstadt Venedig: Umweltgeschichte eines Mythos in der Frühen Neuzeit* (Cologne: Böhlau, 2007).

Matino, Gabriele and Fortini Brown, Patricia (eds.), *Carpaccio in Venice: A Guide* (Venice: Marsilio, 2020).

Mattingly, Garrett, 'No Peace beyond what Line?', *Transactions of the Royal Society*, 13 (1963), 145–62.

Mauny, Raymond, *Les navigations médiévales sur les côtes sahariennes antérieures à la découverte portugaise (1434)* (Lisboa: Centro de estudos históricos ultramarinos, 1960).

McFee, William, *The Law of the Sea* (New York: J. B. Lippincott Co., 1950).

McKechnie, Hector (ed.), *An Introductory Survey of the Sources and Literature of Scots Law* (Edinburgh: Printed for the Stair Society by R. Maclehose & Co., 1936).

McLaughlin, Raoul, *The Roman Empire and the Indian Ocean. The Ancient World Economy and the Kingdoms of Africa, Arabia and India* (Barnsley: Pen & Sword, 2014).

McNeil, Kent, 'The Papal Bulls Dividing the Americas between Spain and Portugal: A Reappraisal', *Journal of the History of International Law*, 26(4) (2024), 351–82.

Mecalister-Smith, Peter and Schwietzcke, Joachim, 'Literature and Documentary Sources Relating to the History of Public International Law: An Annotated Bibliographical Survey', *Journal of the History of International Law*, 1(2) (1999), 136–212.

Meier, Dirk, *Seafarers, Merchants and Pirates in the Middle Ages* (Woodbridge: Boydell Press, 2009).

Meijers, Eduard M., 'Des graven stroom', *Mededelingen der Koninklijke Nederlandsche Akademie van Wetenschappen, afdeling Letterkunde, Nieuwe Reeks* 3(4) (Amsterdam: N.V. Noord-Hollandsche Uitgevers Maatschappij, 1940), 103–205.

Meilink-Roelofsz, Marie A. P., *Asian Trade and European Influence in the Indonesian Archipelago between 1500 and about 1630* (The Hague: M. Nijhoff, 1962).

Mendoça de Albuquerque, Luis, 'El Tratado de Tordesillas e as dificuldades técnicas da sua aplicacão rigorosa', in *El Tratado de Tordesillas y su proyección*, vol. I, Seminario de Historia de America (Valladolid: Universidade de Valladolid, 1973), 119–36.

Meurer, Christian, *The Program of the Freedom of the Seas. A Political Study in International Law* (Nabu Press: Washington, 1919).

Miaja de la Muela, Adolfo, *Internacionalistas españoles del siglo XVI: Fernando Vázquez de Menchaca (1512–1569)* (Valladolid: Cuesta, 1932).

Michalsen, Dag (ed.), *Reading Past Legal Texts* (Oslo: Unipax, 2006).

Mikkelsen, Birger, *Christian IV: A Pictorial Biography* (Copenhagen: Nordisk forlag for videnskab og teknik, 1988).

Mira Caballos, Esteban, *El sistema naval del imperio español. Armadas, flotas y galeones en el siglo XVI* (Madrid: Punto de Vista Editores, 2015).

Mira Caballos, Esteban, *Las Armadas del Imperio. Poder y hegemonía en tiempo de los Austrias* (Madrid: La Esfera de los Libros, 2019).

Mitchison, Rosalind, *A History of Scotland* (New York: Routledge, 2003).

Monaque, Rémi, *Une histoire de la marine de guerre française* (Paris: Perrin, 2016).

Montanari, Massimo, *Storia medievale* (Bari: Laterza, 2002).

Moore, Cameron, *Freedom of Navigation and the Law of the Sea. Warships, States and the Use of Force* (New York: Routledge, 2021).

Morales Padrón, Francisco, 'Descubrimiento y toma de posesión', *Anuario de Estudios Americanos*, 12 (1955), 321–80.

Moréteau, Olivier, Masferrer, Aniceto and Modéer, Kjell A. (eds.), *Comparative Legal History* (Cheltenham-Northampton: Edward Elgar, 2019).

Muir, Edward W., *Civic Ritual in Renaissance Venice* (Princeton: University Press, 1986).

Muldoon, James, 'Papal Responsibility for the Infidel: Another Look at Alexander VI's "Inter Caetera"', *Catholic Historical Review*, 64 (1978), 168–84.

Muldoon, James, *Popes, Lawyers, and Infidels: The Church and the Non-Christian World 1250–1550* (Liverpool: University Press, 1970).

Muldoon, James, *The Expansion of Europe: The First Phase* (Philadelphia: University of Pennsylvania Press, 1977).

Müller, Leos, *Neutrality in World History* (New York: Routledge, 2019).

Muller, Samuel, *Geschiedenis der Noordsche Compagnie* (Utrecht: Gebr. van der Post, 1874).

Muller, Samuel, *Mare clausum: Bijdrage tot de geschiedenis der rivaliteit van Engeland en Nederland in de zeventiende eeuw* (Amsterdam: F. Muller, 1872).

Murdoch, Steve, *Britain, Denmark-Norway and the House of Stuart, 1603–1660* (East Linton: Tuckwell Press, 2000).

Murray, Katherine M. E., *The Constitutional History of the Cinque Ports* (Manchester: University Press, 1935).

Musarra, Antonio, *Genova e il mare nel Medioevo* (Bologna: Il Mulino, 2015).

Musarra, Antonio, *Il grifo e il leone. Genova e Venezia in lotta per il Mediterraneo* (Bari: Laterza, 2020).

Musarra, Antonio, *L'isola che non c'è. Geografie immaginarie tra Mediterraneo e Atlantico* (Bologna: Il Mulino, 2023).

Musi, Aurelio, *L'Italia dei viceré. Integrazione e resistenza nel sistema imperiale spagnolo* (Napoli: Avagliano Editore, 2000).

Musson, Anthony and Stebbings, Chantal, *Making Legal History: Approaches and Methodologies* (Cambridge: University Press, 2012).

Nani Mocenigo, Mario, *Storia della marina veneziana, da Lepanto alla caduta della Repubblica* (Venezia: Filippi Editore, 1935).

Nedkvitne, Arnved, *The German Hansa and Bergen 1100–1600* (Köln: Böhlau Verlag, 2014).

Neff, Stephen C., *Justice among Nations. A History of International Law* (Cambridge, MA: Harvard University Press, 2014).

Neff, Stephen C., *The Rights and Duties of Neutrals: A General History* (Manchester: University Press 2000).

Neff, Stephen C., *War and the Law of Nations. A General History* (Cambridge: University Press, 2005).

Nellen, Henk, *Hugo Grotius. A Lifelong Struggle for Peace in Church and State, 1583–1645* (Leiden/Boston: Brill, 2007).

Newitt, Malyn (ed.). *The First Portuguese Colonial Empire* (Exeter: University Press, 1986).

Newitt, Malyn, *A History of Portuguese Overseas Expansion 1400–1668* (London: Routledge, 2004).

Newitt, Malyn, *Navigations: The Portuguese Discoveries and the Renaissance* (London: Reaktion Books, 2023).

Newton, Arthur P., *The European Nations in the West Indies, 1493–1688* (New York: Barnes & Noble, 1967).

Nieto Olarte, Mauricio, *Exploration, Religion and Empire in the Sixteenth-century Ibero-Atlantic World. A New Perspective on the History of Modern Science* (Amsterdam: University Press, 2021).

Norwich, John J., *A History of Venice* (London: Penguin Books, 2003).

Nothnagle, John, 'Two Early French Voyages to Sumatra', *The Sixteenth Century Journal*, 19(1) (1988), 97–107.

Nowell, Charles E., 'The treaty of Tordesillas and the diplomatic background of American history', in Adele Ogden and Engel Sluiter (eds.), *Greater America: Essays in Honour of Herbert Eugene Bolton* (Berkeley: University of California Press, 1945), 1–18.

Nussbaum, Arthur, *A Concise History of the Law of Nations* (New York: The Macmillan Company, 1947).

Nys, Ernest, 'Une Bataille de Livres, an Episode in the Literary History of International Law', *Juridical Review*, 3.1–3.2 (1891), 131–7.

Nys, Ernest, *Le droit international. Les principes, les théories, les faits*, III (Paris: Weissenbruch, 1912).

Nys, Ernest, *Les origines du droit international* (Bruxelles: A. Castaigne, 1894).

Ober, Frederick A., *Vasco Núñez de Balboa* (New York: Harper & Brothers Publishers, 1906).

Ocker, Christopher et al. (sds.), *Politics and Reformations: Communities, Polities, Nations, and Empires – Essays in Honour of T. A. Brady* (Leiden: Brill, 2007).

Orakhelashvili, Alexander (ed.), *Research Handbook on the Theory and History of International Law* (Cheltenham-Northampton: Edward Elgar, 2020).

Orlando, Ermanno, *Venezia e il mare nel Medioevo* (Bologna: Il Mulino, 2014).

Ormrod, David and Rommelse, Gijs (eds.), *War, Trade and the State: Anglo-Dutch Conflict, 1652–89* (Woodbridge: Boydell Press, 2020).

Ortalli, Gherardo (cur.), *Storia d'Europa, IV, Il Medioevo, Secoli V–XV* (Torino: Giulio Einaudi Editore, 1994).

Ortalli, Gherardo and Puncuh, Dino (eds.), *Genova, Venezia, il Levante nei secoli XII–XIV. Atti del convegno internazionale di studi, Genova-Venezia, 10–14 marzo 2000* (Genova/Venezia: Società Ligure di Storia Patria/Istituto Veneto di Scienze, Lettere ed Arti, 2001).

Ortalli, Gherardo and Scarabello, Giovanni, *Breve storia di Venezia* (Pisa: Pacini Editore, 2003).

Osiander, Andreas, 'Sovereignty, International Relations, and the Westphalian Myth', *International Organization*, 55(2) (2001), 251–87

Ostrogorsky, Georg, *History of the Byzantine Empire* (New Brunswick: Rutgers University Press, 1986).

Oudendijk, Johanna K., *Status and Extent of Adjacent Waters, a Historical Orientation* (Leyden: Sïjthoff, 1970).

Øyrehagen Sunde, Jørn, 'Landslova av 1274 mellom historisk brot og kontinuitet', *Historisk Tidsskrift* 101(4) (2022), 271–85.

Padoa-Schioppa, Antonio, *A History of Law in Europe, From the Early Middle Ages to the Twentieth Century* (Cambridge: University Press, 2017).

Padrón, Ricardo, 'Mapping Plus Ultra: Cartography, Space, and Hispanic Modernity', *Representations* 79 (2002), 28–60

Padwa, David J., *Mare ClausumMare ClausumMare Clausum*sum', *American Journal of International Law*, 54 (1960), 156–9.

Pagden, Anthony, *Lords of All the World: Ideologies of Empire in Spain, Britain and France, 1492–1830* (New Haven, CT: Yale University Press, 1998).

Pagden, Anthony, *Spanish Imperialism and the Political Imagination, Studies in European and Spanish-American Social and Political Theory 1513–1830* (New Haven, CT: Yale University Press, 1990).

Pagden, Anthony, *The Burdens of Empire: 1539 to the Present* (Cambridge: University Press, 2015).

Paine, Lincoln, *The Sea and Civilization, a Maritime History of the World* (London: Atlantic Books, 2014).

Paliaga, Simone, 'Il dominio dell'Adriatico. Sarpi, Giannone e la sovranità contesa tra Venezia, Napoli e Vienna', *Quaderno SISM 2014, Naval History*, Versione Online, [http://www.societaitalianastoriamilitare.org].

Panhuysen, Luc, *Het monsterschip. Maarten Tromp en de armada van 1639* (Amsterdam: Atlas Contact, 2021).

Panikkar, Kavalam M., *Asia and Western Dominance: A Survey of the Vasco da Gama Epoch of Asian History 1498–1945* (Allen & Unwin: London, 1953).

Panizza, Diego, 'Alberico Gentili: vicenda umana e intellettuale di un giurista italiano nell'Inghilterra elisabettiana', in *Alberico Gentili, giurista e intellettuale globale. Atti del Convegno "Prima giornata gentiliana"*, San Ginesio, 25 settembre 1983 (Milano, 1988).

Panizza, Diego, *Alberico Gentili, giurista ideologo nell'Inghilterra elisabettiana* (Padova: La Garangola, 1981).

Pansolli, Lamberto, *La gerarchia delle fonti di diritto nella legislazione medievale Veneziana* (Milano: Giuffrè, 1970).

Pantalacci, Jean-Pierre, 'Le personnel diplomatique vénitien à travers l'Europe, dans la première moitié du XVI siècle, en Cahiers de la Méditerranée' [En ligne], 78/2009, Centre de la Méditerranée moderne et contemporaine, mis en ligne le 15 février 2010.

Paolini, Emiliano, *Filosofia politica e diritto internazionale in Francisco de Vitoria* (Rome: Curcio, 2011).

Paradisi, Bruno, 'Studi e opinioni recenti sulla storia del diritto internazionale', in idem, *Civitas Maxima. Studi di storia del diritto internazionale*, II (Firenze: Olschki, 1974).

Parker, Charles H., *Global Interactions in the Early Modern Age* (Cambridge: University Press, 2010).

Parker, Geoffrey, *Emperor: A New Life of Charles V* (New Haven, CT: University Press, 2019).

Parker, Geoffrey, *Imprudent King: A New Biography of Philip II* (New Haven, CT: Yale University Press, 2014).

Parker, Geoffrey, *Sovereign City: The City-State through History* (London: Reaktion Books, 2004).

Parker, Geoffrey, *The Grand Strategy of Philip II* (New Haven, CT: Yale University Press, 1998).

Parker, Geoffrey, *Un solo re, un solo impero, Filippo II* (Bologna: Il Mulino, 2005).

Parry, Glyn, 'John Dee and the Elizabethan British Empire in its European Context', *The Historical Journal*, 49(3) (2006), 643–75.

Parry, John H., *Europe and a Wider World, 1415–1715* (London: Hutchinson, 1979).

Parry, John H., *The Discovery of the Sea* (Berkeley: University of California Press, 1981).

Parry, John H., *The Spanish Seaborne Empire* (London: Hutchinson, 1971).

Parry, John H., *The Spanish Theory of Empire in the Sixteenth Century* (Cambridge: University Press, 1940).

Parry, John T., 'What is the Grotian Tradition in International Law?', *University of Pennsylvania Journal of International Law*, 35(2) (2014), 299–377.

Pedani, Maria P., *Venezia porta d'Oriente* (Bologna: Il Mulino, 2010).

Penn, Christopher D., *The Navy under the Early Stuarts and its Influence on English History* (Manchester: The Faith Press, 1913).

Pennell, C. R. (ed.), *Bandits at Sea: A Pirates Reader* (New York: University Press, 2001).

Pennington, Ken, 'Ancient, Medieval, and Early Modern Concepts of the *Ius commune*', *Clio@Themis*, 27 (2024), 1–16.

Pennington, Kenneth, *The Prince and the Law, 1200–1600: Sovereignty and Rights in the Western Legal Tradition* (Los Angeles: University of California Press, 1993).

Perruso, Richard, 'The Development of the Doctrine of Res Communes in Medieval and Early Modern Europe', *The Legal History Review*, 70(1) (2002), 69–93.

Petronio, Ugo, 'Civitas Venetiarum est edificata in mari', in Gino Benzoni et al. (cur.), *Studi veneti offerti a Gaetano Cozzi* (Venezia: Cardo, 1992), 171–85.

Petti Balbi, Giovanna, *Una città e il suo mare. Genova nel Medioevo* (Bologna: Editrice Clueb, 1991).

Phillips, John R. S., *The Medieval Expansion of Europe* (Oxford: University Press, 1998).

Piggott, Francis T., *The Freedom of the Seas. Historically Treated* (London: H.M. Stationery Office, 1920).

Pihlajamäki, Heikki, Dubber, Markus D. and Godfrey, Mark (eds.), *The Oxford Handbook of European Legal History* (Oxford: University Press, 2018).

Pillet, Antonio (ed.), *Les fondateurs du droit international* (Paris: Giard & Briére, 1904).

Pin, Corrado (ed.), *Ripensando Paolo Sarpi: Atti del convegno internazionale di studi nel 450° anniversario della nascita di Paolo Sarpi* (Venezia: Ateneo Veneto, 2006).

Pin, Corrado, 'Recensione di: *Fra' Paolo Sarpi, Dominio del Mare Adriatico della Serenissima Repubblica di Venezia*, introduzione di Tullio Scovazzi, Torino: Giappichelli, 2005,' *Studi veneziani*, 50 (2005), 392–6.

Pistarino, Geo, *La capitale del mediterraneo: Genova nel mediterraneo* (Bordighera: Istituto Internazionale di Studi Liguri, 1993).

Placer López, Gumersindo, *Fray Serafín de Freitas, mercedario jurisconsulto portugués* (Madrid: Artes Gráficas, 1956).

Plank, Geoffrey, *Atlantic Wars. From the Fifteenth Century to the Age of Revolution* (Oxford: University Press, 2020).

Pogies, Christian, 'Oceans of cynicism? Norm-genesis, lawfare and the South China Sea arbitration case', in Björnstjern Baade et al. (eds.), *Cynical International Law? Abuse and Circumvention in Public International and European Law* (Berlin: Springer, 2021), 143–62.

Pogies, Christian, 'UNCLOS and the South China Sea Arbitration: Into Lawfare's Abyss?', *The German Journal on Contemporary Asia*, 143 (2017), 93–105.

Pohl, Hans (ed.), *The European Discovery of the World and its Economic Effects on Pre-Industrial Society, 1500–1800* (Stuttgart: Franz Steiner, 1990).

Policante, Amedeo, *The Pirate Myth. Genealogies of an Imperial Concept* (London: Routledge, 2015).

Poot, Anton, *Anglo-Dutch Relations. A Political and Diplomatic Analysis of the Years 1625–1642* (Ph.D. dissertation, Royal Holloway, University of London, 2013).

Porras, Ileana M., 'Constructing International Law in the East Indian Seas: Property, Sovereignty, Commerce and War in Hugo Grotius' *De Iure Praedae – The Law of Prize and Booty*, or "On How to Distinguish Merchants from Pirates"', *Brooklyn Journal of International Law*, 31 (2006), 742–804.

Portuondo, Maria M., *Secret Science: Spanish Cosmography and the New World* (Chicago: University Press, 2009).

Potter, Pitman B., *The Freedom of the Sea in History, Law and Politics* (London: Longmans, 1924).

Poumarède, Geraud, *L'empire de Venise et les turcs, XVIe–XVIIe* (Paris: Garnier, 2020).

Prescott, Hilda F. M., *Mary Tudor: The Spanish Tudor* (London: Phoenix, 2003).

Prestage, Edgar, 'The Anglo-Portuguese Alliance', *Transactions of the Royal Historical Society*, 17 (1934), 69–100.

Preto, Paolo, 'La "congiura di Bedmar" a Venezia nel 1618: colpo di Stato o provocazione?', in *Complots et conjurations dans l'Europe moderne. Actes du colloque international organisé à Rome, 30 septembre-2 octobre 1993* (Rome: École Française de Rome, 1996), 289–315.

Preto, Paolo, *I servizi segreti di Venezia. Spionaggio e controspionaggio ai tempi della Serenissima* (Milano: Il Saggiatore, 2010).

Prétou, Pierre, *L'invention de la piraterie en France au Moyen Age* (Paris: Presses universitaires de France, 2021).

Prodi, Paolo, 'Alessandro VI e la sovranità pontificia', in Carla Frova e Maria G. Ottaviani (cur.), *Alessandro VI e lo Stato della Chiesa. Atti del convegno, Perugia, 13–15 marzo 2000* (Roma: Istituto Poligrafico dello Stato, 2003).

Pryor, John H., *Logistics of Warfare in the Age of the Crusades: proceedings of a workshop held at the Centre for Medieval Studies, University of Sydney, 30 Sept.–4 Oct. 2002* (Farnham: Ashgate, 2006).

Purcell, Kate, 'On the Uses and Advantages of Genealogy for International Law', *Leiden Journal of International Law*, 33(1) (2020), 13–35.

Quaglioni, Diego, 'Treaty of Tordesillas, 1494', in *Encyclopaedia of Diplomacy*, edited by Gordon Martel (New York: John Wiley & Sons, 2018).

Quaglioni, Diego, *La sovranità* (Bari: Laterza, 2004).

Quazza, Romolo, *Storia Politica d'Italia: Preponderanza Spagnuola (1559–1700)* (Milano: Vallardi, 1950).

Queen, David B., *New American World: A Documentary History of North America to 1612, vol. I (America from Concept to Discovery: Early Exploration of North America)* (New York: Arno Press & Hector Bye Inc., 1979).

Quintrell, Brian, 'Charles I and his Navy in the 1630s', *The Seventeenth Century*, 3 (1988), 159–79.

Raestad, Arnold, *La mer territoriale, études historiques et juridiques* (Paris: A. Pedone Éditeur, 1913).

Ramis Barceló, Rafael, *La Segunda Escolástica. Una propuesta de síntesis histórica* (Madrid: Dykinson, 2024).

Ranganathan, Surabhi, 'Decolonization and International Law: Putting the Ocean on the Map', *Journal of the History of International Law*, 23(1) (2020), 161–83.

Ranganathan, Surabhi, 'Global Commons', *European Journal of International Law*, 27(3) (2016), 693–717.

Redding, Benjamin W. D., *The English and French Navies, 1500–1650: Expansion, Organization and State-Building* (Martlesham: Boydell & Brewer, 2022).

Rei, Claudia, *Turning Points in Leadership: Shipping Technology in the Portuguese and Dutch Merchant Empires*. Department of Economics, Vanderbilt University, Working Papers: 1123 (2011).

Reinhard, Wolfgang (ed.), *Empires and Encounters: 1350–1750* (Cambridge, MA: Harvard University Press, 2015).

Renaut, Marie-Hélène, *Histoire du droit international public* (Paris: Ellipses, 2007).

Reppy, Alison, 'The Grotian Doctrine of the Freedom of the Seas Reappraised', *The Fordham Law Review*, 19 (1950), 260–70.

Ribeiro, Marta C., Loureiro Bastos, Fernando and Henriksen, Tore (eds.), *Global Challenges and the Law of the Sea* (Cham: Springer, 2020).

Richardson, Glenn (ed.), *The Contending Kingdoms: France and England, 1420–1700* (London: Routledge, 2008).

Rizzi, Alberto, *I leoni di San Marco: il simbolo della Repubblica Veneta*, III vols. (Caselle: Cierre Edizioni, 2012).

Robbe, Ubaldo, *La differenza sostanziale fra 'res nullius' e 'res nullius in bonis' la distinzione delle 'res' pseudo-marcianea: 'che non ha nè capo nè coda'* (Milano: Giuffrè, 1979).

Rodger, Nicholas A. M. 'The Law and Language of Private Naval Warfare', *The Mariner's Mirror*, 100(1) (2014), 5–16.

Rodger, Nicholas A. M., 'Queen Elizabeth and the Myth of Seapower in English History', *Transactions of the Royal Historical Society*, 14 (2004), 153–74.

Rodger, Nicholas A. M., 'The Naval Service of the Cinque Ports', *English Historical Review*, 111(442), 636–51.

Rodger, Nicholas A. M., *The Safeguard of the Sea: a Naval History of Britain, Volume 1, 660–1649* (London: Penguin Books, 2004).

Roger Lockyer, *Buckingham. The Life and Political Career of George Villiers, First Duke of Buckingham 1592–1628* (Routledge: London, 1981).

Rojas Donat, Luis, 'Dos anális histórico-jurídicos en torno al descubrimiento de las Indias: la accesión y la ocupación', *Revista de estudios históricos-jurídicos*, 19 (1997), 153–66.

Rojas Donat, Luis, 'La potestad Apostólica en las Bulas Ultramarinas Portuguesas y Castellanas', *Revista de estudios históricos-jurídicos*, 29 (2007), 407–20.

Rojas Donat, Luis, 'Papal arbitration? Alexander VI and the Portuguese and Spanish Discoveries of the 15th century', *Imago Temporis. Medium Aevum*, 15 (2021), 363–85.

Rojas Donat, Luis, 'Para una historia del derecho canónico-político medieval: la donación de Constantino', *Revista de estudios históricos-jurídicos*, 26 (2004), 337–58.

Rojas Donat, Luis, 'Potestas ligandi et solvendi: Notas histórico-jurídicas en torno a los orígenes de la primacía del Obispo de Roma', *Revista de estudios históricos-jurídicos*, 27 (2005), 339–51.

Röling, B. V. A., '*Jus ad Bellum* and the Grotian Heritage', in *International Law and the Grotian Heritage* (The Hague: T.M.C. Asser Instituut, 1985).

Romanin, Samuele, *Storia documentata di Venezia* (XIII tomi) (Venezia: Filippi Editore, 1972).

Rosand, David, *Myths of Venice. The Figuration of a State* (Chapel Hill: University of North Carolina Press, 2001).

Rösch, Gerhard, *Venezia e l'impero, 962–1250. I rapporti politici, commerciali e di traffico nel periodo imperiale germanico* (Roma: Il Veltro, 1985).

Rosenthal, Earl, 'Plus Ultra, Non Plus Ultra, and the Columnar Device of Emperor Charles v', *Journal of the Warburg and Courtauld Institutes*, 34 (1971), 204–28.

Rosenthal, Earl, 'The Invention of the Columnar Device of Emperor Charles v at the Court of Burgundy in Flanders in 1516', *Journal of the Warburg and Courtauld Institutes*, 36 (1973), 198–230.

Rossi, Christopher, *Sovereignty and Territorial Temptation: The Grotian Tendency* (Cambridge: University Press, 2017).

Rothwell Donald R. and Stephens, Tim, *The International Law of the Sea* (Oxford-Portland: Hart Publishing, 2023).

Rothwell Donald R., et al. (eds.), *The Oxford Handbook of the Law of the Sea* (Oxford: University Press, 2015).

Rougé, Jean, *Recherches sur l'organisation du commerce maritime en Méditerranée sous l'Empire Romain* (Paris: Sevpen, 1966).

Rubin, Alfred P., 'International Law in the Age of Columbus', *Netherlands International Law Review*, 39 (1992), 5–35.

Rubin, M., 'Sundtoldens Afløning', *Historisk Tidsskrift*, 7(6) (1906), 172–311.

Ruiz-Gálvez, Fernández, 'El totus orbis y el *ius gentium* en Francisco de Vitoria: el equilibrio entre tradición e innovación', *Cuadernos Electrónicos de Filosofía del Derecho*, 35 (2017), 19–43.

Rumeu de Armas, Antonio, *El Tratado de Tordesillas: rivalidad hispano-lusa por el dominio de océanos y continentes* (Madrid: Mapfre, 1992).

Ruoss, Andrew, *Competitive Collaboration: The Dutch and English East India Companies & The Forging of Global Corporate Political Economy (1650–1700)* (Ph.D. Dissertation, Durham, NC: Duke University, 2017).

Russell, Frederick H., *The Just War in the Middle Ages* (Cambridge: University Press, 1975).

Russell, Peter E., 'Some Portuguese Paradigms for the Discovery and Conquest of Spanish America', *Renaissance Studies*, 6(3–4) (1992), 377–90.

Saldanha, Arun, 'The Itineraries of Geography: Jan Huygen van Linschoten's Itinerario and Dutch Expeditions to the Indian Ocean, 1594–1602', *Annals of the Association of American Geographers*, 101(1) (2011), 149–77.

Salom-Franco, Nicolás, 'Vitoria y Grocio frente al mar', *Estudios Socio-Jurídicos*, 3(1) (2010), 93–141.

Salomon Arel, Maria, *English Trade and Adventure to Russia in the Early Modern Era: The Muscovy Company, 1603–1649* (Lahnam: Lexington Books, 2019).

Salomoni, David, *Francis Drake: Il corsaro che sfidò un impero* (Bari: Laterza, 2023).

Salomoni, David, *Magellano: Il primo viaggio intorno al mondo* (Bari: Laterza, 2021).

Salonia, Matteo, 'Encompassing the Earth: Magellan's Voyage from Its Political Context to its Expansion of Knowledge', *International Journal of Maritime History*, 34(4) (2022), 543–60.

Samson, Alexander, *Mary and Philip: The Marriage of Tudor England and Habsburg Spain* (Manchester: University Press, 2020).

San Emeterio Martín, Nieves, 'El debate sobre el dominio de los mares en el imperio español durante los siglos XVI y XVII', *Iberian Journal of the History of Economic Thought*, 7(2), 133–42.

Sánchez León, Pablo, Vieira, Carla and Vieira, Nina (eds.), *Espelhos de Mercúrio. A representação do comércio nas Monarquias Ibéricas, 1500–1800* (Coimbra: Imprensa da Universidade, 2024)

Sánchez Martínez, Antonio, *La espada, la cruz y el Padrón (Soberanía, fe y representación cartográfica en el mundo ibérico bajo la Monarquía Hispánica), 1503–1598* (Madrid: CSIC, 2013).

Sánchez Prieto, Ana B., 'La intitulación diplomática de los Reyes Católicos: un programa político y una lección de historia', in *III Jornadas Científicas sobre Documentación de la Época de los Reyes Católicos* (Madrid: Universidad Complutense, 2004), 273–301.

Sandman, Alison, 'Controlling knowledge: navigation, cartography, and secrecy in the early modern Spanish Atlantic', in James Delbourgo and Nicholas Dew (eds.), *Beyond the New Atlantis: Science and Empire in the Atlantic World, 1500–1800* (London: Routledge, 2008), 31–51.

Santana Pérez, Germán, 'Spanish Maritime Experience in Southern Africa during the Early Modern Period', *International Journal of Maritime History*, 30(4) (2018), 621–33.

Savelle, Max, *The Origins of American Diplomacy: The International History of Anglo America, 1492–1763* (New York: Macmillan, 1967).

Savelli, Rodolfo, 'Un seguace italiano di Selden. Pietro Battista Borghi', *Materiali per una storia della cultura giuridica*, 3(1) (1973), 13–76.

Schama, Simon, *La cultura olandese dell'epoca d'oro* (Milano: Il Saggiatore, 1988).

Schama, Simon, *The Embarrassment of Riches, An Interpretation of Dutch Culture in the Golden Age* (London: Collins, 1988).

Scherillo, Gaetano, *Lezioni di diritto romano, le cose, parte prima: concetto di cosa, cose extra patrimonium* (Milano: Giuffrè, 1945).

Schermaier, Martin J., 'Res Communes Omnium: The History of an Idea from Greek Philosophy to Grotian Jurisprudence', *Grotiana*, 30(1) (2009), 20–48.

Schnakenbourg, Éric, 'La géographie des diplomates: la mondialisation de la diplomatie à l'époque moderne', *Revue d'histoire moderne & contemporaine*, 67(1) (2020), 139–62.

Schnakenbourg, Éric, *Entre la guerre et la paix: Neutralité et relations internationales, XVIIe–XVIIIe Siècles* (Rennes: Presses universitaires de Rennes, 2013).

Scott, Anne M., et al. (eds.) *European Perceptions of Terra Australis* (London: Routledge, 2012).

Scovazzi, Tullio, 'The Evolution of International Law of the Sea: New Issues, New Challenges', in *Recueil des Cours – Collected Courses of the Hague Academy of International Law (Vol. 286, 2000)* (The Hague/Boston/London: M. Nijhoff, 2001), 39–244.

Seifert, Dieter, *Kompagnons und Konkurrenten. Holland und die Hanse im späten Mittelalter* (Cologne: Böhlau Verlag, 1997).

Sellars, Kirsten, *A 'Constitution for the Oceans'. The Long Hard Road to the UN Convention on the Law of the Sea* (Cambridge: University Press, 2025).

Senning, Calvin F., 'The Visit of Christian IV to England in 1614', *The Historian*, 31(4) (1969), 555–72.

Seo, Youngmin, *The South China Sea Dispute as International Law and Politics: Discovering the Role of Law in Times of Power Shift* (Leiden: Brill, 2024).

Sharpe, Kevin, *The Personal Rule of Charles I* (New Haven, CT: Yale University Press, 1992).

Shearer, Ivan, 'Grotius and the Law of the Sea', *ASLP Bulletin*, 26 (1983), 46–65.

Shepard, Jonathan (ed.), *The Cambridge History of the Byzantine Empire, c.500–1492* (Cambridge: University Press, 2008).

Sicking, Louis and van Rhee, Remco (C. H.), 'The English Search for a Northeast Passage to Asia Reconsidered: How 'Flemish' fishermen put the Edward Bonaventure in jeopardy on its return journey in 1554', *The Mariner's Mirror*, 105(4) (2019), 388–406.

Sicking, Louis, 'God's Friend, the Whole World's Enemy. Reconsidering the Role of Piracy in the Development of Universal Jurisdiction', *Netherlands Journal of Legal Philosophy*, 47(2) (2018), 176–7.

Sicking, Louis, 'History of the Hanse: Construction and Deconstruction', *History Compass*, e12798 (2024), https://doi.org/10.1111/hic3.12798.

Sicking, Louis, '*Mare Liberum, Mare Clausum* en de Territorial Wateren. Doctrine en Context van het Zeerecht in de Late Middeleeuwen en de Vroegmoderne Tijd', *Pro Memorie*, 26(2) (2024), 183–210.

Sicking, Louis, 'Naval warfare in Europe, c.1330–c.1680', in Frank Tallet and David J. B. Trim (eds.), *European Warfare, 1350–1750* (Cambridge: University Press, 2010), 236–63.

Sicking, Louis, 'The Pirate and the Admiral: Europeanisation and Globalisation of Maritime Conflict Management', *Journal of the History of International Law*, 20(4) (2018), 429–70.

Sicking, Louis, and Abreu-Ferreira, Darlene (eds.), *Beyond the Catch. Fisheries of the North Atlantic, the North Sea and the Baltic, 900–1850* (Leiden: Brill, 2008).

Sicking, Louis, and Wijffels, Alain (eds.) *Conflict Management in the Mediterranean and the Atlantic, 1000–1800* (Leiden: Brill, 2020).

Sicking, Louis, *Neptune and the Netherlands. State, Economy and War at Sea in the Renaissance* (Leiden: Brill, 2004).

Sicking, Louis, *Zeemacht en Onmacht: Maritieme politiek in de Nederlanden, 1488–1558* (Amsterdam: De Bataafsche Leeuw, 1988).

Sico, Luigi, *Dalla libertà dei mari alla disciplina analitica delle attività di utilizzazione degli spazi marini*, in idem (cur.), *Oltre Montego Bay: nuove tendenze verso il controllo degli spazi marini adiacenti* (Napoli: Editoriale Scientifica, 2009).

Sidney Woolf, Cecil N., *Bartolus of Sassoferrato, his Position in the History of Medieval Political Thought* (Cambridge: University Press, 1913).

Signorotto, Gianvittorio and Visceglia, Maria A. (eds.), *Court and Politics in Papal Rome, 1492–1700* (Cambridge: University Press, 2002).

Simpson, Andrew R. C., and Øyrehagen Sunde, Jørn (eds.), *Comparative Perspectives in Scottish and Norwegian Legal History, Trade and Seafaring, 1200–1800* (Edinburgh: University Press, 2023)

Sines, Ryan, *Norse in the North Atlantic* (Lanham: Hamilton Books, 2020).

Skouteris, Thomas, 'Engaging history in international law', in David Kennedy and José M. Beneyto (eds.), *New Approaches to International Law: The European and American Experiences* (The Hague: T.M.C. Asser Press, 2012), 99–121.

Sobecki, Sebastian I., *The Sea and Medieval English Literature* (Woodbridge: Boydell Press, 2008).

Soly, Hugo (dir.), *Charles V 1500–1558. L'empereur et son temps* (Arles: Actes Sud, 1999).

Sommerville, Johann P., 'John Selden, the Law of Nature, and the Origins of Government', *The Historical Journal*, 27(2) (1984), 437–47.

Somos, Mark and Smeltzer, Joshua, 'Vitoria, Suárez, and Grotius: James Brown Scott's Enduring Revival', *Grotiana*, 41(1) (2020), 137–62.

Somos, Mark, 'Selden's *Mare Clausum*. The Secularisation of International Law and the Rise of Soft Imperialism', *Journal of the History of International Law*, 14 (2012), 287–330.

Southern, Richard W., *Western Society and the Church in the Middle Ages* (London: Penguin Books, 1990).

Spate, Oskar H. K., *The Spanish Lake. The Pacific since Magellan, vol. 1* (Camberra: ANU E-press, 2004).

Stagg, Frank N., *North Norway. A History* (London: George Allen & Unwin Ltd., 1952).

Stapelbroek, Koen (ed.), *Trade and War: The Neutrality of Commerce in the Inter-State System* (Helsinki: Collegium for Advanced Studies, 2011).

Starkey, David J., 'Voluntaries and sea Robbers: A Review of the Academic Literature on Privateering, Corsairing, Bucaneering and Piracy', *The Mariner's Mirror*, 97(1) (2011), 127–47.

Stavrianos, Leften S., *The World Since 1500: A Global History* (Englewood: Prentice Hall, 1966).

Steiger, Heinhard, 'From the International Law of Christianity to the International Law of the World Citizen – Reflections on the Formation of the Epochs of the History of International Law', *Journal of the History of International Law*, 3(2) (2001), 180–93.

Steinberg, Philip E., 'Sovereignty, Territory, and the Mapping of Mobility: A View from the Outside', *Annals of the Association of American Geographers*, 99(3) (2009), 467–95.

Steinberg, Philip E., *The Social Construction of the Ocean* (Cambridge: University Press, 2001).

Steinsson, Sverrir, 'The Cod Wars: A Re-analysis', *European Security*, 25(2) (2016), 256–75.

Stout, Felicity J., *Exploring Russia in the Elizabethan Commonwealth: The Muscovy Company and Giles Fletcher, the Elder (1546–1611)* (Manchester: University Press, 2015).

Stradling, Robert A., 'Catastrophe and Recovery: The Defeat of Spain, 1639–43', *History*, 64(11) (1979), 205–19.

Stradling, Robert A., *Europe and the Decline of Spain* (London: Allen & Unwin, 1981).

Stradling, Robert A., *The Armada of Flanders: Spanish Maritime Policy and European War, 1568–1668* (Cambridge: University Press, 2009).

Straumann, Benjamin, *Roman Law in the State of Nature. The Classical Foundations of Hugo Grotius' Natural Law* (Cambridge: University Press, 2015).

Strootman, Rolf, van den Eijnde, Floris, and van Wijk, Roy (eds.), *Empires of the Sea. Maritime Power Networks in World History* (Leiden: Brill, 2019).

Sturges, Robert S. (ed.), *Law and Sovereignty in the Middle Ages and the Renaissance* (Turnhout: Brepols, 2011).

Subrahmanyam, Sanjay, 'Holding the World in Balance: The Connected Histories of the Iberian Overseas Empires, 1500–1640', *The American Historical Review*, 112(5) (2007), 1359–85.

Subrahmanyam, Sanjay, *The Portuguese Empire in Asia, 1500–1700: A Political and Economic History* (London-New York: Longman, 1993).

Sugden, John, *Sir Francis Drake* (London: Pimlico, 2006).

Susilowati, Endang, 'Coastal Civilization and Maritime Diplomacy in Premodern Southeast Asia', *International Journal of Maritime History*, 30(4) (2018), 649–63.

Tanaka, Yoshifumi, *The International Law of the Sea* (Cambridge: University Press, 2019).

Tandgaard, Iben and Dirckinck-Holmfeld, Gregers, *Christian 4.s København* (København; Politikens Forlag, 2006).

Tarpley, Webster G., *Paolo Sarpi, His Networks, Venice and the Coming of the Thirty Years' War* (Ph.D. dissertation, Washington D.C.: The Catholic University of America, 2009).

Taylor, Harland, 'Trade, Neutrality, and the "English Road", 1630–1648', *The Economic History Review*, 25(2) (1972), 236–60.

Tedeschi, Mario, 'Le bolle alessandrine e la loro rilevanza giuridica', in Simonetta B. Alagna (cur.), *Esplorazioni geografiche e immagine del mondo nei secoli XV e XVI*, Atti convegno Messina 14–15 ottobre, 1993 (Messina: Grafo Editor, 1994).

Tenenti, Alberto, *Piracy and the Decline of Venice* (London: Longmans, 1967).

Tenenti, Alberto, *Venezia e i corsari, 1580–1615* (Laterza: Bari, 1961).

Theutenberg, Bo J., 'Mare Liberum et Mare Clausum', *Arctic*, 37(4) (1984), 481–92.

Thiriet, Freddy, *La Romanie vénitienne au Moyen Age. Le développement et l'exploitation du domaine colonial vénitien (XIIe–XVe siècles)* (Paris: De Boccard, 1975).

Thomas, Jeremy, 'The Intertwining of Law and Theology in the Writings of Grotius', *Journal of the History of International Law*, 1(1) (1999), 61–100.

Thomaz, Luís F., *Cristóvão Colombo o Genovês meu tio por afinidade* (Lisbon: Portuguese Navy Academy, 2021).

Thomaz, Luis Filipe F. R., 'Factions, Interests and Messianism: The Politics of Portuguese Expansion in the East, 1500–1521', *Indian Economic and Social History Review*, 28(1) (1991), 97–109.

Thomaz, Luis Filipe F. R., 'Portuguese control over the Arabian Sea and the Bay of Bengal: a comparative study', in Denys Lombard and Om Prakash (eds.), *Commerce and Culture in the Bay of Bengal, 1500–1800* (New Delhi: Manohar, 1999), 115–62.

Thompson, William R. (ed.), *Great Power Rivalries* (Columbia: University of South Carolina Press, 1999).

Thomson, Erik, 'The Dutch Miracle, Modified; Hugo Grotius's *Mare Liberum*, Commercial Governance and Imperial War in the Early-Seventeenth Century', *Grotiana*, 30 (2009), 107–30.

Thomson, Janice E., *Mercenaries, Pirates, and Sovereigns. State Building and Extraterritorial Violence in Early Modern Europe* (Princeton: University Press, 1994).

Thornton, Helen, 'Hugo Grotius and the Freedom of the Seas', *International Journal of Maritime History*, 16(2) (2004), 17–38.

Thornton, Helen, 'John Selden's Response to Hugo Grotius: The Argument for Closed Seas', *International Journal of Maritime History*, 18(2) (2006), 105–27.

Thornton, John K., *A Cultural History of the Atlantic World, 1250–1820* (Cambridge: University Press, 2012).

Thrush, Derek A., *The Navy under Charles I* (Ph.D. Dissertation, London: University College, 1990).

Tierney, Brian, *L'idea dei diritti naturali* (Bologna: Il Mulino, 2002).

Tierney, Brian, *Liberty and Law* (Washington DC: Catholic University of America Press, 2014).

Tomlinson, Howard (ed.), *Before the English Civil War: Essays on Early Stuart Politics and Government* (Palgrave: London, 1983).

Tommasi, Claudio, 'La "Libertà dei Mari". Ugo Grozio e gli sviluppi della talassocrazia olandese nel primo seicento', *Scienza & Politica*, 9(16) (1997), 42–3.

Toomer, Gerald J., *John Selden, a Life in Scholarship* (Oxford: University Press, 2009).

Tracy, James D. (ed.), *The Political Economy of Merchant Empires* (Cambridge: University Press, 1991).

Trim, David, 'The Secret War of Elizabeth I: England and the Huguenots during the Early Wars of Religion, 1562-77', *Proceedings of the Huguenot Society*, 27(2) (1999), 189–99.

Tröster, Manuel, 'Roman Hegemony and Non-state Violence: A Fresh Look at Pompey's Campaign against the Pirates', *Greece & Rome*, 56(1) (2009), 14–33.

Trujillo, Isabel, *Francisco de Vitoria. Il diritto alla comunicazione e i confini della socialità umana* (Giappichelli: Torino, 1997).

Truyol y Serra, Antonio, *Histoire du droit international public* (Paris: Economica, 1999).

Tucci, Ugo (cur.), *Venezia nel cinquecento* (Roma: Istituto della Enciclopedia Italiana, 1974).

Tuck, Richard, *Natural Rights Theories: Their Origin and Development* (Cambridge: University Press, 1979).

Tuck, Richard, *Philosophy and Government, 1572–1651* (Cambridge: University Press, 1993).

Tuck, Richard, *The Rights of War and Peace: Political Thought and the International Order from Grotius to Kant* (Oxford: University Press, 2001).

Turnbull, David, 'Cartography and Science in Early Modern Europe: Mapping the Construction of Knowledge Spaces', *Imago Mundi*, 48(1) (1996), 5–24.

Ullmann, Walter, 'The Development of the Medieval Idea of Sovereignty', *The English Historical Review*, 64(250) (1949), 1–33.

Ullmann, Walter, *Principles of Government and Politics in the Middle Ages* (London: Mathuen & Co, 1978).

Ullmann, Walter, *The Growth of Papal Government in the Middle Ages: A Study in the Ideological Relation of Clerical to Lay Power* (New York: Taylor & Francis, 1955).

Vadi, Valentina, 'International Law and Its Histories: Methodological Risks and Opportunities', *Harvard International Law Journal*, 58(2) (2017), 311–52.

Vadi, Valentina, 'Perspective and Scale in the Architecture of International Legal History', *European Journal of International Law*, 30(1), 2019, 53–71.

Vadi, Valentina, *War and Peace. Alberico Gentili and the Early Modern Law of Nations* (Leiden/Boston: Brill/Nijhoff, 2020).

Van Caenegem, Raoul C., *An Historical Introduction to Private Law* (Cambridge: University Press, 1992).

van der Wee, Herman, *The Growth of the Antwerp Market and the European Economy, Fourteenth-Sixteenth Centuries* (The Hague: M. Nijhoff, 1963).

van Holk, L. E. and Roelofsen, C. G., *Grotius Reader* (The Hague: Asser Instituut, 1983).

van Ittersum, Martine J., 'Debating the Free Sea in London, Paris, The Hague and Venice: The Publication of John Selden's *Mare Clausum* (1635) and its Diplomatic Repercussions in Western Europe', *History of European Ideas*, 47(8) (2021), 1193–210.

van Ittersum, Martine J., 'Hugo Grotius in context: Van Heemskerck's capture of the Santa Catarina and its justification in *De jure praedae* (1604–1606)', *Asian Journal of Social Science*, 31 (2003), 511–48

van Ittersum, Martine J., 'Knowledge Production in the Dutch Republic: The Household Academy of Hugo Grotius (1583–1645)', *Journal of the History of Ideas*, 72(4) (2011), 523–48.

van Ittersum, Martine J., '*Mare Liberum* versus the Propriety of the Seas? The Debate between Hugo Grotius (1583–1645) and William Welwood (1552–1624) and its Impact on Anglo-Scotto-Dutch Fishery Disputes in the Second Decade of the Seventeenth Century', *Edinburgh Law Review*, 10(2) (2008), 239–76.

van Ittersum, Martine J., 'The Long Goodbye: Hugo Grotius and the Justification of Dutch Exapansion Overseas (1604-1645)', *History of European Ideas*, 36 (2010), 386–411.

van Ittersum, Martine J., *Profit and Principle: Hugo Grotius, Natural Rights Theories and the Rise of Dutch Power in the East Indies 1595–1615* (Leiden: Brill, 2006).

van Veen, Ernst, *An Inquiry into the Portuguese Decline in Asia, 1580–1645. Decay or Defeat?* (Leiden: CNWS Publications, 2000).

Vander Linden, Herman, 'Alexander VI and the Demarcation of the Maritime and Colonial Domains of Spain and Portugal, 1493-1494', *The American Historical Review*, 22(1) (1916), 1–20.

Varela Marcos, Jesús (ed.), *Juan de la Cosa: la Cartografía Histórica de los Descubrimientos Españoles* (Sevilla: Universidad Internacional de Andalucía, 2011).

Vergé-Franceschi, Michel, *Henry le Navigateur: Un découvreur au XVème siècle* (Paris: Éditions du Félin, 2016).

Vergès, Françoise, 'Writing on Water: Peripheries, Flows, Capital, and Struggles in the Indian Ocean', *Positions: Asia Critique*, 11(1) (2003), 241–57.

Verner, Joel G., 'Changes in the Law of the Sea: Latin American Contributions and Rationales', *Social and Economic Studies*, 30(2) (1981), 18–44.

Verzijl, Jan H. W., *International Law in Historical Perspective*, I (Leiden: A. W. Sijthoff, 1968).

Verzijl, Jan H. W., *International Law in Historical Perspective*, VII (Leiden: A. W. Sijthoff, 1971).

Viallon, Marie (dir.), *Paolo Sarpi: Politique et religion en Europe* (Paris: Garnier, 2010).

Vila-Santa, Nuno, 'Diplomacy and Humanism: Ambassador Jean Nicot and the French-Portuguese Maritime Rivalry, (1559–1561)', *Anuario de Estudios Americanos*, 80(1) (2023), 43–77.

Vila-Santa, Nuno, 'Fighting for a *Mare Clausum* and Secret Science: France, England and Spain in the Strategies of Ambassador Dantas (1557–1568)', *Vegueta. Anuario de la Facultad de Geografía e Historia*, 23(2) (2023), 1115–51.

Vila-Santa, Nuno, 'Jan Huygen van Linschoten and the Reys-gheschrift: Updating Iberian Science for the Dutch Expansion', *Historical Research*, 95(265) (2021), 1–22.

Vila-Santa, Nuno, 'Jan Huygen van Linschoten's Itinerario: a decaying commercial portrait of Portuguese Asia?', in Pablo Sánchez León, Carla Vieira and Nina Vieira (eds.), *Espelhos de Mercúrio. A representação do comércio nas Monarquias Ibéricas, 1500–1800* (Coimbra: Imprensa da Universidade, 2024), 261–88.

Vila-Santa, Nuno, *Knowledge Exchanges between Portugal and Europe. Maritime Diplomacy, Espionage, and Nautical Science in the Early Modern World* (15th–17th Centuries) (Amsterdam: University Press, 2024).

Villads Jensen, Kurt, *Crusading at the Edges of Europe, Denmark and Portugal, c.1000–c.1250* (London-New York: Routledge, 2017).

Villar García, Maria B. and Pezzi Cristóbal, Pilar (eds.), *Los extranjeros en la España moderna: actas del I Coloquio Internacional. Celebrado en Málaga del 28 al 30 de noviembre de 2002*, vol. 1 (Málaga: Portadilla, 2003), 73–99.

Villiers, Alan, *The Indian Ocean* (Conran: London, 1952).

Villiers, Patrick, *Les corsaires du littoral: Dunkerque, Calais, Boulogne, de Philippe II à Louis XIV (1568–1713)* (Villeneuve d'Ascq: Presses universitaires du Septentrion, 2020).

Vincent, Bernard, *1492. «L'année admirable»* (Paris: Champs Flammarion, 1997).

Vinogradoff, Paul, *Historical Types of International Law: Lectures Delivered in the University of Leiden* (Leiden: Brill, 1923).

Viñuales, Jorge et al. (eds.), *The International Legal Order in the XXIst Century. Essays in Honour of Professor Marcelo Gustavo Kohen* (Leiden/Boston: Brill/Nijhoff, 2023)

Virga, Vincent, *Cartographia. Mapping Civilizations* (New York, Little Brown & Co., 2007).

Vismara, Giulio, 'Il diritto del mare', in *La navigazione mediterranea nell'alto medioevo* (Spoleto: Centro italiano di studi sull'alto medioevo, 1978), vol. 2, 689–730.

Vismara, Giulio, *Scritti di storia giuridica, 7. Comunità e diritto internazionale* (Milano: Giuffrè, 1989).

Vivanti, Corrado, *Paolo Sarpi* (Roma: Istituto poligrafico e Zecca dello Stato, 2000).

Vivanti, Corrado, *Quattro lezioni su Paolo Sarpi* (Napoli: Bibliopolis, 2005).

Vodola, Elisabeth, *Excommunication in the Middle Ages* (Berkeley: University of California Press, 1986.

Voigt, Christina and Foster, Caroline (eds.), *International Courts versus Non-compliance Mechanisms: Comparative Advantages in Strengthening Treaty Implementation* (Cambridge: University Press, 2024).

Voituriez, Antonio P., *Problemas jurídicos internacionales de la conquista de Canarias* (Las Palmas de Gran Canaria: Universidad de La Laguna, 1958).

Wade, T. C., 'The Roll *de Superioritate Maris Angliae*. The Foundation of the Stewart Claim to the Sovereignty of the Sea', *British Yearbook of International Law*, (1921–1922), 99–108.

Waisberg, Tatiana, 'The Treaty of Tordesillas and the (re)Invention of International Law in the Age of Discovery', *Meridiano. Journal of Global Studies*, 47 (2017), 1–12.

Walton, Nicholas, *Genoa, 'La Superba': The Rise and Fall of a Merchant Pirate Superpower* (London: Hurst & Company, 2015).

Wamberg, Bodil, *Christian IV – en mand under indflydelse* (København: G.E.C. Gad, 1993).

Watkins, Dawn and Burton, Mandy (eds.), *Research Methods in Law* (London: Routledge, 2013).

Weckmann, Luis, *Las Bulas Alejandrinas de 1493 y la teoría política del Papado medieval. Estudio de la supremacía papal sobre islas, 1091–1493* (México: Universidad Nacional Autónoma, 1959).

Weindl, Andrea, 'Grotius's *Mare Liberum* in the Political Practice of Early Modern Europe', *Grotiana*, 30(1) (2009), 131–51.

Westergaard, Waldemar, 'The Hansa Towns and Scandinavia on the Eve of Swedish Independence', *The Journal of Modern History*, 4(3) (1932), 349–60.

Weststeijn, Arthur, 'The VOC as a Company-State: Debating Seventeenth-Century Dutch Colonial Expansion', *Itinerario*, 38(1) (2014), 13–34.

Wiesner-Hanks, Merry E., *Early Modern Europe, 1450–1789* (Cambridge: University Press, 2013).

Williamson, James A., *Hawkins of Plymouth* (London: Adam and Charles Black, 1949).

Willing Balch, Thomas, 'Albericus Gentilis', *American Journal of International Law*, 5(3) (1991), 665–79.

Wills, Garry, 'The Lions of Venice', *The American Scholar*, 68(2) (1999), 45–9.

Wilson, Charles, *Profit and Power: A Study of England and the Dutch Wars* (The Hague/Boston/London: M. Nijhoff, 1978).

Wilson, Eric, 'Erasing the Corporate Sovereign, Inter-Textuality and an Alternative Explanation for the Publication of Hugo Grotius' *Mare Liberum* (1609)', *Itinerario*, 30(2) (2006), 78–103.

Wing, John T., 'Keeping Spain Afloat: State Forestry and Imperial Defense in the Sixteenth Century', *Environmental History*, 17(1) (2012), 116–45.

Wink, Jurriaan and Sicking, Louis, 'Reprisal and Diplomacy: Conflict Resolution within the Context of Anglo–Dutch Commercial Relations c1300–c1415', *Comparative Legal History*, 5(1) (2017), 1–19.

Winstedt, Richard, and De Josselin De Jong, Patrick E., 'The Maritime Laws of Malacca', *Journal of the Malayan Branch of the Royal Asiatic Society*, 29(3) (1956), 22–59.

Winter, Jay M. (ed.), *War and Economic Development. Essays in Memory of David Joslin* (Cambridge: University Press, 1975).

Wolfrum, Rudiger (ed.), *The Max Planck Encyclopedia of Public International Law*, x Volumes (Oxford: University Press, 2012).

Wolter, Hans and Beck, Hans G., *Civitas medievale, secoli XII–XIV*, in Hubert Jedin (dir.), *Storia della Chiesa* (Milano: Edizioni Jaca Book, 1975).

Woodward, David (ed.), *The History of Cartography, Vol. III: Cartography in the European Renaissance*, part 1 (Chicago: University Press, 2007).

Woodward, David (ed.), *The History of Cartography, Vol. III: Cartography in the European Renaissance*, part 2 (Chicago: University Press, 2007).

Wootton, David, *Paolo Sarpi. Between Renaissance and Enlightenment* (Cambridge: University Press, 1983).

Wubs-Mrozewicz, Justyna and Jenks, Stuart (eds.), *The Hanse in Medieval and Modern Europe* (Leiden: Brill, 2013).

Wubs-Mrozewicz, Justyna, 'The Late Medieval and Early Modern Hanse as an Institution of Conflict Management', *Continuity and Change*, 32(1) (2017), 59–84.

Wyatt, Michael (ed.), *The Cambridge Companion to the Italian Renaissance* (Cambridge: University Press, 2014).

Yasuaki, Onuma, 'When was the Law of International Society Born? An Inquiry of the History of International Law from an Intercivilizational Perspective', *Journal of the History of International Law*, 2(1) (2000), 1–66.

Young, Michaela, 'Then and Now: Reappraising Freedom of the Seas in Modern Law of the Sea', *Ocean Development & International Law*, 47(2) (2016), 165–85.

Yun Casalilla, Bartolomé, 'Early Modern Iberian Empires, Global History and History of Globalization', *Journal of Global History*, 17(3) (2022), 1–23.

Zambrano Pérez, Milton, 'Piratas, piratería y comercio ilícito en el Caribe: la visión del otro (1550-1650)', *Historia Caribe*, 12 (2007), 23–56.

Zanetto, Marco, *Venezia e l'Europa, studi storici*, IV (Venezia: Editoria Universitaria, 2004).

Zannini, Andrea, 'L'economia veneta nel Seicento. Oltre il paradigma della "crisi generale"', in *Società Italiana di Demografia Storica. La popolazione nel Seicento, relazione presentata al convegno di Firenze*, 28–30 novembre 1996 (Bologna: CLUEB 1999), 473–502.

Zannini, Andrea, 'Economic and social aspects of the crisis of Venetian diplomacy in the seventeenth and eighteenth centuries', in Daniela Frigo (ed.), *Politics and Diplomacy in Early Modern Italy: the Structure of Diplomatic Practice, 1450–1800* (Cambridge: University Press, 2000), 109–46.

Zemanek, Karl, 'Was Hugo Grotius Really in Favour of the Freedom of the Seas?', *Journal of the History of International Law*, 2(1) (1999), 48–60.

Zendri, Christian, 'Mare passim omnibus patet: il diritto del mare agli inizi dell'età moderna (secc. XV–XVII)', *Archivio Scialoja-Bolla. Annali di studi sulla proprietà collettiva*, 1 (2007), 93–121.

Zendri, Christian, 'Patrimonio ed eredità (secc. XII–XIII)', *Archivio Scialoja-Bolla. Annali di studi sulla proprietà collettiva*, 1 (2016), 205–9.

Zendri, Christian, 'Proprietà collettive e patrimonio nella tradizione giuridica occidentale moderna: appunti per una riflessione', *Archivio Scialoja-Bolla. Annali di studi sulla proprietà collettiva*, 1 (2018), 75–94.

Ziskind, Jonathan, 'International Law and Ancient Sources: Grotius and Selden', *The Review of Politics*, 35(4) (1973), 537–59.

Ziskind, Jonathan, 'The International Legal Status of the Sea in Antiquity', *Acta Orientalia* 35 (1973), 35–56.

Zorzi, Alvise, *La repubblica del leone* (Milano: Bompiani, 2001).

Zorzi, Alvise, *Una città, una repubblica, un impero. Venezia, 697–1797* (Milano: Mondadori, 1989).

Zwierlein, Cornel and Lee, Daniel (eds.), *Sovereignty. European and Global Histories, 1400–1800* (Leiden/Boston: Brill, 2025).

Index of Persons

Index of Places

Index of Concepts

www.ingramcontent.com/pod-product-compliance
Lightning Source LLC
Chambersburg PA
CBHW071335230926
51849CB00002B/403
9789004741393